HARDPRESS.NET
HOME OF HARD-TO-FIND BOOKS

Biographia Borealis
by Hartley Coleridge

Address:
HardPress
8345 NW 66TH ST #2561
MIAMI FL 33166-2626
USA
Email: info@hardpress.net

Biographia borealis

Hartley Coleridge

Published June 1 1833 by F.E. Bingley, 37 Briggate, Leeds

Published June 1, 1857 by E. F. Bingley, 37 Briggate Leeds

BIOGRAPHIA BOREALIS;

OR

LIVES

OF

DISTINGUISHED NORTHERNS,

BY

HARTLEY COLERIDGE.

Hic manus ob patriam pugnando vulnera passi,
Quique sacerdotes casti dum vita manebat,
Quique pii vates et Phœbo digna locuti,
Inventas aut qui vitam excoluêre per artes,
Quique sui memores alios fecêre merendo.
VIRGIL. ÆNID. VI.

LONDON:
WHITAKER, TREACHER, AND CO: AND
F. E. BINGLEY, LEEDS.

1833.

TO THE

RIGHT HONOURABLE

THE EARL FITZWILLIAM,

THESE NOTICES

OF THE

TALENT AND VIRTUE OF THE PROVINCE,

WHICH HE HATH SO LONG HONOURED WITH HIS RESIDENCE,

AND BENEFITTED BY HIS BOUNTY,

ARE,

WITH HIS OWN GRACIOUS PERMISSION,

RESPECTFULLY DEDICATED

BY

HIS SINCERE AND GRATEFUL ADMIRER,

HARTLEY COLERIDGE.

ADVERTISEMENT.

THE Lives contained in this volume were originally intended to form part of a much longer series of provincial Biography. From causes, in *which the Author alone is concerned, and for which he alone is responsible*, the publication is for a time suspended. The sample here offered, is, however, independent and complete in itself: and should it meet with approbation, the Author hopes at no distant period, to resume and fulfil the original design.

He trusts that few inaccuracies or deficiencies will be found in the detail of facts. One or two inadvertencies he takes this opportunity of correcting. The "Mercunis Rusticus" mentioned page 16, was not a Newspaper; but an account of the sufferings of the Episcopal Clergy, during the Commonwealth, written by Bruno Ryves, some time Rector of Acton, and published soon after restoration, probably with a view to justify or filliate the "Bartholoma Act." The dates of Roger Ascham's degrees, were 1534, and 1536, not, as given in his life, 1538, and 1544. It was not the Earl of *Carnarvon* that fell at the battle of Edge-hill, as stated in the life of Roscoe, but the Earl of *Lindsey*. Robert Earl of Carnarvon, was slain at the first battle of Newbury.

As to the principles on which the work has been conducted, and the sentiments which it breathes, explanation is needless, and apology would be base. The Author finds nothing to retract, nothing which he is resolved to dilute into no meaning, and nothing with which any sect, party, or person, can be justly offended.

INTRODUCTORY ESSAY.

WHAT duller looking volume than a Parish Register? What drier commentary on the trite text, *Mors omnibus communis?* What is it, but a barren abstract of the annals of mortality—

> ————Where to be born, and die,
> Of rich and poor makes all the history?

It might, indeed, set on a calculator, or a life-insurance broker, to compute the comparative duration of life in different periods; a Shandean philosopher to speculate on the successive fashions in christian names; a manuscript-hunter to note down the revolutions of penmanship; or a moral economist to infer the progress of corruption from the increase of illegitimate births: but to men whose thoughts and feelings travel in the "high-way of the world," its all-levelling uniformity presents neither amusement nor instruction.

But suppose an aged man to open this same volume, and, seated in the midst of a circle of his fellow-parishioners, run his eye along the time-discoloured pages, and relate his recollections, and his father's, and his great-great-grandfather's recollections of every name in the list, though perhaps few had done more than erect a new dial, or leave the interest of £5 to be distributed on New-Year's Day to twenty poor widows; yet his talk would not be devoid of interest to such as "find a tale in every thing," and that all of whom he spake had been born within hearing of the same church clock, would infuse a family-feeling into his narratives.—He would be a local biographer.

If a few leading characters be excepted, who often owe their exception more to fortune and circumstance than to their intrinsic power, the notices of men in general histories are very much like the Parish Register:—consisting of names and dates, and events in which the bulk of the species are as passive as in their own birth and death. Nor can the majority of readers derive any thing from such histories,

b

better than empty speculations, not quite so trifling, perhaps, but quite as foreign to their " business and bosoms," as those of the virtuosos before mentioned. *Biography* is required, like the old man, to give history a human meaning and purpose.

It is, indeed, frequently asserted, that Biography is a most important *part* of History; and if by history we mean all such knowledge as rests upon testimony—as distinguished from science, which is grounded on demonstration, or on experiment, this is undoubtedly true. But it is more for our purpose, to consider Biography as the *antithesis* of History; to divide the knowledge of the past, founded on testimony, into History and Biography. The distinction we would draw, is not between an inclusive *greater*, and an included *less*, as Geography is distinguished from Topography, but rather such as obtains between Mechanical philosophy and Chemistry; the former of which calculates the powers of bodies in mass,—the latter analyses substances, and explains their operations by their composition.

The facts of the same life may be considered either biographically or historically. If the acts or circumstances of an individual are related only as they bear upon the public interests—if the man be regarded as a state engine, no matter whether he be the steam engine that sets the whole in motion, or one of the most insignificant spindles—if his fortune be set forth, not for any personal interest to be taken therein, but merely as an instance, proof, cause, or consequence, of the general destiny—such an account, though it admitted nothing that did not originate from, or tend towards, a single person, ought not to be called a biography, but a history. Thus Robertson's Charles V. is not a life of Charles V. but a history of Europe in the age of Charles V. On the other hand, the private Memoirs of a public character are no necessary part of public history. Anecdotes of Kings and Ministers, Courtiers and Mistresses, do not explain the state of a nation; they are only so far historical as they indicate the average of morals; and in this point of view they are often extremely delusive,—for the Court is not the dial plate of the national heart. We have been led to state this, though not perhaps in the direct line of our argument, because the substituting a very exceptionable kind of Court biography for true national history is a mistake often practically made, and very mischievous; not only because it bestows the dignity of history on prurient or malignant scandal, but because it breeds a false belief that the welfare and distress of communities are doled out at the discretion of a few fine dressed individuals, who, according to the popular temper, become idols or abominations.

A portion of history does, indeed, enter into all biography. The interests of individuals are so implicated in those of the community, that the life of the most domestic female could not be justly understood without some knowledge of the politics of the time in which she lived. Now what to one age is *Politics*, becomes *History* to all that succeed. The impossibility of writing the annals of a nation without recording the acts, words, and characters of many men in that nation, is obvious. But a philosophical historian always has his eye fixed on an *Event*, or a *Principle*; individual interests and personal characters he considers but as water drops in the "mighty stream of tendency." If he weighs Scipio against Hannibal, it is because they represented Carthage and Rome: if he drops a tear at Philippi, it is not for Brutus, but for the Republic. Whatever diverts attention from the onward course of things, without representing their general aspect, is, in a history, out of place, just as much as anecdotes of physicians and patients, or puffing descriptions of steam-packets, watering places, and the Island of Madeira, in a scientific treatise of medicine. The more interesting such episodes may be, the more they obstruct the historian's legitimate purpose; for the proper interest of history is of a very high abstract quality, and consists chiefly in observing the operation of great principles upon communities in long periods of time; in remarking how the seeming contradictions of facts, tempers, and opinions unite in one result, as this planet, in which there are at every moment so many millions of conflicting motions,—mechanical, chemical, vital, and voluntary, diverging and converging in every possible direction, is still itself moving along the same everlasting way. The motion of the heavens is a sublime contemplation; so are the great, ordained revolutions of empires, magnificent subjects of thought. But to understand either the one or the other; to reduce the multitude of phænomena under a law of unity; and again to trace that law in the infinite detail of its operations; to verify general conclusions by fit inductions; to prove what really is the centre and source of motion and change, and what is inertly and passively moved; is a slow, dry, laborious work of intellect, requiring an intense and continuous attention, which few minds can sustain, and none will find agreeable. For in all abstract processes, besides the strong exertion of one faculty, which as conveying the sense of power, may be pleasurable, it is necessary to keep others under an almost painful constraint. The mind must be held, if the phrase may be allowed, in *decomposition.* No wonder then, if it seize eagerly on the first opportunity of returning to its natural state, and bringing the imagination and sympathies into play. Hence the introduction of biographical, or human interest, into political history, indisposes both reader and writer for the hard passionless spirit of enquiry, so essentially necessary to arrive at those grand principles which convert facts into truths; principles in the light whereof a statesman ought to read the past, and without which history is, for all political application, something worse than an old almanack. For it should be left to the *administrators* of the laws to seek for precedents; the *makers* of laws should regard only principles. Facts, for antiquaries; Examples, for school-boys; Precedents, for lawyers; Principles, for legislators. Let us take an instance, in the reign of our own Elizabeth. Does not our interest in the beautiful Queen of Scotland, interfere with our attention to the interests of the public? and is that interest at all more *historical* in the strict sense of the word, than that we take in the fortunes of Desdemona or Clarissa? Or, to go back a little, are not fair Rosamond, and Jane Shore, in popular recollection, the most prominent characters in their respective epochs; epochs memorable for great changes in society, and rapid development of the constitution? Let us not deceive ourselves after the manner of those that write, or perhaps rather of those that *buy,* pretty books for children. The romance of history only differs from other romances by requiring no invention.

But it will be said, that it is quite natural that we should care more about *persons,* who are our fellow creatures, than about state interests and revolutions, which, in the aggregate, are *brute* forces, as unsympathizing as the lever, the pulley, or the steam-engine; and that most people would find history very tiresome, if it were written according to the idea above proposed. To this we answer, that we do not wish history, for general perusal, to be so written. We only wish to distinguish the peculiar end, object, and function of History from that of Biography.

In history all that belongs to the individual is exhibited in subordinate relation to the commonwealth ; in biography, the acts, and accidents of the commonwealth are considered in their relation to the individual, as influences by which his character is formed or modified,—as *circumstances* amid which he is placed,—as the sphere in which he moves, or the material he works with. The man, with his works, his words, his affections, his fortunes, is the end and aim of all. He does not, indeed, as in a panegyric, stand alone like a statue, but like the central figure of a picture, around which others are grouped in due subordination and perspective, the general circumstances of his times forming the back and fore ground. In history, the man, like the earth on the Copernican hypothesis, is part of a system ; in Biography, he is like the earth in the ancient Cosmogony, the centre and the final cause of the system.

There is one species of history which may with great propriety be called biographical, to which we do not remember to have heard the term applied ;—we mean that wherein an order, institution, or people, are invested with personality, and described as possessing an unity of will, conscience, and responsibility ;—as sinning, repenting, believing, apostatizing, &c. Of this, the first and finest sample is in the Old Testament, where Israel is constantly addressed, and frequently spoken of, as an individual ; and the final restoration of the descendants of Abraham is treated as the redemption of ONE body from disease, of ONE soul from perdition. The scripture *personality* of Israel is something far other, and infinitely more real, than the *personification* of Britannia ; and points at a profounder mystery than human sense can ever interpret.

Much has been said about the usefulness of history, meaning thereby the history of nations ; and hardly too much can be said, if regard be had to the community and its rulers ; for it makes the Past a factor to buy up experience for the Present ; and enables the purged eye to " look into the seeds of time." But if the consideration be private, fireside, *moral* usefulness, we think the benefits of historical reading as a necessary department of education, or a profitable employment of leisure hours, have been very much exaggerated. It may, indeed, do no harm, for the same reason that it does no good, viz. because it takes no hold ; it glides away like globules of crude quicksilver over a smooth surface, or at most is deposited in the shew-room of the memory :—because no conclusions, applicable to common life, can be drawn from it ; because it excites no sense of reality. It is gone through as a task,—by children on compulsion, by *young people* as a merit. The most remarkable thing about your history-reading young ladies, is the self-satisfaction with which they turn over the pages ; and in truth, they might be doing much worse, but might they not also be doing much better ? To make this sort of reading available for any purpose, requires very deep and wide research, and harder thinking than we would gladly see young brows furrowed withal ; for not one man in a thousand, not one woman in a million, is called on to make any use of their politic wisdom when they have got it, and nothing is more likely to delude and puzzle simple persons in the exercise of their political rights, than a superficial acquaintance with the heads of history. But this same politic wisdom itself, even when genuine, and not a puffed conceit, is one of the most unwholesome fruits of the tree of knowledge, and if the mind be not fortified with good and sufficient antidotes, is a moral poison. Why is the "murderous Machiavél" a bye word of abhorrence ? Whence is it, that while the bloody deeds of conquerors shine fair in story and in song, as the wounds of the Faithful in Moslem Paradise, the master-strokes of the subtle politicians, of the Richelieus and Bedomars, only appear as letters of sulphurous flame, writing their own condemnation ? Because the heart of man gives honour to bravery, which is nature's gift, but has no respect for the wisdom which grows of experience in evil ways. Now the study of history in books can give only the same kind of knowledge, and the same habits of mind, as men long versed in public affairs gain by actual experience ; the impression will, indeed, be much fainter, the effect for good or ill much less potent, but it is the same as far as it goes. It is like the knowledge of the world acquired by keeping bad company. Now the study of Biography has at least this advantage, that it enables the student to select his companions. If he chooses Colonel Jack, or Moll Flanders, it is his own fault. But history not only continually exhibits the doings of bad men, but it exhibits only the bad, or at any rate the worse, acts of good ones: for most men are better in their private than in their public relations.

Frail and corrupt as human nature is, it is by no means so hateful, so utterly forsaken of Heaven, as the transactions of kingdoms and republics (there is little difference between the two) would incline us to think. The best part, even of the most conspicuous characters, is that which makes the least shew and the least noise. And after all, the history of nations is only the history of a small portion of the life of a very few men.

We cannot be supposed to censure the study of history : we only wish it to be properly balanced by studies which tend to keep the eye of man upon his own heart, upon the sphere of his immediate duties, of those duties, where his affections are to be exercised and regulated, and which, considering man as a person, consider him as sentient, intelligent, moral, and immortal. For simply to think of a man as a sentient being, is inconsistent with that hard-hearted policy which would employ him, reckless of his suffering or enjoyment, like a wedge or a rivet, to build up the idol temple of a false national greatness; to regard him as intelligent, or rather as capable of intelligence, condemns the system that would keep him in ignorance to serve the purposes of his rulers, as game cocks are penned up in the dark that they may fight the better; to regard him as moral, corrects the primary conception of national prosperity; and to revere him as immortal, commands peremptorily that he shall never be made a tool or instrument to any end in which his own permanent welfare is not included.

It is in all these capacities that the biographer considers his subjects. He speaks of actions, not as mere links in the concatenation of events, but as the issues of a responsible will. He endeavours to place himself at the exact point, in relation to general objects, in which his subject was placed, and to see things as *he* saw them—not, indeed, neglecting to avail himself of the vantage ground which time or circumstances may have given him to correct what was delusive in the partial aspect, but never forgetting, while he exposes the error, to explain its cause.

The work to which these remarks are prefixed is purely biographical.

It professes no more than to introduce the reader to an acquaintance with the several *Worthies* that may drop in upon him during the course of publication.   As it will comprise characters in every profession, of all parties, and many religious denominations, the author cannot in all cases undertake to decide upon the professional merits of those whose lives he has endeavoured to depict ; or to criticise purely professional works, such as relate to physic, engineering, &c. ; but will faithfully detail the judgments which have obtained public credit.   As to matters of opinion, whether political or religious, his rule has been, to make each speak for himself in his own words, or by his own actions, taking care, as far as possible, to represent the opinions that men or sects have actually held, in the light in which they have been held by their pro_ fessors—not in the distorted perspective of their adversaries.   He enters into no engagement to withhold his own .sentiments ; but he will not judge, much less condemn, the sentiments of others.

A work of this nature necessarily borrows much, but wherever original matter was attainable, it has been gladly used, and in the pro_ per place, thankfully acknowledged.   And so far we have discharged our duty as chairman to the combined meeting of the great Counties of Yorkshire and Lancashire.   H. C.

THE LIFE

OF

ANDREW MARVELL.

" Justum et tenacem propositi virum."

HORACE.

" A man in justice grounded, and secure
  In strong allegiance to a purpose pure."

ANDREW MARVELL.

OF Andrew Marvell, a patriot of the old Roman build, and a Poet of no vulgar strain, it is to be regretted that our notices are less ample and continuous than his personal merit deserves, or his exalted walk of public action would induce us to expect. His name, indeed, is generally known—a few anecdotes of his honesty are daily repeated—and a single copy of verses, no adequate sample of his poetic powers, keeping its station in the vestibule of Paradise Lost, records him as the friend and admirer of Milton. But the detail of his daily life—the simple background of the stirring picture—the intermediate transactions which should make up the unity and totality of his story — might indeed be easily supplied by imagination, but cannot be derived from document or tradition.

The mind of Marvell, like the street and the wall of Jerusalem, was built in troublous times. From his youth upwards, he was inured to peril and privation ; and, though he does not appear to have been personally engaged in civil conflict, he could not escape the tyrannous trials of those ' evil days '—reproach and wicked solicitation, and sundering of dearest ties, by violent death, and exile, and crueller estrangement. Yet if his heart was often wounded, it was never hardened. He ever retained and cherished his love of the gentle, the beautiful, and the imaginative. His virtue, firm and uncompromising, was never savage ; nor did his full reliance on his own principles make him blind to perceive, or slow to acknowledge, whatever goodness appeared in men of other faith and allegiance. He was a wit and poet, and as these qualities made him no worse a patriot or christian, so they probably made him a more amiable man.

The father of Marvell, who bore both his names, was a native of Cambridge, and M. A. of Emanuel College, a recent foundation, which was strongly embued with puritanism. Having taken orders, he was elected master of the Grammar School at Hull, and in 1624 became lecturer of Trinity Church, in that town, where his son Andrew was born, Nov. 15, 1620. The elder Marvell was a learned and pious man, who seemed to retain the principles of his college, and possessed a portion of that shrewd humour for which his son was so conspicuous; for Echard, in his history, calls him "the facetious Calvinistical minister of Hull." As Calvinism was then identified with the popular cause, he doubtless instilled into young Andrew's mind the early love of that liberty, to the support of which he devoted his life and talents. Of Andrew's school days little is recorded: at fifteen, an age which would now be esteemed at least two years too soon, he was admitted of Trinity College, Cambridge. His academical progress was proportionate to the growing powers and native energy of his mind. But error, which youth can never wholly escape, peculiarly besets the nonage of an active intellect. And none are more obnoxious to the attacks of the wicked spirits "that lie like truth," than the young and ardent, to whom Truth is a passion, and a Deity. The Jesuits, the subtlest spawn of the subtle serpent, who were then compassing sea and land to make one proselyte, and like all proselytists, religious and political, directed their machinations especially against boys and women, had stolen into the Universities. Young Marvell was a tempting prize; and their plausible equivocations so far prevailed over his inexperience, as to seduce him to London. It was one of the devices of Jesuitism, which held all means indifferent or laudable whereby the power of their church was to be sustained and enlarged, to pretend a zeal for civil liberty, to speak lightly of the *jus divinum,* and to justify resistance. Probably by these means they ingratiated themselves with Marvell, who, in his innocence, might not perceive, that not popular freedom, but the despot_ism of an order was to be substituted for regal prerogative. Moreover, the Catholics, and the Catholic priesthood in particular, were at that time the objects of mob fury and legal pillage; sometimes timidly protected, and sometimes nearly given up by the Court. It is not the least evil of intolerance, that it often sets the martyr's crown on the brow of the bigot and the traitor. But all the Jesuits' craft could not sophisticate the filial piety of young Marvell; though their principles on that head were as lax as those of the Pharisees. He was, therefore, quickly subdued by the remonstrances of his excellent father, who pursued him to the metropolis, and restored him to sanity and his studies.

On the 13th of December, 1638, as appears by his own hand_writing, he was again received at Trinity College, and seems to have steadily applied himself to the pursuit of learning till 1640, when the loss of his revered parent again interrupted his academical course. The circum_stances of the elder Marvell's death are somewhat variously related; but by all accounts he fell a sacrifice to his honour, and sense of duty. The less extraordinary tradition is as follows:—On the banks of the

Humber, opposite Kingston, lived a lady, the only daughter, and main earthly stay of her mother, whose excellent qualities of heart and mind recommended her to the good pastor's especial regard. To perpetuate the friendship of the families, he requested her to become god-mother to one of his children, a relation then supposed to impose great and lasting duties. Her mother, who could scarcely live but in the company of her child, reluctantly consented. The lady came to Hull accordingly, the ceremony was performed, and she became impatient to return to her parent. Coming to the water side, she found the river so rough, and the weather so unpromising, that the watermen earnestly dissuaded her from attempting the passage. But no peril nor persuasion could prevail on her to violate the promise she had made to her mother. The worthy minister, honouring her virtuous resolution, though anticipating a fatal result, resolved to share the danger of which he had been the unwitting cause,—took charge of the duteous female, embarked along with her, and with her perished in the waters.

The other relation is so little in accordance with modern theories, that some apology may be deemed necessary for introducing it into our memoir. But wonderful tales, if not absolutely true, nevertheless are important documents, if they ever were generally believed; for they contribute to the history of opinion. Besides, "there are more things between heaven and earth than are dreamed of in our philosophy."

According to this account, Mr. Marvell's apprehension arose, not from the warning of watermen, nor from the threatenings of the sky, but from that prophetic presentiment, that second sight of dissolution, which, like the shadow on the dial, points darkly at the hour of departure. The morning was clear, the breeze fair, and the company gay; when, stepping into the boat, the reverend man exclaimed—"Ho for Heaven!" so saying, he threw his staff ashore, and left it to Providence to fulfil its awful warning. Of course we ask nobody to believe this unless he chooses, but we should as readily believe it, upon sufficient evidence, as any event in history. So many are the similar cases on record, that he who would reject them all, must be a person of indefatigable incredulity. The prophetic warnings have occurred to young and old, kings and rustics, saints and sinners; to Bentley, the orthodox; to Oliver Cromwell, the fanatic; to Littleton, the rake; to Nelson, the hero; and to Alexander Stephens, the buffoon.

Thus was young Marvell bereft of his natural guardian in his twentieth year, and left to find his way in the troubled world, to decide between warring opinions, and choose amid conflicting parties, unassisted by that voice of authority to which he would have paid most willing deference.* The aged lady, with whose daughter the venerable man had dared to die, sent for his son from Cambridge, acted towards him as a mother, and at her decease bequeathed him her whole property.

The transactions which immediately succeeded this event, are not on record ; but it would seem that Marvell, to whose ardent and liberal mind neither college discipline nor collegiate opinions were likely to be agreeable, became negligent of academic exercises when no longer restrained by parental care ; and, in 1641, he, with four other youths, among whom was Maye, the parliamentary historian and translator and continuator of Lucan, were conditionally dismissed from Trinity College.† Marvell probably never made the required submission, or returned to Cambridge, for soon after we find him on his travels in Italy.

That he was at Rome, appears from his poem, called " Flecnoe an English Priest," which is supposed to have suggested to Dryden his famous satire of Mc Flecnoe, wherein he avenged himself on his old enemy Shadwell, whose politics had gained the Laureateship of which Dryden was deprived at the revolution. Shadwell was fair game ; but Flecnoe seems to have been innocuously dull.‡ At Rome, it is sup-

---

* Marvell thus speaks of his father, in ' The Rehearsal Transprosed : '—" He died before the war broke out, having lived with some reputation both for piety and learning ; and was, moreover, a conformist to the rites and ceremonies of the Church of England, though I confess none of the most over-running or eager in them."

† In the Conclusion-Book of Trinity College, September 24th, 1641, appears the following entry :—" It is agreed by the Masters and Seniors, that Mr. Carter, Dominus Wakefield, Dominus Marvell, Dominus Waterhouse, and Dominus Maye, in regard that some of them are reported to be married, and the others look not after their dayes nor acts, shall receive no more benefit of the college, and shall be out of their places, unless they show just cause to the college for the contrary, in three months."—N.B. A jack tar would probably call the Conclusion-Book the college Log.

‡ The Courtly Laurel has never, in public opinion, recovered from the contamination of Shadwell's brows. Tom was the father of a dynasty of Laureate Dunces, among whom it is grievous to think that such names as Warton and Southey should be numbered ; to wit, Tate, Rowe, Eusden, Cibber, Whitehead and Pie,—

   What though the Courtly Laurel now
   Adorn a true poetic brow,—
   Immortal Bard, as well might'st thou
   Write verses to a huge Dutch Frau,
      As big as all three Graces,
   As well, nay better far by half,
   Make hymns to Jeroboam's calf,
   Or write in sand an epitaph,
   O'er the drown'd world of Mynheer Pfaff,

posed, Marvell first saw Milton, then a young and enamoured roamer in classic lands, who was soon to make " all Europe ring from side to side," already a poet, not of promise merely, but of high atchievement, in the flower of manly beauty, in the vernal warmth of high and generous daring ; not even in the proudest days of her Republic, had Rome to boast two nobler youths than Milton and Marvell. No doubt they sympathised in passionate indignation to see priestcraft throned on the seven hills. D'Israeli has written a book upon the " Quarrels of Authors," why does not he, or somebody else, write one about the " Friendships of Authors ?" Why is it, that the little good that has been on earth has never found an historian ? Whether Marvell ever went the full length of Milton's opinions in Church and State, is not very evident; probably not, for he seems to have been a much more cautious man, and was too young to take any decided part in the civil contest, which by suspending the regal power, made its resumption the

> As waste thy precious Autograph
> Upon the mighty men of chaff
> In lyric periphrases.
>
> TOM BROWN THE THIRD.

Mynheer Pfaff is a famous geologist, and a Neptunian.

Shadwell, though accused by Dryden of "never deviating into sense," was a dramatist of some talent, not wholly valueless, for his plays record the state of manners among certain classes with vivid fidelity, if indeed the records of vice are worth preserving at all. He was the first Englishman who introduced Don Juan upon the stage, and his Tragedy of the Libertine is very good in its own bad kind. His Comedies are resolutely and offensively coarse, and scarcely deserve the trouble of purgation.

As for Flecnoe, it appears that he was not an *English* priest, but a native of the Emerald Isle. Hence Pope :—

> " High on a gorgeous seat that far outshone
> Henley's Gilt-tub—or Flecnoe's Irish throne."
>
> DUNCIAD, BOOK 2d.

Flecnoe having laid aside, (as himself expressed it,) " the mechanic part of priesthood, wrote only to avoid idleness, and published to avoid the imputation of it." Mr. Southey, whose laudable zeal for obscure merit extends both to the dead and to the living, and who seems to entertain a compassion, almost melting into love, for innocent dulness, has dedicated some pages of his *Omniana,* (a miscellany of wonderful learning, and delightful vivacity,) to the vindication of this poor author, and gives some extracts from his poems, which we are afraid, will not plead potently against Mc Flecnoe. Southey ascribes Dryden's antipathy to Flecnoe's just invectives against the obscenity of the stage, for which wickedness Dryden was, if not more infamous, more notorious, than his dull contemporaries. But it is just as likely, that Flecnoe's name, itself a rememberable sound, and apt for composition, had by the attacks of a series of satirists, become, like that of Bavius, of Quarles, of Sternhold, and of Blackmore, a synonyme for extravagant flatness. It is hard for a man to have his name thus memorized, when every thing else about him is forgotten.

more formidable.   In this respect Andrew was a fortunate man, for he partakes fully in the fame of his illustrious friend, as a defender and promoter of true liberty, while he escaped all participation in the more questionable parts of his career.   As tour-writing was not quite so indispensable in the seventeenth century as at present, our account of Marvell's travels is necessarily scanty, the few incidental notices that may occur in his miscellaneous works not being sufficient to compose a regular narrative.   He returned, however, between 1642 and 1643, and while at Paris, on his way homeward, he found occasion to exercise his satirical vein in a Latin Poem upon Lancelot Joseph de Maniban, a whimsical Abbè, who, by a new sort of Cheiromancy, pretended to forbode the fortunes of individuals, not by the lines of the hands, but by those of their hand writing.*

Little information can be obtained of Marvell's proceedings from his return to England, till the year 1652, one of the most important intervals in human history.   How he thought and felt during this period we may easily conjecture, but we are at a loss to find out what he was doing.   It is probable that he acted no conspicuous part, either civil or military, as he is not mentioned in the parliamentary papers, or other public documents, nor does he appear to have employed his pen on either

* The race of the Manibans is not extinct; and, indeed, however absurd it may be to form a *prognosis* of future contingencies from the curves and angles of a MS., we will and do maintain, that a correct *diagnosis* of the actual character of an individual may be drawn from his autograph.   The goodness or badness of the writing contributes nothing to its physiognomy, any more than the beauty or homeliness of a countenance influences its expression.   Expression has nothing to do with beauty; and those who say that a good expression will make the plainest face beautiful, do not say what they mean.   Goodness, shining through ordinary features, is not beautiful, but far better,—it is lovely.   So, too, with regard to the expression of writing; Caligraphy, as taught by writing masters to young ladies, is in truth a very lady-like sort of dissimulation, intended, like the Chesterfieldian politeness of a courtier, to conceal the workings of thought and feeling—to substitute the cold, slippery, polished opacity of a frozen pool, for the ripple and transparency of a flowing brook.   But into every habitual act, which is performed unconsciously, earnestly, or naturally, something of the mood of the moment, and something of the predominant habit of the mind, unavoidably passes:—the play of the features, the motions of the limbs, the paces, the tones, the very folds of the drapery (especially if it have long been worn), are all significant.   A mild, considerate man hangs up his hat in a very different style from a hasty, resolute one.   A Dissenter does not shake hands like a High Churchman.   But there is no act into which the character enters more fully, than that of writing; for it is generally performed alone or unobserved, seldom, in adults, is the object of conscious attention, and takes place while the thoughts, and the natural current of feeling, are in full operation.   D'Israeli, in his " *Curiosities of Literature,*" second series, has two interesting chapters on autographs, writing-masters, and hand-writing.

side. Some incidental notices we may glean from a letter of Milton to the President Bradshaw, that chief of the regicide Judges, who shared with Cromwell, Blake, and Ireton, the honour of being hanged after his death. It is inscribed to the *Honourable* the Lord Bradshaw. No apology can be required for inserting it entire.

" MY LORD,

" But that it would be an interruption to the public, wherein your studies are perpetually employed, I should now or then venture to supply this my enforced absence with a line or two, though it were onely my business, and that would be noe slight one, to make my due acknowledgments of your many favours ; which I both doe at this time, and ever shall ; and have this farder, which I thought my parte to let you know of, that there will be with you to-morrow, upon some occasion of business, a gentleman whose name is Mr. Marvile ; a man whom, both by report, and the converse I have had with him, of singular desert for the state to make use of ; who alsoe offers himselfe, if there be any imployment for him. His father was the Minister of Hull ; and he hath spent four years abroad, in Holland, France, Italy, and Spaine, to very good purpose, as I believe, and the gaineing of those four languages ; besides, he is a scholler, and well read in the Latin and Greek authors ; and no doubt of an approved conversation, for he comes now lately out of the house of the Lord Fairfax, who was Generall, where he was intrusted to give some instructions in the languages to the Lady his daughter. If, upon the death of Mr. Weckkerlyn, the Councell shall think that I shall need any assistance in the performance of my place (though for my part I find no encumbrances of that which belongs to me, except it be in point of attendance at Conferences with Ambassadors, which I must confess, in my condition, I am not fit for,) it would be hard for them to find a man soe fit every way for that purpose as this Gentleman, one who I believe, in a short time, would be able to doe them as much service as Mr. Ascan. This, my Lord, I write sincerely, without any other end than to perform my dutey to the publick, in helping them to an humble servant ; laying aside those jealousies, and that emulation, which mine own condition might suggest to me, by bringing in such a coadjutor ; and remaine,

My Lord,

Your most obliged, and
faithfull Servant,

Feb. 21, 1652. JOHN MILTON."

The silence of this letter as to any diplomatic experience of Marvell sufficiently refutes the statement of certain biographers, that he was employed by the Commonwealth as Envoy to Constantinople. A diligent examination of the epistolary correspondence and private diaries of that eventful period would probably throw some further light on our subject's proceedings. Milton's recommendation to Bradshaw did not gain an appointment for his friend. As the times turned, it is probable that the patronage of the Lord President would rather have been injurious than beneficial to his prospects, for Bradshaw was opposed to Cromwell, by whom he was deprived of the Chief-justiceship of Chester. In 1654, when Milton's famous second defence of the People of England in reply to Salmasius appeared, Marvell was commissioned to present the book to the Protector. How he was received may be conjectured from his letter to Milton on that occasion, which we give entire :—

" HONOURED SIR,

I did not satisfy myself in the account I gave you of presenting your book to my Lord ; although it seemed to me that I wrote to you all which the messenger's speedy return the same night would permit me : and I perceive that, by reason of that haste, I did not give you satisfaction, neither concerning the delivery of your letter at the same time. Be pleased, therefore, to pardon me, and know that I tendered them both together. But my Lord read not the letter while I was with him ; which I attributed to our dispatch, and some other business tending thereto, which I therefore wished ill to, so far as it hindered an affair much better, and of greater importance,—I mean that of reading your letter. And to tell you truly mine own imagination, I thought that he would not open it while I was there, because he might suspect that I, delivering it just upon my departure, might have brought in it some second proposition, like to that which you had before made to him, by your letter, to my advantage. However, I assure myself that he has since read it with much satisfaction.

Mr. Oxenbridge, on his return from London, will, I know, give you thanks for his book, as I do, with all acknowledgment and humility, for that you have sent me. I shall now study it, even to getting it by heart. When I consider how equally it turns and rises, with so many figures, it seems to me a Trajan's column, in whose winding ascent we see embossed the several monuments of your learned victories ; and Salmasius and Morus make up as great a triumph as that of Decebalus ; whom, too, for ought I know, you shall have forced, as Trajan the other, to make themselves away, out of a just desperation.

I have an affectionate curiosity to know what becomes of Colonel

Overton's* business, and am exceeding glad to think that Mr. Skinner has got near you : the happiness which I at the same time congratulate to him, and envy, there being none who doth, if I may so say, more jealously honour you than,

Honoured Sir,

Your most affectionate humble Servant,

Eton, *June* 2, 1654.　　　　　　　　　ANDREW MARVELL.

For my most honoured friend, John Milton, Esq.,

Secretary for Foreign Affairs,

At his house in Petty France, Westminster."

Grace and ease in letter writing is one of the last accomplishments at which literature arrives. Marvell's letters, from which we shall make copious extracts, are not cited as examples of composition, in which respect they are hardly worthy of his talents, but for the historical intelligence they convey, and the testimony which they bear to the writer's integrity. Seldom, however, was he guilty of such bad taste, as in the allusion to Trajan's Column, and never again uttered so uncharitable a surmise as that with regard to Morus and Salmasius. It is some consolation that neither of those grammarians followed the example of the Dacian Monarch, though Milton himself is said to have ascribed the death of Salmasius to chagrin at his defeat. Even good men seldom enter a controversy without making wreck of their peace of mind.

In 1657 Marvell became tutor to Cromwell's nephew. There is extant a letter of his to the Protector, rather more respectful than would please either a royalist or a determined republican. What part he took in the confused passages that ensued on Cromwell's death, we are not informed. He was elected member for his native town in 1660— in that parliament which was destined to see the restoration of royalty. Though it is probable that he corresponded regularly with his constituents from his first election, whatever he may have written previous to the triumphal 29th of May, or in the busy æra of intoxication which followed, has never been discovered. We cannot tell how far he approved the recal of Majesty, which he must have seen it vain to oppose, or whether he laboured to obtain those securities against the encroachments of prerogative which the treacherous counsels of Monk induced the Convention to forego,—what he felt on the violent revulsion of public feeling whereby Charles the Second was enabled to establish a sway which nothing but his own indolence hindered from being despotic,—or how he judged of the vindictive proceedings of the reinstated royalists, which had well

* Overton was Governor of Hull, and became a fifth-monarchy-man.

nigh bereft the world of Milton, and of Paradise Lost. He might not choose to trust his sentiments on such subjects to paper, or he might sedulously reclaim and destroy writings which endangered others as well as himself. It may be necessary to remind the reader, that it was only by the communications of Members, that provincial constituents could then be made acquainted with what passed in Parliament. The publication of debates was at that time, and long after, really and strictly forbidden. Even in Dr. Johnson's day, the standing order was evaded by reports under feigned names or initials. The Doctor himself published (if he did not compose) ' Debates in the Senate of Lilliput.' Has the publication of debates ever yet been legalised by exprsss enactment? We fear not.

Middleton composed his life of Cicero, Jortin, his life of Erasmus, almost entirely from the epistles of their respective subjects. We shall make as free a use, though we cannot construct so regular a narrative, of the parliamentary epistles of Andrew Marvell. The earliest of these is dated November, 1660, in which he laments the absence of his *partner*, Mr. John Ramsden, and tells them he " writes but with half a pen, which makes his account of public affairs so imperfect ; and yet he had rather expose his own defects to their good interpretation, than excuse thereby a total neglect of his duty."

Two of the most difficult questions that occupied the government immediately after the restoration, were, how to dispose of the standing army, which, during the suspension of the monarchy, had become a deliberative and most influential member of the body politic ; and whether to continue or abrogate the excise, a financial offspring of the Long Parliament, which the restored monarch was not unwilling to adopt.

Confiding in the unorganised valour of the English nation, and in the capacity of discipline which exists in every people, he once and for ever opposed a standing army, a species of force, which, had Charles the First possessed, he might have been as despotic as he would ; which Cromwell possessing, kept the realm at nurse for a Prince who, with equal means, could have done more than the worst of his legiti- mate or illegitimate predecessors. The purpose of the Puritans was, to turn the whole blessed island into a Presbyterian Paradise, in which there was to be nothing but churches, and church-yards ;—one to be filled with the living bodies of the saints, and the other with the hanged carcases of their adversaries. The apostate royalists of the Restora- tion would have made England a bear garden, in which all vices were free, and from which nothing but piety was exiled. Marvell had seen a standing army, composed of more respectable materials than could easily be replaced, the instrument of one tyranny ; and most wisely he opposed its continuance, when the same mass, compacted of baser atoms, might perpetuate a tyranny far worse than that which it succeeded. He conceived an army to be a giant body without a directing soul,—a house to let, in which the long-houseless dæmon of despotism might live at a nominal rent.—But hear what Marvell said, nigh 200 years ago :—" I doubt not, ere we rise, to see the whole army disbanded ; and, according to the act, hope to see your town once more ungarrisoned, in which I should be glad and happy to be instrumental to the uttermost ; for I cannot but remember, though then a child, those blessed days, when the youth of our own town were trained for your militia, and did, methought, become their arms much better than any soldiers that I have seen since." Of the excise, he observed prophetically, " He wished it might not be continued too long."*

We cannot but lament that Marvell's correspondence with his constituents, as far as can now be discovered, only commences in November, 1660. He appears to have been first chosen in the short Parliament of 1658—9, summoned after the death of Oliver, during the brief Protectorate of Richard Cromwell, and soon after dissolved to make way for the restoration of the Rump. But it is not certain whether Marvell ever sat in this assembly. The Convention, or *Healing Parliament* met on the 25th of April, 1660, and Marvell paid an early

* The Excise was originally an invention of the Long Parliament, and began in 1673. The Royalist Parliament at Oxford made a similar grant in the King's behalf. Dr. Johnson, in his abhorrence of the Republicans, forgot that Excise, notwithstanding its puritanic origin, had become an adopted and favourite child of Church and King, for he defined it in his Dictionary, " An *odious* tax, levied, not by the officers of Government, but by wretches, &c.;" for which anachronism there were serious thoughts of prosecuting the ultra-royalist lexicographer. A *Fiscal* History of England, or rather of modern Europe, not overloaded with matter purely antiquarian, nor perplexed with speculations of political economy, is a great desideratum, the supplying of which might well engage the attention of the " Society for the Diffusion of Useful Knowledge."

The same letter, the first in the remaining series of Andrew's Public Correspondences, conveys a compliment to the ladies of Hull well worth transcribing, because it shews, first, how much the bonds of domestic duty are relaxed by civil anarchy; and secondly, how necessary the most incorruptible representatives have found it to secure the good graces of their female constituents, who, though not even the advocates of universal suffrage have offered them votes, do for the most part virtually decide the elections. " There is yet brought in an act, in which, of all others,, *your Corporation is the least concerned*; that is, where wives shall refuse to cohabit with their husbands, that in such case the husband shall not be obliged to pay any debts she shall run into, for cloathing, diet, lodgings, or other expenses."

It is highly probable that separations of the nature alluded to frequently arose from religious and political dissentions between husband and wife. The revolt of Milton's first consort is a well-known but not a solitary instance.

attendance ; but what he thought of the Restoration, or how the good townsmen of Hull (the first town which shut its gates against the sovereign, 1642, and which Governor Overton had but a little before refused to surrender till King Jesus should come to claim it) were affected by the revival of royalty, his letters do not inform us. Perhaps it was not thought prudent that any record of his sentiments on that occasion should survive. We may be certain that he never contemplated a fruitless opposition to a measure which was the will of the people, and the necessity of the state ; but surely he would, with the smallest chance of success, have demanded from the royal party such securities as civil and religious liberty required.

The most remarkable feature in his parliamentary dispatches is, that he scarcely ever speaks of himself. He says little or nothing of his own aid or opposition to any particular measure, though it is not difficult to perceive the drift of his opinions. To his private affairs he scarcely alludes, unless it be to thank the corporation for some present or enquiry. He, indeed, manifestly writes under some degree of restraint, knowing that the sanctity of a seal is not always respected by a jealous government in perilous times. The first letters, from November 20th to December 29th, refer chiefly to the settlement of the revenue ; the excise, half of which was given to the King for life, and the other half granted *in perpetuum* to the Crown ; the abolition of the Court of Wards ; the £70,000 per month for the disbanding of the army ; the tonnage and poundage ; the £100,000 to be raised upon lands in the several counties, (the apportioning of which gave rise, as might be expected, to much and angry discussion), which £100,000 was afterwards levied upon the excise of ale and beer ; and the £1,200,000 to be settled upon his Majesty. The Act of Indemnity, and the trial of the regicides, transpired before the commencement of the correspondence, and Marvell makes no allusion to either.* Perhaps he could not have done so without committing both himself and his correspondents. Of ecclesiastical matters he says but little, though he speaks with approbation " of that very good Bill for erecting and augmenting vicarages out of all impropriations belonging to Archbishops, Bishops, Deans and Chapters, or any other ecclesiastical person or corporation, to £80 per annum, where the impropriation amounts to £120, and where less, to one moiety of the profits of such impropriations." He

---

* In his sixth letter, (Dec. 20th, 1660,) he just mentions the " Bill of attainder, against those that had been executed, those that are fled, and of Cromwell, Bradshaw, Ireton, and Pride," but makes no remark, on the pitiful attempt to wreck vengeance on the carcases of the latter, by dragging them on a hurdle to Tyburn, hanging them awhile in their coffins, and burying them under the gallows.

casually mentions, once or twice, the King's Declaration in religious matters, which it was proposed to pass into a law ; but the bill to that effect was lost by 183 against 157. This declaration was intended to satisfy the Presbyterians ; and would, in fact, had it been carried into effect, have grafted the Presbyterian system on Episcopacy, and reduced the Hierarchal power to little more than an honourable presidency.*

On the rejection of this measure, Marvell observes, " so there's an end of that bill ; and for those *excellent things* therein, we must henceforth rely only on his Majesty's goodness, who, I must needs say, hath been more ready to give, than we to receive." In all his earlier letters he speaks respectfully and favourably of Charles and the Royal Family, and seems to have entertained hopes of a just and equal government, a true and comprehensive amnesty of all past offences between Prince and subject, between all sects and parties, between each man and his neighbour.

In speaking of the measures then on foot for establishing the militia, he advises rather to "trust to his Majesty's goodness," than to " confirm a perpetual and exorbitant power by law." This sentiment not only shews that the patriot was not then ill-affected towards the restored line, but proves him to have been a truly wise and liberal statesman ; unlike too many champions of liberty, who, in their dread of prerogative, have unwarily strengthened the tyranny of law, a thing without bowels or conscience, and overlooks the chronic diseases of custom, which slowly but surely reduce the body politic to a condition of impotence and dotage.

Andrew was never so much absorbed by politics as to forget *business*. He paid sedulous attention to the interests of his borough, and of each of his constituents, and watched narrowly the progress of private bills.

We cannot participate the surprise of some of Marvell's biographers at the tokens of respect which he and his partner received from the

* " In this declaration the King promised that he would provide suffragan Bishops in all the large dioceses; that the prelates should all of them *be regular and constant preachers*; that they should not confer ordinations, or exercise any jurisdiction, without the advice of Presbyters, chosen by the diocese; that such alterations should be made in the Liturgy as should render it totally unexceptionable; that, in the mean time, the use of that mode should not be imposed on such as were unwilling to receive it; and that the surplice, the cross in baptism, and the bowing at the name of Jesus, should not be rigidly insisted on."---*Hume.*

It is easy to conjecture what Andrew Marvell considered as the *excellent things* in this declaration. The constant preaching of the Bishops he would freely have left to their Lordships' own discretion : to crossings or bowings he had neither attachment nor antipathy. The *Bulimia* for sermons which afflicted the Puritans was one of the most distressing maladies that ever appeared in Christendom.

worthy corporation of Hull, or suppose that more modern senators would sneer at a cask of ale. Did not Joseph Hume graciously receive a butt of cider? And did not the Orthodox of Cheshire express their admiration of the late Duke of York's Anti-Catholic declaration by presenting him with a mighty cheese? In acknowledging a donation of British beverage, Andrew writes thus (Letter 7th, Dec. 8th):— " We are now both met together, and shall strive to do you the best service we are able. We must first give you thanks for the kind present you have pleased to send us, which will give us occasion to remember you often; but the quantity is so great, that it might make sober men forgetful."

On the 29th of December the King in person dissolved the Parliament with a most gracious speech. All hitherto had gone smooth. The King signified, at parting, a great satisfaction in what had been done, and that it was very shortly his intention to call another Parliament. This dissolution did not interrupt Marvell's correspondence with Hull, neither did he quit London, or take any measures to secure his re-election, which doubtless he knew to be sure enough. His letters during the interval of Parliaments are chiefly taken up with *news,* among which the movements of the King and Royal Family occupy a conspicuous place. It would seem that the Mayor and Corporation of Hull did not take in a newspaper, though several had been issued during the civil war, particularly the Mercurius Aulicus, or Court journal, and the Mercurius Rusticus, the reporter of the Republicans. It was, moreover, the practice of the Puritan clergy, in their prayers, to make a recapitulation of the events of the week, under the form of thanksgiving, or remonstrance. The pulpit, in its bearings upon the people, then exerted the power which now belongs to the periodical press.

Marvell complains of the stoppage of letters, and, that even under ordinary circumstances, the several porters carried them about in their walks, and that so *much time* was lost. The admirable arrangement and dispatch, with the general sacredness of epistolatory communication, is one of the highest blessings which England for many years has enjoyed. It is true that the commerce of the heart is still subject to heavy duties, which we would gladly see diminished, as they might be with advantage to the revenue. Thousands of letters are unwritten from regard to the expense of postage.

In January, 1661, took place the mad insurrection of Venner and the Millenarians. To this Marvell cautiously alludes in his letter of the 12th of January, as *an insurrection of rude and desperate fellows.* It only deserves notice as the first in that series of plots, real and imaginary, Popish, Millnarian, and Republican, which made the reign of the Second Charles as sanguinary as it was licentious.

Reports were already growing rife of conspiracies in various quarters. " Still it is my ill fortune," says Marvell, " to meet with some rumour or other, (as I did yesterday at the Exchange,) of a plot against Hull, (I think indeed those have so that divulge such falsehoods,) but I am not failing to suppress any such thing where I meet with it.   *   *   * I saw, within this week, a letter from a person who dwells not in your town, but near, that your governor was turning out all the inhabitants who had been in the Parliament's service; I believe one is as true as the other." It will not be forgotten, that Hull was a depot in which the Parliament placed much confidence, and where the Presbyterian interest was strong.

The high-church party, who had indeed the plea of retaliation, both for their present suspicions and for their meditated severities, inter-preted the apocalyptic frenzy of Venner and the fifth-monarchy-men, as a sample of Presbyterian loyalty; although in the millenial reign of the saints, there were to be no more Presbyters than Bishops. But any pretext will serve a court to break its word if it be so inclined. It would seem that the good people of Hull, were anxious to retain their old ministers, or at least to have the choice of their new ones. Marvell, their honest counsellor, presses upon them the necessity of unanimity, and the imperative duty of providing, freely and liberally, a mainte-nance for their pastors. He also admonishes them that in case of the excise being *farmed,* they should bid its fair value to Government, and not, by a niggardly offer, put it into the hands of a *foreigner,** "who" says he, " *will not stick to outbid you, so he may thereby be forced to oppress you.*" He takes care to sprinkle his letters with loyalty; whe-ther *sincerely,* or *prudently,* it matters not to enquire. Thus, Jan. 3, 1660-61, " The last of December here was an ugly false report got abroad, that his Majesty was stabbed, which made the guard be up in arms all night. I doubt not the same extraordinary hand that hath hitherto guided him, will still be his protection against all attempts of discontented persons or parties." Jan. 12, "The Queen having embarked, and at sea, was forced to put back, by the Princess Henrietta* falling

---

* Foreigner.—By Marvell spelt Forainer. We do not remember to have met in any more recent author, the word Foreigner used thus merely for one who is not a townsman. We do not think it necessary, in our extracts, to preserve Andrew's orthography, which, like every body's in that age, was extremely irregular; the same word is frequently spelt in different letters on the same page.

* From this Princess Henrietta, married to the Duke of Orleans, is descended the present King of Sardinia, whose contingent relationship to the British crown has been

sick; so the Queen is landed again, and the Princess on shipboard in
the port at Portsmouth, the meazles being thick upon her, and too
dangerous to carry her ashore at present; but we hear that, God be
praised, there is all good hopes of her recovery. *I beseech God to stay
his hand from further severity in that Royal Family wherein the
nation's being and welfare is so much concerned."*

Marvell does not seem to have sympathized with the anti-monarchial
prejudices of Milton. He is said to have written a most pathetic letter
on the execution of King Charles. Could it by no means be recovered?
Certainly he expressed not pity merely, but admiration for that Prince,
and that too in an ode addressed to Oliver Cromwell, but so worded,
that it may pass either for a satire or an eulogy on the Protector. We
shall give some extracts when we come to speak of Marvell as a poet.

The new Parliament met on the 8th of May, 1661. Marvell was
re-elected seemingly without opposition; but instead of Mr. John
Ramsden, (who was probably related to William Ramsden, the mayor
of Hull, to whom the earlier letters are addressed,) his partner was
Colonel Gilby, who seems to have started on the court interest. Some
unrecorded heart-burnings took place between the associates at the election, which ended in an open rupture, which did not, however, prevent
Marvell from co-operating with the Colonel, when the good of their constituents required. April 6th,* (Letter 14th,) he thus acknowledges
his election, which had passed without his appearing or haranguing
from the hustings:—" I perceive you have again" (as if it were a thing
of course) " made choice of me, now the *third* time, to serve you in Parliament; which as I cannot attribute to any thing but your constancy,
so God willing, as in gratitude obliged, with no less constancy and
vigour, I shall continue to execute your commands, and study your service." In his next communication, (May 16th,) he speaks of the bill
for confirmation of ministers in a manner which shews him apprehensive
that the Episcopal party might go to extremes. The inhabitants of
Hull were especially desirous to obtain the patronage of their own

made a bugbear of by those loyal persons who hold that the removal of catholic dis-
abilities annuls the title of the present Royal Family. Certainly her daughter, the
Duchess of Savoy, took care to reserve her own right by protesting against the Act of
Settlement, in 1700.

* In the same 14th letter is a piece of intelligence worth transcribing:—" 'Tis two
days news upon the Exchange, that some French in the bay of Canada, have discovered the long-looked for North-west Passage." This letter also contains an account
of the new peerages to be created in honour of the approaching coronation.
Charles II. was crowned April 13, 1661, nearly a year after his restoration. What
was the reason of so long a delay?

churches. Their indefatigable member forewarns them of the difficulties likely to stand in their way, and of the small support he meets with in his suit. " I believe in this conjuncture I shall be left alone in attempting any thing for your patronage, notwithstanding the assistance you expected from some others, for so they signify to me, and I doubt you will hardly agree about the levying of your minister's maintenance. But in this thing, according as I write to you, you must be very reserved, and rest much upon your prudence. I would not have you suspect any misintelligence betwixt my partner and me, because we write not to you jointly, as Mr. Ramsden and I used to do, yet there is all civility betwixt us ; but it was the Colonel's sense that we should be left each to his own discretion in writing." Yet misintelligence there certainly was, which by some means or other, ripened to absolute division before the 1st of June, when Marvell wrote like a patriot and a gentleman. " The bonds of civility betwixt Colonel Gilby and myself being unhappily snapped in pieces, and in such manner that I cannot see how it is possible ever to knit them again ; the only trouble that I have is, lest by our misintelligence your business should receive any disadvantage. * * * * Truly I believe that as to your public trust, and the discharge thereof we do each of us still retain the principles upon which we first undertook it, and that though perhaps we may differ in our advice concerning the way of proceeding, yet we have the same good ends in general ; and by this unlucky falling out, we shall be provoked to a greater emulation of serving you. I must beg you to pardon me for writing singly to you, for if I wanted my right hand, yet I would scribble to you with my left, rather than neglect your business. In the mean time I beseech you pardon my weakness ; for there are some things which men ought not, others, that they cannot, patiently suffer." Noble and clear as he was, he could not escape calumny ; for in his next he requests his constituents to *believe no little stories* concerning himself, for I believe you to know by this that you have lately heard some very false tales concerning me."

The temper of the new Parliament was different, and much less moderate than that of the assembly by which the King was restored. For though some decided Royalists had found their way into the Convention, the majority, though favourable to the restoration of limited monarchy, were of the Presbyterian party, and attached to the Presbyterian pastors. Hence Charles and his Ministers thought it necessary to temporize, to try their way, to hold out hopes, that a mitigated Episcopacy, an expurgate Liturgy, and an optional compliance with Canons and Rubrics, would leave the *intruding* ministers, (as the strict Episcopalians called them,) who had complied with the Commonwealth, in possession of their benefices. Calamy and Baxter, destined to be among the brightest ornaments of Non-conformity, were even appointed King's chaplains. They, and other leading pastors, were tempted with the offer of Bishoprics ; an offer with which Sharp, in an evil hour for himself, for Scotland and for Episcopacy, complied. But Calamy and Baxter had too much pride, too much virtue, or too ill an opinion of the hand that offered, to accept the mitre. But the second Parliament adopted all the principles, and cherished the resentments, of those high-flying Prelatists, whose ill counsels had rendered the virtues of the first Charles unprofitable. The restoration of the Bishops to their seats in the House of Lords, and to their other temporalities, which considering the manner in which they had been deprived, was indeed an act of justice, had not been proposed to the convention, but was speedily carried by the Parliament of 1661.

The bill of conformity shortly followed, which by a strange coincidence, if it were not really concerted, took effect on St. Bartholomew's day, whereby 2000 ministers, unexpectedly conscientious, were ejected in one day. Were it not that the whole of Marvell's bold and consistent conduct forbids the supposition, it might be conjectured that he declined to contend against measures which he could not successfully have opposed. Between June 1661, and March 1663, there is an hiatus in his correspondence, occasioned by an absence of Andrew's that has never been satisfactorily accounted for. In his letters he speaks of his *private concernments* without specifying what those private concernments were. In the mean while there was talk of supplying his place. Lord Bellasis, the deputy governor of Hull under the Duke of Monmouth, seems to have exerted himself especially on this occasion, but without effect. Of the motives of Marvell's withdrawing we are utterly ignorant ; but we cannot help thinking that he was *glad to be away* from proceedings to which he could not have put an effectual stop, which he saw necessitated a revolution, and could not foresee that it would be a bloodless revolution.

The representations of his constituents, or the apprehension of losing his seat, brought Marvell home perhaps sooner than he intended. He seems not to have taken the interference of Lord Bellasis in good part, for immediately after his return he writes thus :—

"Westminster, April 2, 1663.

Gentlemen,
Being newly arrived in town, and full of businesse, yet I could not neglect to give you notice that this day I have been in the House, and found my place empty ; though it seems that some persons would have been so courteous, as to have filled it for me. You may be assured that

as my obligation and affection to your service hath been strong enough to draw me over, without any consideration of mine own private concernments, so I shall now maintain my station with the same vigour and alacrity in your business which I have always testify'd formerly, and which is no more than is due to that kindnesse which I have constantly experienced from you. So at present, though in much haste, saluting you all with my most hearty respects,

I remain,
Gentlemen, my very worthy friends,
Your most affectionate Friend to serve you,
ANDREW MARVELL."

In the few letters that follow this, previously to the 20th of June, there is little important matter. The hours of the House of Commons were very different then from what they are now, for in the twenty-third letter he mentions it as an unusual thing, that they had sat till six in the evening on the bill for discovery of buying and selling of places. It may be remarked, that notwithstanding the slavish and intolerant principles of that Parliament, they made a firm stand against the progress of corruption, and were by no means lavish in granting the public money. Charles the second was continually in need: his extravagance and indolence prevented him from taking advantage of their niggardly servility, that would have preferred a cheap slavery to an expensive freedom. Had Charles possessed the virtues of his father, and his father's zeal for the Established Church, England would have become the most absolute monarchy in Europe. Providence, ever at work to draw good out of evil, made Charles's mistresses the conservators of British liberty. Yet more are we indebted to the man, whoever he was, that converted James the Second to the Romish communion; for nothing but the dread of Popery would have reconciled the nobility and clergy to that resistance which the people were not yet strong enough to conduct successfully of themselves.

Marvell was not hitherto reckoned among the decided enemies of the court; for we find him appointed, in June, 1663, to accompany Lord Carlisle on an embassy to Russia, Sweden, and Denmark. He tells the Corporation of Hull, " that it is no new thing for members of our House to be dispensed with, for the service of the King and the nation, in foreign parts. And you may be sure I will not stirre without speciall leave of the House, so that you may be freed from any possibility of being importuned or tempted to make any other choice in my absence." Shortly after he thus announces his departure:—" Being this day taking barge for Gravesend, there to embark for Archangel,

so to Moscow, thence for Sweden, and last of all for Denmark, all
which I hope, by God's blessing, to finish within twelve months' time :
I do hereby, with my last and most serious thoughts, salute you, rendering you all hearty thanks for your great kindness and friendship to
me upon all occasions, and ardently beseeching God to keep you all in
his gracious protection, to your own honour, and the welfare and flourishing of your Corporation, to which I am, and shall ever continue, a most
affectionate and devoted servant.   I undertake this voyage with the
order and good liking of his Majesty, and by leave given me from the
House, and entered in the journall ; and having received, moreover,
your approbation, I go, therefore, with more ease and satisfaction of
mind, and augurate to myself the happier success in all my proceedings.
Your known prudence makes it unnecessary for me to leave my advice
or counsell with you at parting ; yet can I not forbear, out of the
superabundance of my care and affection for you, to recommend to you
a good correspondence with the garrison, so long as his Majesty shall
think fit to continue it ; unto which, and all your other concerns, as
Colonel Gilby hath been, and will be, always mainly instrumentall, and
do you all the right imaginable ; so could I wish, as I do not doubt
that you would, upon any past or future occasion, confide much in his
discretion, which he will never deny you the use of.   This I say to you
with a very good intent, and I know will be no otherwise understood
by you."

It is to be regretted that the practice of tour writing was less in
vogue in the seventeenth century than at present.   How interesting
would have been Marvell's observations on the northern courts—on the
deep politics of Sweden, then ruled by the sagacious and unprincipled
Charles the Eleventh—and the barbaric splendour of Russia, which
had hardly begun to be considered as a member of the European
system.   But no notes or letters relative to this period of his life have
been preserved.   One thing is certain ; he had but little reason to be
satisfied with what was doing in England during his absence.   Perhaps
he was not sorry to be spared the pain of witnessing ruinous and treasonable measures which he could not have opposed.   The besotted
Parliament, in treacherous compliance with the King's ill purposes,
had relinquished the Triennial Act without any security except a
powerless clause, "that Parliaments should not be interrupted more
than three years at the most."   In weak complaisance to a popular
clamour, excited by that love of plunder which the English have
inherited from the Scandinavian pirates, and aided by the King's
desire to be fingering the supplies, they had engaged in a needless and
impolitic war with Holland, a state whose friendship we ought to have

cultivated, both from our interest as a mercantile, and our duty as a
Protestant people. But the prosperity of a Republic is an abomination
in the eyes of the liberty-haters even unto this day. We are sorry
that Marvell had, by a satirical piece (published probably during the
Protectorate), contributed to influence the national prejudices of the
vulgar against the Dutch, and what is still worse, he makes the natural
disadvantages which it was the glory of that industrious race to have
surmounted, a topic of ridicule and insult :—

> " Holland, that scarce deserves the name of land,
> As but the offscouring of the British sand,
> And so much earth as was contributed
> By English pilots when they heav'd the lead,
> Or what by the ocean's slow alluvion fell,
> Of ship-wreck'd cockle and the muscle shell.
> This indigested vomit of the sea
> Fell on the Dutch by just propriety :
> Glad, then, as miners who have found the ore,
> They with mad labour fish'd the land to shore,
> And dived as desperately for each piece
> Of earth as if it had been of ambergrease,
> Collecting anxiously small loads of clay,
> Less than what building swallows bear away,
> Or than those pills which sordid beetles roll,
> Transfusing into them their dunghill soul.
> Yet still his claim the injured ocean laid,
> And oft at leap-frog o'er their steeples play'd ;
> As if on purpose it on land had come,
> To shew them what's their *mare liberum.**
> A daily deluge over them does boil ;
> The earth and water play at level coyl.
> The first oft times the burgher dispossess'd,
> And sat, not as a meat, but as a guest ;
> And oft the tritons and the sea nymphs saw,
> Whole shoals of Dutch serv'd up for cabillau.
> Nature, it seem'd, asham'd of her mistake,
> Would throw their lands away at duck and drake ;
> Therefore necessity, that first made kings,
> Something like government among them brings.
> For, as with pygmy's, who best kill the crane,
> Among the hungry he that treasures grain,
> Among the blind the one-ey'd blinkard reigns,
> So rules among the drowned he that drains,
> Not who first see the rising sun commands :
> But who could first discover the rising lands.

---

* According to the work of Grotiu so named, which was answered by Selden in his
Mare Clausum.

"Who best could know to pump an earth so leak,
Him they their Lord and Country's Father speak.
To make a bank was a great plot of state;
Invent a shov'l, to be a magistrate.
Hence some small dyke grave unperceiv'd invades
The pow'r, and grows, as twere, the king of spades."

*   *   *   *   *   *

'Tis probable Religion, after this,
Came next in order, which they could not miss.
How could the Dutch but be converted, when
The Apostles were so many fishermen?
Besides, the waters of themselves did rise,
And as their land, so them did re-baptize.
Though herring for their God few voices missed,
And poor John to have been the Evangelist.

*   *   *   *   *   *

Sure when Religion did itself imbark,
And from the east would westward steer its ark;
It struck, and splitting on this unknown ground,
Each one thence pillaged the first piece he found;
Hence Amsterdam, Turk-Christian-Pagan-Jew,
Sample of sects, and mint of schism grew.
That bank of conscience, where not one so strange
Opinion, but finds credit and exchange.
In vain for Catholics ourselves we bear,
The universal church is only there."

*   *   *   *   *   *   *

Surely this last reproach comes with a very ill grace from an Englishman of Cromwell's days.

Marvell returned to his parliamentary duties in 1665, when the Parliament was sitting at Oxford, on account of the plague then raging in London. On the 23d of October, in that year, he thus writes:— "There is a bill in good forwardnesse to prohibit the importation of Irish cattle ; the fall of lands and rents being ascribed to the bringing them over into England in such plenty." And again, a few days after, he writes :—" Our bill against the importation of Irish cattle was not passed by his Majesty, as being too destructive to the Irish interest." But it appears the bill did afterwards pass, for he writes,—" Our House has returned the bill about Irish Cattle to the Lords, adhering to the word *nuisance*, which the Lords changed to *detriment*, and *mischief*: but at a conference, we delivered the reasons of our adhering to the word *nuisance*."

November 2, he says,—" The bill for preventing the increase of the plague could not pass, because the Lords would not agree that *their houses*, if infected, should be shut up ! ! ! "

The short sessions of 1665 was closed on the 31st of October. Marvell thus enumerates the ten bills passed, to some of which, particularly the five-mile act * as it was called, he must have been strenuously opposed. But the high-church faction had all their own way.—" For £1,250,000 to his Majesty ; for £120,000 to his Majesty to be bestowed on his Royal Highness (*qr*. the Duke of York ?) for attainder of Bamfield, Scott, and Dollman, Englishmen that acted in Holland against his Majesty ; for debarring ejected Nonconformists *from living in or neare corporations, unless taking the new oath and declaration* ; for speedier recovery of rents ; for preventing suits and delays in law (a very inefficient act) ; for taking away damage clear after three years ; *for restraining of printing without license* ; and for naturalizing some particular persons." But with his customary reserve, Andrew makes no allusion to the proposal for making the non-resistance oath obligatory on the whole nation, which was rejected by a majority of three voices only. We may be sure that Marvell was among them.

The autumn of 1666, Dryden's *Annus Mirabilis*, distinguished by several indecisive actions against the Dutch, which the poet magnifies into great victories ; and far more memorably by the fire of London, which was so merciful in its severity, that we are more inclined to attribute it to Divine goodness than to the malice of *Papist* or *Puritan*, seeing that it fairly burned out the plague, and only destroyed six lives,—found Marvell at his post in Parliament, and corresponding as usual with his grateful constituents, whom he has to thank for another present of Yorkshire ale. The principal business transacted in this session was financial. A supply of £1,800,000 was voted, to be raised partly by assessment, and partly by a poll-tax. It may not be wholly

"* It was enacted that no dissenting teacher who took not the non-resistance oath above-mentioned, should, except upon the road, come within five miles of any corporation, or of any place where he had preached since the act of oblivion. The penalty was a fine of fifty pounds, and six months' imprisonment. By ejecting the non-conforming clergy from their churches, and prohibiting all separate congregations, they had been rendered incapable of gaining any livelihood by their spiritual profession. And now, under colour of removing them from places where their influence might be dangerous, an expedient was fallen upon to deprive them of all means of subsistence. Had not the spirit of the nation undergone a change, these violences were preludes to the most furious persecution."—*Hume.*

The spirit of the peers, notwithstanding the presence of the Bishops in their house, was then much more tolerant than that of the Commons. This wicked bill was strongly opposed in the Lords, particularly by the Earl of Southampton, a firm friend of Clarendon. The Lords had also the credit of endeavouring to procure some portion out of the ecclesiastical revenues for the ejected ministers, arguing that they were entitled to the same indulgence which the Commonwealth had granted to the episcopal clergy, *i. e.* a fifth of each living.

D

uninteresting to state how the latter was apportioned.—" Then for the poll-bill the committee hath prepared these votes—that all persons shall pay one shilling per poll ; all aliens two ; all Nonconformists and Papists two ; all servants one shilling in the pound of their wages ; all personal estates for so much as is not already taxed by the land tax shall pay after twenty shillings to the hundred ; cattel, corn, and household furniture shall be excepted, and all such stock for trade as is already taxed by the land tax, but the rest to be liable." Some alterations were subsequently admitted. The Lords, to their great honour, rejected the double taxing of Nonconformists, and made an effort to deliver Aliens also from that oppressive impost. Some discussion took place between the houses on the power of the purse ; the Lords endeavouring to insert a clause, implying a right in the nobility to tax themselves independent of the Commons, which clause the Commons of course rejected. This Parliament, notwithstanding their intolerant and ultra-royalist principles, had a laudable care for the property of the subject, which was indeed very needful in that age of public poverty and court extravagance. The depreciated value of estates and personal effects may appear from the circumstance, that the poll-tax, heavy as it was, was not expected to raise above £540,000. The fire must have ruined thousands ; the Dutch war was doubtless injurious to trade ; the prodigality of the nobility could not be supported without oppressing agriculture ; and the distressful effects of the civil wars were still keenly felt in the country. Never was economy more necessary, and yet the necessary expenses of Government were yearly increasing. England was then at war with Holland, France, and Denmark, and the Scotch Covenanters were once more in arms. The fatal experience of so many years of blood and misery had not taught the nation the folly and wickedness of interfering between man and his Maker. The law against conventicles, sufficiently tyrannical even in England, where a large portion of the population, wealth, and intelligence were sincerely attached to the episcopal church, was forced with additional cruelty and insult upon Scotland, where the best part of the people were dutifully affectionate to their Presbyterian pastors, and where the *curates* or prelatical clergy were, by the admission of all parties, too often low, ignorant, profligate, and brutal. In fact, so mercilessly had the Church of Scotland been stripped at the Reformation, that she could not afford an episcopal establishment. If ever it be lawful to use the sword against the powers that be, the Covenanters of the Raid of Pentland were justified in their resistance ; and it might have been expected that Andrew Marvell would have sympathized with their sufferings, and admired, if he could not approve, their enterprize.

But whatever his real sentiments might be, he did not think fit to communicate them to the corporation of Hull ; for in his letter of the 1st December, 1666, he says,—" For the Scotch business, truly, I hope this night's news is certain of their total rout." But his cautious manner of writing is ever remarkable. He never mentions how he himself or any other member voted ; but speaks of the proceedings of the House as if he had always been of the majority. He even talks in one place of the *princely prudence* of Charles. This might be necessary ; but we are afraid that Andrew entered more heartily than might have been wished, into the scheme of fixing on the *Papists* the guilt of the great fire.

By the 35th letter, which relates to an exchange of prisoners taken in the Dutch war, it would seem that Marvell had renewed his intercourse with Colonel Gilby, for both names are subscribed to it.

The Parliament of 1666—7 was prorogued on the 8th of February, but re-assembled on the 25th of July, to consider the articles of the peace of Breda. The Dutch war, commenced without necessity, and prosecuted, bravely indeed, but with ill-judged parsimony, and a striking want of combination, had closed with a greater disgrace than England had suffered since the days of Bannockburn. The Dutch Fleet entered the Thames, took Sheerness, advanced with six men of war and five fire ships as far as Upnore Castle, where they burned the Royal Oak, the Loyal London, and the Great James, and then fell down the Medway, with almost perfect impunity. Not that the English courage failed ; but improvidence or treachery had left our shores defenceless. The loss was considerable, the consternation fearful, the affront intolerable. Yet was there no reprisal ; for by the end of July the treaty of Breda was concluded, whereby we obtained the territory of New-York, so named from the King's brother. Marvell's correspondence contains scarce an allusion to these occurrences ; but among his poems is a tribute to the memory of Captain Douglas, the commander of the Royal Oak, who, sacrificing life to honour, had refused to quit the vessel when it was in flames, declaring, that " never had a Douglas been known to leave his port without orders." Marvell's address is entitled, " *The Loyal Scot, by Cleveland's* * *Ghost*" upon *the death of Captain Douglas, who was burned on his ship at Chatham.* Like most copies of verses produced on the spur of some public wonder, or last week's heroism, it is very indifferent. There is something humorous, certainly, in putting a panegyric on Scotch loyalty into the mouth of Cleveland, who had been as severe on our northern neighbours

* Cleveland wrote a Poem in Latin and English, called Scotus Rebellis,—the Rebel Scot.

as Churchill or Byron; but almost all that relates to the subject consists of conceits, neither new nor good, and extravagancies strangely out of keeping with the subject.   About the best lines are these:

> That precious life he yet disdains to save,
> Or with known art to try the gentle wave:
> Much him the honour of his ancient race
> Inspir'd, nor would he his own deeds deface;
> And secret joy in his calm soul does rise,
> That Monk looks on to see how Douglas dies.

But their effect is sadly marred by what follows :——

> Like a glad lover the fierce flames he meets,
> And tries his first embraces in their sheets;
> His shape exact, which the bright flames infold,
> Like the sun's statue stands, of burnish'd gold;
> Round the transparent fire about him glows
> As the clear amber on the bees does close;
> And as on angels' heads their glories shine,
> His burning locks adorn his face divine.

We fear that Andrew was more inspired by aversion for prelacy than by admiration for the young Douglas, and only chose the latter for his theme, in order to lay the whole blame of certain national antipathies on the Bishops.   We do not quote the following passages for the reader's approbation, but to shew the utter inefficiency of licencing laws, (for such were then in force,) to restrain the licentiousness of the Pen:

> Prick down the point, whoever has the art,
> Where nature Scotland does from England part,
> Anatomists may sooner fix the cells
> Where life resides, and understanding dwells,
> But *this* we know, tho' *that* exceeds our skill,
> That whosoever separates them does ill.
>
> *   *   *   *
>
> What ethic river is this wondrous Tweed
> Whose one *bank virtue*, t'other vice does breed?
>
> *   *   *   *
>
> 'Tis Holy Island parts us, not the Tweed.
> Nothing but clergy could us two seclude.
>
> *   *   *   *
>
> All litanies in this have wanted faith,
> There's no " Deliver us from a Bishop's wrath,"
>
> *   *   *   *
>
> What the ocean binds, is by the Bishops rent,
> As seas make Islands in the Continent.
> Nature in vain us in one land compiles,
> If the Cathedral still shall have its *isles.*
> Nothing, not bogs, nor sands, nor seas, nor Alps,
> Separate the worlds so, as the Bishop's scalps,
> Stretch for the line their circingle alone,
> 'Twill make a more unhabitable zone;

> The friendly loadstone has not more combined,
> Than *Bishops* cramp't the commerce of mankind.

Though thus severe on the Hierarchy, the poet had not yet lost all respect for the Monarch :—

> Charles, our great soul, this only understands,
> He our affections both, and wills commands.

It must be remembered that Charles had hitherto shewn many good dispositions, and in particular had interfered to save some of the Scotch Nonconformists from the vengeance of Sharpe : notwithstanding the insolent tyranny with which he had himself been treated by the *Kirk* in its days of sovereignty. He had, on several occasions, exerted himself to procure liberty of conscience, both for catholic and protestant dissenters, to little effect indeed, during the influence of Clarendon ; but the secret inclination towards his mother's religion, which probably prompted this insidious toleration, was not yet more than vaguely suspected.

The year 1667 is a great epoch in the history of the human mind, for then was Paradise Lost first given to the world. According to the custom of those times, Marvell accompanied the work of his illustrious friend with a copy of commendatory verses : but it is a truly absurd surmise, that either Marvell's English couplets, or Dr. Barrow's Latin Elegiacs, preserved the production of Milton from obscurity. This is about as probable, as that a sealed and unopened epistle should reach its destination, if directed only in the inside. More plausibly has it been asserted that Marvell united with Sir Thomas Clarges, Mr. Secretary Morrice, and Sir William Davenant to prevent the mighty poet's being excepted out of the act of indemnity ; but is it likely that he, who had himself held office under Cromwell, would possess any influence at Court ?

Though his Parliamentary correspondence continues with little or no interruption, between the years 1667 and 1670, and as a series of historical documents is of high value, yet it throws no light on his private transactions ; nor does it elucidate his personal character, except by affording additional proof of his indefatigable industry ; his unwearied spirits ; his attention to the minutest, as well as to the weightiest matters that came before the House. Rarely does he utter an *opinion* on any subject, unless it bore expressly upon the interests of his constituents. We cannot find any clue to discover, for example, his sentiments on the prosecution of Clarendon, which later historians have represented as a conspiracy between an ungrateful King, and a misguided nation, to ruin the most loyal and immaculate of statesmen ; but it is most probable that he concurred in it. As we are not writing the history of Andrew Marvell's *Times*, we cannot be expected to dilate on all the public measures which he has noticed in his letters, but shall content ourselves with a few extracts which may serve to illustrate the Parliamentary life of the Patriot, or at least the manners, temper, and politics, of the Parliament in which he sat.

Jan. 22, 1766-7:—" Heard the report of the fire of London, full of manifest testimonies that it was by a wicked design, and ordered the report of the insolence of *Papists* to-morrow."

Dec. 22, 1666:—" To-day the Duke of Buckingham and Marquis of Dorchester were upon their petitions freed from the Tower, having been committed for quarrelling and scuffling the other day when we were at the Canary Conference."

Feb 9, 1667 :—"I am sorry to hear of several fires of late in your town, but by God's mercy prevented from doing much harm.   Though I know your vigilance, and have been informed of the occasions, I cannot but, out of the earnestness of mine own sense, advise you to have a careful eye against all such accidents.   We have had so much of them here in the South, that it makes me almost superstitious.   But indeed, as sometimes there arise new diseases, so there are seasons of more particular judgments, and such as that of fires seem of late to have been upon this nation : but God's providence in such cases is well pleased to be frustrated by *human industry*, but much more his mercies are always propitious to repentance."

July 25 :—" Yesternight, at one o'clock, a very dangerous fire happened in Southwark, but blowing up the next house in good time, there were but twelve consumed or ruined.   I cannot but advise you to have especial care in your town of any such accident, or what you will call it; for I am sorry we can yet see no clearer by so many lights."

October 25th :—" This morning several members of our House did in their places move the House to proceed to an impeachment against the Earl of Clarendon, and laid very high crimes to his charge."

Nov. 14 :—" Really the business of the House hath been of late so earnest daily, and so long, that I have not had the time, and scarce vigour left me by night to write to you ; and to-day, because I would not omit any longer, I lose my dinner to make sure of this letter.   The Earl of Clarendon hath taken up much of our time till within this three days.   But since his impeachment hath been carried up to the House of Lords, we have some leisure from that; and now this is the third day that they have, without intermission of any other business, continued upon the question, Whether, upon our desire, to commit him to custody before we sent up (which yet we have not done) the particular articles of our charge against him."—P.S. of the same date:—

" I hear the Lords are at last come to a resolution to desire a conference to-morrow with our House, to show us reason why they should
not commit the Earl of Clarendon before special articles."

" Nov. 23d :—" The Lords and we cannot yet get off the difficulties
risen betwixt us on occasion of our House's demanding the Earl of
Clarendon's imprisonment upon a general charge of treason."

Dec. 3d :—" Since my last to you we have had a free conference with
the Lords, and so a mutual debate on the reasons for, and for not,
committing the Earl of Clarendon on our general charge.   The Lords
yesterday sent a message by Judge Archer and Judge Morton, that,
upon the whole matter, they were not satisfied to commit him, without
particular cause specified or assigned ; whereupon our House, after
very long debate, voted, 'that the Lords not complying with the desires
of the House of Commons in committing and sequestring from their
House the Earl of Clarendon, upon the impeachment carried up against
him, is *an obstruction of the public justice in the proceedings of both
Houses of Parliament, and is the precedent of evil and dangerous consequences.*'   To-day the Lords sent down another message to us, that
they had to-day received a large petition from the Earl of Clarendon,
intimating that he was withdrawn.*   Hereupon our House forthwith

* Clarendon withdrew at the King's express command, who probably knew no other
safe and *easy* means to shield a man whom he could not help revering.

" On the 29th of November, 1667, this illustrious exile embarked in a miserable
boat in the middle of the night, at Erith, and after remaining at sea amidst the
inconveniences and dangers of the worst weather for three days and nights, landed at
Calais.   He left behind him a representation at large to the House of Peers of his
conduct since the Restoration, composed with all the simplicity and modest courage
of conscious innocence and truth : such, however, was the rage of the prevailing
party, that it was presently publicly burned, by order of both Houses."—*Lodge.*

He had built a splendid mansion, to which the populace affixed the nick-name of
Dunkirk House.   In the edition of 1776 are two poems ascribed (we hope errroneously)
to Marvell, one called "Clarendon's House-warming," and the other "Upon his House."
Among other topics of obloquy, they allude pointedly to the misappropriation of certain
building materials, originally set apart for the repair of St. Paul's, but afterwards
diverted to the erection of the Chancellor's palace.   As the second is but short, and
sums up the principal arguments of odium against a venerated name, we shall give it
almost entire :—

> Here lie the sacred stones
> Of Paul . . . .
> Here lie golden briberies,
> The price of ruin'd families.
> The Cavaliers' debenter wall,
> Fix't on an eccentric basis ;
> Here Dunkirk Town and Tangier Hall,
> The Queen's marriage, and all
> The Dutchman's *Templum pacis.*

address his Majesty, that care might be taken for securing all the sea-ports, lest he should pass there. I suppose he will not trouble you at Hull."

March 7, 1668:—"On Wednesday last the House resumed the debate occasioned by the informations of several members concerning the insolencies of Nonconformists in some parts of the nation, disturb-ing ministers in their churches, and setting up their own preachers. The House hereupon came to a resolution, that they would in a body attend his Majesty, desiring him to reinforce by his proclamation the laws against conventicles, and that care might be taken to secure the peace of the nation against the unlawful meetings of *Nonconformists* and *Papists*." With this request Charles, who—half Catholic and half Infidel—hoped, under the mask of toleration, either to be rid of all religion, or to smuggle in that which he found most convenient, was obliged reluctantly to comply, though the petition was meant to imply a severe censure on himself and his favourite, Buckingham, who was now playing the same game with the Nonconformists as Leicester had played with the Puritans under Elizabeth.

Several letters after this are taken up almost entirely with the pro-ceedings against the supposed authors of the miscarriages in the late Dutch war. The public vengeance had better been directed against the authors of the war itself. Of all wars, surely the least profitable have been those which grew out of commercial squabbles.

The privileges and jurisdiction of the two Houses were as undefined as the prerogatives of the crown. We continually find the Peers at variance with the Commons, and their Lordships generally forced to submit at last with no very good grace. An attempt of the Lords to act as a criminal court directly, and not on appeal from the courts below, was strongly resented by the Lower House; and Marvell, though he expresses himself gravely and coolly, no doubt entered fully into the indignation of his fellow members.

May 25, he writes thus:—"I have no more time than to tell you that the Lords, having judged and fined the East India Company, as we think, illegally, upon the petition of one Skinner, a merchant; and they petitioning us for redress, we have imprisoned him that petitioned them, and they have imprisoned several of those that petitioned us; and we, on Monday, send to the Lords severe votes against their pro-ceedings: it is a business of very high and dangerous consequence." On the 9th he informs the Mayor of Hull (then Mr. Anthony Lambert) that there had been a conference between the Houses,—the Commons having voted that the Lords' " taking cognizance and pro-ceeding *originally* upon the petition of Skinner against the East India

Company, was contrary to law. It was Friday in the afternoon before the Lords desired a conference, wherein, with a preamble in writing of a very high and severe sense, they gave us two votes in exchange: that our entertaining a *scandalous* paper of the East India Company, and proceeding thereon, was a breach of the privilege of the House of Peers, and the good union that ought to be betwixt the two Houses: that what the Lords had done upon Skinner's petition was agreeable to law, and consonant to precedents both ancient and modern. We went from thence back to our House, where we sat without intermission *till five o'clock this morning.*" The honest country gentlemen and burgesses had not yet generally fallen into the late hours of the courtiers, and seem to have grown passionate for want of sleep, for they voted, "that whosoever shall be aiding or assisting in the execution of the Lords' sentence or order against the East India Company, shall be deemed a betrayer of the liberties and rights of the Commons of England, and an infringer of the privileges of Parliament." The King adjourned the Houses in consequence, or under pretext, of these differences; but not till the Lords had taken severe measures against Sir Samuel Barnardiston (whom they sentenced to pay £300 on his knees) and other leading members of the East India Company. But it does not appear that Sir Samuel ever submitted to this degrading punishment. Parliament did not meet again for dispatch of business till the 19th of October, 1669. The dissention between the Houses still continued. Marvell records the several stages of the affair, which ended by the two Houses, at the King's desire, erasing "all records in their journals of that matter, that all memory thereof might be extinguished." Feb. 22, 1670.

Every session brought forth some new bill, some forced proclamation, against conventicles. The general disposition of that long-protracted Parliament (which obtained the name of the Pension Parliament) in all things, except its rigid and jealous economy, and severe prosecution of delinquents, coincided with the temper of the better sort of modern Tories. An evil eye on all sectaries, a perfect horror of the Church of Rome, a high devotion to abstract royalty, and to the Protestant Episcopal Church as a vital organ of the state, a vindictive sense of national honour, a restrictive and prohibitory system of commerce,* were, for many years, the leading features of their policy.

* There is scarcely one of Marvell's letters which does not afford some proof that the House in which he sat was no friend to free trade, even between the several parts of the British Empire. We have already seen the bill against the importation of Irish cattle carried against the declared opinion of the King. There was a manifest inclination to exclude French commodities altogether. In enumerating the acts

E

During the years 1668, 69, 70, the public business becoming continually more pressing, and the King's wants more urgent, Marvell's letters
bear more and more on the history of the period, and have less and less
of biographical interest.   Parliament refusing to grant more than
£400,000, to be raised on wines (an imposition very grievous to a
monarch who sympathized with the privations of his wine-bibbing
subjects), the King, dissatisfied with so scanty a supply, and yet more
with the curious inquiries instituted as to the manner in which former
grants had been applied, prorogued the Houses on the 11th of December, on which occasion Andrew piously prays, "God direct his Majesty
further in so weighty resolutions."   Parliament met again on the 14th
of February, 1669—70.   About this time there occur several epistles
from Marvell to his friend William Ramsden, which, though almost
wholly political, express his observations on public affairs with a cir-
cumstantiality, and his opinions with a freedom, which the nature of
his official correspondence precluded.   It may not be unamusing to
compare a few passages referring to the same occurrences : the business-
like brevity and caution of the public document is admirable.   If ever
he takes a little flight, it is to pay a compliment to Majesty, which no
one *need* understand ironically.   Thus of the King's gracious recommendation to put a stop to the differences of the Houses in Skinner's
business.—To *Mr. Humphrey Duncalf*, Mayor :—" Our House thereupon did unanimously vote the entry of this speech in our journal, and
to go in a body on foot to give the King thanks, and to erase the
records in our journal.   A message was forthwith sent to desire leave
to wait on the King, so that we have been twice at Whitehall in one
morning, all infinitely satisfied with the King's justice, prudence, and
kindness in this matter, and I doubt not but all good Englishmen will
be of the same mind."   To Mr. William Ramsden :—" When we began

passed in the session of 1668—9, Marvell mentions a "bill for grazing and tillage,
giving licence to export all corn, and setting an high custom upon foreign corn when
ours is at a good marketable rate."   April 9, 1670 :—" We have sent them up this
morning the bill for prohibition of all foreign brandy, which, though it goes up so
late, I believe will pass before our rising.   The Lords have agreed with the bill of
retrospect upon brandy, to pay 8 pence since 1666.   The Lords have, we fear,
thrown out that part of our bill which provided against men of war trading in
merchandise, truly at an ill season, when so many merchants complain, and the
Turks take prizes in our channels."   The term Turk may here be used as in the
Collect for Good Friday, as synonymous with Mussulman ; for it does not appear that
the Ottoman Emperors or their natural subjects ever practised piracy so far northward.

August 13, 1671 :—" The Lords and we have agreed on an address to his Majesty,
that he wear no foreign manufactures, and discountenance, whether man or woman,
that shall wear them."

to talk of the Lords, the King sent for us alone, and recommended an erasure of all proceedings ; the same thing you know that we proposed at first. We presently ordered it, and went to tell him so the same day. At coming down (*a pretty ridiculous thing*), Sir Thomas Clifford carried speaker and mace, and all members there, to drink the King's health, into the King's cellar. The King sent to the Lords more peremptorily, and they, with much grumbling, agreed to the rasure." Writing to the corporation, he gives the heads of the conventicle bill minutely, in the style of one who saw nothing objectionable in them. To his friend he says,—" The terrible bill against conventicles is sent up to the Lords. They are making mighty alterations in the conventicle bill (which, as we sent it up, is the quintessence of arbitrary malice), and sit whole days, and yet proceed but by inches, and will, at the end, probably affix a Scotch clause of the King's power in externals ;" (*i. e. give the King a dispensing power to make the Parliament malice nugatory*). "So the fate of the bill is uncertain, but must probably pass, being the price of money." During the spring session of 1670, Charles, under pretence of seeking amusement, thought fit to frequent the debates at the House of Lords. This, though not expressly against rule, was against recent custom, and supposed to be a restraint on the freedom of speech. Marvell announces the circumstance to his constituents with some surprise, but without comment, in his letter of the 26th March :—" That which is most extraordinary is, that his Majesty hath for this whole week come every day in person to the House of Lords, and sat there during their debates and resolutions ; and yesterday the Lords went in a body to Whitehall, to give their thanks for the honour he did them therein." To Mr. Ramsden he tells the story more at large :—" The King, about ten o'clock, took boat with Lauderdale only, and two ordinary attendants, and rowed awhile, as towards the bridge, but soon turned back to the Parliament stairs, and so went up into the House of Lords, and took his seat. Almost all of them were amazed, but all seemed so ; and the Duke of York especially was very much surprised. Being sat, he told them it was a privilege he claimed from his ancestors to be present at their deliberations ; that therefore they should not, for his coming, interrupt their debates, but proceed, and be covered. They did so. It is true that this has been done long ago ; but it is now so old, that it is new, and so disused, that at any other but so bewitched a time as this, it would have been looked upon as a high usurpation, and breach of privilege. After three or four days' continuance, the Lords were very well used to the King's presence. The King has ever since continued his session among them, and says it is better than going to a play."

The prospect of public affairs was then sufficiently bad : for Charles, who, like all men whose amiable qualities are not grounded in sound principles, grew worse as he grew old, had now given himself up to the notorious Cabal, and to a set of creatures besides,—French, Scotch, Irish, and, alas, some English, priests and laymen, bigots and atheists, male and female, among whom it is no injustice to say, that Nell Gwyn was considerably the best. But a patriot should never despair of the Republic. He should "brook no continuance of weak-minded-ness,"* but should "hope even against hope." No wonder, however, if sometimes his jaded spirits give way, and he utter the language of despondency. Andrew Marvell more than once verges on this extreme. Many a man, under such circumstances, would have concluded that "the world was made for Cæsar," and since he could do no good for his country, think of doing the best he could for himself. In the private communication from which we have borrowed so much, he gives a character to his fellow representatives which, considering their stern frugality, and bold defence of their own privileges, they do not appear, as a body, to have deserved :—" In this session the Lords sent down to us a proviso for the King, that would have restored him to all civil or ecclesiastical privileges which his ancestors had enjoyed at any time since the conquest. There never was so compendious a piece of abso-lute universal tyranny. But the Commons made them ashamed of it, and retrenched it. The Parliament was never so embarrassed beyond recovery. We are all venal cowards except some few." Now the successful opposition to the Lords' proviso should have convinced him that, though there were some few venal cowards, there were more bold and honest men.†

* Wordsworth.

† Extracts from an "extraordinary black book," said to have been published by Marvell himself, which was perhaps the model of the various muster-rolls of a similar kind that have since appeared.

A Seasonable Argument to persuade all the Grand Juries in England to Petition for a New Parliament ; or, a List of the Principal Labourers in the Great Design of Popery and Arbitrary Power :—

Launceston.—Sir Charles Harbord, surveyor-general, has got £100,000 of the king and the kingdom: he was formerly a solicitor of Staples Inn, till his lewdness and poverty brought him to court.

Devonshire.—Sir Capelston Bamfield, Baronet, much addicted to tippling, presented to the king by his pretended wife, Betty Roberts, the Pall Mall.

Weymouth.—Sir Winston Churchil, was a commissioner of the court of claims in Ireland, now one of the clerks of the green cloth. He profered his own daughter to the Duke of York, and has got in boons £10,000. He has published in print that the king may raise money without his Parliament.

The Parliament, which was prorogued before the end of April, met again on the 2nd of October, 1670. The King, who was now the contented, though concealed, instrument of the French court, partly won over by the arts of the Duchess of Orleans, and her ally Louisa de Queroüaille,* (the Dutchess of Portsmouth,) partly by money in hand, and the promise of French troops, in case that the people's patience should be worn out. A second Dutch war was meditated with the secret purpose of aiding the French to overrun and subjugate the United Provinces. But these designs were not yet ripe for disclosure. A supply was first to be had: £800,000 were demanded, and granted, and more would have been granted, but fresh dissention between the upper and lower Houses, owing to the Lords taking upon them to make amendments in the money bills, occasioned a sudden prorogation, April 22, 1671. If these facts be kept in mind, the following passages, from Marvell's public and private correspondence, will be sufficiently intelligible. October 25.

Newton, in the Isle of Wight.—Sir John Holmes, Sir Ross's brother, a cowardly, baffled, sea captain, twice boxed, and once whipped with a dog whip, as many gentlemen can testify: chosen in the night, without the head officer of the town, and but one burgess, yet voted well elected this last session.

Cambridge Town.—Sir William Hartop, a pension of £200 per annum, and promised to be clerk of the Kitchen: threatens to sue his town for his wages, because he hears they will choose him no more.

Middlesex.—Sir Lancellot Lake, much in debt, has a promise that his elder brother's son shall not be naturalized; a notorious cuckold.

Castle Rising.—Samuel Pepys, Esquire, once a taylour, then serving man to the Lord Sandwitch, now secretary to the admiralty, got by passes and other illegal wages £40,000.

Bath.—Sir William Basset, Henry Seymour's son-in-law, £1,000 given him by Clifford: he has a promise of a place in the law act: always drunk when he can get money.

'The publisher begs pardon of those gentlemen here named, if he has, for want of better information, undervalued the price and merit of their voices, which he shall be ready, upon their advertisement, to amend; but more particularly he must beg the excuse of many more gentlemen, no less deserving, whom he hath omitted, not out of any malice, or for want of good will, but of timely notice; but, in general, the House was, if they please to remember, this last session, by three of their own members told, that there were several Papists, fifty outlaws, and *pensioners* without number; so that upon examination, they may arrive at a better knowledge among themselves, and do one another more right, than we (howsoever well affected) can possibly do without doors.'

* The English, whose organs of speech are notoriously inhospitable to foreign names, found Mademoiselle de Queroüaille's so unacceptable, that they anglicised it into *Carwell,* under which abreviation she is frequently mentioned both in prose and verse. Surely they ought not to complain at King Charles giving her a title so much more accommodated to English pronunciation.

He gives at some length, the preamble of the Lord Keeper's opening speech, (for Charles had still grace enough left to be ashamed of appearing personally as a beggar for money on false pretences,) the most remarkable feature of which is, that the increased power of France is alleged to justify a grant which was to be used in increasing the power of France. Then comes an enumeration of the advantageous treaties which the King had concluded, particularly with Sweden and Holland, (while he knew that the money was wanted to make war upon Holland,) with Spain, whereby we had gained the sovereignty of Jamaica, &c., with Denmark, Savoy, &c. Next his Lordship prepares a spell for that national vanity, which in time past has cost us so dear, alleging " in short that all the Princes of Christendom sought at present to his Majesty, if not for their security, yet as to one without whose friendship they could not promote their affairs." Andrew Marvell was no orator ; it does not appear upon record that he ever made a set speech at all ; yet one might almost wonder that neither he nor any other Englishman got up to remind my Lord-Keeper that whatever consideration his master might have obtained from foreign powers, was taken up solely on old Oliver's credit. But now comes the drift. After touching on the insufficiency of the wine duties to the public occasions ; the expence of the navy since 1660, (£500,000 per annum,) and the King's debts, which were immense and at heavy interest, he desired that the Parliament would supply him (the King) with £800,000 for his navy, as also that they would pay off all those debts which he owed at interest, and that they would finish this before Christmas, as well that he might have time in hand to mature his preparations for the season of the year as that men might attend their own occasions in the country, and make their neighbours taste of their hospitality, and keep up their authority and interest there, which is so useful and necessary to the public." It is a proof that the promises contained in this speech were never intended to be performed ; that neither it nor the King's short introductory address were allowed to be printed.

Several letters follow, containing nothing but lists of the commodities it was proposed to tax, and other devices, for raising the supplies. One of these proposals produced effects so ludicrously characteristic of the brutality of even the highest orders in that reign, that we must extract the passage of Andrew's private correspondence, which contains the story :—

" An accident happened which had like to have spoiled all. Sir John Coventry having moved for an imposition on the play-houses, Sir John Berkenhead, to excuse them, said they had been of great service to the King. Upon which Sir John Coventry desired that gentleman to explain whether he meant the *men* or the *women* players. Hereupon it is imagined that, the House adjourning from Tuesday before till Thursday after Christmas day, on the very Tuesday night of the adjournment, twenty-five of the Duke of Monmouth's troop, and some few foot, laid in wait from ten at night till two in the morning, by Suffolk-street, and as he returned from the Cock, where he supped, to his own house, they threw him down and cut off almost all the end of his nose." Feeble attempts were made by the court to protect the actors in this cowardly piece of loyalty, but the House of Commons displayed a proper spirit, and not only insisted on the punishment of the present offenders, but passed the act which makes cutting and maiming capital without benefit of clergy. From this incident alone, we might credit what Andrew says at the conclusion of his letter—"*the court is at the highest pitch of want and luxury, and the people full of discontent.*" The circumstance is often alluded to in the ballads and epigrams of the time, and is the subject of one which has been given to Marvell. We hope he had too much decency and dignity to have written it, as he certainly had too much wit and good taste to have approved of it. It contains nothing worth extracting, and much that is unfit to be read. Not but what the court *deserved* every word of it.

In another letter, about the same date,* he mentions to Mr. Ramsden, (whom he calls dear Will,) how Monmouth, Albemarle, Dunbane, and seven or eight *gentlemen*, fought with the watch, and killed a poor bedle. They have all their pardons for Monmouth's sake; but it is an act of great scandal." In the same letter :—" The king of France is at Dunkirk. We have no fleet out, though we gave the subsidy-bill, valued at £800,000, for that purpose. *I believe indeed he will attempt nothing on us, but leave us to die a natural death.* For indeed never had poor nation *so many complicated, mortal, incurable diseases.*"

We have more than once had occasion to allude to Charles's disposition to mitigate the rigour of the conformity laws, which may be ascribed part to his good nature, more to his good sense, and most to his secret Romanism. But a letter of Marvell's, (private of course,) suggests a fourth influence, not weaker than the rest :—" The King had

* The letter, containing this information, is in the printed edition, without date; but it must have been written between the end of March and the 22nd of April, 1671; for it mentions the Duchess of York's death, (Ann Hyde's,) which took place March 31, and speaks of Parliament as still sitting, which, on the 22nd of April was prorogued. The King continues to honour the Lords with his presence, against which Lord Clare declared in the royal presence. Lord Lucas also made a " *fervent bold speech*" against the Houses' " prodigality in giving, and the weak looseness of government," the King being present.

occasion for £60,000, sent to borrow it of the City. *   *   *   *
Could not get above £10,000. *The Fanatics, under persecution, served his Majesty.* The other party, both in court and city, would have prevented it. But the King protested money would be acceptable. So the city patched up, out of the chamber and other ways, £20,000. The Fanatics, of all sorts, £40,000." This was just after a sanguinary attack of the " bold train-bands" upon a congregation of non-resisting Quakers, of whom they killed some and wounded many.* But it is more worthy of remark, that the Protestant Dissenters, like the Jews of the middle ages, however harassed by fines, double taxes, and civil disabilities, have always had more ready money than other persons of the same station, and unlike the Jews, have generally been ready to part with it on public occasions.

With all this orthodoxy on one side, and saintship on the other, there was little respect even for the external forms of the established religion. The following would appear, in these days, utterly incredible.—" Feb. 7, 1770—71: Yesterday, upon complaint of some violent arrests made in several churches, even during sermon time, nay, of one taken out betwixt the bread and the cup in receiving the sacrament, the House ordered that a bill be brought in for better observing the Lord's day."

The letters from this time to the prorogation of the 22d of April, are chiefly taken up with financial details, and dissentions between the two Houses, originating in alterations made by the Lords in a money-bill, which the Commons contended was an infringement of their privilege :—" To speak in short, the two Houses were so directly contradictory in their assertions concerning the power of the Lords in altering of rules, &c., that his Majesty (there being no present medium of reconciliation to be found) thought fit to-day to prorogue us, so that the bill of foreign commodities is fallen to the ground." Andrew announces this to his constituents the very same evening ; and this (the 126th) is the last public communication extant before Oct. 20th, 1674, an interruption of nearly three years.

From his letter " to a friend in Persia," we are tempted to make

---

* The following passage of the same letter, (Nov. 28, 1670,) may be interesting to some :—" The other was the trial of Penn and Mead, Quakers, at the Old Baily. The Jury not finding them guilty, as the Recorder and Mayor would have had them, they were kept without meat or drink some three days, till almost starved, but would not alter their verdict, so fined and imprisoned. There is a book out which relates all the passages, which were very pertinent on the part of the prisoners, but prodigiously barbarous by the Mayor and Recorder. The Recorder, among the rest, commended the Spanish Inquisition, saying it would never be well till we had something like it."

some extracts, though we cannot inform the reader who that friend was. It is dated August 9, 1671,—no place specified. It begins in a strain of pious friendship, expressed in terms of the mystic philosophy :—" God's good providence, which hath through so dangerous a disease, and so many difficulties preserved and restored you, will, I doubt not, conduct you to a prosperous issue, and the perfection of your so laudable undertakings, and under that, your own good genius, in conjunction with your brother here, will, I hope, though at the distance of England and Persia, in good time, work extraordinary effects ; for the magnetism of two souls rightly touched, work beyond all natural limits, and it would indeed be too unequal, if good nature should not have at least as large a sphere of activity as malice, envy, and detraction, which are, it seems, part of the returns from Surat and Gombroon.   *   *   * In this world a good cause signifies little unless it be well defended. A man may starve at the feast of a good conscience.   *   *   *   * I know your maxim, *Qui festinat ditescere, non erit innocens.**   Indeed, while you preserve that mind, you will have the blessing both of God and man.   *   *   *   * I am sorry to perceive that mine by the Armenian miscarried. Though there was nothing material in it, the thoughts of friends are too valuable to fall into the hands of a stranger." Scanty as are the notices of Marvell's domestic history, it is delightful to read these issues of a wise and noble heart, not corrupted by the necessity of evil communications, nor hardened by the duty of striving against corruption. But the patriot could not long forget politics, and, as Swift confessed that he could preach nothing but pamphlets, so Marvell declares himself fit for nothing but a *Gazetteer*. It must have been with painful sensations that an Englishman in Persia perused the following account of his *Fatherland :*—" The King having, upon pretence of the great preparations of his neighbours, demanded £800,000 for his navy, (though in conclusion he hath not sent out any,) and that the Parliament should pay his debts, which the ministers would never particularize to the House of Commons, our House gave several bills. You see how far things were stretched beyond reason, there being no satisfaction how those debts were contracted, and all men foreseeing that what was given would not be applied to discharge the debts, which I hear are at this day risen to four millions. Nevertheless, such was the number of the constant courtiers increased by the apostate patriots, who were bought off for that turn, some at six, others at ten, one at fifteen thousand pounds, in money ; besides what offices, lands, and reversions, to others, that it is a mercy they gave not away the whole land and liberty of England. The Duke of Buckingham is again £140,000

---

* i. e. He that is in haste to be rich, shall not be without sin.

in debt, and, by this prorogation, his creditors have time to tear all his lands in pieces. The House of Commons has run almost to the end of their time, and are grown extremely chargeable to the King, and odious to the people. They have signed and sealed £10,000 a year more to the Duchess of Cleveland, who has likewise near £10,000 out of the excise of beer and ale ; £5,000 a year out of the post-office ; and, they say, the reversion of all the King's leases; the reversion of all places in the custom-house ; and, indeed, what not ? All promotions, spiritual and temporal, pass under her cognizance. We truckle to France in all things, to the prejudice of our alliance and honour. Barclay is still Lieutenant of Ireland, but he was forced to come over to pay £10,000 rent to his *landlady* Cleveland." The letter concludes with a brief statement of one of the most extraordinary, if not most important incidents, in English history; one of those stories which we should imagine to be impossible, if we did not know them to be true. " One Blood, outlawed for an attempt to take Dublin Castle, and who seized on the Duke of Ormond here last year, and might have killed him, a most bold, and yet sober fellow, some months ago seized the crown and sceptre in the Tower, took them away, and, if he had killed the keeper, might have carried them clear off. He, being taken, astonished the King and court with the generosity and wisdom of his answers. He and all his accomplices, for his sake, are discharged by the King, to the wonder of all." Andrew does not seem to be very angry with Blood for stealing the crown, nor (what is more extraordinary) with King Charles for pardoning him. In an epigram, found both in Latin and English, he even commends the desperado, but it is for the sake of a stab at an order of men, against whom he entertained an unfortunate prejudice :—

> When daring Blood, his rent to have regain'd,
> Upon the English diadem distrain'd;
> He chose the cassock, circingle, and gown,
> The fittest mask for one that robs the crown :
> But his lay-pity underneath prevail'd,
> And whilst he sav'd the keeper's life, he fail'd.
> With the priest's vestment had he but put on
> The prelates cruelty, the crown had gone.

Whether admiration of " his wise and generous answers" had much to do with Blood's pardon and pension, (for he was rewarded with an estate of £500 in *Ireland*, may justly be doubted. Charles was likely enough to be amused with his audacity, and was as void of resentment as of gratitude. Having persuaded himself that all men, in all their actions, are equally constrained by interest or appetite, he consistently made no difference between friend and foe, and would prefer the man who stole his crown, to him who had preserved it, if the latter happened to be the pleasanter companion. But we suspect something deeper in the favour shewn to Blood than mere caprice. He was rumoured, on good grounds, to be a creature of Buckingham, and, at his instigation, to have made his desperate attempt upon the Duke of Ormond. What motive either could have for seizing the Regalia, it is difficult, at this time, to conjecture, but it is exceedingly probable that Blood, who in England could not be immediately silenced with the bowstring, knew more than it was convenient for either the favourite or the monarch to have known. For though *dead* men tell no tales, *dying* men, even felons at the gallows, may tell horrible tales, and the words of dying men are heard afar, and long remembered, and deeply believed, without much consideration of previous character. Besides, a hanged villain is of no use but to the dissectors: a living one, properly managed, may be of a great deal to a bad government.

One other epistle, addressed to William Ramsden, Esq.,[*] occurs in this interval of Marvell's public correspondence, dated June, 1672. It is short, and not important, though it mentions the assassination of the Pensionary De Wit, and the low state of the Dutch Republic:—"No man can conceive the condition of the state of Holland, in this juncture, unless he can, at the same time, conceive an earthquake, an hurricane, and the deluge." Of the last it did indeed present a pretty tolerable miniature, for the sluices being cut, a great part of the country was under water.

We have not the means of determining whether Marvell's correspondence with the Borough was actually discontinued during these years, whether the papers have been carelessly lost, or, which is most probable, purposely destroyed. For when we consider the character of public measures in that interval, the infamous Dutch war, in which the pensioned Charles and ministers conspired with the French despot to extinguish the poor remains of liberty in Holland, and to destroy the strength of protestantism in Europe, on an implied condition of receiving French assistance to bring about the same end in England,—the prospect of a reign of Jesuits succeeding a reign of harlots,—of absolute power transmitted from the good-natured, unprincipled Charles, to the vindictive, superstitious James,—and the other monstrous abuses of that calamitous

---

[*] William and John Ramsden, Esqrs. were the sons of John Ramsden, who was Mayor of Hull, and died, in 1637, of the plague, and was buried by the Rev. Andrew Marvell, father of our author, who delivered from the pulpit, on this mournful occasion, a most pathetic oration. His eldest son, Mr. John Ramsden, was twice member for Hull. William was a spirited and successful commercial adventurer. Is any of the family left in Hull at present?

æra, we may suppose that even Marvell's caution could not always avoid expressions which might have exposed the town and corporation of Hull to serious inconveniences in the days of Judge Jeffreys and *quo warranto's*. In one letter he hints at a probability of his being employed in Ireland, but we cannot discover that he ever went thither.

Where ever he was there is abundant proof that he was not idle. It was in the year 1672, that he first avowedly appeared in the character of a political satyrist, wherein he gained a high and dangerous reputation, as unblemished as the fame of a *Polemic* can be; but we believe that no man, divine, politician, or critic, ever thought of his controversial writings with calm satisfaction on his death-bed. Yet there are times when the sword must be unsheathed. Whether Marvell's quarrel was just or not, we shall not decide, for it involves theological questions which it were worse than folly to treat extemporaneously and incidentally; but his bitterest enemies were compelled to admire the mixture of brilliant wit and sterling argument which he displayed in the conduct of it.

The circumstances which gave rise to his once famous " Rehearsal Transprosed" were briefly these: Dr. Samuel Parker,* who from a Commonwealth saint had been converted to a High Church and King man, published, in 1670, a book called " Ecclesiastical Polity," the substance of which had been preached at Lambeth, and printed by order of Archbishop Sheldon. We never read it, nor do we know any one that has; and indeed we trust that no enemy of the Church and

---

* Bishop Burnet, (and the word of a *Whig Bishop* neither Whig nor Tory ought to dispute,) says that " Parker was a covetous and ambitious man, and seemed to have no sense of religion, but as a political interest. He seldom went to prayers, or to any exercise of devotion, and was so proud that he was insufferable to all who came near him." Burnet was, however, too credulous of what told against his adversaries. Nor should it be accounted any reproach to the majority of the English clergy, that there have been, and ever will be, so long as the higher preferments are in the gift of the government *protempore*, some time-servers :—

> " Who turn their halcyon beaks
> At every gale and vary of their Master."

Such men will always be more vehement in defence of their last adopted opinions than even true zealots, for they are seldom so utterly devoid of conscience as not to wish to believe themselves, and, if really aware of their own insincerity, they naturally adopt a violence of profession as a safe disguise. The interested suitor always makes love more earnestly than the true lover.

Parker might, however, have a true antipathy to the dissenters, for his father was one of Cromwell's saints. Nothing prejudices the mind so strongly against religion in general, or any form of religion in particular, as having too much of it too early. The mother of Epicurus was the most superstitious of women.

Monarchy will fish it out of Lethe. Of its principles, however, two or three sentences are a sufficient sample :—" It is better to submit to the unreasonable impositions of a Nero or a Caligula, than to hazard a dissolution of the state ;"* and, " that it is absolutely necessary to the peace and government of the world, that the supreme magistaate of every Commonwealth should be vested with a power to govern and conduct the consciences of subjects in affairs of religion." And he asserted that " Princes may with less hazard give liberty to men's vices, than to their consciences." And speaking of the different Sects then subsisting, he lays it down as a fixed rule for all Princes to act by, that " tenderness and indulgence to such men, were to nourish vipers in our bowels, and the most sottish neglect of our own quiet and security."

Well was it said by a Grecian sage—*Beware of the calumnies of your Friends ;* and well might it have been said to the Church of England—Beware of Dr. Samuel Parker's Ecclesiastical Polity. What the church at large thought of this preposterous dressing of old Hobbes's Leviathan in episcopal robes, we know not, for Sheldon's imprimatur only signified the approbation of the court. But as it was manifestly intended to prepare the way for the *King's* religion, we cannot but think that every sincere Protestant with half an eye must have seen through it.

Baxter declining to undertake the defence of the Nonconformists, Dr. Owen replied to Parker in his *" Liberty and Truth vindicated."* Parker made rejoinder next year, in *" A Defence and Continuation of Ecclesiastical Polity, against Dr. Owen ;"* and in 1672 renewed the attack in a preface to a posthumous work of Bishop Bramhall.* This it was which brought on the aspiring divine the perilous wrath of Marvell. " The Rehearsal," that famous comedy of Buckingham's, which has been praised to the full extent of its merit, was then in vogue, and as a tempting title, in literary warfare, is half the battle, Marvell came out with his " Rehearsal Transprosed," of which the full title runs thus : *" The Rehearsal Transprosed; or, Animadversions on a late Book entitled a Preface, shewing what grounds and apprehensions there are of Popery. London : printed by A. B., for the Assignees*

---

* Very possibly, if it were a mere consideration of personal convenience. The only question is, whether resistance to unreasonable impositions in religion is not an absolute duty, not to be neglected :—

" Though Sun and Moon
Were in the flat sea sunk."

What are all States, Thrones, Principalities, and Powers, to a single soul, though it were that of a savage or a new born babe ?

*of John Calvin and Theodore Beza, at the Sign of the King's Indul-
gence, on the South side of the Lake Lemane, 1672."* As we have no
wish to revive the controversy, we shall merely give a few extracts, as
specimens of Marvell's prose style,—of his indefatigable wit, which
approaches in quality to that of Butler, while he has, at times, a
majesty of anger which entitles him to the appellation of a prose
Juvenal. His reading was great and miscellaneous, and he lays it all
under contribution. Of the invention of printing, he writes in the
following cutting train of irony :—" The press (that villainous engine),
invented much about the same time with the Reformation, hath done
more mischief to the discipline of our Chuch than the doctrine can
make amends for. It was a happy time, when all learning was in
manuscript, and some little officer, like our author, did keep the keys
of the library. When the clergy needed no more knowledge than to
read the liturgy, and the laity no more clerkship than to save them
from hanging. But now, since printing came into the world, such is
the mischief, that a man cannot write a book, but presently he is
answered. Could the press but at once be conjured to obey only an
imprimatur, our author might not disdaine, perhaps, to be one of its
most zealous patrons. There have been wayes found out to banish
ministers, to find not only the people, but even the grounds and fields
where they assembled, in conventicles ; but no art yet could prevent
these seditious meetings of letters. Two or three brawny fellows in a
corner, with meer ink and elbow grease, do more harm than a hundred
systematical divines, with their sweaty preaching. And, what is a
strange thing, the very spunges, which one would think should rather
deface and blot out the whole book, and were anciently used for that
purpose, are become now the instruments to make them legible. Their
ugly printing letters look but like so many rotten tooth drawers ;
and yet these rascally operators of the press have got a trick to fasten
them again in a few minutes, that they grow as firm a set, and as biting
and talkative, as ever. O, printing ! how hast thou disturbed the peace
of mankind !—that lead, when moulded into bullets, is not so mortal as
when formed into letters ! There was a mistake, sure, in the story of
Cadmus ; and the serpent's teeth which he sowed were nothing else but
the letters which he invented. The first essay that was made towards
this art, was in single characters upon iron, wherewith, of old, they
stigmatized slaves and remarkable offenders ; and it was of good use,
sometimes, to brand a schismatic ; but a bulky Dutchman diverted it
quite from its first institution, and contriving those innumerable *syn-
tagmes* of alphabets, hath pestered the world ever since, with the gross
bodies of their German divinity. One would have thought in reason,

that a Dutchman might have contented himself only with the wine-press."

For his transferring the name of Bayes from Dryden to his anta_gonist :—" But before I commit myself to the dangerous depths of his discourse, which I am now upon the brink of, I would with his leave make a motion, that, instead of author, I may henceforth indifferently call him Mr. Bayes as oft as I shall see occasion; and that, first, because he hath no name, or at least will not own it, though he him_self writes under the greatest security, and gives us the first letters of other men's names before he be asked them. Secondly, because he is, I perceive, a lover of elegancy of style, and can endure no man's tauto_logies but his own, and therefore I would not distaste him with too frequent repetition of one word ; but chiefly because Mr. Bayes and he do very much symbolize in their understandings, in their expressions, in their humour, in their contempt and quarrelling, of all others, though of their own profession; because our divine, the author, manages his contest with the same prudence and civility which the poets and players of late have practised in their divisions ; and lastly, because both their talents do peculiarly lie in exposing and personating the Nonconformists." (Here, by the way, Andrew identifies Mr. Bayes with Dryden, and so pays the intellects of Parker a high though unintended compliment). " Besides, to say Mr. Bayes is more civil than to say villain and caitiff."

As the Nonconformists were continually and injudiciously opposing to the Church of England the Protestant churches abroad (which had certainly departed further from Rome, whether or no they came any nearer to Heaven), so the High_Church Polemics, with equal lack of temper and judgment, were always reflecting on the foreign reformers and their followers; as if, indeed, the essentials of a church had no where been preserved except in the English episcopal establishment. Parker probably pushed this doctrine to extremes, for which folly he received severe castigation.—" Mr. Bayes, ye know, prefers that one quality of fighting single with whole armies, before all the moral virtues put together ; and yet I assure you he hath several times obliged *Moral Virtue* so highly, that she owes him a good turn wherever she can meet him. But it is a brave thing to be the ecclesiastical Drawcansir : he kills whole nations,—he kills friend and foe. Hungary, Transylvania, Bohemia, Poland, Savoy, France, the Netherlands, Den_mark, Sweden, and a great part of the Church of England, and all Scotland (for these, besides many more, he mocks under the title of Germany and Geneva), may perhaps rouse up our mastiff, and make up a danger worthy of his courage. A man would guess that this giant had promised his comfortable importance a simarre of the beards of all the orthodox theologues in Christendom." "There is risen up this spiritual Mr. Bayes, who, having assumed to himself an incongruous plurality of ecclesiastical offices, one most severe of the penitentiary universal to the reformed churches; the other most ridiculous, of buffoon general to the Church of England, so that he may henceforth be capaple of any other promotion. * * And not being content to enjoy his own folly, he has taken two others into partnership, as fit for his design as those two that clubbed with Mahomet in making the Alcoran. * * But lest I might be mistaken as to the persons I mention, I will assure the reader that I intend not Hudibras; for he is a man of the other robe, and his excellent wit hath taken a flight far above these whifflers: that whoever dislikes the choice of his subject, cannot but commend his performance of it, and calculate, if on so barren a theme he were so copious, what admirable sport he would have made with an ecclesiastical politician."

It is pleasant to read this acknowledgment of an enemy's merits, which shews that Andrew loved wit for its own sake, without looking at the party from which it proceeded. But it must be recollected that his "withers were unwrung." He was no Puritan,—no new-light man. If he inclined to one mode of church discipline rather than another, he chose that which he conceived most favourable to liberty.

Here he rises to a more solemn indignation :—" Once perhaps in a hundred years there may arise such a prodigy in the University (where all men else learn better arts and better manners), and from thence may creep into the church (where the teachers, at least, ought to be well instructed in the knowledge and practice of Christianity); so prodigious a person, I say, may even there be hatched, who shall neither know nor care how to behave himself to God or man; and who, having never seen the receptacle of grace or conscience at an anatomical dissection, may conclude, therefore, that there is no such matter, or no such obligation, among Christians, who shall persecute the scripture itself, unless it will conform to his interpretation; who shall strive to put the world into blood, and animate princes to be the executioners of their own subjects for well-doing."

Of the correctness and elegance of Parker's style, the following passage, which Marvell quotes from page 663 of his Defence (what a book his defence must be!) which Marvell cuts up scientifically, may be a fair specimen:—" There sprung up a mighty bramble on the south side of the Lake Lemane that—such is the rankness of the soil— spread and flourished with such a sudden growth, that, partly by the industry of *his* agents abroad, and partly by *its* own indefatigable pains and pragmaticalness, it quite overrun the whole Reformation." (The bramble, of course, is Calvin). " You must conceive that Mr. Bayes was all this while in an extacy, in Dodona's grove ; or else here is strange work—worse than ' explicating a post,' or ' examining a pillar.' A ' bramble' that had agents abroad, and itself ' an indefatigable bramble.' But straight our bramble is transformed into a man, and he ' makes a chair of infallibility for himself' out of his own bramble timber."

The account of Parker's rise and progress as a chaplain and a popular preacher is rather personal, and too long to be extracted ; but there are some things in it which deserve to be remarked for their universal application : *e. g.* " Having soon wrought himself dexterously into his patron's favour by *short graces* and *short sermons,* and a mimical way of drolling upon the Puritans ; he gained a great authority likewise among the domestics: they listened to him as an oracle, and they allowed him, by common consent, to have not only all the divinity, but more wit too, than all the rest of the family put together." The short graces and sermons, all candidates for preferment will do well to imitate ; but mimical ways should cautiously be avoided. But this is still better :—" Being of an amorous complexion, and finding himself the cock-divine and the cock-wit of the family, he took the privilege to walk among the hens ; and thought it not impolitic to establish his new-acquired reputation upon the gentlewomen's side : and they that perceived he was a rising man, and of pleasant conversation, dividing his day among them into canonical hours,—of reading, now, the common-prayer, and now the romances,—were very much taken with him. The sympathy of silk began to stir and attract the tippet to the petticoat, and the petticoat to the tippet. The innocent ladies found a strange unquietness in their minds, and could not distinguish whether it were love or devotion. * * I do not hear that for all this he had practised upon the honour of the ladies, but that he preserved always the civility of a Platonic knight-errant. For all this, courtship had no other operation but to make him still more in love with himself ; and if he frequented their company, it was only to speculate his own baby in their eyes."

There are some who could not do better than attend to the following : " He is the first minister of the Gospel that ever had it in his commission to rail at all nations. And though it hath long been practised, I never observed any great success by reviling men into conformity. I have heard that charms may even invite the moon out of Heaven, but I could never see her moved by the rhetoric of barking."

But we must make an end of our extracts, (though we could willingly

extend them further,) with a few of those curious thoughts, which consti_
tute the resemblance we have asserted to exist between Marvell and Butler.

Page 57. " This is an admirable dexterity our author has, to correct
a man's scribbling humours without impairing his reputation. He is as
courteous as the lightning, which can melt the sword without ever hurt_
ing the scabbard."

61. "Is, it not strange, that in those most benign minutes of a man's
life, when the stars smile, the birds sing, the winds whisper, the foun_
tains warble, the trees blossom, and universal nature seems to invite
itself to the bridal, when the lion pulls in his claws, and the aspic lays
by its poison, and all the most noxious creatures grow amorously inno_
cent : that even then, Mr. Bayes alone should not be able to refrain his
malignity. As you love yourself, Madam, let him not come near you ;
he hath all his life been fed with vipers instead of lampreys, and scor_
pions for cray-fish ; and if any time he eat chickens they had been
crammed with spiders, till he hath so envenomed his whole substance,
that it is much safer to bed with a mountebank before he hath taken his
antidote."*

140. " Bayes had at first built up such a stupendous magistrate as
never was of God's making. He had put all Princes on the rack to
stretch them to his dimension. And as a straight line continued grows
a circle, he had given them so infinite a power, that it was extended
into impotency. For although he found it not till it was too late in the
cause, yet he felt it all along (which is the understanding of brutes,) in
the effect."

187. " For I do not think it will excuse a witch to say that she con_
jured up a spirit merely that she might lay him, nor can there be a
more dexterous and malicious way of calumny, than by making a need_
less apology for another in a criminal subject. As suppose I should
write a preface shewing what grounds there are of fears and jealousies
of Bayes's being an atheist."

* The germ of this thought, which is borrowed from the fanciful physics of an age
when Shaftesbury consulted astrologers, Dryden cast nativities, and Buckingham
sought for the philosopher's stone, is to be found in Hudibras:—

> The Prince of Cambay's daily food
> Is Asp, and Basilisk, and Toad,
> Which makes him have so strong a breath
> Each night he stinks a Queen to death.

Marvell was manifestly much addicted to light reading; a proof that he did not sym_
pathize with the sour, imagination-killing austerities of those separatists, whose cause
it fought so ably, when it was become the cause of conscience and liberty. His allu_
sions to romances, plays, and poems, are very numerous and apposite. This taste is
often observable in men of business, statesmen, and philosophers.

Though our quotations have already extended too far, we cannot leave behind the following passage, because it states the just principles of the patriot in the clearest point of view. Speaking of Laud's unhappy attempt to force a form of worship upon the Scotch, and the consequent insurrection, he says, " Whether it be a war of religion or of liberty, is not worth the labour to enquire. Whichsoever was at the top, the other was at the bottom ; but considering all, I think the cause was too good to be fought for. Men ought to have trusted God ; they ought and might have trusted the King with the whole of that matter. The arms of the church are prayers and tears, the arms of the subject are patience and petitions. The King himself being of so accurate and piercing a judgment would soon have felt where it stuck. For men may spare their pains when nature is at work, and the world will not go the faster for our driving. Even as his present Majesty's happy restoration did itself, so all things else happen in their best and proper time, without our officiousness."

Such an attack may naturally be supposed to have called forth a host of answers, some of which attempted to vie with the quaintness of Marvell's title.

As Marvell had nicknamed Parker *Bayes*, the quaint humour of one entitled his reply " Rosemary and Bayes ;" another, " The Transproser Rehearsed, or the Fifth Act of Mr. Bayes's Play ;" another, " Gregory Father Greybeard with his Vizard off." " There were no less than six scaramouches together upon the stage, all of them of the same gravity and behaviour, the same tone, and the same habit, that it was impossible to discern which was the true author of ' The Ecclesiastical Polity.' I believe he imitated the wisdom of some other Princes, who have sometimes been persuaded by their servants to disguise several others in the regal garb, that the enemy might not know in the battle whom to single."

Parker certainly did answer, or attempt to answer, his adversary, in " A reproof of the Rehearsal Transprosed," in which he hints the propriety of Marvell's receiving a practical reproof from the secular arm. About the same time Andrew found in his lodgings an anonymous epistle, short as a blunderbuss :—" If thou darest to print any lie or libel against Dr. Parker, by the eternal God, I will cut thy throat," which pious expression of High-church zeal was adopted as the motto to the " Second part of the Rehearsal Transprosed," printed in 1673. From this second part we must be content with a single extract. Parker had reproached Marvell with the friendship of Milton, then living, in terms calculated to draw fresh suspicion on the aged poet, in an age when many would have deemed it a service to the church, if not to God, to assassinate the author of Paradise Lost. Of his great and venerable friend, Marvell speaks thus honourably :—

"J. M. was, and is, a man of great learning and sharpness of wit as any man. It was his misfortune, living in a tumultuous time, to be tossed on the wrong side, and he writ, *flagrante Bello*, certain dangerous treatises of no other nature than that which I mentioned to you writ by your own father,* only with this difference, that your father's, which I have by me, was written with the same design, but with much less wit or judgment. At his Majesty's happy return, J. M. did partake, even as you yourself did, of his regal clemency, and has ever since lived in a most retired silence. It was after that, I well remember it, that being one day at his house, I there first met you accidentally. But there it was, when you, as I told you, wandered up and down Moorfields, astrologizing on the duration of his Majesty's government, that you frequented J. M. incessantly, and haunted his house day by day. What discourses you there used he is too generous to remember."

Perhaps it was well for Marvell, that Milton could not read this, and we hope no one was so injudicious as to read it to him, for he would most angrily have spurned at anything like an *extenuation* of deeds in which he never ceased to glory. The very constitution of Milton's mind, his defect and his excellence, forbad him to conceive himself to have been in the wrong : in this, as in all else, but his genius and his nobility of soul, he was the very antipodes of Shakspeare. He that relented not, when he saw Charles the First upon the scaffold, was little likely to turn royalist, when he heard of Charles the Second in his haram.

Marvell, in all his authentic works, speaks with respect and tenderness of Charles the First, whose errors and misfortunes he attributed mainly to the rash counsels of the Prelates. In religion, he appears to incline to the Calvinistic doctrines, but without bitterness against the contrary opinions. He was truly liberal without indifference.

In October, 1674, his correspondence with his constituents was resumed, (or rather from this date it has been preserved,) and continued

---

* Controversy is pitch; none can meddle with it and be clean. How little worthy of Marvell was it to reproach Parker with what his father had written; was it his fault that his father was one of Oliver's committee-men, or that he wrote a book in defence of " the government of the people of England," with a most hieroglyphical title of emblems, motto's, &c., enough, as Andrew says, to have supplied the mortlings and achievements of this godly family ?

Parker died Bishop of Oxford, and it is asserted, on the very dubious credit of Jesuits, that he would have openly professed Popery under James the Second had he not been married. He died 1687, at the President's lodge of Maudlin College, Oxford. His versatility of principle does not seem to have enriched his family, for one of his daughters was reduced to the necessity of begging her bread.

to within a few month's of his death. The first letter of this renewed series has been often quoted as an instance of his incorruptibility and caution. The people of Hull had thought fit to propitiate with a present their governor, the Duke of Monmouth, then highly popular, and the hero, if not head of a certain party, who, to avert the dangers of a catholic succession, would gladly have washed the stain of illegitimacy from Charles's favourite offspring, though neither the law nor the Church of England permitted this *ex post facto* legitimation. They manage these things better at Rome. However Monmouth was the man of the day, and Marvell was to officiate in offering to the Duke the good town's oblation. But let him tell his own story :—" To-day I waited on him, and first presented him with your letter, which he read over very attentively, and then prayed me to assure you, that he would, upon all occasions, be most ready to give you the marks of his affection, and assist you in any affairs that you should recommend to him ; with other words of civility to the same purpose. I then delivered him the six broad pieces, telling him I was deputed to blush on your behalfe for the meanness of the present, &c. ; but he took me off, and said he thanked you for it, and accepted it as a token of your kindness. He had, before I came in, as I was told, considered what to do with the gold ; but that I by all means prevented the offer, or I had been in danger of being reimbursed with it. I received the bill which was sent me on Mr. Nelehorpe ; but the surplus of it exceeding much the expense I have been at on this occasion, I desire you to make use of it, and of me, upon any other opportunity."

As these letters relate wholly to the confused and unhappy politics of the time, and do not throw any new light on what is generally known, much less lead to the discovery of what is obscure, we shall make no further selections from them. We do, however, earnestly desire to see them republished in a convenient form, with whatever historical elucidation they may require to render them intelligible. It is right to mention that they testify favourably to the general accuracy of Hume, with whose account of the same transactions we have had occasion to compare them. The last date is June 6th, 1678, about two months before his death. He died, perhaps happily for his fame, before the explosion of the Popish plot.

In the latter years of his life Marvell frequently appeared as a political writer, and perhaps excited more animosity in that capacity, than by his firmness as a senator. In 1675 was seen the novel spectacle of a Bishop (and one who had been a confessor for his church) assailed by a plain priest, for over-toleration, and defended by a Calvanistic layman. Dr. Herbert Croft, Bishop of Hereford, had published a book called the "Naked Truth, or the true state of the Primitive Church," which, unlike most theological tracts in the seventeenth century, was in a moderate spirit, and of a moderate size, being no more than a quarto pamphlet of four or five sheets. As it was hostile to the high pretensions of the Hierarchy, as well as against the forcible interposition of the civil power in matters of belief or worship, it propably was resented by the more violent clergy as the treason of a false brother. Dr. Francis Turner, Master of St. John's College, Cambridge, published his "Animadversions on the Naked Truth," wherein, unluckily for himself, he indulged in a sort of prim facetiousness not quite in unison with the subject. Marvell had already made one divine "sacred to ridicule," by a dramatic nick-name: he now anabaptized Dr. Turner as "Mr. Smirke, or the Divine in Mode," alluding to a chaplain in Etherege's comedy,—"Sir Fopling Flutter, or the Man of Mode,"—thus holding him up as the model "of a neat, starched, formal and forward divine." There is a passage near the commencement which we must transcribe for the benefit of all *would-be-wits* in orders :—

"And from hence it proceeds, that, to the no small scandal and disreputation of our church, a great arcanum of their state hath been discovered and divulged; that, albeit wit be not inconsistent and incompatible with a clergyman, yet neither is it inseparable from them. So that it is of concernment to my Lords the Bishops henceforward to repress those of them who have no wit from writing, and to take care that even those that have, do husband it better, as not knowing to what exigency they may be reduced; but however, that they the Bishops be not too forward in licensing and prefixing their venerable names to such pamphlets. For admitting, though *I am not too positive in it*, that our episcopacy is of apostolical right, yet we do not find, among all those gifts there given to men, that Wit is enumerated ; nor yet among those qualifications requisite to a Bishop. And therefore should they, out of complacency for an author, or delight in the argument, or facility of their judgments, approve of a dull book, their own understandings will be answerable, and irreverent people, that cannot distinguish, will be ready to think that such of them differ from men of wit, not only in degree, but in order. For all are not of my mind, who could never see any one elevated to that dignity, but I presently conceived a greater opinion of his wit than ever I had formerly. But some do not stick to affirm, that even they, the Bishops, come by theirs, not by inspiration, not by teaching, but even as the poor laity do sometimes light upon it,—by a good mother. Which has occasioned the homely Scotch proverb, that " an ounce of mother wit is worth a pound of clergy." And as they come by it as do other men, so they possess it on the same condition : that they cannot transmit it by breathing, touching, or any natural effluvium, to other persons ; not so much as to their most domestick chaplains, or to the closest residentiary. That the King himself, who is no less the spring of that, than he is the fountain of honour, yet has never used the dubbing or creating of wits as a flower of his prerogative ; much less can the ecclesiastical power conferre it with the same ease as they do the holy orders. That whatsoever they can do of that kind is, at uttermost, to impower men by their authority and commission, no otherwise than in the licensing of midwives or physicians. But that as to their collating of any internal talent or ability, they could never pretend to it ; their grants and their prohibitions are alike invalid, and they can neither capacitate one man to be witty, nor hinder another from being so, further than as they press it at their devotion. Which, if it be the case, they cannot be too exquisite, seeing this way of writing is found so necessary, in making choice of fit instruments. The Church's credit is more interested in an ecclesiastical droll, than in a lay chancellor. It is no small trust that is reposed in him to whom the Bishop shall commit *omne et omni modum suum ingenium, tam temporale quam spirituale*; and, however it goes with excommunication, they should take good heed to what manner of person they delegate the keys of laughter. It is not every man that is qualified to sustain the dignity of the Church's jester, and, should they take as exact a scrutiny of them as of the Nonconformists through their dioceses, the numbers would appear inconsiderable upon this Easter visitation. Before men be admitted to so important an employment, it were fit they underwent a severe examination; and that it might appear, first, whether they have any sense ; for without that, how can any man pretend—and yet they do—to be ingenious ? Then, whether they have any modesty ; for without that they can only be scurrilous and impudent. Next, whether any truth ; for true jests are those that do the greatest execution. And lastly, it were not amiss that they gave some account, too, of their Christianity ; for the world has hitherto been so uncivil as to expect something of that from the clergy, in the design and style even of their lightest and most uncanonical writings."

Few Bishops seem to have honoured Marvell with their correspondence : but Dr. Croft did not think it derogatory to the mitre to thank his sarcastic avenger. We must give his letter, though it is not the ideal of epistolary or episcopal composition. Marvell's work, it must be remembered, was published under the name of Andreas Rivetus, Jun.:

SIR,

I choose to run some hazard of this (having no certain information), rather than incur your censure of ingratitude to the person who hath set forth Mr. Smirke in so trim and proper a dress, unto whose hands I hope this will happily arrive, to render him due thanks for the humane civility and christian charity shewed to the author of Naked Truth, so bespotted with the dirty language of foul-mouthed beasts, who, though he feared much his own weakness, yet, by God's undeserved grace, is so strengthened, as not at all to be dejected, or much concerned with such snarling curs, though sett on by many spightfull hands and hearts, of a high stamp, but as base alloy. I cannot yet get a sight of what the Bishop of Ely (Turner) hath certainly printed; but keeps very close, to put forth, I suppose, the next approaching session of Parliament, when there cannot be time to make a reply; for I have just cause to fear the session will be short. Sir, this assures you, that you have the zealous prayers and hearty service of the author of Naked Truth, your humble Servant,   H. C.

July, 1676.

In answer to this letter from Bishop Croft, Marvell says :—

" MY LORD,

Upon Tuesday night last I received your thanks for that which could not deserve your pardon; for great is your goodnesse to profess a gratitude, where you had a justifiable reason for your clemency; for notwithstanding the il-treatment you received from others, 'tis I that have given you the highest provocation. A good cause receives more injury from a weak defence, than from a frivolous accusation; and the ill that does a man no harm, is to be preferred before the good that creates him a prejudice : but your Lordship's generosity is not, I see, to be reformed by the most exquisite patterns of ill nature; and while perverse men have made a crime of your virtue, yet 'tis your pleasure to convert the obligation I have placed upon you into a civility.

Indeed, I meant all well, but 'tis not every one's good fortune to light into hands where he may escape; and for a man of good intentions, less than this I could not say in due and humble acknowledgment, and your favourable interpretation of me; for the rest, I most heartily rejoice to understand, that the same God who hath chosen you out to bear so eminent a testimony to his truth, hath given you also that Christian magnanimity to hold up, without any depression of spirit, against its and your opposers : what they intend further, I know not, neither am I curious; my soul shall not enter into their secrets; but as long as God shall send you life and health, I reckon our church is indefectible ;

may he, therefore, long preserve you to his honour, and further service, which shall be the constant prayer of,

My Lord,

Your Lordship's most humble

and most faithful Servant,

London, July 16, 1676.   ANDREW MARVELL."

To this work of Marvell's was added a short " Historical Essay con-concerning general Councils, Creeds, and Impositions, in Matters of Religion, by Andreas Redivivus, Jun., 1671, quarto." Of Turner, it is but fair to say that, whether his opinions were right or wrong, he proved his integrity under severe and repeated trials. He was among the seven Bishops who were imprisoned for refusing to authorize the Declaration of Liberty of Conscience ; yet he stuck to James in his adversity, and died a Non-juror and an Exile.

These strong and deep-thoughted satires gained for Marvell the reputation of a wit, even in the court where wit was one of the few good things admissible. Charles himself forgave the Patriot for the sake of the Humourist. Loving ridicule for its own sake, he cared not whether friend or foe, church or conventicle, were the object of derision. Burnet, who vilifies Marvell by calling him the " liveliest droll of the age," declares, that "his books were the delight of all classes, from the King, to the tradesman :" a sentence which accidentally points out the limits of reading in those days. As neither wits nor poets have been always remarkable for moral firmness, and are as vulnerable in their vanity and fears as politicians in their avarice and ambition, no means were omitted to win over Marvell. He was threatened, he was flattered, he was thwarted, he was caressed, he was beset with spies, and, if all tales be true, he was way-laid by ruffians, and courted by beauties. But no Dalilah could discover the secret of his strength : his integrity was proof alike against danger and against corruption ; nor was it enervated by that flattery, which, more frequently than either, seduces those weak, amiable ·creatures, whom, for lack of better, we are fain to call good. Against threats and bribes, pride is the ally of principle ; but how often has virtue pined away to a shadow, by too fondly contemplating its own image, reflected by insidious praise ; as Narcissus, in the fable, consumed his beauty by gazing on its watery shade. In a Court which held no man to be honest, and no woman chaste, this soft sorcery was cultivated to perfection ; but Marvell, revering and respecting himself, was proof against its charms.

There is a story told of his refusing a bribe, which has been heard and repeated by many, who perhaps did not know in what king's reign he lived, and which has been so often paralleled with the turnips of Curius, and the like common places, that some sceptical persons have held that there is as little truth in the one as in the other. However, we believe it to have been founded in fact, and that the mistake has been in the dulness of those who took a piece of dry English humour for a stoical exhibition of virtue. At all events, a life of Andrew Marvell would be as imperfect without it, as a history of King Alfred without the neat-herd's cottage and the burnt cakes. It is related with various circumstances, but we shall follow the narrative of a pamphlet printed in Ireland, A. D., 1754:—" The borough of Hull, in the reign of Charles II., chose Andrew Marvell, a young gentleman of little or no fortune, and maintained him in London for the service of the public. His understanding, integrity, and spirit, were dreadful to the then infamous administration. Persuaded that he would be theirs for properly asking, they sent his old school-fellow, the Lord Treasurer Danby, to renew acquaintance with him in his garret. At parting, the Lord Treasurer, out of *pure affection*, slipped into his hand an order upon the treasury for £1000, and then went to his chariot. Marvell, looking at the paper, calls after the Treasurer, " My Lord, I request another moment." They went up again to the garret, and Jack, the servant boy, was called. " Jack, child, what had I for dinner yesterday?" " Dont you remember, sir? you had the little shoulder of mutton that you ordered me to bring from a woman in the market." " Very right, child." " What have I for dinner to-day?" " Dont you know, sir, that you bid me lay by the *blade-bone to broil.*" " 'Tis so, very right, child, go away." " My Lord, do you hear that? Andrew Marvell's dinner is provided; there's your piece of paper. I want it not. I knew the sort of kindness you intended. I live here to serve my constituents: the ministry may seek men for their purpose; *I am not one.*"

One mark of authenticity the story certainly wants:—it has no date. As, however, it mentions Lord Danby as treasurer, it must have occurred within the last four years of Marvell's life: for Sir Thomas Osborne, afterwards first Duke of Leeds, was not appointed treasurer till the 19th of June, 1673; nor was he created Earl Danby till the 27th of June, 1674. The fact of his having been Marvell's school-fellow rests, as far as we have discovered, upon the Irishman's credit alone, though it is not impossible, as his family estates lay in Yorkshire and Lancashire.

In addition to the circumstances mentioned above, it has been customary to enhance the merit of Marvell by relating how, after refusing the King's thousand pounds, he was obliged to borrow a guinea of his bookseller. But the story is better without this heightening touch. The very familiarity with which the word guinea is employed, points to a period when a guinea was the lowest sum which a gentleman could think of accepting. Now guineas were first coined in 1673, and it is by no means likely that the term became immediately familiar. Marvell was more likely to have borrowed a broad piece. Borrowing of a bookseller is an expedient very likely to occur to an author of later days; but Andrew Marvell never was a bookseller's author, nor were booksellers likely to be liberal lenders, when the copyright of Paradise Lost was transferred for £15.

Marvell was far from affluent, but there is no ground for supposing that he ever was, in the proper sense of the word, *poor*. His paternal estate, though small, was unimpaired: his mode of living simple and frugal, but not sordid. His company was sought by the great, as well as the witty; notwithstanding his politics, he was admitted into the company of the merry Monarch, (but so to be sure was Colonel Blood,) and he was on so intimate a footing with Prince Rupert, than whenever the Prince dissented from the court measures, it was usual to say " he has been with his tutor." It is said, that when Marvell had become so obnoxious to the Court, or rather to the Duke's party, that it was dangerous for him to stir abroad, Rupert visited him at his humble apartment, in a Westminster attic.

That Marvell was exposed to assaults from the drunken insolent followers of the Court, such as those that revenged the cause of Nell Gwyn on Sir John Coventry's nose, is almost certain. Homicide, in a midnight scuffle, was then esteemed as venial as adultery. The habit of bloodshed, contracted in civil warfare, had choked up the natural remorse of hearts which had either no religion, or worse than none. But that any settled design of assassinating him was meditated by any party, cannot be proved, and therefore ought not to be believed.

So long indeed, as he condescended to write in masquerade, and to veil his serious purpose with a ridiculous vizard, it seems to have been the wish of the government to let him escape. But when at last he dared to be once for all in earnest, and set forth the dangers of the constitution plainly and without a parable, the ruling powers were afraid to laugh any longer, and began to think of prosecuting. In the early part of 1678, appeared " An Account of the growth of Popery and arbitrary Government in England," ostensibly printed at Amsterdam, which though without his name, was well known to be the work of Marvell, for none else could and would have written it. Shortly after, the following proclamation appeared in the Gazette.

" Whereas there have been lately printed and published, several seditious and scandalous libels, against the proceedings of both Houses of Parliament, and other his Majesty's Courts of Justice, to the dishonour of his Majesty's government, and the hazard of the public peace : These are to give notice, that what person soever shall discover unto one of the Secretaries of State, the printer, publisher, author, or hander to the press, of any of the said libels, so that full evidence may be made thereof to a jury, without mentioning the informer ; especially one libel, entitled " An Account of the growth of Popery," &c., and another called " A seasonable Argument to all Grand Juries," &c. ; the discoverer shall be rewarded as follows :—he shall have £50 for the discovery of the printer, or publisher, and for the hander of it to the press, £100," &c.

So little was Marvell alarmed at this movement, that he writes to his friend Popple in a strain of jocular defiance about it. The letter is dated 10th of June, 1678, and is perhaps the latest of his extant writings :—" There came out, about Christmas last, a large book, concerning ' The growth of Popery and arbitrary Government.' There have been great rewards offered in private, and considerable in the Gazette, to any who would inform of the author. Three or four books, printed since, have described, as near as it was proper to go, the man, Mr. Marvell, being a member of Parliament, to have been the author ; but if he had, surely he would not have escaped being questioned in Parliament, or some other place." No prosecution, however, ensued, but dark and desperate menacings hovered round him ; he was obliged to be cautious of going abroad, and was sometimes obliged to secrete himself for several days. Perhaps he found it prudent to absent himself from Town, and seek security among his constituents ; for in an extract from the books of the Corporation of Hull, we find this notice : " This day, 29th July. 1678, the court being met, Andrew Marvell, Esq. one of the burgesses of Parliament for this Borough, came into court, and several discourses were held, about the Town affairs." We know not, whether like his father, he was possessed with a presentiment of approaching mortality, and felt that this was to be his last visit to the scenes of his childhood ; but certain it is, he was destined to see them no more. He returned to London, and with scarce any previous illness, or visible decay of constitution, on the 16th of August, he expired.

No wonder if so sudden a decease, in an age when all were disposed to believe, and too many to execute, the worst that evil thoughts suggest, were ascribed to the effects of poison ; but since all men are liable to be called away every hour, it is better not to add horrid surmises to the woeful sum of horrid certainties.

It is somewhat singular, that the Parliament, in which Marvell had sat so long, itself the longest which ever sat under the monarchy, survived him but one session, as if its dissolution were deferred as long as it numbered one righteous man. The pension Parliament was dissolved on the 30th of December, 1678.

It has been said that Marvell was the last member that received wages from his constituents. Others, however, his contemporaries, maintained the *right*, and suffered their arrears to accumulate as a cheap resource at the next election. More than once in the course of Marvell's correspondence, he speaks of members threatening to sue their boroughs for their pay.

Aubrey, who knew Marvell, and may be trusted when he describes what he saw, says that he was " of a middling stature, pretty strong set, roundish cheeked, hazel eyed, brown haired. In his conversation he was modest, and of very few words. He was wont to say he would not drink high, or freely, with any one with whom he would not trust his life." Heaven be praised, we live in times when such a resolution would seldom interfere with the circulation of the bottle. If a gentleman take care that the liquor does not injure him, he need apprehend no *bodily* hurt from his compotators.

As a Senator, his character appears unimpeachable. He was a true representative of his constituents ; not slavishly submitting his wisdom to their will, nor setting his privilege above their interests. How he would have acted, had he been a member of the Long Parliament, which presumed to command the King in the name of the nation, and levied forces against the Monarch, under his own Great Seal, we can only conjecture. The sphere of his duty was far different ; for the Commons, on the Restoration, necessarily resumed their pristine character, which was not that of a ruling Committee, but a simple representation of the third estate. There was then no need of a monarchical, or of an aristocratical party in the lower House, for the monarchy and aristocracy still retained ample powers of their own. A member of Parliament had therefore only one duty to attend to, as a counsellor is only obliged to serve the interests of his clients, leaving to the Judge and Jury the justice of the general question. We are convinced, that a restitution of the tribunitial power, originally vested in the Commons, should be accompanied with the restoration of the just prerogatives of the Peerage, and of the Crown. " Give the King his own again," and the people will get their own too.

Of his poetic merits, we would gladly speak at large, but our limits allow not of immoderate quotation, and his works are too little known, and in general too inaccessible, to be referred to with confidence. It is disgraceful to English booksellers, (we say not to the English nation,) that they find not a place in our popular collections. The writer of this notice can truly say that he met with them only by accident, and was astonished that they were not familiar as household words. But probably the same causes which retarded the poetic fame of Milton, went nigh to extinguish that of Andrew Marvell. The classical Republicans were few and inefficient. The Puritans would not read poetry. The High-Church Bigots would read nothing but what emanated from their own party. The common-place roystering Royalists were seldom sober enough to read, and the mob-fanatics did not know their letters.

Moreover, the mere celebrity of a man, in one respect, sometimes throws a temporary shade over his accomplishments in a different line. Milton had produced Poems in his youth, that alone would place him high among Poets, yet no one remembered that the author of the " Defensio populi Anglicani" had ever written Comus ; and Roscoe was perhaps the first to remind the people of England, that Lorenzo di Medici ranks high among the bards of Italy. It is not without effort that we remember that Cæsar's Commentaries were written by the same man who conquered at Pharsalia. And what reader of Childe Harold thinks of Lord Byron's speech about the Nottingham Frame-breakers? Lord John Russell's Tragedies are obscured by the lustre of his Reform Bill, and should Paganini produce another Iliad, it would only be read as the preposterous adventure of a fiddler. Hence we may fairly conclude that Marvell's fame would have been greater, had it been less ; that had he been as insignificant a being as Pomfret, or Yalden, Dr. Johnson might have condescended to rank him among the Poets of Great Britain.

We took occasion to allude to Marvell's sentiments on the death of Charles the First, expressed in his Horatian Ode to Oliver Cromwell. The lines are noble :—

AN HORATIAN ODE
UPON CROMWELL'S RETURN FROM IRELAND.

*   *   *

> Though justice against fate complain,
> And plead the ancient rights in vain :
>   But those do hold or break,
>   As men are strong or weak.
> Nature, that hateth emptiness,
> Allows of penetration less;
>   And therefore must make room
>   Where greater spirits come.
> What field of all the civil war,
> Where his were not the deepest scar?

And Hampton shows what part
He had of wiser art:
When twining subtle fears with hope,
He wove a net of such a scope,
 That Charles himself might chace
 To Carisbrook's narrow case;
That thence the royal actor borne,
The tragic scaffold might adorne,
 While round the armed bands,
 Did clap their bloody hands:
He nothing common did, or mean,
Upon that memorable scene;
 But with his keener eye,
 The axe's edge did trye.
Nor call'd the Gods with vulgar spight,
To vindicate his helplesse right:
 But bow'd his comely head
 Downe, as upon a bed.
This was that memorable houre,
Which first assured the forced power;
 So when they did designe
 The capitol's first line,
A bleeding head where they begun
Did fright the architects to run.

The poems of Marvell are, for the most part, productions of his early youth. They have much of that over-activity of fancy, that remoteness of allusion, which distinguishes the school of Cowley; but they have also a heartfelt tenderness, a childish simplicity of feeling, among all their complication of thought, which would atone for all their conceits, if conceit were indeed as great an offence against poetic nature as Addison and other critics of the French school pretend. But though there are cold conceits, a conceit is not necessarily cold. The mind, in certain states of passion, finds comfort in playing with occult or casual resemblances, and dallies with the echo of a sound.

We confine our praise to the poems which he wrote for himself. As for those he made to order, for Fairfax or Cromwell, they are as dull as every true son of the muse would wish these things to be. Captain Edward Thomson, who collected and published Marvell's works in 1776, has, with mischievous industry, scraped together, out of the state poems, and other common sewers, a quantity of obscene and scurrilous trash, which we are convinced Marvell did not write, and which, by whomsoever written, ought to be delivered over to condign oblivion.

With less injury to Marvell's reputation, but equal disregard of probability, Captain Thompson ascribes to him the hymns or paraphrases, " When all thy mercies, Oh my God," " The spacious firmament on high," which were published in the Spectator, and afterwards in the works of Addison, to whom they undoubtedly belong. He was not the man to claim what was not his own. As to their being Marvell's, it is just as probable that they are Chaucer's. They present neither his language, his versification, nor his cast of thought.

We cannot better conclude, than with the following beautiful extract from a letter to a friend in affliction, which is novel on a trite subject,—that of consolation :—

HONOURED SIR,

Having a great esteem and affection for you, and the grateful memory of him that is departed being still green and fresh upon my spirit, I cannot forbear to enquire, how you have stood the second shock, at your sad meeting of friends in the country. I know that the very sight of those who have been witnesses of our better fortune, doth but serve to reinforce a calamity. I know the contagion of grief, and infection of tears ; and especially when it runs in a blood. And I myself could sooner imitate than blame those innocent relentlings of nature, so that they spring from tenderness only, and humanity, not from an implacable sorrow. The tears of a family may flow together like those little drops that compact the rainbow, and if they be placed with the same advantage towards heaven, as those are to the sun, they, too, have their splendour ; and like that bow, while they unbend into seasonable showers, yet they promise that there shall not be a second flood. But the dissoluteness of grief—the prodigality of sorrow—is neither to be indulged in a man's self, nor complied with in others. Though an only son be inestimable, yet, it is like Jonah's sin, to be angry at God for the withering of his gowrd. He that gave his own son, may he not take ours ? It is pride that makes a rebel ; and nothing but the overweening of ourselves, and our own things, that raises us against Divine Providence. Whereas, Abraham's obedience was better than sacrifice. And if God please to accept both, it is indeed a farther trial, but a greater honour. 'Tis true, it is a hard task to learn and teach at the same time. And where yourselves are the experiment, it is as if a man should dissect his own body, and read the anatomy lecture. But I will not heighten the difficulty, while I advise the attempt. Only, as in difficult things, you would do well to make use of all that may strengthen and assist you ; the word of God, the society of good men, and the books of the ancients : there is one way more, which is, by diversion, business, and activity, which are also necessary to be used in their season."

RICHARD BENTLEY, D.D.

THE life of BENTLEY is not a pleasing retrospect. It affords a painful proof that peaceful pursuits are not always pursued in peace—that the irascible passions may be excited, no less by controversies of literature, than by disputes of politics ; and that mean, and malignant interests are as busy in academic shades, as they can be in " high-viced cities;"—that power is as eagerly, and unscrupulously grasped at by the scholar, as by the courtier ; and that money was once as unrighteously worshipped in Trinity College, Cambridge, as now in Threadneedle Street, or Capel Court.

> " Ingenuas didicisse fideliter artes
> Emollit mores nec sinit esse feros."

> Of liberal learning 'tis the choicest fruit
> To make a gentleman of clown or brute.

So says Ovid. This is one of the first apothegms that poor little Latiners are doomed to learn ; and a beautiful one it is ; displaying the value of classical learning in the clearest light. There is but one small objection to it :—it is not true.

It were well for great authors, poets, philosophers, scholars,—may be also for divines, if their memory lived only in their works—if their books were like the pyramids, which are admired the more, because we know not by whom, or for what, they were erected. Happiest, as the first and greatest of poets, is HOMER, of whose corporeal existence, not a record survives. So utterly are the footsteps of his mortal pilgrimage obliterated, that certain irrefragable doubters deny that he ever appeared in the body, and maintain that the *Iliad* is a meteor formed of the exhalations of a national mind, a unison of many voices, blended by the distance of a remote age ; and it is pleasanter to believe even this, than to think that his life was spent in petty squabbles, and *qui tam* litigation : or that, according to one tradition, he drowned himself from vexation, because he could not guess a miserable riddle.

It may not be an unfitting introduction to the biography of England's first *Hellenist*, if we attempt to fix the just value of that literature, to which BENTLEY dedicated those hours, which were not engaged in litigious feuds, from which no distraction of affairs, no peril of estate, or reputation, ever diverted him.   In the ceaseless ebb and flow of opinion, what has been unduly exalted by one age, is oft times as unjustly depreciated in the next, and so it has happened, that a minute acquaintance with the niceties of two dead languages, which has been honoured with the exclusive name of scholarship, and regarded as the sole type and symbol of a liberal education, is now considered by the most influential movers of popular judgment, as the specious disguise of self complacent ignorance, the fruitless blossom of indefatigable idleness, at best a frivolous accomplishment, and not seldom, an insidious abettor of privileged prejudice, and of " creeds outworn." But in truth there is no more wisdom, and far less amiability, in running along with a new folly, than in sitting still in the shadow of an old one.

In the wide circuit of human capacity, there is room for every art, and every science. As that liberty which infringes on another's birthright is usurpation, so that knowledge, whatever it be, which allows not space for all knowledge to expand, is merely learned ignorance. Neither the exact sciences, which are part and parcel of the pure reason ; nor the practical arts of life, which good sense constructs out of experience, are any wise defrauded, by the attention which certain intellects choose to bestow, on the remains of antiquity. It is a very useless enquiry—what kind of knowledge, or what line of occupation is best— all are good, and in a complex system of society, all are needful. The community will best be served, if each do strenuously what he can do best, without troubling himself about the comparative worth or dignity of his vocation. When we consider the excellence to which Sciliger, Bentley, Heman, Heyne, attained in their art, we cannot reasonably doubt, that the All-giver endued them with peculiar faculties, fitted to their peculiar object, and that devoting themselves to that object, they obeyed the will of him who bestows on each man according to his divine pleasure. When we see a beautiful picture, we know that its maker was bound by special duty to paint. When we read an acute and elegant criticism, we are sure that its author is right in being a philologer. Wherever we find any branch of learning cultivated to the detriment of general information, we say not " this is overrated," but " other things are underrated," the fabric of learning has been built on too narrow a basis, and without that symmetry and inter-dependence of parts which is no less indispensable to intellectual soundness, than to visible beauty. But though the commonwealth of mind requires universal erudition, yet for the individual it is sufficient that he be wise in his own craft— the division of labour allows and demands that particular functions should appropriate particular agents—all will go well for each and all, if there be not wanting some few overlooking and ruling geniuses, some master intellects, some architectonic sages, to keep the operatives to their work, and to restrict them to their province.

The question is not, therefore, whether critical learning be not useful and ornamental to the individual, not whether a Bentley employed, or misemployed, his faculties, but whether the predominance assented by classical studies over all other human knowledge, is rightfully conceded. Never for a moment would we allow it to be disputed that *Mozart* and *Handel* were glorious beings, who well fulfilled these duties to nature and to society; for be it remembered, that we speak not of those higher duties to God and the soul, which are essentially the same for all degrees, ranks, ages, sexes, and capacities. Their excellence proves irrefragably that they laboured in their appointed path; nevertheless we would not willingly constitute the *music masters* a committee of general instruction, nor do we very highly approve the fashion, which confines every female not born to manual labour, and too many of those that have no secure or honorable prospects of exemption from servitude or toil, hour after hour to a *Piano-forte*, for six days in the week, if the seventh be kept holy—wasting her happy spirits in the weary iteration of sounds, in which she delights not herself, and by which therefore she cannot delight others. By parity of argument the excellence of Virgil's verses does not demonstrate the propriety of compelling every boy, who is not sent to a ship or a factory, to be a Latin versifier, nor will the well-earned reputation of PORSON and BLOMFIELD, justify that arrangement, which measures the fitness of any man to form the mind of youth, and to tend over the souls of the poor, by his skill in deciding the priority of Greek readers, and his zeal for the abdicated rights of the Æolic Digamma.

In the history of *classical* learning in England, the most conspicuous name is that of RICHARD BENTLEY, who was one of the most prominent characters of the age to which he belonged. He was equally distinguished for the vigour of his intellect, the extent of his erudition, and the violence of his conduct. His life was long and active, and certainly not spent in an even tenor. From the manner in which it was occupied, his natural element appears to have been that of strife and contention. His literary controversies, not few in number, were conducted with much ferocity; nor was his name more familiarly known in the classical haunts of the Muses, than in the unclassical Court of King's Bench, where he had *six* law-suits in less than *three* years. The name of Bentley occupies a very prominent place in the works of Pope, Swift, and other contemporary satirists, and is familiarly known to multitudes who have no knowledge of his writings, or of his real character.

Of this most learned and pugnacious individual, the present Bishop of Gloucester *(Dr. Monk)*, who has cultivated similar studies, has written a most elaborate life. From the Bishop's ample details, and other sources of information, we shall endeavour to give a condensed and accurate view of Bentley's personal and literary history.

RICHARD BENTLEY was born at *Oulton*, a village near Leeds, in Yorkshire, on the 27th of January, 1662. His lineage was neither so high, nor so low, as it has sometimes been represented. His progenitors were of that respectable class which has supplied every profession with many of its brightest ornaments, the higher description of English yeomen. They had been settled for some generations at *Heptonstall*, a village about eight miles from Halifax, where they possessed property. During the civil wars, his grandfather, James Bentley, a captain in the Royal army, was taken by the enemy, and died a prisoner in Pontefract Castle. His father, Thomas Bentley, possessed a small estate at *Woodlesford*, in the parish of Rothwell. In the year 1661, he married Sarah, daughter of *Richard Willie*, a stone-mason, at Oulton, and the first offspring of their union was the subject of this memoir.

For the first elements of classical learning, he is said to have been indebted to his *mother*, who is represented to have been a woman of an excellent understanding. He was then sent to a day-school in the neighbouring hamlet of *Methley*, and afterwards to the grammar school at Wakefield. *Cumberland* says, that " he went through the school with singular reputation." It appears that Mr. Jeremiah Boulton was the master of Wakefield school until April, 1672, when a Mr. John Baskerville succeeded him. Of this gentleman, to whom the principal credit of Bentley's education must belong, nothing is known, but that he was of Emmanuel College, Cambridge, and presided in the school at Wakefield till his death, in 1681. Not to name the school, or the masters of men illustrious for literature, has been justly called by Dr. Johnson, " a kind of historical fraud, by which honest fame is injuriously diminished." For the place of his education, Bentley testified throughout life the greatest attachment, and extended to persons coming from that seminary, his encouragement and patronage.

At the time of Bentley's birth, his father was considerably advanced in life, but his mother was only nineteen. They had four children younger than himself, of whom only two, *Ann* and *Joseph*, survived their infancy. When he was thirteen years old his father died, leaving his property at Woodlesford to his eldest son, *James*, the offspring, as it appears, of a former marriage. Richard was committed to the care of his grandfather *Willie*, who determined upon sending him to the University. He was. admitted, at Cambridge, a Subsizar of St. John's

College, under the tuition of the *Rev. Joseph Johnston.* The master of the college was *Dr. Francis Turner*, afterwards Bishop of Ely. Of the peculiar direction of Bentley's academical studies, no record has been preserved. That he then laid the foundation of his accurate and extensive knowledge of the classics, and attained that nice perception of their poetical measures, for which he stands unrivalled, cannot be doubted.

The academical prizes which now serve to stimulate the exertions of students, had, at that period, no existence ; but it is necessary to recollect, that a mind constituted like that of Bentley's required no stimulus of this nature. Youthful genius, when it enters upon its proper career, proceeds with an impulse that seems to be instinctive ; and not unfrequently nourishes a secret contempt for all those objects which are most attractive to minds of a *secondary* mould. Bentley, who was never oppressed with a distrust of his own powers or attainments, must speedily have felt a consciousness of superiority over all his classical instructors ; and, like every other scholar who makes any bold excursions beyond the common limits, he must, to a great extent, have been his own preceptor.

Having continued at college for upwards of two years, he became a scholar on the foundation of Dr Downman, and at the expiration of the third year, he succeeded to one of the Yorkshire scholarships, founded by *Sir Marmaduke Constable.* At the regular period he commenced Batchelor of Arts, in company with a greater number of students than have ever taken their degree at the same time, till the last two or three years. In the list of honours, his place corresponds with that of third wrangler, according to the present distribution. From a fellowship of his college he was excluded by a provision in the statutes, which prohibits more than *two* fellows being chosen from the same county. He was, however, appointed head master of the Grammar-school at *Spalding*, in Lincolnshire. The commission of so important a trust to a youth, who had only completed the *twentieth* year of his age, is not merely a testimony of his scholarship, but implies an opinion favourable to his general character. On attaining the age of majority, he disposed of his interest in the Oulton property to his brother James, and the money thus procured he devoted to the purchase of *books*, which are not less necessary to a scholar, than tools to a carpenter.*

The office of a country schoolmaster generally fixes the destiny of

* For particulars relative to the Oulton property, Bentley's ancestors, and other matters connected with the place of his nativity, Dr. Monk acknowledges himself indebted to his friend *John Blaydes, Esq., Jun.*, whose father is possessed of the property in question.

its possessor for life, and forces him to be contented with the humble, but honourable fame to be acquired in the discharge of its duties. But Bentley was designed for a different sphere : he did not preside over the school more than a twelvemonth,—too short a period to afford means of estimating his merits as an instructor, and scarcely sufficient to place his name upon record in that capacity.

He next accepted the office of domestic tutor to the son of *Dr. Edward Stillingfleet*, Dean of St. Paul's. For this appointment he was indebted to St. John's College, of which the Dean had been a Fellow. To a young man of talents and merit, hardly any situation could have been more advantageous. It was not only favourable to the cultivation of his talents, but to the views of advancement in the clerical profession.

Bentley took his degree of Master of Arts in July, 1683, after which his personal connection with Cambridge was discontinued for the space of seventeen years. In the mean time, prosecuting his studies with all the advantages of books and literary society, he amassed and digested that *prodigious* fund of knowledge, which displays itself in his earliest publications.

The Revolution of eighty-eight, among various greater and lesser consequences, produced a new batch of Bishops, to supply the sees vacated by the scrupulous *Non-jurors*, who, though of stout spirits, were of timid consciences, and, after braving the wrath of a bigot in prosperity, preserved unbroken allegiance to a monarch in exile, spite of the metaphysical figment of the original contract, and the audacious falsehood about the warming pan. Many may doubt whether they acted wisely ;—none will deny that they thought nobly. Well had it been, had this secession, or deprivation, produced no worse effects than the promotion of Stillingfleet to the diocese of Worcester, for he was a man whose massive erudition, and sound book-mindedness, were edified by piety, and illumined by good sense. About the same time, Bentley, with his pupil, the younger Stillingfleet, removed to Oxford, and was incorporated Master of Arts, July 4th, 1689, being admitted of Wadham College. Whatever of living learning Oxford had then to boast, was doubtless assiduously sought out by Bentley, but his favourite companions were the MSS. of the Bodleian, and its weighty volumes,—the silent language of the dead.

In the ardour of youthful ambition, Bentley projected editions of the Greek grammarians, and Latin poets. The project which he contemplated as the foundation of his fame, was a complete collection of the fragments of the Greek poets ; " an undertaking," as Dr. Monk remarks, " the magnitude and difficulty of which those only can appreciate, who have endeavoured to collect the quotations of any *one* poet, scattered through the whole range of classical authors, as well as of grammarians, scholiasts, and lexicographers." This work, however, he never executed, but of his competency for such a task, he has left sufficient evidence in his collection of the fragments of *Callimachus*, afterwards communicated to *Grævius*. At the suggestion, as it is supposed, of the very learned Bishop Lloyd, he undertook the stupendous task of publishing a complete edition of the Greek Lexicographers ; but where so much is attempted, little is often accomplished. The general design, which was too vast to be properly executed by *one* individual, appears to have been abandoned after a short' interval ; but it is much to be regretted that he did not publish an edition of *Hesychius*, an author in whom he professes to have made upwards of *five thousand* corrections. Of his familiarity with this lexicographer, he exhibited a sufficient specimen in his earliest publication, subjoined to *Dr. Hody's* edition of the chronicle of *Joannes Malela Antiochenus*, which was printed at Oxford in the year 1691. " The various and accurate learning, and the astonishing sagacity displayed in his epistle to Mill," says Dr. Monk, " attracted the attention of every person capable of judging upon such subjects. The originality of Bentley's style, the boldness of his opinions, and his secure reliance upon unfailing stores of learning, all marked him out as a scholar to be ranked with Scaliger, Casaubon, and Gataker." Such was the production which established the fame of Bentley, at the age of *twenty-nine*, in the highest rank of literary eminence ; and from that moment the eyes of every scholar in Europe were fixed upon his operations. " Great is the number of persons who have since appeared with success in this department," continues Dr. Monk, " it would not be easy to name a critical essay, which for accuracy, ingenuity, and original learning, can take place of the " Appendix to Malelas."

Bentley's next appearance before the public was in the character of a *divine*. He had received deacon's orders from Compton, Bishop of London, in the year 1690, and soon afterwards was appointed one of the Bishop of Worcester's chaplains.

The Honourable ROBERT BOYLE died on the 30th of December, 1691. Wishing that at his death, he might promote the same cause to which he had devoted his life, he bequeathed by his will, a salary of £50 a year, to found a lectureship for the defence of religion, against *infidels*. The lecturer was to be chosen annually, and to deliver *eight* discourses in the year, in one of the churches of the metropolis. The care of the trust was bequeathed to four trustees, who forthwith nominated Mr. Bentley lecturer for the first year. We can hardly conceive a greater compliment to the merits of a young man only in deacon's orders, than the selection of him from the whole clerical profession, as the champion of the faith delivered down by the Apostles. He mentions this distinction at different periods of his life, in such terms as to shew that he considered it the greatest honour with which he was ever invested. The eight discourses which he preached in consequence of this appointment, are in a great degree directed against the principles of Hobbes and Spinoza. According to Dr. Monk, " Bentley claims the undoubted merit of having in these sermons been the first to display the discoveries of NEWTON, in a popular form, and to explain their irresistible force in the proof of a Deity." Before he ventured to print his lectures, he consulted that great philosopher, respecting some of the arguments he had founded upon those discoveries ; and his different queries were answered in four letters. Newton's Letters on this occasion have been long before the public ; they commence with two remarkable declarations, the object of which he had in view while writing his immortal work, and a disavowal of that *intuitive genius* for which the world gave him credit ; he says, " when I wrote my treatise about our system, I had an eye upon such principles as might work with considering men, for the belief of a Deity, and nothing can rejoice me more than to find it useful for that purpose. But if I have done the public any service this way, it is due to nothing but *industry* and *patient* thought."

Bentley's reputation for talent and learning was greatly augmented by the publication of his lectures ; of which the *sixth* edition, including other three discourses, was printed at Cambridge in the year 1735. The lectures were translated into Latin by *Jablouski*, who was himself a writer of distinguished learning. Nor did the merit of the author remain without its reward : in the year 1692, soon after he had taken priest's orders, he obtained a *Prebend* in the cathedral of *Worcester* ; and in the course of the following year, he succeeded *Henry de Justel*, as keeper of the King's Library. Such was the auspicious commencement of *Boyle's Lectures*, an institution to which we owe some of the ablest theological pieces in our language ; among which we may mention " Clarke's Discourses on the Being and Attributes of God," and " Newton's Dissertation on the Prophecies."

The reputation which Bentley had now acquired was not unattended with its usual consequences, envy and detraction. The envy produced by Bentley's endowments, was increased by a certain haughtiness discoverable in his conversation and demeanour. There was a traditional anecdote current during his life, which shews the opinions prevalent upon this subject. It is that " a nobleman dining at his patron's, and happenning to sit next to Bentley, was so much struck with his information and powers of argument, that he remarked to the Bishop, after dinner, " My Lord, that chaplain of yours is certainly a very extraordinary man." " Yes," said Stillingfleet ; " had he but the gift of *humility,* he would be the most extraordinary man in Europe." *

In 1694 he was again appointed to preach Boyle's lectures ; but this series of discourses his friends could never prevail upon him to publish, nor has it been ascertained that the manuscript is preserved. He had now made great progress in preparing editions of *Manilius* and *Philostratus.* He appeared to have been chiefly deterred from sending them to press, by the increased expense of paper and printing in England. He was induced, by the cheapness of German typography, to adopt the plan of printing his edition of the Greek sophist at *Leipzig,* and there one sheet was actually printed as a specimen ; but he was so disgusted with the meanness of its appearance, that he resolved his learned animadversions should not be exhibited in so unsuitable a dress. "It may be remarked," says Dr. Monk, "that Bentley always placed a high value upon typographical elegance, and was more fastidious upon this head, than might have been expected, from one who so well understood the *intrinsic* merits of a book." In this respect we are, however, more inclined to commend, than to censure his taste ; the elegance of typography is, in most cases, a harmless luxury; nor do we perceive any difficulty in supposing that a competent judge of good printing, may also be a competent judge of good writing.

It was in a great measure owing to his zeal and perseverence, that the Cambridge University Press, which had never recovered the shock of the civil wars, was restored to respectability. A sufficient sum having been raised for defraying the necessary expenses, the charge of providing types was solely entrusted to Bentley. We are expressly informed, that the subscriptions were principally procured by his exertions. The types were cast in *Holland* ; and some well-known books, which afterwards issued from that press, particularly *Taylor's Demosthenes, Kuster's Suidas,* and *Talbot's Horace,* afford sufficient evidence of the commission having been placed in proper hands.

In the year 1695, his patron, the Bishop of Worcester, gave him the

---

* Very likely :—the gift of humility would make any man *extraordinary,* though he should possess "small Latin, and less Greek." The modesty to decline, the pride to disdain an invidious display of talents or acquirements—the good sense that soberly appreciates the abilities of self—the candour and generosity that does willing justice to the merits of others—are frequent, though not constant accompaniments of true genius, and of genuine learning. But true humility is something very different from all these : it is not a gift, but a *grace,*—only bestowed on such as have made the soul a temple for the Father of light and love. C.

rectory of *Hartlebury*, to be held till his pupil should arrive at the canonical age. This preferment he retained for the space of three years: the interest of the same prelate had, about that period, procured him the nomination of Chaplain in ordinary to the King. It was also about this period that he was elected a Fellow of the Royal Society. We must here record it as an instance of scandalous ingratitude, that when the Bishop's grandson, Benjamin Stillingfleet, was left an *orphan*, and was sent, in the humble capacity of sizar, to Trinity College, Bentley refused to give him a fellowship, and preferred several competitors of inferior attainments.

At the commencement of the year 1696, he ceased to reside in the Bishop's house, in Park-Street, Westminster, and took possession of the librarian's apartments in St. James's Palace; and in the month of July, he was created Doctor of Divinity, at Cambridge. He was appointed to preach the commencement sermon, and the subject which he selected was that " of Revelation, and the Messias ;" a subject which he treated in a manner not unworthy of his reputation.

Dr. Bentley was now making a rapid approach to the full height of his literary fame, and his principal efforts were more the results of accidental excitements, than of his own deliberate plans. In the year 1692, Sir William Temple, one of the most fashionable writers of the age, had published " An Essay on Ancient and Modern Learning," in which he strenuously opposed the opinions of *Fontenelle* and *Perrault*, who had given a very decided preference to the *moderns*. Sir William had caught the contagion of the then prevalent literary controversy, in which the first scholars in Europe were engaged, and he was of opinion that the *ancients* possessed a greater force of genius, with some peculiar advantages; that the human mind was in a state of decay; and that our knowledge was nothing more than scattered fragments saved out of the general shipwreck. But Temple's learning was of that gentle-manlike quality which fitted him rather to admire than to judge; and his preference of the ancients probably arose more from long familiarity, and pleasant associations, than from a fair estimate of comparative value. Had he advanced the names of Shakspeare, Milton, Bacon, Newton, he would have furnished his French antagonists with powers they knew not of. The fables of *Æsop*, and the epistles of *Phalaris*, which he believed to be the most ancient pieces of prose written by profane authors, doubtless appeared much more to the purpose.

Dr. Aldrich, the learned dean of Christ Church, was accustomed to employ some of his best scholars in preparing editions of classical works; and of these publications, which were generally of a moderate compass, it was his practice to present a copy to every young man in his college.

The task of editing the epistles of *Phalaris* was committed to the HON. CHARLES BOYLE, a young gentleman of pleasing manners, and of a relish for learning, creditable to his age and rank. He had profited by the tuition of DR. GALE, the dean of York, who had long cultivated Grecian literature ; and on his admission at Christ Church, he was under the tuition of ATTERBURY, who, if not a profound, was at least an elegant scholar. In his editorial labours he was aided by his private tutor, *John Freind*, then one of the junior students, and afterwards a physician of no small celebrity. The editor of Phalaris wished to procure the collation of a manuscript belonging to the Royal library ; but, instead of making any direct application to the librarian, he had recourse to the agency of *Thomas Bennett*, a bookseller, in St. Paul's Churchyard, who appears to have executed his commission with no extraordinary degree of zeal, or despatch. In order to conceal his own negligence, he is supposed to have misrepresented the entire trans- action to his employers at Oxford ; and the preface to Mr. Boyle's edition of Phalaris, published in the year 1695, contains a sarcastic reflection on Bentley for his want of civility. To the editor he imme- diately addressed a letter, explaining the real circumstance of the case ; but, instead of receiving an answer in the spirit of conciliation, he was given to understand he might seek his redress in any way he pleased. It is, however, dangerous to take a lion by the beard.

. DR. WOTTON had recently engaged in a controversy respecting the comparative excellence of the ancients and moderns, and after he had sent to the press his " Reflections upon Ancient and Modern Learning," Bentley happened to state, in a conversation, that the epistles of Phalaris were spurious, and that we have nothing now extant of *Æsop's own composing*. This casual remark led to a promise that he would furnish a written statement of his opinions, to be added to the second edition of the Reflections.

A new edition of the " Reflections on Ancient and Modern Learn- ing " being called for, Wotton claimed his friend's promise, that he would demonstrate Phalaris's epistles and Æsop's fables, to be forgeries. Bentley desired to excuse himself, alleging, that circumstances were altered since the promise was made, as the treatment which he had received in the preface to the Oxford Phalaris, would make it impos- sible for him to write his dissertation, without noticing the calumny propagated against him in that work. This excuse not appearing sufficient, his friend exacted the performance of the engagement. This is his own account, which we find unequivocally corroborated by Wot- ton. Accordingly, he undertook a dissertation, in the form of letters, to Wotton, in which the main object was, to demonstrate that the author of " Phalaris' Epistles," was not the Sicilian tyrant, but some sophist of a more recent age ; reserving to the conclusion his remarks on Boyle's edition, and the personal reflection upon himself.

There still remained the Æsopian fables, the other great object of Sir William Temple's admiration ; and to dispossess the old Phrygian fabulist of the credit, or rather the discredit, of having written the collection, was no difficult task. " This section of Bentley's perform- ance," says Dr. Monk, " exhibits little novelty or research, and bears greater marks of haste than any other part of the dissertation. It is probable that the printer was too urgent, or his friend Wotton too impatient, for the publication of the book, to allow more time for the Appendix. The history of the fables, though not generally known, had in fact been told before, and Bentley only contributed greater precision and accuracy, together with a few additional circumstances."

On the publication of this joint work, the sensation in the literary and academical circles was without parallel. In the large and dis- tinguished society of Christ Church, it produced a perfect ferment. The attack upon the Phalaris was considered an affront to the dean, under whose auspices it was published, and the college, for whose use it was designed. It was therefore resolved that the audacious offender should experience the full resentment of the body whom he had provoked ; and the task of inflicting this public chastisement devolved upon the ablest scholars and wits of the college. The leaders of the confederacy were FRANCIS ATTERBURY and GEORGE SMALRIDGE, both of them, in process of time, members of the Episcopal bench. Each was nearly of the same age as Bentley, and they were regarded as the rising lights of the University. Mr. Boyle, in whose name and behalf the controversy was carried on, seems to have had but a small share of the actual operation, having then quitted academical pursuits, and entered upon the theatre of active life. But as Bentley's opponents were likely to obtain little triumph in matters of erudition, they determined to hold up his character to ridicule and odium ; to dispute his honesty and veracity ; and, by representing him as a model of pedantry, conceit, and ill manners, to raise such an outcry as should drive him off the literary stage for ever. Accordingly, every circum- stance which could be discovered respecting his life and conversation, every trivial anecdote, however unconnected with the controversy, was caught up, and made a topic either of censure or ridicule.

Rumours and conjectures are the lot of contemporaries. Truth seems reserved for posterity, and, like the fabled MINERVA, is born at once. The secret history of this volume has been partly opened in one of WARBURTON's letters. Pope, it appears, was " let into the secret."

The principal share of the undertaking fell to the lot of Atterbury. This was suspected at the time, and has since been placed beyond all doubt, by the publication of a letter of his to Boyle, in which he mentions that " in writing more than half the book, in reviewing a good part of the rest, and in transcribing the whole, half a year of his life had passed away." The main part of the discussion upon Phalaris was from his pen. That upon Æsop was believed to be written by *John Freind*, and he was probably assisted in it by *Alsop*, who at that time was engaged on an edition of the fables. But the respective shares cannot now be fixed with certainty. In point of classical learning, the joint stock of the confederacy, bore no proportion to that of Bentley: " their acquaintance with several of the books upon which they comment," observes Dr. Monk, " appears only to have begun upon this occasion ; and sometimes they are indebted to their knowledge of them from their adversary ; compared with his boundless erudition, their learning was that of schoolboys, and not always sufficient to preserve them from distressing mistakes. But profound literature was at that time confined to few ; while wit and railery found numerous and eager readers.* It may be doubted whether BUSBY himself, by whom every one of the confederate band had been educated, possessed knowledge which would have qualified him to enter the lists in such a controversy."

There was another individual in whom Bentley's dissertation excited a still deeper feeling of resentment. Sir William Temple had already been chagrined at the favourable reception of Wotton's reflections, the work of a young and unknown author, but his mortification was increased tenfold by Bentley's appendix, which it must be confessed placed him in an uncomfortable predicament. He now saw it demonstrated by arguments, not one of which he could refute, that the two productions believed by him to be the oldest, and pronounced to be the finest in existence, were the fabrications of some comparatively recent hand.

It was at this time that JONATHAN SWIFT made his first attack upon Bentley, in the " Tale of a Tub." The greater part of this celebrated piece of humour had been composed, as the author informs us, in the preceding year. The first design of the tale was only to ridicule the corruptions and extravagances of certain religious sects. The sections containing his ridicule of criticism, and of whatever else he disapproved in literature, were written upon the appearance of Wotton's and

---

* Wit and invective obtained an apparent triumph. "The bees of Christ Church," as the confederacy was called, rushed in a dark swarm upon Bentley, but only left their stings in the flesh they could not wound. He merely put out his hand in contempt, not in rage. Doubtful whether *wit* could prevail against *learning*, they had recourse to *personal* satire.

Bentley's joint publication. Swift was at that time living under the protection of Sir William Temple, at Moor Park, and regarded his patron with the utmost attachment and veneration. Perceiving the uneasiness of the Baronet at the awkward situation in which this controversy had placed him, he determined to avenge his cause by those weapons, against which no learning, and no genius, is entirely proof. This celebrated piece succeeded at the time in obliging and gratifying Sir William Temple, and in exciting a high opinion of Swift's talents among private friends, to whom the manuscript was shewn, but for some reason several years passed before it was given to the public.

About this time Bentley formed a club, or evening meeting, of a few friends, who were amongst the greatest intellectual characters that the history of mankind can produce : this society, which met once or twice a week, in the librarian's apartment at St. James's, consisted at its foundation, of Sir Christopher Wren, John Evelyn, Isaac Newton, and John Locke.

The attack from Christ's Church commenced with the new year. The honour of leading on the assault was given to Alsop, who published a selection of Æsop's fables, as the dean's present to his students. At length appeared the performance of the confederate wits, which was to extinguish for ever the fame and pretensions of Bentley : it was a book of about three hundred pages, with a motto sufficiently menacing :

> " Remember Milo's end,
> Wedg'd in that timber which he strove to rend."

This work, which once enjoyed an extravagant popularity, is now little known, except through the fame of him whom it was intended to crush.

JOHN MILNER, a veteran schoolmaster at Leeds, engaged in the dispute on Phalaris, and took part against Bentley. DR. GARTH, his contemporary at Cambridge, who was related to the Boyle's, published about this time his well known poem, " The Dispensary," and pronounced his judgment upon the merits of the two combatants in this simile :—

> " So diamonds take a lustre from their foil,
> And to a Bentley 'tis we owe a Boyle."

A couplet which is, perhaps, more frequently quoted than any other in the poem, and always to the disparagement of the author's judgment. At Cambridge, a caricature was exhibited of Phalaris putting the unfortunate critic into his brazen bull ; and, as it was thought that a member of St. John's College could not properly make his exit without a pun, he was represented saying " I had rather be roasted than Boyled."

Of all the attacks upon Bentley written at this period, the only one which continues to be known by its own merits, is " Swift's Battle of the Books," a piece exhibiting, perhaps, more than any of his writings, the original vein of humour which distinguishes its author. Like its predecessor the " Tale of a Tub," it was composed to soothe the mortified feelings of his patron Sir William Temple. This work continues to be read and laughed over by thousands, who would have turned a deaf ear to the eloquence of the English *Memmius*, and all the combined wit and learning of Christ Church.

The facetious Dr. King, also, seems to have been one of those rabid wits, who fastens on his prey, and does not hastily draw his fangs from the noble animal. At one of those conferences which passed between Bentley and the bookseller, King was present, and being called upon by Boyle to bear part in the drama, performed it quite to the taste of " the bees." He addressed a letter to Dean Aldrich, in which he gave one particular ; and to make up a sufficient dose, dropped some corrosives. He closed his letter thus :—" that scorn and contempt which I have naturally for *pride* and *insolence,* makes me remember what otherwise I might have forgotton." Nothing touched Bentley more than reflections on his " pride and insolence." Our defects seem to lose much of their character, in reference to ourselves, by habit and natural disposition ; yet we have always a painful suspicion of their existence, and he who touches them without tenderness is never pardoned. The invective of King had all the bitterness of *truth.*

Bentley nicknames King, *Humty Dumty,* through the progress of the controversy, for his tavern pleasures, and accuses him of writing more in taverns, than in his study. He little knew the injustice of the charge against a student who had written notes to 22,000 books and MSS. But all this was not done with impunity. An irritated wit only finds his adversary cutting out work for him. A second letter, more abundant with the same pungent qualities, fell on the head of Bentley. King says of the arch-critic,—" he thinks meanly, I find, of my reading ; yet for all that, I dare say I have read more than any man in England, besides him and me, for I have read *his book all through."* A keen repartee this !

Men of genius are more subject to " unnatural civil war," than even the blockheads whom Pope sarcastically reproaches with it. Bentley's opinion of his own volume seems equally modest and just. " To undervalue this dispute about Phalaris, because it does not suit one's own studies, is to quarrel with a *circle* because it is not a *square.* If the same question be not of vulgar use, it was writ therefore for a few ; for even the greatest performances, upon the most important subjects, are no entertainment at all to *the many of the world."*

Bentley, although the solid force of his mind was not favourable to the lighter sports of WIT, yet was it not quite destitute of those airy qualities; nor does he seem insensible to the literary merits of " that odd work," as he calls Boyle's volume; and conveys a good notion of it, when he says, " it may be very useful as a common-place book, for ridicule, banter, and all the topics of calumny." With equal dignity and sense, he observes, on the ridicule so freely used in that work,—" I am content, that what is the greatest virtue of his book, should be counted the greatest fault in mine."

His reply to " Milo's End," and the torture he was supposed to pass through, when thrown into Phalaris's bull, is a piece of sarcastic humour, which will not suffer by comparison with the volume more celebrated for its wit. " The facetious ' Examiner ' seems resolved to vie with Phalaris himself in the science of PHALARISM; for his revenge is not satisfied with one single death of his adversary, but he will kill me over and over again. He has slain me twice, by two several deaths! one in the first page of his book, and another in the last. In the title-page I die the death of Milo, the Cretonian; the application of which must be this :—that as Milo, after his victories at six several Olympiads, was at last conquered and destroyed in wrestling with a tree; so I, after I had attained to some small reputation in letters, am to be quite baffled and run down by *wooden antagonists*. But, in the end of his book, he has got me into Phalaris's bull, and he has the pleasure of fancying that he hears me begin *to bellow*. Well, since it is that I am in the bull, I have performed the part of a sufferer. For as the cries of the tormented in old Phalaris's bull, being conveyed through pipes lodged in the machine, were turned into music for the entertainment of the tyrant; so the complaints which my torments express from me, being conveyed to Mr. Boyle by this answer, are all dedicated to his pleasure and diversion. But yet, methinks, when he was setting up to be *Phalaris junior*, the very omen of it might have deterred him. As the old tyrant himself at last bellowed in his own bull, his imitators ought to consider that, at long run, their own actions may chance to overtake them."

Bentley meanwhile remained calm under this merciless storm, relying upon the goodness of his cause, and a conviction that the public judgement, however strangely it may be perverted for a time, will at length come to a just decision upon every question. WARBURTON tells an anecdote upon the authority of Dr. S. (whom we apprehend to be Smallbroke, Bishop of Lichfield and Coventry,) who meeting Bentley at this period, and telling him not to be discouraged at the run made against him, was answered, " indeed I am in no pain about the matter for it is a maxim with me, that no man was ever written out of reputation but by himself." He had now, however, to experience the most painful of all circumstances attending popular outcry ; the desertion, or coldness of some friends, whose regards were influenced by fashion. That he felt uneasiness at this situation may well be believed, indeed he confesses as much in one of his letters to *Gravius ;* but instead of expressing this to the world, he applied himself to write such an answer as should effectually turn the tide of popular opinion, and make the weapons of his enemies recoil upon their own heads. His sentiments at this time are expressed in a letter to his unshaken friend EVELYN, who appears to have stood up alone as his defender, and to have recommended the public to wait and hear the other side, before they pronounced his condemnation. He feels gratefully this proof of Evelyn's friendship ; and assures him that he shall very shortly be able to refute all the charges, and all the cavils of his enemies, so fully " both in points of learning, and of fact, that they themselves would feel ashamed."

That Bentley did not immediately reply to his adversaries must be regarded as fortunate, not only for himself, but for the whole learned world. " Although there is no doubt," says Dr. Monk, " but that such a publication, as he meditated, would have put him in possession of the victory, and settled the whole controversy, so perfectly was he master of all parts of the question, yet a hasty performance could not have supplied us with so valuable a treasure of wit and learning, as appeared at the beginning of the following year ; a piece which by the concurring testimony of all scholars has never been rivalled. The Boyleans had pursued a course calculated to display their adversary to the greatest advantage, and to raise to the highest pinnacle the reputation which they designed to overthrow. In their efforts to confute his reasonings about Phalaris, they had introduced a variety of new topics, which the writers, from whence they drew their knowledge, had treated either erroneously, or slightly. This imposed upon Bentley the necessity of explaining and elucidating them ; in doing which he was able to develope stores of learning, more than either his friends hoped, or his enemies apprehended. It was fully believed that his first dissertation had been the elaborate result of more than *two years* attention to the subject ; that his bolt was now shot, and that his learning and objections were exhausted. So far was this from being the case, that it was in fact a hasty sketch, the sheets of which were sent to the press as fast as they were written. When the famous reply appeared, the public found to their astonishment, that the former piece had consisted only of the *sprinklings* of immense stores of learning, which might almost be

L

said, like his talents, to expand with the occasion that called them forth. Before he submitted his case to the world, Bentley was careful to arm himself with a full refutation of those charges upon his personal behaviour.

This work was given to the public in the beginning of the year 1699; the appearance of which is to be considered as an epoch, not only in the life of Bentley, but in the history of literature. The victory obtained over his opponents, although the most complete that can be imagined, constitutes but a small part of the merit of this performance. Such is the author's address, that while every page is professedly controversial, there is embodied in the work a quantity of accurate information relative to history, chronology, antiquities, philology, and criticism, which it will be difficult to match in any other volume. The cavils of the Boyleans had fortunately touched upon so many topics, as to draw from their adversary a mass of learning, none-of which is misplaced or superfluous: he contrives with admirable judgment to give the reader all the information that can be desired upon each question, while he never loses sight of his main object. Profound and various as are the sources of his learning, every thing is so well arranged, and placed in so clear a view, that the mere novice in classical literature, may peruse the book with profit and pleasure, while the most accomplished scholar cannot fail to find his knowledge enlarged. Nor is this merely the language of those who are partial to the author: the learned DODWELL, who had no peculiar motive to be pleased with a work, (in which he was a considerable sufferer, and who, as a *Non-juror*, was prejudiced against Bentley's party,) is recorded to have avowed, " that he had never learned so much from a book in his life." This learned volume owed much of its attraction to the strain of humour which makes the perusal highly entertaining. The advocates of Phalaris having chosen to rely upon wit and railery, were now made to feel in their turn the consequences of the warfare which they had adopted. Even Bishop Warburton, who was not well disposed to Bentley's reputation, admits, that " he beat the Oxford men at their own weapons."

Sir William Temple was spared the mortification of beholding the result of a controversy, upon which he had so imprudently staked his credit for taste and discernment. He died a few weeks before the appearance of the dissertation, which was to annihilate for ever the pretensions of this Sicilian hero to the fame of authorship. His Christ Church allies did not feel easy under the report that a reply from Dr. Bentley was in preparation, and they seemed to have thought in earnest of executing the threat denounced in the gaiety of their hearts, that if the Doctor was not quiet, " they would put forth a book against him every month as long as he lived."

Bentley, who was now only in the 38th year of his age, was left to enjoy the triumph of his great learning and sagacity, to which even the most averse were compelled to pay homage : and what was a still more important result of his book, he had silenced, and put so shame, the slanderous attacks made upon his character. Upon the various matters of this celebrated controversy, his victory was complete and final, and he was left in undisputed possession of the field. A declaration was indeed made by his adversaries of their intention to publish a complete reply to his book ; but this was all an empty vaunt ; they felt their inability to renew the conflict upon questions of learning, and it was the course of prudence, not to recal public attention to the dispute. It may be remarked that not one of the Boylean confederacy ever again appeared before the world as a critic. Atterbury, their leader, immediately found business of a different character.

We now enter upon difficult ground. Hitherto we have contemplated Bentley as a scholar, disputing with would-be-scholars, in a field, where his scholarship gained a dear, a difficult, and a glorious victory. In the Phalaris controversy he was a knight, clad in impenetrable mail, condescending to defeat a conspiracy of fencing-masters at their favourite ' tierce and carte,' and then crushing them, all and several, by the blows of his invincible mace. Standing on the vantage ground of truth, he despised their pitiful cries of " foul play," and demonstrated himself as stainless in honour, as he was redoubtable in prowess. It is really mortifying to see the armed champion sinking into a petty litigant, and to find him contending, not for the unstained virginity of antique learning, but for miserable quibbles of college etiquette, and yet meaner matters connected with " the three denominations" of pounds, shillings, and pence.

Posterity, (who and what is it?) have been constituted a court from which there is no appeal. Before this imaginary tribunal every great man is called to account for his deeds committed in the flesh. His biographer is presumed to be at once advocate and judge, while in fact he should be no more than witness. DR. MONK, the only authentic biographer of Bentley, is doubtless an admirable witness, but as an advocate, he lays himself open to the charge alleged against a certain great jurist, in the case of poor *Peltier,* of sacrificing his client to his own reputation for impartiality ; and as a judge, he takes especial care not to prejudice the jury in favour of the *panel.* He has elaborately stated all that Bentley did to offend the college, and as little about what the college did to offend Bentley. He has given the original

Latin, (and what Latin!!) of the statutes which Bentley was accused of violating ; but he has not impressed, by any pains taking of his own, the good and sufficient reasons for which Bentley disregarded the letter of the law, in order to vitalize its spirit.

People at this time of day will not care much whether the statutable *onus* of a few hundreds lay upon the master of Trinity college, or upon the fellows. Be it recollected, that we are not speaking of sums drawn from the people ; but of an estate, entrusted to certain hands for certain purposes. Bentley conceived that the trustees were diverting too large a portion of this estate to their personal uses ; that the fellows of trinity had a strong inclination to turn the college funds into a snug sinecure. To correct this growing evil he resorted to his magisterial prerogative. He found himself at the head of a royal foundation, and took upon him the authority of a king, perhaps unconstitutionally, but still for the benefit of the whole, of a permanent body, as contra-distinguished from individual interests.

The foundation of Trinity college, Cambridge, is said to have been " the first-fruit of the Reformation." HENRY VIII, about a month before his death, appropriated to the establishment of that college a part of the revenues of the spoliated monasteries. " The price of a dog, and the hire of a harlot," say the Rabbins, " shall not be put to any holy purpose," and even the Jewish priests, who murdered the Lord of life, refused to put the price of blood into their treasury. But the price of much blood, the hire of much spiritual prostitution, constituted the original treasury of that corporation, whose *name* now being utterly disconnected with all religious associations, and giving rise to innumerable irreverend puns, might very fitly be changed. Its first days were dark and turbid, no wonder, yet it received a body of statutes from EDWARD VI. that blossom of royalty, whose beautiful youth, and timely death, preserved the house of Tudor from utter execration, who, happily for himself, if not for England, was called away before his mother's milk was well out of his veins, and before any of his father's venom was ripened. Queen Elizabeth, who united the best and worst of both sexes, her grandfather's craft and frugality, her father's courage and cruelty, and her poor mother's vanity, gave another set of statutes, and from the apparent discrepancy of these codes, much of the long enigma of Bentley's litigations was compounded. The college flourished mightily. At one time, the two archbishops and seven bishops were its *alumni*. It could boast of COKE and BACON, of BARROW and NEWTON. Nor ever, till this time, has it lacked pupils who glory in its name, and in whose names it well may glory.

Contrary to the constitution of most colleges, Trinity is obliged to accept a master at the appointment of the crown. WILLIAM III. during the life of his queen, devolved all literary and religious patronage upon her, who was regarded, even by the conforming clergy, as the true sovereign, while her consort was considered as little more than commander-in-chief. Even the royal library was called the Queen's library. After Mary's death, William, displaying herein the rare knowledge of his own ignorance, committed to six prelates the responsible task of recommending fit persons for all vacant bishoprics, deaneries, and other ecclesiastical preferments, as well as headships and professorships in the royal patronage. It was a wise act, and had it been followed in spirit by his successors, the church had never been, as now, a loose card in the hands of state gamblers. The original members of this commission were TENISON, Archbishop of Canterbury; SHARP, of York; LLOYD, Bishop of Litchfield and Coventry; BURNET, of Saram; STILLINGFLEET, of Worcester, and PATRICK, of Ely. On the death of Stillingfleet, in 1699, MOORE, Bishop of Norwich, was advanced to his place; and Dr. MONTAGUE being promoted to the deanery of Durham, Bentley was recommended by them to the vacant headship of Trinity college, Cambridge.

The result of Bentley's appointment proves the inexpediency of giving an office to a man, simply because he deserves it, without considering whether it is fit for him, or he fit for it. It has been said, of CHARLES I. that had he been an absolute king, he would have been the best of absolute kings. So of Bentley, we may assert, that he was the fittest of all men to be the Autocrat of a college, for of all men he best understood, and best loved, the ends for which colleges were founded. Being put over a venal, turbulent aristocracy, he pursued his end, regardless of the means, and hence only derived the credit of profiting as adroitly by the ambiguities and corruptions of law, as he had done, and continued to do, by the subtleties of verbal criticism. Tradition says, that being congratulated upon a promotion so little to have been expected, by a member of St. John's, he replied in the words of the Psalmist, " by the help of my God, I have leaped over the wall." Another anecdote, preserved in Dr. Bentley's family, relates that Bishop Stillingfleet said, " we must send Bentley to rule the turbulent fellows of Trinity College ; if any body can do it, he is the person ; for I am sure he has ruled my family ever since he entered it."

On the first of February, 1700, Bentley was installed Master of Trinity College,—looked upon by Europe as her first scholar, and by England as the tutor of her future sovereign. But the hand of Providence was heavy on the house of Stuart. William, Duke of Gloucester, died July 29, 1700, and so prevented Bentley from sharing the honours of FENELON, as the preceptor of a possible good king, or the disgrace of SENECA, as the instructor of an actual Nero.

His first step on entering into the office was of a very inauspicious description. A dividend from the surplus money had been fixed in December 1699, to be paid agreeably to the custom of the college, to the Masters and Fellows for the year ending at Michaelmas. The Master's share, amounting to £170, was clearly due to Dr. Montague, whose resignation took place in November, but by some accident it had not been disbursed to him. Bentley immediately upon his admission, claimed this sum, as being profits accruing during the vacancy, and therefore payable to the new master, and by terrifying the treasurer, who declined paying it, with a threat of bringing him before the Archbishop of Canterbury, he actually obtained the money.*

It so happened, that, at Bentley's accession, the Master's lodge, at Trinity, was very much in want of repair. He, who was a member of the same club with SIR CHRISTOPHER WREN, and whose spirit was a sojourner in Athens, must needs have had magnificent ideas of architecture ; and if he had very inadequate calculations of the expense attending the realization of such ideas, the errors of his arithmetic ought not to impugn the integrity of his principles. Yet the expensiveness of these improvements,—the long bills he ran up with masons, carpenters, *glaziers*,† &c., and the violent means whereby he enforced payment at the college expense, were the chief ostensible pretexts of the quarrel between Bentley and his college! Its real causes however we believe to have lain much deeper.

In the first year of his mastership, Bentley became Vice Chancellor, being chosen agreeably to the custom of the University, as a senior in degree among the Heads of houses, who had not already

* With all our admiration of Bentley, we are constrained to admit that, in money matters, he displayed neither the indifference of a scholar, the liberality of a gentleman, nor the exactness of an honest man. Very possibly, he had suffered in his youth from inattention to these things; and there are never wanting prudent friends to persuade a man that, because he is a genius, or learned, all the world are in a conspiracy to rob him. No man was ever long honest, who habitually distrusted the honesty of others; for who will labour to attain or preserve a virtue which he does not believe to exist? Money squabbles, however, are a most unfortunate commencement of any connection between individuals or societies. The civil list is *a wet blanket* on a young king's popularity; and a contested point in the marriage articles, though quite forgotten in the ardour of the *honey moon*, often proves a rankling thorn in the side of matrimonial felicity.   C.

† Glaziers. This respectable trade is not rashly called in question. The insertion of *sash windows* in the lodge, was one of the grounds upon which Bentley was prosecuted.   C.

served in that office. Owing, probably, to his inexperience in University business, very few matters of importance were transacted during the year of Bentley's vice chancellorship. One of its duties seems to consist in giving of dinners, which, owing perhaps to the unfinished state of his lodge, he did not fulfil to general satisfaction. Yet, considering that he was then engaged in the important business of winning and marrying a wife, he might fairly have been exempted from the charge of inhospitality. He had long cherished an attachment to MRS. JOANNA BERNARD, a lady who had been a visitor in Bishop Stillingfleet's family. She was daughter of Sir John Bernard, in Huntingdonshire. Being now raised to a station of dignity and competence, he succeeded in obtaining the object of his affections, and was united to her at Windsor, having previously obtained a royal dispensation, under the Great Seal, for deviating from Queen Elizabeth's statutes, which enjoined celibacy to the master as well as to the fellows of Trinity College. This marriage appears to have been eminently happy. The lady, who continued the partaker of his joys and sorrows for nearly forty years, is described as possessing the most amiable and valuable qualities. She had a cultivated mind, and was sincerely benevolent and religious. WHISTON relates, that Bentley was in danger of losing her during his courtship, from insinuating doubts of the authority of the book of Daniel; a story exceedingly improbable, which, if it ever had any foundation, has been distorted from the truth, according to the practice of that hearsay narrator.* The alliance with Mrs. Bentley, whose family connections were numerous and distinguished, was the means of securing him powerful protection at critical periods of his life; while the excellence of her disposition tended to soften the animosity of his opponents. We find her mentioned with applause and sympathy, in publications written for the purpose of injuring the character and fortune of her husband.

In the course of Bentley's year of office, he had an opportunity of displaying his spirit and decision, in upholding the rights of the

---

* The truth may be, that Bentley stated that such doubt might have existed,—an admission quite enough to alarm a lady's orthodoxy; for a good simple hearted woman cannot conceive the possibility of any one denying what to her is " stuff of the conscience." Bentley might be disposed to take up the question as a point of criticism rather than as a point of faith, but he was not the man to commit himself, his love, and his preferment, for any heresy, new or old. Such heterodox Quixotism he left to Whiston, who forfeited brilliant prospects in the Church, to scruples which he deemed conscientious, though the orthodox believers account them damnable, and the no-believers ridicule them as insane. He was an honest wrong-headed Arian, far too credulous of tales that told ill for his opponents, but, I believe, incapable of intentional falsehood.   C.

University against the mayor and corporation of Cambridge, who had given permission and encouragement to players to perform at *Sturbridge* fair, without the sanction of the Vice Chancellor, and in defiance of his authority.   His vindication of these privileges granted by charters and acts of parliament, was essential to the discipline of the place, and we may judge from the practice of subsequent times, that the prompt interference of Dr. Bentley on this occasion, was productive of good and permanent effects.

A Greek prelate, *Neophytos*, Archbishop of Philippopoli, visiting England at this time, came to Cambridge, and was admitted doctor of divinity by the University.   On this occasion, the Vice Chancellor, with great good nature, directed that he should be presented by the Greek Professor, JOSHUA BARNES,* who was thus gratified with the opportunity of delivering a Greek oration, a copy of which is still preserved.

Before the end of his year of office, Bentley had the gratification of declaring his political sentiments, and those of the University, in an address presented to King William, upon Louis XIV. acknowledging the son of James II. as King of England.   The address was undoubtedly composed by the Vice Chancellor, who expressed his opinion on public affairs in clear and uncompromising terms.

On the death of DR. SAYWELL, Bentley was collated to the Archdeaconry of *Ely,* a dignity which, besides his rank in the Church, was endowed with the two livings of *Haddenham* and *Wilburton.*   He had the honour of receiving this preferment from BISHOP PATRICK, one of the most learned and exemplary prelates that ever graced the Bench. As the archdeaconry conferred a seat in the lower House of Convocation, then at high discord with the Bishops, it seems probable that a wish to call into action, on the other side, such talents and spirits as Bentley's, might have occasioned this appointment. · He was regular in his attendance at the synod as long as it was permitted to meet and deliberate, and he took a share in the debates.

It has already been stated, that the Master of Trinity is a nominee of the crown.   The heads of almost every other college are elected by the Fellows.   Hence it is likely that the appointment of every headmaster, will much resemble the placing of a Scottish minister in those days, when the Covenanters had not fully submitted to the yoke of

---

* Of Joshua Barnes, who wrote a tract to prove that the real author of the *Iliad* was no other than *Solomon,* Bentley declared, " that he understood Greek as well as an Athenian cobler."   We are inclined to believe that an Athenian cobler would have puzzled Bentley himself.   Yet the observation is witty, and well expresses the distinction, between extensive learning, and critical scholarship.   C.

patronage. Whatever his personal merits may be, he wants the sanction of an harmonious call. Were he even the very person whom they would have elected, they will not immediately forget that they did not elect him, and if, instead of the longest approved member of their own society, an alien, and a junior is set over their heads, the implied declaration of their insufficiency to the purposes of self-government, will strengthen shyness into antipathy; an antipathy easily enough overcome if the stranger take pains to make himself, as the phrase is, "one of us;" but sure to ferment into deadly hatred, if he assume the port and authority of a conqueror. Bentley seems to have behaved towards his fellows as a Norman lord to Saxon boors; to have treated their perquisites, and privileges, as if they were mere conditional concessions, voluntary and temporary abatements of his prerogative, dependent upon good behaviour. But, worse than all, he did not associate with them, he would not be "one of us" among them, and of all crimes which any man can commit against mess, common-room, corporation, or coterie, of which he is an enrolled member, this is the most grievous, and the more grievous in proportion to his admitted superiority.

Bentley, however, when at Cambridge, chose to live with a small party of friends, among whom, Davis, whose classical pursuits resembled his own, was the most respectable; and Ashenhurst, a young physician, who practised in the university, the most devoted. Yet was the critic always accessible to scholars, and alert in promoting the interests of literature, of which he gave an instance in his patronage of KUSTER,* a learned German, whose edition of *Suidas*, he procured to be printed at the Cambridge press.

* LUDOLF KUSTER, an erudite Westphalian, whose treatise on the Greek Middle Verb, has made his name familiar even in grammar schools, was appointed by FREDERIC, first king of Prussia, professor of an academy at Berlin, and obtained leave to visit foreign Universities. In his youth, forbearing to insult the ear of antiquity, by clapping an *us* to the end of his Teutonic sirname, he followed the practice of Erasmus, Melancthon, Scapula, and other early scholars, publishing under the signature NEOCORUS, the nearest Greek translation of Kuster, which in German signifies a *sexton*. He was by the veteran GROEVIUS, introduced to the notice of Bentley, and having while at Paris, collated three MSS. of *Suidas*, he undertook an edition of that lexicographer, which, as related in the text, was printed at Cambridge. It was a hurried, and therefore ill-digested work, which did not escape severe animadversions. SUIDAS was a compiler of the tenth century, whose whole, or chief value arises from the fragments of ancient authors embedded in him, like grains of porphyry in sand; a weak and credulous man, to whom we owe many of the scandalous tales which libel the old philosophers and poets; in the amendment of whose corruptions, and in the confutation of whose errors, Bentley himself would have been usefully employed, albeit that POPE obliquely reproaches him with " poaching in

M

At the general election, in November, 1701, Cambridge returned to parliament MR. ISAAC NEWTON. Never can she hope again to be so represented. Yet the philosopher must have felt rather out of his element among the squires and courtiers in St. Stephen's. It is needless to say that Bentley voted for his illustrious friend.

Returning with ardour to his interrupted studies, in the following summer, the great critic announced his intention of publishing an edition of *Horace,* the most popular (if the term may be allowed) of all the Latin poets, and the only one of which nine tenths of those who enjoy a classical education have any remembrance.

Suidas for unlicensed Greek." Anno 1706, Kuster's three folios of the lexicon being completed, the editor returned to Berlin, and, by the management of Bentley, his introduction to his royal master was particularly auspicious. The University of Frankfort, on the Oder, having resolved to celebrate the centenary anniversary of its foundation with secular solemnities, invited various other Universities to assist by their deputies at this ceremony. The invitation sent to Cambridge was courteously accepted, and a deputation was nominated by the senate, consisting of representatives in the different faculties. The King of Prussia presided at the solemnities, and Kuster being attached to the delegation, was presented to him attired in the scarlet robes of a Cambridge doctor, and received in the gracious manner which his merits and character demanded. There exists a curious letter from him to Bentley, in English, giving a detailed account of this academical jubilee: See *Monk's Life, p.* 149. Here permit me to remark a peculiar use and beauty of classical literature, in giving a common language, a common interest, a co-patriotism to the scholars of different countries, and thereby promoting a free intercourse, which, breaking down the barriers of national prejudice, confers a real benefit on those that have no tongue but that their mothers taught them, softening the horrors of war, and preparing the earth for universal peace. Perhaps it is a further advantage, that the common language is no longer that of any existing nation, it puts all upon an equality.

Kuster was too eminent not to be envied, too proud, or too petulant, to be a court professor, so he left Berlin hastily, either oppressed by his rivals, or disgusted with his livery. With the king's permission, he returned to *Utrecht,* resigned his situation, and proposed an edition of *Hesychius,* the most important of the Greek lexicographers, relying on the assistance of Bentley, who was known to have turned his attention particularly to that author. Bentley made a liberal offer of his emendations, but saddled with a condition, that the work should be printed at Cambridge. We cannot help wishing, that our English Aristarch had not insisted on this proviso, whereby much delay was interposed, and the *Hesychius* finally postponed till too late, for Kuster never lived to complete it. Methinks the shade of the lexicographer might arise and say, with the Miltonic Satan :—

> " What matter where, if I be still the same,
> And what I should be?"

Kuster engaged in an edition of *Jamblichus's* life of Pythagoras; one of the attempts of declining paganism, to produce miracles and revelations, in opposition to those of christianity. He afterwards put forth an *Aristophanes,* which met with success, but all these labours did not preserve their author from restlessness and

For Bentley's purpose, however, Horace was not, perhaps, the best book to be chosen; for Bentley, with erudition unbounded, and understanding strong as subtle, had not a spark of poetry in his nature, and seems to have allowed the poet no privilege above the proseman, except the burdensome distinction of verse. Metre was the only peculiar quality of poetry of which he had any feeling; nor was he aware, that to criticise a poet, something more is necessary, besides a general mastery of the language in which he writes. Moreover, Horace was not corrupt enough to furnish employment for Bentley's powers. With him,—

> Greek and Latin were intended
> For nothing else but to be mended.—

as Butler says of puritanic religion.

His critical skill was like those detergent acids, which are excellent for removing stains, when such exist, but if applied needlessly, are apt to eat holes. It was not his humour to let well alone.

poverty, which compelled him to hurry his works into the world scarcely half made up. It was his object, as soon as he could scrape together £600, to purchase a life annuity. For this he toiled, and dedicated, and besought the interest of Bentley; and, by his advice, offered his Aristophanes to *Montague*, Lord Halifax, who had succeeded to the office of Dorset and Somers, as receiver-general of dedicatory adulation. Kuster is said to have painfully earned the £60 which was then thought a sufficient remuneration for such addresses. It must be conceded, that they read rather better in Latin than in English; but we may rejoice that literature is no longer disgraced by such hyperbolical sycophancy. The annuity was purchased, but the poor scholar had no luck with it. His banker failed, and threw him once more on his resources. He re-visited England, for the double purpose of engaging with booksellers for the publication of Hesychius, and of obtaining a loan from his friends. This was in 1712. BISHOP MOORE and others, gave him promises: Bentley, under the delicate form of lending, gave him money, with little chance of repayment. Shortly after, he received a tempting offer from the *Abbè Bignon*, librarian to the King of France. He was invited to reside at Paris, with a pension of 2000 livres, a further appointment as a Member of the *Académie des Inscriptions*, and all the consideration which his learning was sure to command among the French *savans;* but for this it was required that he should renounce *heresy*, or, as the French Abbé probably termed it, Hugonotism. Let not protestant indignation outrun christian charity, if we relate that a poor book-worm shrunk from the slow martyrdom of starvation, or that an English divine continued to correspond with him after his apostacy. Whatever he gained by his change of religion, or rather say, of communion, he did not long enjoy it; dying suddenly, in 1716, of a strange disorder, which modern physicians attributed to intense application, in an unhealthy attitude. Time was, when it would have been ascribed to supernatural vengeance. A cake of sand was found in his lower abdominal region. His apostacy, however, can scarce have exposed him to the wrath of Pope, who nevertheless has insulted his memory in the *Dunciad*. Pope found it easier to translate Greek, than to construe it.

Dr. Monk regrets that his hero did not devote himself to Greek rather than to Latin editorship; but may we not ask, were there no objects to which such powers and such acquirements might have been applied, more important than disputed readings, dislocated sentences, points misplaced, and accents turned the wrong way? Might not the knowledge which convicted Phalaris of forgery, by such extensive collection, and skilful collation, of evidence, have thrown clear daylight on the obscure of ancient history—have elucidated the origin, the genealogy, and the kindred of nations—have shown how the growth and revolutions of language illustrate the growth and changes of society? Or, could he not have expounded the principles of Greek and of Roman speech by the laws of universal logic, and raised Philology to Philosophy?—But let us return to our narrative.

The year 1702 was marked by the death of Grœvius, a venerable scholar, whose admiration of Bentley was almost idolatrous.

During the first five years of his mastership, the Doctor made several innovations in college discipline, some of which, though reluctantly received at first, are still maintained with advantage. He improved the system of examinations for fellowships and scholarships, and abolished the truly electioneering custom which obliged the candidates to keep open hospitality at a tavern during the four days. He extended the penalty of three-half-pence, for absence from chapel, which had been exacted from under-graduates only, to the lower half of the sixty fellows. He altered the hour of the Saturday evening Latin declamations, much to the scandal of some of the seniors, and decreed that the head lecturer, and four sub-lecturers, should be fined eight pence and four pence respectively, according to statute, if they neglected to lecture and examine daily in the hall. Another, and very unpopular exertion of his authority, certainly, seemed to reflect on the Fellows in a very tender concern. A pecuniary mulct was appointed by statute on any person leaving table before grace. Now the Fellows, not relishing the surveillance of a number of impatient youths upon the protraction of their repast, were in the habit of permitting the younger students to leave hall at pleasure, and laying a fine of two pence weekly on all, whether present or absent. This imposition, the master, by his sole prerogative, annulled, and gave free permission to depart before grace, without punishment; alleging, as his ground, " the unreasonable delays at meals, at some of the Fellows' tables."—After a feast comes a fast. There had been no supper allowed in hall on Friday. Bentley, overruling the scruples of the superstitious, ordered that there should be a flesh-supper in hall on that day, in order to prevent the youths from satisfying their appetites in more exceptionable places. He also obliged the Noblemen and Fellow-Commoners to attend chapel, and perform college exercises, as well as the other students. In all this, there was nothing objectionable; but Bentley carried all with a high hand, scarcely deigning to consult the eight seniors, his statutable advisers.

He also took upon himself to expel a member of the college, who had been twice detected by the proctor at a house of ill-fame, and sundry times at a dissenting meeting-house. In dismissing a profligate hypocrite, the master would surely have met with the support of his fellows; but there was an informality in the manner of doing it, which hereafter furnished matter of complaint.

Meanwhile, a question was discussing, which, though of little public interest, concerned the college deeply. It was disputed, whether absolute seniority could take place of seniority of degree;—whether, for instance, a Master of Arts, ranking 50 in the list of Fellows, should have preoption of chambers or livings, over a Doctor of Divinity ranking only 49. Bentley generally contended for priority of degree; alleging, that the disuse of divinity degrees had caused a neglect of study in the college. And most true it is, that when a man is once Fellow, though he has all the opportunities in the world for acquiring learning, he has no further incentive. As far as the University is concerned, he has attained his *ultimatum:* no subsequent examination displays his maturer acquirements—elicits how much he may have acquired, or exposes how much he may have forgotten. In Bentley's reign, the preparatory exercises for a Doctor's degree were not absolutely formal. They showed at least that the candidate could still speak Latin. As to the matter of the theses and disputations, as orthodoxy only allowed one conclusion, and one decision, it never could be much varied. The battle was sold, and who cares how scientific the sparring might be? But Bentley wished that the Fellows of Trinity should graduate in the higher faculties, i. e. law, physic, and divinity; and certainly, the words of the statute do, in our disinterested opinion, clearly define the highest graduate, not the senior member, as having the right of preoption. It is a pity that college statutes are not written in English, or Latin, or some other intelligible language. At present, they are in a *lingo* that never was spoken on earth, and which can only be justified on the principles of those enthusiasts, who think a language clearly divine, because it was never human.

Bentley seems to have entered on his government with the worst of all possible disqualifications—a contempt for those whom he was called to govern. Not content with a lawless sway, he accompanied every exertion of his prerogative with wanton insult, and made the college books the standing records of his overbearing antipathy. Bishop *Hacket*, a confessor of episcopacy during the Commonwealth, retaining in his honoured age an honourable affection for the place of his youthful studies, had, in 1667, given twelve hundred pounds to rebuild that ruinous fabric entitled Garret's Hostel, with a proviso, that the rents of the chambers therein should for ever be appropriated to the improvement of the library. The new library being completed at an expense of eighteen thousand pounds, something was still requisite, to furnish it with desks, book-cases, and other appurtenances, and the college resolved that the money advanced for this purpose should be repaid out of the rents of the Bishop's chambers. This arrangement, though not inconsistent with the statutes, and approved by the bishop's executor, did not please the master. He insisted that all the sums so applied, amounting to about £50 a year, had been " intervented;" insisted that they should be restored, and devoted to the purchase of books ; with an assertion, "that the college had been robbing the library, and putting the money in their own pockets." Truly, he treated his subjects like worms, and forgot that a worm will turn if you tread upon it. This is said to have given cause to the first misunderstanding between Bentley and the seniority. In demanding the restitution, he might be self-justified ; but the reproach was gratuitous. Whenever a head is to be appointed to a society of christian gentlemen, the first question to be asked should be,—is he a christian ? the second,—is he a gentleman ? A spontaneous insulter is neither.

So passed the first five years of Bentley's mastership. Meanwhile, *King William*, whose merits as a deliverer were soon forgotten when it was found that a parliamentary king was rather more expensive than a *jure divino* monarch, had died, and *Queen Anne*, deservedly the favourite of the clergy, and of the Universities, succeeded to the undivided allegiance of a then loyal people. She had already gladded Oxford with her presence, and in 1705, she conceded to Cambridge the costly honour of a royal visitation. A royal visit to a University, is, or might be called, *dunce's holiday*, for then degrees are conferred on all whom royalty appoints, without the statutable qualifications and exercises. Upon this occasion NEWTON knelt down, plain mister, and arose SIR ISAAC. It is the glory of knighthood that such a man deigned to accept it, but it must have been a whimsical spectacle to see a woman holding a sword in an assembly of parsons, to bestow upon a man of peace, an order essentially military.

About this time, Parliament purchased the library of SIR ROBERT COTTON, a useful collector, whose name is connected with some of the rarest treasures of literature. Bentley, as royal librarian, was entrusted with this welcome charge. Apartments were fitted up for him in Cotton House. He spent a considerable part of every year in town, where his talents obtained admission to the highest circles, and his advancement to the bench was regarded as certain; and certain it might have been, had he possessed the requisite pliancy of temper, for in no age, was mere talent of whatever kind, at so high a premium. When we recollect that nothing but the conscientious scruples of Queen Anne herself, (and blessed be her memory therefore,) prevented *Swift* from being a bishop, we might almost wonder that the first scholar in Europe, a chosen and successful champion of religion, and a peculiar favourite of the pious Queen, was not, while his laurels were yet unmildewed, advanced to the top of his profession. Perhaps the richer sees were all bespoken, two or three deep, and Bentley preferred a wealthy certainty, which incurred little expense, to the higher dignity of a poor bishopric, entailing an enlarged expenditure, and the misery of hope deferred. At a later period, 1709, he was a candidate for the see of Chichester, but the change of ministry gave it to DR. JOHN ROBINSON, who afterwards figured as plenipotentiary at the treaty of Utrecht. Perhaps the odium, justly or unjustly, attached to that negociation, made him the last ecclesiastic whom the English government have employed in diplomacy. Yet later, Bentley refused the poor bishopric of Bristol, and on being asked "What sort of preferment he would desire?" answered, " that which could leave me no wish to change."

That the character of our subject was still accounted stainless in the great world, is evinced by the fact, that persons of rank and reputation were anxious to place their children under his immediate care. During the year 1707, Edward Viscount Hinchinbrooke, Lord Kingston and his brother, and Sir Charles Kemys, were his private pupils, and inmates of the lodge. For the head of a college to take pupils is a thing now scarcely known, and perhaps never usual. Probably the Fellows felt quite as much aggrieved at the injury done to themselves, as at the degradation of the Master's dignity. The tutorship of a noble youth is generally the first step in the ladder of preferment ; a good thing in hand, (for such as possess the necessary assiduity and suppleness,) and a bill upon the future which seldom fails to be honoured. It is not wonderful, therefore, that the fellows of Trinity murmured at the expense incurred on account of the Master's pupils. What they had to pay was probably a trifle, but what they lost in expectation, (and every college tutor would set down to his own creditor account, the whole possible gain of each titled or honourable pupil, even to the contingency of a mitre, as sure and personal loss,) was as large as their hopes or their wishes. At all events, this measure of

Bentley's excited much clamour.   It would shock a mother of the present water-drinking day, to be informed that the residence of those young gentlemen in the lodge occasioned an alarming increase in the consumption of college ale.   That it interrupted the progress of Bentley's Horace, was not half so annoying to the seniority.   To be serious,—the money part of this business strongly illustrates the absurdity of adhering to ancient usages, when the circumstances that gave rise to them are changed.   When colleges were first founded, the master of each was presumed, indeed necessitated, to be a bachelor. Provisions were cheap, money was scarce.   It was therefore an obvious convenience to supply him with necessaries from the college stock in kind, especially as his attendants were supposed to be poor scholars, who might almost literally subsist on the crumbs that fell from his table.   A married master, with hungry children, and a train of beer-bibbing hirelings, was not even contemplated in hope, as a single seed of time.   Every thing about a college savours of celibacy.   For the accidents of married life, there is no provision.   There are college libraries, kitchens, (noble ones,) cellars, ample and well stocked, gardens, bowling-greens,—even in some instances, private theatres, (for the Fellows of Trinity were obligated, by statute, to present *Comedies* at certain stated feasts,) but whoever heard of a college nursery? when was there a degree taken in midwifery ?

From these and other causes, complaints against Bentley became louder and louder, and he was openly taxed with greediness and meanness, in saddling the college with the support of his own boarders, with whom he received not more than £200 a year.   He attempted to silence all murmurs by extolling the honour done to the society by these young patricians (which honour, by the way, he pretty well monopolised himself), and by referring to three sash windows which he had put into their apartments at his own expense !   Verily, it is heart-sickening to find a man, whom one would fain venerate, engaged in such squabbles, and worse still, to find him so often in the wrong.

Still, however, the feuds of Trinity College were confined within its own walls; and Bentley was known to the world only as a scholar, and a patron of scholars.   His fame was European.   Veteran plodders either veiled their eyes in adoration, or confessed, by impotent detraction, their sense of his superiority.   It can hardly be said that he bore his faculties meekly; yet, in the literary world, if he used his giant's strength like a giant, it was like a good-natured giant.   To the weak, he was merciful ; and to the young, as one that chasteneth whom he loveth.   He was rude, not malicious : he growled, and shook his mane, and sometimes gave an ugly bite, but he never stung.   He left his

enemy crest-fallen, but not heart-broken. An instance of his rough
way of doing a good turn, occurred in his correspondence with Tiberius
Hemsterhuis, or Hemsterhuisius, as he latinised his name, making
thereby as near an approach to the sonorous majesty of Roman nomenclature, as his tatooed highness of the Sandwich Islands, in a naval
uniform coat, and no breeches, doth to the English court dress. This
young Dutchman, in his eighteenth year, was engaged to complete an
edition of the Onomasticon of Julius Pollux, a curious work, from which
almost all our direct information on the in-door arrangements of the
ancients is derived. Of course it is the production of a comparatively
recent age, for books are seldom written about common matters till
they begin to grow obsolete; whence it arises, that the very things
which everybody knows in one generation, are those which nobody
knows a few generations after. Julius Pollux, therefore, may take rank
somewhere between Captain Grose and Dr. Kitchener. His principal
value depends on the illustration which he affords to the comic writers;
and with fragments of the comic writers his text abounds, and on the
correction and explanation of these fragments, young Tiberius particularly prided himself. Before the work was out of the press, he ventured to write to Bentley, as the highest living authority, for his
opinion and assistance respecting certain passages; a mark of deference
from a rising genius, which must have highly delighted our Aristarchus, and deserved, what it obtained, a prompt and satisfactory reply.
Hemsterhuis's thanks for this condescention, though despatched immediately, were never delivered till the spring of 1708, nearly three years
after his original communication, and when the Julius Pollux had been
some time before the Public. The gratitude of the youthful editor, and
his fears lest the involuntary delay of his acknowledgments should be
ascribed to disrepect, were very affecting. Bentley, who saw immediately the strength and the weakness of his disciple, promptly relieved
him from his apprehension of having offended, and fairly complimented
his diligence and learning, but at the same time, made him so keenly
sensible of his deficiency in the *res metrica*, (where after all, the youth
only partook of the general ignorance of continental scholars,) and so
completely upset his supposed emendations of the fragments, that the
aspirant was absolutely disheartened, and thought for a time of relin-
quishing classical pursuits altogether. But he thought better of it, and
lived to acquire a rank in criticism, second only to Bentley's own; and,
what was far more to his honour, remembered the exposure of his
youthful errors with gratitude, and often related the anecdote to his
pupils, when he would impress upon them *how much they had to learn*.
Hemsterhuis kept Bentley's two Epistles till his death, when they were

N

published by David Ruhnken, his pupil and admirer. There have been men, who would have burned them.

Bentley, at this period, corresponded with many of the most learned men in Europe, and received from them all that homage which his wide spreading reputation demanded. From one of these letters it appears that, in 1708, his candlelight studies had injured his sight, which was restored by an application of the insects called multipedæ. To this benefit he pleasantly alludes, in two latin elegiac couplets :—

> Quod liceat Veli doctas mihi volvere chartas
> Ponitur hæc vobis, gratia Multipedæ
> At vobis maneat crebris, precor, imbribus uda
> Subque cavo quercus cortice tuta domus.

> That learn'd Deveil's deep page I may peruse,
> Ye things of many feet, to you I owe,
> Moist be your darkling cells, with frequent dews
> And safely snug, the rough oak's rind below.

The cure of which the things of many feet obtained the credit, was so effectual, that to his remotest old age, Bentley's sight remained unimpaired, notwithstanding the intense exertion of his eyes in reading small type, and decyphering scarce legible manuscripts.

However regardless of the feelings and purses of the then population of Trinity, Bentley was indefatigable in promoting the glory and welfare of the college as a state. In one year, (1706,) he laid the foundation of an observatory, and of a chemical laboratory. The first was destined to assist the observations of Roger Cotes, first Plumian Professor of Astronomy, of whom, after his early decease, Newton said " If Cotes had lived, we should have had something." The laboratory was devoted to the researches of the Veronese Vigani, an ingenious foreigner, who cultivated a science but just beginning to deliver itself from the avaricious quackery of the alchemists. Vigani may be called the first Cambridge Lecturer on Chemistry ; and no successor was appointed for some years after his death. It was Bentley's design to make his college the focus of all the science and information in the kingdom ; and, to make it an edifice worthy of the learning he wished it to contain. But even the most obvious improvements were regarded with an eye of suspicion ; and his taste for architecture, which he gratified unscrupulously at the college expense, incurred great and not altogether unfounded odium. His own lodge he had repaired, or rather re-edified, at a cost originally calculated at £200, but which amounted to somewhere about £1000, exclusive of a new stair-case, which he erected in defiance of the direct refusal of the Bursar, (the academic chancellor of the exchequer,) and unsanctioned by the Seniors. For this stair-case, the Fellows absolutely denied payment. But Bentley had, as he expressed it, "a rusty sword, wherewith he subdued all opposition." This was an obsolete statute, compelling the whole body of Fellows to almost perpetual residence. Were all corporations invested with a power to accommodate their institutes to ever-changing circumstances, and did they make a wise and provident use of that power, law would not so often be the power of iniquity. By the terrors of the "rusty sword," and other threats of a like nature, the autocrat of Trinity at length enforced the discharge of a debt of £350, incurred against the consent of those who had to pay it. Nor were the stretches of his authority confined to matters of finance. In the distribution of honours, offices, and preferments; in the infliction of penalties, even to confiscation and exile, (so far as he could inflict them,) he was equally arbitrary. Whoever opposed him was certain to be excluded from every reward of merit, and to receive something more than justice for the first alleged offence. That his severer measures were absolutely and substantially unjust is by no means clear; but he proceeded to extremities without either consulting his legal assessors, or even waiting for legally convicting evidence. Of two Fellows, whom he expelled in 1708, the guilt admits of little doubt, for one of them, John Wyvil, confessed to the fact of purloining and melting down the college plate; the other, John Durant Breval, hereafter designed to figure along with Bentley himself in the Dunciad, was more than suspected of what (christian) men call adultery, and (heathen) Gods, a platonic friendship for a married lady. But they were both punished unconstitutionally, by the Master's sole prerogative, and their offences were forgotten in the danger of liberty.

We cannot, therefore, be surprised, that Bentley met with opposition, or faint support, even when he stepped forward as the enlightened patron of learning, and of learned men; that schemes really magnificent, such as his renovation of the chapel, were cited as fresh instances of rapacity,—that innovations, which might be improvements, were only regarded as precedents of oppression,—and that the Fellows of Trinity only waited for a tangible pretext, and a bold leader, to throw off that allegiance which they conceived to be forfeited by lawless tyranny. The pretext occurred, in Bentley's project for a new division of the college funds. The leader appeared in the person of Miller, a lay Fellow, and a rising Barrister, who was accustomed to visit his University friends at the Christmas vacation, and chanced to come just when this revolutionary proposal of the Master's had struck "a panic of property."

In order to comprehend the nature and extent of the change contemplated, it is necessary to state, that the original endowment allotted to each Fellow, free chambers and commons, with stipends varying according to their degrees, viz.:—for a Doctor of Divinity, £5 : a Batchelor of Divinity, £4 ; a Master of Arts, £2 13s. 4d. These, with a small sum for dress, were the whole emoluments of a Fellowship. As these sums became insufficient, through the depreciation of money, and as the college funds increased, several alterations had taken place in the distribution, not necessary to be here recounted ; in particular, the advance in the value of a Fellowship was made to depend upon standing solely, without any regard to superiority of degree, which removed one great incentive to graduate in the higher faculties. Now it was Bentley's plan to restore the original ratio, by multiplying the sum mentioned in the statutes by ten, so as to give £50 to a Doctor, £40 to a Batchelor of Divinity, and £26 13s. 4d. to a Master of Arts : —but of course the Master's own stipend was to be settled according to the same proportion. Now the original foundation allotted the Master £100 for stipend and commons together, without specifying how much should be reckoned as stipend alone. Bentley chose to state it as £85 ; but as a demand for £850 "at one fell swoop" was rather too alarming, he offered to content himself with £800. This being resisted, he lowered his claims to £400, and then to £200, which, of itself, was not unreasonable ; and had it covered the whole of his estimates, it is probable that the measure might have been carried, and peace restored to the society. But the worst was behind.—By regular custom, the Master was supplied with certain articles, as bread, beer, coals, candles, oil, linen, &c., from the public stock, and no definite limit had been set to his consumption. Bentley's enormous demands in these particulars, which really seem incredible, had given rise to much clamour, and must have been intended to reconcile the college to any mode he might suggest of getting rid of a burden at once exorbitant and uncertain. He offered, therefore, to accept £700 a year in lieu of all allowances. The mere amount of the demand was not the only objection. It tended to make him altogether independent of the seniority. The *budget*, therefore, when first introduced, in 1708, had a very cold reception. He had recourse to various methods to procure its adoption ; altered several details, but always came to the same conclusion as to the sum total. The fellows continued to demur. He endeavoured to promote a petition in favour of his budget among the Junior Fellows,—a measure not likely to conciliate the Seniority. At length he had recourse to the violent expedient of stopping the supplies, and was just proceeding to extremities, when Miller arrived, at the conclusion of 1709, to raise the standard of open revolt. He declared the Master's demands to be altogether unreasonable, and suggested the possibility of obtaining redress, by appealing to a higher authority. Bentley was not the man to yield to menace.—Conference followed conference. Ill blood and ill language ensued. The Master denounced Lawyers as the most igno- minious people in the universe—told one senior Fellow that he would die in his shoes, and called another "the college dog;" and finally pronounced his fatal malediction,—" From henceforward, farewell peace to Trinity College." So saying, he set off for London.

No sooner was he gone, than Miller, conceiving that the Master intended to petition the Queen in council, advised his comrades to have the first word, and lay their complaints before a competent authority. He drew up a statement of grievances, which was subscribed by the sixteen Senior Fellows present in college, and by eight of the Juniors; notwithstanding some objection from DR. COLBATCH, Professor of Casuistry, who, as he was the slowest to enter into the quarrel, was the most perseverent in prosecuting it. No sooner was Bentley informed of this unexpected step, than he hastened back from town "with the speed of a general who hears of a mutiny among his troops during his absence, and resolves to arrest its progress by making a summary example of the ringleaders." On the 18th of January he caused Miller's name to be struck off the college boards. On the 19th it was restored by the Vice-Master and eight Seniors; and on the 24th it was again struck off by Bentley. Compromise became hopeless, and both parties flew to arms.

For all important disputes which can arise in the different colleges about 45 in number, which compose the English Universities, the final appeal lies to the Visitor. In the present case a difficulty arose as to who was visitor. The statutes of EDWARD VI. appoint the bishop of Ely to that function. Those of Elizabeth are silent as to the general right of visitation, which might therefore be presumed to abide in the crown as representative of the founder; but by the 40th article, the bishop of Ely is appointed Visitor in case of misconduct on the part of the Master. To this prelate, then bishop Moore, an early friend of Bentley, and munificent patron of literature, a petition was addressed, containing a summary in 54 articles, in the form of interrogatory, of Bentley's real and supposed misdemeanors, signed by the vice master and 29 fellows. Many of the counts may be fairly pronounced frivolous and vexatious. We should scarce have expected to find marriage alleged as a crime against a protestant dignitary, or that the fellows of the richest college in Europe should have complained of their Master's wife keeping a coach. But if many of the articles were not worth answering, there were those which Bentley could never satisfactorily answer, especially his tyrannical interference with all college appointments and elections, and his reckless expenditure of the college funds. Prudence and delicacy would have recommended a private reference to the visitor as arbitrator ; but the passions of the parties were too much excited for prudence, and to delicacy none of them seem to have had the slightest claim.   The articles were published under the form of a pamphlet, and Bentley replied in a printed address to the bishop, whose jurisdiction he nevertheless denied, a composition of more acerbity than elegance, containing more recrimination than explanation, and throwing the onus of the quarrel on the sottish habits and jacobite politics of his oppugners.

In his political allusions, Bentley made what is vulgarly called a bad shot.   The people were tired of the Whigs, sick of a war, in which, according to the invariable custom of England, they gained nothing but debt and glory, and perhaps secretly pining for the restoration of the exiled family, from which the worst men expected the reward of secret adherence, and the best the blessing of God on a fearless act of justice.   In this humour of the public, Sacheverel became the idol of the mob for doctrines which in these days would have exposed his barns to arson and his life to violence.   He was, like most mob orators, a man of middling character and mediocre talents, thrust forward by the high church party as a tool, whose proceedings they might acknowledge or deny, according to their success.   His sermons, which are utterly worthless, were not supposed to be his own composition, and his defence, which was masterly, is known to have been the production of Atterbury, assisted by Smalridge and other of Bentley's Christ church adversaries. The popular ferment attending his ill-judged prosecution, coincided with the Queen's personal bias towards the Tories, and the machinations of Mrs. Masham, a new favourite, who is said to have resented some personal slight of the haughty dutchess of Marlborough, that great but unhappy woman, so admirably described by Pope under the name of Atossa, to oust the Whig ministry.   But what Bentley lost by the defeat of his nominal party, was more than supplied by the influence of his wife, who was connected both with Mr. Masham, the favourite's husband, and with St. John, the new secretary of state, and afterwards Lord Bolingbroke, no very creditable patron for a divine, but who had talents enough to know that the name of Bentley looked well on the ministerial list.   Now it happened that some of Bentley's accusers were full as much addicted to Venus and Bacchus as to Minerva.   The Doctor had not scrupled to assert that the poverty which the Fellows of Trinity ascribed to his exactions, was wholly owing to the additional tax on claret ; and his lady did not fail to take the advantage which a female reign always affords to scandal in the guise of morality. But the main manager in the matter was Harley, the Lord-treasurer, a circuitous fine gentleman, to whom Bentley addressed a *projet* of a royal letter, in which every point was decided in his own favour, and the Master enjoined " to chastise all licence among the Fellows." But such downright dealing did not accord with the views of the wily politician. It is uncertain whether this bold stroke came to the ears of the enemy, but certain it is, that on the twenty-first of November, Bentley received a peremptory summons to answer the articles against him by the eighteenth of December.

Bentley, being thus at bay, at first thought of appealing to Convocation ; but, finding that he was likely to be anticipated in that quarter, and perhaps expecting little favour from his brethren of the clergy, he resolved on a petition to the Queen, setting forth, that her Majesty, as representative of the royal founder, was the rightful Visitor, and that the assumption of the visitatorial functions by a subject was an invasion of her prerogative ; finally throwing himself and his cause on her Majesty's protection. This petition met with immediate attention. Mr. Secretary St. John directed the Attorney and Solicitor General to examine the allegations on both sides, and make a report thereon with all convenient speed. At the same time the Attorney General was to signify to the Bishop of Ely her Majesty's pleasure, that all proceedings be staid till the question should be decided in whom the right of visitation lay. Bishop Moore, in his reply, expressed a cheerful acquiescence and confidence that her Majesty would never deprive him of any right belonging to his see. The second of January, 1710—11, was appointed for hearing of the cause. Sir Peter King, afterwards Lord Chancellor, and Mr. Miller, appeared as counsel for the Fellows. No less than five months elapsed before the law officers could make their report to Government. This document, which Dr. Monk has given at length in the appendix, contains a full and impartial statement of the facts of the case, and delivers a cautious opinion on the point at issue—to wit, that, whether the statutes of Edward the Sixth were or were not virtually abrogated by those of Elizabeth, the *master is*, by either code, subject to the jurisdiction of the Bishop of Ely ; leaving to her Majesty and to Dr. Bentley, the course of moving for a prohibition in a court of law, if either thought fit to contest this opinion.

This decision was far from pleasing to Bentley, who wanted not the expensive privilege of litigation, and that, too, in face of the highest legal authority, but a direct interposition of the crown in his own favour. He therefore determined to address the Prime Minister, Harley, who was then just recovering from the wound inflicted on him by the French assassin, Guiscard, and had been created Earl of Oxford, and Lord High Treasurer. This application was severely censured, as a desertion of the Whigs, in whose lists the Doctor's name had hitherto, for fashion's sake, been borne, though he was never a very devoted or factious politician, and seldom alluded to public matters at all, except in order to throw suspicion upon his enemies. As the memorial is artful and characteristic, we shall give a few extracts from it :—

Cotton House, July 12, 1711.

Right Honourable,

After my hearty thanks to God for the wonderful preservation of your most valuable life from the stabs of an assassin, and my sincere congratulation for your new station of honour, so long and so well deserved ; I humbly crave leave to acquaint your lordship, that at last I have received from Mr. Attorney General the report, sealed up and directed to Mr. Secretary St. John, a copy of which is here inclosed. Your lordship, when you read it, will please to observe, that all the facts alleged in my petition are here confirmed :—that the statute of Edward, which once constituted the Bishop of Ely visitor, was rejected and left out in the two later bodies of statutes, those of Philip and Mary, and those of Elizabeth, now only in force ;—that the crown has, for a century and a half, been in sole possession of the visitatorial power ;—that no Bishop of Ely, all that while, ever heard of his being visitor, or ever once pretended to act as such, till this present Bishop ; and as for the 40th statute of Elizabeth, which *obiter* and incidentally styles the Bishop of Ely *visitator*, my counsel largely proved—first, that it was *ipso facto* void ; and secondly, that, supposing it to be now in force, it was in the power of the crown to vacate it at pleasure. It is clear, that if her Majesty will maintain her prerogative, it is but saying the words, and vacating the 40th statute : on the contrary, if she will abandon it to the Bishop, she may give him a new corroborating statute, if this be too weak. However, to give more satisfaction about both the points in question, I have permission to inclose the opinion of the learned Sir Nathaniel Lloyd, her Majesty's Advocate-General and Vice Chancellor of Cambridge ; which he is ready, if occasion were, to maintain in a public manner, by report or by pleading. He, indeed, humbly conceives, that even Mr. Attorney's present report is sufficient for her Majesty's prerogative, though the former point be waived ; and it is so much the more so, by what I have heard last post, that those Fellows—the minor part of the whole society—that are complainers against me, have subscribed a petition to her Majesty, that she will please to take this matter into her own hands. My Lord, I very readily close with this, and desire nothing more, than that her

Majesty would send down Commissioners with full power to set every thing right, and to punish where fault may be found. I only beg, and most humbly hope, that such persons may be nominated as are lovers of learning, and men of conscience and integrity, above the influence of party, and then I fear not but that I shall be both honourably acquitted, and merit the public approbation. I am easy under every thing but loss of time by detainment here in town, which hinders me from putting the last hand to my edition of Horace, and from doing myself the honour to inscribe it to your Lordship's great name; which permission is most humbly asked and intreated by

Your Lordship's most obedient and obliged Servant,

RICHARD BENTLEY.

The result of this communication was an order from the Minister, that the report of the Attorney and Solicitor General be laid before the Lord Keeper, Sir Simon Harcourt, and all the crown lawyers; and a letter from Secretary St. John to Bishop Moore, signifying her Majesty's desire that all proceedings should be staid. Thus the leaning of Government was sufficiently obvious, and Bentley secured sufficient respite to set the last hand to his Horace.—We hear no more of the college quarrels during the remainder of 1711; nor did the prosecution advance much more rapidly in the course of 1812. The crown lawyers, after more than seven months' deliberation, decided, January 9, that the crown was Visitor General of the College, but that the Bishop of Ely possessed, under the 40th statute, the power of hearing and deciding upon the charges against the Master; adding, that it was in the power of the crown, with consent of the college, to alter the Visit. atorial authority. This opinion, subscribed with many eminent legal names, was opposed by the plain common sense of Sir Joseph Jekyl, a worthy man, whose old-fashioned consistency gained a witty panegyric from Pope:—

> "A horse laugh, if you please, at honesty:
> A sneer at Jekyl, or some queer old Whig
> Who never chang'd his principle or wig."

To honest Jekyl, lawyer as he was, it appeared as it must do to every honest man who is not a lawyer, that, if the 40th statute of Elizabeth were valid at all, it clearly recognized the Bishop of Ely as Visitor once for all, to all intents and purposes; especially as the same statutes make no mention of any other visitatorial authority. Indeed, Bentley's own assertion, that the 40th statute was *ipso facto* void, as contradicting the general drift and spirit of the code, and probably proceeding from a mere inadvertence in the reviser, is, in reason, much more tenable than the

o

distinction which his adversaries attempted to draw. The absence of any express appointment of a general Visitor, and the circumstance that this particular regulation *De Magistri amotione** is conveyed in the very words of the earlier statutes, favours the idea, that the visitatorial

---

* Cap 40: De Magistri, si res exigat, amotione.

Quoniam capite gravi aliquo morbo laborante, cætera corporis membra vehementer quoque vexari solent, idcirco statuimus et ordinamus, ut si Magister Coll. in suo officio obeundo admodum negligens et dissolutus repertus fuerit aut de inhonesta vitæ ratione aut incontinentia suspectus fuerit, per Vice Magistrum et reliquos septem seniores, aut per majoren partem eorum quorum conscientiam in hac re quantum possumus oneramus, sicut Domino Jesu rationem reddituri sunt, cum omni modestia et lenitate admoneatur; quod si hoc modo admonitus non se emendaverit, secundo similiter admoneatur; sin autem neque tum quidem resipuerit, Vice Magister et reliqui seniores, vel major pars eorum rem omnem Visitatori Episcopo Eliensi, qui pro tempore fuerit aperiant, qui et eam diligenter cognoscat et cum equitate definiat. Cujus sententiæ Magistrum sine *ullâ appellatione* omnino parere volumus; sub pœnâ loci sui in perpetuum amittendi.

Porro si dictus Magister corame dicto Visitatore aliquando examinatus, et vel hæreseos, vel Læsæ Majestatis crimine, vel de Simonia' Usura, Perjurio coram Judice commisso, furto notabile, homicidio voluntario, incestu, adulterio, fornicatione, dilapidatione bonorum Collegii vel de violatione Statutorum ejusdem vel denique de alio quovis consimili crimine notabili, coram prædicto Visitatore legitime convictus fuerit sine morâ per eundem Vice Magistrum Officio Magistri privetur: neque ullam ei Appellationem aut ullum aliud Juris remedium permittimus: sed quæcun que in hâc causâ tentaverit irrita esse volumus, et decernimus ipso facto.

(TRANSLATION.)

Chapter 40.—Of the removal of the Master, if need require.

Whereas, if the head be disordered, the whole body and its members must be afflicted together; therefore we order and appoint, that if the Master be found very negligent or remiss in the discharge of his office, or be suspected of ill life, or inconti-nency, let him be rebuked with all moderation and gentleness, by the Vice Master and seven seniors, on whose conscience we charge this matter, as they shall answer the same before the Lord Jesus; and if, being thus admonished, he amend not, let him be rebuked a second time in the same manner: but if neither then he be brought to consideration, the Vice Chancellor and senior Fellows, or the majority thereof, shall lay the whole matter before the Visitor, the Bishop of Ely, for the time being; who shall diligently examine and equitably decide the same. By whose sentence it is our will that the Master do abide absolutely, and without any appeal, under penalty of perpetual forfeiture of his office.

Furthermore, if the Master aforesaid, being at any time examined before the afore-said Visitor, and by the aforesaid Visitor lawfully convicted of heresy, high treason, simony, usury, perjury in the presence of a judge, notorious theft, wilful murder, incest, fornication, adultery, dilapidation of the college estate, or violation of its statutes, or, in fine, of any other the like notorious crime—let him be, without delay, by the aforesaid Vice Master, deprived of his office: nor do we permit him any appeal, or other remedy at law; and whatsoever he may essay in this sort, we will to be null and void, and so we do, *ipso facto*, declare it to be.

power was meant to beresumed by the crown ; and that the words casually referring to the Bishop of Ely, were carelessly transcribed from King Edward's cartularies. But that Queen Elizabeth meant herself and her successors to visit the college at large, and to devolve upon his reverend Lordship of Ely the task of castigating the Master, is a supposition which neither good sense nor the plain laws of interpretation can admit. Still, there the statute was, and the easiest way would appear to have been, either to confirm or abrogate, by order in council, or (if needful) by act of parliament, according to Bentley's suggestion.

As however, the Bishop was acknowledged by the legal authorities on all hands to have jurisdiction in the present question, it was generally believed that the prohibition would be taken off, and that the long suspended cause would proceed. Still the interdict continued, and it was long supposed that the Master owed this respite to the good offices of his wife with Lady Masham and St. John. But certain letters of Lord Oxford's collection, give a different colour to the affair.

The Treasurer had, in fact, been holding communications with both parties, had given to each a hope of his countenance. Whether straight forward measures were so alien to his habits, that he was necessitated to play false, even when he had no personal stake in the game, or whether he was really well disposed towards Bentley, and wished to keep his alleged misdemeanors from public exposure, till an opportunity should occur of removing him to some less obnoxious station of dignity, certainly it was his advice, perhaps his sincere and judicious advice, that both parties should submit their differences to the arbitration of the crown. Probably he suffered the Fellows to conclude that they would speedily be delivered from the burden of an unpopular head. Reports were circulated that Bentley was actually appointed to the Deanery of Litchfield.*

---

* The rumour of this appointment had reached the ears of Kuster, who mentions it in two letters to his true brother in the muses, with no small exultation. We subjoin the following extract, both to shew how a German scholar can write English, and to prove that Greek does not absolutely annihilate the grateful affections :—

" Aug. 5, 1712. P. S. After I had written this letter, which I kept from one post day to another, waiting for Mr. Hemsterhuis's letter to be inclosed in myne, there came to see me some English gentlemen, and amongst them one of your college, Nomine Town, a physician, (qui magni te facit,) who brought me the good news that you were made Dean of Litchfield. Ego plane erectus fui hoc nuncio; and afterwards I drank first your health, and afterwards, upon the confirmation of this news. I can assure you, sir, that I shall long heartily to have the confirmation of this from you, because nobody of your friends can take more part in your prosperity than I do, having found that I have no truer friend than you. Mr. Hemsterhuis's desseins to write this same day, Vale." Again, in a latin epistle, " gratulor tibi ex animo de

This however proved unfounded. It might have been a hazardous experiment to bestow conspicuous favour on a man against whom such discreditable charges were pending. Conciliation and procrastination were the ruling principles of Harley, and doubtless he wished Bentley, at least to make a shew of concession. But this was what the Doctor would not do. The only approach he ever made to pacification, was by detaching some few of his adversaries from the common cause. *Divide et impera*, a politic maxim, of which even the worldly expediency is very doubtful, when applied to large communities, is an effectual rule for maintaining supremacy in small factious republics, as the history of the Italian cities too often evinces, and Bentley made the most of it in Trinity College.

But finding this method too slow for his impatience, he determined to starve the combinators to a surrender, and to shew the Fellows, that if they were not content to receive what he chose, in such proportion as he chose, and allow him to appropriate as much as he chose, they should have nothing at all. Having manœuvred poor old Stubbe, the senior of his opponents, out of the Vice-mastership, and put a more manageable person in his place, he proceeded, at the winter audit, 1712-13, to interdict a dividend, unless his plan of distribution was accepted. Thus writes the aged Ex-Vice-master to the Earl of Oxford :—" Dr. Bentley, I hear, at the auditing of our college accounts, refused to vote a dividend of the remaining money, in order to starve the poor members into an acquiescence under his base and unworthy measures. Our College, my Lord, though it be dutiful and silent, is in a very wretched condition ; and if your Lordship please to look upon it with compassion, you will be a second founder to us. My Lord, I cannot ask pardon for this without remembering my former offences of this nature ; but I cannot doubt either of your Lordship's pardon, or of the success of my petition, when I consider that I speak for a nursery of learning to my Lord of Oxford." Whether Harley, who prided himself in the reputation of a Mecænas, was touched with compassion, or cajoled by flattery, to interest himself for the starving Fellows, or whether he only prescribed patience, a cruel prescription to the hungry, we know not. Certainly Bentley's expectations of submission from his opponents, and of protracted interposition from the minister, were disappointed. Miller would be put off no longer, and resolved to bring the matter before the Court of Queen's Bench. Stubbe* apprised the Treasurer that all

nova hæc dignitate, et gaudeo eo magis, quo magis id inimicis tuis doliturum esse *novi*." This shews that Bentley's litigations were heard of over the channel.

* Stubbe must at one time have stood high in Bentley's good graces, for his nephew had, through the Master's influence, been pre-elected to a fellowship, contrary to cus-

endeavours to prevent the cause coming to a hearing would probably be vain, as the court would not allow the validity of the royal, or in good sooth, ministerial prohibition, while the discussion of a point of prerogative could do little good to a tottering administration: which argument, whether urged by the Ex-Vice-master or not, determined the ministry to take off the embargo, and Secretary St. John, now Lord Bolingbroke, wrote to Bishop Moore, " giving him the Queen's permission to proceed as far as by law he was empowered." Before the end of the Easter Term, 1713, the affair of Trinity College was first brought into court, by Mr. Page* obtaining a Rule for the Bishop to shew cause why a Mandamus should not issue to compel him to discharge his judicial functions. After a full year's delay, arising partly from forms of law, of which delay appears to be the only assignable object, and partly from the avocations of the Judges, and the disturbed state of the nation, in the Month of May, 1714, the trial of Bentley actually commenced. The large hall of Ely house was converted into a Court of Justice;

tom, and without the claim of merit, being a worthless and profligate young man, whom Bentley himself afterwards declared " the worst man that ever entered a college." Whiston, who antedates the proceeding three years, alludes to this as Bentley's first deviation from rectitude, and asserts that the Master himself allowed that in this case he departed from the rule—Detur Digniore. It is also said that this Edmund Stubbe was to marry a niece of Bentley's, in which case, his uncle's fortune, not less than £10,000, was to have been settled on the young couple. We can scarce suppose, if this be true, that young Stubbe's vices were then notorious, though it sometimes will happen, that those who have the disposal of young ladies, are as blind to the faults of a wealthy suitor, as the young ladies themselves to the defects of a handsome lover. This is not the only occasion on which Bentley has been accused of match-making. He was said to have bestowed some small preferment on a young B. A. on condition that he should marry Mrs. Bentley's maid. This was probably an unfounded surmise; but the condition of the working clergy was then so depressed, and attendance on the higher classes so much esteemed, that the marriage of a small vicar with a lady's maid would not be accounted a misalliance, and happy was the poor curate, who could obtain for his daughter the enviable situation of Mrs. Honour. For some curious particulars on this head, consult " Echard on the Contempt of the Clergy and of Religion, 1670." Parson Adams is no exaggeration.

* This Page was afterwards a Judge of " hanging" notoriety, whom Pope has " damn'd to everlasting fame."

> " Poison, or slander dread, from Delia's rage,
> Hard words, or hanging, if your Judge be Page."
> IMITATIONS OF HORACE.

> " And dies if dulness gives her Page the word."   DUNCIAD.

In Johnson's Life of Savage, some specimens of this man's eloquence are preserved. Let us rejoice that the dynasty of the Pages is at an end.

where written evidence was produced in support and refutation of the
54 articles against the Master of Trinity College.   The counsel for the
prosecution were Sir Peter King, (Is opposition to church dignitaries
hereditary in his family?) Sir John Cheshyre, Mr. Serjeant Page,
Dr. Paul, the civilian, and Edmund Miller, who probably pleaded with
more sincerity on this occasion than advocates generally obtain credit
for, and a mastery of the facts and bearings of the case, which few advocates have the means of acquiring.   Bentley's* counsel were the Hon.
Spencer Compton, (afterwards Speaker, and Earl of Wilmington,) Mr.
Lutwych, and Dr. Andrews, the civilian.   Bishop Moore had chosen as
his Assessors, Lord Cowper, the Ex-Chancellor, and Dr. Newton, an
eminent civilian.

Though the principle grounds of complaint have been already related
in the order of their occurrence, it may promote perspicuity if the important heads of the 54 articles be gone over, premising, that being in
an interrogatory form, they read sometimes rather ludicrously.   As
e. g. conceive the following questions put by a learned Judge, or Reverend Bishop, to a Doctor of Divinity, a public guardian of the morals,
manners, and orthodoxy of ingenuous youth ?   32. "Why did you
use scurrilous words and language to several of the Fellows, particularly
by calling Mr. Eden an ass, and Mr. Rashleigh the college dog ; by
telling Mr. Cock he *would die in his shoes,* and calling many others
fools and *sots* and other scurrilous names?"   Or, 33. "Why did you pro-
fanely and blasphemously use and apply several expressions in the
Scripture? As "he that honours me, him will I honour."   "I set life or
death before you, choose you whether," or to that effect."   Or, 12.
"When by false and base practices, as by threatening to bring letters
from court, visitations and the like, and at other times by boasting of
your great interest and acquaintance, and that you were the genius of
the age . . . . why &c.?"   Or, 10. "Why have you, for many years
past, wasted the college bread, ale, beer, coals, wood, turf, sedge, charcoal, linen, pewter, corn, flour, brawn, and bran, viz. 40,000 penny
loaves, 60,000 half-penny loaves, 14,000 gallons of ale, 20,000 gallons

---

* " In a loose paper, which I found in the treasury of Trinity College, there is the
following account of the performances of four of these gentlemen.   The writer seems
to be some Fellow who was present at the trial :

Spencer Compton.   He hath been heard to say afterwards that he never was so
ashamed of any cause in his life.

" Sir J. Cheshyre.   He used Dr. B. very much in his own way.

Serj. Page.   He hummed and haw'd, and stumbled, so his clients were very much
ashamed of him.

" Mr. Miller.   Was very exact as to dates and quotations, but otherwise very dull
and heavy.—*Dr. Monk.*

of beer, 600 chaldron of coals, 60,000 billets of wood, 1000 hundreds of turf, 100 load of sedge, 500 bushel of charcoal, 100 ells of Holland, 400 ells of diaper and other linen, 5000 ounces of pewter, 200 bushels of corn, 400 bushels of flour, 300 bushels of bran, and other goods to the value of £3000 or other great sum, in expending the same, not only on yourself, but upon your wife, children, and boarders, and that in a very extravagant manner, by causing your servants to make whole meals upon the said college bread and beer only, (you not allowing them either flesh, cheese, or butter, with the same) and by many other ways?" We presume that these counts were not read aloud in Ely house in the presence of the accused, as the whole business was conducted by written affidavits, whereof no less than twenty-seven were sworn against the Master, nor does it appear that any one of the complainants relented, and declined to support his signature upon oath.

The first and second articles refer to the Master's appropriation of certain sums, which of right belonged to his predecessor, and to the misapplication of the said sums. The third, fourth, fifth, sixth, and seventh, to the expenditure in rebuilding and fitting-up the Lodge— which is roundly stated at £1500—and to the unwarrantable means taken to inforce payment of the same. The seventh goes so far as to charge Bentley with obtaining money under pretence of paying work-men, and diverting it to other purposes.

The ninth, absurdly enough, asks Dr. Bentley why he married; and why, having married, he brought his wife into college.—It is wonderful that some of his prosecutors should hazard a question which might have been retorted with such bitter effect upon themselves; and somewhat remarkable how unwillingly Queen Elizabeth permitted the marriage of the clergy.

The tenth, thirtieth, thirty-first and forty-fourth, relate to waste of the college goods, and exorbitant demands upon its funds. The twelfth and thirteenth, to the staircase business (a discreditable job altogether). The fourteenth, to the allotment of college chambers—(*seems* frivolous at this distance of time, but might be very serious at the commencement of the last century). The fifteenth, to unlawful interference with the appointment of officers, in which the Master appears to have been culpable and inconsistent. The seventeenth, eighteenth, nineteenth, twentieth, twenty-first, twenty-sixth, and twenty-seventh, to punishments inflicted without due conviction, or the consent of the seniority. The twenty-second regards the expulsion of Miller. The twenty-third, fortieth, and fifty-second, allege certain irregularities and omissions in the chapel service (which, for any spiritual benefit derived from it, might as well be omitted altogether). As for the "founder's prayers," Bentley was quite right in letting them alone ; for they are a mere apology for masses, and where the belief of purgatory does not obtain, have no meaning whatever. The forty-third and forty-fourth articles relate to the new scheme of dividends. The thirty-seventh and forty-seventh, to the bowling green, and another plot of ground, which Bentley had used according to his pleasure, asserting himself "to be Lord of the soil." The fifty-third complains of the observatory ;—one or two others, of the expense incurred in renovating the chapel, and purchasing an organ; and the rest relate either to mere repetitions of former offences or to matters of college regulation—such as the Friday's supper, the declamations in chapel, the permission to quit table before grace, and the like

On a dispassionate review of these articles, it appears that they amount to a sort of accumulative treason against the state and liberties of Trinity College. By far the greater part of them are trifling,—yet, altogether, they prove, beyond contradiction, that Bentley's views extended to absolute sovereignty—that he deemed himself irresponsible —treated the college estate as if no individual but himself had a free-hold therein—and did not condescend to observe those formalities which, by a true college man, are regarded as essential to academic existence.

At the commencement of the trial, public opinion was strong in his favour. Admitted on all hands to be the first scholar in his country, a gifted champion of christianity, connected by friendship or alliance with some of the highest characters of the nation, the man to whom Stillingfleet had committed the care of his son, whom Locke, and Evelyn, and Wren, and Newton had called friend, whom Samuel Clark addressed in terms of veneration, and whom the most erudite foreigners regarded as first among the first, he stood opposed to a knot of comparatively obscure men, to answer upon points in which the great world took little interest, before a judge devoted to literature, who had once been his companion. He had also the reputation of court favour ; he had befriended the existing government in an anxious crisis ;* he had adorned his *alma mater*, not only by his own learning,

* In June, 1812, a furious attack was made upon the Tory ministry, respecting the pending negotiations at Utrecht—the Whigs denouncing them as traitors, who were intriguing with the common enemy, to betray the allies, either in the hope of restoring the Stuarts, or from mere spite and envy at Marlborough's glory. The House of Lords was the scene of contest, and so high did whiggish expectation soar, that, according to Swift (Journal to Stella), the opposition desired their friends to bespeak places, to see the Lord Treasurer carried to the Tower. Though the Ministers obtained a Majority, yet it was especially desirable that every possible expression of

but by that which he imported; even his expensive architecture was, at worst, a magnificent offence, which the public might enjoy without paying for it; and, what was no small prepossession with the many, he had always maintained the port of an innocent man. But, as the cause opened, public opinion took alarm, and the Bishop's own sentiments were altered. So little had Bentley anticipated this—so great was his contempt of his opposers, or his confidence in himself—that, on one hearing, when the Bishop expressed an opinion favourable to his accusers, his nerves were unable to stand the unexpected shock, and he actually fainted away. The trial continued six weeks, and would doubtless have ended in convicting the Master of violating the statutes, and wasting the goods of the college. The Visitor, having consulted

national confidence should be tendered, to embolden their supporters. Bentley managed an address from the University of Cambridge to the Queen, declaring the fullest reliance on the wisdom of her councils, and thanking her for the prospect of a speedy pacification. With that well-weighed caution which appears in all his political conduct, he made the University express their attachment to the Hanoverian succession, terming that house "her Majesty's relations," a phrase not very consonant to Queen Anne's personal predelections, as there can be small doubt that she would willingly have bequeathed her crown to nearer relations; but it neither committed himself nor the Ministry. He had the honour of presenting it to her Majesty with his own hands.

Nothing could be more *politic* than the whole course of Bentley's politics. He was the supporter of government—not of government by one party, or the other—and never fairly laid himself open to the charge of tergiversation. To be sure, he dedicated his Horace to Harley, and reminds him, that Horace was not the less acceptable to Mecænas, because he had borne arms with Brutus and Cassius:—but who ever looked at a dedication for any thing but neat flattery? His moderation in this respect contrasts strangely. with his imprudent violence as Master of Trinity. Perhaps there was no situation in the world for which he was so unfitted, as the headship of a college. Even his learning was not of that quality which is required in a preceptor, or guide of juvenile studies; for his mind was too rapid to wait upon the slow developement of ordinary comprehensions. He had an exquisite tact, an intuitive perception of the possibilities of language, but he had little feeling for the beauties of thought and imagery, and still less sympathy for the minds of others. He had probably quite forgotten what it was to be a learner, and could not sympathetically discover the cause of a difficulty arising from the intellectual constitution of an individual, though, as in the case of Hemsterhuis, he would infallibly indicate a deficiency of positive knowledge on any given topic. In a word, he could point out what was to be learned, but he could not teach.

How different a being was Aldritch, the very ideal of a college head, who made those who would not have loved learning for its own sake, love it for his, who was better pleased to elicit the talents of others, than to display his own—who made even logic amiable, by proving that it was no foe to good fellowship—who regulated conviviality by making himself its moving principle—planned the Peck-water, loved his pipe, and composed "the bonny Christ-Church bells."

P

his assessors, who are said to have dissented, prepared a sentence of ejectment, which it was not decreed that he should pronounce : for before the day of passing judgment arrived, he was himself called to the last assize, just one day before his sovereign lady—that truest friend of the English Church, who has given name to Queen Anne's Charity ; a charity, indeed, which, if there were merit in human works, might partly atone for the unprofitable bloodshed of Marlborough's Victories. Bishop Moore died July 31st ; Queen Anne, August 1st, 1714.

That the Bishop had decided against Bentley, is proved by a sentence, or decretum, in anti-ciceronian latin, found among his papers after his death. But Dr. Monk believes that this was only provisional, and not intended to have been put in force, till all milder measures had failed. Moore was a munificent prelate, and deserved a better end than to die of a cold, caught while listening to heart-breaking allegations against one whom he had long esteemed, and never could cease to admire.

As the decease of the Visitor rendered all previous proceedings null and void, the case of Trinity College might either die a natural death, or had to be commenced de novo. Having arrived at the end of the first stage of this protracted contest, let us take a rapid retrospect of Bentley's literary life during the period of these turmoils. It has been noted by his enemies, and lauded by his eulogists, that whenever the tide of accusation was strongest against him, he was sure to come out with some book which turned the public attention from his delinquencies to his abilities, and indisposed the world to believe that so much learning could lack honesty. But it is by no means evident that this coincidence of his classical publications with the climacterical æras of his fortune was the result of design. Strife and trouble seem to have been congenial to his faculties : controversy was a stimulus without which he would have slumbered. He was naturally a bird of tempest. But as almost all his works were occasional—called forth by the publications of others, we can hardly suppose that all the half-learned of Europe delayed their lucubrations till the precise moment when Bentley was to make a diversion, by holding them up to scorn ; or that the evil genius of Le Clerc and Collins were in collusion with the good genius of the Master of Trinity College. Yet the coincidence, which certainly did exist, furnished Arbuthnot with a good hit, in a squib published long after the period we speak of—a palpable and professed imitation of Swift's manner—which Dr. Johnson would have called " the echo of an unnatural fiction." *

* "An Account of the State of Learning in the Empire of Lilliput, together with

The commencement of the Horace has been already mentioned. This seems to have been his professed engagement from August 1702, to

the History and Character of Bullum, the Emperor's Library Keeper." The passage alluded to is as follows:—

"Bullum is a tall raw-boned man, I believe near six inches and a half high. From his infancy he applied himself with great industry to the old Blefuscudian language, in which he made such a progress, that he almost forgot his native Lilliputian; and at this time he can neither write nor speak two sentences without a mixture of old Blefuscudian. These qualifications, joined to an undaunted forward spirit, and a few good friends, prevailed with the Emperor's grandfather to make him keeper of his library, and a Mulro in the Gomflastru, though most men thought him fitter to be one of the Royal Guards. These places soon helped him to riches, and upon the strength of them he soon began to despise every body, and to be despised by every body. This engaged him in many quarrels, which he managed in a very odd manner: whenever he thought himself affronted, he immediately *flung a great book at his adversary*, and, if he could, felled him to the earth; but if his adversary stood his ground, and flung another book at him, which was sometimes done with great violence, then he complained to the Grand Justiciary, that these affronts were designed to the Emperor, and that he was singled out only as being the Emperor's servant. By this trick he got that great officer to his side, which made his enemies cautious, and him insolent.

"Bullum attended the court some years, but could not get into a higher post; for though he constantly wore the heels of his shoes high or low, as the fashion was, yet having a long back and a stiff neck, he never could, with any dexterity, creep under the stick which the Emperor or the chief minister held. As to his dancing on a rope, I shall speak of it presently; but the greatest skill in that art will not procure a man a place at court, without some agility at the stick."

Swift never renewed the attack upon Bentley, after the " Tale of a Tub," and " The Battle of the Books." Perhaps he was ashamed of having, in the Phalaris' Controversy, taken the wrong, that is to say, the losing side. Perhaps he abstained cautiously from whatever might connect him with the " Tale of a Tub," under the impression that but for that offspring of youthful imprudence, (which like most of the *Disowned*, is as like its father as his worst enemies could desire,) he might have been an English Bishop instead of an Irish Dean. Those who love not the church, and, alas! they are too many, and those who amuse themselves with experiments upon human nature, may possibly wish that Gulliver had attained a mitre. It would be curious to see what sort of a Bishop a high-churchman, whose christianity was contempt for Infidels, and whose orthodoxy was hatred of Dissenters, would have made. Yet the Dean had many worse things to answer for, than writing the Tale of a Tub.

What, however, he would not do himself, he found others to do for him. Never was literary band so closely united by harmonious dissimilitude as that which comprized Swift, Pope, Gay, Arbuthnot, and Parnell: they were a perfect co-operative society, and might be said, almost without a metaphor, to feel for each other. But Swift *thought* for them all:—his was the informing mind, and exercised over his associates that supremacy which philosophic power, however perverted, will always maintain over mere genius, though elegant as Pope's—over simple erudition, though extensive as Arbuthnot's. Moreover, whenever a limited number of men form a

December 1711 ; but in that interval he found several opportunities of displaying his acquirements, either in assisting friends or provoking enemies. He contributed some highly esteemed emendations to Davies's "Tusculan Questions," supported by able notes, and a body of conjectural alterations to Needham's edition of Hierocles on the golden verses of Pythagoras. It is to be wished that Bentley had given a critical opinion upon the date and real author of the Golden Verses themselves. If they could be proved to be of high antiquity, they would form a most valuable document of heathen, we had almost said, patriarchal morality. In 1709, he succeeded in procuring a reprint of the Principia of his illustrious friend, by engaging Cotes, his own protegé, to superintend the publication at the University press. Nearly three hundred letters between Newton and Cotes are preserved in Trinity College. Well may we ask, with Dr. Monk, why are they not given to the world ? In this letter-publishing age, when something is really wanting to preserve epistolary composition from the anathema of disgusted common sense, that these treasures should be withheld, is shameful. Sir Isaac was then detained in town by his office as Master of the Mint. It is infinitely to Bentley's honour that he used his influence to promote learning, in branches other than his own ; but in Newton's Principia he had a sort of personal interest, as having been the first to employ their discoveries in the popular defence of religion.

In 1710, just after the college quarrel had come to an open rupture, and while disputing the visitorial rights of the Bishop of Ely, he seemingly volunteered a literary rencounter with a *universal genius*, who had impudently ventured on his peculiar ground. The celebrated John Le Clerc, having written and reviewed himself into a reputation for all sorts of knowledge, except Greek criticism, in an evil hour thought he could " play the lion too," and ventured forth as editor of the Fragments of Menander and Philemon, though his knowledge of Greek is said to have been acquired at a late age, and never to have exceeded the modicum of a " high-school" boy. What could have tempted him to make this display of his insufficiency is hard to guess ; as Greek editorship is not the stage for versatile audacity to play on. Cleverness, eloquence, variety of attainment, will do nothing. The defect of scholarship cannot be hid. But in Le Clerc's youth, *critical* scholarship can scarce be said to have existed, and perhaps, like other great men, he was ignorant of the change of times. That precise determination of the rules and licences of the ancient dramatic measures which has

league or union, it is ten to one that the least amiable will be the most influential. When, therefore, Pope or Arbuthnot attack Bentley, we may suspect that they were little more than Swift's doubles, if they did not actually father what he writ.

guided conjecture to certainty, and enabled the commentator to discern the just outline of an original picture through successive coatings of false colour, was, in the days of Grotius, as little anticipated by the great readers, as a law to regulate the occultations of Jupiter's Satellites was expected by those antique rustics, who assembled with clang of pots and clash of platters to drive away the monster that was smothering the eclipsed moon. Whatever is known on this subject, is owing to Bentley, for he first pointed to what was wanted, and shewed how it was to be obtained.

When Hemsterhuis exposed his lack of metrical experience, Bentley was content to make him sensible of his deficiency, by encouraging him to supply it, and even this kind severity was inflicted in the privacy of a post letter. When Barnes, by an edition of Homer, in which he had embarked his little all, proved that his Greek was more in bulk than value, Bentley through a private communication to a common friend, let the veteran understand that he could have demolished him, and then dismissed him as loathe to spoil his fortune. " There is room enough in the world for thee and me."

To Le Clerc he was not equally merciful, and several anecdotes have been circulated to account for his severity to the Swiss Literateur. Perhaps he thought that a reviewer wants the condition of obtaining mercy. With his usual extemporaneous rapidity, of which he never forgot to boast, he struck off his Emendations in *Menandri et Philemonis reliquias ex nupera editione Johannis Clerici,* under the name of Phileleutherus Lipsiensis, a work of high reputation, in the sending forth of which he affected a mystery for which it is difficult to assign a reason. The MSS was committed with a charge of secrecy to Burman, the bitterest enemy that Le Clerc's review had made, and printed in Holland. But the purpose of concealment if it really existed, was defeated by the indiscretion of Dr. Hare, then chaplain general to the army in the Netherlands, to whom the conveyance of the pacquet was intrusted. While the sheets were yet in the press, the report that Burman was about to launch the thunderbolts of Bentley against the editor of the Fragments reached the ears of Le Clerc himself; who forthwith despatched a menacing epistle to the English Aristarch, calling upon him to disown, by the next post, the authorship of the forthcoming attack, and denouncing his personal hostility if the work were avowed or an answer refused. Bentley without either owning or denying the performance, responded in a cool caustic epistle, exhibiting that perfect self-possession which naturally attended him when he was in the right, and did not always forsake him when he was in the wrong. With the most provoking civility, he exposed the ignorance of his antagonist as a Grecian editor, and the still more egregious folly of supposing his blunders sacred, and of expecting to silence criticism by bullying. As soon as the " Emendations" appeared, the author was immediately detected amid the small band of Greek scholars. Most likely he only disguised his name for the pleasure of hearing it guessed. It was agreeable to be told that he must have written the book because nobody else *could* have written it. In ·three weeks not a copy remained unsold, a proof of popularity almost unparalelled in the annals of classic lore ; which arose less from the merit of the work itself, great as it may be, than from the delight which the literati experienced in the humiliation of one whose critical censures they had long dreaded. Yet if Le Clerc had few friends, Bentley had many enemies. Old Gronovius, who impartially hated both, issued a diatribe, entitled " Infamia Emendationum in Menandrum nuper editarum." Bergler, whose Greek learning was really considerable, reviewed the controversy in the Leipsic Acta Eruditorum, in a mild conciliatory spirit, and John Cornelius de Paúw, of Utrecht, an unfortunate scholar, whose name we have never seen, in latin or English, uncoupled with terms of vituperation, reviled Phileleutherus in a production to which, in allusion to the grasping disposition of his adversary, he subscribes the subriquet of Philargyrius Cantabrigiensis,—Love-Gold, of Cambridge. To this composition, which is said to be abusive even beyond the usual measure of scholastic virulence, Le Clerc, who would have acted wisely to withdraw from a contest in which he could never recover his laurels, added a preface, and Salvini, the Florentine, appended some feeble notes. To none of these retorts did Bentley deign a reply.

At length, on the 8th of December, the great critic put the last hand to his Horace, just in time to lay it at the feet of Lord Oxford, in a dedication, which formed the first public proof of his adherence to the victorious tories. It was originally intended for Lord Halifax, but before the time of publication, Halifax had ceased to be a minister, and Harley had succeeded to the vacant place of patron, which then seemed essential to the formation of a cabinet.

To Harley, then, was Horace given, with an address, not much more adulatory than custom authorised. In one respect, the topic of compliment was well chosen. Harley, not content to owe his earldom of Oxford to his political service, claimed descent from the Veres and Mortimers, the feudal possessors of that peerage, and Bentley took care to humour him in this vanity. Whether the genealogical pretensions of the Lord Treasurer were just or not, is of little consequence : certainly Bolingbroke, the colleague of his triumph, and partaker of his subsequent persecutions, treated them with ridicule—"as mere jovial inspirations from the fumes of claret;" but perhaps Harley was rather the honester man of the two. This change in Bentley's political connexions did not escape chastisement from Pope, or his understrapper, the annotator of the Dunciad, who makes it the ground of a most unprovoked attack on his nephew Thomas, who is thus mentioned in the remark on verse 205, Book 2 :—

> "Bentley his mouth with classic flattery ope's,
> And the puff'd orator bursts out in Tropes.

"Not spoken of the famous Doctor Richard Bentley, but of one Thomas Bentley, a small critic, who aped his uncle in a little Horace. The great one was intended to be dedicated to Lord Halifax, but the ministry changing, it was given to Lord Oxford. So the little Horace was dedicated to his son, the Lord Harley." It may be added, that this sarcasm propably asserts an untruth ; ten to one, it was Richard Bentley whom Pope intended all the while.

The appearance of Horace was the signal for a fresh list of animadverters to direct their shafts against the editor. Among these, the most humourous was his old adversary, Dr. King, a very small poet, whose vulgar trash still occupies a place in collections from which Sidney, Marvell, and a hundred worthier names are excluded. His tirade on this occasion is not void of drollery. It describes Horace as visiting England according to his own prophecy, and taking up his abode in Trinity College, where he puts all to confusion,—consumes immoderate quantities of college bread and ale, and grows immensely fat. *Epicuri de greqe porcus.* But Bentley had more formidable antagonists.—John Ker, and Johnson of Nottingham, two schoolmasters, attacked his Latinity, which, though vigorous and Roman in the mould of the sentences and cast of thought, sometimes admitted words and expressions of doubtful purity. Alexander Cunningham, a learned Scotchman, resident at the Hague, at a later period, directed his attacks, which were not to be despised, against the temerity of Bentley's Emendations. Few persons will be much interested in the origin, the ins and outs, or even the right and wrong of these paper wars. For poor Schoolmasters, like Ker and Johnson, it was a good mode of advertising their academies, to appear before the world as adversaries of Bentley. Ker, moreover, was a dissenter, and, as such, apprehensive of the high church party, to which Bentley had just proclaimed his adhesion.

If however, the publication of the Horace exposed the editor to much ridicule and some just criticism, it procured him the most flattering testimonials from the learned both at home and abroad. Among others, Atterbury, the old antagonist of our critic, then dean of Christ Church,

was among the first to offer his congratulations in a neat and brief epistle, in which, after thanking Bentley for his "noble present," and
expressing his obligations for the great pleasure and instruction he had
received from that excellent performance, he confesses "the uneasiness
he felt when he found how many things in Horace there were, which
after thirty years acquaintance with him, he did not understand."
Atterbury was a courtier, and knew well how much flattery man will
bear. It is pleasant to remark that the Phalaris controversy, so profitable to literature, left no rankling stings in the minds of those by whom
it was conducted. Among all the pamphlets, which for more than
twenty years were levelled at Bentley's fortune and reputation, not one
can be ascribed to a member of the Christ Church league. The battle
had been honourably fought and fairly won: the prowess of the knights
was proved, and thenceforth they lived on terms of courtesy, if not
of friendship.

On the merits and defects of Bentley's Horace, none but the accomplished scholar can expatiate, and none but professional scholars could
feel much interest in the discussion. The intrusion of the conjectural
readings into the text has been censured as altogether unwarrantable.
Many of them go to crop the most delicate flowers of Horatian fancy,
and sheer away the love-locks which the world has doated on. The
value of the work consists in the extraordinary display of learning and
ingenuity which the defence of these innovations called forth, in the
skilful allegation of parallel passages; in the wonderful adroitness with
which every line and every letter that supports the proposed change is
hunted out from the obscurest corners of Roman literature, and made
to bear on the case in point, and in the logical dexterity with which
apparent objections are turned into confirmations. Vast as was Bentley's reading, none of it was superfluous, for he turns it all to account;
his felicity in fixing his eye at once on what he needed, in always finding the evidence that he wanted, often where no one else would have
thought of looking for it, is almost preturnatural. His learning suggested all the phrases that might be admitted in any given passage;
but his taste did not always lead him to select the best.

Shortly after the completion of the Horace, the Doctor's erudition
was employed in a service of more general interest, and more intimately
connected with his sacred profession. A certain small party were
industriously conspiring to bring out infidelity in a more pleasing and
popular form than it had hitherto assumed. The reveries of the Italian platonists, and the metaphysical subtleties of Bruno and Spinoza,
were too refined and learned to be widely mischievous; the slavish
politics of Hobbes made his hard-headed materialism unfashionable

after the revolution, and the obscene, blaspheming Atheism of Charles the Second's revellers condemned itself to execration. Still Deism, which even under the reign of the Puritans had secretly leagued itself with Republicanism, found too many advocates ; some hovered on the confines of latitudinarianism and unbelief, and others, seduced perhaps by excessive admiration of heathen writers and heathen institutions, persuaded themselves that Christianity, whether true or false, was not necessary either to the perfection of the individual, or the welfare of society. Well knowing that if the conscience were once relieved from the obligation of believing, no proof nor evidence would long constrain the understanding to assent, the revolters against revelation took upon themselves the title of Free-thinkers, and wrote and spoke to set forth the duty and expediency of liberating the thinking faculty from the tyranny of creeds and dogmata. They also dwelt much upon the intrinsic excellence, the bliss and loveliness of virtue, and its fitness to the nature of man, the *necessary* benevolence of the Deity, and the like topics, which do not *read* so very unlike Christianity, as to alarm the simple pious, though they do implicitly destroy the foundations, by disowning the necessity of the Christian scheme. Such at least were the doctrines of Shaftesbury, the most elegant writer, and the most philosophic mind of the whole fraternity; whose opinions, on subjects purely philosophic, are worthy of respect. Others, there doubtless were, who addressed themselves to a lower rank of intellect, and maintained the natural indifference, or the irresponsible fatality of actions. Among those *free-thinkers,* who prided themselves on keeping terms with morality, was Anthony Collins, a man of fortune and fashion; and unlike the herd of modern infidels, a gentleman altogether presentable ; whose plausible address and ready talents had formerly gained the confidence of Locke. He had also a shewy second-hand acquaintance with the ancient writers, which made him the oracle of a small society which met at the Grecian Coffee-house, near Temple-bar. Early in 1713, appeared Mr. Collins's " Discourse of Free-thinking, occasioned by the Rise and Growth of a Sect called Free-thinkers." The book created a great sensation. It was, of course, extolled by such as openly professed, or covertly inclined to the opinions of the author, and was probably even more admired by the cowardly and unwilling believers ; for there is nothing so great as an infidel in the eyes of those that would be infidels if they dare. Even sound christians are apt to exaggerate the talents of their opponents : and moreover there is always a strong prejudice in favour of audacity ; and ever will be, as long as fear—not love,—slavish acquiescence, not rational conviction, (which pre-supposes *true* free-thinking,)—are made the basis of moral and religious education. Collins's

Q

book is said, by those who have read it, to be discreditable in a literary point of view; composed of rash assertions and flimsy sophisms, thickly fenced with garbled quotations and misinterpretations of Plato, Cicero, and other ancient writers, whom by a most absurd anachronism, or yet absurder equivoque, he would prove to have been *free-thinkers*. It was this affectation of reading and scholarship that called Bentley into the field.* Under his old signature of Phileleutherus Lipsiensis, he encountered and demolished the infidels, and made the Christian alarmists ashamed of their fears.

Bentley had in fact, but little to do. For a scholar, to whom every relic of antiquity was familiar as *Propria quæ Maribus* to a Master of the lower form, to convict a half learned and dishonest smatterer of false citation and misapplication, was child's play. But, in the course of his examinations, he had an opportunity of doing Christianity a real service. The recent labours of Dr. Mill to rectify the text of the Greek Testament had brought to light a body of thirty thousand various readings; a discovery by which many of the weak brethren were frightened, as if a fatal flaw had been detected in the title deeds of their everlasting inheritance. It is easy to conceive what use a Collins would make of these discrepancies; and Protestantism would not submit to an authority like that of the Council of Trent, which gave an *ex-post-facto* sanctity to the Vulgate, with all its errors on its head. But Bentley re-assured the faith of the fearful, by shewing that an immense majority of these variations did not affect the sense at all, and that none disturbed any cardinal doctrine. Collins was not even an honest man, for he reprinted his work in Holland, purified from the gross cases of ignorance exposed by Bentley, and then circulating this expurgate edition, (which he had taken care to mask by a false title page,) in England, he persuaded his party that the passages in question were forgeries of

---

* Besides Bentley, Collins was answered by Hoadley, and by Whiston; the pretence of free-thinking was exposed by Berkeley, (afterwards Bishop of Cloyne,) in the third number of the Guardian; and Ibbot, a chaplain to Arch-bishop Tenison, made the confutation of his discourse the subject of his Boylean Lectures. Swift, who probably despised Antony's shallowness, more than he abhorred his irreligion, gave an "Abstract," in which the arguments of Collins, and his invectives against the high-church clergy are exhibited in an improved style, and without the pedantic quotations which fill more than half of the original work. This plain statement, which displays the tenets of the free-thinkers in their true and naked proportions, he delivers in the character of a Whig, thus identifying Whiggism and Infidelity, in order to cast odium on his political opponents: a most unfair manœuvre, though executed with the Dean's accustomed success.

A full examination and exposure of Collins's book may be found in Leland's "Deistical Writers."

Bentley's. On such an offender, what severity could be too severe ? Of the temper in which Bentley executed vengeance however, we may judge from the fact, that he afterwards refused to continue his Reply, when requested by Caroline, Princess of Wales: conceiving himself discountenanced by the Court, he protested that he would do nothing to gratify those who had behaved no better than his declared enemies. But sound arguments in behalf of Christianity are not the worse because the man who urges them may be but an indifferent Christian. Even in the primitive church, St. Paul bears testimony that " Some preached Christ even of envy and strife ;" but notwithstanding every way, he rejoices, that " Christ was preached."

The reply to Collins was the last published work of Bentley, previous to the trial at Ely-house, so unexpectedly terminated by the death of Bishop Moore, and brings the literary annals of our subject to a chronological accordance with his civil—we might almost say—his militant history. To Trinity College we must now return. As all proceedings were by the decease of the Visitor rendered null and void, the parties now stood *in statu quo ante bellum ;* and a fair opportunity offered to conclude a lasting peace on the basis of mutual concession. No less than six of the original prosecutors had died during the progress of the suit, and of those that remained, few possessed vigour, talent, funds, or influence, to contend against the Master. Middleton, the ablest subscriber of the original petition, had ceased to be a Fellow, and was yet unknown beyond the circle of his acquaintance, who perhaps, little expected that " Fiddling Conyers," as Bentley contemptuously called him, would atchieve a high name in English literature. A temporary pacification was concluded. The scheme of dividends and compensation was allowed to drop, but for all besides, Bentley was as despotic as ever. All offices were bestowed at his discretion: to oppose him, was to forswear promotion. After the death of Dr. Smith, Modd, a convenient nonentity, who had not taken the statutable degrees, was made Vice-Master; Bathurst, who was almost blind, Bursar ; and Hanbury, whom the Doctor himself had charged with drunkenness, was appointed to superintend the morals of the students, in the quality of senior Dean. In thus advancing notoriously incompetent persons to posts of responsibility, he not only excluded such as he could less easily manage, but in effect, got the whole college administration into his own hands. Modd had nothing to do but respond Amen to *his* master's propositions, and as Bathurst *could* not see the accounts, and nobody else was allowed to look at them, it followed that the whole power of the purse, without check or limit, was in the Doctor's hands.

As however, he could not think his reign secure while Miller remained a member of the College, he sought a fresh pretext to oust the lawyer. On a former occasion, he had cut his name out of the buttery-boards, because not being a physician, he held a medical fellowship. Now he urged, with more shew of justice, that Miller, possessing a pretty estate, fell under the statute which excludes all persons holding any ecclesiastical preferment whatever, college preacherships excepted, or any property to the amount of £10 a year, from the benefit of the college. But unluckily it happened that Bentley, not long before, had refused to accept the resignation of a gentleman of £10,000 a year, say-ing, that people of property were very useful members of the society. Miller met this attempt with a petition, and a new set of articles, differ-ing little from the former ; but the new Bishop of Ely, Fleetwood, refused to take cognizance of the case, unless his right to be general Visitor was ascertained. He would . not visit the Master, unless he might visit the Fellows also, and so for a time the matter rested. A little while before this, Bentley had delivered a visitation charge, in his capacity of Archdeacon of Ely, in which he did not quite satisfy the passionate admirers of the new dynasty ; for though he called King George Antoninus, he admitted that it was impossible for a foreign prince, newly imported, not to commit *some* errors. Miller, who was an intolerant Whig, represented this as sedition, and a sufficient ground of expulsion ; but there was no getting Bishop Fleetwood to stir. The expression, however, did the Archdeacon no good at court, where his enemies made the most of his dedication to Harley, now in the Tower on a charge of high treason. But Bentley managed his political relations with great skill, and availed himself of every feasible opportunity to express his loyalty to the Government *de facto,* whether it were Whig or Tory. His arch-deaconry had, about two years before, exposed him to the wrath of the University, whose privileges and per-quisites, with regard to the probate of wills, were conceived to be infringed by his officer, Dr. Brookbank, in consequence of which misun-derstanding, a decree was passed, by acclamation, that no Arch-deacon of Ely, or his official, should be eligible to the office of Vice-Chancellor. (Oct. 10, 1712.) At the close of 1714, this slur was removed by the mediation of Sherlock,* afterwards the most eminent of Bentley's ene-mies, the decree rescinded, and the thanks of the University voted to Dr. Bentley for his able defence of the Christian religion against the Free-

---

* Sherlock and Waterland were both elected Heads of Houses in the course of 1714, the former of Catharine Hall, the latter of Magdalen College. They are among the greatest ornaments of the Church of England. Waterland continued friendly to Bentley. Sherlock soon took an active part against him.

thinkers, with a request that what remained of the work might be speedily finished, with which Bentley never thought fit to comply. At this period the disposition of the academical public seems to have been favourable to the Great Critic; and had he possessed a more complying temper, and a nicer sense of integrity in pecuniary dealings, he might have lived in peace and honour, and risen to the highest dignities of his profession. The political contingencies of the times furnished him with frequent occasions of serving the government, which was looking at the Universities with an ominous eye of suspicion. Oxford, retaining a traditionary affection for the grandson of Charles I., almost approved the conduct of her Chancellor, the Duke of Ormond, who had joined the *Pretender*, by electing his brother, the Earl of Arran, in his room. Cambridge, less devoted to the exiles, was yet coldly affected towards the Whig domination, and reinstated her Tory representatives at the general election of 1715. Riots took place on the *Pretender's* birthday, and again on that of King George, and some young gownsmen broke windows, and cried "No Hanover." This the Vice Chancellor prudently considered merely as a breach of discipline; but it was judged expedient that the Senatus Academicus should express their attachment to constitutional monarchy, in the Protestant line, by a formal act. An address was got up, declaring that they had ever acknowledged King George as their rightful sovereign, reminding him of his promises, and engaging in turn to train up the youth in the way they should go, "that they might shew in their conduct an example of that loyalty and obedience which this University, *pursuing the doctrines of our church*, has ever maintained." This testimonial seems to have been well timed, for it gained from the king a present of Bishop Moore's magnificent library, consisting of 30,000 volumes, which, at Lord Townsend's suggestion, had been purchased by the crown for £6,000, while the sister University was insulted by being placed under military surveillance. On this occasion appeared the well-known epigram by an unknown hand :

> " King George, observing with judicious eyes
> The state of both his Universities,
> To Oxford sent a troop of horse, and why ?—
> That learned body wanted loyalty :
> To Cambridge books he sent, as well discerning
> How much that loyal body wanted learning."

Retaliated by Sir W. Browne, founder of the prizes for odes and epigrams :—

> " The King to Oxford sent a troop of horse,
> For Tories own no argument but force ;
> With equal skill to Cambridge books he sent,
> For Whigs admit no force but argument."

Bentley seems at this time to have been considered as a Whig luminary ; for a tract, inordinately whiggish (that is, Hanoverian), called " *University Loyalty Considered*," is subscribed Philo-Bentleius and Philo-Georgius. We hope the Doctor was not at the bottom of this.

When the heir of Stuart made his first effort to recover the throne which his father could not keep, Bentley, on the 5th of November, preached before the University against Popery, in a style of tremendous eloquence, which proves what he might have done, had he chosen to cultivate his native language.*

* Sterne, who availed himself unscrupulously of whatever suited his purpose, has borrowed—or, as some would say, stolen—a striking passage of this discourse, and inserted it into the sermon read by Corporal Trim—(see Tristram Shandy). We cannot resist inserting it, along with the preceding paragraphs.

After speaking of the various corruptions introduced into Christianity by the Romish clergy with a view to make their trade profitable—as purgatory, pardons, relics, &c., he proceeds :—" I might now go on to shew you a more dismal scene of impostures—*judicia Dei*—the judgments of God, as they blasphemously call them, when no human evidence could be found—their trials by ordeal—by taking a red hot iron in the hand—by putting the naked-arm into hot boiling water—by sinking or swimming in pools or rivers, when bound fast, hand and foot—all of them borrowed or copied from pagan knavery and superstition ; and so managed, by arts and sleights, that the party could be found guilty or innocent, as the priests pleased, who were always the tryers. What bribes were hereby procured ? What false legacies extorted ? What malice and revenge executed ? On all which, if we should fully dilate and expatiate, the tragedy of this day, which now calls for our consideration, would scarce appear extraordinary. Dreadful indeed it was,—astonishing to the imagination : all the ideas assemble in it of terror and horror. Yet, when I look on it with a philosophical eye, I am apt to felicitate those appointed for that sudden blast of rapid destruction, and to pity those miserables who were out of it, the designed victims to slow cruelty, the intended objects of lingering persecution. For since the whole plot (which will ever be the plot of popery) was to subdue and enslave the nation, who would not choose and prefer a short and despatching death, quick as that by thunder and lightning, which prevents pain and perception, before the anguish of mock trials—before the legal accommodations of goals and dungeons —before the peaceful executions of fire and faggot ? Who would not rather be placed direct above the infernal mine, than pass through the pitiless mercies, the salutary torments, of a popish inquisition—that last contrivance of atheistical and devilish politic ? If the other schemes may appear to be the shop, the warehouse of Popery, this last may justly be called its slaughter-house and its shambles. Thither are haled poor creatures (I should rather have said rich, for that gives the most frequent suspicion of heresy), without any accuser—without any allegation of fault. They must inform against themselves, and make confession of something heretical, or else undergo the discipline of the various tortures ;—a regular system of ingenious cruelty, composed by the united skill and long successive experience of the best engineers and artificers of torment. That savage saying of Caligula's, horrible to speak or hear, and fit only to be writ in blood—" *Ita feri ut se mori sentiat*"—is here heightened and improved. " *Ita se mori sentiat, ut ne moriatur*," say these merciful inquisi-

About the same time, while the Jacobites were regarded with more than usual alarm, and many of the parochial clergy—the poor and discontented ones especially,—were more than suspected of a leaning towards the proscribed House,—the decease of Dr. George Hickes, the Saxon scholar, an honest Yorkshireman, who had been deprived of the Deanery of Worcester as a Non-juror, led to the discovery of certain papers in his hand-writing, of so very High-Church a tendency, as not only to unsettle the foundations of the Hanoverian government, but to exclude a great majority of the people from the Christian covenant. According to this relic, all the conforming clergy were schismatic: orders conferred by Bishops under the new regime were invalid, and consequently baptism, performed by the schismatic divines, illegal, and of no saving efficacy. Of course, it was the understood purpose of the Jacobites, on their expected return to power, to eject the usurping clergy from their benefices, and to debar the laity from the sacred ordinance, till the priest should be re-ordained, the layman re-baptized, by hands of unpolluted orthodoxy. Nothing could be more opportune for the government than the publication of these papers; for they helped to undeceive some well disposed persons, who thought that civil obedience would be assured by restoring the *jure divino* succession, and religion less imperilled by Catholic power, than by Low-Church politics. But when it appeared that the designs of the plotters would unsettle all ecclesiastical property, interfere with the rights of patronage, dissolve the bands of matrimony, make the child of holy vows at once unregenerate and illegitimate, and brand the chastest matron as neither maid, wife, nor widow (for the marriages performed by schismatics would be as voidable as the baptisms), all the moderate church party were panic-struck, and many an honest vicar began to pray sincerely for King George. Bentley neglected not to improve this juncture of affairs. As Archdeacon of Ely, he summoned the clergy of that diocese (among whom were some suspicious characters) to a visitation,

---

tors. The force, the effect, of every rack, every agony, are exactly understood. This stretch, that strangulation, are the utmost nature can bear; the least addition will overpower it: this posture keeps the weak soul hanging on the lip, ready to leave the carcase, and yet not suffered to take its wing: this extends and prolongs the very moment of expiration—continues the pangs of dying, without the ease and benefit of death. O pious and proper method for the propagation of faith! O true and genuine Vicar of Christ, the God of mercy and the Lord of peace!"—*Bentley's Sermons, 6th edition, page 360.*

Well might the Corporal express his feeling of the tremendous energy of this passage, by saying "he would not read another word of it for all the world." It is a wonder that Dr. Ferriar of Manchester, who took so much pains in detecting the plagiarisms of Sterne, should have overlooked this.

regardless of the foul roads and interrupted festivities of December, and in a clear, forcible, and argumentative charge, insisted upon the necessity of giving support to the established government; exposed the folly of expecting security for a Protestant church under a Catholic head; and, availing himself of poor Hickes's projected purgation of the Temple, set forth how absolutely the preferments and spiritual character of the majority among them would lie at the mercy of a triumphant and exasperated party, should the Stuarts be allowed to re-ascend the throne.   This, it has been observed, is the only composition of the Doctor's which can strictly be called political (though, in the various pamphlets of business which his litigations called forth, he did not omit to impute disaffection to his adversaries, or to ascribe his own unpopularity to his zeal for the powers which be).   It seems to have been couched in temperate and respectful terms, avoiding personal reflections on those whose opinions he condemned.   It is probable that it answered its purpose.   As might be expected, it was highly lauded by the adherents of his own side, and not much relished by the devotees of the other; among whom was Thomas Hearne, the antiquary, who probably regarded divine right and indefeasible succession as venerable *antiquities*; though the antiquity of these, like that of Phalaris' Epistles, is shrewdly suspected of being spurious.   But the Bentley of political criticism has not yet arisen.   Both sides content themselves with blank assertion, vague deductions of possible consequences, and mutual recrimination.   Be it as it may, most antiquaries are Ultra-Tories, but very harmless and useful in their way.   Bentley was perhaps as little the better for the extravagant praise of Oldmixon, the Whig historian, of Dunciad notoriety, as the worse for the notice in Hearne's MSS. Diary, purporting, that the charge *"proves Dr. Bentley to be (as he is) a rascal, and an enemy to the King, and to all the King's friends."*   It was obvious enough whom Tom Hearne held to be King.   He partook the political sentiments of his Alma Mater, where it was customary (within the memory of persons not long deceased) to drink to the *King over the water.*

On the 15th of April, 1716, Bentley, in a letter to Wake, Archbishop of Canterbury, first broached his famous scheme for restoring the text of the Greek Testament " exactly as it was at the time of the Council of Nice," without the difference of " twenty words," or even " twenty particles."   This magnificent promise, the apparent presumptuousness of which exposed him to much obloquy, he never lived to execute, though he lived more than six and twenty years after its first promulgation.   Yet he certainly did make it in earnest, and never abandoned his purpose till old age overtook him.   We cannot better convey a notion of the method which he proposed to adopt, than in the words of the erudite reviewer of Dr. Monk's Life, in Blackwood's Magazine. —"Compressed within a few words, his plan was this:—Mill, and other collectors of various readings, had taken notice only of absolute differences in the *words*, never of mere variations in their order and arrangement ; these they conceived to be purely accidental. Bentley thought otherwise ; for he had noticed, that, whenever he could obtain the genuine reading of the old authorised Latin version, technically called the *vulgate*, the order of the words exactly corresponded to the order of the original Greek. This pointed to something more than accident. A sentence of St. Jerome ripened this suspicion into a certainty. Hence it occurred to him, that if by any means he could retrieve the true text of the Latin Vulgate, as it was originally reformed and settled by St. Jerome, he would at once obtain a guide for selecting, amongst the crowd of varieties in the present Greek text, that one which St. Jerome had authenticated, as the reading authorised long before his day. Such a restoration of the Vulgate, Bentley believed to be possible by means of MSS. of which the youngest should reach an age of 900 years. How far this principle of restoration could have been practically carried through, is a separate question ; but for the principle itself, we take upon ourselves to say, that a finer thought does not occur in the annals of inventive criticism. It is not a single act of conjectural sagacity, but a consequential train of such acts."

The passage of St. Jerome to which Bentley owed the suggestion above mentioned, is to this effect,—that in translations from one language into another, it is sufficient if the sense be preserved, except in the case of the Sacred Scriptures, " *ubi et verborum ordo mysterium est*," where the very order of the words is a mystery. But it is very doubtful whether this single expression of a very florid and vehement writer, is sufficient basis for so important a superstructure of hypothesis, or whether the discovery of the Vulgate, were it possible, in Jerome's Autograph, would contribute much to the purity of the holy writings : for Jerome was deeply tainted with the monastic superstition, then in the fervour of pristine mania ; and as he is known to be a very licentious and mystical expositor, it is not likely that he was a very faithful translator. There is nothing, however, in Bentley's scheme, that need have excited the angry passions to such a pitch, as the pamphlets on this occasion betray. It is fearful to think that a proposal to cast new light on the books, which are the written bond of peace, should on any man living have operated as a summons to malignant warfare.

As whatever illustrates the history of the Sacred Writings possesses a lasting interest, superior to any curiosity which can attach to the

R

squabbles of Trinity College, we will here pursue the project of Bentley's New Testament, free as he boasted even from literal errors, from its rise to its final disappearance. As early as 1713, Dr. Hare, in his " Clergyman's thanks to Phileleutherus Lipsiensis," a work seemingly intended to give Bentley a lift on to the Bench, suggested a revision of the divine Text, a task to which he asserted no man but Bentley to be equal. James Wetstein, a Swiss scholar, then chaplain in the Dutch army, and afterwards destined to perform the work which Bentley's feuds, and growing years, intercepted, urged the same undertaking. In 1716, appeared the letter to Wake above mentioned ; from that time to 1720, the public heard little of the new edition, and our Critic's enemies did not omit to insinuate, that the proposition was a mere artifice to curry favour with the Primate, who had himself laboured honourably in the field of Biblical criticism. Nevertheless, Bentley found time amid all his turmoils, to collate and to promote collations. His assistants, James Wetstein, and John Walker, obtained access to several valuable MSS., both of the Greek and Latin Text, and the Benedictines of St. Maur, among whom were ranked the distinguished names of Montfaucon and Sabatier, though catholics, did every thing in their power to forward a work, which Protestantism constrains us to confess, tended to the overthrow of the monastic system. For the collation of a single MS. at Heidelburg, Wetstein was paid £50, which no one, who ever underwent the toil of reading, even a printed sheet, with a view to literal accuracy, will think too much. That indefatigable scholar, who really seems to have read his Bible with no other purpose but to discover Variæ Lectiones, found in the King's library at Paris, a MS. of the whole Scriptures in Greek Capitals written on vellum, and *superscribbled* with certain writings either of, or about, St. Ephraim the Syrian.

Here we may incidentally mention that the high price or scarcity of writing materials contributed full as much to the destruction of ancient books, as either " Christian bigotry," or " Gothic fire." That either the Goths or the Saracens destroyed books *wilfully*, is uncertain. That the Christian Bishops, in the age when the incestuous alliance of Church and State was first contracted, exerted their influence to annihilate the monuments of heathen genius, and the records of heathen history, is indubitable, because the perpetrators of this worse than robbery, have boasted of their conscientious crime. Pagan literature was the Venus to whom the world had assigned the prize of beauty, and whom that jealous Juno, the State; and the new Goddess of new wisdom, that leaped, equipped in murderous panoply, from the brain of Constantine, (the state religion to wit,) in pure spite vainly endeavoured to despoil of immortality. Yet it is fearful to think how much priests and barbarians have destroyed : and when we recollect that, but for the PRESS, the Puritans might have annihilated Shakspeare, and the High-church-men certainly would have extinguished Paradise Lost,* we cannot but think that a yearly thanksgiving for the invention of print-ing might be very advantageously substituted for certain courtly services in the Liturgy, which were always base and blasphemous, and now are utterly unmeaning.

But perhaps this vice-society sort of conduct eventually saved more than it caused to perish : manuscripts were hidden under the earth, in holes and corners, in chinks and crannies, in all manner of places where no one but a rat or an inquisitor would think of looking for them ; from whence they came forth, at the revival of literature, like flies on a warm winter day, or words released from congelation in the arctic air. But there can be no doubt that many and many a good author was obliterated by the monks for the sake of the parchment on which he was written. Had the pictures of Raphael then existed, they would have been daubed over with apocryphal saints, hideous allegories, and ghastly topographies of damnation. A manuscript thus abused, is technically called a Palimpsest ; and by the unconquerable industry of classic scholars, many portions of ancient literature have been detected beneath monkish manuals and legends ; even as Alpine flowers preserve their vegetable vitality beneath a nine months' covering of snow. So precious were books esteemed in the long winter of their scarcity, that

* That this is not an idle surmise is demonstrated by the fact, that an epitaph, written by Atterbury upon Cyder Philips, in which the said blank verse costermon-ger Philips is impiously designated " Uni Miltono secundus," second to Milton alone, (Oh merciful fishes!!!) was by a Bishop of London, forbidden to be inscribed in West-minster Abbey, not for the abominable falsehood which it contains, but because for-sooth, the name of Milton, which is written in characters of everlasting light in the Heaven of Heavens, was unfit to appear in an Episcopal Church. Verily, if we had not somewhat more than a Bishop's confidence in the divine goodness, which can and will transform all things to its own likeness, we would say with a slight alteration of Shakspeare's words :—

> I tell thee, churlish Priest,
> That my sweet *Poet* shall a ministering angel be,
> When thou liest howling.

Cyder is pleasant cool tipple, but far too thin a potation to furnish out any poem beyond the dimension of a sonnet, and Philips's cyder dissolved a portion of lead in the process of pressing, and might bring on the Devonshire colic. Because Paradise was lost by an apple, Philips, writing about apples, thought he was writing another Paradise lost. Philips was one of the cockney sparrows, that exhibited their poetic parts to Bentley. Mallet was another. Poor creatures !—At tune homo audes occidere Caium Marium ?

the donation of a pious volume to a convent, was thought a good bid for salvation ; and (what is more extraordinary) the monks of some monasteries, as early as Charlemagne, were allowed to kill deer, on condition that they used the hides for book covers.

In 1720, he issued his proposals in form, in a paper which only enlarges a little on his letter to the Archbishop, and was accompanied by the twenty-second chapter of the Apocalypse, as a specimen, not of the type, or paper, which were to be the best that Europe afforded, but of the method and arrangement. Nothing was to be altered, either in the Greek or Latin text, from mere conjecture ; the common readings were to be noted in the margin, and, whatever criticism might suggest as an improvement, was to be mentioned in the Prolegomena. The subscription for the two folio volumes was three guineas, small paper copies, five for the large ; no great sum, if the work had really proved, as he designated it, a κειμήλιον, an everlasting possession, a charter, a Magna Charta, to the whole Christian Church : a true restoration of the famous exemplar of Origen, which was the standard of orthodox faith in the fourth century, and of Jerome's refined Vulgate, the rule of the Western Churches, purified from 2000 errors of the Popes, Clement VIII. and Sixtus V., and as many of the Protestant Pope, Robert Stephens.*

The boastful, and almost irreverend tone, of these proposals, which were, by his own confession, drawn up in one evening by candle light, and the peculiar crisis at which they were published, excited a prejudice against the author, of which his enemies were not backward in availing themselves. Middleton, who seems to have personally hated Bentley, and had then (in 1720,) peculiar motives of resentment, attacked the proposals in a pamphlet of extreme virulence. Not content to expose the uncertainty of Bentley's hypothesis, or to argue a case of learning upon learned grounds, he accuses him in plain terms of dishonourable dealing towards his assistant John Walker, ("to whom he allotted half the profit and almost all the trouble of this work, yet reserved all the reputation of it to himself,") of ingratitude to Dr. Mill, and inconsistency with his own opinions expressed in the reply to Collins, and the Sermon on Popery. Most unfairly, he imputes meanness to Bentley's mode of publishing by

---

* So Bentley called the worthy Printer, in allusion to the deference paid by Protestants to his Testament, printed in 1550, from which all subsequent texts have been taken. The Professor once said, to his sometime friend Hare, " I am your Pope. Your only Greek Testament is with me." Which ridiculous escape of vanity, was afterwards reported, much to his disadvantage.

subscription, (of which **Dr. Middleton** did not scruple to avail himself in his life of Cicero.) " We find," says he, " in these two paragraphs, such paltry insinuations, such low and paltry higgling to squeeze our money out of us, &c., that it puts me in mind of those mendicants in the streets, who beg our charity with a half sheet of proposals pinned to their breasts." In allusion to the South Sea mania, then at its height, he says, " But indeed, most people are agreed in opinion that he has borrowed his scheme from Change Alley, and in this age of bubbles took the hint to set up one of his own, for having invented a sure secret to make paper more durable than parchment, and a printed book, however used and tumbled about, to outlast any manuscript preserved with the greatest care, he instantly takes in a partner, opens books for subscriptions, and does not in the least question but that Bentley's bubble will be as famous and profitable as the best of them." With all this vituperation, Middleton did not make out a single case against the veteran critic ; he must have been hard run when a verbal misquotation of a single word, (ubi *ipse* verborum ordo, for, ubi *et* verborum ordo,) which makes not the least alteration in the sense, furnishes occasion for three pages of bitterness. But the most discreditable feature of the attack is Middleton's appealing to religious prejudices, of which he did not partake, and which he knew to be founded in ignorance. He could not but know, that the Textus Receptus, which had become a sort of conscience with Protestant Christians, was only that which Stephens, the printer, had selected out of a number of MSS., some of them of late date, and little authority, and that many helps and much material, and far superior critical skill, had been brought to light since the first printed editions of the Scriptures appeared. The tendency of Conyers' mind was not to implicit faith, but he knew that to meddle with a settled standard, is always to excite the fears of many, and to these fears, weak and superstitious as in this instance they were, he appealed against the authority of Bentley.

This brochure, being published without a name, was not immediately laid at the right door, and succeeded, not so much by exposing Bentley's scheme, as by inciting him to expose the defects of his temper, which he did most woefully in his reply. Though he well knew the book to be the composition of Middleton, he unjustly suspected that the first mover of it was Colbatch, now leader of the college opposition, and on this groundless surmise, directed such a torrent of abuse against the supposed aggressor, whom, though he does not name, he sufficiently indicates, as was never uttered by a critic in his vernacular tongue. " Cabbage-head, insect, worm, maggot, vermin, gnawing rat, snarling dog, ignorant thief," are the epithets applied by one Doctor of Divinity to another. To this most disgraceful production we shall have occasion to revert when we proceed with the belligerent part of Bentley's history. It should be reprinted by the Society for the Diffusion of Useful Knowledge, for the instruction of such as imagine that the licence and *personalities* of the press, are a *peculiar* disgrace of the nineteenth century. Let it be recollected, that all this evil speaking was introduced into a work of which the ostensible purpose was to illustrate and restore the New Testament, being entitled, "*Doctor Bentley's proposals for printing a new edition of the New Testament, and St. Hierom's Latin Version.*" As usual, in his later controversial writings, the Doctor speaks of himself in the third person.

The proposed *New* Testament gave rise to several other pieces, one or two of which it may not be amiss to mention. Zachary Pearce, a young Fellow of Trinity, then Chaplain to the Lord Chancellor, afterwards Bishop of Rochester and of Bangor, and editor of Longinus, in two elegant Latin epistles, signed Phileleutherus Londinensis, took a fair view of the question, and made an estimate of Bentley's qualifications and disqualifications. This tract is chiefly memorable as recording the unfavourable effect of the South-sea speculation upon literature, and the universal thirst for sudden wealth then pervading all classes of society. Another "Letter" appeared, in vindication of the disputed verse, 1 John, v. 7, which it was apprehended that Bentley would condemn, and probably exclude from his edition. It was erroneously attributed to Middleton, and is printed as his in Sir Walter Scott's republication of Lord Somers' Tracts. The real author was Smalbroke, afterwards Bishop of St. David's. These flying papers at this age would have appeared as articles in the periodical reviews: but a second assault from Middleton, called "Further Remarks on the proposals, &c." was so superior to his former publication in learning, style, and argument, and found the public mind so ill disposed towards his adversary, that a notion long prevailed, that it actually forced Bentley to abandon his project by putting a stop to the subscription. But this opinion, which contradicts all that is known of the great critic's character, is sufficiently confuted by facts. The subscriptions amounted to £2,000; and the business of collating was carried on wherever the learning of Bentley had interest among scholars. As late as 1725 and 1726, his nephew, Thomas Bentley, was examining manuscripts at Paris, Rome, Naples, and Florence. Through the agency of Philip de Stosch, a learned German Baron, well known to virtuosos for his splendid publication of antiques, and secretly employed by the British government as a spy on the exiled family then resident at Rome, access was procured to that famous MS. called, *par excellence*, the Vatican, which had never before been used for the purpose of correcting and fixing the sacred text.*

Another report states, that Bentley gave up his scheme because the Treasury refused to permit the paper for its publication, to be imported duty free. That this penny wisdom of the government excited his indignation there can be no doubt ; but that indignation would operate upon him as a stimulus, not as a sedative. His first determination would be, " to shame the rogues, and print it ;" and accordingly we find him borrowing a valuable manuscript of the Ex-Minister, the Earl of Oxford, a few days after the alleged repulse, and employing David Casley, his deputy in the King's and Cottonian libraries, to examine the various important MSS. in the Bodleian and other collections at Oxford. Fairly, therefore, we may conclude, that neither direct opposition, nor want of public encouragement rendered this great design abortive. But the continual turmoil in which he lived till protracted age, his unquiet secular engagements, and the number of literary undertakings into which he was provoked by competition, so interrupted his *opus magnum*, of which he once spoke as if he considered it a solemn duty imposed on him by divine authority, and so diverted and divaricated his mind, that at length the labour lost its charm, and no longer supplied that excitement which was necessary to set the wheels of his mind a going. With all his energy, with activities that brooked not rest, with spirits nothing could unnerve, he was not the man to execute great works of patient toil and long delay. The revision of the Greek Scriptures, upon the plan which he so ingeniously conceived, would, if pursued uninterruptedly, have been too long and too slow for his impatience. The money advanced upon the subscription was ultimately returned.

We left Trinity College in the year 1714, still divided against itself ; but the determined refusal of Bishop Fleetwood to act as Visitor, cut off the discontented party from all hope of redress, and Bentley's main endeavours were directed to the exclusion of Miller, whom he regarded as the ringleader of the malcontents, who would do every thing in his power to keep alive the spirit of resistance. But absolute as he was, he could not forcibly expel the obnoxious serjeant, though he withheld all the emoluments of his fellowship.

---

* It was a long-prevalent opinion among biblical scholars, that the Vatican MS. was among those sent from Italy to Alcala, in 1514, to aid in forming that famous Polyglot Bible, edited under the auspices of Cardinal Ximenes, the earliest impression of the sacred writings in their original languages, commonly known as the Complutensian Bible. But the learned Bishop has proved satisfactorily, from the great variations between the MSS. and the Complutensian text, that the editors had never had recourse to it.—"*Notes on Michaelis,*" *vol.* 3.

Three men, of very different tempers, talents, and principles, seem to have been ordained to oppose the supremacy of Bentley. These were Miller, Middleton, and Colbatch. Of these the first was a lawyer and a politician, with a political conscience, who espoused the cause of his college with an eye to the advantage which an important suit always affords to a rising counsel, and to the eclat which an ambitious man derives from opposition to an unpopular authority. Middleton, who, ceasing to be a Fellow in the very earliest stage of the process, had no personal interest in the quarrel, was probably incited to make it his own by some private pique at the Master, who used to call him " Fiddling Conyers," and probably evinced little respect for his talents, great as they afterwards proved. Of all Bentley's literary opponents he was the most formidable, and the least scrupulous; he was a man of the world. Dr. John Colbatch was a dry, grave, honest man, with a *strong*, rather than a *fine* sense of rectitude; an inflexible stickler for right, a strict and literal expounder of the moral law, a zealous advocate for the *letter* as well as the *spirit*; somewhat of a Martinet in matters of discipline, whose resolutions, once taken, became part and parcel of his conscience, and who never forgave an offence against himself, if he deemed it an offence against justice. His naturally saturnine temperament had been darkened by successive disappointments; for after holding the honourable station of Chaplain to the British Factory, at Lisbon, and gaining the approbation of Queen Mary by a work on the religion and literature of Portugal, he became, by especial request, a private tutor, first to the son of Bishop Burnet, and afterwards in the family of the " proud Duke" of Somerset: yet at forty was obliged to return to his college with no other subsistence than his Fellowship, and a Prebend of Salisbury, of £20 value. If, however, as Middleton asserts, his virtue was deemed " too severe," and had " something disagreeable about it," it was no wonder if he failed to profit by the acquaintance of the great. To make available the patronage of courtly Bishops, and *proud* Dukes, other qualifications are necessary, besides severely disagreeable virtue. He considered himself an injured man, for speaking of the neglect he had experienced, he said, " that the hardships he suffered were aggravated by some circumstances which must lie infinitely heavier, and sink deeper into an ingenuous mind, than any temporal loss or inconvenience whatever." Perhaps he sometimes mistook a personal resentment for righteous indignation. The University made him some amends by appointing him, in 1707, Professor of Casuistry, and had he not come in collision with Bentley, he would probably have grown grey in the study of civil law and ecclesiastical antiquity, his favourite researches, produced profound and unreadable treatises, and died a senior Fellow.

In his opposition to the Master, there is every reason to think that he was strictly conscientious. He was slow to enrol himself among the Remonstrants; for his principles, which were High-Church in religion, and Tory in politics, made him averse to appeals against constituted authority. He supported Bentley in some of his strongest reforms during the first years of his Mastership, and though he signed the petition of 1710, it was with an expressed proviso, that his sole object was an amicable arbitration. As he had an ill opinion of Miller, who was a violent Whig and Low-Churchman, he kept much aloof from the Prosecutors so long as the Counsellor was their main mover, and rather sided with those who thought his Fellowship vacated by his unstatutable income. It was not till 1715 that he entered into the quarrel with all his heart, and with all his mind, and with all his soul, and with all his strength, and devoted to it a perseverance worthy of a martyr: it became the *primum mobile* of his soul, the spring of his actions, the regulator of his principles: urged, as he thought, doubtless, by "the strong antipathy of good to bad," he would have sacrificed life, as well as health, ease, and fortune, to the cause.

It often happens, that the immediate occasion of a rupture is a comparative trifle, and the world are disposed to wonder that men who have submitted to so much for the sake of peace, should buckle on their armour at last for so little; not remembering, that each successive demand, be it large or small, goes to prove the inutility of concession; that human patience has but a certain capacity; and that the last drop makes the cup overflow. Thus, it was a mere informality in disposing of a piece of college land situate in Kirby Kendal, where no substantial injury was done to any party, that produced the first personal conflict between Colbatch and the Master. Bentley does not appear to have resented this opposition, for shortly after he made Colbatch an offer of the Vice Mastership, which he declined, as not having attained the requisite standing. Perhaps he suspected a sinister purpose in the offer itself; for had he accepted it, in violation of the letter of the law, he would virtually have assented to the dispensing power of the Master, and acknowledged his right in the absolute disposal of offices and emoluments.

It was Bentley's determination to be himself the fountain of honour and profit to all his subjects. He did not even allow a gradation of patronage, but interfered as decidedly in the appointment of college servants, as in the elections to Scholarships and Fellowships. He made his own coachman porter, and afterwards bestowed the same office (the importance and pickings of which no one who has not had the benefit of a University education can calculate) on that coachman's son, a lad of fifteen.　　　　s

Attached to the foundation of Trinity College, are twenty *pauperes*, or beadsmen, endowed with a yearly salary of £6, and a suit of livery, which was once a respectable competence, and would still be a valuable assistance to a decayed housekeeper of respectable character.   Bentley bestowed one of these pensions on an ale-house keeper, who could scarce be supposed to want it, and another on one Joseph Lindsay, a notorious blackguard, and leader of the Tory mob in the riots on the Pretender's birth-day.   It is difficult at this distance of time to assign the motive to such a flagrant abuse of a commendable charity.   The Doctor said that henceforward the mob would do no harm, a fetch of policy that has been imitated on a larger scale, by statesmen less sagacious than Bentley.   Whether he thought that in any conceivable emergence it might be useful to have the mob on his side, we cannot say; but the supposition is not impossible, if it be true that, on a subsequent occasion, he proposed to Zachary Pearce,[*] then candidate for a Fellowship, to bring down a strong party of Westminster boys, to exclude Miller forcibly from the place of election.   We fear that England's greatest scholar was not above *making unto himself friends with the mammon of unrighteousness.*   It is, however, most probable that the uproarious champion of High Church and Hereditary Right was a protegé of Ashenhurst, the most obsequious and unhesitating of Bentley's supporters in and out of college.   Ashenhurst was so good a Tory, that he is said to have compounded with his conscience, for taking the oaths to King George, by never taking fees of the Nonjurors.   However it might be, there is not a more disgraceful passage in the whole history of Bentley's malversations; for what can be worse, than to turn the provision intended for the virtuous poor into a bounty on outrage and insubordination?[†]   Yet so obstinate was he in his purpose, that he declared he

* This incredible anecdote is related on the credit of Zachary himself, who afterwards became a Bishop, and was no enemy of Bentley.   Perhaps the Doctor rather suggested it as what *might* be done, than as what *ought* to be done.   Pearce was a Westminster scholar, and the *esprit de corps* was then, and ever continues, remarkably strong in that seminary.   If, indeed, the youths of Westminster partook the Tory politics of their Master, Dr. Robert Freind, they would have highly enjoyed an expedition which, to the ordinary attractions of a *row*, united the opportunity of insulting so black and sour a Whig as Sergeant Miller.   Though the disciples of our public schools have never yet taken so decided a part in state affairs as those of *L'Ecoles Polytechnique, du Droit, du Medicin,* and others in the French metropolis, and though the students of our Universities are not so much addicted to constitution making as the German Burschen, yet in all our great schools and colleges there is a bias, and we are sorry to say it is inordinately aristocratic.   At the period of which we write, however, the Whigs were the placemen and pensioners—the court party; and the Tories, or country party, the men of the people.

† It is but fair to suggest a possible motive, which *might* induce Bentley to favour

would carry it, though every Fellow but Mr. Brabourn were opposed. Mr. Brabourn was a person of deranged intellect, whose vote ought never to have been asked or accepted.

The statutes direct that no lease shall be sealed, nor the presentation to any preferment made out, but in presence of the sixteen senior Fellows or their representatives. Two small livings falling vacant about the same time, Bentley disposed of them, not only without observing the above-mentioned form, but contrary to routine, and, it was asserted, for private considerations.

A heavier cause of complaint was, his never submitting the college accounts to the inspection of those whose right and duty it was to overlook and check them ; asserting, either that it was too early, or that the time was past—averring statute against custom, or custom against statute, or expediency and his own prerogative against both, as suited his purpose. There was an ancient ordinance, that, if the eight seniors (the legal council of the Master, without whose consent none of his acts were esteemed of more validity than those of the King, apart from his council, in the English constitution) were divided among themselves (*in plures partes divisi sunt*), the question should be decided according to the vote of the Master. This could only have been intended to give the Master a casting vote in case of an equal division : but the lax clumsiness of its expression gave Bentley a pretext for asserting that, unless the eight were unanimous against him, his proposal, if singly seconded, must prevail. By this means it became almost morally impossible to oppose him : draught after draught on the college treasury was paid, and yet there was no end of his demands ; and as he was not less liberal or able to reward those who aided his purpose, than he was sure and powerful to crush whatever intercepted his path, the small band of recusants met with few recruits among their immediate juniors, and the new Fellows introduced by Bentley had little sympathy with the aggrieved elders. They were, for the most part, either his own connections and dependents, or young men of high classical attainments, whom a community of studies naturally inclined to his interests. Thus the old Fellows were somewhat in the situation of an aboriginal people driven from their ancestral possessions by an intruding colony. In vain did Colbatch protest and remonstrate, and call out for a Visitation. The *vis inertiæ* of Bishop Fleetwood was not to be overcome.

this man. He *might* think Lindsay harshly treated, and refused employment for an ebullition of zeal, and account it better to remove him out of temptation, than to let him steal or starve. Dispositions extremely tyrannical when opposed, are sometimes even weakly compassionate, where power is not at stake, for compassion almost implies a sense of superiority.

By a statute of Queen Elizabeth it is ordered, that one third of the college rents shall be reserved in corn or malt, or a sum equivalent to the price current of those articles, in order that the college revenues might in some measure keep pace with the fluctuations in the value of money. Bentley took upon him to grant two leases, without any regard to the provisions of that statute, whereby he obtained larger fines for the benefit of the existing society, at the probable expense of their successors. This measure, which he carried with his accustomed despotism, was particularly grievous to Colbatch, whose college was his country and his family, and the Fellows of Trinity, for all generations to come, as his own offspring and inheritors. He addressed two letters to the Bishop of Ely, who adhered to the non-interference system.

But at this desperate juncture the state of the foundation attracted the attention of Archbishop Wake, who had just been advanced from the see of Lincoln to the Primacy. This prelate, who had distinguished himself in a controversy with Bossuet, and has been uncharitably censured for a well-meant but impracticable project of Union between the English and Gallican Churches, was in habits of intercourse with Philip Farewell, a junior Fellow of Trinity, who corresponded with Colbatch. Through him, the primate was informed of the lamentable discord, and consequent relaxation of discipline, in the largest academical institution of Britain, and saw the necessity of bringing the case before some competent authority. He therefore, by the intermediation of Farewell, suggested the propriety of a petition to the King, to be signed by a respectable number of Fellows, simply praying that the Visitatorial right might be ascertained, that it might be known of whom redress was to be sought, promising to support such petition in his place at the Council-board. The petition was soon in readiness, subscribed by nineteen Fellows. Though specially cautioned to keep their cause separate from that of Miller, which in fact only regarded his own Fellowship, yet, in an evil hour, they were persuaded to intrust it to his management.

A few days before this movement Bentley, who knew well enough what was afloat, addressed to Archbishop Wake his proposals for restoring the New Testament: no wonder then, if his adversaries called the whole project a *ruse de guerre*. If so, it was an unsuccessful one, for Wake was heard to declare, within three weeks after, that " Dr. Bentley was the greatest instance of human frailty he had ever known, with his parts and learning, to be so insupportable." But Wake's own influence was not great with a government that regarded Mother Church with most unfilial coldness, and knew the worth of Bentley, as head of the ministerial party in Cambridge, and the rate at which he prized his services, too well to trouble themselves with troubling him. Accordingly, though the petition did obtain a tardy hearing, being read in Council on the 26th of October, 1716, more than five months after its presentation, nothing more came of it than an offer of Bishop Fleetwood to resign the Visitatorial Power to the Crown, and a reference of the question to Attorney-General Sir Edward Northey, who took time to consider of it. Before he had made up his mind, a change took place in the Cabinet, and Sir Edward went out of office, carrying the papers in his bag. At least for three years, they were not forthcoming, and there was no chance of getting another petition so powerfully signed. Thus did the concatenation of events conspire to protect Bentley, who acted as if, like another despot, he deemed the star of his destiny invincible. His great object was still to rid himself of Miller. He had procured the provisional election of David Humphreys, on condition that the proceeds of the Fellowship be stayed till the King should decide whether or no Miller was entitled to hold it. The King, however, did not interfere. The Fellowship was still in abeyance, and what concerned the Master more, the time was approaching when the useful Ashenhurst, not being in orders, would be superannuated, unless the physic-fellowship, held by the obnoxious Serjeant, could be cleared for his reception.

The regular election coming on in September, Miller arrived with the determination to exercise his rights as a Fellow. Bentley, failing in the notable scheme before mentioned, of a sortie from Westminster, had recourse to a couple of constables, who forced Miller from the Lodge, and detained him in custody till the election was over. Then, adjourning to the chapel, Bentley and his voters proceeded to fill the five vacancies. In his appointments on this occasion, he displayed the opposite points of his character, his honourable love of learning, and his reckless partiality and favouritism. Three of his nominees were young scholars, whose riper years fulfilled the promise of their early proficiency, Leonard Thomson, Zachary Pearce, and John Walker, the last of whom has been repeatedly named as Bentley's assistant in the New Testament. The number was filled up with a nephew of Mrs. Bentley's, and a nephew of Dr. Hacket's. The Nepotism of the first nomination may easily be forgiven ; but the second has very much the air of a job. Dr. Hacket, a senior Fellow, who owed his own election solely to his relationship to the great benefactor Bishop Hacket, was a very serviceable man to the Master, and knowing that the Master could not do without him, raised his price accordingly. It was said that there had been elected three Fellows and two Nephews.

Colbatch, conceiving all the proceedings to be nullified by the violent exclusion of Miller, withdrew from the chapel while the election went forward, and afterwards returned and protested.   This was his regular practice for many years, by which he gained nothing but a salvo for his own conscience, and a fresh article of accusation against the Master. Violent altercations took place in the college chapel, and from that time forth, the common forms of civility ceased to pass between the two Doctors.   Colbatch having now arrived at the required standing, laid claim to the Vice-mastership, for which Modd, being only M.A. was not qualified; but Bentley, in reference to the words of the statute, reminded him that after the events of the last week, his appointment would not only be *incommodum*, but *incommodissimum*.

The violence used against Miller had served no useful purpose, and the customary means of annoyance were unavailing against a man who did not reside in the college, and was not dependant upon its favours. Bentley, therefore, took to smoother courses, and while the disappearance of the Fellows' petition along with Sir Edward Northey, occasioned a suspension of hostilities on that side, he made overtures of peace to the Serjeant, or to speak plainly, attempted to buy him off. It was proposed that Miller should be paid all arrears up to July 1715, and his law expenses to boot, if he would resign his Fellowship, and withdraw his petition.   But he was then sore with the recent insult, and sanguine in his expectations of vengeance, so he refused to make terms with his enemy, and did just what his enemy might have prayed for—he wrote a book. Indeed the Doctor was not more felicitous in timing his own publications, than lucky in the mistiming of what was written against him.   By some strange fatality, whoever attacked Bentley was sure to give gratuitous offence to some higher power. Among the measures which the new Ministry were expected to bring forward in the session of 1717, were two Bills, one to ascertain the power of the King over the Church, and the other to regulate the Universities; both expressly levelled at the High-church party.   Elate with expectation of a movement which was to lay the Hierarchy at the feet of the civil power, Serjeant Miller put forth " *A humble and serious Representation of the Present State of the University of Cambridge,*" intended, no doubt, to press upon Parliament the necessity of a prompt and decisive interposition ; filled with such statements of the abuses, disorders, and disaffection of his *Alma Mater*, of course not overlooking Trinity College, or forgetting to give Dr. Bentley his full share of vituperation, that the whole University was put in commotion, every dutiful son of Granta felt himself personally insulted.   A public censure was passed, and inserted in the newspapers, declaring the "Humble and serious Representation" " to be a false, scandalous, and malicious libel on the good government and flourishing state of the University," and Miller was deprived of the Deputy-high-stewardship.

In the course of the same year (1716) Bentley signalized his attachment to the existing government, and displayed his own influence over the academical public, with singular dexterity. A congratulatory address to the King on the suppression of the rebellion had been proposed, and, on some pretext of informality, rejected. Though there was no really disloyal design in this, it had an ill appearance. Bentley prepared another address, and, by a series of able manœuvres, carried it by surprise, in such a manner as to get the main credit of it himself.

The English have always been famous for improving upon the inventions of others. The series of Latin authors, " in usum Delphini," was a fair challenge to English scholarship. The year 1716 was distinguished by a ministerial project to rival the Delphine Classics. It is said that the judges, Parker and King, suggested to Lord Townshend the propriety of employing Bentley in a similar series, " in usum Principis Frederici." Bentley shrunk not from the labour, though he alone was to be tasked with what the whole learning of France was barely sufficient to perform. But he demanded £1000 a year during the performance of the work, and Lord Townshend would only guarantee for £500, a very insufficient remuneration to the first scholar of the world, for what must needs have been the business of his life, when the instruction of a Prince was the object. Some one proposed that the editor should be remunerated per sheet, which proposal Bentley coolly rejected, saying, " that he or any man could fill a sheet fast enough." A schism took place in the ministry : Lord Sunderland supplanted Lord Townshend, and the Frederician Classics were heard of no more. Bentley could have done nothing in his own way without doing good ; but it is very doubtful whether he would have succeeded in an edition for the use of schools, and such, of course, the Frederician was intended to be. He would have made difficulties where schoolboys never suspected any, and left all the difficulties that a boy would stumble at, *in statu quo.* He was too learned to teach,

The year 1617 brought, as usual, its triumphs and its turmoils. Bentley had long been looking, with a vulture's eye, at the Regius Professorship of Divinity ; for Dr. James, the Regius Professor, was not expected to live—in short, he died. But Bentley was not, according to the intention of the foundation, eligible, for he was himself one of the electors. By the charter of their institution, the three Royal Professors (those of Hebrew, Greek, and Divinity) are to be chosen by the Vice Chancellor, the Master, and two senior Fellows of Trinity, and the Heads of King's, St. John's, and Christ's. As no substitute

was appointed in case of the Master of Trinity being himself a candidate for the office, it may be supposed that the founder meant the
situations to be incompatible.   But a rule which might exclude the
fittest person from the chair was wisely dispensed with, and in fact
there were two precedents of the Divinity Professorship having been
held by Masters of Trinity.   But a more substantial objection to the
union of the functions is, that the Master, conjointly with the other
electors, is to take cognizance of the Professor's conduct, and, on just
occasion shewn, after due admonition, to remove him from the chair.
But obstacles of this kind were no obstacles to our hero, (for if an
invincible will, that decrees its own effect, and makes every faculty
subservient to its purpose—a faith in inward power that vanquishes all
circumstances, be heroism, Bentley was a hero,*—a term often strangely
misapplied to love-sick Narcissus's and pensive students.

Though he knew that six out of the seven electors would oppose him,
that the only vote he could command in the conclave was his own—
though he had seen the routine of succession broken through in order
to exclude Dr. Bradford, an eminent man, and afterwards Bishop of
Bristol, from the Vice Chancellorship, simply because suspected of being
a Bentleian, and Dr. Grigg appointed, as it were, purposely to keep
him out; though his own name had been proposed for the mere pleasure
of rejecting him, "he bated not one jot of· heart or hope."   His first
scheme was to defer the election beyond the statutable period, in order
that the appointment might lapse to the crown, in which case he
thought himself secure.   His Majesty's return from Hanover, and the
prevention of the Swedish invasion, carried the Vice Chancellor to
London, with an address, just in time to enable Bentley to assert that
the lapse had taken place.   This, however, was over-ruled.   But his
arts were not exhausted.   Dr. Grigg was a most obsequious chaplain to
the *proud* Duke, who was then Chancellor of the University of Cambridge.   Bentley contrived that the Duke should send his Chaplain a
seasonable summons, and that he should be himself appointed *locum
tenens.*   He insinuated to the government, that the surest way to make
the ministerial cause triumphant in the seats of learning—in other
words, to get the church into the power of the cabinet—was to countenance himself and Waterland ; and laboured, not wholly in vain, to
affix the stigma of disaffection upon all who opposed him ; and as it
was certain that all Jacobites abhorred Dr. Bentley, politician's logic
would readily infer, that all who did not vote for Dr. Bentley were
Jacobites.   But still it is probable that the Doctor's ambition would
have been balked, but for one lucky article in the foundation statutes,

* It is a moot point with the critics whether a hero ought to be an honest man.

that, if any of the Electors were Vice Chancellor at the time of election, the number should be filled up by the head of Queen's College. Now the head of Queen's was Bentley's idolater, Davies: Bentley himself represented the Vice Chancellor, and was also Master of Trinity: of the two senior Fellows, Mr. Cock (of whom Bentley had prophesied that he would die in his shoes) was bed-ridden, and poor Stubbe had never shewn his face in Cambridge since his extrusion from the Vice Mastership; their places were therefore supplied by Modd and Bathurst, and well supplied, as far as the Master's interest was concerned, for thus he could reckon four good votes, his own inclusive. The day was set, the electors were summoned, Bentley and his friends were ready: the heads of King's, St. John's, and Christ's did not choose to be present at what they esteemed a mockery of election, and perhaps thought to invalidate the proceedings by their absence. After waiting an hour, Dr. Bentley offered himself as a candidate: no other appearing, the formalities were gone through, and by the first of May, 1717, he was Regius Professor of Divinity. Do the annals of electioneering contain any thing parallel? *

For his prælection on this occasion, he chose the disputed text in St. John's Epistle, " For there are three which bear record in Heaven, the Father, the Word, and the Holy Ghost, and these three are One." The discourse has never been printed, nor is it known whether it be in existence. His enemies ridiculed it as savouring more of verbal criticism, than of sound theology; but perhaps with little justice. The authenticity or spuriousness of any passage, appearing in any author, can only be decided in two ways, either critically or historically, by internal or external evidence. Bentley in his prælection probably considered the verse *critically;* examined whether it harmonized with the general style of its author, and the manner of speaking in his age: in his projected restoration of the Sacred Text, he engaged to consider it *historically,* and to admit or exclude it, as the number and weight of manuscript authorities, and testimonies of the Fathers' should preponderate

---

* Not the least remarkable feature in this strange transaction, is the supineness and infatuation of Bentley's adversaries. Had they possessed the true electioneering spirit, old Cock would have been brought in his bed to the Hustings, as we see in Hogarth's admirable print of the Tollbooth. Hearne, whose unfriendly disposition towards the Professor we have more than once had occasion to remark, thus notices the business:—" Dr. Bentley is elected Regius Professor. He was opposed by Dr. Ashton, Master of Jesus, who had got it, if Bentley had not used knavery. Ashton was best qualified.—MS. Diary." Why is this Diary of Hearne's a MS.? *Non cuivis contigit adire Corinthum.*

> Not all mankind, nor even all the godly,
> Can get at book in library of Bodley.

T

for or against. It would certainly argue strongly against the verse, should it appear that it was not cited at the Council of Nice, wherein Arianism was condemned, nor referred to by any Father of the first four centuries. Yet it may be doubted whether Arius, who denied not the Divinity or Filiation, but the Coeternity and Consubstantiality of the Son, would have thought it conclusive against him. " You endeavour to prove," says Bentley, in reply to a letter of a *layman*, whose name has not transpired, " You endeavour to prove, (and that's all you aspire to) that it *may* have been writ by the Apostle, being consonant to his other doctrine. This I concede ; and if the fourth century knew that verse, let it come in in God's name, but if that age did not know it, then Arianism in its height was beat down, without the aid of that verse ; and let the fact prove as it will, the doctrine is unshaken." If Arianism had not been beaten down without it, it would not have been beaten down with it. It is just as evasible as twenty others, and twenty others as conclusive as it. The preponderance of outward testimony seems to be against it, but the logic, the connection of thought, the very *architecture* of the passage speaks strongly for it. If the seventh verse be rejected, the eighth should be rejected also. But this is no place to discuss the question. Bentley is said to have decidedly condemned the verse in his prælection.*

The duties of the Divinity Professor are important, though from the almost total neglect of the old scholastic Theology and Logic, many of them, if not altogether discontinued, have become mere matter of routine. He should moderate in the disputations in the schools, lecture twice a week, create Doctors of Divinity, and preach in Latin before the University on certain stated days. The stipend, as fixed by Henry VIII. was only forty pounds, but a change of times having rendered this salary utterly inadequate, King James I. endowed the Professorship with the three livings of Colne, Pidley, and Somersham, in Huntingdonshire, altogether about £300 annually, which Bentley, by taking the great tithes into his own hands, and letting the small tithes to rent to his Bailiff, expected to raise to £600.

But it cannot be supposed that the chiefs of the University were easy under the trick which had given them a Professor of his own

---

* In some of the earlier Protestant Translations, the verse in question was distinguished with a different type, the discontinuance of which distinction was severely censured by Emlyn, an Arian, who was prosecuted for a work entitled " A humble enquiry into the Scripture account of Jesus Christ." Our knowledge of this fact is due to Dr. Monk, but we think it probable that the early translators rather meant to dignify the verse, than to bastardize it. Surely the Red Letter Days are not meant to be rejected out of the year.

choosing, who scarcely deigned to tender the formal respect due to their station. They only waited for an opportunity of marking their indignation, confident that the violence of Bentley would not let them wait long.

Cutting short the monotonous relation of college despotism, of which our readers must be heartily tired; not detailing how the Divine Professor turned the old dove-cote into a granary for his Somersham tithe corn, and compelled the college to pay for doing the same; how he obliged the college brewer to take his tithe malt at full price, though damaged by the insect called weevil, to the great disparagement of the fair fame of Trinity *audit* ale; how either he or his bailiff Kent effected a collusive sale of wheat, in order to raise the college rents, and make the college pay an unreasonable price for its own bread; how he made his humble servant, Richard Walker, Junior Bursar, and how Richard Walker * paid away the public money at his sovereign's discretion; how the Master of Trinity built and planted, and erected barns, and summer-houses, and villas, and how the poor Fellows bore the burden of all—we will pass to the month of October, 1717, when his Majesty, George 1st, being at Newmarket, was invited by a gowned

* There is something almost affecting in the blind devotion, the canine fidelity, of this man to Bentley. He seems to have asked for nothing but the means of serving his master. He was possessed with the passion of loyalty; and, we doubt not, would have been proud to encounter want, blows, scorn, prison, pillory, or death itself, for his liege lord. While Hacket, Ashenhurst, and others of Bentley's instruments might be suspected of being " super-serviceable knaves," Walker should be discharged of all such suspicion. What is extraordinary is, that he was not a man of scholastic pursuits, and perhaps knew more about books from handing them to the Master, than from his own studies. There was not between Bentley and Walker, as between my Uncle Toby and Corporal Trim, the bond of a common hobby-horse. But there are—at least, there were—some minds, to whom servitude is congenial; in whom submission is not servility, but instinct; who are pleased to annihilate their own will and individuality, and exist as mere instrumental members of another. Their glory is in their humiliation, and therefore it is no mystery that they seem the more inveterately attached the worse they are used. We cannot accord to this temper the approbation of reason. There is but one Being to whom such unconditional obedience, such self-abasement, is due. All submissions of man to man are but the steps of God's altar, or they are essentially idolatrous. Still, if there be such a thing as an amiable weakness, it is this excess of loyal affection. This slight tribute we thought due to *Frog* Walker, as in that age and place of nicknames he was called, from having held a curacy among the fens. The place of Junior Bursar was like that of Ædile at Rome, the first step in the ladder of office; and like that, too, was charged with the care of the public buildings, &c., and the disbursements pertaining thereto. The appointment of Walker to this office enabled Bentley to give full swing to his architectural mania. This was hardly honest; but Richard's ideal of right was constituted by the Master's dictum.

deputation to honour the University with his presence, and was graciously pleased to appoint Sunday, the 6th, for that purpose; which, considering the toil, bustle, vanity, and expense, the unnecessary cooking and dressing, and all the pomp and worldliness attendant on a royal visitation, was little better than the Head of the Church commanding sabbath-breach. No wonder that no good came of it. To Bentley fell the two-fold task of creating the Royal Doctors of Divinity (who, as we have already stated, were created at the royal fiat, without either undergoing the statutable examinations, or keeping the statutable terms), and of entertaining the King and his suite at Trinity Lodge. The visit of another great personage, the Duke of Somerset, gave Vice Chancellor Grigg, the Duke's chaplain, who had been so notably outmanœuvred in the Professorship business, an opportunity of annoying Bentley in a small way, by bringing his patron to Trinity Lodge at a most unseasonable and unexpected time of the morning, without any previous announcement, so as to surprize the Master in his dressing-gown, in the agony of preparation for the royal guest. It would require the imagination and the pencil of a Hogarth to portray how the proud Duke must have looked, and how the Master of Trinity looked, and how Dr. Grigg must have enjoyed his sullen apologies and angry confusion. Not content with this, the duty of conducting his Majesty from St. Mary's to Trinity College devolving upon Grigg, as Vice Chancellor, he, under some pretence or other, led the King to a back gate, which had been closed to keep out the mob, and kept his anointed sovereign standing in a most filthy and unsavoury lane till intelligence of the matter could be conveyed to the great gate, where the Master was waiting in all due form to receive his illustrious visitor. If all this was intended to make Bentley appear awkward in the royal presence, it was unsuccessful; for the King, declining to partake of the magnificent banquet laid out in Hall, dined privately with a few Noblemen at the Lodge, as if he had rather be Bentley's guest than the University's. The Doctor was afterwards complained of for monopolizing the honour of the royal visit, but considering the sentiments of some of the leading characters in Cambridge, it is no wonder that King George should keep aloof from indiscriminate society there.

This concerted chapter of accidents was but the omen of more serious misunderstandings. Next day, October 7th, a congregation was held in the Senate-house to finish the creation of the Royal Doctors, of whom only three, Grigg, Davies, and Waterland, as Heads of Houses, had been made in the royal presence, just to let the King see how it was done. Bentley refused to perform his office, except at the unusual rate of a four guinea fee. Many candidates demurred. One Professor would not act, except on his own conditions. It was ruled that his agency was not indispensable. Dr. Bardsey Fisher, Master of Sidney, prompted by the Beadle, performed, for the old regulation fee of a broad piece, certain forms which were to qualify certain persons to write D. D. after their names, to wear a scarlet gown over a black coat, and to hold a plurality of benefices.

When it is considered that a Doctor's degree is either a mere luxury, or the qualification for considerable emolument ; that these royal Doctors were, after all, considerable savers in time, toil, and pocket, by the King's visit, which must have caused the Regius Professor a great expense in all three ; and that the mere operation of qualifying them for pluralities, must have taken up many hours of Bentley's *day*, a day always devoted to the advantage of mankind, when not employed to the injury of the Fellows of Trinity College, Cambridge, we really think, not that Bentley was quite right in claiming the four guineas, but that it would have been much better if the new Doctors had paid it without more ado, for any man who can afford to be a D.D. can afford to pay four guineas.

But Conyers Middleton, who was one of the Doctors to be created, thought otherwise, not because he grudged the guineas, but because he hated Bentley, so instead of going for his investiture to Dr. Bardsey Fisher, as a man who thought the head inn too expensive, would take up his quarters at the most respectable pot-house in a village, he paid his four guineas to Dr. Bentley, with a proviso that they should be repaid if the King decided against the claim. We cannot help thinking that Middleton acted with a presentiment, or rather with a rational calculation, that he was paying four guineas for an advantage over his enemy. The detail of the business would be little interesting. Month after month passed, and the King did not interfere, and Bentley kept the money ; at last Middleton brought an action in the Vice-chancellor's court, a decree was issued to arrest Bentley for the sum. Clarke, an Esquire Beadle, was sent to serve the process ; he got into the Lodge, but could not see the Master ; he was locked up in a room for some hours, and then discharged, without having effected the arrest. Various preliminaries were gone through in the Vice-chancellor's court, to none of which Bentley attended. At last the Vice-chancellor pronounced him to be in contempt of the University Jurisdiction ; suspended his degrees, summoned three several courts to give him an opportunity of making his submission, and then finding him still obdurate, resolved to merge his own act in a decree of the University at large. A *grace* was proposed to the Senate, the representative body of the University, to strip him of all his degrees. A vain attempt was made by Ashenhurst to interrupt their proceedings, by tendering the votes to Dr. Otway, a suspected nonjuror, but it was not allowed to pass. On the 17th of October, 1718, the Senate of the University of Cambridge passed a grace, by which the Master of Trinity and Regius Professor of Divinity, was degraded *ab omni gradu suscepto,* and, to speak technically, reduced to the condition of a mere *Harry Soph.*

It is difficult to find any parallel to the predicament in which Bentley and the University were placed by this unprecedented act. The ruler of the first college was without a vote in the ruling assemblies, the highest Teacher of Theology was forbidden to enter the University pulpit. It somewhat resembled the case of the Duke of Norfolk, during the continuance of the Catholic disabilities; the first Peer without a seat in the House of Peers, the Hereditary Earl Marshall prohibited from discharging his functions. Strange, however, as his position was become, Bentley was not a whit daunted, when informed of his degradation, he said, " I have rubbed through many a worse business," and forthwith drew up a petition to the King, as supreme Visitor, laying open the circumstances of the case, and urging the injustice with which, without hearing or summons, he had been suspended from all his degrees by the Vice-chancellor, and inhibited from discharging his duty, as Divinity Professor, the precipitation with which the Senate had passed the grace of degradation, and the Vice-chancellor's refusal to administer the oaths to Dr. Otway. (He never neglected to direct suspicion towards the politics of his opponents.) Of course the petition closed with a prayer for redress of grievances. It met with speedy attention : was read in Council on the 30th of October, and produced an order that the Vice-chancellor should attend at the Board on the 6th of November with an account of the proceedings. The office of Vice-chancellor terminates annually on the 4th of November. It was therefore of the utmost importance to Bentley's adversaries, with whom the academical body corporate was now identified, not to let the chief magistracy pass into dangerous hands. According to established order, it would have fallen to Dr. Davies, President of Queen's, the only college-head who had voted in Bentley's favour. To make sure of excluding him, Dr. Gooch, the Vice-chancellor of the preceding year, who was the originator of the whole measure, was re-elected by a majority of two to one. To London then the re-elected Doctor went, not over well pleased with his own situation, and eager for any opening to an escape. On presenting his statement before the King in council, he attributed the suspension of Bentley to his non-appearance in the action for debt, which all the world knew was not the true ground, but was most industrious in shifting the responsibility from his own shoulders, reminding his

Majesty that the suspension was sunk in the degradation, and that the Vice-chancellor humbly conceives that he is not personally responsible for an act of the body corporate of the University of Cambridge, of which he is but one member." Nothing was immediately concluded in council, but after sometime the matter was referred to a Committee, and the general surmise was, that a Royal Commission, that hope of the Whigs and terror of the Tories, would be appointed to visit the University, and redress all grievances. Among the paradoxes of the times not the least surprising was that the Tories were disputing the extent of the royal power, and Oxford literally deliberating on the propriety of resist-ing the King, should he attempt to interfere with her rights of self-government.

Every thing in England takes the shape and hue of politics. You may form a very likely guess at an Englishman's political sentiments from hearing his opinions upon poetry, his comparative estimate of clas-sical and mathematical learning, his preference of physical or metaphy-sical science, or even his judgment in a dispute between two neighbour-ing families. No wonder then, if a question, involving such important interests as that of Bentley's degradation, out of which grew so much discussion with regard to the limits of clashing jurisdictions, and in which the rights of the Church, so closely implicated in those of the Universities, were not remotely concerned, become a matter of party, and was variously judged according to the political predilections of dif-ferent men. Pamphlets flew thick. Arthur Ashley Sykes, a low-church divine, and indefatigable Polemic, led the way. Dean Sherlock, the strength of the High-church men, responded in defence of his Univer-sity. Conyers Middleton followed. His refusal of the four guinea fee had produced effects beyond all that he hoped for, and now he came for-ward with the professed intention of vindicating the steps of which he had been the primary mover, but with far more desire of holding up Bentley to public odium. In 1719, at the ripe age of thirty six, the future Biographer of Cicero first appeared as an author. Shakspeare's *maiden* essay was a scurrilous ballad, Middleton's was " A full and im-partial account of all the late proceedings in the University of Cambridge against Dr. Bentley." He possessed the talent of being severe without being scurrilous. He did not call names, (a practice to which his adver-sary was unfortunately addicted, both *viva voce* and in print,) and if he did not always conceal his malice, he never betrayed his irascibility. He took advantage of the alarm felt by certain persons at the prospect of a royal visitation, to impute the report of such a movement to Bentley's presumption, if not the design to his insinuations. The passage is as follows :—" But even this will hardly seem strange from him who dares to give out that the King and his Ministry will interpose to reverse our statutable proceedings against him ; that for the sake of a single person so justly odious, so void of all credit and interest amongst us, his Majesty will set a mark of his displeasure upon his famous and loyal University.   But it is to be hoped that an insolence so apparently tending to alienate the affections of his people from his Majesty, may meet with the just severity and chastisement of the law." Contrary to his inclination, Conyers complimented his antagonist, and prophesied the defeat of his own party in a single sentence "He has ceased to be Doctor, and may cease to be Professor, but he can never cease to be Bentley."

The literary warfare continued during 1719.   Middleton produced a second and a third pamphlet.   These and all the others published in the course of the controversy were anonymous; and as Middleton was a new writer, poor Colbatch, whose fate it was to bear the blame of others' lampoons, received for a time the credit or discredit of his compositions.

So violent was the excitement of the controversy, and so deep the mutual hatred of the parties, that the most improbable rumours found credit ; and the antagonists of Bentley scrupled not to impute to his partisans the purpose of assassination. It was currently reported that Dr. Gooch was shot at through a window of his lodge, and more than hinted whence the bullet came.   In some recent repairs of Caius College, a bullet was actually found in the wainscot.   Of course it is not intended to ascribe to Bentley any privity to a murderous design ; but if he or Ashenhurst extended patronage to many such men as Joseph Lindsay, it is not impossible that some of them may have taken this unwarrantable mode of displaying gratitude.

Meantime, Colbatch, and the other Remonstrants in Trinity, were suffering all the miseries of hope deferred.   It does not appear that they had taken any part in the decisive proceedings of the University against their Master ; and perhaps they had not much reason to rejoice at his *degradation*, which did not diminish his power over them, and was very unlikely to mollify his exercise of it.   Archbishop Wake was, indeed, a true, but not an efficient friend ; for he seems to have been a righteous Bishop ; and the Church, though it has the opportunity of *purchasing* great interest by leaguing with the government, has very little authority of its proper own.   The Minister, Lord Sunderland, and the Chancellor, Lord Parker (afterwards Earl of Macclesfield), deceived them with fair words.   All this while their petition was, as it were, in a state of suspended animation, in Sir Edward Northey's pocket.   After three years, it was resuscitated by the persevering representations of Colbatch, read at the Council board a second time on the 26th of May, and referred to the Committee.

The Royal Visitation was daily expected, and the hopes of the malcontents began to revive, when Bentley, by a stroke of policy which may share the commendation bestowed on the unjust steward, cut the ground from beneath them, and at once redoubled their cause of complaint and deprived them of their last apparent chance of redress. We have already mentioned the proposal for a compromise with Serjeant Miller, and its rejection. That learned lawyer having stumbled into the ill graces of the University, where he was as little beloved, and nothing like so much feared, as Bentley himself, seeing those Bills, on the strength of which he had expressed such premature and offensive exultation, postponed *sine die*, seeing his own blunders exposed by the ex-doctor's formidable pen in a manner not at all conducive to his professional advancement, in fine, having failed in a frivolous prosecution of Walker for some unintelligible illegality with regard to taking a pupil, began to consider that as revenge was not to be had, money was not to be despised. The re-appearance of the Petition produced a renewal of overtures on the part of Bentley, which found Miller in the humour of Shylock, when, finding that the bond did not allow him any blood, he offers to take his principal. In this extraordinary treaty it was considered that the Serjeant, on condition of receiving half his dues as a Fellow since 1715, together with his room rent, and £400 for his law expenses, should resign his Fellowship, and withdraw both his own petition, and that of Colbatch. To make the College pay the lawyer for betraying its cause was a bold thought, but Bentley's design was bolder still. He demanded of the college, payment of his own costs, and by the college they were paid. At the very time while Bentley had not a degree in the University, when a decided interposition of Government was looked for to put a stop to the blended anarchy and despotism of his rule, he succeeded in extorting £500 for the charges of his defence. This was effected through the agency of Baker, who gained over a majority out of the total list of Fellows, by which the resistance of five out of the eight seniors was overborne. The pretence was that such payment was the only means of restoring peace. Miller went off with £528 of the college money, to which perhaps he was *legally* entitled, had he not forfeited all claim on his clients by treacherously abandoning their cause. Though no longer an honest man he continued a Whig, and became member for a borough, in which honourable capacity he distinguished himself, by speaking, in 1725, against the bill for enabling Lord Bolingbroke, who had been attainted, to succeed to the family inheritance, after he had received the King's pardon. Though this partial reversal of the attainder was advocated by Walpole himself, Miller's opposition seems not to have displeased the Ministry, for shortly after he was appointed one of the Barons of the Exchequer for Scotland. Enough of him, and his rewards, and honours.

And now the prospects of Trinity College, at least of the discontented party in it, were worse than ever, for there was no chance of obtaining a Visitor from the Crown, since the petition was withdrawn from the council, and as the Bishop of Ely refused to act in that capacity, though informed by Colbatch and Ayloffe, of all the circumstances of the bargain with Miller, and the Master's extraordinary demand, there was even less probability of his departing from his secure neutrality in any possible emergence. Wake, their only friend, had no longer the power to assist them ; and it was the understood intention of the Court to screen the Master.

Passing over some minor events at Cambridge, we will proceed to give a brief account of a new series of litigations, in which the triumphs of Bentley were such as to inspire a belief in the superstitious, that the demon of law-suits was his familiar spirit. The sole consolation and only hope of his late prosecutors was in the press, and to the press they appealed, not quite despairing of shaming the superior powers into interference. Middleton was the chosen champion, for his popular style made his services the most effective, while his situation protected him from all apprehension of Bentley's wrath. With the assistance of Colbatch's memorials he produced a keen invective, entitled " *A true account of the present state of Trinity College, in Cambridge, under the oppressive Government of their Master, Richard Bentley, late D.D.*" Of the spirit of this composition the motto, taken from one of Cicero's orations against Verres, is at once an omen and a sample :—" *Prætermittam minora omnia quorum simile forsitan alius quoque aliquid aliquando fecerit : nihil dicam nisi singulare ; nisi quod si in alium reum diceretur incredibile videretur.*" * The book was in strict accordance with this promise. It was what it was intended to be, a *libel*, whether true or false, upon Bentley. But it also proved what it was not intended to be a libel on the King's Government. Bentley, who fixed an inevitable eye on the errors of his opponents, directly perceived his advantage. In the absence of Colbatch, at whose door, as usual, the libel was laid, he procured, notwithstanding the opposition of Ayloffe, Jordan, and Bouquet, the signature of the college to a ready made censure of the book and his author, and a power of attorney under the college seal, to prosecute the said author, its printers and publishers.

* " I will pass over all lesser matter, whereto possibly at some time or other, some person or other may have done something somewhat similar. I will mention nothing but what is unique ; nothing but what, if alleged against any other criminal, would appear incredible."

Having accomplished this purpose, he proposed to remove Colbatch from the seniority, a measure in which he was supported by the crazy Brabourn and the unconscientious Baker; but Modd and Barwell, though they had little courage, had still some conscience, and refused to participate in the oppression of a friend and brother, whose character they probably admired for the very points in which it differed from their own. Defeated in this design, he commenced an action against Bickerton the publisher. This produced an immediate avowal of authorship by Middleton, who also would have added to his confession the articles of accusation, drawn up by Colbatch to be laid before a Visitor, but the bookseller declined publishing what might be considered another libel. He could therefore only declare that he was the author of the work, that his sole purpose in writing it was to bring about a Visitation, and that he was ready, should the Master, or any of his friends, answer it in print, either to defend every allegation, or publicly to recant.

But Bentley had observed a passage in the book which served his ends much better than a paper controversy, or even a public recantation. At page 5 of the " True Account" were these words :—" While the liberty of Englishmen is so much the envy of other nations and the boast of our own, and the meanest peasant knows where to find redress for the least grievance he has to complain of, it is hardly credible that a body of learned and worthy men, oppressed and injured daily in every thing that is dear and valuable to them, should not be able to find any proper court of justice in the kingdom that will receive their complaints."

At this day, these words would scarce be deemed libellous. They were rather aimed at the Bishop of Ely, or the King's Ministers, than at the Courts of Law, if indeed they were any thing more than an exclamation of indignant surprise at the unfortunate position in which Trinity College was placed by the uncertainty of the Visitatorial power. But at that time the Courts were exceedingly jealous of their jurisdiction. An information was laid against Conyers Middleton in the King's Bench, on the joint behalf of the King and Richard Bentley.

This was at the beginning of 1720. The law's delay protracted the trial for a year and a half. In Trinity term, 1721, the cause was tried in the Court of King's Bench, and Dr. Middleton found guilty of a Libel. Still, judgment was deferred, and Conyers kept in an agony of suspense, which Bentley, whose resentment was not mitigated by the two pamphlets published by Middleton at the commencement of this suit, on the project of the New Testament, did not take any means to abridge. To heighten his distress, his friends, even those for whose sake he had braved the wrath of one who was never to be offended with impunity, gave him little support or countenance. Colbatch alone administered to his necessity, exerted himself to procure affidavits in his favour, and sent him fifty pounds, no small donation from a poor clergyman, whose means must have been cruelly narrowed by the expenses of the college disputes. Middleton at times was apprehensive of a fine beyond his means to pay, which would have consigned him to a jail, a comfortable abode even then, for the knave that would not pay, but a miserable den for the poor man that could not. By the mediation of one of the University representatives, he gained access to some great personage, (supposed to be the Lord Chancellor,) who, being a man of infinite promise, engaged to mollify the Chief Justice, and procure a lenient sentence. So the term passed away and the long vacation succeeded, and Middleton was still left to suffer perhaps more than the severest sentence would have inflicted. The unwearied Colbatch employed this vacant time in preparing a tract in Middleton's favour, to be entitled " *The case of Richard Bentley against Dr. Middleton considered, and a Question arising thereupon discussed ; viz. how far it may be lawful to publish the notorious crimes of any wicked man.*" But his bookseller shewed the MS. to Counsellor Ketelbey, who pronounced that it would infallibly be accounted a libel, and reminded the bibliopole that " Bentley now knew the way into Westminster Hall;" so the work still remains unprinted. Dr. Monk speaks highly of the ability and earnestness of its execution. As there is now no danger of Bentley's ever finding his way into Westminster Hall again, we importune those in whose hands it may be, to give it to the world, at least so much of it as bears upon the liberty of the press in general. As a revision of the libel laws cannot and will not be long deferred, the arguments of the sturdy casuistical Professor may throw some light on a subject of the highest importance, concerning which there is a lamentable want of clear ideas.

The bursting of the South-sea bubble, which awakened thousands from dreams of countless wealth to the sober certainty of ruin, and exhibited a degree of baseness, falsehood, peculation, and depravity in high places, which English history has never since rivalled, brought about a change of administration. Lord Townshend, a liberal statesman, clear of all participation in the abominable thing, who had been supplanted, in 1716, by the intrigues of the Sunderland party, was recalled to the King's councils. Parliament having mitigated the popular resentment by giving up some gross and palpable peculators as examples, thought proper to screen the rest by an act of grace. A promise to introduce a clause which should apply to Middleton's case was made and broken by the Lord Chancellor Macclesfield. The gloomy month of November found Conyers again in attendance at the Court of King's

Bench, still tormented with expensive delays, and reduced at last to make vain offers of compromise to his prosecutor. Failing there, he directed his own counsel to move for judgment upon the verdict. Chief Justice Pratt, (father to the first Earl of Camden,) immediately observed, " that he had hoped to hear no more of this affair, but that two Doctors of Divinity," (the learned Judge either forgot or did not choose to acknowledge Bentley's degradation,) " to avoid the scandal justly given by such personal quarrels, would have found someway of making it up between themselves." At last Middleton was persuaded to admit " that as far as he had offended the law in what he had done, he was sorry for it, and asked the Master's pardon." Whether such a guarded apology ought to satisfy the honour of a gentleman, we leave it to the learned in the laws of the *Duello* to decide. Certainly it did not immediately satisfy the anger of a Divinity Professor, nor is the logic of it absolutely irrefragable. If he were only sorry for having offended the Law, it would seem more reasonable that he should apologise to the Court by whom the Majesty of the Law is represented, than to his adversary. Bentley, however, demanded that he should subscribe a paper owning that he had wronged and abused the whole society. To that Middleton would not bend, but moved once more for judgment by his counsel the following day.

The Chief Justice, an honest man, animadverted with some severity on the unforgiving and exorbitant temper of Bentley, and sarcastically asked, " Whether the Society would not have the paper stuck up at the Exchange, and have Dr. Middleton led through Westminster Hall, with it printed to his hat." Seeing no chance of obtaining any thing more in the present disposition of the Court, Bentley condescended to accept the apology, and the defendant paid the prosecutor's taxed costs, which perhaps amounted to more than any fine that would have been levied. In order, in some degree, to recompense him for such charge and vexation incurred in their common cause, and perhaps likewise to mortify the Divinity Professor, the prevailing party in Cambridge established a new office of *Proto-bibliothecarius*, or head librarian, to which Doctor Middleton was triumphantly promoted, spite of the resistance of Bentley's partisans, who called the business a scandalous job. The grace was proposed on the 14th of December, 1721, and carried by a majority of 112 to 49. So high did party spirit run, that the only two members of St. John's, who voted against the appointment, were hissed all the way from the schools to their own college.

Our narrative must now retrograde a little, to record a few incidents, that formed the episodes of this restless drama. Of these the most refreshing is the defeat of Bentley in an attempt to keep Colbatch out of the Rectory of Orwell, vacant by the death of Dr. Stubbe, in October

1719, to which, as senior Doctor, he was entitled by statute. A dissention among the Master's supporters frustrated the unjust machinations to deprive Colbatch of his right. It is but just to add, that the failure of this plot was a subject of general congratulation.

The inconvenience and absurdity of suffering the Divinity Professorship to become a sinecure in the hands of a man prohibited from discharging its duties were so apparent, that the leaders of the University made serious efforts to put an end to this state of things by stripping Bentley of the office.

The long expected Royal Visitation coming to nothing, all expectation of remedy from that quarter died away. Dr. Gooch, who was, in November, 1720, elected Vice-chancellor the third time, had threatened, while pronouncing Bentley's suspension, to deprive him of his Professorship, if he did not make due submission and satisfaction for his contumacy. But in order to carry this menace into effect, it was necessary to obtain the concurrence of the Master of Trinity, who was by no means likely to assist in his own deposition. In Trinity term, 1720, a rule of the Court of King's Bench was obtained, calling upon the electors to shew cause why a mandamus should not be issued calling upon them to fill an alleged vacancy of the chair, of course on the ground of illegality and collusion in the election of Bentley, who was therefore assumed not to be, and never to have been, Professor of Divinity at all,—*ergo*, that the chair had been vacant ever since the death of Dr. James. This was a very weak invention. It was met by affidavits from Modd, Davies, and Bentley. In Michaelmas term the rule was discharged.

In January 1720-21, appeared the pamphlet to which we have already alluded, in which Bentley, without either justice or decorum, abuses Colbatch for what he knew to be the work of Middleton. It is true he did not name the object of his vituperation, but the Professor of Casuistry was surely designated by the terms " Casuistical Drudge," " Plodding Pupil of Escobar," &c.,* yet more rudely by descriptive allusions to Colbatch's dark complexion and rigid features, and most cruelly, by an insinuation that he partook of the family derangement of his brother, who *had taken a fancy from a vow, or a vision, to wear a beard to his girdle sufficient for a Greek Patriarch.*"

Colbatch did not bear " a cheek for blows," and here was provocation that might have stirred a much more " milk-livered man." Yet even

---

* Anthony Escobar Mendoza, a celebrated Spanish casuist, born at Valladolid in 1589, entered the society of Jesuits at fifteen, was for many years a popular preacher, and died in 1669. His works, the principal of which are his Moral Theology, and Cases of Conscience, extend to forty folios. Well might a pupil of his be a plodder.

in his anger he remembered the statutes, for which he had an almost superstitious reverence. In compliance with the letter of the law, he applied to Modd, the Vice Master, to take cognizance of the affair between the Master and himself. From Modd, however, he neither obtained nor expected redress ; but, the first time Bentley was in town, he exhibited the libel to a college meeting, and obtained from the majority a vote, that it was " false, scandalous, and malicious," and a resolution, that, should it really prove to be a member of the college, he should be proceeded against according to statute. Though there was no likelihood of this resolution being carried into effect (for there was no doubt as to its author), it expressed the society's conviction of Colbatch's innocence. Brabourn, who concurred at first in the censure, probably from not well knowing what it meant, afterwards recanted, in equal ignorance of what he was doing, and it was never entered in the college register. But by applying to the heads of colleges, Colbatch obtained what he would have done well to consider ample satisfaction—a declaration, that the book was " a most virulent and scandalous libel, highly injurious to Dr. Colbatch, contrary to good manners, and a notorious violation of the statutes and discipline of the University ;" and though they could not, on a mere moral certainty, assume it as *legally* proved that the Master of Trinity was the author, they resolved, " that the author of the libel, as soon as he was discovered, should receive such censure as the statutes did in that case appoint." This was to all intents and purposes equivalent to censuring Richard Bentley by name ; and with this full and honourable vindication of his own character, Colbatch ought to have been content. But he had caught the epidemic of the time: he would stand for law, and was doomed to find, that whoever entered the courts with Bentley was a certain victim. He prosecuted Crownefield, the University bookseller, in the Vice Chancellor's Court, for selling the obnoxious pamphlet. The various stages of this suit are too much entangled in the technicalities of the civil law, and the peculiarities of University jurisdiction, to interest the general reader ; suffice it to say, that the delays of the Vice Chancellor's court (in which it worthily imitates courts of greater business), protracted the cause till the Act of Grace put a stop to all criminal processes. But Colbatch was a sort of amateur civilian, and fancied that he understood cases of law as well as cases of conscience. There still remained a process, unknown to the common law, which he thought the government pardon did not prevent—an enquiry into the authorship of the libel " in the office of a judge," which he thought might oblige Bentley to be examined as a witness, and compel him to criminate himself.

On the 24th of November, 1721, the very day on which Middleton was finally summoned before the King's Bench to atone for his libel, Colbatch, regardless of professional advice, entered the Vice Chancellor's Court to call Bentley to account for *his*.   Certain preliminaries past, Bentley was cited to give evidence, but not one of the officers was willing to serve the citation upon him.   It was like "belling the cat."   They remembered the treatment which Clarke had experienced three years before.   Atwood at last undertook the enterprize, and was agreeably disappointed at his civil reception.   But in truth the circumstances were materially altered.   In 1718 the Doctor was taken by surprise, and was undetermined what to do : his detention of Clarke, and refusal to submit to the arrest, were mere artifices to gain time ; and he probably expected a more decisive interference in his favour than a vacillating and unpopular government dared to extend.   In the present instance his measures were all determined, and incivility could only have disturbed them.   He simply asked, "Whether the summons related to Colbatch's business?" and left the beadle to suppose that it would be attended to :—nothing could be further from his purpose. The court to which he was cited was fixed for January 17, 1722.   As soon as the college audit, and the usual altercations thereat were over, he went to London, consulted counsel, and obtained an opinion that the proceedings on foot against him were illegal, "*as partaking of the nature of a general inquisition*," and might be resisted in the Court of King's Bench.   But the King's Bench would not be sitting before the day of appearance.   What then !   He negotiated with one of his brother chaplains to give him his turn of attendance at St. James's.   The Vice Chancellor and his court assembled on the appointed day.   "Richard Bentley, Master of Trinity College, was three times summoned by name:"—no answer, except that Lisle, a Proctor, and one of the Master's noisiest partisans, produced a letter from the Lord Chamberlain, the Duke of Newcastle, stating that Dr. Richard Bentley was absent on the King's service.   This the Vice Chancellor was compelled to acknowledge as a sufficient excuse.   Proceedings were adjourned to the 16th of February ; before which time, the Court of King's Bench granted a rule for the Vice Chancellor to shew cause, &c., on the second day of the following term, and staying proceedings in the interval.

This interference of the Common Law Courts with what the High-Churchmen considered a canonical and spiritual authority, excited great indignation, and brought Colbatch into more difficulties than ever. By mere obstinacy, and conceit of his own legal acumen, he had exposed the University to something like a public rebuke ; and now he set about to defend it in a way that gave his and the University's maligners a long-wished-for advantage against both. He produced a treatise, entitled *Jus Academicum*, which is said to show a deep acquaintance with the laws and constitutions of academic establishments, and an able defence of their necessary rights and privileges. Unfortunately, Colbatch understood—at least had studied—the Canons, Decretals, and Pandects much better than the laws of his native land. Not so had Bentley, as the sequel shewed. He simply directed his counsel to read certain passages of the Jus Academicum before the Court of King's Bench, and to move them to take cognizance of contempt of their jurisdiction. Among the most offensive was the following:—

" There is a strange doctrine got into Westminster Hall, where it hath prevailed for above these hundred years past, as it is like to do for these hundred years to come, unless my lords the Bishops shall think fit to take notice of it in Parliament, viz. : that the King's pardon shall put a stop to any process carried on in the spiritual courts, for the reformation of manners, and the salvation of a man's soul." This was enough to alarm the Lords Justices, who were then, and ever, extremely jealous of any attempt to set up the authority of the spiritual courts against their own. But other sentences hinted at the possibility of resistance on the part of the University, and seemed to accuse the King's Government of evil designs against liberty. Yet so little aware was the author of his work containing any thing libellous, that he had sent a presentation copy to every judge on the bench, except Pratt and Fortescue. Most likely they never read it.

A rule of court was granted for Wilkin, the publisher, to shew cause why an attachment should not issue against him. As the interrogatories to which the person attached would be subjected would oblige him to discover the author, Colbatch's friends bestirred themselves to make intercession for him with the great. Dean Sherlock and Dean Hare used their interest with Lord Townshend ; and Dr. Freind, Master of Westminster School, applied to Lord Carteret. The Ministers seem to have really wished to do their best for him ; but, unluckily, Colbatch, who was in every thing the victim of Fortune and his own mistakes, relied chiefly on the Lord Chancellor, who, while sustaining him with hope and fair words, was actually cooling his friends and heating his enemies. Had Earl Macclesfield, however, been sincere in his good offices, it is doubtful whether they could have done the unfortunate divine any real service. Pratt was an inflexible judge, possessed with a high sense of the sanctity of his own office, and a just apprehension of government interference. The Ministers, indeed, promised much. Lord Carteret, in particular, told Dr. Freind, that, " if the Doctor

(Colbatch) were sent to prison, here—(brandishing his pen)—here is Mercury's wand, which will soon fetch him out." Gradually this tone of assurance was exchanged for a style of cautious admonition. For some cause, or for none, the treacherous Macclesfield wilfully misadvised him; and the sole effect of his weary and tantalizing attendance on these true courtiers was, to exasperate the minds of Pratt and the other justices of the King's Bench against him. At length, on the 14th of May, 1723, he moved the court for judgment, was committed *pro forma*, and, after little more than a week's confinement, was brought up to petition for his discharge; whereupon Sir Littleton Powis, the senior puisne judge, made an exposure of combined ignorance, pedantry, and insolence, that must have set gravity at defiance. The motto of the Jus Academicum was that everlastingly-quoted scrap of Horace,— *Jura negat sibi nata, nihil non arrogat,*—which the unlearned judge chose to read *nihil non ABrogat,* and insisted upon it that it was meant to apply to the court. Colbatch would have done well had he suffered his Lordship to proceed without correction; for by arguing the point, and repeatedly contradicting Sir Littleton on the very seat of justice, he became guilty of a contempt, and instead of *one mark,* which would originally have satisfied the court, he incurred a fine of £50.

While Bentley was thus revenging himself on one of his enemies, another furnished him with an opportunity of like satisfaction, by a course exactly similar. Middleton, in quality of chief librarian, had written a Latin tract upon the method of arranging the public library, and especially the books contained in the King's magnificent present, a subject seemingly as safe as any author could handle. But the hatred of Bentley was then the ruling principle of all Middleton's thoughts, words, and works. Unwarned by the example of Colbatch, he introduced into his dedication a passage explicitly denying the authority of the common law courts to overrule the academical courts, and implicitly calling the King's Bench *forum prorsus alienum et externum,* a court altogether strange and foreign. It was not to be expected that this would escape the critical eye of Bentley, or the animadversions of his Majesty's justices. On the very day (May 14th) on which Colbatch moved for judgment, Sergeant Cheshyre moved for an information against Middleton's bookseller. The same process which the King and Richard Bentley had been conducting against Colbatch, was repeated against Middleton, with the same result, but with far less delay and mortification; for Conyers learned, at his friend's cost, not to trust in courtiers' promises, nor to degrade himself by fruitless solicitations. He was accordingly committed for five days, brought up on the 20th of June, fined £50, and discharged, after giving securities for his good behaviour for a twelvemonth.

While Bentley's enemies were thus smarting under the lash of the law, he was successfully availing himself of the same mighty power to recover the station of which he had been deprived. It would be tedious to relate the details of the suit, which terminated in a complete reversal of all the University proceedings against the Master of Trinity. On the 14th of February, 1724, a peremptory mandamus was issued to the Chancellor, Masters, and scholars, " to restore Richard Bentley to all his degrees, and to every other right and privilege of which they had deprived him." Thus was it decreed, that every attempt to bring that unconquerable man to account for his deeds, should end in the distress and discomfiture of his adversaries, and afford to himself the gratification of a triumphant display of great and various abilities. The natural effect of this extraordinary success must have been to remove from his mind every shade of doubt with respect to the rectitude of his cause, and to encourage him to proceed boldly as he had begun. Six law suits prosecuted to a successful issue within three years, were enough to make any man, not endowed with a double portion of humility, fancy himself the minion of Justice. Yet he was not quite satisfied with the length of time during which the doubts of lawyers and the uncertainty of the law had deferred his victory. Notwithstanding that the greater part of the costs had fallen on his antagonists, his own share was more than he found it convenient to pay. His feelings on this head he expressed, *suo more*, the first assizes after his restoration, when the judges visited Trinity Lodge, and one of them observed, " Dr. Bentley, you have not thanked us for what we have done for you." The Doctor answered, " What am I to thank you for ? Is it for only doing me justice after a long protracted lawsuit ? Had you indeed restored me to my rights at once, I might have expressed my obligations ; but such have been your delays, that if I had not been an economist in my youth, I must have been ruined in the pursuit of justice." The judge must have felt that he was not on the bench.

The events of the four years succeeding 1724 are neither numerous nor important. Though it can hardly be said that even temporary tranquility prevailed, Colbatch himself seems to have despaired of successful resistance. He withdrew to his Rectory at Orwell, and doubtless lived in hope of better times. The restored Professor, whose public functions had been discontinued during the suspension of his degrees, now entered upon the duties of his Professorship with zeal, and took a leading part in the University politics, presided at the theological disputations, and appeared frequently in the University pulpit.   From these officea, however, he desisted in 1727, and made Dr. Newcome, the Margaret Professor of Divinity, his substitute.   His liability to severe colds, the consequence of intense study, and neglect of exercise, rendered his attendance in the schools extremely dangerous.

The years 1724, 25, and 26, were distinguished by a display of literary rivalry, not wholly unprofitable to the interests of literature, but little becoming the sanctity of two dignified clergymen, one of whom had passed his grand climacteric.   We have more than once had occasion to mention Dr. Francis Hare, at one time a most fervid admirer and professed friend of our Aristarch ; but the friendships of the ambitious are seldom lasting, and Bentley found, or fancied, occasion to suspect Hare of undermining his credit in several instances, and particularly in the business of the Frederician Classics.   Still no absolute rupture had taken place ; for Bentley chose, in his own words, —*amicitiam dissuere, non disrumpere,*—to *unstitch,* not *tear asunder friendship.*

But the dishonest vanity of Hare gave a pretext for more decisive hostility.   During the period of their intimacy, the two scholars had held much conversation on classical subjects, and Bentley, who in all that regards the *res metrica* is an absolute discoverer, had communicated and explained a method of reducing the apparent lawlessness of the Latin Comic Metre to something like regularity.   Hare produced an edition of Terence, in which he availed himself of the instruction thus obtained to appropriate the credit of Bentley's metrical discoveries without any acknowledgment.   This Aristarch considered, not without good grounds, as an invasion of his patent, and, though he might well have spared whatever reputation the plagiarism might detract from him ; perhaps he was not to be blamed for laying claim to his own, especially as his sometime friend and flatterer, had not spared insinuations to the discredit of his moral character, even while lauding his intellectual qualifications.

Bentley's Terence was undertaken with the express purpose of stopping the sale and destroying the credit of Hare's work, and though carried through the press with almost breathless haste, is said by a high authority to be the most useful, elegant, and accurate of all our critic's editions.   The text is corrected in upwards of a thousand places.   The metrical system perfectly elucidated, and the surreptitious half-knowledge of Hare exposed with merciless severity.   Bentley's triumph would however have been more complete, had he known where to stop. But seeing that his rival had announced an intention of editing Phædrus, he determined to anticipate him, and published that Fabulist along with the Terence. For this work he had made no adequate preparation, nor did he allow himself time to defend his emendations, which are numerous, rash, and dogmatical, by argument or authority. The crudities of this hurried performance gave Hare an opportunity of retorting in an *Epistola critica*, chiefly remarkable for unsaying all the praises which he had himself uttered in the " Clergyman's Thanks." Well might Sir Isaac Newton remark that it was a pity two such Divines should spend their time in quarrelling about a play-book.

Meantime Dr. Middleton having returned from Italy, revived the suit respecting the four guineas in the Vice-chancellor's court. It does not appear that Bentley defended the action ; the guineas were repaid with twelve shillings costs. The whole proceeding was discreditable to all parties concerned.

Bishop Fleetwood was now no more ; and his see was held by Bishop Greene. This change gave some faint hopes to the opposition party in Trinity College, for Dr. Greene was willing to act as Visitor provided that his right was legally determined, and his expenses guaranteed. Bentley was more absolute than ever. Many of his prosecutors had now joined the ruling party. Modd had been succeeded in the Vice-mastership by Baker. Walker held the power of the purse ; the Master continued to appoint to Fellowships by his own sole authority, and had recently nominated his own son Richard, though no more than fifteen years of age. With far more reprehensible partiality, he let a college estate, situate in Petergate, York, to his brother James, on a lease of twenty years, upon considerations manifestly insufficient. Yet regardless of the clamour which this job excited, he afterwards renewed the lease to Priscilla Bentley, his brother's widow, for a fine of only £20. But these details are devoid of interest, and it is time that we proceed to the renewal of those hostilities of which these and other malversations were the pretext if not the cause.

The great odium arising from the Master's alleged ingratitude in refusing a Fellowship to the grandson of his early patron, Stillingfleet, once more put Colbatch in motion. His first application was to Gibson, who then filled the see of London, before whom he laid a glowing account of the deplorable state of his college, and the urgent necessity for a Visitor. Gibson expressed indignation, but could promise no other assistance than his support at the council board, in case of a petition respectably signed. He suggested that the Bishop of Ely might act as Visitor under the statutes, leaving it to Bentley, if he pleased, to apply for a prohibition from the Courts at Westminster. But things were not in train for either of these courses. The indefatigable Colbatch next endeavoured to interest the Dean and Chapter of Westmin-

ster in the cause, by pointing out certain letters patent, giving a right
of preference to Westminster scholars in all elections, the provisions of
which had never been fully complied with, and were now utterly disregarded.   But this intrigue, which tended to turn Trinity into a close
college, came to nothing, except that it procured to the Rector of
Orwell the honour of having his health drank at the Westminster anniversary, in connection with "*restoration to Trinity College.*"   It cannot,
indeed, be supposed, that he had any object in the suggestion, but to
bring the college affairs under discussion, and in this he did not entirely
fail.   Legal authorities began to doubt the soundness of the opinion
given by Queen Anne's lawyers in 1712, which decided that the general
power of Visitation had been transferred to the crown by Queen Elizabeth's statutes.   In the latter part of 1727, a set of questions were proposed to five leading counsel, among whom was Sir Philip Yorke, the
Attorney-General.   All agreed that King Edward's statute *De Visitatore*, was still in force, that by its provisions, the Bishop of Ely was
entitled to hold a triennial Visitation, and that the 40th statute of
Queen Elizabeth was corroborative of the former.   While these points
were under consideration, the King, George the Second, paid a visit to
Cambridge, which was near proving fatal to Bentley.   The fatigue of
creating fifty-eight D.D.'s of royal appointment brought on a dangerous
fever ; but by the strength of his constitution, the medical skill of
Mead, and a few week's use of the Bath waters, he recovered.   This
was the last time that Cambridge has been honoured with the presence
of royalty, April 25, 1728.

   The right of the Bishop of Ely being now affirmed to the fullest
extent, it was determined once more to bring the Master of Trinity to
his trial.   Colbatch laboured with his usual perseverance to promote a
petition, but at first could only procure the support of three Fellows,
and those Juniors—Parne, Ingram, and Mason, the last a man celebrated
for uncouthness of manner, and mathematical proficiency ; these were
soon after joined by Johnson, a Fellow of higher standing, to whose
merits Bentley had been inattentive.

   In order to keep their proceedings secret, they held their meeting in
Dr. Colbatch's Rectory-house, at Orwell, which thence obtained the
name of *Rye House*.   But the plot was not long concealed from Bentley.
Knowing his own interest in high places, he determined to anticipate
the Fellows with a petition, in which he described their design as a conspiracy to deprive the crown of the Visitatorial right.   To this document, spite of the opposition and protests of Colbatch and his party,
who raised a tumult in the chancel, the college seal was affixed.   It was
presented to the King, at Hampton Court, by commissary Greaves, who

afterwards became Bentley's main legal adviser. The Fellows presented counter-petitions, and urged the Bishop of Ely to a visitation. The Bishop petitioned the Privy Council to be heard in support of the rights of his see. Bentley's counsel prayed for postponement, and so 1728 past away.

The commencement of 1729, brought forth a pamphlet from Bentley, and a reply from Colbatch. In March, the cause came to a hearing before the Privy Council, who determined that they could not advise the King to interfere in the matter, but that the Bishop was at liberty to act according to his own discretion. As soon as this decision was made, the complainants took steps to prosecute their charges. The state of Colbatch's health not allowing him to make any great exertion, it was arranged that Johnson should be the prosecutor or promoter. A new ally joined the malcontents in the person of Edward Smith, who, being a man of some property, undertook to bear a large portion of the expenses. For while the Master had all his costs allowed from the college stock, the prosecutors had to carry on the war at their own charge.

For several years, the cause made no real progress. The resources of Bentley, his knowledge of all the ambiguities, shifts, and defences of the law, and his expedients of procrastination, appeared to be endless. The narrative of these contests would furnish an admirable study for a young barrister, but cannot be sufficiently divested of technicalities to be generally interesting or even intelligible. We can therefore only give the main turns of the question in a sort of chronological abridgment.

1729. April 1. The articles of accusation, 64 in number, being drawn up in form, Bishop Greene cited the accused to appear and answer, at Ely house, on the 5th of May.

May 3rd. Bentley moved the Court of King's Bench for a prohibition, on the ground that by the 40th statute of Elizabeth, it was required that he be twice admonished by the Vice-master, before the Visitor was empowered to act. Could he have gained the sanction of the court to his interpretation, he had been safe, so long as he had the choice of the Vice-master in his own hands. May 7th, the court granted a rule for the Bishop to shew cause. May 12. The Bishop's counsel shewed cause, and the court decided, that the premonitions of the Vice-master and Seniors were only required in case of negligence or lighter delinquencies, and that the Bishop was at liberty to proceed as Visitor. The Bishop forthwith sent the accused a copy of the 64 articles. On the 10th of June, Bentley appeared at Ely house in a purple cloak, and objected, by his proctor, to the articles severally and generally ;—1st. That a great number of them were mere cases of negligence ; 2nd. That what was done by the Master and Seniority was the act of the college, and therefore not within the meaning of the 40th statute ; 3rd. That whatever passed previous to 1721, was included in the act of grace. All these objections were overruled by Bishop Greene.

Bentley's counsel advanced the same objections in the Court of King's Bench, as ground for a writ of prohibition. The court granted a rule to shew cause, and stayed proceedings. Trinity term passed away. The long vacation brought about an enforced truce ; and now we hear, for the last time, of Bentley's New Testament. It is supposed only to have waited for the collection of the Vatican and of the Dublin Greek MSS. The antiquity of the latter had been much exaggerated. But Michaelmas term came on with a rule made absolute, and discussions of counsel. The court remarked, (as well they might,) that no such cause had ever been tried before them, and declined to pronounce judgment till it had been argued by way of " declaration and answer." In 1729, it came to a close, and with it all rumour of the projected New Testament. It might have been pleasant to read the annotations of the litigants of Trinity College, on the 6th chapter of the 1st to the Corinthians, 7th and 8th verses.

1730 passed like its predecessor. The Bishop sued for a writ of consultation : Bentley, after delaying as long as he could, put in his replication, which was " immaterial." The Bishop demurred : Bentley, who, in this process, was plaintiff, was forced to " join in demurrer ; " but by neglecting to make up " the paper book," or copy of proceedings, and then objecting to the defendant's doing it for him, he protracted the business to the end of Trinity Term, and so another legal year passed away. During these proceedings, a report was rife that Bentley was about to be removed to the Deanery of Lincoln, which much alarmed his supporters at Cambridge, who might not have found their situation improved under a new regime. No wonder, then, that they exulted in the success of his dilatory tactics. On his return to Cambridge, they went forth to meet him at Bourn Bridge, and conducted him in triumph to his college, which was adorned for his reception as it had been for the entertainment of the Sovereign.

At the public commencement, the Doctor once more appeared as Divinity Professor, moderating and opposing the theological exercise in the new Senate House, then opened for the first time.

Without following the trial step by step through this and the following year, or detailing some arts of annoyance which the Master was able to practice upon his prosecutors in Cambridge, we will merely state, that, in Easter Term, 1731, the judges of the King's Bench, having overruled Bentley's three objections, overthrew the hopes of his opponents, by starting another of their own. This was, an inaccuracy in the Bishop's citation, which described him as " specially authorised and appointed Visitor," by the 40th statute of Queen Elizabeth, whereas he was only recognized in that capacity; and upon the strength of this flaw, the court determined to continue the prohibition. So ended this act of the forensic drama, the exhibition of which cost Colbatch and the other prosecutors £1000, besides their share of £1300 paid for the Master's expenses out of the college chest. It might be thought that they must have been heartily sick of law, and every thing connected with it: but no ;—either conscience, wrath, or shame, or perhaps the inveterate habit of litigation, which is as difficult to cure as any other sort of gaming, incited them to try one stake more. No doubt they received pecuniary aid from divers sources, though the particular sums or donors are not to be discovered. The court of King's Bench had acknowledged the validity of King Edward's statutes, and the general and absolute right of the Bishop of Ely to act as Visitor. There were hopes, therefore, of an immediate Visitation. Colbatch drew up a new set of articles, which he expected would avoid all cavils. Bentley, after some tampering with the Bishop, applied to the Attorney General for a fiat, prohibiting the Bishop's Visitation, on his old ground, that the crown only was Visitor. This was refused. The prosecutors, too impatient to await the natural removal of a Master now in his 70th year, resolved to appeal, by writ of error, to the House of Peers; and here, after long delays and warm debates, in which Bishop Sherlock took a decisive part against Bentley, the judgment of the court of King's Bench was reversed, by a majority of 28 Peers against 16, May 8th, 1732.

Still, the mode of proceeding was to be ordered. Each one of the 64 articles was discussed, and it was not till February, 1733, that it was finally arranged, that the Bishop should try the Master of Trinity on 20 out of the 64, which nevertheless included only eight really distinct heads of accusation:—1st, the Master's habitual absence from chapel, where he had scarce been seen, in the morning, for twenty years; and, during the last ten, almost as seldom in the afternoon:—2, his non-appointment of lecturers on the catechism:—4, using the college seal at meetings which did not consist of the statutable number of sixteen:—4, the sale of a piece of land belonging to the college in Kirby Kendal:—5, extravagance in building upon the Master's premises:—6, erecting a country house for himself at Over:—7, the wasteful extravagance of his household:—8, the bargain with Sergeant Miller. The consideration of these articles occupied the Bishop and his assessors

Y

from the 13th of June, 1733, to the 27th of April, 1734, when the Bishop solemnly declared, "that Dr. Richard Bentley was proved guilty, both of dilapidating the goods of his college, and violating its statutes, and had thereby incurred the penalty of deprivation appointed by those statutes: accordingly, he pronounced him to be deprived of the Mastership of Trinity College."

And now the world expected that Richard Bentley, in his seventy-third year, driven from the lodge which he had adorned, and from the walks which he had planted, must *peep about* to find himself a "dis-honourable grave." But the world was mistaken: he had still a strong hold and a stout garrison. An inadvertence, or perhaps a mere *lapsus plumæ*, in that same formidable 40th statute so often mentioned, enabled him to set Colbatch and the Bishop at defiance, and close his days in the scene of his warfare. The execution of the sentence of deprivation was by that statute committed to the Vice Master,—*sine mora per eundum Vice-Magistrum officio Magistri privetur.* Now, if the King, and not the Bishop, were *general* Visitor, the Bishop had no means of punishing the Vice-Master in case he should neglect this, or any other part of his duty. If, therefore, Bentley could but procure a Vice-Master who would neglect or refuse to expel him, he and the Vice-Master alike were secure from the Bishop's penal power. Baker, who, though untroubled with scruples, might not have deemed it prudent to resist episcopal authority, was no longer a Fellow, but reposed from his honourable labours, as incumbent of Dickleborough. Hacket was Vice Master, when Bishop Greene, having pronounced the sentence of deprivation, sent three copies thereof, one directed to Dr. Bentley, a second to be affixed to the college gates, and a third to Vice Master Hacket, with a mandate for its execution. Hacket, whose policy was delay, returned for answer, that he would take legal advice; probably purposing to take the largest bribe. But his time-serving allegiance was not what Bentley, in the present juncture, required. He could not long be induced to undergo the present frowns of Colbatch, and the far-off fulminations of the Visitor. He contentedly resigned his office at the Master's desire, and Richard Walker was appointed in his place, May 17, 1734. Walker would have dared or suffered any thing, rather than be the instrument of his sovereign's deposition; but he had a quiet plausible pretext for not undertaking so disagreeable a service: he was not, *idem* Vice-Magister,—not the *same* Vice-Master in whose term of office the sentence had been passed. This must appear to every one a mere quibble, but he who objects to quibbling in matters of statute, might as well object to homicide in warfare.

Had the Bishop acted upon King Edward's statutes (the validity of which had been affirmed by the highest judicial authority), as Visitor-General of Trinity College, there is little doubt but that he might have compelled the execution of his sentence, maugre the ingenuity of Bentley, and the repugnancy of Walker. But he seems to have been ill qualified to cope with such adversaries. He hesitated till the Parliament broke up. Application to the House of Lords, which, in maintaining his rights, would have asserted its own, became, for the present, impossible. Perhaps, after all, the prelate was satisfied with having done what *he* could call his best, and was not anxious to drive the famous old man from his home. There is something in dauntless perseverance, however exercised, that overawes the weak, and gains the respect of the noble. Yet, after an interval of months, in January, 1735, the Bishop did send his mandate to Dr. Walker, but Walker did not even acknowledge the receipt of it. Colbatch, as senior Fellow, called to enquire whether the Vice-Master had done his duty, but he could not extort a reply. The prosecutors, having learned from dire experience all that Westminster Hall would do for them, resolved, contrary to the *natural* and legal advice of counsel, to seek justice direct from the House of Peers. But whether from informality in the form of their petition, or disinclination on the part of their Lordships to meddle further, the debate ended with *leave* being given—that the petition be withdrawn. Before the next step could be determined on, a compromise took place between Bentley and several of the prosecutors, which left Colbatch to carry on the war, if he were so disposed, with his own resources. Smith was now his sole confederate: yet hostilities did not immediately cease. Three mandamuses were obtained against Walker, and all three quashed ; the last, on April 22d, 1738, few will care how, or why. It is probable that Colbatch would not yet have desisted, but a final close was put to the contest by the decease of Bishop Greene (May 28), who died like his predecessor, Moore (though after a much greater interval), without seeing his authority confirmed by the execution of his sentence. From this time Bentley, if not triumphant, was secure. And thus ended the *ten years'* war, which, like other wars, had been ruinously expensive, having cost the college, on the Master's account alone, nearly £4000, or double its annual income. How Colbatch and the other prosecutors stood it out, is hard to say ;—and still stranger, that the Master of Trinity, as Archdeacon of Ely, should have thought proper to sue the Rector of Orwell for three shillings and sixpence. Colbatch defended the suit, but lost, and consoled himself with writing a book to prove that he ought to have won. Dr. Monk has read it ! ! !

Having thus brought the history of our subject's litigations to an end, we must briefly mention that, during these latter years, he was engaged in two great works, one of which he never finished, and the other he had done well never to begin. These were his Homer, and his Paradise Lost. First, of the latter.

His design of restoring Milton originated in 1731, and was completed on the first day of the following year, and is said to have been suggested by Queen Caroline. He executed it with his usual reckless audacity, and not without a portion of his usual ingenuity. But between Bentley editing Horace, and Bentley editing Milton, there is a wide difference. Of ancient poetic genius he perhaps knew as little as of English,—as little as any body else; but of the Greek and Latin languages he knew more than all men of his time,—of the English language not much more than any tolerably educated woman. To English criticism, therefore, he brought his defects without his excellence. In commenting on the ancient classics, he brought so much collateral knowledge, and discovered so many acute analogies in defending his alterations, that his very errors were instructive. But for applying his *hook* to Milton he made no such amends. His acquaintance with early European literature was scanty; he was little, if at all, versed in modern foreign tongues. The romantic and allegorical compositions of the middle ages were out of his track of reading; nor was he deeply imbued with that Hebrew lore, through which Milton derived his highest inspirations. Of the Rabbinical writings he probably knew absolutely nothing. He was therefore incompetent to the task of illustrating Milton, and had no particular aptitude for correcting him. Yet his egregious failure in this instance ought not to detract from the fair fame he earned in provinces more peculiarly his own.

As no conceivable errors of hand or press could justify such deviations from an established text, as he was determined to venture upon, he protected his mutatious excisions and interpolations by the hypothesis of a reviser or amanuensis, who had availed himself of Milton's blindness to do, what Dr. Bentley was then doing, to make alterations, *ad libitum*, and to publish his own forgery as the genuine production of the poet. This critical fiction of Bentley's has excited more moral indignation than the case called for. No deception was produced, and none could have been intended. It was only an exorbitant piece of impudence.

As Homer was blind as well as Milton, the same sort of an editor would have served to screen whatever castigations, extrusions, or intrusions, the slashing critic thought necessary, in order to make the Iliad just what Homer ought to have made it. These would not have been a few, for he proposed to reject all lines that would not admit the Æolic Digamma

in every word where that "something greater yet that letter"* is ever to
be found. Had he lived to execute this purpose, he would doubtless have
displayed great learning, and no small absurdity. The hypothesis
seems to be utterly untenable. The pronunciation of language is in
continual flux, and at all times there are many words which are uttered,
or accented, according to the choice or judgment of individuals, after
an older or a newer fashion. Poets, (especially when and where there are
no critics,) will use either at discretion, as suits their metre, and often
avail themselves of both for the sake of variety. Yet Bentley considered
the revived Digamma, as the child of his old age; and in the brief
interval between the conclusion of his long struggle, and his death,
was fond of discussing the point with those young scholars who came to
visit him, as the patriarch of Helenic learning. But the publication of
the digammated Homer was prevented by a paralytic affection, which
seized the venerable scholar in the course of 1739, just after the appearance of his Manilius, a work of his earlier years; of this, and the
Lucan, which was first printed fourteen years after his death, at the
Strawberry-hill press, nothing need be said.

Thus have we brought the active life of Bentley to a conclusion.
We must be more brief than we could wish in pourtraying his familiar
history, though the picture is extremely pleasing.

In his domestic relations, Bentley was not only blameless, but exemplary; and domestic virtue always brings its own reward. Whatever
brawls disturbed him without, " he still had peace at home," nor did he
carry his despotic rule and contumelious language to his own fire side;
if he called his children names,—they were names of fondness. If he
erred, it was in too partial a regard to his kindred or dependents. For
forty years he was the affectionate husband of a virtuous wife, who
never had reason to complain that his controversies or his law-suits had
soured his temper. Mrs. Bentley was the mother of four children, of
whom one died in his infancy. Richard, the surviving son, discovered
such uncommon talents, that he was entered at Trinity College at ten
and made Fellow at fifteen. He was bred to no profession, and suffered
severely in after life from neglect of economy. Elizabeth, the eldest
daughter, married Mr. Humphrey Ridge, of Hampshire, and in less

---

* Of the Digamma nothing is settled, after all the learning that has been employed
about it, except that its form is that of a Roman F, though sometimes it rather
resembled G, and that it was either a W or a V, or something between both. It is
only found on some old marbles, and on coins of the Greek town of Velia, in Italy.
However pronounced it must have been an offence to the ear. The Greeks were
right in dropping it, and we are wrong in puzzling about it.

than a year, was a widow. Joanna, who married Mr. Dennison Cumberland, and became mother to Cumberland, the dramatist, was a beauty celebrated from her very infancy.* After Mrs. Bentley's death, both her daughters spent much time in the lodge, and supported by filial attentions, such as only a daughter can render, the declining years of their father, who spent the evening of his long and stormy day as peacefully as if all his life had been gentleness.

The author of the *West Indian* gives a most charming account of his grandfather in old age, though Bentley died when Cumberland was but ten years old. Between old age and childhood there is a strong and holy sympathy; nor is there the least reason to suspect Cumberland's picture of false colouring, because he is not always accurate in facts and dates.

The favourite companion of the great Critic, in his latter years, was the faithful Walker, with whom he used to smoke his pipe, (a habit he only indulged in after his seventieth year,) and discussed his port, a liquor for which he entertained an orthodox respect, while he expressed an anti-gallican contempt for claret, saying that *it would be port if it could.* He continued to the last to amuse himself with reading, occasionally shewing picture books to his grandchildren, never harshly correcting them when their noisy gambols interrupted his studies. Such at least are the reminiscences of his grandson, and it is good for the heart to believe them.

But we must hasten to a close. Bentley is said to have had a presentiment that he should reach his eightieth year, and not exceed it. "It was an age long enough," he would remark, "to read every thing worth reading."

Et tunc magna mei sub terris ibit Imago.

In January, 1742, he completed his eightieth year. In June he was well enough to preside at the examination for University scholarships; shortly after he was seized with a brain fever, and on the 14th of July, 1742, he expired. He was the first of Critics, and might have been among the first of men, if he could have endured contradiction.

---

* The pretty pastoral, published in the 8th volume of the Spectator,

> My time, Oh ye shepherds, was happily spent,
> When Phœbe went with me wherever I went,

is said to have been composed by Byrom, then a young B.A. of Trinity, in honour of *Jug* Bentley, (as Aristarchus used to call his darling child,) when she was but eleven years old. Some prudent mothers, and still more Aunts, will look grave at the publication of such a compliment to so very young a lady, but we never could learn that Miss Joanna was the worse for it.

THOMAS LORD FAIRFAX.

In narrating the lives of Lord Fairfax, and the famous Earl of Derby, we shall have occasion to redeem our pledges of strict political impartiality. Both fell on the same evil days—the same mighty interests agitated both, but they viewed them from different positions, or through the medium of different prejudices. They took opposite sides, and fought, it may be, with equal merit, but not with like success. Fame has reversed the judgment of Fortune, since Derby stands unchallenged in the first rank of the martyrs of loyalty, while Fairfax follows in the rear-guard of the confessors of republicanism. But which was in the *right*, or which least in the *wrong*, is a question for neither Fortune nor Fame to decide, nor shall we pronounce the verdict. It belongs to history, not to biography. We will endeavour to do justice to the acts of both, without approving or condemning the cause in which either acted.

Thomas Lord Fairfax was of an ancient and renowned family, long settled at Denton, in the parish of Otley, in Yorkshire. A military and a poetical spirit had characterised the house of Fairfax for many generations. Thomas Fairfax, great-grandfather to our present subject, engaged, after the manner of aspiring youth in that age, in the wars of Charles V. and Francis I., as a voluntary, and was with Bourbon at the sack of Rome, in 1527. In 1577, or 1579, he was knighted by Queen Elizabeth. His son Thomas received the same martial honour from the more appropriate hand of Henri IV., for his valour displayed before Rouen, in the English force sent to the assistance of the French Protestant cause; and afterwards signalized himself in the German wars against the house of Austria. He was the first Lord Fairfax of Cameron, and elder brother to Edward Fairfax, the translator of Tasso.* A third brother, Charles, was a Captain under Sir Francis

---

* Edward, second son of Sir Thomas Fairfax and Dorothy his wife, was born at Denton, but the year of his birth has not been ascertained; neither are we informed of the place of his education. That his youth was studious, appears by his early proficiency; and he continued all his days a man of books and of peace, living a country life, familiar with the beauties of nature, and devoting much time to the

Vere, at the battle of Newport, fought in 1600; and in the three years' siege of Ostend, commanded all the English in that town for some

culture of his children and nephews (the sons of the Lord Fairfax), who grew up under his tuition in all liberal and godly learning. Though possessed with that shy fantastic melancholy which some have deemed the proper complexion of poets, he kept old English hospitality, yet impaired not, but rather improved, his estate. And so, having attained a good old age in credit and good-will, he died in 1632, at his house called New-hall, in the parish of Fuyistone, between Denton and Knaresborough, happy in being spared the necessity of choosing a side in the sad contest that ensued.—*Chalmers' Bio. Dic. Vol. XIV.*

The translation of Tasso's Jerusalem, by which alone he is remembered, was the work of his youth, and was dedicated to Queen Elizabeth. So long as the Italian models continued in vogue, and the rich, various, long-drawn, linked sweetness of our early versification was understood and enjoyed, Fairfax's Tasso was read and admired, as a fair exotic transplanted by a skilful hand into a congenial soil. King James delighted in it (and the King's prerogative then extended over the realms of the Muses), and it solaced the prison hours of Charles 1st, to whom it must have been strangely fascinating, since the name of Fairfax could not hinder him from loving it. Waller acknowledged himself indebted to the English Tasso for the melody of his own numbers; and Dryden mentions Fairfax as coæqal with Spenser. Even under the detestable tyranny of French criticism, when it became fashionable to talk of the Elizabethan writers as rude stammerers in an unpolished language and unmanageable metres, the wits of the new school allowed him such modicums of praise as they were wont to accord to the poets of better times; always, however, objecting to his stanza, the *ottava rima*, as unfitted to the English tongue. In fact, their ears, accustomed to the narrow compass, quick recurring rhimes, and balanced structure of the couplet, were incapable of perceiving a prolonged and suspended harmony. The present race of critics have a much juster sense of poetic music; and though it is unlikely that Fairfax will ever again be generally read, he is no longer liable to be insulted by invidious comparisons of his stanzas with the couplets of a Mr. Hoole, of the India House, who *traduced* (to borrow an expressive French phrase) Tasso and Ariosto in the English heroic verse. Fairfax was, it must be confessed, an unfaithful translator, who, if he sometimes expanded the germ of his author to a bright, consummate flower, just as often spoiled what he was trying to improve. Besides his version of the "Jerusalem Delivered," he wrote the "History of Edward the Black Prince," and Eclogues, composed in the first year of James 1st, said by his son to be so learned, that no man's reading but his own was sufficient to explain the allusions in them. This filial praise does not promise much poetry. Probably the Eclogues are "allegorical pastorals." Now, as pastoral, *per se*, is the silliest of all compositions, so, with due deference to Mantuan and Spenser, the allegorical is the absurdest of all pastorals. Still, they must be curious; and it is to be regretted that, excepting the fourth, which appeared in Mrs. Cooper's "Muses Library," 1737, they have never been printed.

Collins says of Edward Fairfax, that "himself believed the wonders that he sung." There is more truth in this than might be wished. He was so much affected with the superstitions of his age, as to fancy his children bewitched, and that on so very weak grounds, that the poor wretches whom he prosecuted for this impossible crime were actually acquitted. Yet even the verdict of a jury, little disposed as juries then

time before it surrendered. In this service he received a severe wound in the face from a splinter of a French Marshal's skull. He was slain in 1604.

Sir Thomas Fairfax, brother of the poet, created, A.D. 1627, Baron Fairfax, of Cameron, in the Kingdom of Scotland, married Helen, daughter of Robert Ask, Esq., and by her left two daughters and five sons, of whom the eldest, Ferdinando, succeeded to the title, and, by Mary, daughter of Edmund Sheffield, Earl of Mulgrave, was father to Thomas, afterwards third Lord Fairfax, the Parliamentary general.

Heralds, who amid the darkness of unrecorded antiquity, seldom miss of finding what they seek, have stretched the Fairfax pedigree beyond the Ultima Thule of the Norman Conquest. Francis Nichols, in his " British Compendium," asserts that the original seat of the family was at Towcester, in Northumberland, whence they removed into Yorkshire. Certainly the name signifying, *fair-locks*, (*Sax.* Feax Hair,) indicates a Saxon derivation, though quaintly Latinized in their motto *Fare, Fac, Say Do*, after the fashion of *canting heraldry*. But the more credible account of Whitelock ascribes the first elevation of the house to the law ; though its martial and poetical propensities plead strongly for the Heralds.

Thomas, afterwards Lord Fairfax, was born at the family seat of Denton, January, 1611. We have no information concerning his childhood, nor the place of his school education ; but, as his father was a zealous Puritan and disciplinarian, and his own character was stern and unbending, we may conclude that the rod was not spared. He studied

---

were, (or dared be,) to favour witches, does not seem to have disabused his senses, for he left behind, in manuscript, " Dæmonologia : a discourse of Witchcraft, as it was acted in the family of Mr. Edward Fairfax, of Fuyistone, in the County of York, in the year 1621." This has never been printed. A copy was in possession of the late Isaac Reed, Esq. As an important document in the history of human nature, it ought assuredly to be given to the world. It must be remembered that Fairfax in this instance only coincided with the spirit of his age, and bowed to the wisdom of his ancestors. To have doubted of the existence of witches, would then have exposed him to the imputation of atheism ; and as certain disorders were uniformly attributed to diabolical agency, an anxious parent might be excused for mistaking the symptoms in his own offspring. We need not doubt that he spoke sincerely, when he said, in this very treatise, " For myself, I am in religion neither a fantastic Puritan, nor a superstitious Papist ; but so settled in conscience, that I have the sure ground of God's Word to warrant all I believe, and the commendable ordinances of our English church to approve all I practice ; in which course I live a faithful Christian and an obedient subject, and so teach my family."

We trust that none will object to these notices of a poet, who, though too little known to be the subject of a separate article, is nevertheless, one of the *Yorkshire Worthies.*

z

sometime at St. John's College, Cambridge, to which he was afterwards
a benefactor, and acquired a love of learning which never forsook him,
and made him, in some of the darkest passages of the civil war, an
intercessor for learned books and learned men. He is said to have been
deeply versed in the history and antiquities of England, a line of study
which for the most part disposes the mind to an almost superstitious
reverence for royalty. On Fairfax it does not seem immediately to
have taken this effect, though perhaps it had its weight before the close
of his career.

The long peace, which James the First so prided himself in preserving, was unable to extinguish the warlike quality of English blood.
The noble youth sought action in foreign campaigns; and many of
lower grade, or desperate fortunes, adventurers who had spent all,
" younger sons of younger brothers, and the like," "cankers of a calm
world," adopted, in countries not their own, the mercenary trade of war,
which perhaps after all, is neither more sinful nor less honourable, than
the gentlemanly profession of arms. At least it has as much of " the dignity of danger." But it is a great neglect in the policy of any state to
suffer its subjects, at their own discretion, to adopt a foreign service;
and a great error in a monarch, to keep his dominions so long in peace,
that the art military is forgotten, and the military habits of unconditional obedience, and undeliberative execution become obsolete. " No
Bishop, no King," was the favourite maxim of the *Rex Pacificus*. " No
Soldier no King," is the doctrine of historic experience. Monarchy, at
least the feudal monarchy, established on the downfall of the Roman
Empire, is an institution essentially military. A crown is a bauble
without a helmet; the true sceptre is the sword. Under the feudal
system, the whole constitution of society was military; all rank
was military; to bear arms was the distinction of free-birth, to be a
*lay*man of peace, was to be a churl, a knave, a villain, a slave.

While this system continued in vigour, the pride of heraldry retained
a meaning, and the throne was respected as the fountain of honour even
when the king was persecuted, deposed, or assassinated. But when the
constitution of general society grew pacific, it became necessary that
the power of the sword should centre in permanent bodies, more immediately devoted to the sovereign, wherein by an obvious and intelligible
necessity the monarchical principle is preserved untainted, and which
may supply at once a safe channel for the ambition of enterprising youth,
and a regular occupation for those unruly natures among the commonalty, for whom the ordinary restraints of civil life are as insufficient, as
the engagements of humble industry are irksome, those choice spirits,
in a word, that would rather fight than work. The policy, perhaps the

religion of the First James, (for there appears no good ground for suspecting him of disgraceful cowardice, and the strongest reason for believing, that amid all his strange vanity and vicious infatuations, he still retained a conscience,) made him averse to war : the interests of the nation, (considered as distinct from those of the monarch,) allowed and required peace, and the learned King fondly imagined that by maintaining the monarchical principle in the church, he was raising around the throne a host of bloodless champions, who would secure the allegiance of the nation by all the fears of eternal punishment ; not considering that, while he bound the Hierarchy to himself, he was setting them at an incommunicable distance from the people, and leaving a gap, for the disaffected, who were sure to make a dangerous use of the favour and attention which the multitude always bestow on those who persuade them that they are not taught or governed as they should be. He found the church divided into two parties, and thought by his regal authority, to give the victory to the anti-popular side. Thus he hastened the schism which might yet have been prevented ; arrayed all the discontent of the country against the doctrines which he patronized, gave to the demagogue preachers the *speciem libertatis*, the shew of freedom and the glory of daring, and brought upon the court ecclesiastics the odium of flatterers and self-seekers. The best arguments of the Arminians and Prelatists were disregarded, because they had too visible an interest in their tenets, while the wildest declamation of the Puritans passed for Gospel, because they declaimed at the risk of their ears.

Meanwhile the youth and valour of the kingdom engaged as volunteers in the contests of Holland, France, and Germany were imbibing principles, and acquiring habits, by no means favourable to the state of things which the King was desirous to establish and uphold. Even the few expeditions undertaken by command, or with the countenance of the state, were all in behalf of revolted nations ; and the assistance afforded to the United Provinces, to the French Hugonots, and to the German Protestants, was a practical acknowledgment of the right of resistance. The alliance of France with the insurgent Americans contributed not more to the French revolution, than the alliance of England with the continental Protestants to the temporary suspension of English monarchy. The Dutch, adopting a republican government, consistently adopted a presbyterian church ; and though the German Lutherans retained the name of Episcopacy, the Lutheran Bishop fell so far short of the wealth, pomp, aristocratic rank, and apostolical pretensions of the English prelate, as to bear a much nearer resemblance to the plain, if not humble Presbyter. There were no doubt very good and sufficient reasons for the difference, but they are not reasons likely to occur to a young man, whose slender stock of theology was derived from Scripture and his own unlearned judgment, not perhaps wholly unbiased by that love of novelty, which is as endemic a disease of youth as poetry or love. And the hot-blooded gallants, *who cared for none of these things*, at all events lost some of their attachment to ancient custom ; the line of their associations was broken ; if on their return, they proved ever so loyal, they were lawless in their loyalty : and under all suppositions, they had been habituated to separate the idea of military from that of civil obedience ; to obey, where they owed not a subject's allegiance, and to command, without their sovereign's commission.

Thus the country was stocked with soldiers of fortune, whose knowledge of the technicals of war, though perhaps not very profound, or extensive, was formidable to a government, which, busying itself with matters far better left to the decision of public opinion, had neglected to maintain that military strength and science, without which, no regal government can be secure.

We have hazarded these observations, not with an intent of entering into the causes, or detailing the progress of that civil war in which our subject bore so conspicuous a part, but because these circumstances belong as it were to the education of young Fairfax's mind ; and because the operation of foreign service upon the martial spirit of the gentry has not been sufficiently taken into the account by those who have treated of this extraordinary period.

Fairfax inherited the warlike tendencies of his ancestors, sought for opportunities of distinction as a volunteer in Holland, under the command of Horatio Lord Vere,* with whom also the Earl of Essex, and other of the Parliamentary chieftains, were instructed in martial affairs. It was probably during his campaigns, that Fairfax became acquainted with his future wife, Anne, fourth daughter of the Lord Vere, who was educated in Holland, and there contracted religious sentiments which made her have *"less veneration for the church of England than she ought to have had."* It is supposed that her zeal for the Presbyterian cause had great influence on her husband's subsequent conduct. Perhaps she told him when to stop, but not till too late. Returning to England in 1634, or 1635, he married, and retired to his father's seat in Yorkshire. And

* This Horatio was fourth son of John de Vere, fifteenth Earl of Oxford, of that family; and by King Charles I., Anno 1625, was advanced to the title of Lord Vere, of Tilbury. He long served in Holland, with great valour and reputation, jointly with his brother, the brave Sir Francis Vere, governor of the Briel. In 1620, Sir Horatio commanded the expedition sent to the assistance of the Elector Palatine. It was about 1632 or 1633, that Fairfax served under him, and was at the taking of Bois le Duc from the Spaniards." *Kippis.*

from this time we hear little of him, till the breaking out of the war in 1642. With a wife who had learned her religion and politics in the Dutch Republic, and a father "actively and zealously disaffected to the King," he did not long hesitate in choosing his side, but gave the benefit of his valour, which was great, and of his military experience, which was enough to be terrible to commanders who had none, to that Parliament who were looked upon by their adherents, not only as the trustees of civil liberty, and champions of Christian discipline, but as *bona fide* the only legitimate government remaining. For strange as it may now appear, there can be little doubt, that thousands believed that the King was absolutely a captive in the hands of the malignants, deluded and overruled, and that the Parliament army was raised as much for his rescue and protection, as for the defence of the country against the traiterous attempts of courtiers and Irish Papists. We know not whether Fairfax actually partook of these imaginations, or whether he persuaded himself that he was justified in vindicating the office of the King (the King which can do no wrong, and which never dies) against the mortal and fallible representative of that office, (a supposition in which there is no *logical* absurdity, though in the use made of it by the revolted Parliament, there was a very gross dishonesty). If we may believe himself, he never was an enemy to monarchy in the abstract: indeed, he was too much a mere man of action; he possessed not the requisite boldness and subtlety of intellect to be a true republican. He was more likely, as a porer over old records and chronicles, to be misled by false precedents, such as the compulsory obtaining of Magna Charta, and other like securities, from the Plantagenets, the Parliamentary deposition of Edward II. and Richard II., the transfer of the crown to the House of Lancaster (which, if it had been a legal act, would certainly imply a supremacy of the national council over the regal authority), or by the false analogy of the Princes of Germany in his own time, at war with their liege Lord the Emperor, than by theories or first principles. He was not one, like Milton, to dive into the depths of his own nature, for the model of a perfect commonwealth. But many an honest dull man has lost the guidance of his common sense by reading History. The examples of the past seem to be intended for beacons; but too often, like the fallen Pharos of Alexandria, they lie under water, and those who peer out for their light are wrecked upon their ruins, for want of knowing that the course of the stream is changed. Of all politicians, the most erring are those who rely solely upon the instructions of the past.

That Fairfax erred in judgment (unless he designed the abolition of monarchy from the beginning) none will deny. The event proved it.

Yet the King's conduct had given plausible ground for believing that the levying of forces by the Parliament was a purely defensive measure. While we fully acquit him of all guilty share in the atrocities of the Irish massacre, it is by no means certain that the rebels were not persuaded that they were acting with his approbation. As he was continually accused of *Popery* by his enemies, it is probable that his friends of the old church readily believed what they wished to be true, especially as the Queen's attachment to the Catholic priesthood was as notorious and ostentatious as her power over her husband.* Of the persons who enjoyed the most of the King's countenance and conversa-

* This beautiful and unwise lady, whose best apologist is Vandyke (for the painter will not let you think ill of her), was no example of the prudent management recommended by Pope, in his character of the good woman :—

"She who ne'er answers till a husband cools,
And if she rules him, never shows she rules."

She was not content with governing unless all the world knew that she governed, and in this weakness the King too fondly indulged her. "The King's affection to the Queen was of a very extraordinary alloy,—a composition of conscience, and love, and generosity, and *gratitude* (qr.), and all those noble affections which raise the passion to the greatest height; insomuch that he saw with her eyes, and determined by her judgment, and did not only pay her this adoration, but desired that all men should know that he was swayed by her, which was not good for either of them.— *Clarendon.*

Charles and Henrietta exhibited the singular spectacle of a young couple quarrelling in the honey-moon, making it up, and conceiving in wedlock a passion romantic and violent as first love. Partly owing to the machinations of her French attendants (the priests especially), and partly to the ill offices of Buckingham, she was provoked on her first arrival to a degree of sullenness which obliged the King to use her with something like peremptory harshness; but after her French followers were sent back, and Buckingham removed by assassination, he thought he could not make her sufficient amends, and allowed her a dominion over himself and his affairs which she too often exerted more like an artful mistress than a dutiful wife. That she should love sway was natural; but that, as Clarendon says, "she did not more desire to be possessed of this unlimited power, that all the world should take notice that she was the entire mistress of it, was foolish." When she departed for France for the last time before her consort's death, she exacted two promises of him;—one, that he would receive no person into his favour who had at any time injured him, without her consent; the other, that he would make no peace with the rebels but through her interposition and mediation, that the kingdom might know the share she had in procuring it---*Lodge.*

It is well known that Henrietta exerted her influence to raise supplies from the English Catholics, for the royal cause. She probably injured the King's interest more than she strengthened it by this means. It would perhaps have been wise to decline the money or service of a Catholic, if freely offered; for whatever might be the case with a few sincere republicans, and a greater number of factious malcontents, it was fear for the Protestant religion that arrayed the nation against its sovereign.

tion, if there were some like Falkland, whose characters no ingenuity of malice can stain, there were others whom he would have done well to keep at a distance. Indeed he never seems to have recovered from the ill effects of his boyish affection for the romantic profligate Buckingham. Others, too, there were, like Laud, whom no virtue could in that age have saved from popular hatred ; for they were Bishops. At the instigation of these perhaps well-meaning churchmen, he had exercised certain severities upon the Puritans, too slight to overawe, but amply sufficient to provoke, which the more fearful and the more violent represented as the earnest of a sweeping persecution. He thought that after a few examples had been made of the most refractory, the rest of the people would be quietly preached and catechised into uniformity of religious profession ; a purpose which nothing but the slow operation of a Spanish Inquisition, or the exterminating sword of a Joshua ever can or will effect in the present state of the world. But his great and suicidal error was his authoritative interference with the Scotch churches. Had the Scotch had no religious scruple or prejudice, still their nationality would have forbad them to pray in words composed by English prelates. Thence arose the Covenant, the precedent of armed and successful resistance ; the necessity of a Parliament ; the exposure of Charles's want of military strength and art ; and, directly or indirectly, all the train of evils that ended in the overthrow of the church and monarchy.

We cannot find that Fairfax sat in any Parliament previous to the breaking out of the war. When the King, having refused to part with the command of the militia, retired northward, and, arriving at York, set about raising a guard for his person (following therein the example of the Commons), Fairfax appeared at the head of a multitude of 100,000, with a petition, praying, or more properly commanding, his Majesty to desist from raising an army against his people, and to return and hearken to his Parliament. The King attempted to decline receiving this remonstrance, but was overtaken and surrounded on Heyworth Moor, where Sir Thomas laid hold of the pommel of his saddle, and thrust the petition into his hand. This, it must be owned, was a strange way to persuade the King that guards were unnecessary to his safety.

It was in Yorkshire that the first demonstration of actual hostility took place. The body-guard, which Hume only estimates at 600 men, but which popular apprehension exaggerated to 3000, was alleged in proof of the traiterous designs of the malignants; and the insolent conduct of some common soldiers, which Charles did every thing in his power to suppress and punish, was related in evidence on the King's trial, to convict him of making war against his people. Charles arrived in York in March, 1642. On the 23d of April, 1643, the gates of Hull were shut against him. As this was naturally deemed an act of rebellion, Charles, attended by the flower of the Nobility, collected hastily what troops he could, and, after vainly attempting to buy off Sir John Hotham, made warlike demonstrations before that fortress. Sir John Hotham, though he rejected the violent measures proposed by his council of war, who advised that the royalists should be allowed to approach as if they were to be admitted into the garrison, and then cut off, resolved to hold out, and letting in the sea, laid the country for three miles round under water. The seige of Hull commenced on the 7th of July, and seems to have been raised about the 30th, when Charles returned to York. War being now inevitable, the Yorkshire gentry who were attached to the royal cause, wishing to remove the scene of action as far from their own estates as possible, prevailed on the King to march southward. Accordingly, after rejecting a proposal of the Commons, which amounted to little less than the abolition of of monarchy, and receiving a cargo of arms and ammunition, purchased by the Queen in Holland, he advanced to Nottingham, and there set up his standard, August 22.

By this time the Parliament had placed the command of the militia, and authority to raise forces in every county, in such hands as they esteemed trustworthy. The majority of the northern Peers were attached to the King's party, and probably Ferdinando Lord Fairfax was the most powerful adherent of the Parliament in those parts. Accordingly, he received their commission (still running in the King's name) to be General of the forces in the north, and his son, Sir Thomas, was appointed General of Horse under him.

We believe it was Marshall Scomberg who advised Bishop Burnet, in his history of his own times, to say as little as possible of fighting matters, lest he should expose his ignorance to the ridicule of military men. It was very good counsel, and we shall follow it in this and every other life where military transactions are to be related. Where any thing characteristic occurs,—any thing that denotes the intrepidity, perseverence, generosity, or sagacity of our subjects, in connection with their military employments, we shall set it in as clear a light as pos-sible; but in all that belongs to tactics we must be necessarily brief, and follow our guide's simplicity. Neither can we undertake to trace every movement of the forces under our General's command; for the purport and effect of these minute operations can only be estimated by an experienced eye, capable of representing to itself the relative position of all the numerous small bodies on both sides, whose stations dotted, and whose motions intersected the country, and even then, unless the nature of the ground were faithfully depicted, which cannot be done in words, no adequate judgment could be formed.

Lord Fairfax left behind him " Short Memorials," not intended for the public eye, but for the satisfaction of his own relations, which, nevertheless, were published in 1699, by Bryan Fairfax, Esq., to prevent a surreptitious edition. They are not particularly creditable to his talents as an autobiographer, being written in a heavy, ungainly style, and interspersed with religious phrases, which though characteristic of that age, when men sang hymns to jigs, and marched to battle to psalm tunes, sound strange to modern ears, amid a recital of blood and rapine. But Fairfax doubtless believed that he was wielding " the sword of the Lord and Gideon," and appears to have died in the same comfortable faith. Unfortunately, these memoirs contain no account of any thing previous to the commencement of the war ; beginning with a narrative of some petty actions in the autumn of 1642. His first exploit was driving a small detachment of royalists from Bradford to Leeds, whither in conjunction with captain Hotham, he marched a few days after, and compelled the enemy to retire upon York. In order to secure the West Riding, from whence the principal supplies were derived, he advanced to Tadcaster, with a design to guard the pass of Wetherby, which he maintained against an ineffectual attempt of Sir Thomas Glenham. Cavendish, Earl of Newcastle, and Clifford, of Cumberland, united their forces at York, to the number of 9000, and resolved to fall on Tadcaster, which fort being judged untenable, the Fairfax's, father and son, risked an engagement ; but, notwithstanding the advantage of ground, were worsted, after six hours hard fighting, and withdrew, in the night, to Selby. But the royalists always lost by want of discipline and vigilance what they gained by valour. Sir Thomas, three days after, by a night march, in the course of which he passed by several posts of the enemy, gained Bradford, and there intrenched himself. This was at the close of 1642, the first year of that memorable contest, which, though comparatively insignificant, as to the number of men engaged, the blood shed, and the martial deeds achieved, far exceeds all other civil wars, in the greatness of its moral interests and the noble qualities, both of head and heart, which it developed in all parties. We know not any portion of history which discloses so much of human nature, which detects so many of " the spirits that lie like truth," none from which rulers and subjects may derive so much wisdom, none which so emphatically asserts that " the wrath of man worketh not the righteousness of God."

In most of the conflicts which have divided nations against themselves, one side or other have been so wicked, or both so worthless, or

the points at issue so personal and valueless, that the recital of their
progress and results merely amuses by variety of incident, or disgusts
by sameness of depravity ; but in the principles and the fortunes of the
Cavaliers and the Roundheads, we still experience a real and vital con_
cern.   The warmth of passions, though abated, is not extinguished.
We feel as if our own liberty, our own allegiance, our own honour and
religion, were involved in the dispute.

At the opening of the year 1643, the King's affairs wore an aspect by
no means unpromising.   In the preceding summer, when he withdrew
from the Metropolis, and found the gates of his own *good* town of Hull
shut against him, he had neither ships nor men, nor money : every port
in the kingdom, Newcastle excepted, was in the hands of his enemies ;
the Lord Lieutenants, in whom the immediate power of raising troops
was vested, were all their creatures ; the power of the purse had been
taken from him, and though the law was really on his side, yet so com_
pletely was the administration of it intercepted by the Parliament, and
so skilfully had they turned the forms of law to their own purposes,
that simple persons were not quite sure whether it was not rebellion to
obey their sovereign.   And here we may be permitted to remark how
completely the unprovided condition in which Charles was found in this
extremity confutes the assertions and the fears of those who justified
their proceedings, upon rumours of armies, and martial preparations in
England and Ireland, while in truth the King's adherents had scarce a
weapon but the sword worn for fashion by their sides, or the antiquated
furniture of their ancestral armories.   That Charles *wished* to be free of
Parliamentary controul there can be no doubt, any profession of his own
notwithstanding ; for he was a man, a King, and a High_church_man ;
but that he was plotting to make himself absolute by force of arms,
there is no better proof than the reports of spies, the wild talk of a few
hot_brained drunken Cavaliers, and the apprehensions of some who had
indeed occasion to dread the exercise of his lawful prerogative.   To
these weak grounds of suspicion, we perhaps may add the secret insinu_
ations of foreign states, particularly France and Sweden, then respec_
tively governed by Richlieu and Oxenstierna, two of the *profoundest
politicians* that ever lived.

Thus destitute was Charles when he refused to resign to the Parlia_
ment his right in the militia " even for an hour."   The deep-headed
leaders of the *movement,* who were not frightened with their own noise,
anticipated no obstacle to their ambition, and thought, by forcing the
sovereign to a base submission, above all, by involving his name in their
purposed vengeance on his advisers, to deprive him at once of authority,
friends, honour, and reputation, and would then have been satisfied to

propitiate the *popular superstition* in favour of royalty, by-keeping him as a pensioned pageant, as helpless and as useful as the automaton idol of a pagan priesthood, that nods and shakes its head as the manager pulls the string, and seems to utter what the ventriloquist squeaks out of its mouth. But it was not so ordered. It was ordained that their victory should be purchased with much blood ; that the Constitution should rather suffer a stab, and suspended animation, from which its tenacious vitality soon recovered, than a shameful wound that would have emasculated and degraded its nature. The majority of the nobles, the country gentlemen, the agricultural population in those districts that were remote from the contagion of the metropolis, the episcopal clergy, and the Universities, together with the Catholics, and a pretty large minority of the mob, who loved bear-baiting and May games, and " cakes and ale," better than fasts and sermons, still clung to the King. The train-bands of some counties were raised for his service. The nobility armed their tenants and retainers, the gentry formed themselves into troops, the Prince of Orange induced experienced officers to take command of his levies, the colleges sent their plate to be coined for his use ; light vessels, freighted with arms and ammunition, purchased abroad by the Queen, running into the shallow creeks, where the Parliament's ships could not follow, landed and disposed of their cargoes much after the manner that contraband goods are run in our times. Charles soon found himself in a condition to face the army of Essex, whom the Parliament had appointed their General-in-Chief, swearing " to live and die with him." A slight skirmish near Worcester, and the indecisive battle of Edge-Hill, were followed by the advance of the royal army upon London. Banbury and Reading were taken ; Oxford joyfully received the host of the " Defender of the Faith." A treaty was proposed, and it is not improbable, that in the panic, reasonable terms might have been obtained. But while matters were in train for a conference, and the ruling party had prohibited their troops from acting on the offensive, a rash attack on the regiment stationed at Brentford, ascribed by the royalist historians to the unruly impetuosity of Prince Rupert, gave colour to a suspicion of treachery, and extinguished the last sparks of loyalty in the City, which had all along been the head quarters of disaffection. After this the King retired to Oxford, and a negociation actually commenced, which could have been only intended by each party to throw the guilt of blood on their antagonists ; for the conditions proposed by the Parliament were such as no one could expect a King, with a devoted and increasing army, to accept, nor could the King have expected that any better would be offered.* When once the sword is

* It was during this abortive negociation, that the Puritan Parliament first

drawn, in civil fight, it can never be sheathed, till it has fairly proved who is the strongest.

We cannot esteem these statements an irrelevant digression, because they help to shew the steps whereby men like Fairfax, who if bigotted, were not fanatical, and certainly not disposed to extremities, were led to wage war on the King, while they wished the conservation of the monarchy. First taking up arms to keep the peace, in the belief that the royal party were too weak to resist, they afterwards refused to lay them down, because the King was too formidable, and too much exasperated to be trusted.

The hostilities in Yorkshire never seem to have been suspended either by the winter or the negociations. It will be recollected that we left Sir Thomas intrenched at Bradford. According to his own account he had only three troops of horse, and about eight-hundred foot, but, upon summoning the country, he made up the latter twelve or thirteen hundred, " too many to lay idle, and too few to be on constant duty."

In a war of posts and parties, boldness and the first blow is more than half the battle. A hot engagement on the 23rd of January, made him master of Leeds, with all the stores and ammunition laid up there. Soon after he defeated Colonel Slingsby at Gisborough, and received in the name of the King and Parliament, the submission of Wakefield and Doncaster. All hopes of adjustment being over, Ferdinando Lord Fairfax, and his son, Sir Thomas Fairfax, were proclaimed traitors by the Earl of Newcastle, to whom the King had entrusted the command of the four northern counties, and who was, in return, proclaimed traitor by the Parliament. About the same time the Hothams, father and son, who had displayed the first overt act of opposition to the sovereign, deserted the Parliamentary cause. Though their defection was not yet

---

demanded, in express terms, the abolition of Episcopacy. This was clearly what neither they, had they been, which they were not, a legitimate representative Parliament, had any right to demand, nor Charles, had he been as absolute a monarch as he was accused of seeking to be, could have had any right to grant, as long as there was one congregation in the empire, who deemed Episcopacy essential to a Christian church, and therefore, in their view, essential to covenanted salvation. The people have, in these matters, no more just authority than the King, nor the King than the people, nor the gentry than the mob, nor the learned than the ignorant. No man, no community, has a right to deny to any portion of the community, what that portion esteem necessary to their eternal well-being. The state may determine the political rank and functions of religious ministers, and over church property it has the same prerogative, be it more or less, as over other property; for property, under whatever denomination, is of the things that be Cæsars. But over the religious character of ministers, the state has no lawful sway. It may deprive a Bishop of his barony, but not of his orders.

fully declared, they much inconvenienced the elder Fairfax by denial of succours, compelling him to retire from Selby towards Leeds. On his march he was intercepted by Newcastle, who lay with his army on Clifford-moor, whereupon he summoned his son to join him, with what forces he could raise, at Sherburn, to make good his retreat. After some inconsiderable operations at Tadcaster, Sir Thomas was twice defeated by the Lord Goring, at the head of twenty troops of horse and Dragoons, so mightily had the royal force increased. The first action was on Bramham-moor, the second on Seacroft-moor. After an embarrassed retreat, he reached Leeds, where his father had safely arrived an hour before him. Leeds and Bradford were then the only places of strength held by the Parliamentarians northward of Hull, which the Hothams were then plotting to deliver into the hands of the Royalists. Fairfax determined by a bold enterprize to revive the spirits of his party, then much dejected by the King's successes in the West.

He attacked and recovered Wakefield, captured the elder Goring, took 1400 prisoners, 80 officers, and a large store of ammunition. Thus encouraged, the father and son formed a junction, and resolved to engage the Earl of Newcastle, who was advancing to the siege of Bradford, though their united forces did not exceed 3000, while those of the Earl were 10,000, armed and appointed as nobly as the wealth and magnificence of Cavendish could afford, animated by his chivalric spirit, and directed by the experience of King, his Lieutenant, a veteran Scot, long practised in the continental wars. The result of this temerity was the defeat of Atherton Moor, June 30, 1643. Two thousand were slain or taken in the field, and two thousand more surrendered the next day. The situation of the Fairfaxes was now most perilous, and had the royalists known how to make use of their victory, the North might have been secured to the King, the communication between the Scotch and English rebels cut off, and perhaps the House of Stuart would still be reigning over the British Isles.

The elder Fairfax withdrew to Leeds on the night of the battle, having commanded his son to remain in Bradford with 800 foot and 60 horse, at a great strait, scarce knowing which way to turn, for there was no garrison to receive his scattered troops. Halifax and Beverley were evacuated, and Sir John Hotham had declared, that should he retreat towards Hull, the gates should be shut against him. But at this very juncture, the treason of the Hothams exploded. The son was seized in the town, and the father made his escape through a postern. One of the cannon which he had himself directed to oppose his sovereign's entrance, was discharged after him without effect. Attended with six guards only, he made for his house at Scorbro', near Beverley,

which he had secretly fortified and stored.   But meeting with unexpected obstacles, he turned his steps to Beverley, where Colonel
Boynton, his own nephew, was already apprised of his approach, and
ready to apprehend him.   So well had the Colonel kept his counsel,
that his troops knew not for what service they were called out, and
when Sir John, riding unawares into the town, found seven or eight
hundred armed men lining the street, he boldly put himself at their
head, and bad them follow him, and they, uninformed of his apostacy,
were about to obey, when his nephew laid hold of his bridle, and, with
suitable apologies, arrested him as a traitor to the Commonwealth.   He
and his son were sent to London, committed to the Tower, and, after a
considerable interval, executed on Tower-hill.   We cannot reckon this
among the crimes of the Parliament.   The son might well have been
spared, for his offence was filial obedience ; but the father was a double
traitor, and there is reason to think that his secession from the parliamentary interest was owing to envy at the higher promotion of
Fairfax, rather than to returning loyalty.

These events took place at the very time that the battle of Atherton
Moor was fighting, and the news arrived just in time to relieve the
Lord Ferdinando from his despondency.   Thus writes his son :——
" Whilst the Lord Fairfax was musing on these sad thoughts, a messenger was sent unto him from Hull, to let him know the townsmen
had secured the Governor ; that they were sensible of the danger he
was in, and if he had any occasion to make use of that place, he should
be very readily and gladly received there."

Meanwhile, Sir Thomas, with his little remnant, was surrounded in
Bradford by the vastly superior force of the royalists.   It was a woeful
time, when women and young children were fain to be dragged along
with flying or pursuing squadrons, feeling less horror amid shot, and
fire, and savage gashes, and "strange images of death," than in the desolation of their once happy homes, and silent expectation of all imaginable villanies.   The wife and children of Fairfax were at his side
when, with dauntless courage, and a religious confidence in his cause
which they who least approve his cause must admire, he determined to
cut his way through the enemy.   Of the peril and capture of his lady
he speaks feelingly in his memorials :——" I must not here forget my
wife, who ran the same hazard with us in this retreat, and with as
little expression of fear ; not from any zeal, or delight in the war, but
through a willing and patient suffering of this undesirable condition.

I sent two or three horsemen before, to discover what they could of
the enemy, who presently returned, and told us there was a guard of
horse close by us.   I, with some twelve more, charged them : Sir Henry

Fowles, Major General Gifford, myself, and three more, broke through. Captain Modd was slain, and the rest of our horse being close by, the enemy fell upon them and soon routed them, taking most of them prisoners, among whom was my wife, the officer, Will Hill, behind whom she rid, being taken. I saw this disaster, but could give no relief, for after I was got through, I was in the enemy's rear alone; those who had charged through with me went on to Leeds, thinking I had done so too, but I was unwilling to leave my company, and staid till I saw there was no more in my power to do, but to be taken prisoner with them."

Arriving at Leeds, he found all in great distraction: the council of war resolved to abandon that place and take refuge in Hull, which was full sixty miles distance, and several of the King's garrisons intervening. With singular skill or good fortune he thridded his way through the numerous detachments hovering round Leeds, and gained Selby in safety, intending to cross the ferry, and make for the parliamentary post at Cawood. But before he could accomplish this purpose, he was overtaken by a company of horse, and received a shot in the wrist, which made the bridle fall out of his hand, and occasioned so great a loss of blood, that he had like to have fainted. But overcoming nature by a strong effort of will, he siezed the reins in his sword hand, and withdrew from the meleé: his intrepidity gave resolution to his followers; the enemy, perhaps gladly, suffered a brave man of an ancient house to escape, and after a most harrassing march, attacked on every side, he arrived at Hull.—But we must give his own account of this adventure:—" I had been twenty hours on horseback after I was shot, and as many hours before: and as a further affliction, my daughter (afterwards Duchess of Buckingham), not above five years old, endured all this retreat a horseback, being carried before her maid; but nature not being able to hold out any longer, she fell into frequent swoonings, and in appearance was ready to expire her last. Having now passed the Trent, and seeing a house not far off, I sent her with her maid only thither, with little hopes of seeing her any more alive, though I intended the next day to send a ship from Hull for her. I went on to Barton, having sent before to have a ship ready against my coming thither. Here I lay down to take a little rest, if it were possible to find any in a body so full of pain, and a mind yet fuller of trouble and anxiety. Though I must acknowledge it as the infinite goodness of God, that my spirit was nothing at all discouraged from doing still that which I thought to be my duty. I had not rested a quarter of an hour before the enemy came close to the town. I had now not above a hundred horse with me: we went to the ship, where, under security of our

ordnance, we got all our men and horse aboard, and crossing Humber,
we arrived at Hull, our men faint and tired. I myself had lost all,
even to my shirt, for my clothes were made unfit to wear with rents
and blood. Presently after my coming to Hull, I sent a ship for my
daughter, who was brought the next day to the town, pretty well
recovered of her long and tedious journey. Not many days after, the
Earl of Newcastle sent my wife back in his coach, with some horse to
guard her; which generous act of his gained him more reputation than
he could have got by detaining a lady prisoner on such terms." There
is something amiable in this extract. It is pleasing to observe that
even civil war does not extinguish a parent's tenderness. Perhaps it
had been better for the poor little girl to have died then, than to have
lived to be the wife of Villiers. We like Fairfax, too, for calling his
wife by that plain, homely, kindly, *Christian* appellation. Nothing is
more heartless than to hear Sir, and Madam, and my Lord, and my
Lady, between husband and wife. Still more odious are such titles of
honour passing between parents and children.* The names of father,
mother, husband, wife, brother, sister, which the Almighty himself has
appointed, are far, far more venerable, as more holy, than any which
the feudal system has left behind. We do think, however, that Fairfax
should have acknowledged Newcastle's generosity with something more
than a flat truism.

Though the immediate danger was thus passed through, the situation of the Fairfaxes in Hull was extremely critical. The Parliament,
intent on watching the personal movements of the King, whom they
yet hoped to drive into a compromise which might amount to a virtual
surrender of sovereignty, seem hitherto to have neglected the support

---

* Let it not be supposed that we recommend the example of Philip Egalité, or
advocate a substitution, by Act of Parliament, of the titles Citoien, and Citoienne,
for *your Grace*, and *your Highness* Conventional forms of respect are useful enough
where there is no substance of natural duty, or heart-affection. Let them be observed
as rigidly as may be in the court, the ball-room, the quarter sessions, the formal
dinner party; but let them be expelled from the family fire-side. So far from being
actuated by any jacobinical or levelling principle, we are pleading in behalf of, and
in pure affection for, the Aristocracy, who are the only persons subject to these
restrictions, and in a much worse condition, in all that regards their in-door affections, than any part of society but the brutally oppressed and ignorant. It is related
of the Proud Duke of Somerset, that when his second Duchess tapped him fondly on
the shoulder with her fan, he turned round haughtily, and said, "Madam, my first
Lady was a Percy, and she never took such a liberty." In what a desart must that
man's heart have dwelt;—of how much innocent pleasure must he have deprived himself, without the benefits of religious mortification.

We have always had a good opinion of King James I. ever since we learned that he
used to call his son *Baby Charles.*

of their most faithful adherent in the north ; but now the Scotch were pressed to advance with 20,000 men, and the Earl of Manchester's army was directed to march northward. Fairfax, on his own part, was indefatigable in supplying his losses.—"Our first business," says he, "was to raise new forces, and in a short time we had about 1500 foot, and 700 horse. The town (Hull) being little, I was sent to Beverley with the horse, and 600 foot ; but my Lord of Newcastle now looking upon us as inconsiderable, was marched into Lincolnshire with his whole army, leaving some few garrisons. He took in Gainsborough and Lincoln, and intended to take in Bolton, which was the key of the associated counties ;* for his orders (which I have seen) were, to go into Essex, and block up London on that side. Having laid a great while still, and being now strong enough for those forces which remained in the country, we sent out a good party to make an attempt upon Stamford Bridge, near York But the enemy, upon the alarm, fled thither, which put them also in such fear, that they sent earnestly to my Lord of Newcastle, to desire him to return, or the country would again be lost. Upon this he returned again into Yorkshire, and not long after came to besiege Hull. I being at Beverley, in the way of his march, and finding we were not able to defend such an open place against an army, I desired orders from my father to retire back to Hull, but the committee there had more mind of raising money than to take care of the soldiers. And yet these men had the greatest share in command at this time, and would not let any orders be given for our retreat, nor was it fit for us to retreat without an order. The enemy marched with his whole army towards us : retreat we must not, keep the town we could not, so to make our retreat more honourable and useful, I drew out all the horse and dragoons towards the enemy, and stood drawn up by a wood side all that night. Next morning our scouts and theirs fired on one another. They marched on with their whole body, which was about 4000 horse and 12,000 foot. We stood still till they were come very near to us. I then drew off, having given

* The associated counties were Hertford, Essex, Cambridge, Huntingdon, Norfolk, Suffolk, and Lincoln. These were placed by the Parliament under the charge of Edward Montagu, second Earl of Manchester, better known as Lord Kimbolton, a man once the companion of Charles in his romantic visit to the Spanish Princess, but whom a Puritan wife in the first instance, and afterwards the imprudence of Charles, who selected him, out of all the disaffected of the Upper House, for impeachment along with Hampden, Pym, Hazlerig, Hollis, and Strode, on the memorable fourth of January, had made one of the most active partizans of Parliament. N. B. The title by which, during his father's life time, he was called to the House of Peers, was properly Baron Montagu, of Kimbolton, in the county of Huntingdon.

directions before for the foot to march away towards Hull, and thinking to make good the retreat with the horse. The enemy, with a good party, came up in our rear; the lanes being narrow, we made shift with them till we got into Beverley, and shut the gate, which we had scarce time to do, they being close to us." It is manifest, from these accounts, how little art there was on either party. Indeed the whole history of the civil war during the earlier campaigns, exhibits not only a deficiency of technical knowledge, which neither side had enjoyed the opportunity of acquiring, but a striking want of unity and co-operation in the general arrangements, which, considering the great talents engaged on each party, is rather to be wondered at. The republican armies, however, did acquire these things: the royalists, relying on their impetuous courage, never improved.

But to return. Fortune now smiled deceitful on the King's affairs. Newcastle returned rapidly from his successful incursion into Lincolnshire, and on the 28th of August, Beverley was carried, after a stout and bloody defence. Fairfax and the wreck of his troops, overpowered by numbers, were driven to the very gates of Hull. The plunder of Beverley is said to have amounted to £20,000, and the Earl (now Marquis) of Newcastle drove all the cattle from the fields in its vicinity to victual the garrison of York. It is hard to say what the necessities of war may not justify: but as the inhabitants of Beverley had been passive sufferers throughout the contest, and, according to Whitelock, even showed an inclination to the King's side, this rapine was at best a cruel necessity. The best excuse that can be offered for it is, that the Parliament having possessed themselves of all the regular sources of revenue, the royalists were obliged in some measure to make the war maintain itself.

On the second of September the Marquis of Newcastle sat down before Hull, now the only parliamentary garrison north of the Humber. The horse being worse than useless in the beleagured town, they were despatched under Fairfax's command into Lincolnshire, to join that army, nominally the Earl of Manchester's, but of which the directing spirit was Oliver Cromwell. Having effected a union, they attacked and defeated a body of 5000 royalists at Horncastle; while at the same time the besieged in Hull made a desperate sally, and repulsed the besiegers. In consequence of these mishaps, the Marquis hastily raised the siege of Hull; and that good town, which was strongly and sincerely attached to the Parliament, was not again assailed during the war. There were some thoughts of turning the church of Beverley into a royalist fortress, but this was abandoned, and the whole of that part of Yorkshire was freed.

The fighting season of 1643 was now drawing to a close. The royal cause had on the whole been eminently successful. The Queen, early in the year, had landed on the coast of Yorkshire, with arms and equipments for a considerable force; and having escaped the shot of four puritanical vessels which bombarded the house in which she lay all night, was conducted to York by the gallant Newcastle, whose attachment to her was so notorious, that his troops were scornfully called "the Queen's army," and "the Catholic army." Such was the unexhausted might and loyalty of the north, that although her influence was dreaded by the graver royalists, she quickly mustered thirty troops of horse, and 3000 infantry, at the head of which she rode as commander to join her royal husband at Oxford. Large reinforcements had been raised in Wales by the exertions of the Marquis of Hertford. The counties of Cornwall, Devonshire, and Somerset, were almost entirely the King's. Bristol had surrendered to Prince Rupert. The battles of Bradoc Down, Stratton, Lansdown, and Round-a-way Down, had been won by the chivalric valour of the royalist gentry; and though the siege of Gloucester was raised by the skilful advance of Essex, and the drawn battles of Chalgrave Field and Newbury were claimed by the opposite party, the honour, if not the advantage, rested equally upon the adherents of Charles. These victories, it must be remembered, were almost all achieved over superior numbers. The enthusiastic honour and high mettle of the Cavaliers out-dared the dogged resolution of the Puritans, among whom there had not yet arisen a leader to make profit of their zeal by partaking and inflaming it. Had the strange proposal of Essex, to trust the whole cause, after the analogy of the old judicial combats, to the decision of a single battle, been accepted, the champions of the crown and mitre would probably have prevailed. The Parliament still contained so much of the old leven, that it had intrusted all its armies to members of the aristocracy, and of these Fairfax alone seems to have combined with valour and military knowledge, a sincere, hearty, and conscientious devotion to the business.

But the royal fortunes had reached their highest ascension, and from this period began to decline. The Parliament applied to Scotland for succour, and it was given on condition that England should adopt the Presbyterian discipline, establish a uniformity of worship throughout the kingdoms, and take the solemn League and Covenant. With these conditions the Parliament complied; took the Covenant themselves, and enforced it as far as their influence extended. Fairfax took it, no doubt zealously, and observed it better than most of its subscribers. One of the articles, which provides for the inviolability of the King's person, though fearlessly broken by some, was a terror to others, who were more apprehensive of infringing the Covenant, than of shedding innocent blood.

Fairfax was next employed against a man whose Norman name has since contracted other associations than those of unsuccessful loyalty, the Lord Byron,* first of his ancient house that bore that title, who was then besieging Nantwich, in Cheshire, with an army of Irish. In the depth of a severe winter, Sir Thomas set forth from Lincolnshire, on the 29th of December, and marching across the island, was joined by Sir William Brereton ; on the 21st of January, the armies met near Nant. wich. Byron was routed with great loss. Of 3000 foot, which he commanded, more than 2000 were slain or captured. The horse, amounting to 1800, mostly escaped. Probably Fairfax was deficient in that branch of the service. The Parliament had voted that no quarter should be given to the Irish catholics in any engagement ; but it does not appear that Fairfax rigorously executed these orders. There can be little doubt, however, that the multitude of Irish, who began to join the royal standards after Charles had made truce with the rebels in Ireland, aggravated the miseries of the civil war, and tended fatally to exasperate the people against their sovereign. In this battle Monk, afterwards the restorer of monarchy, was taken prisoner; after being confined some time in the Tower, he entered the Parliament's service, was successfully employed in Ireland, and laid the foundation of that military reputation, which enabled him to perform so conspicuous a part in subsequent history.

In the middle of March, Fairfax, in obedience to his father's orders, marched back into Yorkshire. The father and son united their forces at Ferrybridge, and on the 11th of April, 1644, they defeated, at Selby, Colonel Bellasis, the royalist governor of York, who had advanced to prevent their junction. The Lord Ferdinando, by a circuitous march, arrived just in time to support Sir Thomas. The attack was made in three divisions; the first led by the elder Fairfax, the second by Sir John Meldrum, and the third by Colonel Bright. Young Fairfax commanded the horse. The battle was obstinately disputed till our Fairfax, with the cavalry, forced a passage into the town and routed his

---

* " In the year 1643, Sir John Byron, great grandson of him who succeeded to the rich domains of Newstead, was created Baron Byron, of Rochdale, in the County of Lancaster: and seldom has a title been bestowed for such high and honourable ser vices as those by which this nobleman deserved the gratitude of his royal master. Through every page of the history of the civil wars, we trace his name in connection with the varying fortunes of the King, and find him faithful, persevering, and disin. terested to the last."—MOORE'S BYRON.

No less than seven brothers of the name of Byron fought at Edge-hill.

antagonists. This victory made him once more master of the midland parts of Yorkshire, and he now, by order of his masters at Westminster, prepared to march into Northumberland, to support the Scotch army, which to the number of 20,000, under the command of Lord Leven, after vainly summoning the town of Newcastle, then commanded by Sir Thomas Glenham, passed the Tyne on the 22nd February, and faced, without venturing to attack, the Marquis's army. Harassed by continual skirmishes, pinched by the severity of the weather, and almost destitute of forage and provisions, these covenanted warriors, whether allies or invaders of England, were reduced to great extremities, and had they been left to their own resources, and the undivided power of Newcastle directed against them, the day of Neville's cross might have been emulated, perhaps on the same field.

But before either Fairfax could join his auxiliaries, or Newcastle bring them to an action, the clamorous solicitation of the city of York, which the defeat of Bellasis had left much exposed, induced the Marquis to fall back to its relief, and thus to leave the way clear for the Scots, at the very time when their necessities were about to force them either to fight or retire. They joined the Lord Fairfax, at Wetherby, on the 20th of April, and proceeded to besiege York, into which the royalists had betaken themselves. As the besieging forces were not sufficient for the regular investment of a place of such extent, divided by a river, and the art of attacking towns was then in a manner unknown to the British, no great progress or impression was made, but an irregular blockade was maintained, diversified with occasional assaults on the out-works. In one of these, Sir Thomas had an opportunity of rendering an important service to literature. St. Mary's Tower, wherein lay many foundation charters and other documents relating to the monasteries, in Yorkshire and other northern counties, accidentally blew up: the younger Fairfax, whose attachment to antiquities we have already had occasion to mention, preserved as many of them as he could, and liberally rewarded such soldiers as brought any of them to him. There he employed that painful antiquary Roger Dodsworth, to copy, allowing him an annuity of £40 for life, by which means they were saved from destruction, and make a part of the Monasticon Anglicanum.

While the siege, or rather blockade, of York was in hand, some flattering advantages had befallen the royal side ; and, in particular, Rupert, who was for carrying all by dint of valour, and for this knightly temper, added to the tie of blood, was much more trusted by the King than his haste and inexperience made prudent, had by a sudden movement relieved Newark, and defeated a considerable force before that town. His very rashness, in this enterprize, stood him in good

stead. " He undertook it," says Lord Clarendon, " before he was ready
for it, and so performed it." Advancing with his horse only, and out-
stripping his infantry by four miles, he encountered and dispersed
a numerous advanced guard of the enemies' cavalry, and then in the
strength and ardour of success, fell upon the main line, and gained
a more decided victory than any which the war had yet produced.
Then marching through Lancashire, he captured several posts of the
Parliamentarians by the way, raised the siege of Latham House, (of
which we shall have to speak in the next life,) and so penetrated into
Yorkshire. Sir Thomas Fairfax and Major-general Desley, with 6000
horse and dragoons, and 5000 foot, marched out to intercept his progress,
but he evaded them by fetching a compass with his army, and joined
the Marquis of Newcastle.

The forces of Leven and Fairfax, now united with the Earl of Manchester's army, of which Cromwell was Major-general, immediately
broke up the siege, which they were beginning to press with vigour,
and withdrew to Hessey-moor. A council of war was held, in which
there arose a difference of opinion between the two nations. The Scotch
were for retreating, the English for fighting. The former prevailed,
and they fell back to Tadcaster. Great jealousies and strong national
antipathies prevailed ; which if the royalists had possessed but a little
patience, might have terminated in a decided rupture. The Marquis
of Newcastle counselled delay ; but the unmanageable Prince Rupert
would scarce listen to his advice. By a weakness, perhaps deserving of
a harsher name, the King had given his hot-headed cousin, (who was
alike unskilled to command and repugnant to obey, and fitter for a night
attack or marauding excursion, than for the arrangement and execution
of combined and extensive operations,) precedence in command of the
noble Newcastle, who had served him so wisely, so bravely, and so successfully, in a manner at his own private cost. But the Prince had
some private pique against the Marquis, who, on his part, was not fully
satisfied with the treatment of the court, and was only waiting for a
season when he might retire with honour. Prince Rupert, pretending,
perhaps truly, the peremptory commands of the King, drew almost the
whole garrison from York, leaving only a handful of men with Sir Thomas Glenham, and sought the allied armies of the rebels, who were
arrayed on Marston-moor, eight miles from the ancient city, so that the
report of the cannon, and the contradictory rumours, ever and anon
arriving, must have kept its inhabitants in restless agony. For many a
dear life was that day at deadly hazard, many a wife knew not if she
were a widow, and many a venerable man, who had grown old in the
service of that beautiful Minster, muttered with trembling affection the

petitions of the Liturgy, which a near and mighty foe had sworn to efface, even with blood. With what strange, what conflicting prayers, was Heaven besieged that day.

Fifty thousand subjects of one king stood face to face on Marston Moor. The numbers on each side were not far unequal, but never were two hosts speaking one language of more dissimilar aspects. The Cavaliers, flushed with recent victory, identifying their quarrel with their honour and their love, their loose locks escaping beneath their plumed helmets, glittering in all the martial pride which makes the battle day like a pageant or a festival, and prancing forth with all the grace of gentle blood, as they would make a jest of death, while the spirit-rousing strains of the trumpets made their blood dance, and their steeds prick up their ears : the Roundheads, arranged in thick dark masses, their steel caps and high crown hats drawn close over their brows, looking determination, expressing with furrowed foreheads and hard-closed lips the inly-working rage which was blown up to furnace heat by the extempore effusions of their preachers, and found vent in the terrible denunciations of the Hebrew psalms and prophecies. The arms of each party were adapted to the nature of their courage : the swords, pikes, and pistols of the royalists, light and bright, were suited for swift onset and ready use ; while the ponderous basket-hilted blades, long halberts, and heavy fire-arms of the parliamentarians were equally suited to resist a sharp attack, and to do execution upon a broken enemy. The royalists regarded their adversaries with that scorn which the gay and high-born always feel or affect for the precise and sour-mannered : the soldiers of the covenant looked on their enemies as the enemies of Israel, and considered themselves as the elect and chosen people,—a creed which extinguished fear and remorse together. It would be hard to say whether there were more praying on one side or swearing on the other, or which, to a truly Christian ear, had been the most offensive. Yet both esteemed themselves the champions of the church, there was bravery and virtue in both ; but with this high advantage on the parliamentary side, that while the aristocratic honour of the royalists could only inspire a certain number of *gentlemen*, and separated the patrician from the plebeian soldier, the religious zeal of the Puritans bound officer and man, general and pioneer, together, in a fierce and resolute sympathy, and made equality itself an argument for subordination. The captain prayed at the head of his company, and the general's oration was a sermon.

In the morning of the second of July the battle commenced. The charge was sounded, and Prince Rupert with his gallant cavalry dashed in upon the Scots, who quickly took to flight, perhaps sincerely, but had their running away been a concerted manœuvre it could not have answered better, for by this means the right wing of the royalists, with Rupert, was drawn away in the pursuit of the runaways, and left the main body exposed to the steady disciplined troops of Manchester and Cromwell. The royalists never seem to have learned, till too late, that a pitched battle is not a hunting day. Advancing to the charge with the same light hearts, and pursuing their game with as little consideraration, as if the business were a chace, in which the danger only went to enhance the pleasure, they were no match for serious fighters like Oliver and Fairfax. The centre of the King's army was left with its right flank unguarded, to oppose the individual valour of the men who composed it, to the combined strength of a multitude, made one by "a discipline the rule whereof was passion."* The republicans (for such the troops of Cromwell were then become) withstood the onset of the royalists like a rock, and rolled back upon them like a rock tumbled from its basis by an earthquake. The horse, commanded by the quick-witted dissolute Goring, wheeled round to meet the returning squadrons of Rupert; the infantry fled fighting, and fought flying. The Marquis of Newcastle alone, with his own regiment, composed of his old tenants and domestic retainers, would not give an inch. Newcastle's infantry were slain almost to a man, and their corpses lay side by side, an unbroken line of honourable dead.

Meanwhile Sir Thomas Fairfax, who, with Lambert, commanded in the left, committed an error similar to that of Prince Rupert. With that impetuosity which came upon him always in the field, and was so strongly contrasted with the saturnine gravity of his habitual character, he broke the line of the royalists, and unwarily separating himself and his immediate followers from the main body, joined the victorious centre in the pursuit of the fugitives. Lucas, the King's leader in that quarter, closed his ranks, and made so fierce a charge on the parliamentarian cavalry, that it was driven back on the infantry, and the whole wing put to rout. Thus in this battle there had been three separate engagements, in two of which the royalists had prevailed. Each party now thought itself secure of victory, when Cromwell returned from the pursuit, and the contest was renewed with redoubled obstinacy, each party occupying the ground where its adversary stood in the morning. But the sword of Cromwell was cast into the balance, and all the valour of the royalists was outweighed. After a bloody and terrible conflict, the royal army was pushed rather than driven off the field, and all the artillery, baggage, and other material fell into the victor's hands. Rupert and Goring retreated rapidly through Lancashire. The Mar-

* Lord Brook.

quis of Newcastle, weary of a charge which little suited his elegant and studious habits, and long since mortified by the malign influences which made Charles most suspicious of his best friends, set sail for Hamburgh, with King and other of his followers, and continued abroad till the Restoration.* His noble estates were sequestrated by the Par-

* That Newcastle had found or fancied causes of disgust some months before the flight of Marston Moor, appears from the following letter of Charles, equally honourable to the heart and head of the writer:

"Newcastle,

By your last despatch I perceive that the Scots are not the only, or it may be said the least, enemies you contest withall at this time; wherefore I must tell you in a word, for I have not time to make long discourses, you must as much contemn the impertinent or malicious tongues or pens of those that are, or profess to be, your friends, as well as you despise the sword of an equal enemy. The truth is, if either you or my L. Ethin leave my service, I am sure at least all the north (I speak not all I think) is lost. Remember, all courage is not in fighting; constancy in a good cause being the chief, and the despising of slanderous tongues and pens being not the least ingredient. I'll say no more, but let nothing dishearten you from doing that which is most for your own honour, and the good of (the thought of leaving your charge being against both) your most assured, real, constant friend,

Oxford, April 5, 1644.   CHARLES R.

Newcastle has been rather harshly treated by Clarendon, among whose virtues or weaknesses the love of the elegant and poetical was by no means so conspicuous as in his royal master. According to the noble historian, "he was a very fine gentleman, active and full of courage, and most accomplished in those qualities of horsemanship, dancing, and fencing which accompany a good breeding, in which his delight was. Besides, he was amorous in poetry and music, to which he indulged the greatest part of his time, and nothing could have tempted him out of those paths of pleasure, which he enjoyed in a full and ample fortune, but honour and ambition to serve the King when he saw him in distress. He liked the pomp and absolute authority of a General, and preserved the dignity of it to the full; and for the discharge of the outward state and circumstances of it, in acts of courtesy, affability, bounty, and generosity he abounded. But the substantial part and fatigue of a general he did not in any degree understand (being utterly unacquainted with war), nor could submit to, but referred all matters of that nature to his Lieutenant-General, King. In all actions of the field he was still present, and never absent in any battle, in all which he gave instances of an invincible courage and fearlessness in danger, in which the exposing himself notoriously did sometimes change the fortune of the day when his troops began to give ground. Such actions were no sooner over than he retired to his delightful company, music, or his softer pleasures, to all which he was so indulgent, and to his ease, that he would not be interrupted upon any occasion whatsoever, insomuch that he sometimes denied admittance to the chiefest officers of the army, even to General King himself, for two days together."

Those who would see the life and character of this nobleman depicted by a kinder, softer hand, should consult his memoirs written by his Duchess, the high-souled Margaret of Newcastle, said to be the most voluminous of authoresses, who, with a vanity pardonable, if not amiable, in woman, had all her tomes impressed with her armorial

liament in 1652, which, at little more than five years' purchase, produced £112,000. The battle of Marston Moor was a blow which the royal cause never recovered. Poor as the King was, the capture of his arms and ordnance, and the death of so many brave men, was what he could ill afford; but in an army like his, of which not only the spirit and direction, but the physical strength, was derived from the highest and smallest class, every gentleman slain was a loss that could not be repaired.

The three parliamentary Generals, Fairfax, Lesley, and Manchester, now sat down before York, which surrendered on the 15th of July, so that the whole country north of the Trent, with the exception of a few scattered garrisons, was in the hands of the ruling party. In reducing these remnants of royalism, Sir Thomas seems for some time to have been principally employed; a service of little glory and much danger, for he had to do with men determined to sell their lives as dear as possible. Twice was he in imminent peril of death; first, in the assault of Helmsley Castle, where he received a shot in the shoulder, which threatened to prove fatal; and again, before Pomfret Castle, where he narrowly escaped a cannon ball, which passed betwixt him and Colonel Forbes so close that both were knocked down with the wind of it, and Forbes lost an eye.

The elder Fairfax now made York the seat of a standing committee, whereby the affairs of the whole county were controuled. So absolute was the power exercised by this junto, that when, in 1644, the corporation of Beverley had re-elected Mr. Robert Manbie, a royalist, to their mayoralty, the committee, in the name of the Parliament, commanded them to annul the election,* and to elect such person as they should approve.

bearings. To this, Pope, who never could omit an opportunity of insulting a woman, living or dead, alludes in his description of Tibbald's library, afterwards preposterously transferred to Cibber:—

"There, stamped with arms, Newcastle shines complete."

Langbaine reckons up eight folios of her Grace's: she is an especial favourite with Charles Lamb: we need add nothing more in her commendation.

* Quinto die Augusto, 1644. A true coppie of an order sent from the standinge committee at Yorke unto the governors and Burgisses of the Towne of Beverley."— Scaum's Beverlac. Vol. I., Page 365.

The principle charges against Manbie are, that he was unduly elected, contrary to the charter of the town, and " that after he was soe chosen Mayor he betrayed the trust in him reposed, and deserted his place and office and went to Yorke, being then a garrison towne, and held by the Lord Newcastle against the Parliament," that he had taken away the town plate and mace, misapplied " diverse soomes of mooney" due to the ministers and preachers of the town, that he had laid fines and impositions

From this time, till the passing of the self-denying ordinance, Sir Thomas Fairfax does not appear to have been engaged in any of the greater actions. He had probably enough to do to check the risings of the defeated party in the Northern counties, while the mass of the Parliamentary troops were employed, for a while, with very ill success, in the western and midland regions. Sir William Waller, whom the Houses had once called " their conqueror," was worsted at Cropredy-bridge, near Banbury, (that noted seat of Puritanism.) Essex, driven into the extremity of Cornwall, escaped with some difficulty in a small boat, while his troops under Skippon, without striking a blow, delivered up their arms, ammunition, artillery, and baggage to the King. But so far were the Parliament from desponding, or putting on a face of dejection for these reverses, that the committee of the two kingdoms voted to Essex, in the moment of his defeat the thanks of the nation for his zeal, fidelity, courage, and conduct. Yet it is probable, that at this very time, they were secretly determined upon his removal. His forces were soon rearmed and recruited, and, united with those of Manchester, Cromwell, Middleton, and Sir William Waller, fought on the 27th of October, 1644, the second battle of Newbury, which like the first was bloody and indecisive. In none of these actions was Fairfax engaged, but it is necessary thus passingly to allude to them, because they tended to produce that change of system, to which he owed his elevation. In the first place, a desperate schism took place between the Earl of Manchester and his major-general Cromwell, the latter accusing his superior, in plain terms, of cowardice or treachery, in not doing his utmost to destroy the King's army at Newbury. Waller and Essex had long been at secret variance, and the Parliament, which now began more openly to assume the aspect of a republican senate, was in danger of mis-carrying through the disagreements of its commanders. But this danger was effectually averted by the famous self-denying ordinance, whereby all members, of either House, were made incapable of holding command in the army, which was to be recruited and new-modelled according to the democratic system, now begining with the rise of the Independents, to gain ascendancy. By this means, without the odium or apparent ingratitude of depriving officers, against whom they had no specific complaint, by name, they ridded themselves of aristocratic spirits, who would, if longer entrusted with military power, very likely have turned it against their employers, when they perceived that the success of their cause involved the downfall of their order.

on *well-affected* (i. e. Parliamentarian) persons during the siege of Hull by the royalists, &c. Manbie was compelled to deliver up the mace to the committee, and of course it was not restored to the town but upon *conditions*.

Essex, Waller, Warwick, Manchester, and Denbigh, were thus
obliged to lay down their commissions, and Fairfax, almost alone among
the aristocracy, remained qualified for command.   As the representative therefore, of the ancient nobility, and of the Presbyterian interest,
Fairfax might be said to succeed to the vacated generalship, by the just
and established rules of promotion.   Of all the patrician supporters of
the popular side, he had displayed the most conscientious devotion to the
cause ; and however blameable he may appear in the eyes of many good
and wise men in the choice of his party, it is certain that in taking up
arms against the King, he neither gratified the selfishness of disappointed ambition, nor violated the ties of private gratitude.   He had
received no favour from the King, he had asked none ; he sought no
vengeance, he had nothing to hope from the subversion of the
ancient regime.

It has been argued, idly enough, that if Fairfax had withdrawn from
the contest at this juncture, when the remodelling of the army strongly
indicated the purpose of maintaining a standing force, unconnected with,
and uncontrouled by, the regular constitutional authorities, his name
would have descended to posterity stainless, as that of a warrior for law
and liberty.   But surely, whatever reasons determined his conduct in
1642, they were equally strong, or stronger, in 1645.   There were the
same grounds for suspecting Charles's intentions.   If he were not to be
trusted at one time, (and his alleged want of faith was the colourable
pretext of the war,) it was very unlikely that he had grown more trustworthy at the other.   If it was apprehended, that at the first opportunity, he would revoke his concessions, made in peace, to a legitimate
Parliament, was it supposable that he would pay, that he was morally
bound to pay, more regard to concessions yielded by compulsion of the
sword, to men whom he could not think legally possessed of any political
character ?   In truth, the time when a wise man ought to have sided
with the sovereign, was before the war commenced.   When the star-
chamber and high-commission court were abolished, the King had conceded all that he had a right to concede, and to attempt to strip him of
a power which all acknowledged to be inherent in his crown, upon a
mere contingent probability of his abusing it, was justifiable on no principle but that of bare-faced tyranny.   But when the opposite factions
were once blooded, all hope of saving the constitution was at an end ;
nothing remained but the choice between absolute monarchy and an
absolute republic, to which a nominal King would be a useless, expensive appendage, an ornament grosly out of taste.   In a word, if Fairfax
was right in entering upon the war, he was bound in honour and conscience to persevere in it so long as the power which he had acknow-

ledged for sovereign thought proper to trust him. Moreover, so exasperated were the royalists become, and so full was the land of men of blood, that there was no hope of peace, no security for life, but in the complete victory and undisputed authority of one side or other. Men may make war when they choose, but they can only make peace when Heaven chooses.

Though the self-denying ordinance was not formally passed till the 3rd of April, 1645, two days after which Essex resigned his commission, yet Fairfax received the appointment of commander-in-chief on the 21st of January, and was immediately summoned from the North to receive his investiture. He came up to London very privately, arrived on the 18th of February, and the next day was brought up by four members to the House of Commons, where he was highly complimented by the Speaker, and received his commission as general-in-chief. A few days before an ordinance had been formed, importing that there should be forthwith raised, for the defence of the *King* and of the Protestant religion, and the laws and liberties of the kingdom, an army consisting of 6600 horse, to be distributed into eleven regiments; 1000 dragoons, in ten companies, and 14,000 foot, in twelve regiments; each regiment of foot to consist of 1200, distributed into ten companies. For their maintenance there was imposed on nineteen of the counties and cities of England, a monthly cess of £53,456, to be raised by a land-tax. It is wonderful how, amid the suspension of trade and industry necessarily consequent on civil discord, the general insecurity of property, and the successive ravages of both parties, the Roundheads plundering in the name of the law, and the Cavaliers by the law of the sword, such sums could possibly be raised. The Long-Parliament were no economists, according to the modern notion of the term, for they voted the Earl of Essex a retiring pension of £10,000. But it must be recollected, that they had, under the name of sequestration, confiscated the estates of most of the gentry opposed to them. These were, in some instances, sold, but more generally the owners were allowed to compound for them. The revenues of the church were also in a great measure diverted, nor were the plate and ornaments of churches spared.* But a nation will generally pay and suffer more in the hope of change, than for the support of *things as they are.*

To Fairfax the Parliament granted the extraordinary privilege of selecting his subordinate officers out of all the Parliamentarian armies, at his own discretion, subject to the approbation of the House. On the

* " Nov. 1643. The rebels seize the regalia and plate in Westminster Abbey, and being desired to leave one single cup for the communion, answered " *a wooden dish would serve the turn.*"—Salmon's Chronological Abridgment.

25th of March, £1500 were voted to him as a present. On the 3rd of April, he departed for Windsor, where he had appointed the general rendezvous; and there, with the assistance, or rather under the directions of Cromwell, he set about new-modelling the army. The discharged officers acquired the name of Reformados.

While the business of the self-denying ordinance, and consequent changes in the army, were proceeding, an ineffectual treaty was going on at Uxbridge. Nothing could have been seriously intended by the heads on either side, except to satisfy their respective adherents, which, in both parties, were growing clamorous for peace, of their conciliatory disposition. As this disposition was shewn by the Parliament, in a reiteration of the old demands respecting the militia, (which they now, however, only asked to command for seven years,) and the abolition of episcopacy, with a yet harder condition, that forty English, nineteen Scotch, and all Catholics who had born arms for the King, should be attainted and excepted from a general pardon; it cannot be wondered that the commissioners separated, after twenty days discussion, without effecting any thing; especially as the temporary success of Montrose in Scotland inspired the royalists with delusive hope.

The war, which had never been wholly suspended, even in the immediate neighbourhood of the negociators, revived with more than its former vigour in this, the fourth, campaign.

The character of the forces on both sides was materially altered. The chivalric humanity of the royalists was in a great measure lost " by custom of fell deeds." The good example of Charles could not prevent the camps of his followers from becoming the abode of riot; and the keen privations, which alternated with excessive indulgence, gave his soldiers the reckless and rapacious character of banditti. The republicans, on the other hand, began to exchange their sobriety of manner for the strangest antics of imaginary inspiration: the high-wrought enthusiasm of a few philosophic minds infected the mass with the most mischievous fanaticism, even to the supposing themselves above all ordinances, not only human, but divine, and as free from the moral, as from the ceremonial law.

In the spring of 1645, " the disposition of the forces on both sides was as follows: part of the Scottish army was employed in taking Pomfret, and other towns in Yorkshire: part of it besieged Carlisle, valiantly defended by Sir Thomas Glenham: Chester, where the Lord Byron commanded, had long been besieged by Sir William Brereton, and was reduced to great difficulties. The King, being joined by the Princes Rupert and Maurice lay at Oxford with a considerable army, about 15,000 men. Fairfax and Cromwell were posted at

Windsor, with the new-modelled army, about 22,000 men. Taunton, in Somersetshire, defended by Blake, (afterwards the famous Admiral,) suffered a long siege from Sir Richard Granville, who commanded an army of about 8000 men, and though the defence had been obstinate, the garrison were now reduced to great extremity. Goring commanded in the West, an army of about the same number." *

The first actual service in which Fairfax was employed in his new capacity of Commander-in-Chief was the relief of Taunton, a town whose fidelity and suffering in the parliamentary cause made its deliverance an object of honour and gratitude no less than of policy. But it was a consideration of first-rate importance to retain the military talents of Oliver Cromwell, who, though he was the secret mover of the self-denying ordinance, was, according to the strictness of its operation, himself disqualified by it, for he was a member of the lower house for the borough of Huntingdon. But this difficulty was easily overcome by the craft of Oliver, and through the instrumentality of Fairfax. Before the day appointed for the officers dismissed under the ordinance to deliver up their commissions, Cromwell, who was raised to the second command under Fairfax, was already on the march. Orders, never meant to be obeyed, were despatched by the House, requiring his immediate attendance in Parliament, and empowering the new General to put some other officer in his place. A ready compliance was feigned, but, a few days after, Fairfax sent a request that he might be allowed to retain Lieutenant-General Cromwell, as his advice was needed in filling up the vacancies. This request was shortly afterwards enlarged, so that Cromwell received permission to serve for that campaign. It would have been no easy matter to have dismissed him by any ordinance after the campaign was ended.

This matter settled, Fairfax, with 8000 horse and foot, hastened to the relief of Taunton. He began his march on the 1st of May, and reached Blandford, in Dorsetshire, on the 7th, when the northward movements of the King, who had succeeded in raising the siege of Chester, occasioned a change of orders from the committee of both kingdoms appointed for the management of the war. He was now directed to observe the King's motions, and, if expedient, to lay seige to Oxford, which the King's absence left exposed. Having despatched Colonel Weldon to the west with 4000 men, he retraced his steps, arrived at Newbury on the 14th, rejoined Oliver Cromwell and General Brown ; after a rest of three nights faced Dennington Castle, took a few prisoners, and determined to deprive the monarch of his Zoar, by assailing Oxford. But the fate of that loyal and learned University

* Hume.

was deferred yet a while. Scarcely had Fairfax sat down before it, when news arrived that Charles had taken Leicester by storm, May 31st, and was menacing the eastern associated counties, the possession of which might have been followed by that of London itself.   No time was to be lost : Fairfax broke up the siege of Oxford on the 5th of June, marched through Buckinghamshire into Northamptonshire, without any certain knowledge of the course which the King was taking. It is even asserted, that the armies were within six miles of each other before either knew of the other's approach.

Fairfax had refreshed his troops at Gilsborough, in Northamptonshire, from the 11th to the 14th of June, on which day the fortune of the war was decided at Naseby.   The King was strongly dissuaded from risking a battle. Gerrard, who lay in Wales, was expected shortly to join, and Goring, whose desperate courage, and quickness both of thought and execution, were as serviceable in actual combat as his debauchery and cruelty were mischievous to the general interests of the cause, was to bring up his powers as soon as Taunton, the walls of which were battered to pieces, and the whole town in ruins, should be carried. An interesting book might be written on the mighty events that have been determined by the delay or miscarriage of letters. Goring had written to the King, informing him that in three weeks he expected to be master of Taunton, and should then hasten with all the forces of the west to join the main army, and intreating him to avoid a general action in the interim.   This letter, which, had it arrived at its proper destination, might have prevented the defeat of Naseby, was unwarily intrusted to a fellow who, being no other than a spy of Fairfax's, of course carried it forthwith to his employer, who thus became acquainted with the real circumstances and intentions of the royal party.   So the King had no counter-authority to oppose to the impetuosity of Prince Rupert, backed by the young nobles and gentry, who, after all the mischances of the war, still continued to throng his camp, and who were naturally as impatient of fatigue as they were fearless of danger.

On the 14th of June, 1645, the action commenced. The King led on his centre in person. Prince Rupert commanded on the right. Sir Marmaduke Langdale on the left. The forces of the republic were thus disposed.   Cromwell was opposed to Langdale on the right ; Fairfax and Skippon faced the King in the centre ; and Ireton, Cromwell's son-in-law, was to encounter Rupert on the left. Prince Rupert, who had been appointed General-in-Chief of the royal horse, incorrigible in his rashness, ruined his too confiding uncle * by falling precisely

* The Princes Rupert and Maurice were the sons of Elizabath, daughter of James

into the same error whereby he lost the victory at Edge-Hill and caused the overthrow of Marston Moor. The fury of his onset bore down the left wing of the enemy, notwithstanding the stout resistance of Ireton, who was wounded and taken prisoner. As usual, Rupert detached himself from the main battle to hunt the fugitives as soon as they *broke cover*; an indiscretion savouring more of blood-thirstiness than courage: nay, with more than his usual absurdity, he wasted precious time in summoning the parliament artillery, which was strongly guarded, and set him at defiance. Surely he might have employed his powers better in supporting his royal kinsman, who, on this occasion, "displayed all the conduct of a prudent general, and all the valour of a stout soldier." * A flank movement upon the adverse centre, executed at the right moment, when the infantry were giving way, might have given a prosperous issue to the fight. But of the possibility of such a manœuvre it is not for us to judge.

The attack of the royal main body had broken the van of the parliamentarian centre: the troops fell back upon the rear in disorder: Skippon was severely wounded, and was requested by Fairfax to leave the field, but this he refused, declaring that he would keep his post as long as one man maintained his ground. But now was the time that the skill and courage of our hero shone forth conspicuous. At the critical minute he brought up the body of reserve, and the battle raged anew. Not content to exercise the functions of a Captain, he grappled personally with the foe, galloped through the thickest of the fray, encouraged with his dauntless example the brave, and shamed, by the risk of his own life, those who were inclined to yield. Though his

and sister of Charles I. by Frederic Elector Palatine. This lady was highly celebrated by the flowery *euphuistic* pens of the time, and was called, even in her husband's camp, the "Queen of Hearts." Sweetness of disposition, and condescending grace of manners, she might well possess, for she was a Stuart, and the ancestress of the present royal family of England; but her portrait, in Lodge's Series, from a picture by Hornthorst, gives no exalted idea of her beauty. It seems to have been taken when she was in years, and deeply furrowed with the afflictions which her husband's ambition had brought upon her. Contrary to his father-in-law's advice, he accepted the crown of Bohemia, was crowned at Prague in November 1619, defeated at Prague in November 1620; deprived at once of Bohemia and the Palatinate, long an exile and wanderer, vainly soliciting assistance from various powers, amused with false hopes by several, he died just after the battle of Lutzen, where the heroic Gustavus Adolphus, from whose victories the unhappy Frederic began to look for restoration, was slain. He left his wife in absolute poverty.

Rupert is said to have been the inventor of Mezzotinto, the hint of which he took from a soldier burnishing his musket with a file.

* Hume.

2 D

helmet was beat to pieces, he continued to ride about bare-headed,—to mark, with his experienced eye, where an advantage was to be gained, and where a weak point was to be strengthened. While thus engaged, he came up to his body-guard, commanded by colonel Charles Doyley, who respectfully rebuked him for thus hazarding his person, wherein lay the safety of the whole army, and of the *good cause*, to be riding bareheaded among the showering bullets," and offered him his own helmet ; but Fairfax, who was not a man of many words, put it by, saying, " 'Tis well enough, Charles." There was wisdom as well as gallantry in this. Soldiers, even regular soldiers, seldom fight with hearty good will for a general who betrays by superfluous caution, an over consciousness of his own value ; but an army of predestinarians, who persuaded themselves that the bloody work they were about was actually " the good fight of faith," would have ascribed any anxiety for self-preservation to a distrust of the promises of Heaven.

The battle of the centres was still doubtful, when Cromwell, having defeated the left wing of the royalists, and pursued them just far enough to prevent their rallying, adding prudence to valour, did what Prince Rupert ought to have done, brought up his triumphant force to the aid of his struggling chief, and falling on the weary infantry of Charles, put them to instant rout. One regiment alone preserved its order unbroken. Twice was it assailed by Fairfax, twice it repulsed the assailants, but in vain, for the general, directing Doyley to make a third charge in front, simultaneously attacked the stubborn body in the rear. The ranks were pierced in all directions. Fairfax slew an ensign with his own hand, seized the colours, and gave them to a common soldier to hold. The soldier, inheriting the spirit of ancient Pistol, afterwards boasted of the trophy, as if he had won it himself, for which he was severely complained of to the general : " Let him keep them," said Fairfax, " I have to-day acquired enough besides."

When too late, Prince Rupert, desisting from his fruitless attempt on the artillery, rejoined his uncle, with his men jaded, his horses blown, and the time for effective aid gone by. Charles, whose infantry was now utterly discomfited, made his appeal to this body of cavalry, " One charge more and the day is ours," but the appeal was disregarded. The King could only save his own person by precipitately leaving the field. The victory of the republicans was complete, but dearly purchased, and by a remarkable casualty, the victors lost more men than the vanquished. The slain of the royalists did not exceed 800, that of the Parliamentarians was 1000. This was perhaps owing to the havoc made by Rupert's cavalry among Ireton's men in the commencement of the action. Thus Naseby cannot be called a bloody battle. Seldom indeed has the temporary possession of three kingdoms been determined at so small an expense of life. But 500 officers, 4000 private captives, with all the King's artillery and ammunition, remained in the hands of the conquerors ; the mass of the royal army was broken up, and there was neither heart nor means in the country to recruit it.

The haste with which Charles was at last compelled to fly, as well as his little expectation of such a necessity, may be inferred from the fact, that his private cabinet or escrutoire fell into the hands of his adversaries. Thence were taken—rather say, stolen—those letters between Charles and his Queen, which were afterwards published under the title of "The King's Cabinet opened," the common-place book of all after historians who have been unfriendly to Charles's fame. The expressions of amorous tenderness with which these epistles abound were peculiarly offensive to the rigid Puritans, who would have condemned a mother caressing her babe for *creature love* : * but cooler heads have deduced proofs from this correspondence, that all Charles's concessions and advances to a pacification were mere artifices to gain time, and get rid of the Parliament. The truth seems to be, that Charles was as sincere as the political morals of the day required ; nor were his adversaries at all stricter in their adherence to truth. Simplicity of speech was not the virtue of that age. Perhaps it is the rarest as the most difficult of virtues in all ages. †

* Perhaps these stern critics would have been better pleased with the connubial doctrine of Charles the Eleventh of Sweden, who, when his consort ventured to hint an opinion, said, in a very kingly manner, " Woman, I want you to bear me children, not to give me advice."

† "The Athenians, having intercepted a letter written by their enemy, Philip of Macedon, to his wife Olympia, so far from being moved by a curiosity of prying into the secrets of that relation, immediately sent the letter to the Queen unopened. Philip was not their sovereign, nor were they inflamed with that violent animosity against him which attends all civil commotions."---*Hume.*

We do not remember whether Mitford, whose dread of republicanism made him a bitterer enemy to the good name of Athens than ever Philip was to her political existence, mentions or gives credit to this story. But the Athenians were a people of genius, and genius, however unprincipled, always has fits of generosity, or if not, vanity sometimes serves as well.

The laws of war *authorise*, if they do not *justify*, the interception, detention, examination, and publication of all documents of a purely public nature,—as letters to and from ambassadors, commanders, &c. Hence we pass no censure upon Fairfax for availing himself of Goring's letter to Charles, or for the means he used to possess himself of it. But private correspondence, like private property, should always be sacred in war as in peace,---most especially the correspondence of husband and wife; and not the less so, because the husband and wife happen to be a King and Queen. It was a most ungentlemanlike act fo the weekly-fast-ordaining Parliament or their

As Goring's letter had fully informed Fairfax of all the plans of the royalists, he was not at a loss how to follow up his victory. It might seem to have been the easiest course to pursue the King immediately. No article in his instructions forbad it; for while Essex's commission ran in the name of the King and Parliament, his was in that of the Parliament only, and contained not the clause which enjoined regard to the King's person. But however it was, Charles escaped on the evening of the 14th of June to Ashby-de-la-Zouch, from whence he passed to Hereford, and thence to Abergavenny, in Wales, with little or no molestation.

Sir Thomas Fairfax first recovered Leicester, which surrendered after two days' seige, on the 18th. Then taking a westward route, he passed through Warwick to Marlborough, where he received the Parliament's orders to relieve Taunton. But when he arrived at Blandford (July 2), he was informed that Goring had withdrawn his horse from before Taunton, and betaken himself to Langport on the Parret, a central town of Somersetshire. Thither Fairfax hastened, attacked the royalists in that post, beat them from it, killed 300, and took 1400 prisoners. Goring fell back upon Bridgewater, which capitulated on the 22d, but not till the outer town had been stormed. Bath fell on the 30th, and Sherborne Castle on the 15th of August. Bristol was now the last hope of the royal cause in the west: Prince Rupert was the governor, and whatever forces the shattered fortunes of royalty could raise, were at his discretion. He boasted that he would hold it at least four months, if there were no mutiny. It was well victualled and well fortified. There was abundant time to repair all deficiencies, for Fairfax, who seems to have been cautious of leaving hostile garrisons in his rear, did not sit down before Bristol till the 22d of August. The King, who relied much upon contingencies, hoped that before Bristol was subdued something would fall out in his favour. But the defence of a town was the worst service in which Rupert could possibly have been engaged; for it requires the most patience, the strictest discipline, the greatest endurance of privation. No sooner had the besiegers carried the outer lines by storm, than he capitulated, rather, it may be supposed, in ill humour, than in fear, sick of the tediousness and confinement of his duty, on the 10th of September.

The anger and disappointment of the King on this hasty abandonment of the best strength of his declining cause, are forcibly and feelingly expressed by the King in his letter to his headstrong and fickle nephew, dated from Hereford, 14th September, 1645. As there is a great deal

agents to open Charles's letters to his wife, and all historians who make use of them to blacken his character ought to forfeit the character of gentlemen.

of *heart* in it, we shall give it for the benefit of those who ignorantly imagine that Kings have no hearts :—

" Nephew,

Though the loss of Bristol be a great blow to me, yet your surrendering it as you did is of so much affliction to me, that it makes me not only forget the consideration of that place, but is likewise the greatest trial of my constancy that hath yet befallen me ; for what is to be done, after one that is so near me as you are, both in blood and friendship, submits himself to so mean an action. I give it the easiest term ; such—I have so much to say that I will say no more, only, lest rashness of judgment be laid to my charge, I must remember you of your letter of the twelfth of August, whereby you assured me, that if no mutiny happened, you would keep Bristol for four months. Did you keep it four days ? Was there any thing like a mutiny ? More questions might be asked, but now I confess to little purpose. My conclusion is to desire you to seek your subsistence until it shall please God to determine my condition somewhere beyond sea, to which end I send you herewith a pass, and I pray God to make you sensible of your condition, and give you the means to redeem what you have lost ; for I shall have no greater joy in a victory, than in a just occasion to assure you of my being your loving uncle, and most faithful friend,   C. R.

It is obvious enough from this letter, that Charles suspected either treachery or pique in the surrender of Bristol. But there is no just ground for accusing Rupert of dishonest tampering with the enemy. Charles had only himself to blame for trusting so important a post to one whose imprudence and ungovernable temper had already injured his cause so deeply, and who had not the least experience in the kind of duty he undertook so confidently. But we can hardly suppose Rupert to have been cajoled by the plausible terms in which Fairfax addressed his first summons. If they then expressed Sir Thomas's own sentiments, he must have been strangely blind to what was doing even in his own camp.—" Sir, the crown of England *is* and *will be* where it ought to be ; we fight to maintain it there. But the King, misled by evil counsellors, or through a seduced heart, hath left his Parliament, under God, the best assurance of his crown and family : the maintaining of this schism is the ground of this unhappy war on your part, and what sad effects it hath produced in the three kingdoms is visible to all men. To maintain the rights of the crown and kingdom jointly ; a principal part whereof is, that the King, in supreme acts, is not to be advised by men of whom the law takes no notice, but by his Parliament, the great counsel of the kingdom, in whom (as much as man is capable of) he hears all his people as it were at once advising him, and in which multitude of counsellors lies his safety and his people's interest ; and to see him right in this hath been the constant and faithful endeavour of the Parliament. And to bring those wicked instruments to justice that have misled him is a principal ground of our fighting." The vindictive spirit of this last sentence nullifies the favourable impression of the constitutional notions contained in the former passages, which, though they do not historically describe what the English constitution had been, point out clearly what it ought to be. The Parliament, in their legislative quality of guardians of the constitution, were in duty bound to insist on whatever was requisite for its utmost practicable perfection, according to the wants and capacities of the time being, without tying themselves to the measure of times past. Truly absurd, *pace tanti viri*, is the argument of Hume, that, because the English were content under the semi-despotism of Elizabeth, they might very well have rested under the milder rule of Charles 1st. As plausibly might it be asserted, that the adult youth ought not to repine at being denied a steed, and should be thankful if he is allowed a donkey, because, while he was in petticoats, he was particularly proud of a rocking-horse. But then every advance in freedom should be accompanied with an *amnesty* ; at least no man should be called to account for infringement of popular rights which have not been achieved, realised, chartered, and made law. For there is, or certainly there should be, no such thing as a political crime, which is not a demonstrable breach of a positive existing law. But independent of these considerations, the eagerness to search out and punish delinquents, whether it proceeds from malice or cowardice ; whether the pretext be retribution or security ; whether it exist in a " high court of justice," or a committee of public safety, is alike inconsistent with the true idea and sincere love of liberty ; for it always implies or induces a lawless lust of power, and where that is there can be no liberty. He that would not have all men as free as they are capable of being, does not deserve, and therefore cannot enjoy, freedom himself. But we are digressing too far.

It were little interesting to detail the several military expeditions in which our subject was engaged between the surrender of Bristol, and the final reduction of the kingdom. As little remained to do, but to subdue the scattered garrisons which held fast their integrity in spite of despair, several of which were private mansions, in which old age and womanhood endured all extremities of famine and toil, and sleepless peril, for a King who could neither reward fidelity nor punish desertion, it would perhaps conduce more to the honour of Fairfax, to say where he was not concerned, than where he was. It is agreeable, therefore, to record that he had no share in the atrocious massacre of the garrison of Basing-house; a gallant few, who with slight succours from head-quarters at Oxford, maintained the ancient hall of the Marquis of Winchester for more than two years, (from August 1643, to October 1645.) This bloody execution was done by Cromwell's troops alone, but it is very uncertain whether Oliver himself could have stopped it, had he been so minded; for the garrison were for the most part, like the Marquis, tainted with the inexpiable sin of *Popery,* and to spare them, would have been as the rebellion of Saul. The habit of blood-shed however acquired, must corrupt and harden the heart; but we do not ascribe, to the military saints of Cromwell, any natural cruelty; we even believe that their consciences often reproached them with lenity, and that they were always as humane as their religion allowed them to be. We are happy who live in times when religion, under all diversities of form and doctrine, is the law of gentleness and love; and scarcely can credit, when we read of zealous religionists, men of prayer and fasting, who searched the Scripture for precedents of slaughter, said grace as devoutly before cutting a throat as before carving a fowl, and dreamed that the times were at hand when the meek shall inherit the earth, never doubting that themselves were of the number. Strange it is, that when they opened their bibles, (as was their custom,) to determine their conduct by the first text that struck their eyes, they never stumbled on those words of the Saviour, " *Ye know not of what spirit ye are.*"

In these woeful aberrations Fairfax had little part. He continued to the end, as he began, a solemn sturdy Presbyterian, too dull for enthusiasm, too sober-minded for fanaticism, too unimaginative to perceive the beauty of the established worship, and too proud to submit his private judgment to tradition.

After the taking of Bristol, Fairfax and Cromwell divided their forces. Cromwell marched towards the east. Fairfax hastened to complete the subjugation of the West. After possessing himself of some minor posts, he commenced the blockade of Exeter, towards the end of October. That loyal city held out with great determination for several months, during which he took Dartmouth by storm on the 18th January, 1646, and defeated Lord Hopton, at Torrington, on the 16th February. On the 24th February, the Parliament voted £50,000 for his army, out of the excise. He pursued Lord Hopton into Cornwall, and after taking Mount Edgecomb and Fowey, so completely hemmed him round in Truro, that he was fain to capitulate on terms which, to Fairfax's honour, were far from severe: to wit, that all soldiers, whether

English or foreign, should have liberty, on delivering up their arms and horses, either to go over seas, or return to their homes in England, only engaging not to serve against the Parliament; that officers and gentlemen of quality should be allowed to depart with horses for themselves and one servant, or more, according to their rank, and arms befitting a gentleman; that troopers and inferior horse officers, on delivering up their arms and horses, should receive twenty shillings to carry them home; and that English gentlemen, of considerable estate, should have the general's pass and recommendation to the Parliament for moderate composition.

Before the signing of the treaty, the Lord Hopton, with Arthur Lord Capel, the Prince of Wales, Sir Edward Hyde, (afterwards Earl of Clarendon,) and other royalists of distinction, passed over to Scilly, and thence to Jersey. Exeter surrendered on articles, April 13th.

The West being thus clear of an enemy, Fairfax hastened to besiege Oxford. Before he lay down before that city, the King had withdrawn thence in disguise, and having now no place of strength to retire to, and no army a foot,* and the Parliament refusing all offers of accommodation, he took the resolution of casting himself on the generosity of the Scotch army, whose head quarters were then at Newark. This was a singularly unfortunate step. Had he negociated with the English army, while Fairfax retained his influence in it, he would probably have met at least with more sincerity. The siege of Oxford commenced on the 1st of May, and it capitulated on the 24th of July; happy, under its hapless destiny, in falling into the hands of Fairfax, whose honourable regard to learning and learned men should never be forgotten by those who would judge most unfavourably of his public conduct. The consideration with which he treated the University, exposed him to the bitter censure of the "Root and Branch Men;" but it has procured him a good word from that truly quaint and honest antiquary, Antony-a-Wood, one of the many glories of Merton College, who was little enough inclined to praise King Charles's enemies. Yet he testifies to the good conduct and discipline of Fairfax's soldiers, and to the general's care of the Bodleian library, which, he confesses, had suffered much more from the King's garrison, than it did from the Roundheads. Fairfax shewed his affection for that inestimable treasure by bequeathing to it the voluminous MSS. of Roger Dodsworth, amounting to 122 volumes, all in Roger's

---

* The last force that took the field in the King's favour, commanded by Lord Astley, and consisting of 3,000, were defeated at Stowe, on the 22nd of March, by Colonel Morgan, and thus all hopes of relieving or strengthening the King at Oxford, were frustrated. Astley, when the affair was over, said to his captors "You have done your work, and may go play, unless you choose to fall out among yourselves."

own writing, besides original MSS. which he had obtained from several hands, making altogether 162 folios.

The next important engagement in which our general was concerned was the taking of Ragland castle, the seat and fortress of the Marquis of Worcester. This mansion, wherein the King had found refuge for some time after the battle of Naseby, and where, according to one account, the old Marquis made a strong effort to convert him to the Catholic faith, had been beset early in the spring, by a portion of Fairfax's army, under Morgan. It was gallantly, though hopelessly, defended; but when Fairfax approached in person, the Marquis rightly thought it was better to surrender to him than another. Honourable terms were obtained for the garrison, but the aged Marquis, then in his 84th year, was treated by the Parliament, (probably on account of his religion,) with a most disgraceful rigour, to which we hope Fairfax was nowise accessary. As the influence of Cromwell and the Independent party increased in the army, that of Fairfax and the Parliament declined. In the personal violence inflicted on the King, Fairfax had no actual share; but he was employed by the Parliament to convey to the Scotch army, the price of the King's blood. In the course of his northward march, on the 15th of February, 1647, he met the King, then a captive in the charge of Parliamentary Commissioners, just beyond Nottingham, and his Majesty stopping his horse, Sir Thomas alighted and kissed his hand; and afterwards mounted and discoursed with him as they rode along.

The Parliament were beginning to find that they had raised an army to overawe themselves, and took measures for disbanding the supernumeraries. On the 5th of March, after a long and stormy debate, Fairfax was voted general of the forces that were to be continued. On the 12th of the same month he came to Cambridge, where the honorary degree of Master of Arts was conferred upon him. The Latin speech made on these occasions, generally contains a summary of merits, similar to that in a Peer's patent of creation. We hope the orator who presented Fairfax did not forget Roger Dodsworth and the Bodleian.

As the self-denying ordinance had no prospective operation, Sir Thomas Fairfax was, about this time, elected member for Cirencester: probably with a view of being a mediator between the Parliament and the army. But he had no talents for intrigue, and quickly found that the soldiers, who as long as there was an enemy in the field, had preserved the strictest discipline, now began to imitate their superiors in rebellion. And indeed it was little to be expected, that men, long accustomed to blood and plunder, who had moreover the conceit that they were the elect and the salt of the earth, and many of whom had risen from the

2 E

lowest grades of society to high offices, would return to their ploughs and looms, and live peaceably under an authority as illegal as that they were themselves determined to assume.   Cromwell had done his work ; he was particularly formidable to the Presbyterians, and he had exhibited symptoms of a disposition to close with the King.   The Parliament wished to send him to Ireland, but it did not suit his purposes to go thither.   The council of agitators, a sort of political union among the soldiers, arose, and Fairfax found that he was no more master.   He saw through their designs, he deliberated on laying down his commission, but he was persuaded to retain it, for his name had still great weight with all parties.   In political matters, however, he never had much judgment of his own, and for a time suffered himself to be an active instrument of the military democracy, which the people looked upon as the bulwark of liberty ; and it may be said with truth, that however violent the acts of the army, their principles were more liberal, more tolerant, and more consistent than those of the assembly at St. Stephen's. To be short, Fairfax seems to have concurred in all the measures of the army, till the seizing of the King's person by cornet Joyce, on the 3rd of June.   At this, according to his own account, in his memorials, he " immediately sent two regiments, commanded by colonel Whaley, to set all things again in their *due course and order.*"   Whaley overtook the King on his way towards Cambridge, and signified that the general (Fairfax) was much troubled at those insolencies which were committed by the soldiers about his Majesty's person, " and as he had not the least knowledge of them before they were done, so he had omitted no time in seeking to remove that force," which Whaley had orders to see done, and therefore he desired his Majesty to return to Holmby, where all should be settled on its former footing.   But Charles either thinking any change for the better, or deluded with an opinion, that the army were really in his favour, would not comply with this request.   Fairfax waited on him at Sir John Cutt's house, near Cambridge, but could not obtain his confidence, nor persuade him to return to Holmby.   He also made an ineffectual attempt to call a council of war, to proceed against Joyce, whose proceedings no one would either own or disavow.   This difference did not immediately dissolve Sir Thomas's connection with the mutinous army.   He joined in the march to St. Albans, and on the 15th of June, was a party to a charge against eleven of the members of the House of Commons, among whom were Denzil Hollis, Sir John Clotworthy, and Sir William Waller, the heads of the Presbyterian party. When the army were encamped on Houndslow Heath, he received the Earl of Manchester, and Lenthal, the Speakers of the two Houses, who with sixty-six members thought proper, under pretence of personal danger, to put themselves under the protection of the military, which was perhaps preferable to the tyranny of the London apprentices, by whose riotous interference the Parliament was now controuled. On the 6th of August, he entered London, in defiance of the Parliament's order that the army should not approach them within fifteen miles, replaced the Speakers in their seats, and voted for the expulsion of the eleven accused. Perfect order was preserved, and private property respected. In all these acts, he persuaded himself that he performed the part of one " who was no enemy to monarchy and civil government :" he never departed from the outward respect due to the *presence* of Majesty. Even while an army, nominally under his command, was dragging the King's person along with them in all their movements, he declared in his letters to the Parliament, in behalf of himself and his officers, " that they conceived that to avoid all harshnesses, and afford all kindnesses to his Majesty, consistent with the peace and safety of the Kingdom, is the most christian, honourable, and prudent way ; and that tender, moderate, and equitable dealing towards his Majesty, his family, and party, is the most hopeful course, to take away the seeds of war and feuds amongst us and our posterity, and to procure a lasting peace." Is it credible, that Fairfax still believed that any remnant of monarchical power could be retained without a counter-revolution ? It is commonly said, that he was at this time the tool of Cromwell. The truth rather seems to be, that both he and Cromwell were equally hurried along by the despotism of Fate, working in the wild humours of the army.

When the King fled from Hampton Court, and, for no assignable reason, put himself into the hands of Hammond, governor of Carisbrook Castle, some shew of negociation took place between him and the Parliament, which of course proving abortive, a vote was passed, at the nod of the army, that no more addresses be made to the King, nor any letters or addresses sent to him, and that it should be treason for any one, without the leave of the two houses, to have any intercourse with him. The army, with Fairfax's concurrence, went a step beyond this, not only agreeing to the resolution, but resolving to stand by the Parliament in whatever further should be necessary for settling and securing the Parliament and kingdom, *without* the King, and against him. Thus, " though Fairfax wished nothing that Cromwell did, he contributed to bring it all to pass."

On the 13th of March, 1648, Ferdinando Lord Fairfax dying at York, Sir Thomas succeeded to all his estates and titles, and was appointed Governor of Pontefract Castle, and Custos Rotulorum in his room.

A re-action was now commencing in the nation, and the royalists attempted several risings, which served no purpose but to ensure their own destruction, and precipitate their master's doom. In suppressing these insurrections, Lord Fairfax exerted his customary skill and valour. On the 9th of April he quelled a riot of the London apprentices, who had declared for God and King Charles. He sent powerful reinforcements to subdue the troops revolted in Wales under Langhorne, Poyer, and Powell. A rash enterprise had been undertaken in Essex and Kent, without much concert, by Goring Earl of Norwich, Lord Capel, Sir Charles Lucas, and others. It was against these that Lord Fairfax performed his last important military services. He had been commanded to march to the north, where an invasion from Scotland, under Hamilton, was daily apprehended, and where Carlisle and Berwic were once more in the hands of the royalists. But before he was many days on his route, he received counter orders to march into Kent, to oppose Goring and his sometime fellow-commander, Sir William Waller.

Though severely indisposed by the gout, he displayed his usual vigour and courage, with his usual success, and defeated a considerable body of insurgents at Maidstone on the 2d of June. Though requested not to expose his own person, he mounted with his gouty foot wrapped up, and led on the men to the very brunt of the action. Such of the royalists as escaped passed over the river, and being joined by several companies under Capel and Lucas, shut themselves up in Colchester on the 12th of June. Fairfax came to the same place on the 13th of that month, attempted vainly to storm it, and then commenced a blockade, which continued for eleven weeks. The royalists were reduced to great extremities of hunger, and for five weeks fed upon horse flesh; all their endeavours to set on foot a general treaty being, as might be expected, ineffectual. To their proposals of this nature Fairfax answered, "that such a treaty, and for such a peace, was not the proper work of himself, or the armies, but theirs that had employed him, and the best terms that he would grant, were, that the common soldiers, if they laid down their arms within twenty hours, should have free leave to depart to their homes, and the officers passes, to go beyond sea." It would have been well for Fairfax's reputation if these terms had been accepted; for the brave perseverance of the loyal handful exasperated him to severities, which remain a lasting blemish to his name. Colchester surrendered on the 28th of August. Sir Charles Lucas and Sir George Lisle were dishonourably butchered for *example's sake*, for which cruelty his memorials give no better excuse than that they were soldiers of fortune, which was not true, and if it had been, could not extenuate the cold-blooded execution of brave gentlemen, who had not violated the laws of war. Lucas was first shot; Lisle went up and embraced the body, and then presented himself to the executioners. Perhaps apprehensive of being mangled, he bad the soldiers approach nearer : one of them replied, " I warrant, Sir, we'll hit you ; " to which he rejoined, " Friends, I have been nearer to you when you have missed me." This execution over, Fairfax went to the Town-ball, where the rest of the prisoners were confined, and addressing himself to the Earl of Norwich and the Lord Capel, told them " that, having done that which military justice required, all the lives of the rest were safe, and that they should be well treated, and disposed of as the Parliament should direct." But the Lord Capel had not so soon digested this so late barbarous proceeding as to receive those who caused it with such return as his condition might have prompted to him, but said that they should do well to finish their work, and execute the same rigour to the rest ; upon which there were two or three such sharp and bitter replies between him and Ireton as cost him his life in a few months after."*

When a bill of attainder against Lord Capel was brought into the House of Commons, he pleaded that Fairfax had not only promised him his life, but had expressly acknowledged that promise in a letter to the House. Lord Fairfax was called on to explain his meaning in that letter. He had then the chance at least of saving a brave man's life, but he merely said, " that his promise did not extend to any other but the military power, and that the prisoners were, notwithstanding, liable to trial and judgment by the civil power." A very similar case, our readers will recollect, occurred after the battle of Waterloo.

We have anticipated the order of time a little, to bring all the trans- actions connected with the surrender of Colchester under one point of view, for the attainder of Capel did not take place till after the execu- tion of Charles. Fairfax, having reduced Colchester, and laid a heavy fine of £12,000 on the inhabitants, who seem to have been passive in the whole business to excuse them from being plundered, he made a sort of triumphant progress through Ipswich, Yarmouth, St. Edmund's_ bury,—for what purpose does not appear. He returned to London in December. Some degree of mystery hangs about his participation in that violent measure called " Pride's Purge," when all the members known to be hostile to the abolition of monarchy were excluded by sol- diers placed for the purpose, and only the most decisive Independents permitted to enter the House. While Whitelock asserts expressly that it was done by special order from the Lord General, (Fairfax,) and the council of the army ; he declares, no less positively, that he had not the least intimation of it till it was done, and appeals to several members, with whom he was at that very time discoursing, for the truth of his

* Clarendon.

asseveration," which is also affirmed by Clarendon. The probability is, that he had never been told what was on foot, that he had never been consulted about it, that he did not *choose* to know it; but that it was anything more than he expected, is absolutely incredible, except on the supposition that he was the most gullible of mankind.

When the "High Court of Justice," was formed, his name was placed first on the list of judges, but he declined to act as such. There was a great deal of irresolution, not to say prevarication, in his proceedings on this occasion. His lady shewed a far manlier spirit. When the regicide court first assembled, and the crier, calling over the names of the judges, came to "Thomas Lord Fairfax,"—no answer. A second time the summons was uttered—"Thomas Lord Fairfax." A voice from the crowd replied,—" he has more wit than to be here." A moment's pause:—some one asked who spake, but there was no reply. The court resumed. When the impeachment was read, running in the name of "all the good people of England," the same voice exclaimed, " No, nor the hundredth part of them." Axtel, the officer, commanded the soldiers to fire at the box from whence the voice proceeded. The guns were levelled, when it was perceived that it was the Lady Fairfax that spake so boldly.

If we are to believe Anthony Wood, Fairfax had resolved to prevent the execution of the King at the head of his own regiment, but was duped by Cromwell, who directed him "to seek the Lord," and that he was actually "seeking the Lord," in Harrison's apartments at Whitehall, while the bloody deed was doing. But this is utterly incredible, and needs no refutation. He certainly had no active participation in the King's death; but so perfectly supine was he during the whole transaction, that his neutrality is rather to be ascribed to some private scruple than to any clear perception of the iniquity of the deed. Wood, to make the story still more wonderful, adds, that "when his Majesty was beheaded, and his corpse thereupon immediately coffined, and covered with a black velvet pall, Bishop Juxon, who attended him on the scaffold, and Thomas Herbert, the only groom of the chamber that was then left, did go with the said corpse to the back stairs, to have it embalmed; and Mr. Herbert, after the body had been deposited, met with the General Fairfax, who asked him How the King did? whereupon Herbert, looking very strangely upon him, told him that the King was beheaded, at which he *seemed very much surprised.*" We will not—we do not—believe that Lord Fairfax was guilty of such unfeeling hypocrisy, such despicable affectation. But he lived in an age when scarcely any man dealt fairly with his own conscience. Certain it is, that he did not immediately break off his connection with the regicide party, who were indeed now become the de facto government, and as such, perhaps, entitled to obedience, but not to co-operation, from those who condemned the steps whereby they had risen. On the 15th of February, just fifteen days after the King's death, he was nominated one of the new council of state; and though he refused to subscribe the test appointed by the Parliament for approving all that had been respecting the King, and kingly power, he was, on the 31st of March, voted General-in-Chief of all the forces in England and Ireland.

In May he made an excursion into Oxfordshire, where he put down the Levellers, who were growing very troublesome, and was made a Doctor of Laws,—a whimsical custom of the Universities to invest with academical dignities the men of the sword. He continued his tour southward, and inspected various forts, &c. in the Isle of Wight, Southampton, and Portsmouth; and near Guildfold had a rendezvous of the army, whom he exhorted to obedience. He must have had some difficulty in determining whom, under existing circumstances, they ought to obey.

On the 4th of June he and other officers dined with the city of London, who testified their gratitude by a present of a large and weighty bason and ewer of beaten gold. The wildest levellers are not ignorant of the *negociable* value of rank. The most abandoned acknowledge the moral influence of character, and the most passionate enthusiasts (if they are not physically mad) think it well to have some common sense in their service; just as the most devoted Bacchanalians insist upon their servant's keeping sober enough to carry them home, and see them to bed. No wonder, then, that the new republic were anxious to keep Lord Fairfax, who was almost the only man who brought title, property, character, and a cool brain into their councils. Perhaps, too, they hoped to make him a *set-off* against Cromwell. But he was weary, disappointed, no longer young: his wife, who had shared his perils and promoted his efforts while she imagined that he was fighting for the establishment of a Christian church, and an effective Christian discipline, was vexed in spirit to see him led about at pleasure by *sectaries*, who agreed with her in nothing but a hatred of prelates and surplices. Her pride, if not his own, forbad him to be General of troops whom he could not restrain; and therefore, having found out at last, that he had no power for good, and no inclination to further evil, he resigned his commission in June, 1650, when the Scots declared for King Charles II. The Presbyterians then hoped that the re-establishment of monarchy would bring about the establishment of their church, but Fairfax prudently declined either to oppose or assist the enterprize.

He resigned his office on the 26th of June; the government gave him a pension of £5000 a year, and he retired to his seat at Nun-Appleton, in Yorkshire. From that time, we hear nothing of him, (except that he always prayed for the restoration of the royal family,) till after the death of Cromwell. When Monk appeared in the field to deliver the Parliament, (which then resumed its functions,) from Lambert and his soldiers, Lord Fairfax once more took the field; the Yorkshire gentry gladly obeyed his summons; on the 3rd of December, 1659, he appeared at the head of a body of gentlemen, his friends and neighbours. His name and reputation induced the Irish brigade, of 1000 horse, to join him, which gave Monk a decided advantage. He took possession of York, on the 1st of January, 1660. On the 29th of March, he was elected one of the knights of the shire for the county of York, in the short healing Parliament he gave his glad consent to the restoration of the monarchy, which he had so great a hand in destroying, and was at the head of the committee appointed to wait on the King at the Hague. Charles received him with his accustomed graciousness, and, it is said, that in a private interview, he asked pardon for all past offences. From this time to his death, he lived at his country seat in great privacy, giving himself up to study and devotion, without taking any part whatever in public affairs. The most remarkable action that has been recorded, of his last eleven years, was his presenting to King Charles a copy of verses, of his own composition, *to* or *about* the horse on which his Majesty rode to his coronation, which horse was of his own stud, and given by him to the placable monarch, as a peace-offering. We regret that we cannot give the verses intire. Lord Fairfax died on the 12th of November, 1671, in the 60th year of his age, and is buried in the aisle adjoining to the south side of the chancel of Bilburgh church, near York. He left no male issue. He was after his kind, a poet, or at least a versifier of Scripture. In Mr. Thoresby's Museum are his MS. version of the Psalms, Canticles, and other portions of the Bible. He was, upon the whole, a very honest man.

JAMES, EARL OF DERBY.

"SANS CHANGER."

Such is the motto of the noble house of Stanley, and well was it fulfilled in the steadfast loyalty of this brave man, and his heroic spouse.
Their story, as far as it has been recorded, is but short, and we shall tell
it simply ; singling their acts and sufferings from the chaos of contemporary occurrences, and relating them, by themselves, " unmixt with
baser matter."

James, seventh Earl of Derby, was the eldest son of William, the sixth
Earl, by Elizabeth, daughter of Edward Vere, seventeenth Earl of Oxford,
and of Anne, daughter of the "great Lord Burleigh." Neither Collins,
nor Lodge, mention the date of his birth, nor the place of his education,
but there can be no doubt that he was instructed in all such polite and
liberal learning as was supposed, in that age, to become his rank. Hardly
a record remains of his youth and early manhood, except that he was
one of the many Knights of the Bath appointed at the coronation of
Charles First, and that he was summoned to Parliament on the 13th of
February, 1628, by the title of Lord Strange. Calling the eldest sons
of Peers to the Upper House, during their father's life time, was not
unfrequent during the reigns of the first Stuarts. We hear nothing of
his travels, though it is not probable that he omitted what was then, as
now, esteemed essential to the accomplishing a complete gentleman, especially as his wife, to whom he was early united, was a French lady,
related to the blood royal of France. This famous woman was Charlotte
de la Tremouille, daughter of Claude, Duke of Thouars. She may,
however, have come over in the train of the beautiful and unfortunate
Henrietta.

Derby was no frequenter of the court. He lived among his tenants,
dividing his time between his English estates and his little kingdom of
Man, which he was anxious to improve and civilize. But peaceful
years and charitable deeds make little shew in the memorial page, and
Derby owes his place in history, not to the virtues which sprang out of
his own good will and choice, but to those which were elicited from him,

2 F

like fire from flints, by the blows of fortune. Scarcely had his father's death put him in possession of his ample domains, when the approach of civil war obliged him to exchange the garb of mourning for a coat of mail, and the kind superintendence of a good landlord over his paternal dependants, for the duties of a military commander.

When King Charles retired to York in the beginning of 1642, Derby was one of the first nobles who joined him. He was almost immediately despatched back into Lancashire to array the military force in that county, of which he was Lord Lieutenant, for the King's service. It was the original intention of Charles to hoist his standard at Warrington; a situation which would have rendered Lord Derby's powers in the highest degree available: but through the weak or selfish suggestions of certain in the council, he was induced to set up the signal of war at Nottingham. This was a great disappointment to Derby, who actually mustered 60,000 men on the three heaths of Preston, Ormskirk, and Bury, and was proceeding to use the same efforts in Cheshire, and North-Wales, where also he was Lord-Lieutenant, when a special letter from his Majesty required his presence at head quarters, with such troops as he could equip directly. The Lancashire men, thinking themselves slighted, or like all irregular forces, intolerant of delay, went sulkily home, or joined the opposite party, to which they were of considerable aid in seizing Manchester. But the Earl, though mortified, was not changed; from his personal friends, and his tenantry, he raised three regiments of foot, and as many troops of horse, which he clothed and armed at his own cost. With these he waited on the King at Shrewsbury. He was straightway ordered back, with orders to attempt to surprize Manchester. He returned, hastened his preparations, fixed the very hour and mode of the assault, when the very night before the enterprize was to have been executed, he received counter-orders to repair to the King immediately. He obeyed, and was rewarded by having his trusty powers taken from him, and placed at the disposal of others, while he was once more remanded into Lancashire to raise fresh men as he could. Treatment like this, and a course of management enough to ruin any cause, would have made many a man retire in disgust, if not actually change. But

> Loyalty is still the same
> Whether it lose or win the game,
> True as the dial to the sun
> Although it be not shone upon.

Derby's loyalty was of that exalted, pure, and simple character, which was ready to suffer all things not only *for* the King, but *from* the King. Though the royal interest in Lancashire, was sunk very low, he had influence to raise a force sufficient to storm Lancaster and Preston, in which undertakings he shared and more than shared the utmost personal dangers, and was preparing for an attack on Manchester, when this new levy was called away to the main army; and nothing was left for him to do but to fortify his mansion at Lathom, and hold it out till better times.   But before he had put the last hand to his work of restoring his home to the martial condition for which in former centuries all baronial residences were designed, he received intelligence that the King's enemies and his were planning an invasion of his little sovereignty of Man.   To save this island which might serve for a retreat should the King come to the worst, he determined to sail thither in person, and to intrust his lady with the completion and command of the half-finished works at Lathom.   The place had great capabilities of defence: little was wanting to make it tenable against a considerable force.   The Earl placed a few soldiers within the walls, with what arms and ammunition he could collect or spare.   And so, leaving perforce his wife and children to the perils of a siege, he hastily departed. He was just arrived in the Isle, when the Countess received certain intimation that she was to be attacked in her own house.   No time was lost.   The ancient fabric was fortified to the best of known art and present means.   The little garrison was strengthened by such recruits from the midling and lower classes of neighbouring people, as gratitude made trustworthy; and these were admitted singly, or in small parties.   Beloved as the Countess and her husband were, she had less difficulty in procuring stores and provisions than generally beset the defenders of royalty.   Out of the troops left by the Earl, the recruits from the neighbourhood, and the family servants, she formed six divisions, called Regiments, at the head of which she placed so many country gentlemen, and gave the chief command to Captain Farmer, a Scot, and an old Low-country soldier, afterwards slain at Marston-moor.   With such secrecy were these arrangements made, that the enemy approached within two miles of Lathom before they were aware that they would be resisted.

On the 28th of February, 1644, Fairfax and his men arrived, and sent a trumpet to desire a conference with the Countess, to which she agreed; and in order to impress the foe with a notion of her power, "she placed her inefficient and unarmed men on the walls and tops of towers, and marshalled all her soldiers in good order, with their respective officers, from the main guard in the first court to the great hall, " in which she calmly awaited the visit of the adverse leader.   There is no need to say that the meeting was ceremonious, for where no kindness is, there must be ceremony, or there will be no courtesy; and

Fairfax, whether patriot or rebel, was still a gentleman. He offered the Countess a safe and honorable removal, with her children, retinue, and effects, military stores excepted, to the Familyse at Knowsley park: where she might reside without molestation, with the moiety of the Earl's estate for her support. She answered that she was under a double trust—of faith to her husband, and allegiance to her Sovereign," and desired to have a month to consider. This being refused, she told the general that "She hoped then he would excuse her if she preserved her honour and obedience, though perhaps to her own ruin."

It was now matter of hesitation with the assailants whether to proceed by storm or blockade. By a stratagem of one of the Earl's Chaplains, who persuaded the rebels that there were only fourteen days provision in the house, the latter method was determined on. After a fortnight, Fairfax sent formally to demand a surrender. The Countess replied that "She had not yet forgotten what she owed to the Church, to her Prince, and to her Lord, and that till she lost her honour or her life, she would still defend that place." The besiegers then begun regularly to form their trenches. On the 24th of March, the Heroine ordered a sally of 200 men, who slew 60 of the enemy, with a loss of only two lives. Fourteen weeks past before the besiegers could complete their lines, so constantly were they interrupted by the sallies of the besieged. But when this was done, they approached nearer and nearer to the moat, and succeeded in erecting a strong battery, with a mortar of large calibre, from which a shell was thrown that fell into the room where the Countess and her children were at dinner. Providentially it exploded harmless, and the noble woman, whose courage raised, not quailed, at danger, bid her faithful soldiers issue forth with a voice that might have shamed a coward to heroism. Sword in hand, they drove the rebels from their battery, spiked the guns, or tumbled them into the moat, and bore off triumphantly the mortar into the house, on the very 29th of April, appointed by the enemy for a general assault, in which it was resolved to give no quarter. Some days past before the works could be repaired.—The pioneers and engineers had no quiet in their labours; and when it was done, the unconquerable band sallied forth again, dispersed the men, slew a hundred, and spiked the cannon, with the loss of only three men. We are at a loss to account for such disgraces of men, certainly not cowards, whatever else they might be, unless it were that such more than manly daring in a high-born and delicate female appeared to minds unacquainted with the inner might of magnanimity, which is of no sex, but purest in the pure, and fairest in the fair, like a supernatural visitation. The noble lady was still present in the most perilous adventures, that none might seek a safety which she scorned. She stood among the smoke, and fire, and bullets, as if she bore a " charmed life." But the sole enchantment that she used was prayer and thanksgiving, her only spells were conjugal affection and dauntless loyalty.

Three months had the siege continued : the besiegers had left 2000 men under the walls of a single dwelling. Fairfax, who had not commanded in person, suspected mismanagement, and sent Colonel Rigby to supersede the officer who had hitherto conducted the operations. The Colonel had a private pique against Derby, which manifested itself in the affronting terms wherein he couched his summons to surrender. Though the garrison was now in great streights for ammunition, their corn spent, and their horses nearly all killed for food ; yet did Charlotte of Tremouille, with her own voice, reply to the insulter, " Trumpet, go tell that insolent rebel, Rigby, that if he presume to send another summons within this place, I will have the messenger hanged up at the gates." How much longer she could have maintained this lofty port, or kept a starving garrison in order, was not put to the trial ; for even then the royal banners were gleaming in the distance ; and the cloud of dim dust, set afar from the battlements of Lathom, announced that deliverance was nigh. The Earl, having put his insular territories in a state of defence, hastened back to the aid of his Countess, and arrived at the critical moment when Rupert was unsuccessfully endeavouring to recover Bolton-le-Moors, a town in the midst of Derby's patrimony. In the Prince's host were some companies of Derby's own men, who had been so strangely taken from under his command at the commencement of the war. No sooner did these honest yeomen recognize their hereditary chief, than they joyfully ranged themselves at his orders. In half an hour Bolton was the King's, and Derby was the first man that entered it. This done, the whole force of Rupert marched towards Lathom, with intent to engage the enemy, but before they were well in sight, Rigby broke up the siege without a blow, May 27, 1644.

The Earl and his Countess now returned together to the Isle of Man, leaving to a subordinate officer the charge of Lathom house. We shall not relate in detail how the siege was renewed after the battle of Marston Moor, nor how, after a long and gallant defence, it was surrendered at the express desire of the King, who would not have loyal blood wasted in hopeless obstinacy. For Derby and his consort, the following years were years, not of peace, but of comparative inaction. Cooped up in their diminutive kingdom, where they were honoured as patriarchal princes, they bad defiance to the fleets, the threats, and the persuasions of the Parliament. Even when their children, whom they had sent into England on the faith of a pass from Fairfax, were detained in captivity by the ruling powers, though repeated offers were made to restore them, with the whole of the English estates, if the Earl would give up his island: he constantly answered, that much as he valued his ancestral lands, and dearly as he loved his offspring, "he would never redeem either by disloyalty." Nor did they change their resolution even when the King, for whom they held their rocks and little fields, was no more, and his son a wandering exile. Angry at solicitations which implied an insult to his honour, Derby returned the following reply to that fierce republican, Ireton, who had urged the old proposal with renewed earnestness :—

"I received your letter with indignation, and with scorn I return you this answer: that I cannot but wonder whence you should gather any hopes from me, that I should (like you) prove treacherous to my Sovereign; since you cannot be insensible of my former actings in his late Majesty's service; from which principle of loyalty I am no way departed,

I scorn your proffers; I disdain your favours; I abhor your treasons; and am so far from delivering this island to your advantage, that I will keep it to the utmost of my power to your destruction.

Take this final answer, and forbear any further solicitations; for if you trouble me with any more messages upon this occasion, I will burn the paper, and hang the bearer.

This is the immutable resolution, and shall be the undoubted practice, of him who accounts it the chiefest glory to be,

His Majesty's Most Loyal and Obedient Subject,
Castle Town, 12 July, 1649.   DERBY.

He remained in the isle till 1651, when the younger Charles entered England at the head of a Presbyterian army, governed by Presbyterian preachers, with which it was impossible for the English royalists cordially to co-operate. But Derby's loyalty had no reservations: his oath of allegiance contained no proviso for the case of a King bringing the *solemn league and covenant* along with him. At the request of Charles (who sent him the order of the Garter) he left the island and landed in Lancashire, to join in as unpromising an enterprise as ever threw away good lives. His charge was to raise the county power if possible;—if not, to follow the main army (which, with the titular King, was pressing on by forced marches to Shrewsbury) with the small body of two hundred horse which were left with him for safe conduct. Having sent forth trusty emisaries in all directions to announce his arrival, and call his cavaliering friends and neighbours from their retreats, two or three days after he parted with the King he fixed his quarters at Wigan, to wait the coming up of the musters. But the next morning he was unexpectedly attacked by a large body of militia and regulars under Lilburn, whom Cromwell had detached to hang upon the King's rear, and prevent the junction of stragglers. Derby's "band of brothers" were set upon in an irregular street, which enabled them to make a prodigious stand against over-running numbers. "Three thousand veterans, practised in war's game," were barely sufficient to cut to pieces, and trample under foot, two hundred loyal English gentlemen. In this skirmish the Earl received seven shot in his breast-plate, thirteen cuts in his beaver, and five or six wounds in his arms and shoulders, and had two horses killed under him. Yet his time was not yet come. He escaped almost singly, and found his way through Shropshire and Staffordshire, to join the King at Worcester.

Of the result of the third of September, and the subsequent wanderings and escapes of Charles, who in this land of oaks is ignorant? It was Derby that with cold and bleeding wounds led the King in secrecy to St. Martin's gate, and directed him to the concealments of White ladies and Boscobel, where he himself had found shelter not many days before. He then made for his own country, though sick of heart, and wounded sore ; but scarcely had he gained the borders of Cheshire when he was overtaken by a party under Major Edge, to whom he surrendered, under a promise of quarter. He was led prisoner to Chester. The Parliament sent down a commission to nineteen persons, selected from the military, who formed a sort of court-martial, styled, "A high court of Justice," in order "to try the Earl of Derby for his treason and rebellion."

> Treason never prospers. What's the reason?
> Why when it prospers none dare call it treason.

Of course the Earl was found guilty, and condemned to die, but by an unnecessary aggravation of cruelty, the execution was appointed to take place in his own town of Bolton-le-Moors, where, a few years ago, he appeared a conqueror. He was beheaded on Wednesday, the 15th of October, 1651. Two days before his death, he wrote a letter to his Countess, which we shall give entire :—

"MY DEAR HEART,

I have heretofore sent you comfortable lines, but alas I have now no word of comfort, saving to our last and best refuge, which is Almighty God, to whose will we must submit ; and when we consider how he hath disposed of these nations and the government thereof, we have no more to do but to lay our hands upon our mouths, judging ourselves, and acknowledging our sins, joined with others, to have been the cause of these miseries, and to call upon him with tears for mercy.

The governor of this place, Colonel Duckenfield, is general of the forces which are now going against the Isle of Man; and, however you might do for the present, in time it would be a grievous and troublesome thing to resist, especially those that at this hour command the three nations, wherefore my advice, notwithstanding my great affection to that place, is that you would make conditions for yourself, and children, and servants, and people there, and such as came over with me, to the end you may get to some place of rest, where you may not be concerned in war, and taking thought of your poor children, you may in some sort, provide for them: then prepare yourself to come to your friends above, in that blessed place where bliss is, and no mingling of opinion.

I conjure you, my dearest Heart, by all those graces that God hath given you, that you exercise your patience in this great and strange trial. If harm come to you, then I am dead indeed: and until then I shall live in you, who are truly the best part of myself. When there is no such thing as I am being, then look upon yourself and my poor children; then take comfort, and God will bless you. I acknowledge the great goodness of God to have given me such a wife as you;—so great an honour to my family,—so excellent a companion to me,—so pious,—so much of all that can be said of good,—I must confess it impossible to say enough thereof. I ask God pardon with all my soul, that I have not been enough thankful for so great a benefit; and where I have done any thing at any time that might justly offend you, with joined hands I also ask your pardon. I have no more to say to you at this time, than my prayers for the Almighty's blessing to you, my dear Mall, and Ned, and Billy.—Amen, sweet Jesus!" *

It now behoves us to say a few words of the subsequent fate of the woman to whom this writing was addressed. After her husband's death she still held out her domain of Man, ruling it with a broken fortune, broken health, broken heart, but unbroken spirit, till those Christians to whom the Earl at his leave taking had committed the care of his wife and children, and of the island forces, betrayed it to the government. Then was the Countess for a time a captive, and after-

---

* Like many of the nobility of that period, the Earl of Derby possessed literary talents. In the Desiderata Curiosa may be found "The History of the Isle of Man, by James, Earl of Derby and Lord of Man, interspersed with large and excellent advices to his son; and one of the Sloane MSS. in the British Museum is a sort of historical common-place book, written with his own hand."—*Lodge.*

wards a wanderer, subsisting on such kindness as the poor can bestow on the poorer still. At the restoration, the estates reverted to her eldest son, and she spent the short remnant of her days at Knowsley Park. It is needless to say that the adventures ascribed to her in a popular novel are purely fictitious. Her portrait, by Vandyke, by no means corresponds with the regal description of the novelist. It is the round *sonsy* visage of a good wife and mother, but neither beautiful nor impressive. She had seven children;—three sons, of whom only one survived her, and four daughters. She died in 1662.

Mr. Bagaley, one of the Earl's gentlemen, who was allowed to attend him to the last, drew up a narrative of his dying hours, the manuscript whereof still remains in the family; but a large portion of it is printed in Collins' Peerage, from whence we have transcribed it:—

"Upon Monday, October 13th, 1651, my Lord procured me liberty to wait upon him, having been close prisoner ten days. He told me the night before, Mr. Slater, Colonel Duckenfield's chaplain, had been with him from the governor, to persuade his Lordship that they were confident his life was in no danger; but his Lordship told me he heard him patiently, but did not believe him; for, says he, "I was resolved not to be deceived with the vain hopes of this fading world." After we had walked a quarter of an hour, he discoursed his own commands to me, in order to my journey to the Isle of Man, as to his consent to my Lady, to deliver it on those articles his Lordship had signed: with many affectionate protestations of his honour and respect of my Lady, both for her birth, and goodness as a wife, and much tenderness of his children there.

Then immediately came in one Lieutenant Smith, a rude fellow, and with his hat on; he told my Lord he came from Colonel Duckenfield, the governor, to tell his Lordship he must be ready for his journey to Bolton. My Lord replied, "When would you have me to go?" "To-morrow, about six in the morning," said Smith. "Well," said my Lord, "commend me to the governor, and tell him by that time I will be ready." Then Smith said, "Doth your Lordship know any friend or servant that would do the thing that your Lordship knows of? It would do well if you had a friend." My Lord replied, "What do you mean? Would you have me find one to cut off my head?" Smith said, "Yes, my Lord, if you could have a friend." My Lord said, "Nay, Sir, if those men that would have my head will not find one to cut it off, let it stand where it is. I thank God, my life has not been so bad, that I should be instrumental to deprive myself of it, though he has been so merciful to me, as to be well resolved against the worst terrors of death. And for me and my servants, our ways have been to

prosecute a just war by honourable and just means, and not by these
ways of blood, which to you is a trade." Then Smith went out, and
called me to him, and repeated his discourse and desires to me. I only
told him, my Lord had given him an answer. At my coming in again
my Lord called for pen and ink, and writ his last letter to my Lady,
to my Lady Mary, and his sons, in the Isle of Man. And in the mean
time Monsieur Paul Moreau, a servant of my Lord's went and bought
all the rings he could get, and lapped them up in several papers, and
writ within them, and made me superscribe them to all his children and
servants. The rest of the day, being Monday, he spent with my Lord
Strange, my Lady Catherine, and my Lady Amelia. At night, about
six, I came to him again, when the ladies were to go away; and as we
were walking, and my Lord telling me he would receive the sacrament
next morning and on Wednesday morning both, in came the aforesaid
Smith, and said, "My Lord, the governor desires you will be ready to
go in the morning by seven o'clock." My Lord replied, "Lieutenant,
pray tell the governor I shall not have occasion to go so early; by nine
o'clock will serve my turn, and by that time I will be ready: if he has
not earnester occasions, he may take his own time." That night I staid,
and at supper my Lord was exceeding chearful and well composed; he
drank to Sir Timothy Featherstone (who was a gentleman that suffered at Chester a week after in the same cause) and said, "Sir, be of
good comfort, I go willingly before you, and God hath so strengthened
me, that you shall hear (by his assistance) that I shall so submit, both as
a Christian and a soldier, as to be both a comfort and an example to you."
Then he often remembered my Lady Mary, with my Lady his wife,
and his sons, and drank to me and all his servants, especially Andrew
Broom; and said, he hoped that they that loved him would never forsake his wife and children, and he doubted not but God would be a father to them, and provide for them after his death.

In the morning my Lord delivered to me the letters for the island,
and said, "Here, Bagaley, deliver these, with my tender affections, to
my dear wife and sweet children, which shall continue, with my prayers for them, to the last minute of my life. I have instructed you as
to all things for your journey. But as to that sad part of it (as to
them) I can say nothing: silence and your own looks will best tell your
message. The great God of heaven direct you, and prosper and com-
for them in their great affliction! Then his Lordship took leave of Sir
Timothy Featherstone, much in the same words as over night. When
he came to the castle gate, Mr. Crossen and three other gentlemen, who
were condemned, came out of the dungeon (at my Lord's request to
the marshal) and kissed his hand, and wept to take their leave. My

Lord said, "God bless and keep you, I hope my blood will satisfy for all that were with me, and you will in a short time be at liberty; but if the cruelty of these men will not end there, be of good comfort, God will strengthen you to endure to the last, as he has done me: for you shall hear I die like a Christian, a man, and a soldier, and an obedient subject to the most just and virtuous Prince this day living in the world."

After we were out of town, the people weeping, my Lord, with an humble behaviour and noble courage, about half a mile off, took leave of them; then of my lady Catherine and Amelia, upon his knees by the coach side (alighting for that end from his horses) and there prayed for them, and saluted them, and so parted. This was the saddest hour I ever saw, so much tenderness and affection on both sides.

That night, Tuesday the 14th of October, 1651, we came to Leigh; but in the way thither, his Lordship, as we rode along, called me to him, and bid me, when I should come into the Isle of Man, to commend him to the archdeacon there, and tell him he well remembered the several discourses that had passed between them there, concerning death, and the manner of it; that he had often said the thoughts of death could not trouble him in fight, or with a sword in hand, but he feared it would something startle him, tamely to submit to a blow on the scaffold. "But," said his Lordship, "tell the archdeacon from me, that I do now find in myself an absolute change as to that opinion; for I bless God for it, who hath put this comfort and courage into my soul, that I can as willingly now lay down my head upon the block, as ever I did upon a pillow."

My Lord supped a competent meal, saying "he would imitate his Saviour: a supper should be his last act in this world;" and indeed his Saviour's own supper before he came to his cross, which would be to-morrow. At night when he laid him down upon the right side, with his hand under his face, he said, "Methinks I lie like a monument in a church, and to-morrow I shall really be so."

As soon as he rose next morning, he put on a fresh shirt, and then said, "This shall be my winding-sheet, for this was constantly my meditation in this action." "See," said he to Mr. Paul, "that it be not taken away from me, for I will be buried in it."

Then he called to my Lord Strange to put on his order, and said, "Charles, once this day I will send it you again by Bagaley, pray return it to my gracious Sovereign, when you shall be so happy as to see him; and say, I sent it in all humility and gratitude, as I received it, spotless, and free from any stain, according to the honourable example of my ancestors."

Then we went to prayer, and my Lord commanded Mr. Greenhaugh to read the Decalogue, and at the end of every commandment made his confession, and then received absolution and the sacrament ; after which, and prayers ended, he called for pen and ink, and wrote his last speech, also a note to Sir E. S.

When we were ready to go, he drank a cup of beer to my Lady, and Lady Mary, and Masters, and Mr. Archdeacon, and all his friends in the island, and bid me remember him to them, and tell the Archdeacon he said the old grace he always used, &c. Then he would have walked into the church, and seen Mr. Tildesley's grave, but was not permitted, nor to ride that day upon his own horse ; but they put him on a little nag, saying they were fearful the people would rescue his Lordship.

As we were going in the middle way to Bolton, the wind came easterly, which my Lord perceived, and said to me, " Bagaley, there is a great difference between you and me now, for I know where I shall rest this night, in Wigan, with the prayers and tears of that poor people, and every alteration moves you of this world, for you must leave me, to go to my wife and children in the Isle of Man, and are uncertain where you shall be ; but do not leave me, if possibly you can, until you see me buried, which shall be as I have told you."

Some remarkable passages in my Lord's going to the scaffold, and his being upon it, with his last speech and dying words.

Betwixt twelve and one o'clock on Wednesday (October 15th), the Earl of Derby came to Bolton, guarded with two troops of horse and a company of foot ; the people weeping and praying all the way he went, even from the castle, his prison, at Chester, to the scaffold at Bolton, where his soul was freed from the prison of his body. His Lordship being to go to a house in Bolton, near the cross, where the scaffold was raised, and passing by, he said, "This must be my cross." And so going into a chamber with some friends and servants, had time courteously allowed him by the Commander-in-Chief till three o'clock that day, the scaffold not being ready, by reason the people in the town refused to strike a nail in it, or to give them any assistance ; many of them saying, that since these wars they have had many and great losses, but none like this, it being the greatest that ever befel them, that the Earl of Derby should lose his life there, and in such a manner. His Lordship, as I told you, having till three o'clock allowed him, I spent that time, with those that were with him, in praying with them, and telling them how he had lived, and how he had prepared to die ; how he feared it not, and how the Lord had strengthened him and comforted him against the terrors of death ; and after such like words, he desired them to pray with him again; and after that giving some good instructions to his son, the Lord Strange, he desired to be in private, where we left him with his God, where he continued upon his knees a good while in prayer. Then called for us again, telling how willing he was to die and part with this world; and that the fear of death was never any great trouble to him never since his imprisonment, though he had still two or three soldiers with him night and day in the chamber; only the care he had of his wife and children, and the fear what would become of them, was often in his thoughts; but now he was satisfied that God would be a husband and a father to them, into whose hands he committed them; and so taking leave of his son, and blessing him, he called for the officer, and told him he was ready. At his going towards the scaffold, the people prayed and cried, and cried and prayed. His Lordship with a courteous humbleness said, "Good people, I thank you all; I beseech you pray for me to the last. The God of heaven bless you; the Son of God bless you; and God the Holy Ghost fill you with comfort." And so coming near the scaffold, he laid his hand on the ladder, saying, "I am not afraid to go up here, though I am to die there;" and so he kissed it, and went up, and walking a while upon the scaffold, settled himself at the east end of it, and made his address to the people thus, viz.:—

" I come, and am content to die in this town, where I endeavoured to come the last time I was in Lancashire, as to a place where I persuaded myself to be welcome, in regard to the people thereof have reason to be satisfied in my love and affection to them; and that now they understand sufficiently. I am no man of blood, as some have falsely slandered me, especially in the killing of a captain in this town; whose death is declared on oath, so as the time and place now appears under the hand of a Master in Chancery, besides the several attestations of a gentleman of honour in the kingdom, who was in the fight in this town, and of others of good report, both in the town and country; and I am confident there are some in this place who can witness my mercy and care for sparing many mens lives that day.

" As for my crime (as some are pleased to call it) to come into this country with the King, I hope it deserves a better name; for I did it in obedience to his call, whom I hold myself obliged to obey, according to the protestation I took in Parliament in his father's time. I confess I love monarchy, and I love my master Charles, the second of that name, whom I myself proclaimed in this country to be King. The Lord bless him and preserve him: I assure you he is the most goodly, virtuous, valiant, and most discreet King that I know lives this day; and I wish so much happiness to this people after my death, that he may enjoy his right, and then they cannot want their rights. I profess here in the presence of God, I always sought for peace, and I had no other reason; for I wanted neither means nor honours, nor did I seek to enlarge either. By my King's predecessors mine were raised to an high condition, it is well known to the country; and it is well known, that by his enemies I am condemned to suffer by new and unknown laws. The Lord send us our King again, and our old laws again, and the Lord send us our religion again.

"As for that which is practised now, it has no name, and methinks there is more talk of religion than any good effects of it.

"Truly, to me it seems I die for God, the King, and the laws, and this makes me not be ashamed of my life, nor afraid of my death."

At which words, *The King*, and *Laws*, a trooper cried, We have no King, and we will have no Lords. Then some sudden fear of mutiny fell among the soldiers, and his Lordship was interrupted; which some of the officers were troubled at, and his friends much grieved, his Lordship having freedom of speech promised him. His Lordship, seeing the troopers scattered in the streets, cutting and slashing the people with their swords, said, "What's the matter, gentlemen? where's the guilt? I fly not, and here is none to pursue you?" Then his Lordship, perceiving he might not speak freely, turned himself to his servant, and gave him his paper, and commanded him to let the world know what he had to say, had he not been disturbed; which is as follows, as it was in my Lord's paper under his own hand :—

"My sentence (upon which I am brought hither) was by a council of war, nothing in the captain's case alleged against me; which council I had reason to expect would have justified my plea for quarter, that being an ancient and honourable plea amongst soldiers, and not violated (that I know of) till this time, that I am made the first suffering precedent in this case. I wish no other to suffer in the like case.

"Now I must die, and am ready to die, I thank my God with a good conscience, without any malice, or any ground whatever; though others would not find mercy upon me, upon just and fair grounds; so my Saviour prayed for his enemies, and so do I for mine.

"As for my faith and my religion, thus much I have at this time to say :

"I profess my faith to be in Jesus Christ, who died for me, from whom I look for my salvation, that is, through his only merit and sufferings. And I die a dutiful son of the church of England, as it was established in my late master's time and reign, and is yet professed in the Isle of Man, which is no little comfort to me.

"I thank my God for the quiet of my conscience at this time, and the assurance of those joys that are prepared for those that fear him. Good people, pray for me, I do for you; the God of heaven bless you all, and send you peace; that God, that is truth itself, give you grace, peace, and truth. Amen."

Presently after the uproar was ceased, his Lordship, walking on the scaffold, called for the headsman, and asked to see the axe, saying, "Come, friend, give it me into my hand, I'll neither hurt it nor thee, and it cannot hurt me, I am not afraid of it;" but kissed it, and so gave it the headsman again. Then asked for the block, which was not ready; and turned his eyes and said, "How long, Lord, how long?" Then putting his hand into his pocket, gave him two pieces of gold, saying, "This is all I have, take it, and do thy work well. And when I am upon the block, and lift up my hand, then do you your work; but I doubt your coat is too burly (being of great black shag) it will hinder you, or trouble you." Some standing by, bid him ask his Lordship for-giveness, but he was either too sullen, or too slow, for his Lordship forgave him before he asked him. And so passing to the other end of the scaffold, where his coffin lay, spying one of his chaplains on horse-back among the troopers, said, "Sir, remember me to your brothers and friends; you see I am ready, and the block is not ready, but when I am got into my chamber, as I shall not be long out of it (pointing to his coffin) I shall be at rest, and not troubled with such a guard and noise as I have been;" and so turning himself again, he saw the block, and asked if it was ready, and so going to the place where he began his speech, said, "Good people, I thank you for your prayers and for your tears; I have heard the one, and seen the other, and our God sees and hears both. Now the God of heaven bless you all, amen." And so bow-ing turned himself towards the block, and then looking towards the church, his Lordship caused the block to be turned, and laid that ways, saying, "I will look towards the sanctuary which is above for ever." Then having his doublet off, he asked, how must I lie, will any one shew me, I never yet saw any man's head cut off; but I will try how it fits: and so laying him down, and stretching himself upon it, he rose again, and caused it to be a little removed; and standing up, and look-ing towards the headsman, said, "Remember what I told you; when I lift up my hands, then do your work."

And looking at his friends about him, bowing said, "The Lord be with you all, pray for me;" and so kneeling on his knees, made a short and private prayer, ending with the Lord's prayer. And so bowing himself again, said, "The Lord bless my wife and children; the Lord bless us all." So laying his neck upon the block, and his arms stretched out, he said these words aloud:

Blessed be God's glorious name for ever and ever.   Amen.
Let the whole earth be filled with his glory.   Amen.

And then lifting up his hands, was ready to give up the ghost, but the executioner, not well observing, was too slow.   So his Lordship rose again, saying (to the headsman) " What have I done that I die not ? Why do not you your work ?   Well, I will lay myself down once again in peace, and I hope I shall enjoy everlasting peace."   So he laid himself down again, with his neck to the block, and his arms stretched out, saying the same words :

Blessed be God's glorious name for ever and ever.   Amen.
Let the whole earth be filled with his glory.   Amen.

And then lifting up his hands, the executioner did his work, and no manner of noise was then heard, but sighs and sobs."

" The Earl of Derby," says Clarendon, " was a man of unquestionable loyalty to the late King, and gave clear testimony of it before he received any obligations from the court, and when he thought himself disobliged by it.   This King in his first year sent him the Garter ; which, in many respects, he had expected from the last.   And the sense of that honour made him so readily comply with the King's command in attending him, when he had no confidence in the undertaking, nor any inclination to the Scots ; who, he thought, had too much guilt upon them in having depressed the crown to be made instruments of repairing and restoring it.   He was a man of great honour, and clear courage ; and all his defects and misfortunes proceeded from his having lived so little time among his equals, that he knew not how to treat his inferiors, which was the source of all the ill that befell him ; having thereby drawn such prejudice against him from persons of inferior quality, who yet thought themselves too good to be contemned, that they pursued him to death."

Helene pinx.   J. W. cook, sculp.

From the original in the collection of
His Grace the late Duke of ....

Published Oct. 1 1842 by E. P. Bowles, 87 Briggate, Leeds.

ANNE CLIFFORD,

COUNTESS OF DORSET, PEMBROKE, AND MONTGOMERY.

John Knox, during his second residence at Geneva, put forth " The first blast of the trumpet against the monstrous *regiment** of women." It was aimed at that Mary of England who was persuaded by priests and other ill-disposed persons to attempt the re-establishment of what she conceived to be *the* CHURCH, by the exertion of her secular power. John Knox ought to have written " against the monstrous regiment of priests," which in kingdoms as in private families, is always most powerful over women, because women are more docile, more confiding, have a much greater yearning after Heaven than men. Moreover, they are almost sole patentees of the virtue of self-denial, and if once they can be convinced that humanity, pity, toleration, or what you will, is a self-indulgence, and a self-seeking, it follows as necessarily as U after Q, that cruelty, hard-heartedness, and intolerance, are a mortification of the flesh, meritorious exactly in proportion as it is painful.

The priests of some religions undertake, for a *consideration*, to bear the sins of such of the laity as put trust in them. They may perhaps find, at last, that they have spoken more truth than they meant to do. It is no small portion of the sins of the earth, of which priests shall bear the blame, and the *whole* blame ; for the reluctant obedience of those who accepted them for the sake of the Lord, whose commission they had forged, shall not lose its reward. He that said that a cup of cold water, given for *his* sake, should not be given in vain, would take no exception, if for his sake, it were ignorantly given to Judas Iscariot.

We have been induced to sound this " Counter-blast" to the " first blast of the Trumpet," because we believe that women, when they *do* err, err far more frequently from superstition, than from passion, and that their worst errors proceed from too great a distrust of their common sense and instinctive feelings, and too great a reliance on *men*, or *serpents*, or *priests*, who promise to make them wise. Under the name priest, we comprehend all creatures, whether Catholic or Protestant,

* i. e. Government.

clerks or laymen, who either pretend to have discovered a byeway to heaven, or give tickets to free the legal toll-gates, or set up toll-gates of their own; or, either explicitly or implicitly discredit the authorised map, and insist upon it, that no one can go the right way, without taking them for guides, and paying them their fees.

We then conclude, that the main disqualification of women to rule, arises from the easiness with which they are ruled, and their proneness to give the reins into dishonest and usurping hands; a fault so nearly allied to the christian virtues of humility, docility, and obedience, so germane to that gentle, confiding spirit, which is at once their safety and their peril, their strength and their weakness, that we doubt whether the defining power of words can fix the land-mark between the good and the evil. It must be " spiritually discerned."

But no good woman *wishes* to rule. Ambition, a far deadlier sin, than the world conceives, and a degrading vice into the bargain, makes worse havoc in a female heart than in a male's. For the graces of womanhood are all womanly,—shy, timid, apt to fly from the most distant approach of harm. In man, many virtues sometimes consort with a giant vice, as we read in the book of Job that there was a meeting of the sons of God, and that Satan came also among them. But in woman the dominance of any one evil passion is as the " abomination of desolation sitting where it should not ;" as the unclean spirit in the empty house that took seven spirits worse than itself, and dwelt with them. There are few instances in which ambitious women have even retained the conservative virtue of their sex. We do not recollect more than one virgin Queen in authentic history. But what is yet more fearful, ambition perverts, where it does not extinguish, the maternal affection, and makes the holiest of feelings a mighty incentive to crime. Semiramis, Agrippina, and Catherine de Medici, are not the only instances that might be adduced of women who have not merely scrupled no wickedness for their sons' advancement, but actually corrupted the minds of their offspring, and plunged them into excess of sensuality, that themselves might govern in their names. But we need not look so high to see the mischief at work. There is no situation on earth more undesirable than that of a portionless beauty with an ambitious mother. The manœuvres, the falsehoods, to which parents who are poor and proud, will sometimes condescend, in order to bring about what is called a great match for a daughter, (that is to say, a connection with a family by whom she will most likely be despised, even now, and in the good old times, might very probably have been poisoned,) far exceed the utmost ingenuity of novelists to devise. And though it is to be hoped that such intrigues and plottings are comparatively rare in the cultivated part of society, yet how often is the happiness of young hearts sacrificed, and virtuous unions forbidden, on a vague expectation of a higher offer? Nor are the influences of ambitious women on their husbands less injurious. It is a hard thing for a married statesman to be honest, if a coronet may be obtained by tergiversation. If " Nolo episcopari," was ever sincerely uttered, it must have been by a celibate clergyman.

Yet, although the *desire* of ruling is thus pernicious to feminine goodness, it by no means follows, that when Providence imposes the *duty* of ruling on a woman, she is to shrink from the responsibility. When the law of succession or the course of events throws dominion into a lady's hands, the same ordaining Power that makes the duty can qualify the person for its performance. There is no intellectual unfitness for sway in the sex : and whatever of moral or physical weakness may pertain to it, may be more than compensated by fineness of tact, purity of inclination, and the strength of good resolve. Indeed, when we consider how few women have attained sovereignty, and how large a proportion of those few have been great sovereigns (we wish more of them had been good women), we might almost conjecture that the politic faculties of the women were greater than those of the men. But the apparent superiority arises from the greater necessity for exertion and circumspection which the sex imposes, and the impossibility of weak women, in dangerous junctures, keeping possession of the seat at all.

Are these reflections irrelevant to Biography? We trust not. At least they were freely suggested by the portrait of that noble lady, whose character we are about to depict. She was one who, with many disadvantages of time and circumstances, after enduring in no slight measure the sufferings to which her sex is exposed from its dependency, during the long residue of her life, happily combined the graces and charities of the high born woman, with the sterner qualifications of a ruler ; the faith and hope of a Christian crowning and harmonizing all. Her sway was little less than regal—we would rather say patriarchal; and long was she remembered in the vales of Westmorland, and among the cliffs of Craven, as a maternal blessing.

As the name of Clifford has so long been connected with the " North Countree," and brings along with it so many historical, poetical, and romantic associations, we shall enter somewhat more than usual into the annals of the family, which, as they must have formed no small part of the education, so are they an important portion of the history of the Lady Anne herself, who made a digest of the family records, with the assistance of Sir Matthew Hale. We regret to say, that from the specimen we have seen, the learned judge seems to have contrived to

shed a sombre, judicial dulness over the composition.   He was much
more interested about the tenures, leases, and other legal antiquities,
than about the wild adventures, loves, and wars of the ancient house.
Some beautiful notices of the Cliffords are to be found in "Southey's
Colloquies," a book that ought to be in every gentleman's and clergyman's library in the kingdom.   In the happily balanced mind of Mr.
Southey, the liveliest fancy serves to stimulate the most accurate
research, and to give a vividness and reality to the past, which the
mere historian, who is not also a poet, hardly *wishes* to bestow.   For the
facts which follow, we are mainly indebted to Dr. Whitaker's History
of Craven.

The original seat of the Cliffords seems to have been in the Marches
of Wales : they afterwards acquired a princely property in Westmorland.   Robert, son of Roger de Clifford and of Isabella, co-heiress of the
Viponts, born about 1274, was the first who connected the family with
Yorkshire. "The situation of his estates on the confines of the Western
Marches, the military character of his family, and the period of turbulence and war which followed the death of Alexander the Third of
Scotland, contributed to form him for an active and strenuous life.   He
was only nine years old at the death of his father, and about thirteen at
the demise of his grandfather Roger, a long-lived and famous Baron in
the reign of Henry the Third, and the earlier years of his son."   "From
his infancy," saith Sir Matthew Hale, " he was educated in the school
of war under King Edward I., as good a master for valour and prudence
as the world afforded ; for by the record of the plea of the 14th Edward
I., it appears that when he was not above nineteen years of age, *stetit
in judicio regis juxta latus suum*, the great business of the claim of the
King of England to the superiority of Scotland being then in agitation,
which doubtless was a time of high action, and fit to enter a young
counsellor, courtier, and soldier.   And this King, who well knew how
to judge of men fit for action, was not wanting to supply this young
Lord with employments befitting the greatness and towardness of his
spirit.   And as it appears by the honours and possessions conferred
upon him from time to time by this Edward, the wisest of English
kings, so he retained the like favour with his son Edward of Carnarvon,
who, in the first year of his reign, granted him the office of Earl
Marshall of England.   And by a fresh charter, dated at Carlisle 24th
Sept. 25 regni sui, the King, having entered Scotland, and seized the
lands of his opposers, grants unto him and his heirs the castle of Car-
lavrock, in Scotland, and all the lands thereunto belonging, which were
Robert Maxwell's, and all the lands thereunto belonging, which were

* Whitaker.

William Douglas's, the King's enemy's, upon Mary Maudin's day, 26 Edw. I., at which time he (Douglas) was taken and imprisoned ; and this was in satisfaction of £500 per annum land in Scotland, with an agreement, that if it did not arise to so much, it should be made good out of other lands in Scotland, and if not, to defaulk. But these acquisitions of land in Scotland were not such as our Robert could build much upon : as they were gotten by power, so they could not be preserved or kept without difficulty. Peace or war between the two nations might be fatal to these his purchases. The latter might make the retaining of them difficult or casual, and the former might occasion a restitution of such prizes. Robert, therefore, not willing to build any great confidence on these debateable acquisitions, in the beginning of the reign of Edward II. cast his eye upon a more firm possession, and "this was the castle, and house, and honour of Skipton."

So far for a sample of Sir Matthew's style, which is neither elegant nor particularly lucid. Robert de Clifford married Matilda, one of the daughters and co-heirs of Thomas de Clare. He was concerned in several of the invasions of Scotland, and probably as successful as any of the other marauders. In 1297 he entered Annandale with the power of Carlisle (of which he was Governor), and slew 308 Scots near Annan Kirk. In 1301 he signed the famous letter from Edward II. to Pope Boniface VIII.,* claiming the seignory of Scotland, by the name of Chatellain of Appleby. In 1306, immediately after the coronation of Robert Bruce, he entered Scotland with the Earl of Pembroke, and defeated Bruce at St. John's town. But he went upon his neighbour's land once too often, and was slain at Bannockburn, June 25th, 1314 ; the most

* No small part of the power assumed by the Popes in disposing of Kingdoms was authorised by the conduct of Kings and nations themselves, who admitted or denied that right as suited present convenience, without ever looking to remoter consequences. Monarchs and factions played off the papal authority against each other. No Pontiff carried his pretensions higher than Boniface, who assumed the title of Master of all Kings, caused two swords to be carried before him, and added a second crown to the Tiard. Had he, however, always judged over Kings as justly as he did in the case of Scotland, the powers he claimed might well have been conceded to the then acknowledged head of the Christian Church. The Scotch had solicited his interference in their favour, which was virtually acknowledging his right to dispose of kingdoms. . Hereupon he wrote a severe expostulation to Edward, commanding him to desist from his oppressions, and demonstrating the rightful independence of the Scotch, as well by arguments of ancient history, as by the allowances and concessions of English Kings. To this letter Edward, who had ever been a rigorous dealer with the Church, replied in a bold strain, deriving his seignory over Scotland from the Trojan Brutus, and the times of Ely and Samuel, and appealing to Heaven with the usual insolence of regal hypocrisy. A hundred and four Barons assembled in Parliament at Lincoln set their seals to this instrument, in which they take care to inform

disastrous day which England ever saw, but for which every true Briton, whether born north or south of the Tweed, is thankful. His body was sent by the victor to Edward II., at Berwick, but the place of its interment is uncertain, though Dr. Whitaker conjectures Bolton Abbey. Of this Robert, first Lord of Skipton of the Cliffords, Sir Matthew Hale observes that " he always so kept the King's favour, that he lost not the love of the nobility and kingdom, and by that means had an easy access to the improvement of his honours and great-ness. He was employed upon all occasions, in offices of the highest trust, both military and civil, having the advantage of a most close education in his youth, under a Prince most eminent for both. He lived an active life, and died an honourable death in the vindication of the rights of his Prince and country." It will be remarked, that Sir Matthew, in asserting the *rightfulness* of a usurpation unparalleled till the partition of Poland, only used a mode of speech familiar to former times, when it was always taken for granted that the claims of the English were just. Our elder poets, historians, and jurists always speak of the Scotch and of the French who adhered to their native princes as rebels.*

Roger, second Lord Clifford of Skipton, joined the Earl of Lancas-ter's insurrection against Edward II., was severely wounded and taken prisoner at the battle of Boroughbridge, March 16th, 1322, and sen-tenced to death, along with Lancaster, and the other Lords, whom the

---

Boniface, that though they had justified their cause before him, they did not acknow-ledge him for their judge.—*Hume.*

* As late as the reign of Elizabeth, the people cherished a hope that the right of the English crown in France was not dead, but sleeping. The adored memory of the fifth Harry, the Lancastrian hero, tended to keep alive a feeling that the *fleurs de lys* were not barren ornaments in England's escutcheon. The poets and dramatists flat-tered the delusion, as must be evident to all who have read Drayton's Battle of Agin-court, and his spirit-stirring ballad on the same subject. Shakspeare, in his Henry the Fifth, not only falls in with the same prejudice, but takes the pains to versify from the Chronicles a long speech of the Archbishop of Canterbury against the Salique Law, which no audience could have heard out, who did not feel something more than a poetical interest in the question. There can be no doubt that many people then attended the theatre for the purpose of learning the history of their country, and " held each strange tale devoutly true." These auditors listened as patiently to " a muster roll of names," or dates, in blank verse, as litigants will do to unintelligible law jargon, which they suppose to explain their title to a disputed field or pathway. How else could Shakspeare have ventured to set on end near sixty such lines as the following :—

Nor did the French possess the Salique law,
Until four hundred one and twenty years
After defunction of king Pharamond,

issue of that day had made traitors, " so that all the lands were seized into the king's hands as forfeited ; but by reason of his great wounds being held a dying man, the execution was respited for that time, and after the heat of the fury was over, his life was spared by the said king, so as he died a natural death, in the 1st year of King Edward III. He died childless and unmarried." Robert de Clifford being his brother and heir, Robert, the third Lord, regained his lands, by the general act of restitution of all the Earl of Lancaster's party, passed in the Parliament of the 4th Edward III. Nothing very remarkable is mentioned concerning him, nor of his two immediate successors, Robert and Roger, of whom the former died young and childless. The latter was engaged in the French and Scottish wars of Edward III., but of his exploits no record remains. " The chain of feudal dependence reached from the cottage to the throne." Accordingly we find that Roger Lord Clifford retained Sir Thomas Mowbray, " for peace and for war," at a salary of £10 yearly, and was himself retained by the Earl of March, for service in Ireland, for which he was bound to provide five Knights Bachelors, thirty-four squires, and forty mounted archers, properly equipped for one year, for which the said Roger was to receive wages at the rate of ten marks a man, passage outward and homeward, to be provided by the said Earl of March, who was to share in the prisoners and other prizes of war, according to the customary proportion, &c. Such at least appears to be the signification of an ancient indenture, in obsolete French, dated London, the 25th Sep., in the third year of Richard II. It is not without interest, as throwing light upon the inter-dependencies of military service in those days ; but Dr. Whitaker should not have concluded that all his readers would understand half-anglicised French of the 14th century, but should have explained the document in plain terms.

Thomas, the sixth Lord, lived not much more than two years after his father's death. He died beyond seas. His daughter, Maud, was second wife to that Richard, Earl of Cambridge, who suffered the penalties of treason, in the reign of Henry V. His son John " was a soldier, and he lived under a martial prince, who by indenture, dated Feb. 8, 4th Henry V., retained him in his service for the war in France for one year : the contract was to this effect, that this Lord, with fifty men at arms, well accoutred, whereof three to be knights, the rest Esquires, and one hundred and fifty archers, whereof two parts to serve on horseback, the third on foot, should serve the king from the day he should be ready to set sail for France, taking for himself four shillings for every knight ; for every Esquire, one shilling ; for every archer, six-pence per

Who died within the year of our redemption
Four-hundred fifty-six.

diem." According to the general computation of the value of money in those days, this rate of payment seems enormously high.

Sir Matthew continues, " This was the usual means whereby Kings in those times furnished their armies with men of value ; and it was counted no dishonourable thing for persons of honour upon this kind of traffic, to make themselves an advantage ; indeed it was in those martial times the trade of the nobility and great men." This *trade* indicated a gradual decay of the genuine feudal system, and prepared the way for standing armies. This John Clifford fell at the seige of Meause, in the last year of Henry V. and was buried in Bolton Abbey.

The next Lord Clifford was slain at St. Albans, May 22, 1455, fighting for his sovereign, in whose service the family was destined to perform and to suffer much. He is first of the line whose name is familiarised to the general reader, being the subject of some powerful lines in the second part of " King Henry the Sixth."

> " Wast thou ordained, dear father,
> To lose thy youth in peace, and to achieve
> The silver livery of advised age,
> And in thy reverence and thy chair days thus
> To die in ruffian battle ? Even at this sight !
> My heart is turn'd to stone : and while 'tis mine
> It shall be stony.   York not our old men spares,
> No more will I their babes : tears virginal
> Shall be to me even as the dew to fire ;
> And beauty that the tyrant oft reclaims
> Shall to my flaming wrath be oil and flax.
> Henceforth I will not have to do with pity."

The " younger Clifford," by whom this dreadful resolution is sup-posed to have been made, has been recorded as the most merciless in a merciless time.   But such is the appetite of man for horrors, that the facts even of civil war are not bad enough to satisfy it without aggrava-tion.   The Clifford who fell at St. Alban's was not a very old man, being only in his forty-first year, nor was Rutland, whom the son of that Clifford is said to have butchered with his own hand, after the battle of Wakefield, a child, but a youth of nineteen, who had probably killed his man before he was killed himself.   Yet John, the ninth Lord Clif_ford, must have been a wholesale homicide to be distinguished as he was, since Leland says, " that for slaughter of men at Wakefield he was called the Boucher."   Shakspeare, or whoever was the author of King Henry VI., has palliated his thirst of blood by ascribing it to filial ven-geance ; but if the father fell only by the chance of war, the son could not be entitled, even by martial morality, to pursue his revenge beyond the measures of war.   It was to his tent that King Henry, when taken captive, at the second battle of St. Albans, by the party which used his name, was brought to meet his victorious Queen, and there he knighted his young Edward, then a boy of eight years. Seldom has a Prince so meek been entertained by a subject so ferocious. Clifford was slain the day before the battle of Towton, after the rencountre at Ferrybridge. Having put off his gorget, he was struck in the throat with a headless arrow, and so was sent to his own place, wherever that might be. This happened in the small valley of Dittingdale, or *Deidingdale*, between Towton and Scarthingwell. The place of his interment is uncertain, but he was not gathered in the tomb of his forefathers. The common report was that he was flung into a pit with the crowd of carcases, and none thought fit to seek for his bones. So detestable is cruelty, even to a cruel generation, that nobody esteemed *black-faced* Clifford too good to rot omong his fellow cut-throats of the " swinish multitude."

John, Lord Clifford, though dead, was attainted, and his estates, castles, &c., forfeited in the 1st of Edward IV. The castle, manor, and Lordship of Skipton, were granted to Sir James Stanley, and afterwards, in the 10th year of King Edward IV., to Richard, Duke of Gloucester, according to the terms of the grant " for the encouragement of piety and virtue in the said Duke," who retained it till his death.

Thus was the house of Clifford driven from its possessions, and deprived of its rank. The children of the ruthless warrior sought and found a refuge among the simple dalesmen of Cumberland. Who has not heard of the *good* Lord Clifford, the *Shepherd Lord?* He that in his childhood was placed among lowly men for safety, found more in obscurity than he sought,—love, humble wisdom, and a docile heart. How his time past during his early years, it is pleasanter to imagine, than safe to conjecture ; but we doubt not, happily, and since he proved equal to his highest elevation, his nurture must needs have been good. His mother Margaret, with whom came in the barony of Vescy, was married to Sir Lancelot Threlkeld, who extended his protection over the offspring of her former husband. Much of Henry Clifford's boyhood is said to have been passed in the village named after his kind step-father, which lies under Blencathara, on the road between Keswick and Penrith. The only extant document relating to the Cliffords during the domination of the House of York, " is a deed of arbitration between Lancelot Threlkeld, knight, and Lady Margaret, his wife, the Lady Clifford, late the wife of John Lord Clifford, on the one part, and William Rilston, one of the executors of the will of Henry de Bromflete, Lord Vescy, deceased, in which the said Lancelot and Margaret promise " to be good master and lady to the said William, and to move the children of the said John, late Lord Clifford, to be loving and tender to the said William." It would seem by this, that the attainder did not deprive the Cliffords of their interests in the barony of Vescy.

The " Shepherd Lord" was restored to all his estates and titles in the first year of Henry VII. He was a lover of study and retirement, who had lived too long at liberty, and according to reason, to assimilate readily with the court of the crafty Henry. By the Lady Anne, he is described " as a plain man, who lived for the most part a country life, and came seldom either to court or to London, excepting when called to Parliament, on which occasion he behaved himself like a wise and good English nobleman." His usual retreat, when in Yorkshire, was Barden-tower; his chosen companions the Canons of Bolton. His favourite pursuit was astronomy. He had been accustomed to watch the motions of the heavenly bodies from the hill-tops, when he kept sheep; for in those days, when clocks and almanacs were few, every shepherd made acquaintance with the stars. If he added a little judicial astrology, and was a seeker for the philosophers-stone, he had the countenance of the wisest of his time for his learned superstition. It is asserted that at the period of his restoration he was almost wholly illiterate. Very probably he was so; but it does not follow that he was *ignorant*. He might know many things well worth knowing, without being able to write his name. He might learn a great deal of astronomy by patient observation. He might know where each native flower of the hills was grown, what real qualities it possessed, and what occult powers the fancy, the fears, or the wishes of men had ascribed to it. The haunts, habits, and instincts of animals, the notes of birds, and their wondrous architecture, were to him instead of books; but above all, he learned to know something of what man is, in that condition to which the greater number of men are born, and to know himself better than he could have done in his hereditary sphere. Moreover, the legendary lore, the floating traditions, the wild superstitions of that age, together with the family history, which must have been early instilled into him, and the romantic and historical ballads, which were orally communicated from generation to generation, or published by the voice and harp of the errant minstrel, if they did not constitute sound knowledge, at least preserved the mind from unideaed vacancy. The man " whose daily teachers had been woods and rills," * must needs, when suddenly called to the society of " knights and barons bold" have found himself deficient in many things; and that want was exceeding great gain, both to his tenantry and neighbours, and to his own moral nature. He lived at

* See Wordsworth's " Song at the Feast of Brougham Castle," a strain of triumph supposed to be chaunted by a minstrel on the day of rejoicing for the " good Lord's

Barden with what was then a small retinue, though his household accounts make mention of sixty servants on that establishment, whose wages were from five to five and twenty shillings each.   But the state of his revenues, after so many years, of spoliation, must have required rigorous economy, and he preferred abating something of ancestral splendour, to *grinding the faces of the poor*.   This peaceful life he led, with little interruption, from the accession of the house of Tudor, till the Scotch invasion, which was defeated at Floddenfield.   Then he became a warrior in his sixtieth year, and well supported the military fame of his house on that bloody day.*   He survived the battle ten years, and died April 23, 1523, aged about 70.   By his last will he appointed his body to be interred at Shap, if he died in Westmorland; at Bolton, if he died in Yorkshire.   He was twice married, first to Anne, daughter of Sir John St. John, of Bletsho, and secondly to Flo-

restoration, in which the poet has almost excelled himself.   Had he never written another Ode, this alone would set him decidedly at the head of the lyric poets of England.

* The enumeration of his followers in the old metrical history of Floddenfield, is curious enough to justify its insertion in a work treating of local heroes:—

> From Penigent to Pendle Hill,
> From Linton to long Addingham,
> And all that Craven coasts did till,
> They with the lusty Clifford came;
> All Staincliffe Hundred went with him,
> With striplings stout from Wharle'dale;
> And all that Hauton hills did climb,
> With Longstroth eke and Litton dale,
> Whose milk-fed follows, fleshy bred,
> Well brawnd with sounding bows upbend,
> All such as Horton Fells had fed
> On Clifford's banner did attend.

Let any person, with a tolerable ear, read these lines aloud, before or after the similar catalogues in Homer, Virgil, Milton, or other poets who have borrowed their nomenclature from the ancient languages, and he will become aware how much our poetic feelings are under the dominion of sound.   Of the places mentioned in Homer's catalogue, a very considerable number were quite as insignificant as Longstroth or Long Addingham; and yet it is obvious that Homer's self could never make Long Addingham as poetical as Amphigeneia.

It may be worth remarking, that the epithet " milk-fed" applied to the Longstrothians and Litton-dale's-men, (who were no milk-sops notwithstanding,) is strictly Homeric.   In the commencement of the thirteenth book of the Iliad, it is applied, with special commendation, line 5th of the original, to the Thracian tribe of Hippe molgi, (milkers of mares,) whom he distinguishes as the longest lived and the most righteous of mankind.   Mare's milk is to this day a principal article of diet among the equestrian Tartar tribes.

rence, daughter of Henry Pudsay, of Bolton, Esq., and widow of Sir Thomas Talbot, of Bashall.

The old age of this good man was sorely disturbed by the follies and vices of a disobedient son. It is not often that a parent complains publicly of his offspring. The sorrow of a despised father seeks concealment, not pity ; and what injury will not an old man endure before he asks redress against his child? Clifford's affliction must have been great indeed, before he was brought to write to a privy counsellor such a letter as the following; which we give unaltered, except as to the spelling. It may serve to shew what sort of creature was the *graceless* of the 16th century.

"I doubt not but ye remember when I was afore you with other of the King's highness's council, and there I shewed unto you the *ungodly* and *ungudely* disposition of my son Henry Clifford in such wise as it was abominable to hear it : not only despiting and disobeying my commands, and threatening my servants, saying that if ought came to me he would utterly destroy all, as apppeareth more likely, in striking, with his own hand, my poor servant Henry Popely, in peril of death, *which* so lieth, and is like to die ; but also he spoiled my houses, and feloniously stole away my proper goods, which was of great substance, only of malice, and for maintaining his inordinate pride and riot, as more speedily did appear when he came out of the court and into the country, apparelled himself and his horse in cloth of gold and goldsmith's work, more like a Duke than a poor Baron's son as he is. And moreover, I shewed unto you at that time his daily studying how he might utterly destroy me, his poor father, as well by slanders shameful and dangerous, as by daily otherwise vexing and disquieting my mind, to the shortening of my poor life. And notwithstanding the premises, I, by *the King's command*, and your desire, have since given to him £40, and over that my blessing upon his good and lawful demeanor, desiring also that he should leave the dangerous and evil counsel of certain evil disposed persons, as *well young Gents* as others, which have before this given him dangerous counsel, whose counsels he daily followeth ; and where I shewed unto the King's grace and you, that if his shameful dispositions were not looked upon, and something promised by his Highness, to bring him to dread (as the beginning of all wisdom is to dread God and his Prince), he should be utterly undone for ever, as well bodily as ghostly, as appeareth at large not only by the increase of his evil dispositions, but also seeking further to great Lords for maintenance, wherein he hath taken more boldness, saying, that he shall cast down one of my servants, though they be in my presence ; and yet moreover he in his country maketh debate between gentlemen, and troubleth divers houses of religion to bring from them their tythes, shamefully beating their servants and tenants, in such wise as some whole towns are fain to keep the churches both night and day." We are not informed whether the King or his counsel took any means of reclaiming this aristocratic young robber, who in due time succeeded to his poor father's estates and honours. He is said, however, to have reformed like his namesake Henry the Fifth, whom he probably made his pattern. -

We hope his father lived to see his reformation.* Perhaps, after all, he was not *much* worse than the licence of his age and rank was supposed to allow. To plunder the defenceless habitations of their inferiors might be a privilege of gentle blood in the reign of the Eighth Harry, as to ruin and desert any woman whose male relatives were not entitled to gentlemanly satisfaction has been accounted in more recent times. Aristocratic morals are as accommodating in one case as the other. The violence of Clifford and his associates points to the effects of a long civil war, and an imperfect civilization.

Within two years after his father's death Henry Clifford was advanced to the dignity of Earl of Cumberland. A very minute

* The Rev. Rector of Whalley seems to have almost forgotten his cloth when he speaks thus slightly of this *prodigal son* and his sacrilegious robberies :—" Indeed the extravagances of a gay and gallant young nobleman, cramped in his allowance by a narrow father, under the influence of a jealous step-mother, were likely to meet with more than sufficient allowance from the world. The method which this *high-spirited young man* took to supply his necessities is characteristic of the times : instead of resorting to Jews and money-lenders, computing the value of his father's life," (he seems to have computed it at very little) " and raising large sums by anticipation, methods which are better suited to the calm unenterprising dissipation of the present age, young Henry Clifford turned outlaw, assembled a band of dissolute followers, harrassed the religious houses, beat their tenants, and forced the inhabitants of whole villages to take sanctuary in their churches." How lamentably dissipation has fallen away from the reverend antiquary's good graces!

As for Dr. Whitaker's conjecture, that Henry Clifford was the hero of the *Notbrowne Mayd*, because that beautiful ballad was first printed in 1521, and containing the word *spleen* could not have been composed much earlier, and because the hero of it pretends to be an outlaw, and afterwards describes Westmoreland as his heritage, we neither cordially embrace, nor scornfully reject it. The *great lynage* of the lady certainly may agree with Lady Percy (whom Henry Clifford married), "and what," asks the Doctor, " is *more* probable, than that this wild young man, among his other feats, may have lurked in the forests of the Percy family, and won the lady's heart under a disguise, which he had taken care to assure her concealed a Knight ? " What is of more importance, Dr. Whitaker cannot suppose that he continued his irregular course of life after his marriage. Of course he lived as virtuously after marriage as the agreeable Rouet of a comedy is presumed to do after the close of the fifth act.

account of his expenses on this occasion is printed in the history of Craven, which may be highly useful to those who investigate the comparative prices of commodities at different periods, as well as to such as are curious about the manner of life among our ancestors.

The expense of his Lordship riding to London with thirty-three servants was £7 16s. 1d. Drunkenness was not among his vices, for his wine for five weeks cost only 3s. 4d.* Nine pounds a week were sufficient for the whole establishment of thirty-four men and horses in London. But the mention of these items would not only be tedious to the general reader, but delusive also; for not only were the prices different from what they are now, but the intrinsic value of the coins greater. It is rather more interesting to find that my Lord, on being created an Earl, gave a new livery to his chaplain, the parson of Guisely. The luxury of apparel in that age was excessive, and continually called down the unavailing denunciations, the *bruta fulmina* of the pulpit; but the parson of Guiseley was plainly dressed enough, nor was the Earl by any means extravagant in arraying his lady, albeit she was a Percy. In alms and offerings he was very economical: in hounds, hawks, and all that pertained to the sports of wood and field, he treated himself like a gentleman. The fee of a physician in 1525 was one pound. In this there has been little rise. A friar received four pence for singing mass. My Lord Derby's minstrels had three and four pence. Well might the clergy preach against those profane ballad-mongers, who were so much better paid than themselves.

The first Earl of Cumberland had the address or fortune to retain the favour of Henry VIII., whose youthful comrade he had been, till the end of his life. Seven years after his advance to an earldom he was honoured with the Order of the Garter; and a little before his death, on the final dissolution of monasteries, he received a grant of the priory of Bolton, with all the lands, manors, &c. thereunto pertaining, and otherwise shared in the church's spoils. This gift may have been intended as a reward for his loyalty and valour displayed in that alarming rebellion, of which the plunder of the religious houses, and the favouritism of low-born persons (a glance at Lord Cromwell, the principal promoter of the suppression), were, if not the causes, the most plausible pretexts. Aske and his followers laid siege to Skipton Castle, and were joined by many retainers of the house of Clifford; but the Earl held it out.

It was but nineteen days before his death that Clifford became

---

* The price of two gallons of sack in Shakspeare's time was 5s. 8d. But the prices of all commodities had increased almost two-fold between the accession of Henry VIII. and the decease of Elizabeth.

formally possessor of the lands and remains of Bolton. How far his participation in the division of the spoil contributed to the comfort of his departure it is not for us to say. He expired April 22, 1542, aged 49, and was buried in the vault of Skipton Castle.

The peaceful life of his successor, also called Henry, was happy in furnishing few materials for the biographer. When only sixteen years old he was made a Knight of the Bath, at the coronation of Queen Anne Bullen. He married the Lady Ellenor Brandon, niece to King Henry VIII., and daughter of Mary, the widow of Louis XII., a woman to be held in everlasting honour; for she dared, in the sixteenth century, to unite herself to the man of her choice. Thus the Clifford family became closely united with the blood royal. Great matches are seldom quite so prudent as they appear. The expenses attending this lofty alliance were such as to compel the Earl to alienate the oldest manor remaining in the family; but after the death of the Lady Ellenor he retired into the country, and, by judicious retrenchment, more than repaired the breach in his estates; in which laudable design he was assisted by his second wife, Anne, daughter of Lord Dacre, a very domestic woman, who was never at or near London in her life. In the interval between his marriages he was seized with a sickness, which for a time suspended all appearances of animation, so that the physicians thought him dead. His body was stripped, laid out upon a table, and covered with a hearse cloth of black velvet, when some of his attendants, by whom he was greatly beloved, perceived symptoms of returning life. He was put to bed, and by the use of warm applications, internal and external, gradually recovered. But for a month, or more, his only sustenance was woman's milk, which restored him completely to health, and he became a strong man.[*]

Of this Earl his grand-daughter states, " that he had a good library, and was studious of all manner of learning, and much given to alchemy." No wonder, as his principal study was to retrieve his fortune, that he spent a little time and money in the pursuit of the philosopher's stone. It would have been very convenient to turn lead into gold, if the secret could have been kept. On the whole, the second Earl seems to have been—

A frugal swain,
Whose only care was to increase his store.

He would, had he lived much longer, have found it very difficult "to "keep his son at home." After his first lady's death he was only three times at court: first, at the coronation of Queen Mary; secondly, at the marriage of his daughter to the Earl of Derby; and thirdly, to

* Whitaker, from the Appleby MS.

congratulate Queen Elizabeth on her accession. The only military transaction in which he appears to have been engaged was a few months before his decease, when he assisted the Lord Scroop in fortifying Carlisle against the rebels of 1569, when the Earls of Westmorland and Northumberland planned " the Rising of the North," which was ultimately so beneficial to the Clifford family, by enabling them to appropriate the lands of the Nortons. He died just five days after he had finally concluded a match between his son George, then in his eleventh year, and the daughter of Francis Russel, second Earl of Bedford. The poor children, when they attained puberty, were obliged to stand by the impious and unnatural bargain. We need hardly say that the union was eminently unhappy. Yet a father busied himself on his death bed in bringing it about, and reckoned it not among things to be repented of.*

* It was no unusual thing in those times to which, by certain writers, we are referred for lessons of wisdom and examples of holiness, to contract marriages between contingent children, whose sex and very existence were yet undetermined. So completely was the first ordinance of God perverted to the purposes of ambition. The effects upon general morality may be easily conjectured.

The following document, relating to a former Lord Clifford, (the Lord Thomas, who was slain at St. Alban's,) is so curious, that we need not apologize for its insertion a little out of chronological order :—

" Be it known to all men, that for as Much as it is meritorie and medeful for every true christian man to testify and bare true wituess in every true matter or cause; therefore we, William Ratcliffe, being the age of five score yeres; Nicholas Whitfield, of 98 yeres; and John Thom, of 80 years, will record and testify, for verrey trawthe, that the Lord, Sir Thomas Clifford, marryed Elizabeth, his doghter, unto Robert Plumpton, the eldest son and heir of Sir William Plumpton, when she was but six yeres of age, and they were wedded at the chappel within the castell, at Skypton, and the same day one John Garthe _bare her in his armes_ to the said chappel. And also itt was agreed at the same tyme that yf the foreseid Robert dyed within age, that then the said Lord Clifford should have the second son of the said Sir William Plumpton, unto his second doghter. And they were bot three years marryed when the said Robert dyed; and when she came to the age of twelve yeares she was marryed to William Plumpton, second son to the foresaid Sir William, and the said Sir William promised the said Lord Clifford that they should not ligg togedder till she came to the age of sixteen yeres; and when she cam to eighteen yeres she bare Margarete, now Lady Roucliffe. And how as hath bene evydent imbeseled, or what as hath been doon syns, we cannot tell, but all that ys afore rehersed in thys bill we wyll make yt gode, and yf nede be, deeply depose the King and hys counsell, that yt is matter of trawthe, in any place wher we shal be comanded, as far as it is possible for such olde creatures to be carried to. In witness whereof, we, the said Wm. Nicholas and Iohn have sett our seales the XXVIth of October, in the XIX yere of the reane of Kynge Henrie the VIIth. (A. D. 1503).

Contrary to our usual practice and intention, we have in this transcript preserved the original orthography, as given by Dr. Whitaker, contractions excepted, that the

George Clifford, third Earl of Cumberland, succeeded to the title, which he memorized, and the estates, which he was near spending, in 1569, when only in his eleventh year. The wardship of wealthy minors was then an important and oppressive prerogative of the crown, which was usually let out to favourites or powerful persons whom it was desirable to influence ; but the charge of young Clifford was naturally and properly given to his father-in-law, Francis Earl of Bedford, though his education was chiefly conducted by Viscount Montague, who had married his mother's sister, and with whom he resided for some time in Sussex. At the customary age, (then three years earlier than now,) he was sent to Cambridge, where he was entered of Peter House. His tutor was Whitgift, afterwards Archbishop of Canterbury. He was so passionately devoted to the mathematics, (which were not then, as now, the staple commodity of Cambridge,) that he rather neglected logic and theology, greatly, no doubt, to the displeasure of his pious preceptor. But perhaps the thoughts of the youth were already upon the ocean, and he cared for no learning but what might serve mariner

> To steer the bold bark o'er the new-found main,
> To the new land of glory, blood, and gain.
> Not on the still height of the sylvan tower
> He lov'd to wait the planetary hour;
> Nor wrought in fire the secret to unfold,
> Of youth perpetual, and transmuted gold.
> He from the dizzy mast the stars survey'd,
> That point to realms where gold is ready made.

To do anything like justice to the life of this high-born adventurer would require a volume.* Perhaps the main incidents cannot be more concisely related than in the words of his daughter, inscribed upon the famous family picture at Skipton Castle :—" This is the Picture of George Clifford, third Earl of Cumberland, in the male line of his family, the fourteenth Baron Clifford, of Westmorland, and Sheriff of that county by inheritance ; and, in the same descent, the thirteenth Lord of the honor of Skipton, in Craven, and also Lord Viscount and Baron Vescy. He was born son and heir apparent to H. Earl of Cum-

"air of ancient simplicity" may not be impaired. The paper would be interesting if it were only for the great age of the honest Craven men by whom it is witnessed. In what a strange morbid state of mind this little Elizabeth, this virgin widow not yet in her teens, must have been kept, especially when the character of nurses and waiting women in that age is considered, of which Juliet's nurse is doubtless a fair and somewhat flattering sample.

* Had the Lord George been born at Skipton we would have given him a separate article ; but he chose to be born in Westmorland, and lived very little in Yorkshire.

2 K

berland, by his second wife Anne, daughter to William Lord Dacre, of the North ; he was born in his father's castle of Bromeham, in Westmorland, the 8th of August, 1558. At the age of eleven years and five months, lying then in the house called Battell Abbey, in Sussex, he came to be Earl of Cumberland by the decease of his father, who died in the said castle of Bromeham, about the 8th or 10th of January, 1570, as the year begins on New-year's-day. When he was almost 19 years old he was married in the church of St. Mary Overs, in Southwark, June 24, 1577, to his virtuous and only lady, the Lady Margaret Russell, third daughter and youngest child to Francis, second Earl of Bedford, by his first wife, Margaret St. John, by whom he had two sons and one daughter, Francis and Robert, who being successively Lords Cliffords, died young, in their father's life-time ; and the Lady Anne Clifford, who was just fifteen years and nine months at her father's death, being then his sole daughter and heir. He performed nine voyages by sea in his own person, most of them to the West Indies, with great honour to himself, and service to his Queen and country, having gained the strong town of Fiall, in the Zorrous Islands,* in the year 1589 ; and in his last voyage the strong fort of Portorico, in the year 1598. He was made Knight of the Garter by Queen Elizabeth, and counsellor of state by King James. He died in the Duchy-house, in the Savoy, London, the 30th of October, 1605, being then of age 47 years and 3 months wanting 9 days. His bowels and inner parts *was* buried + in Skipton Church, in Craven, in Yorkshire, the 13th of March following. By his death the title of Earl of Cumberland came to his only brother, Sir Francis Clifford. But the ancient right to his baronies, honours, and ancient lands descended then to his only daughter and heir, the Lady Anne Clifford, for whose right to them her worthy mother had after great suits at law with his brother Francis, Earl of Cumberland. This Earl George was a man of many natural perfections; of a great wit and judgment, of a strong body, and full of agility ; of a noble mind, and not subject to pride or arrogance ; a man generally beloved in this kingdom. He died of the bloody flux, caused, as was supposed, by the many wounds and distempers he received formerly in his sea voyages. He died penitently, willingly, and christianly. His only daughter and heir, the Lady Anne Clifford, and the Countess, her mother, were both present with him at his death."

* The Azores.

+ Something is evidently wanting in the inscription here. The sentence was probably written thus :—His bowels and inward parts ".was" buried in the church of Savoye, and his body in Skipton church.—*Whitaker.*

The many naval expeditions in which Lord George engaged were undertaken chiefly at his own cost, and were attended with great loss as well as suffering. His first appearance as a military adventurer was in Holland, whither he went with a party of noble volunteers, in the hope of relieving Sluys, then besieged by the Prince of Parma. The design proved abortive. About the same time he fitted out, at his own charge, a fleet of three ships and a pinnace, the latter commanded by Sir Walter Raleigh, for a voyage of discovery and privateering. Contrary winds detained this little squadron till August, 1586, when it bent its course towards the South Sea, reached the forty-fourth degree of south latitude, and then returned. The crew endured severe hunger, only partially mitigated by the capture of a few trifling Portuguese vessels.

In the memorable year of the Armada, the Earl commanded the Elizabeth Bonaventure, and highly distinguished himself in the action fought off Calais. Disinclined to rest, and perhaps little loving a home embittered by a forced marriage, which the virtues of his lady only made more grievous, by adding self-reproach to dissatisfaction, (for there are none in whose company men find themselves so ill at ease as those whom they feel they ought to love, and yet cannot love,) he projected a second voyage to the South Seas as soon as the Armada was destroyed. England and England's Queen were now eager for reprisal upon Spain, whose golden lands in the New World offered at once revenge, renown, and booty. Clifford received his sovereign's commission, and the loan of a royal ship, the Golden Lion, which he nevertheless had to fit out at his private expense. But the sea, which he wooed for his bride, was to him a cruel mistress. Baffled by storms, and compelled by stress of weather to cut his main-mast by the board, he could hardly clear the channel, and put back without effecting anything. But though hardly dealt with by the winds and waves, he was not cast down. Tranquillity was not for him. On the 18th of June, 1589, he sailed once more toward the Western world, with three small vessels, headed by his flag-ship the Victory. On this cruise he took and dismantled Fiall, in the Azores, (as mentioned by his daughter,) and captured twenty-eight vessels of various burdens, valued at more than £20,000. These prizes were dearly purchased. In an engagement between the Victory and a Brazil ship, he was wounded in several places, and scorched by an explosion of gunpowder; but this was nothing to what he and his crews suffered by famine and thirst on their homeward voyage, and almost within sight of Ireland; contrary winds preventing their coming to land. More perished by thirst than had fallen either by war or disease during the whole expedition.

> Water, water, every where,
> And all the boards did shrink,
> Water, water, every where,
> Nor any drop to drink.
>
> THE ANCIENT MARINER.

At length a change of wind enabled the survivors to land in Bantry-bay, on the 2nd of December. What a spectral company they must have been!

But neither danger, want, nor pain, can uproot an instinct, or change that native bias of the mind which is destiny. In May 1591, Clifford was at sea cruising with small success in the Mediteranean. The following year he fitted out a fleet for the West Indies, which he did not accompany in person. This was much the most fortunate of his ventures, yet not the less unfortunate for himself. His ships fell in with, and captured, a Spanish Caraque, valued at £150,000; but the admiralty courts, or what then supplied their place, decided, that not having been himself engaged, he had no legal claim to any part of the prize. Instead of receiving, therefore, that high interest for his money that he expected as his just due, he was obliged, to save himself from extreme embarrassment, to accept £36,000 of the Queen, as a boon. Elizabeth was far from wealthy, and, except in her dress, sternly economical, therefore this donation shews either that Clifford was personally in her good graces, or that she thought he had been treated with palpable injustice. By the portraits that remain of him, he appears to have been a man well suited to win the eye of a woman certainly not devoid of passion, for he was a model of masculine comeliness, with a countenance of more expression than usually belongs to a handsome man, and a person formed alike for strength and agility, accomplished in all knightly exercises, splendid in his dress, of romantic valour, and a tongue to speak eloquently

> Of all the wonders of the mighty deep,
> Tales that would make a maiden love to weep,
> Of perils manifold and strange, of storms,
> Battle, and wreck, and thousand feller forms,
> Which Death, careering on the terrible sea,
> Puts on to prove the true Knight's constancy.

Neither the Queen's favour, nor his own losses, could extinguish his passion for nautical adventure. But the occurrences of his latter voyages are not striking enough to require a place here. Altogether he must be denominated an unfortunate speculator on the chances of maritime war. We cannot call him a Sea-Quixote, for a degree of cupidity mingled with his restlesness. The long war, and the enormous wealth of the Spanish settlements, had revived in the English character the Scandinavian spirit of piracy: few of Elizabeth's warriors emulated the stainless honour and humanity of Sir Philip Sidney. Drake and Raleigh themselves were little better than Gentlemen Buccaneers.

A few words may here be admitted on Clifford's deportment as a courtier. Unfit for political business, he was favoured without being trusted. Elizabeth, who seldom suffered her personal partialities to interfere with the distribution of office, and sagaciously discovered the native vein of each man's faculties, found easy means to fix his attachment, and gratify her own vanity at the same time. "She knew—perhaps admired—his foibles, and certainly flattered them." * In 1592 she invested him with the Garter, which he wears in the Skipton picture. A scarce whole-length portrait, engraved by Robert White, preserves another little circumstance, which, trifle as it is, is characteristic; and it is only fair to record of him what he would diligently have recorded himself. At an audience, after his return from one of his expeditions, the Queen dropped her glove: Clifford took it up, and presented it on his knees. Graciously she bad him keep it for her sake. He had it richly set with diamonds, and wore it ever after, on ceremonial occasions, in the front of his hat.

On the super-annuation of Sir Henry Lea, K. G., he was appointed her Majesty's peculiar champion at all Tournaments. Sir William Segar, in his treatise "Of Honour, Military and Civil," has memorialized the order of his admission to this office, for which he was so admirably qualified by taste and nature. Doubtless he wore that suit of tilting armour which now hangs "in monumental mockery" at Appleby castle, the helmet of which no living shoulders could support. "But he must have been of a stature well adapted for bearing great weights, for the whole suit measures only five feet nine inches from the cone of the helmet to the ground. The perpendicular posture may, however, have occasioned some contraction in the leathern ligaments of the joints.† It is pleasant to gaze in imagination on the pageantry of antique times. In all that pertains to parade and ceremony, we are a most degenerate people. Not that we have lost the love of show, but shows with us have no meaning. In the chivalric ages every observance was significant, historical, or allegorical. We love to read of these things in romance. They had a charm for the sweet Spenser and the noble

* Lodge. † Whitaker.

Sidney ; and Milton himself, republican as he was, caressed them in fancy, and disdained not the towered cities where—

> Throngs of Knights and Barons bold,
> In weeds of peace high triumphs hold ;
> With store of ladies whose bright eyes
> Rain influence, and adjudge the prize
> Of wit, or arms, while both contend
> To win her grace, whom all commend.
> There let Hymen oft appear,
> In saffron robe, with taper clear,
> And pomp, and feast, and revelry,
> With mask and antique pageantry ;
> Such sights as youthful poets dream,
> On summer eve by haunted stream.—L'ALLEGRO.

If any utilitarian require further reason for our particularity on this head, we assure him that the expense of these pageants was a great means of ruining the nobility, and compelling them to alienate their estates ; whereby the neck of the feudal power was broken, and room was made for the middle gentry to rise.   Hence the increased importance of the House of Commons, and its natural consequence,—the abridgment of monarchical prerogative, and aristocratic privileges.   But listen to Sir William Segar :—

 "On the seventeenth day of November, anno 1690, this honourable gentleman," (Sir Henry Lea) "together with the Earl of Cumberland, having first performed their service at arms, presented themselves unto her highness at the foot of the stairs, under her gallery window, where at that time her Majesty did sit, accompanied with the Viscount Turyn, ambassador of France, many ladies, and the chiefest nobility. Her Majesty beholding these armed knights coming towards her, did suddenly hear a music so sweet and secret, as every one thereat greatly marvelled.   And hearkening to that excellent melody, the earth as it were opening, there appeared a pavilion, made of white taffeta, containing eight score ells, being a proportion like unto the sacred temple of the Virgins Vestal.   This temple seemed to consist upon pillars of porphyry, arched like unto a church : within it were many lamps burning : also, on the one side, there stood an altar, covered with cloth of gold, and thereupon two wax candles, burning in rich candlesticks : upon the altar also were laid certain princely presents, which, after, by three virgins, were presented unto her Majesty.   Before the door of this temple stood a crowned pillar, embraced by an eglantine tree, whereon was hanged a table, and therein written, with letters of gold, this prayer following : *—Elizæ, &c. Piæ, potenti, fælicissimæ virgini,

* "To Eliza, the most pious, potent, and fortunate virgin, the lady-champion of

fidei, pacis, nobilitatis vindici ; cui Deus, Astra, Virtus summa devo-
verunt omnia. Post tot annos, tot triumphos, animam ad pedes posi-
turus tuos sacra senex affixit arma. Vitam quietam, imperium 'æter-
num, famam æternam precatur tibi, sanguine redempturus suo. Ultra
columnas Herculis Columna moveatur tua, Corona superet coronas
omnes, ut quam Coelum felicissime nascenti coronam dedit beatissime
moriens reportes Coelo Summe, Sancte, Æterne, audi, exaudi, Deus.

*   *   *   *   *   *

" These presents and prayer being with great reverence delivered into
her Majesty's own hand, and he himself* disarmed, offered up his
armour at the foot of her Majesty's crowned pillar ; and kneeling upon
his knees, presented the Earl of Cumberland, humbly beseeching she
would be pleased to accept him for her knight, to continue the yearly
exercises aforesaid. Her Majesty graciously accepting of that offer,
this aged knight armed the Earl, and mounted him upon his horse :
that being done, he put upon his own person a side-coat of black velvet,
pointed under the arm, and covered his head, in lieu of a helmet, with
a buttoned cap."

Besides his addiction to the ancient exercises of nobility, Lord George
was much given to horse-racing, a sport or game of more recent introduction. He kept splendid hospitality, and gave princely entertain-
ments ; his toils and his pleasures were alike costly. No wonder then,
that having " set out with a larger estate than any of his ancestors, in
little more than twenty years he made it one of the least," and that his
muniment room is full of " memorials of prodigality, sales, mortgages,
inquietude, and approaching want ;" but his pride preserved him from
running deeply into debt : he preferred alienating his property to borrowing on usury, and it was found at his death, that his debts did not
exceed £700. He died at the Savoy in London ; but his remains were

---

faith, peace, and nobleness; to whom God, her stars, and her virtue, have sworn to
give all sovereignty, After so many years, so many triumphs, the Aged, who would
lay his life at thy feet hath hung up his dedicated arms. He implores for thee
quiet life, everlasting dominion, everlasting fame, which he is ready to purchase with
his own blood. May thy crown excel all crowns : that crown which Heaven
most auspiciously gave thee at thy nativity, mayest thou, most blessed, at thy death
bear back to Heaven. O thou supreme, holy, eternal God, hear and give ear."

The peculiar brevity and compact collocation of the Latin tongue gives a beauty
and satisfactoriness to lapidary or epigrammatic writing wholly unattainable in any
other language. The introduction of a prayer on an occasion of mere pageantry---
a prayer addressed to the supreme God, in which there is mention of Hercules; in
which the Divinity is classed with the stars, and an abstract human quality---is very
characteristic of the age and taste of Elizabeth.

* Sir Henry Lea.

conveyed to the seat of his forefathers, and he lies in the vault of Skipton castle. The entry of his interment in the parish register of Skipton is as follows :—" 1605. Oct. 29. departed this life, George, Earl of Cumberland, Lord Clifforde, Vipounte, and Vessie, Lord of the honor of Skipton in Craven, Knight of the most noble order of the Garter, one of his highness privie counsell, Lord Warden of the cytie of Carlell and the West Marches, and was honorably buried at Skipton, the XXIX of December, and his funerall was solemnized the XIIIth day of Marche next then following." The custom of that day in regard to hearsing up of corpses, must have been even more dilatory and expensive than the present fashion. The body is kept above ground more than two months, and then is buried privately, we are to suppose ; then more than two months after, his funeral is publickly solemnized. A like double celebration of marriages, and of christenings, was not unusual at the same period. The Earl was little more than forty seven.

This extraordinary man, who saw, and did, and suffered so much, has left no account of his voyages and perils ; but Dr. Whitaker discovered among the family evidence, a MS. journal of the expedition of 1586, (which the Earl did not himself accompany,) apparently written by an ordinary pilot, or inferior officer, intituled as follows :—" A Voyage pretended to the India, set forth by the good Earl of Cumberland, with two ships and a pinnace, Mr. Wytherington being captain of the admiral, and Mr. Lister of the vice-admiral." One passage only is extracted by the Doctor from this journal ; but it is worth repeating :— " Nov. 5. Our men went on shore and *fet rys*,* and burn't the rest of the houses in the *Neger's* town ; and our boat went down to the outermost" uttermost, " point of the river, and burnt a town, and brought away all the rice that was in the town. The 6th day we served God, being Sunday." The account of the voyage of 1589, and its horrible distresses and privations, was drawn up by Edward Wright, a famous mathematician, who was himself in the fleet. His narrative may be found in Hackluyt. Several letters of the Lord George are preserved ; but they throw little light on the most interesting part of his life, though they sufficiently testify his pecuniary difficulties. One is addressed to the Lord Treasurer Buleigh, requesting the loan of £10,000 from the Queen. It is dated 22nd September, 1586, when he was engaged in his first expedition. Another to Sir Francis Walsingham, respecting a Spanish ship, wrecked on the coast near Plymouth, in the time of the Armada, which it was falsely rumoured that the

---

* Probably intended for *fetched rice ;* the more than usual irregularity of spelling in this MS. proves it to be the work of an uneducated man, e. g. vyag for voyage, vys athmerrall for vice-admiral.

Duke of Medina Sidonia, the Spanish admiral, was aboard. A third relates to the action off Calais, in which Clifford bore so considerable a part. It is dated 20th February, and inscribed to Lord Burleigh. We shall quote but one, addressed also to Lord Burleigh, and dated April 26, 1597. It expresses little satisfaction with the reward of his services, or the profit of his ventures.

" To my very good Lord the Lord Treasurer of England.

"MY GOOD LORD,—As I have ever found your Lordship willing to do me kindness, so I beseech you, (now in the time when much it may pleasure me both in my reputation and estate,) to give me your best furtherance. I hear her Majesty will bestow the Isle of Wight upon some such as shall there be resident: To which condition willingly I would, as is fitting, tie myself, not with such humours to sea journeys, as heretofore has carried me on, but, by just discourage, settle myself to what shall neither get envy, nor give colour to false informations. I protest to your Lordship, desire of enabling myself for her Majesty's service, chiefly drew me with greediness to follow those courses all this year, as your Lordship knows there hath been likelyhood of my employment, and generally spoken of. Now I hear it is otherwise determined, to which I willingly submit myself ; but so sensible of the disgrace, that if her majesty does not shew me some other token of her favour, I shall as often wish myself dead as I have hours to live. But my fitness to govern that island I leave to your Lordship's judgment: but this I vow, he lives not, that with more duty and care shall keep and defend it than I will, and if by your Lordship's good means it may be obtained, I shall think her Majesty deals most graciously with me, and ever acknowledge myself most bound to your Lordship, whom I commit to God, and rest your Lordship's to command—GEORGE CUMBERLAND."

But the only writing of this high-born sea-wanderer that can be considered as a literary composition, is a speech delivered at some masque or spectacle in the character of the melancholy Knight. It is curious, and throws over his real discontents but a thin veil of fiction. It is long, and in a quaint, conceited style ; but some passages are curiously biographical, and others whimsical for the excess of allegorical adulation.

" This Knight, (*Fairest* and Happiest of Ladies) removing from castle to castle, now rolleth up and down in open field, a field of shadow, having no other mistress but night shade, nor gathering any moss but about his heart. This melancholy, or rather desperate retiredness, summons his memory to a repetition of all his actions, thoughts, misfortunes, in the depth of which discontented contentedness upon one leaf he writes, *utiliter consenesco,* and masters up all his spirit to its wonted courage: but in the same minute he kisseth night-shade and embraceth it, saying, *solanum solamen.* Then having no company but himself, thus he talks with himself: That he hath made ladders for others to climb, and his feet nailed to the ground not to stir: That he is like *him* that built the anchor to save others, and *themselves* to be drowned. That when he hath outstript many in desert, he is tript up by Envy, until those *overtake* him, that *undertook* nothing. He on the confidence of unspotted honour, levelled all his actions to nurse those twins, Labour and Duty, not knowing which of these was eldest, both running fast, but neither foremost. Then, casting his eyes to Heaven, to wonder at Cynthia's brightness, and to look out his own unfortunate star: with deep sighs he breathes out a two-fold wish, that the one may never wain while the world waxeth; that the other may be erring, not fixt. There is no such thing as night-shade; for where can there be mist or darkness where you are, whose beam wraps up clouds as whirlwinds dust? Night-shade is fallen off, sinking into the center of the earth, as not daring to show blackness before your bright-ness. I cannot excuse my Knight's error, to think that he should cover himself obscurely in any desolate retiredness where your Highness beauty and virtue could not find him out. He now grounds all his actions neither upon hopes, counsel, nor experience; he disdains envy, and scorns ingratitude. Judgment shall arm his patience, patience confirm his knowledge, which is that,—yourself being Perfection, know measure, number, and time to cause favour where it should, and where you please, being only wise and constant in weighing with true steadi-ness both the thoughts of all men, and their affections, upon which he so relies, that whatsoever happen to him you are still yourself, wonder and happiness, to which his eyes, thoughts, and actions are tied with such an indissoluble knot, that neither Death, nor Time that triumphs after Death, shall, or can unloose it. Is it not, as I have often told you, *that after he had thrown his lard into the sea, the sea would cast him on the land for a wanderer?* He that spins nothing but Hope, shall weave up nothing but repentance. He may well entertain a shade for his mistress, that walks the world himself like a shadow, embracing names instead of things, dreams for truths, blind prophecies, for seeing verities. It becomes not me to dispute of his courses; but yet none shall hinder me from wondring to see him, that is not, to be, and yet to be—that never was. If ye think his body too strait for his heart, ye shall find the world wide enough for his body." The allusions to his own circumstances in this speech are obvious: the rest of it, is not very intelligible, or particularly worth understanding.

We have before stated, that his union with the Lady Margaret Russel was eminently unhappy. But though a cold, negligent, and unfaithful husband, he is not accused of domestic tyranny. Yet the sorrows of his wife were doubtless large enough ; and it is said that his attachment to a Court-lady, occasioned a separation : perhaps a *desertion*, would better express the truth. To this entanglement, his daughter, who speaks of him, as a good daughter should do of an indifferent father, thus feelingly alludes, " But as good natures through human frailty are often misled, so he fell in love with a lady of quality, which did by degrees draw and alienate his affections from his so virtuous and loving wife ; and it became the cause of many sorrows." But it is rather to be thought that he had little conjugal affection to alienate, and that his wife, who married him without love, loved him no more than duty could constrain from an unwilling heart. Yet, whatever secession may have taken place during the Earl's life, prevented not his consort from attending his dying hours, for we have the testimony of the Lady Anne, that she and her mother were with him a few hours before his decease.

Three children were the produce of that family compact, which only deserves to be called a marriage, insomuch as it was sanctified by the pious submission of the most suffering party. Two sons, Francis and Robert, and the daughter, for whose sole sake we have given these notices of her forefathers, *one only* of whom was worthy to be progenitor to such a child. But God alone is the Father of souls.

Both Francis and Robert died while their father, who cared little for them, was at sea. Of Francis, the elder, his sister says " that he was admired by those who knew him for his goodness and devotion, even to wonder, considering his childish years: his brother Robert and the Countess their mother, were in Skipton Castle at his death, where the same Countess was great with child with her only daughter, whom she was delivered of in that Skipton Castle, the 30th of January following: she that was the Lady Anne Clifford, and came to be the only child to her parents. When this Lord Francis died, his said father was then beyond seas, in the north parts of Ireland, whither he was driven on land, by great extremity of tempest, in great hazard of life, ten days before the death of the said son, when that Earl was on his return from the isles Azores in the West Indies." So Clifford's eldest child died just when its father was near dying of hunger. The second son, Robert, in like manner, never lived to be a man, yet was he " a child endowed with many perfections of so few years, and likely to have made a gallant man." His sorrowful mother, and his then little sister were in the house when he died, "which Lady Anne Clifford, was then but a year and four months old, by the death of her said brother Robert Clifford, she came to be the sole heir; and when this young Lord Robert died, his father, George, Earl of Cumberland, was in one of his voyages on the seas toward Spain and the West Indies."

Of her mother she says, "That the death of her two sons did so much affect her, as that ever after the book of Job was her constant companion. The good and afflicted lady had troubles in her widowhood, which a male heir would have prevented; but the life of a virtuous daughter, and the memory of two sons that lived not long enough to be wicked, (to whom, therefore, she could ascribe as many *possible* virtues as she chose,) were better to her than any son would have been.

In the remarkable family picture to which we have already adverted, the Countess, Margaret is represented standing by her husband's side, with one arm extended towards her two sons; and some have plausibly imagined that she is soliciting the Earl to stay at home and take care of them. She has a most amiable countenance, being more like a good woman of the present day, than most female portraits of her time. Her dress, which is high up to the throat, and opens in front, with wide hanging sleeves, would not be much out of fashion now; but her little boys, linked arm in arm, and inveterately staring at nothing, are rather too like miniature doctors of divinity. Their long dresses completely concealing their feet, are more like cassocks than anything else; and they have surcingles round the waist. It is pleasant to see how children were drest in the seventeenth century.

Before we enter upon our account of the Lady Anne, we will give her description of herself as a letter of introduction:—"I was" says she "very happy in my first constitution, both in mind and body; both for internal and external endowments; for never was there a child more entirely resembling both father and mother than myself. The colour of mine eyes was black, like my father's, and the form and aspect of them was quick and lively, like my mother's. The hair of my head was brown and very thick, and so long that it reached to the calf of my legs when I stood upright; with a peak of hair on my forehead, and a dimple on my chin: and an exquisite shape of body, like my father. But now time and age have long since ended all those beauties, which are to be compared to the grass of the field: (Isaiah xl. 6, 7, 8; 1 Peter i. 24.*) For now, when I caused these memorables of myself to be written, I have passed the sixty-third year of my age. And though I

* Isaiah xl. 6, 7, 8: "The voice said cry; and I said what shall I cry?—All flesh is grass, and the goodliness thereof is as the flower of the field; the grass withereth, the flower fadeth, because the Spirit of the Lord bloweth upon it—surely the people

say it, the perfections of my mind were much above those of my body : I had a strong and copious memory, a sound judgment and a discerning spirit ; and so much of a strong judgement and a discerning spirit ; and so much of a strong imagination in me, as at many times even my dreams and apprehensions *proved* to be true."

Lady Anne Clifford was born, as she herself testifies, on the 30th January, 1589-90, at Skipton Castle. With a Shandean exactness, very unusual among female autobiographers in these days, she begins her memoirs of herself nine months before her nativity, for the sake of introducing a beautiful quotation from the cxxxix. Psalm, 12th, 13th, 14th, 15th, and 16th verses, "Thou hast covered me in my mother's womb : I will give thanks unto thee, for I am fearfully and wonderfully made : marvellous are thy works, and that my soul knoweth right well. My substance was not hid from thee when I was made in secret, and curiously wrought in the lowest parts of the earth. Thine eyes did see my substance, yet being imperfect ; and in thy book all my members were written, which in continuance were fashioned, when as yet there was none of them."

Her governess was Mistress Taylor ; her tutor, that excellent man— "the well languaged Daniel." The disagreements of her parents, and the embarrassed condition of the family estates, obliged her education to be conducted on the strictest principles of frugality ; but luckily the best knowledge is not the dearest ; and to the housewifely habits imposed upon her youth, and her comparative seclusion from expensive vanities, many of her best virtues may be ascribed. Her improvement was in no particular neglected ; but above all, she was nurtured in the precepts and practice of economy, self-denial, domestic order, and

"Pure religion, teaching household laws." *

is but grass. The grass withereth, the flower fadeth, but the word of our God shall stand for ever." 1 Peter i. 24 : For all flesh is as grass, and all the glory of man as the flower of grass."

* Wordsworth. Perhaps I ought to apologize for quoting this poet so often, but to promulgate by any means such a line as the above, surely needs no apology. Mr. Wordsworth will, I doubt not, excuse me, if, admiring above measure the poetry of the sublime sonnet which it concludes, I venture to object to the querulous spirit which it breathes. That we are much worse than we ought to be, is unfortunately a standing truism, but that the "stream of tendency" is *recently* diverted from good to evil, I confidently deny. Having said this much, it is better to give the sonnet at once, for I am afraid that some one of my readers may not have a copy of Wordsworth's poems in his pocket, or even on his parlour window.

Written in London, 1802.
"O friend, I know not which way I must look
For comfort, being as I am opprest,

To all such book-learning as could edify or adorn her young mind she
was skilfully and honestly guided by her Preceptor Daniel, who, in

> To think that now our life is only drest
> For show: mean handy-work of craftsman, cook,
> Or groom. We must run glittering like a brook
> In the open sunshine, or we are unblest:
> The wealthiest man among us is the best.
> No grandeur now in nature or in book
> Delights us. Rapine, avarice, expense,
> This is idolatry, and these we adore.
> Plain living and high thinking are no more
> The homely beauty of the good old cause
> Is gone,—our peace, our fearful innocence,
> And pure Religion, breathing household laws."

Seldom has the same feeling, which is expressed so often, been expressed so beautifully; but is not the feeling itself a delusion, or rather, in minds like Wordsworth's,
a voluntary *illusion?* Greater virtues were rendered visible by the trials of the past, than
by the security of the present, but it was not the *goodness* of the times that called those
virtues into act. Had there been no persecutors there would have been no martyrs:
war and oppression make patriots and heroes; and wherever we hear of much alms-
giving, we may be sure that there is much poverty. If Anne Clifford had not had a
bad father and two bad husbands, and a long weary widowhood, and lived in days of
rebellion, usurpation, and profligacy, she perhaps would have obtained no other
record than that of a sensible, good sort of a woman, upon whose brow the coronet
sat with graceful ease. Nay, it is possible, that the same disposition which her adver-
sities disciplined to steady purpose, meek self-command, considerate charity, and
godly fortitude, might, under *better* circumstances, have produced a most unamiable
degree of patrician haughtiness. From reading the memoirs of her, and such as her,
an imaginative mind receives a strong impression of the superior sanctity of former
generations; but a little examination will prove that these high examples have
always been *elect exceptions,* called out of the world---no measures of the world's
righteousness. No period produced more saintly excellence than that in which
Anne Clifford lived: in none were greater crimes perpetrated; and if we look to her
later years---never, in a christian age, was the average of morals so low. But the age was
characterised more by the evil than the good, as Rochester's poems were much more
characteristical of Charles the second's times than Milton's.

One thing is obvious, that if we are not better than our ancestors, we must be
much worse---if we are not wiser than the ancients, we must be incorrigible fools.
God forbid that I should glory, save in the glory of God. God forbid that I should
flatter the men of my own generation, or detract one atom from the wise or good of
ages past. What we are we did not make ourselves; whatever truth perfumes our
atmosphere, is the flower of a seed planted long ago. We do not, we need not do
more than cultivate and improve our paternal fields. But to deny that we *are*
benefitting by the labours of our forefather, morally as well as physically, would be
impious ingratitude to that Great Power which hath given, and is giving, and will
give the wish, and the will, and the power, and the knowledge, and the means to do
the good which he willeth and doeth.

Much, very much, remains to do. It is no time to sit down self-complacently, and

his address to another noble Lady—Lucy, Countess of Bedford, has so well set forth the use of books, what they can, and what they cannot do:

And though books, Madam, cannot make the mind,
(Which we must *bring* apt to be set aright)
Yet do they rectify it in that kind;
And touch it so as that it turns that way,
Where judgment lies: and though we cannot find,
The certain place of truth, yet do they stay
And entertain us near about the same;
And give the soul the best delight that way,
Enchant it most, and most our spirits inflame
To thoughts of glory, and to worthy ends:
And therefore in a course that best became
The clearness of your heart, and best commends
Your worthy powers you run the rightest way
By which when all consumes, your fame shall live.

If Anne could read all the books represented in the picture where she is portrayed as a damsel of thirteen, she must have been a learned little lady indeed—for among them are Eusebius, St. Augustine, Josephus, and Sir Philip Sidney's Arcadia. But

Pictoribus atque Poetis
Quidlibet audendi semper fuit æqua potestas.

as Horace has it—thus quaintly Englished by Tom Brown the third,

To Bards or Limners there is no denying
An equal privilege of dauntless lying

Yet as her funeral panegyrist asserted she could discourse well upon all subjects—from predestination to Slea-Silk—we may conclude that she studied the fathers in the original languages.

Among the papers at Skipton Castle is an original book of accounts, filled with memoranda relative to this young lady's education, from 1600 to 1602, from which Whitaker has given copious extracts. We shall select such items as are most characteristic, or throw light on the

count our gains; but neither is it a time to stretch out our arms vainly to catch the irrevocable past. We can neither stand still nor go backward, but striving to go backward, we may go lamentably astray. There is one line in Mr. Wordsworth's sonnet, against which, for *his own* sake, I must enter my protest:

" No grandeur *now* in nature or in book
Delights us."

If by "us," he means the numerical majority of the population, I answer, that many more are awake to the grandeur and beauty of nature now than at any former æra: if he means that the mind and soul of England is insensible to the sublime, in the visible or in the intellectual world, let him only consider the number of young, and pure, and noble hearts, that have joyfully acknowledged the grandeur of his *book*, and let him unsay the slander.

habits and economy of Elizabeth's latest days. All books, whatever the
subject, were then introduced with a text or an ejaculation. The
same was the case with the old metrical romances, which regularly
begin and conclude with addresses to the Saviour, the Virgin or the
Saints: often strangely inconsistent with the matter which they preface. Stage-plays also, were finished with a prayer. No wonder that
grave citizens guarded their ledgers with scripture, and still less that
a young female's pocket book should commence with a petition to be
used on entering church: "O Lord increase our faith, and make us
evermore attentive hearers, true conceivers, and diligent fulfillers of thy
heavenly will." After come these lines, supposed to be in the hand-
writing of Daniel:—

> To wish and will it is my part,
> To you good lady, from my heart
> The years of Nestor, God you send,
> With happiness to your live's end.

She was at this time in London, under the care of Mistress Taylor;
the whole receipt for the two years amounting only to £38. 12s. 1d.,
and the disbursements to £35. 13s. 3d. The extravagance and neglect of the Earl her father, who is never mentioned in this book, reduced
the good Countess her mother, to a state, bordering on poverty. Nor
had he anything to spare for his daughter. But better fathers than
George Clifford, were, in that age, often careless and unaffectionate to
their female children. The want of a male heir is a great mortification
to an aristocratic family. What, however, was deficient in the allowances of her parents, was supplied in some measure, in presents from noble
ladies, particularly the Countesses of Northumberland, Derby, and Warwick, who used to fetch her to visit them in their own coaches, and
sent her donations, sometimes in gold, sometimes silver groats,
threepences, &c. in small silver barrels, often in trinkets, venison,
(what would a young lady of these days think of a whole stag at a
time,) fruit, fish, &c. The mother's directions for her dress and
management are numerous and minute. But to proceed with our
extracts.

Item. A reward for finding her Ladyships golden picture lost, 15s.
Rather high.

By some unaccountable syncope of memory or understanding, Dr.
Whitaker asks upon this article—"Were there any miniatures at this
time?" Has he forgotten Portia's Caskets? Has he forgotten, or did
he never read a play called Hamlet, written near the time which he is
inquiring about? If the pictures Hamlet shews to the Queen were not
miniatures, but full length portraits, yet there is another passage which

puts the question to rest at once,—"It is not very strange ; for my uncle is king of Denmark, and those who would have made mouths at him while my father lived, give twenty, forty, fifty, and a hundred ducats a piece for his *picture in little*." The wearing of miniatures, richly set in gold, pearls, or diamonds was a fashion in the courts of Elizabeth and the first Stuarts. Hiliard, and the elder Oliver, the first Englishmen, who could be called artists, were both miniature painters, and both living in 1600. Another item, in her Ladyship's accounts is, an ivory box to put a picture in, xii d. Now surely a picture contained in a twelve-penny box of ivory,* must have been as minute as any of Petito's, famous as he was for inserting portraits into rings, bracelets and seals. Possibly the Doctor has confounded miniature in general, with miniature in enamel.

It is afflicting to think how the free and graceful motions of childhood have been constrained and distorted by the absurdities of fashion. The Lady Anne did not wholly escape. We find among her memoranda 7s. to a French woman for a Rabato wyre: this by its high price must have been a new-fangled torture: and again 5s. 11d. for a Verdingale and Verdingale wyre. The purpose of the Rabato or ruff was to prevent the natural turn and fall of the neck : and how would a maiden trip it on the elastic turf, or fragrant heather of a mountain side, if her steps were impeded by a Verdingale stiffened with wire? Some other items there are which seldom enter the bills of a modern lady's education ; for example, "15s. for a masque." "Item 10s. to musicians for playing at my Lady Anne's masque." Masques indeed, were then worn as an article of dress—a piece of superogatory modesty which gave license to much impudence. But the *masque*, at which the musicians played must have been, not a modern masquerade, but one of those *allegorical pastorals*, which were so much in vogue at the courts of Elizabeth and James, and particularly patronized by Anne of Denmark, with whom the daughter of Clifford was a special favourite. Who will censure a fashion which gave birth to Comus?

Of printed books, there is no mention ; we find a pair of writing tables charged at 11s., and two *paper* books; one for *accompte*, and another to write her catechism in. The Church catechism is probably meant, for Pinnock's Catechisms, then were not. Yet it is rather remarkable that in an age so *very* religious, a young woman so well tutored, should, in her eleventh year, require a book to write down, what every

* Is there not an error in transcription here? When almost all foreign commodities (wines excepted) were much dearer than at present, it is very unlikely that an ivory box, however tiny, should not cost more than one shilling.

village child can say by heart at seven. Perhaps some more advanced system of theological instruction is intended.* The only article from which we can derive a hope that she was not quite forgotten by her father, is the following " Item to Captain Davis's man when he shall come to my Lady with Indian clothes." These Indian clothes might be part of the Earl's booty.

We should not have expected, at a time when *"filthy worsted stocking knave,"* was a Shaksperian epithet of contempt, to find an Earl's daughter wearing green worsted stockings. Some little matters rather go beyond our antiquarian knowledge; for instance, " twelve little glasses of *coodinecks*;" "eleven bunches of *glass* feathers;" two dozen *glass* flowers, &c. We are aware that glass is sometimes spun into a very close resemblance to ostrich feathers; but was this practised at the commencement of the seventeenth century?

After all, it must be acknowledged that these accounts give little information as to the more solid parts of Lady Anne's breeding. The most pleasant intelligence which they supply is, that she was not

---

* " I wish it were a part of modern education in the same rank to require young ladies either to write or read their Catechism. But modern education takes a different course, and therefore produces no such characters as Lady Anne Clifford."— WHITAKER.---Fudge ! As an antiquary, we can well allow the Doctor to cling as fondly to the relics of old times, as ivy to a ruin. Let him praise old poets, old sermons, old books, old manners, old wine, rites, ceremonies, superstitions, as much as he pleases, we can sympathise with him to any extent. But when the Catechism is the topic, he ought to speak, not as an Antiquary, but as a Divine, and should not have suffered his fanciful partiality for things, which after all, would not charm if they were not obsolete, to seduce him into a vulgar, jacobinical sneer at all the female rank of his own days. Young ladies of Lady Anne's station do not now usually repeat the Catechism to the Curate "*after the second lesson at evening prayer,*" nor can we find that such was ever the custom; but are we thence to conclude,that their religious instruction is neglected? So far from it, if ever religion was in *fashion* it is at the present day. Young men, educated at classical or commercial seminaries do sometimes exhibit a most disgraceful, heathenish ignorance, not only of the doctrines and constitution of the Church to which they are supposed to belong (not belonging to any other) but of the plain historical facts of Christianity---because in these establishments, the only attention paid to Christian instruction, consists, or did very lately consist, in a compulsory attendance at a Chapel, where though something *might* be learned, nothing *is*. It is but justice to acknowledge that considerable improvement has been made in this particular within the few last years. But such exposures of ignorance in the other sex are comparatively rare.

Let it be remembered that we are not speaking of what would emphatically be called " a *religious* education," for it is manifest that Lady Anne's was not of that character; inasmuch as she learned dancing, and the use of the cross-bow, and took part in private theatricals.

debarred from healthful recreation.　There is nothing to be objected to but the wire.

With what gratitude she received the instructions of Daniel, is testified by the monument erected at her cost in the church of Beckington, Somerset, with this inscription—

" Here lies, expecting the second coming of our Lord and Saviour, Jesus Christ, the dead body of Samuel Daniel, Esq., that excellent poet and historian, who was Tutor to the Lady Anne Clifford in her youth. She was daughter and heir to George, Earl of Cumberland, who in gratitude to him erected this monument to his memory a long time after, when she was Countess Dowager of Pembroke, Dorset, and Montgomery.　He died in October, anno 1619."

She has also introduced the likeness of her Tutor into the family picture at Skipton.*　He had doubtless laboured, not in vain, to inspire

---

* " Samuel Daniel, the most noted Poet and Historian of his time, was born of a wealthy family in Somersetshire, and at seventeen years of age, became a Commoner of Magdalen Hall, where he continued about three years, and improved himself in mathematical learning by the help of an excellent Tutor.　But his *Geny* being more prone to easier and smoother studies, than in pecking and hewing at Logic, he left the University without the honour of a degree, and exercised it much in English History and Poetry, of which he then gave several ingenious specimens.　He was afterwards for his merits made gentleman extraordinary, and afterwards one of the the grooms of the privy chamber to Anne the Queen Consort of King James I, who being for the most part a favourer and encourager of his muse (as she was of John Florio, who married Samuel Daniel's sister) and many times delighted in his conversation not only in private but in public, was partly for these reasons held in esteem by the men of that age for his excellencies in Poetry and History, and partly in this respect, " *that in writing of English affairs whether in prose or poetry, he had the happiness to reconcile brevity with clearness, qualities at great distance in other authors.*" Daniel had also a good faculty in setting out a mask or play, and was wanting in nothing that might render him acceptable to the great and ingenious men of his time: as to Sir John Harrington the poet, Cambden the learned, Sir Robert Cotton, Sir H. Spelman, Edmund Spenser, Ben Jonson, John Stradling, *Little* Owen the Epigrammatist."---*Antony Wood's Athenæ Oxonienses.*

We feel rather strange to find John Stradling and *little* Owen the Epigrammatist mentioned as great and ingenious men, along with Spencer and Ben Jonson. Daniel's poems, though included in the collections of Anderson and Chalmers, are less read and known than they deserve to be.　His longest work, " *Of the civil wars between the Houses of Lancaster and York,*" in six books, is unreadably tedious, though it is written in an excellent vein of pure English, with many deep political reflections, and some few passages of considerable pathos; but his epistles, sonnets, and moral pieces, if they contain not much high poetry, have a calm wisdom, a beauty of sentiment, and a propriety of expression which make them highly valuable.　There have been few Poets so fitted to conduct the education of a noble female as Samuel Daniel.

her with a love of poetry, and a regard for poets, which she displayed in erecting or renewing the tomb of Spenser in Westminster Abbey.

Though by her father's death, she hardly can be said to have lost a father's care, nor her mother to have been bereft of a husband's love, yet are the widow and the orphan exposed to numberless mortifications and petty indignities, which rarely befal the wife and daughter of a living brave man, however negligent of his domestic duties. A young Heiress, indeed, is generally beset with professing followers; an amiable woman seldom is without true friends; but though wealth draws courtship, and goodness will conciliate affection, it is power alone that commands the world's respect. But the widow and daughter of George Clifford, from the moment of their destitution, were opposed in their nearest rights, by him to whom they would naturally have looked for protection. Margaret, Countess of Cumberland, had but just time to bury her deceased Lord, when she was called to defend her daughter's inheritance.

The Earldom of Cumberland descending in the male line only, fell undisputed to Francis, second brother to the late Earl, a man as easy and indolent as his predecessor was active and restless. But the greater part of the estates were, by an ancient entail, inheritable by the Lady Anne. A long series of law proceedings followed, of which Sir Matthew Hale has drawn up " an accurate and technical account." Though opposed by the Court, and subjected to divers annoyances, the Dowager Countess (whose own right of jointure in the Westmorland property does not appear to have been called in question), continued for many years to uphold her daughters claim, by all the weapons which the law's armoury offers for sale. It would be difficult, and not very amusing, to narrate the several stages of a cause turning upon entails, fines and recoveries, reversions, &c. &c. But the drift of the question was, whether the limitation of descent to the heirs male, effected by Henry, second Earl of Cumberland, cut off the unlimited entail of Edward II. Though the King's award of the 4th March, 1617, was in favour of Earl Francis, (by whom about the same time the said King was magnificently entertained at Brougham castle,) yet the matter never rested, nor did Lady Anne recover possession of what she deemed her right till after the death of the last Earl of Cumberland in 1643. Thus, to use the words of Sir Matthew Hale, who never expresses himself so well, as when he utters an honest feeling : " oftentimes it falls out that the vanity of men in studying to preserve their name, though to the total disherison of their own children, is crossed, or proves unsuccessful to the end designed."

At a very early age, Lady Anne was united to Richard, third Earl of Dorset of the Sackvilles. He was a man of spirit and talent; but a licentious spendthrift, who continually tormented her to give up her inheritance for ready money. But her principles of obedience were not so slavish, as to permit him to involve herself and her offspring in ruin: a miserable life she must have led with him, yet she speaks gently of his memory: perhaps her second marriage taught her sincerely to regret him, for he was a man of sense, and a man of sense, though a profligate, is less insupportable, though more inexcusable, than a profligate fool.

While the Dowager Countess of Cumberland survived, the suits at law appear to have been conducted solely in her name, and she is accused of denuding the Westmorland property of wood out of pure revenge: but were it not more charitable to suppose, that the expenses of litigation compelled her to this course? The Lady Anne received no support from her husband in the prosecution of her title: perhaps could take no direct method to do herself right. Her mother still continued her protector, and displayed in her behalf the spirit of a Russel.* This virtuous but unhappy woman, was finally released on the 24th of May, 1616, "in the chamber wherein her Lord was born into the world, when she was fifty six years old, wanting six weeks, and that very day twenty-five years after the death of her son Robert, Lord

---

* Among other persecutions, the Lady Margaret did not escape the pest of impertinent counsellors. Nor was she quite free from the weakness of wishing to hear her own character from others. In the family papers is a letter from a Sir John Bowyer to the Earl Francis, wherein the little squire, wishing to curry favour with the great Lord, and to shew his own importance at the same time, gives a minute account of how he (Sir John Bowyer) had been visiting "my honorable Lady of Cumberland," and what was said and done on the occasion. It would have been diverting to *hear* him *tell* the story. What an admirable mixture for this world, is conceit and servility— Hear him. " At my departure I told her *Ladyship* that I did intend, God willing, to ride over, and do my duty to your *Lordship;* wishing that it would please God that all differences between your *Honour* and her *Ladyship* were well composed; which reconciliation was also generally wished and expected in the south parts, and would, no doubt be soon brought to pass, if some that made profit of your *Honour's* differences, and loved to fish in troubled waters, were not the impediments of it. Her *Honour* desired and enjoined me to say plainly, what was generally spoken hereof, and *what the world conceived* of her. I was loath, but, being commanded, used words to this effect: Your Ladyship is held to be very honorable, much devoted to religion, very respective unto ministers and preachers, very charitable unto the poor: yet under favour, some do tax your *Honour* to be too much affected to *go to law.* That is said my Lady, that I am contentious and over-ruled by busy wrangling fellows. (I did humbly crave pardon for my plainnesss.) Sir, I do like you much the better for your plainness: and if my Lord of Cumberland will make me any honourable offers, I will deceive the world, or them that think me given to law."

Clifford." She was, by her daughter's testimony, "of a great natural wit and judgement, of a sweet disposition, truly religious and virtuous, and indowed with a large share of those four moral virtues, Prudence, Justice, Fortitude, and Temperance.—By industry and search of records she brought to light the then unknown title which her daughter had to the ancient Baronies, Honors, and Lands of the Viponts, Cliffords, and Vescys. So as what good shall accrue to her daughter's posterity, by the said inheritance, must next under God, be attributed to her." Some notion may be formed of the common course of a noble and pious lady's studies, in those days, from the books depicted over the Countess's portraits, to wit, "A written hand book of Alkimee, Extractions of Distillations, and excellent medicines. All Senekae's works translated out of Latine into English. The Holy Bible, the old and new Testament."*

"On the 14th of March, 1617, the King took upon himself the awarding of a long difference betwixt the male and female branches of the House of Clifford, and ordered that Lady Anne the Countess of Dorset, and the Earl her husband, should make a conveyance of the Honor of Skipton, and other the ancient baronies, honors, and Lands of the Viponts, Cliffords, and Vescys remainder to his first, and other sons intail, remainder to the Countess for life, remainder to her first, and other sons, remainder to her remainders; and £20,000 to be paid by the Earl of Cumberland to the Earl of Dorset. To this award the two Earls subscribed; but notwithstanding the potency of the Earl of Cumberland, the will of the King, and the importunity of a husband, the Countess refused to submit to the award." †

The few years immediately ensuing, past heavily enough for the Countess, but without furnishing any memorable grief for history. She was now become a mother. She was successively bereaved of three boys; and, considering the temper of the man and of the times, it is probable that her maternal affliction was rather insulted by her husband's reproaches, than lightened by his participation. For the failure of heirs male, though the Church would not allow it for a ground of divorce, was often made by royal and noble spouses a ground of neglect and ill-usage. And she might look on her two little daughters, with somewhat of the feeling of the Indian woman, who justified herself to the missionary for destroying her female child, by recounting the manifold miseries from which she was delivering it. Yet she speaks of him as if she never ceased to feel pride in his manly faculties and accomplishments. "He was," she tells us "in his nature of a just mind, of

* Inscription on the family picture.---Ibid.   † Sir Matthew Hale

a sweet disposition, and very valiant ; that he excelled in every sort of learning all the young nobility with whom he studied at Oxford ; and that he was a true patriot and an eminent patron of scholars and soldiers." She does not however scruple to record the uneasiness which she sustained from his extravagant waste of his own estates, and from his eagerness to sign away her patrimonial rights for present accommodation. Such was his "excess of expense in all the ways to which money can be applied," according to Clarendon " that he so entirely consumed almost the whole great fortune which descended to him, that when he was forced to leave the title to his younger brother, he left in a manner nothing to him to support it." He died in 1624, leaving two daughters, of whom the eldest Margaret, married John Tufton, Earl of Thanet, through whom the ancient possessions of the Clifford's in Westmorland and Craven have descended. The younger, Isabella, was married to Compton, Earl of Northampton. Horace Walpole mentions among the M.S. relics of Lady Anne—Memoirs of the Earl of Dorset, her first husband ; but no such work has yet come to light, nor is it to be supposed, that she would willingly record the misdoings of one, whom pride, if not tenderness, would forbid her to expose, and of whom truth forbad her to be an eulogist.

Little is written or remembered of her six ensuing years of widowhood. As her uncle, the Earl Francis, by virtue of the King's award, kept possession of her lands and castles in the north, she probably resided much with her maternal relatives the Russels. She took care, however, still to assert her claims, for it is on record, that in 1628, and afterwards in 1632 she made *her entries into the lands* ; a legal recipe for rescusitating a right from a state of suspended animation, the method of which we do not precisely understand.

At the mature age of forty-one, she entered a second time into the marriage state, being wedded on the third day of June, 1630, to Philip Herbert, Earl of Pembroke and Montgomery. We regret that we cannot detail the place and particulars of their courtship, or in any satisfactory manner account for a wise and staid matron, not inexperienced in conjugal trials, and the mother of two children, throwing herself away upon one who has come down to posterity in the character of an ingrate, an ignoramus, a common swearer, a bully, and a coward. Perhaps the natural defects of this eccentric person have been exaggerated by the royalist writers, for his ingratitude to his royal master, and the odious offices in which he served the Parliament, made him hateful to many, and contemptible to all. At the period of his marriage with the Lady Anne, he was considered as a rising courtier, being Lord Chamberlain of the King's Household, and Warden of the Stanneries in the former of which capacities he broke, with his official wand, in the precincts of the Palace of Whitehall, the head of Thomas Maye, the Poet and Parliamentary Historiographer; and in the latter, he was near driving the people of Cornwall and Devon (then, as now, the most loyal of counties) into rebellion, by his oppressions and extortions. He was of a most distinguished family: his mother was the sister of Sir Philip Sidney;[*] his brother and predecessor was Chancellor, and a great benefactor of the University of Oxford,—Lord Herbert of Cherbury, and the pious George Herbert were among his kindred; yet is he said to have been so illiterate, as hardly to know how to write his name. But he had a handsome person, which he was an adept at adorning. Though his temper was liable to escapes and sallies which beget a suspicion of insanity, he possessed, in his lucid intervals, the art and mystery of disguise in great perfection, so that an old gossiping writer[†] calling him the "young worthy Sir Philip," and remarking his sudden favour with King James, observes, "that he carries it without envy, for he is very humble to the great Lords, is desirous to do all men good and hurt none." He was the spoiled child of the court, where he made his appearance in his sixteenth year, "and had not been there two hours but he grew as bold as the best." According to Osborn, he was notorious for "breaking wiser heads than his own;" not always however with impunity, for "having the gift of a coward to allay the gust he had in quarrelling," he received, and did not revenge, a public and personal castigation at a horse-race from Ramsay, afterwards Earl of Holderness.—These certainly were the follies of his youth; and in 1630 he was a widower of forty-five. His large estate, and the reputation of great court interest might induce the Lady Anne to give ear to his addresses, in the hope that he would be the means of recovering her ancestral possessions. But so it is, that men, endued with no other talent, do sometimes possess extraordinary power over the best and wisest women, and not least over those whose youth is fled. What happiness the Countess enjoyed in her new connection, is manifest from the following letter, addressed to her uncle Edward, Earl of Bedford, preserved in the Harleian Collection.—

"MY LORD,—Yesterday by Mr. Marshe I received your Lordship's letter, by which I perceived how much you were troubled at the report of my being sick, for which I humbly thank your Lordship. I was

---

[*]This Lady was the Countess of Pembroke to whom her brother addressed his "Arcadia"---not the Lady Anne Clifford, as has been absurdly asserted. Sir Philip Sidney was killed three years before Anne was born. What a murderer of pretty tales is that same chronology!

[†] Rowland White.

so ill as I did make full account to die; but now, I thank God, I am something better. And now, my Lord, give me leave to desire that favour from your Lordship as to speak earnestly to my Lord for my coming up to the town this term, either to Bainarde's Castle, or the Cock-pitt; and I protest I will be ready to return back hither again whensoever my Lord appoints it. I have to this purpose written now to my Lord, and put it enclosed in a letter of mine to my Lady of Carnarvan, as desiring her to deliver it to her father, which I know she will do with all the advantage she can, to further this business; and if your Lordship will join with her in it, you shall afford a charitable and a most acceptable favour to your Lordship's cousin, and humble friend to command.   ANNE PEMBROKE."

Ramossbury, this 14th of January, 1638.

" If my Lord should deny my coming, then I desire your Lordship I may understand it as soon as may be, that so I may order my poor business as well as I can without any one coming to town; for I dare not venture to come up without his leave, lest he should take that occasion to turn me out of his house, as he did out of Whitehall, and then I shall not know where to put my head. I desire not to stay in the town above ten days, or a fortnight at the most."

Yet in her memoirs she speaks of him as a good wife should ever speak of a deceased husband, were it but for her own credit—just hints at his faults, and magnifies his merits, for she tells us he had a very quick apprehension, a sharp understanding, and a discerning spirit, with a very choleric nature, and that he was, " in all respects one of the most distinguished noblemen in England, and well beloved throughout the realm." There could be no purpose of deception here, (for these memoirs were never meant to meet the public eye;) unless she wished to exten- uate her unlucky choice to her own posterity.

It is an amusing, if not a very useful speculation, to imagine how certain persons *would* have acted and thought, under certain circum- stances and opportunities, in which the said persons never happened to be placed. We could for instance, compose a long romance of the heroic actions which Anne Clifford *would* have performed in the civil war, had she been possessed of her broad lands and fenced Castles. She *might* have made Skipton or Pendragon, as famous as Lathom and Wardour. She was a firm royalist; for though she had small reasons to love Kings or Courts, she was a true lover of the Church. But at the breaking out of the conflict, her northern holds were in the feeble, though loyal hands of her cousin Henry; and when, at the death of the last Earl of Cumber- land, her title became undisputed, Skipton was already in a state of siege, and it was long before the hostile parties left her lands free for her entrance. Whatever assistance she may have given to the royal cause, must have been in direct contradiction to her husband's will, for he, in revenge for the loss of his Chamberlain's staff, of which he was deprived for raising a brawl in the House of Lords, carried the power of his wealth, and the disgrace of his folly, to the Roundhead faction. By some means or other he was, on the attainder of Laud, appointed Chancellor of Oxford; and though most deservedly stripped of that honour by King Charles, who set the noble Marquis of Hertford in his place; yet, on the prevalence of the Presbyterian party, to which he professed great devotion, he was restored; and conducted, with what courtesy and gentleness may well be conjectured, the expulsion of the Episcopalians from their colleges. No wonder that he was contemptuously hated by the royalists; or that this hatred broke out in keen and bitter libels (if truth be libellous) immediately after his death; for those were not days when rancour respected the sanctity of the tomb. He just outlived the monarchy, and divesting himself of the rank which he disgraced, accepted a seat in the Rump Parliament for Berkshire. He died January 23, 1649-50.

We can hardly call the following a *jeu-d'esprit*, for it is not in a very playful spirit. It has been attributed to Samuel Butler, and was printed in one sheet, fol. under the title of "The last Will and Testament of Philip &c."

"I, Philip, late Earl of Pembroke and Montgomery, now Knight for the County of Berks, being, as I am told, very weak in body, but of perfect memory (for I remember this time five years I gave the casting voice to dispatch old Canterbury; and this time two years I voted no address to my master; and this time twelvemonth brought him to the block) yet, because death doth threaten and stare upon me, who have still obeyed all those who threatened me, I now make my last Will and Testament.

"Imprimis, for my soul: I confess I have heard very much of souls, but what they are, or whom they are for, God knows, I know not. They tell me now of another world, where I never was, nor do I know one foot of the way thither. While the King stood, I was of his religion, made my son wear a cassock, and thought to make him a Bishop: then came the Scots, and made me a Presbyterian; and, since Cromwell entered, I have been an Independent. These I believe are the kingdom's three Estates, and if any of these can save a soul, I may claim one. Therefore, if my Executors do find I have a soul, I give it him that gave it me.

"Item, I give my body, for I cannot keep it; you see the Chirurgion is tearing off my flesh: therefore bury me. I have church-land enough. But do not bury me in the church porch; for I was a Lord, and could not be buried where Colonel Pride was born.

"Item, my will is to have no monument; for then I must have epitaphs, and verses; but all my life long I have had too much of them.

"Item, I give my dogs, the best curs ever man laid leg over, to be divided among the council of state. Many a fair day have I followed my dogs, and followed the states, both night and day: went whither they sent me; sat where they bid me; sometimes with Lords, sometimes with Commons; and now can neither go nor sit. Yet, whatever becomes of me, let not my poor dogs want their allowance, nor come within the ordinances for one meal a week.

"Item, I give two of my best saddle horses to the Earl of Denbigh, for I fear ere long his own legs will fail him: but the tallest and strongest in all my stables I give to the Academy, for a vaulting horse for ALL LOVERS OF VERTU. All my other horses I give to the Lord Fairfax, that when Cromwell and the states take away his commission, his Lordship may have some Horse to command.

"Item, I give my hawks to the Earl of Carnarvon. His father was Master of the Hawks, to the King; and he has wit, so like his father, that I begged his wardship, lest in time he should do so by me.

"Item, I give all my deer to the Earl of Salisbury, who I know will preserve them, because he denied the King a buck out of one of his own parks.

"Item, I give my chaplains to the Earl of Stamford, in regard he never used any but his son the Lord Grey, who, being thus both spiritual and carnal, may beget more Monsters.

"Item, I give nothing to the Lord Say, which legacy I give him because I know he'll bestow it on the poor.

"Item, to the two Countesses, my sister and my *wife*, I now give leave to *enjoy their estates*. But my own estate I give to my eldest son, charging him on my blessing to follow the advice of Michael Oldworth; for, though I have had thirty thousand pounds per annum, I die not in debt, above four score thousand pounds.

"Item, because I threatened Sir Harry Mildmay, but did not beat him, I give fifty pounds to the footman who cudgelled him.

"Item, my will is that the said Sir Harry shall not meddle with my jewels. I knew him when he served the Duke of Buckingham, and, since, how he handled the crown jewels, for both which reasons I now name him the knave of diamonds.

"Item, to Tom May, whose pate I broke heretofore at a masque, I give five shillings: I intended him more, but all who have read his History of the Parliament think five shillings too much.

"Item, to the author of the libel against ladies, called news from the New Exchange, I give threepence, for inventing a more obscene way of scribbling than the world yet knew; but, since he throws what's rotten and false on divers names of unblemished honour, I leave his payment to the footman that paid Sir Harry Mildmay's arrears; to teach him the difference 'twixt wit and dirt, and to know ladies that are noble and chaste from downright roundheads.

"Item, I give back to the assembly of divines, their classical, provincial, congregational, national: which words I have kept at my own charge above seven years, but plainly find they'll never come to good.

"Item, as I restore other men's words, so I give to Lieutenant-General Cromwell one word of mine, because hitherto he never kept his own.

"Item, to all rich citizens of London; to all Presbyterians, as well as cavaliers, I give advice to look to their throats; for, by order of the states, the garrison of Whitehall have all got poignards, and for new lights have bought dark lanthorns.

"Item, I give all my printed speeches to these persons following, viz.—that speech which I made in my own defence when the seven Lords were accused of high treason I give to Sergeant Wild, that hereafter he may know what is treason, and what is not: and the speech I made extempore to the Oxford scholars I give to the Earl of Manchester, speaker, *pro tempore*, to the House of Peers before its reformation, and Chancellor, *pro tempore*, of Cambridge University since the reformation. But my speech at my election, which is my speech without an oath, I give to those that take the engagement, because no oath hath been able to hold them. All my other speeches, of what colour soever, I give to the academy, to help Sir Balthaser's Art of well speaking.

"Item, I give up the ghost."

We trust there is no harm in being amused at this Testament, though no possible provocation could justify such profane scoffing at the nakedness of a soul. It were better, at least no worse, that we were ignorant or forgetful of immortality,—never thought of death but as the bursting of a bubble, or the ceasing of a sound,—than that we should turn "the judgment to come" into an argument of malice, and meditate on the dissolution of a fellow sinner, without fear of God, or charity for man. But this truly *sarcastic* composition was produced in an angry, persecuting, and persecuted time, and persecution produces more zeal than piety on all sides.

Lady Anne, who for some years had been separated from her husband, now entered on her second widowhood, with an ample fortune, and the consolation of reflecting, that her late spouse's politics had preserved her estates from sequestration. Though she could hardly have much loved a man, whom it was impossible for her to esteem, she heard not of his death with indifference. To any feeling heart, there is a peculiar sadness in the decease of those, that have once been dear, and afterwards estranged. Caldecott, the Earl of Pembroke's Chaplain, informed her of his master's interment in a letter, which has not been perfectly preserved, but which shews, that *she* retained no resentment against the dead, though perhaps no clerk in Oxford had received such cruel injuries at his hands.

Here may properly be inserted the Lady's own account of her wedded life,—" I must confess with inexpressible thankfulness, that, through the goodness of Almighty God, and the mercies of my Saviour Jesus Christ, Redeemer of the world, I was born a happy creature in mind, body, and fortune; and that those two Lords of mine, to whom I was afterwards by *divine Providence* married, were in their several kinds as worthy noblemen as any there were in this kingdom; yet it was my misfortune to have contradictions and crosses with them both. With my first Lord, about the desire he had to make me sell my rights in the land of my ancient inheritance for a sum of money, which I never did, nor ever would consent unto, insomuch, that this matter was the cause of a long contention betwixt us; as also, for his profusion in consuming his estate, and some other extravagancies of his: and with my second Lord, because my youngest daughter, the Lady Isabella Sackville, would not be brought to marry one of his younger sons, and that I would not relinquish my interest I had in five thousand pounds, being part of her portion, out of my lands in Craven. Nor did there want malicious ill-willers, to blow and foment the coals of dissention between us; so as in both their life times, the marble pillars of Knowle, in Kent, and Wilton in Wiltshire, were to me oftentimes but the gay arbours of anguish; insomuch as a wise man, that knew the insides of my fortune, would often say that I lived in both these my Lords' great families as the river Roan, or Rhodanus, runs through the lake of Geneva without mingling any part of its streams with that lake; for I gave myself up wholly to retirement as much as I could in both those great families, and made good books and virtuous thoughts my companions, which can never discern affliction, nor be daunted when it unjustly happens; and by a *happy genius* I overcame all those troubles, the *prayers of my blessed mother* helping me therein."

From the self satisfaction with which she discloses the sources of her troubles, it is evident that however much her peace might be disquieted, her heart was never bruised. Had she ever loved either of her Lords, she would not have found her *genius* so potently happy to sustain their unkindnesses. She considered marriage as a necessary evil—a penalty of womanhood; and expecting no felicity, suffered no disappointment.

The demise of the Earl of Pembroke, left her free and uncontrouled mistress of the ancient fees and estates which had been legally hers ever since 1643. But her property was in the most dilapidated condition. Six of her castles,—Brough, Brougham, Pendragon, Appleby, Barden, and Skipton, were wholly or partially in ruins, and Skipton, her birth-place, after changing hands twice, and undergoing two sieges, had been dismantled* by command of the Parliament, its roofs broken in, the lead and timber sold, and the venerable tapestry, the antique furniture, and embossed plate, destroyed or scattered; her parks, her farms, her woods, and her tenants, all melancholy witnesses to the miseries of civil discord. But she was not cast down by the sight of desolation; it only furnished her with congenial employment. From her second widowhood to her death, she

---

* The severity with which Skipton was dismantled, or, as the phrase was, *slighted* by the Rump-Parliament, is to be ascribed to the difficulty of maintaining it as a place of defence, owing to its being commanded by two heights, while it afforded a temptation and temporary shelter to the loose marauding parties of Cavaliers. It was not till after its seizure by, and recovery from, the Royalists of Duke Hamilton's expedition, that it was thus hardly dealt with.

resided almost wholly on her northern domains, " where she went about doing good," little interrupted by the successive governments that preceded the Restoration. Yet she extended her protection to the distressed royalists, particularly the learned and the clergy ; nor does it appear that she ever withdrew from the communion of the church of England. Perhaps it was not till after the return of Charles that she planted in the Bailey of Skipton castle, an acorn from the Oak of Boscobel " as a symbol of the ancient loyalty of her house." It grew up to be a noble tree, and long survived the fortunes of that regal family, whose deliverance it was meant to commemorate.

The life of a widowed female, chiefly occupied in repairing the damages of war, of law, of neglect, and of waste; in the regular duties of a landholder; and in orderly deeds of beneficence; does not furnish much incident. We may, therefore, rapidly sum up the actions of her latter years, by no means, however, undertaking to enumerate all her charities. She set herself vigorously to restore the ancient castles and churches, a work which was her delight and her pride, of which she took care not to lose the credit with posterity. As long as stone or marble can perpetuate the memory of the just, her's will continue in Westmorland and in Craven. The inscriptions which record her re-edifications, are all nearly the same, as far as relates to herself. That upon Skipton Castle may suffice for a specimen :—

" This Skipton Castle was repaired by the Lady Anne Clifford, Countess Dowager of Dorset, Pembroke, and Montgomerie, Baroness Clifford, Westmorland and Vescie, Lady of the Honour of Skipton in Craven, and Sheriffesse by inheritance of the County of Westmorland, in the years 1657 and 1658, after this maine part of it had lain ruinous ever since December 1648, and the January following, when it was then pulled down and demolished, almost to the foundation, by the command of the Parliament then sitting at Westminster, because it had then a garrison in the civil wars in England. God's name be praised ; Isaiah, Chap. 58. Thou shalt raise up the foundations of many generations, and thou shalt be called—The repairer of the breach, the restorer of places to dwell in." The same text is set over the entrance of Barden.

Almost immediately upon her widowhood, she repaired to Skipton, which she found scarred and riddled through and through with shot, and little more than the bare roofless walls remaining. The steeple of the adjoining church was nearly demolished by random balls in the two sieges. But the long gallery, built in the days of the first Earl for the reception of the *Lady Ellenor's Grace*, was still entire, and here she spent some days, making her bed-room the octagon chamber. Such minutiæ she delighted to record of herself, and we cannot think them altogether uninteresting, since she thought them worthy of preservation. We know not whether it was on this or some subsequent visit that she erected " The Countess' Pillar," a stately obelisk, on the Roman road called the Maiden-way, the remains of which still mark the spot, where she parted with her mother for the last time.

As she was not one to " dwell in ceiled palaces, while the Lord's House lay waste," she soon repaired the church of Skipton ; renewed the tombs of her two little brothers, and erected a magnificent marble monument to her father, adorned with the armorial bearings of the various noble families whose blood mingled in his veins. On this she inscribed a long epitaph, chiefly remarkable for the assurance that it contains, that he died penitently, meaning that he had much to repent of, and that she herself was his sole surviving *legitimate* offspring, an innuendo which the delicacy of a modern daughter would have avoided. But Anne could never forget her mother's injuries. There are yet families in Craven, which might claim a sinister descent from George, Earl of Cumberland. Lady Anne has been much and justly commended for her care of her first husband's spurious offspring ; but we are not told how she behaved to her brothers and sisters of the half-blood.

In honouring the remains of her father, she acted from the combined feelings of pride and duty ; but the marble statue which she raised at Appleby to her mother, was the offering of pure affection. Her deep and reverential love for that good parent seems to have been the warmest feeling of her soul ; it breaks out in every page of her memoirs. Whatever good she obtained or achieved, whatever evil she escaped or surmounted, she attributes to her mother's prayers. In one passage she makes a long enumeration of the perils she had gone through from fire, from water, from coaches, from fevers, and from excessive bleedings, simply to ascribe her deliverance to the prevailing holiness of her mother.

Her general residence was at Brougham or Appleby, but she visited all her six castles occasionally, and describes the particulars of her movements with rather tedious minuteness. Shortly before the restoration, the existing powers insulted her by placing a garrison in her renovated mansion of Skipton ; yet this did not prevent her from going thither early in 1658, and passing some weeks among these uninvited guests. " Thus removing from castle to castle, she diffused plenty and happiness around her, by consuming on the spot the produce of her vast domains in hospitality and charity. Equally remote from the undistinguishing profusion of ancient times, and the parsimonious elegance of modern manners, her house was a school for the young, and a retreat for the aged ; an asylum for the persecuted, a college for the learned, and a pattern for all." *

She was not without a touch of superstition ; but her superstition never infected her religion. It was rather the result of her circumstances than of her convictions. It consisted in believing herself the charge not only of a divine providence, but of a personal destiny. We have already seen her writing of her " happy Genius." Now, the term Genius, was then seldom or never used in its modern sense, (though the kindred words Geny, and Ingene sometimes were so,) but in its original Roman acceptation, of a presiding and directing power. It is plain too, that she had a leaning towards judicial astrology, in which her father, who as the *melancholy knight*, complains that he has been deceived by *prophecies*, also partook, as may appear from these words :—" So as old Mr. John Denham, a great astronomer, that sometime lived in my father's house, would often say, that I had much in me in nature to shew that the sweet influences of the Pleiades, and the Bands of Orion, mentioned in Job, were powerful both at my conception and nativity." But this is only one form of a belief which all mankind, in spite of themselves, entertain,—the one thing in which the devout and the atheist agree.

It was probably about her sixty-third year that she employed some nameless artist to compile the famous family picture. Its merit as a work of art may not be very high, but it need not have exposed the Countess to reproach for parsimony for not engaging the pencil of Vandyke or Mytens, which a learned author gravely assures us were at her command. Vandyke had been dead more than a dozen years before the earliest possible date of this picture. Nor would any painter, who was above practising the mechanical part of his business, have willingly undertaken a work which was to include so many coats of arms, so many written pedigrees. A fine composition was not what the Lady wanted, but a plain prose representation of the lineaments of those most dear to her. She was a patroness of poets and a lover of poetry, yet we do not read that she employed a bard for her land-steward, or that her leases were in rhyme.

The picture, besides several detached half-length portraits, such as those of Daniel and of Mrs. Taylor, her tutor and governess, consists of a centre and two wings ; the centre representing her father, mother, and brother, and each of the wings her own likeness at different periods of life,—the one, as a maiden of thirteen ; the other, as a widow in her grand climacteric. In the latter she is depicted as clothed in a black

* Whitaker.

serge habit, with sad-coloured hood, the usual habiliments of her declining years. Books are introduced into both, as if purposely to shew that the love of reading acquired in her youth had lasted to her old age; which was so true, that when the decay of her sight forbad her to read for herself, she employed a regular reader. But it appears that, as she grew older, she limited her studies more within the range of her practical duties; for while her youthful effigy is attended by Eusebius, Godfrey of Bulloigne, and Agrippa de Vanitate Scientiarum, the maturer image has only Charron on Wisdom, a Book of Distillations and rare Medicines, and the Bible.

To have revived the martial and festal magnificence of the past would have accorded neither with her means nor her mind: but she maintained all that was best in the feudal system; the duteous interdependence of superiors and inferiors, the lasting ties between master and servant, the plain but ample hospitality, and the wholesome adherence to time-honoured customs. Large as her revenues were, her expenditure, especially in building, was such as to leave little for idle parade. She rebuilt or repaired six castles and seven churches, and founded two hospitals. So strictly did she earn the character of a restorer, that finding an ancient yew in one of the courts of Skipton destroyed by the besiegers, she took care to have another planted precisely in the same place, which some years ago was standing, and a noble tree.

The Restoration made no improvement in her fortunes (except that she was no longer saddled with garrisons), and no alteration in her mode of life. In the court of Charles her virtue would have been as little recommendation as her grey hairs. She took little interest in the politics of any kingdom but her own; for while she noted down every thing, however minute, that related to her own household or estates,—as repairs, boundary ridings, death or marriage of domestics, entertaining of judges at assizes, &c., she seldom mentions any thing of the general affairs of the country, but such as everybody must have known. Yet it is to a supposed political transaction that the revival of her celebrity was owing. Though few have not heard of her reply to the Minister, who had attempted to interfere with her rights of nomination in the late borough of Appleby, of blessed memory, it is necessary to insert it here :—

"I have been bullied by a usurper, I have been neglected by a court, but I will not be dictated to by a subject. Your man shan't stand.

Anne Dorset, Pembroke, and Montgomery."

This letter was first published in the periodical called "The World," in 1753. The paper in which it appears is imputed to Horace Walpole,

who has introduced Lady Anne among the " Royal and Noble Authors,"
for the sake of repeating it. The original has never been produced,
nor does the writer in the "World" explain how he came by it.
Recently, a considerable degree of doubt has arisen with regard to its
authenticity. It is argued that, " fond as the Countess was of recording
even the most insignificant affairs of her life, there are no traces of it,
nor of the circumstance which is said to have occasioned it, in her
memoirs ; nor does the work in which it first appeared condescend to
favour us with any hint of reference to the original authority from
which it was derived. The measured construction and the brevity of
each individual sentence,—the sudden disjunction of the sentences
from one another,—the double repetition, in so small a space, of the
same phrase, and the studied conciseness of the whole, are all evidently
creatures of modern taste, and finished samples of that science of composi
tion, which had then (I mean when the Countess acquired her habits of
writing) scarcely dawned on English prose. No instance, I think, can
be found of the verb "stand" having been used at that time in the
sense to which it is applied to this letter, nor was the quaint and coarse
word "bully" known but as a substantive." * We cannot enter into
the minutiæ of this criticism, but we agree in the main, that the letter
is a very weak invention, and very much out of character. Such
laconic abruptness, such angry contempt of official dignity, belonged
not to the stately Anne Clifford. Had the epistle, *mutatis mutandis*,
been ascribed to Queen Elizabeth, it would have had much greater
dramatic propriety. But there is another difficulty. The letter is
addressed to Sir Joseph Williamson, Principal Secretary of State. Now
Sir Joseph Williamson was not Secretary of State till the 11th of
September, 1674, when Lord Arlington was advanced to be Chamberlain of the King's household. Lady Anne Clifford died 22d March,
1675. Now those who wish to legitimate or bastardize the letter, may
possibly take the trouble to ascertain whether there was a vacancy in
the representation of Appleby within that period. There certainly was
no general election. If the Countess did write this famous composition,
it must have been nearly the last act of her life, which would account
for no mention of it occurring in her memoirs. But we have little
doubt that it is spurious, were it only on one ground. The Lady Anne
never forgot, however she might forgive, King James's award, and the
detention of her estates. Had she had a mind to enumerate her
grievances, she would not have begun with the usurpation.

Though in her childhood and youth she suffered much sickness, and

* Lodge.

soon after the death of her first husband was in great danger from the small-pox, yet she attained the unusual age of eighty-six with few infirmities. And as her latter life was peaceful and active, so was her last end peace. She died at Brougham Castle, March 22d, 1675, and was buried the 14th of April following, in the sepulchre which she had herself erected at Appleby; choosing rather to lie beside her beloved mother, than with her martial ancestors at Skipton. Her funeral sermon was preached by Rainbow, Bishop of Carlisle, from Proverbs, xiv. 1 :—" Every wise woman buildeth her house." One sample of this oration must suffice, and with that we conclude our sketch of this excellent woman.

" She had," says he, " a clear soul, shining through a vivid body. Her body was durable and healthful, her soul sprightful ; of great understanding and judgment ; faithful memory, and ready wit. She had early gained a knowledge, as of the best things, so an ability to discourse in all commendable arts and sciences, as well as in those things which belong to persons of her birth and sex to know. She could discourse with virtuosos, travellers, scholars, merchants, divines, states- men, and with good housewives, in any kind, insomuch that a prime and elegant wit, well seen in all human learning (Dr. Donne), is reported to have said of her, that she knew well how to discourse of all things, from predestination down to slea-silk. If she had sought fame rather than wisdom, possibly she might have been ranked amongst those wits and learned of that sex, of whom Pythagoras, or Plutarch, or any of the ancients, have made such honourable mention ; but she affected rather to study with those noble Bereans, and those honourable women, who searched the scriptures daily ; and, with Mary, she chose the better part, of learning the doctrine of Christ."

In our brief notice of George, Earl of Cumberland, we alluded to the narrative of his third voyage, drawn up by Wright, the mathematician, and included in Hakluyt's collection. From this account we shall select a passage, which Lord Byron must have read before he composed the Ship-wreck in Don Juan. After relating their vain attempts to reach the coast of Ireland, and the rapid reduction of the crew's allowance from half a pint to a quarter pint of water daily, then to a few spoon- fuls of vinegar, or squeezings of wine-leas, to each meal, he proceeds thus :—

" With this hard fare, (for by reason of our great want of drink, we durst eat but very little,) we continued for the space of a fortnight, or thereabout, saving that now and then we feasted for it in the mean

time, and that was when there fell any hail or rain, the hail-stones we
gathered up and did eat them more pleasantly than if they had been
the sweetest comfits in the world.   The rain-drops were so carefully
saved, that so near as we could, not one was lost in all the ship.   Some
hung up sheets tied with cords by the four corners, and a weight in the
middle, that the water might run down thither, and so be received into
some vessel; some that wanted sheets hung up napkins and clouts, and
watched them till they were wet through, then wringing and sucking
out the water.   And that water which fell down and washed away the
filth and soiling of the ship, trod underfoot, as runneth down the kennel
many times, when it raineth, was not lost, but watched and attended
carefully, yea sometimes with strife and contention, at every scupperhole
and other place where it ran down, with dishes, pots, cans, and jars,
whereof some drank hearty drafts as it was, without tarrying to cleanse
it.   Some indeed tarried the cleansing, but not often, as loathe to lose
such excellent stuff.   Some licked with their tongues, like dogs, the
boards under feet, the sides, rails, and masts of the ship; others, naturally more ingenious, fastened girdles or ropes about the masts, daubing
tallow betwixt them and the mast, that the rain might not run down
between, in such sort that those ropes or girdles hanging lower down on
one side than the other, a spout of leather was fastened to the lower part
that all the rain drops that came running down the mast might meet
together at this place and there be received.   *Some also put bullets of
lead into their mouths to slake their thirst."*

        * All except Juan who, throughout abstain'd,
          Chewing a piece of Bamboo and some lead.

                                        CANTO II. 80.

ROGER ASCHAM.

" Gladly would he learn, and gladly teach."—CHAUCER.

THERE was a primitive honesty, a kindly innocence, about this good old scholar, which give a personal interest to the homeliest details of his life. He had the rare felicity of passing through the worst of times without persecution and without dishonour. He lived with princes and princesses, prelates and diplomatists, without offence and without ambition. Though he enjoyed the smiles of royalty, his heart was none the worse, and his fortune little the better. He had that disposition which, above all things, qualifies the conscientious and successful teacher ; for he delighted rather to discover and call forth the talents of others, than to make a display of his own.

Roger Ascham, the friend of Jane Grey, and the tutor of Queen Elizabeth, was born at Kirby Wiske, near Northallerton, A. D. 1515. His father discharged with diligence and fidelity the office of steward in the family of Scrope. His mother Margaret was more highly connected. He had two brothers and several sisters. His parents, having lived forty-seven years together as man and wife should live, expired in one day, and almost at the same hour.

It was the fashion of that time, that youth of respectable connections and small fortune were received into the houses of the great, and educated along with the scions of nobility. Roger, before his father's death, was taken into the family of Sir Anthony Wingfield, and brought up with the two sons of his patron, under the care of their tutor, Mr. Robert Bond.* For an humble, dutiful, steady and studious temper, no situation could be more advantageous. Such was Roger's. By living in a wealthy mansion he obtained access to more books than his

* " To conclude, let this, amongst other motives, make schoolmasters careful in their place,—that the eminences of their scholars have commended their school-masters to posterity, which otherwise in obscurity had been altogether forgotten. Who had ever heard of R. Bond, in Lancashire, but for the breeding of learned Roger Ascham, his scholar ? "---*"Fuller's Holy and Profane States."*

father could have purchased for him, and became an ardent reader almost as soon as he knew his letters: there, too, we may suppose he acquired that simple courtesy, that reverend kindliness of manner, which enabled him to win and retain the good graces of three royal females so dissimilar as Lady Jane Grey, Queen Mary, and Queen Elizabeth. Perhaps by secretly assisting his fellow-students, the young Wingfields, he first opened in his own mind that extraordinary aptitude for tuition which he afterwards displayed, and observed some of the facts which led him to think so deeply and so rightly on the culture of the human intellect.

In the year 1530, when he had attained his fifteenth year, he was sent, at the charges of his good patron, Sir Anthony, to St. John's College, Cambridge, where his studies neither went astray for lack of guidance, nor loitered for want of emulation. St. John's was then replete with all such learning as the time esteemed. The hard-headed dialectics and divinity of the schoolman was interchanged with the newly-recovered literature of Greece and Rome. The mind of Europe, divided between the rigidity of the old scholastic discipline and the inquisitive imaginations of the Italian Platonism, which brought poetry and philology in its train, might be likened to an old hawthorn stock, white with the blossoms of the spring; and if credit be given to Ascham's panegyrist, St. John's was a brief abstract, containing fair samples of every kind of excellence.*

Ascham's tutor was Hugh Fitzherbert, Fellow of St. John's, a man of learning and merit, and if we may judge of his sur-name, of high descent on one side at least. Whether related to Sir Anthony Fitzherbert we cannot tell. Among his contemporaries or immediate seniors are enumerated some whose names are immediately recognized,

---

* "Yea, surely, in that one college, which at that season, for number of most learned Doctors, for multitude of erudite philosophers, for abundance of eloquent orators, all in their kind superlative, might rival or outvie all mansions of literature on earth, were exceeding many men, most excellent in all politer letters, and in knowledge of languages." But English is not the speech of compliment or panegyric. No translation can come up to the issimuses and errimorums of old Rome. Here is the original, from Grant's " Oratio de vita et obitu Rogeri Ascham : "---

Imo certe in hoc uno collegio, quod eâ ætate singula totius orbis literarum domicilia et doctissimorum Theologorum numero, eruditissimorum Philosophorum turbâ, eloquentissimorum oratorum multitudine, vel juste adaequare, vel longe superare posset, erant complurimi homines omni politiori literatura linguarumque cognitione præstantissimorum. Quorum ille provocatur exemplis, et literarum imbibendarum ardore incensus, brevi propter admirabilem ingenii vim et indefessam in studiis industriam, tantos in Græcis Latinisque literis progressus fecit, ut omnes aequales, si non superaret, certe unus singulus adæquaret.

and others, perhaps, deemed equal or superior in their own day, whose existence is only discovered by antiquaries, and whose works derive their value from their scarcity. In the list are George Day, John Redman,* Robert Pember, Thomas Smith, John Cheek, Nicholas Rid-

* "John Redman, or Redmayne, descended from those of his name in Yorkshire, was near allied to Cuthbert Tunstall, Bishop of Durham, by whose advice he from childhood became conversant with the study of learning. At the first foundation of Corpus Christi College, (Oxford,) he was a student there for some time, under the care and government of Mr. J. Clayton, the first president: then he went to Paris, where he improved his studies till he was twenty one years of age. Afterwards returning to his native country of England, he settled in St. John's College, in Cambridge, where by his and John Cheek's example of excellency in learning, of godliness in living, of diligence in studying, of counsel in exhorting of good order in all things, were bred up so many learned men in that one college, as it was thought by one," i. e. Roger Ascham, "that the whole University of Louvain, in many years, was never able to afford. In 1537, he commenced Doctor of Divinity, and about that time was made public orator of that University, and afterwards the first Master, or Head, of Trinity College, and a dignitary in the church. But that which is most observable is, that when he first came to that University, being then very well versed in the Greek and Latin tongues, and adorned with knowledge by the reading of Cicero, it so fell out, that John Cheek and Thomas Smith, (being at that time young men, but afterwards knights,) were stirred up with a kind of emulation of his parts, and the honour that was daily done unto him. Whereupon, being very desirous to follow that which he had gained and then did possess and teach; they threw aside their sordid barbarisms, and applied themselves to the eloquence of Plato, Aristotle, and Cicero. The truth is, that by Redman's profound knowledge in the Tongues, Humanity, and Divinity, he obtained many admirers, and thereby gained proselytes, to the great advantage and refinement of the Greek and Latin Tongues in the University of Cambridge. He was esteemed the most learned and judicious divine of that time."—WOOD.

Hear this, ye men of Oxford, with what candour your noble old antiquary, who loved his Alma Mater almost to idolatry, and whose old age ye did persecute so shamefully, can speak of a man who carried the glory of his learning to the sister University.

Redman was, of course, an author, but the works published under his name have shared the too general oblivion of old divinity. If we may judge by the title of one of them, he must have been a Latin sacred versifyer. It is " Hymnus in quo Peccator justificationem quærens rudi imagine describitur." " A Hymn in which a sinner seeking Justification is rudely sketched off." He was also one of the divines employed in compiling the Liturgy of 1549. He died in 1551. He is thus honourably mentioned in Strype's Memoirs of Cranmer: " This year, (1551,) died John Redman, Master of Trinity Coll. in Cambridge, one of the greatest lights of that University, by bringing in solid learning among the students. He was a person of extraordinary reputation among all for his learning, and reading, and profound knowledge, so that the greatest divines gave a mighty deference to his judgment."

Of the " perfidious Prelate," Edmund Grindal, we shall say no more than that he obtained the praise of Spenser, who in one of his theologico-allegorical pastorals designated him, by an easy transposition of syllables, the good Shepherd Algrind.

ley, Edmund Grindal, (afterwards Archbishop of Canterbury, named of High-church-men the "perfidious Prelate,") Thomas Watson, Walter

Others have stigmatized him as the careless Shepherd that let the wolves of Geneva into the fold.

Non nostrum est tantas componere lites.

The following notice of Thomas, afterwards Sir Thomas Wilson, occurs in " Dib. din's Library Courpanion:"

" Sir Thomas Wilson is worthy of the phalanx of knights, in which he is here embodied," (Sir Thomas Elyote, Sir Anthony Fitzherbert, Sir Thomas More, &c.) "and will be long remembered as a philologist, rather than as a statesman or divine. His slender little volume, entitled *Epistola de vitâ et obitu duorum Fratrum Suffolciensium, Henrici et Caroli Brandon,* 1552, 4to., is a volume to rack the most desperate with torture, as to the hopelessness of its acquisition. The Bodleian library possesses it; so does the Museum, and so does Earl Spencer. Another copy is not known to me. Wilson's Art of Logic, 1551, 8vo., and of Rhetoric, 1553, 4to., are among his best performances, and highly commended by Tom Warton. Wilson was also among our earliest translator's from the Greek, having translated three orations from Demosthenes, &c., 1540, 4to. In fact, as an assistant of Sir Francis Walsingham, one would be glad to know a great deal more of the life of this eminent man, and especially to get at the contents of some of his correspondence. I take this to be the Wilson thus noticed by Roger Ascham, in his third letter to Edward Raven: "I trust Will. Taylor, John Bres, and *Thomas Wilson,* will not be behind. I pray God I may find these good Fellows at Cambridge, for there is the life that no man knows, but he that hath sometimes lacked it, and especially if one be able to live plentifully there."

Ridley, the companion of Latimer at the stake, is too well known as a reformer and a martyr to need commendation here. Thomas Watson was, in his youth, a polite scholar, poet, and Latin dramatist, " and gained great commendation for his Antigone out of Sophocles, by the learned men of his time; who have further avowed that as George Buchanan's tragedy called Jephtha has among all tragedies of that time, been able to abide the touch of Aristotle's precepts, and Euripides' examples; so also, hath the tragedy of this Thomas Watson, called Absalom, which was in a most wonderful manner admired by them, yet he would never suffer it to go abroad, because in *locis paribus* Anapæstus is once or twice used for Iambus," as Roger Ascham testifies. Here we may observe an approximation to the delicacies of modern scholarship, in the same college, which was destined to produce Bentley. The representation of Latin plays was then a stated exercise of the students of the Universities, and great schools, while the Inns of Courts exhibited masques and allegories, and even the parish clerks of Clerkenwell got up a Mystery of the Creation and History of the whole world, the representation whereof was continued, (with occasional adjournments, no doubt,) for nine days. This would not, in Antony's opinion, *be able to abide the touch of Aristotle's precepts.* The profane absurdity of many of those Scripture mysteries was such as to be incredible to persons only slightly acquainted with ancient manners. In one, performed in the *Cathedral* at Chester, wherein we may suppose the singing men and clerks were the actors, are the following stage directions:— " Enter *God,* creating the world." " Adam and Eve discovered, *naked,* but not ashamed."

Haddon, James Pilkington, R. Horn, John Christopherson Bishop of Chichester, Thomas Wilson, John Seton, and several other men, who afterwards appeared to great advantage in church or state.

Watson was afterwards Master of John's College, and chaplain to Gardiner Bishop of Winchester, by whom he was appointed, with other Doctors and learned men of Cambridge, to hold a disputation at Oxford, with Cranmer, Ridley, and Latimer, on matters of religion, Anno 1554. In 1557, he was consecrated Bishop of Lincoln. Deprived at the commencement of Elizabeth's reign, for refusing the oath of supremacy, he presumed to pronounce the sentence of excommunication against his sovereign, and passed the remaining years of his life in various prisons. Died 1584, in Wisbech-castle, Cambridgeshire. A man of much learning, but an ill temper.

Robert Horne, of a Cumberland Family, was Dean of Durham in 1551, in which capacity he scandalized the Catholics and antiquaries by removing the image of St. Cuthbert from its place in the cathedral; deprived by Queen Mary, 1553, took refuge at Strasburg, along with Jewel and other Protestants, returned in 1558, was made Bishop of Winchester in 1560. He is characterised by the apostolic vicar, Milner, as " a dilapidator of the property of his Bishopric, and a destroyer of the antiquities of his cathedral." He died 1579.

Day was a Bishop of Chichester, deprived in the reign of Edward VI., restored by Queen Mary.

James Pilkington, Batchelor of Divinity, born of a knightly family at Rivington, in the parish of Bolton, in Lancashire. Was a voluntary exile for the Protestant cause in the reign of Queen Mary, and succeeded Tonstal in the see of Durham in 1561: founded a free-school at his native place of Rivington, *sub nomine et auspiciis Elizabethæ Reginæ*: wrote comments on Nehemiah, Haggai, and Obadiah, and died at Bishop's Aukland in 1575. Buried in the cathedral of Durham. On his tomb were sculptured a monody by Dr. Laurence Humphrey, and an epicedium by Fox the martyrologist, both long since obliterated.

Walter Haddon was a doctor of civil law, who, though a Cantab, was made by a royal mandate President of Magdalen College, Oxford, contrary to statute. But he was a zealous promoter of the Reformation. Pity that Reformers should ever take illegal advantage of the royal prerogative, but so it was. He was obliged to withdraw at the accession of Mary, and concealed himself in privacy, but re-appeared at the rising of Elizabeth, and was made one of her Masters of Requests, and employed in several embassies. He wrote books both in prose and verse, which few persons now living ever heard of; among the rest, an oration on the death of Master Bucer. Anthony Wood ascribes to him an Epistle " de vita et obitu fratrum Suffolciensium Henrici et Caroli Brandon." The " Fratres Suffolcienses " were doubtless the two sons of Charles Brandon, Duke of Suffolk, by his last wife, Catherine, daughter of Lord Willoughby of Eresby, who died both on the same day, of the sweating sickness, at the Bishop of Lincoln's palace at Bugden, A.D. 1551. So remarkable a catastrophe in a family connected with royalty was sure to set all the muses a weeping. Walter Haddon died 1571.

John Seton, Prebendary of Winchester, was one of the disputants against Cranmer and Latimer, in 1554, and was famous for the brief and methodical Book of Logic which he composed for the use of junior scholars.

2 P

At the age of eighteen, when the youth of our generation are just composing their *Vales* at Eton or Harrow, Ascham commenced B.A., 28th of February, 1538-9, and, on the 23rd of March following, he was elected Fellow, chiefly, as himself has gratefully and modestly recorded, by the interest of Dr. Nicholas Medcalf, then Master of the college. His account of this transaction, and his grateful tribute to his departed

Thomas, better known as *Sir* Thomas Smith, was eminent in his day both as a philologer and a statesman; born at Saffron Waldon, in Essex; sent into Italy to finish his education at the King's charge; made on his return public orator of Cambridge, Regius Professor of Greek, and Professor of Civil Law. Under Edward VI., or rather under the Protector Somerset, he was one of the principal secretaries of state, Sir William Cecil, afterwards Lord Burleigh, being the other. At this time also he was knighted, endowed with the spoils of the Deanery of Carlisle, and, though a layman, appointed Provost of Eaton. Though Queen Mary deprived him of these preferments, he suffered no other molestation during her reign, but enjoyed a pension of £100, saddled with the condition that he should not quit the kingdom. In the beginning of Queen Elizabeth he was called again to the service of the commonwealth, was restored to his Deanery, was present with the divines at the framing of the liturgy, and employed in several embassies. He was also restored to the Secretary's office, made Chancellor of the order of the Garter, and frequently sent in the House of Commons, where he became " very useful to the commonwealth of learning," by certain regulations he was the means of bringing about in regard to the corn-rents of college property. He died in the climacterical year of his age, in the month of July, 1577, and was buried in the church of Heydon Mount, in Essex. All his Greek and Latin books he bequeathed to Queen's College, Cambridge, as well as a large globe of his own construction, and founded two exhibitions for natives of Saffron Waldon. He is the author of several historical and political works, which must be highly curious and instructive, particularly, " *The Commonwealth of England, and the manner and government thereof, in three books.*" Black letter, 1583, several times reprinted, and twice translated into Latin. " *The authority, form, and manner, of holding Parliaments,*" not printed till 1685, and by some doubted to be Sir Thomas Smith's. " *De re nummaria,*" probably an essay on the coinage. But he is best remembered (in Cambridge at least) for the part he took in the controversy respecting the true pronunciation of Greek, and for his endeavours to rectify and fix the orthography of the English Language. This never-yet-achieved adventure has excited the ambition of many philologers, as may be seen in the preface to Todd's Johnson's Dictionary. Among those who have essayed to reconcile spelling to pronunciation, may be reckoned Alexander Gill, Master of St. Paul's School, (who, with yet greater audacity, wrote a satire on Ben Jonson,) Mitford, and Landor. A similar experiment was tried, yet more hopelessly, upon the French, by Jean Antoine de Baif, a poet of the sixteenth century, so voluminous, that no man was ever known to have read his works through. Of Pember and Christopherson no more need be said at present, than that they were correspondents of Roger Ascham. Sir John Cheek, tutor to King Edward VI., and one of the great restorers of Greek literature in England, is so well known, that it were superfluous to give so short a notice of him as our limits would allow in this place. Of his contest with Bishop Gardiner, mention will be made in the text. His sister was the first wife of Cecil.

superior, must be given in his own words. " Dr. Medcalf," he says, " was a man meanly learned himself, but not meanly affectioned to set forth learning in others. He was partial to none, but indifferent to all ; a Master of the whole, a father to every one in that college. There was none so poor, if he had either will to goodness, or wit to learning, that could lack being there, or should depart thence for any need. He was a papist indeed ; but would to God that among *all us Protestants* I might once see but *one*, that would win like praise, in doing like good for the advancement of learning and virtue. And yet though he were a Papist, if any young man given to *New Learning*, (as they termed it,) went beyond his fellows in wit, labour, and towardliness, even the same neither lacked open praise to encourage him, nor private exhibition to maintain him. I myself, one of the meanest of a great number in that college, because there appeared in me some small shew of towardness and diligence, lacked not his favour to further me in learning. And being a boy, new Batchelor of Arts, I chanced among my companions to speak against the Pope ; which matter was then very much in every body's mouth, because Dr. Hains and Dr. Skip were come from the court to debate the same matter, by preaching and disputation in the University. This happened the same time when I stood to be Fellow there. My talk came to Dr. Medcalf's ear. I was called before him and the Seniors, and after grievous rebuke, and some punishment, open warning was given to all the Fellows, none to be so hardy to give me his voice at that election. And yet, for all those open threats, the good father himself privily procured, that I should be even then chosen Fellow. But the election being done, he made countenance of great discontent thereat. This good man's goodness and fatherly discretion used towards me that one day, shall never be out of my remembrance all the days of my life. And for the same cause have I put it here in this small record of learning. For, next to God's Providence, surely that day was by that good father's means, dies Natalis unto me for the whole foundation of the poor learning I have, and of all the furtherance that hitherto elsewhere I have obtained."

The human heart is capable of no more generous feeling than the genuine gratitude of a scholar to his instructor. It is twice blessed ; honourable alike to the youth and to the elder, and never can exist where it is not just. But it is at the same time a melancholy instance of the pride of fallen nature, that this feeling is seldom uttered except where the pupil has, by general consent, excelled the master. Intellectual benefits are more reluctantly acknowledged than any others. For kindness, for encouragement, for maintenance of studies, for exhortation, even for salutary correction, our thanks are generally ready, and

often sincere; but who is willing to own, even to himself, how much of
his knowledge, how much of his mental power, has been communicated
by a teacher? How many of his *thoughts* are mere recollections?
However much we may profit by the wisdom of others, it is as much as
most of us can do to forgive them for being wiser, or earlier wise, than
ourselves. The utterance of grateful sentiments is wonderfully facili-
tated when it can be accompanied with certain qualifying clauses and
admissions. Thus Ascham evidently dwells with the more satisfaction
on his obligations to Medcalf, because the latter was a man meanly
learned, and a *Papist*.

Ascham, however, had rightly a very moderate estimation of that
sort of learning which can be taught by voice or book, and passively
received into the memory. With as little of pugnacity or indocility
as ever belonged to a lively and enquiring mind, he held fast the truth,
that it is only by its own free agency that the intellect can either be
enriched or invigorated;—that true knowledge is an act, a continuous
immanent act, and at the same time an operation of the reflective faculty
on its own objects. How he applied this idea to the purposes of
education, his " Schoolmaster," written in the maturity of his powers,
and out of the fulness of his experience, sufficiently shows. But the
idea, though undeveloped, wrought in him from his earliest youth:
his favourite maxim was *Docendo disces*. The affectionate wish and
strenuous effort to impart knowledge is the best possible condition for
receiving it. The necessity of being intelligible to others brings with it
an obligation to understand ourselves; to find words apt to our ideas,
and ideas commensurate to our words; to seek out just analogies and
happy illustrations. But, above all, by teaching, or more properly by
reciprocal intercommunication of instruction, we gain a practical
acquaintance with the universal laws of thought, and with the process
of perception, abstracted from the accidents of the individual constitution: for it is only by a sympathetic intercourse with other minds that
we gain any true knowledge of our own. Of course we speak of free
and friendly *teaching*, not of despotic *dictation*, than which there is no
habit more likely to perpetuate presumptuous ignorance.

The study of the Greek language was at that time new in western
Europe, and in England a mere novelty. To Ascham it was as " the
trouble of a new delight:" every lesson which he gained he was eager
to impart: he taught Greek, he wrote Greek, he talked Greek, no
wonder if he dreamed in Greek. There might be a little vanity in
this: but whatever vanity he possessed (and he certainly loved to talk
of himself) was so tempered by modesty, and blended with such candour, such glad acknowledgment of others' merits, that the sternest

judgments could hardly call it a foible. By this industrious communication and daily practice he acquired, at a very early period, such a command of the Greek vocabulary, and so vernacular a turn of phrase, that his Senior, Robert Pember, to whom he had addressed an epistle in that tongue, assures him that his letter might have been written at Athens. But the critical nicety of modern scholarship was then unknown, and it is very unlikely that Pember himself felt or understood that perfect *atticism* upon which he compliments his young friend. Pember's epistle of course is in Latin, interspersed with Greek, and curious enough to be worthy of translation. It is to this effect:— " Dearly beloved Roger,— I render thee thanks for thy Greek epistle, which might seem to have been indited at ancient Athens, so exactly hast thou attained the propriety of Greek phrase : of exquisite penmanship it is, as are all thine. *Use diligence, that thou may'st be perfect, not according to the stoical, but to lyrical perfection, that thou may'st touch the harp aright.* Continue to read Greek with the boys, for thou wilt profit more by one little fable of Æsop, read and explained by thyself, than if thou shouldst hear the whole Iliad expounded in Latin by the learnedest man now living. Peruse Pliny, in which author is the greatest knowledge of things, along with the most florid opulence of Latin speech."*

In this letter we may notice, first, the testimonial to the beauty of Ascham's penmanship, which proved a principal mean of his advance-

* I wish young scholars paid attention to this recommendation. Pliny is never read at school, and very seldom at college ; yet 1 have the high authority of Southey for saying, that he is the most instructive of all the Roman authors. The extent of his knowledge is almost marvellous; his veracity, where he speaks from personal observation, is daily approved by modern experiment and discovery ; and even his credulity adds to his value, by disclosing more fully the actual state of physical science in his age and country. It is surely quite as interesting to know what properties the passions or the imaginations of men have ascribed to a plant or animal, as to count its stamina and petals, or ascertain the number of its vertebræ. Both are very useful. But the highest recommendation of Pliny is his moral wisdom, his almost christian piety, his intelligent humanity. Of all the Romans he was the least of a Roman, and approximated nearest to the pure idea of man.

Many of the most useful of the Greek and Roman authors are wholly excluded from the common course of education, under the absurd notion that they are not classical. One might imagine that the purity of Latin speech were as seriously sacred as a virgin's chastity. Cardinal Bembo declined reading the scriptures (in the vulgate translation) for fear of corrupting his Latinity; and I have heard with my own ears a young student of divinity give a similar reason for not reading St. Augustine. The feeling is at bottom an aristocratical one. From causes not necessary to be discussed in this place, classical erudition is not only esteemed the befitting ornament of a born gentleman, but has the power to "gentle the condition" of *puddle blood,* an efficacy never ascribed to any other kind of knowledge.

ment: secondly, a proof that he was actually engaged in the tuition of *boys* : thirdly, that in his plans, both for his own improvement, and for that of his pupils, he diverged from the common routine of lectures: fourthly, that his friend, well discerning the bent and purpose of his genius, urged him to proceed with those humane and elegant studies, on which some austerer judgments looked with an evil eye. From one passage of this epistle, certain dull, literal brains have told us, that " Mr. Robert Pember advised him to learn instrumental music, which would prove a very agreeable entertainment to him after his severer studies, and was easy to be attained by him, as he was already a great master of vocal music." It is certainly very possible, that Pember may have given him such advice, but it is nevertheless certain, that he does not give it in the letter in question. There is no allusion to recreation at all. The whole drift of the writer is an exhortation to perseverance in a course of study already commenced ; and surely Mr. Pember, however he might approve of music as a relaxation, (which, by the way, Roger Ascham did not,) had more sense than to advise a young man, intended for the church, *dare operam*, to devote all the energies of his soul, to make a perfect fiddler of himself. But it is not for every one to interpret parables. *

So far was Ascham from devoting himself to music with that intensity which Pember has been supposed to recommend, that he appears to have had no manner of taste, but rather a platonic antipathy for it, even as an amusement. Nor would he be well pleased with the present course of education in his University, if we judge by the sentiments which he expresses in his Schoolmaster, and Toxophilus.

" Some wits, moderate enough by nature, be many times marred by over much study and use of some sciences, namely, music, arithmetic, and geometry. These sciences as they sharpen men's wits over much, so they charge men's manners over sore, if they be not moderately mingled, and wisely applied to some good use of life. Mark all mathematical heads, which be wholly and only bent to those sciences, how solitary they be themselves, how unapt to serve in the world. This is not only known by common experience, but uttered long before by wise men's judgment and sentence. Galen saith, much music marreth men's manners, and Plato hath a notable place of the same thing, and excellently translated by Tully himself. Of this matter I wrote once more

---

* The words of the original are—" Da operam, at sis perfectus, non Stoicus, ἀλλὰ Λυρικὸς, ut belle pulses lyram." No doubt in the same sense that Socrates was commanded by the Oracle to make music; or, to appeal to a far higher authority, as David " shewed a dark speech on the harp," i. e. opened and exalted the understanding by the aid of the imagination.

at large, twenty years ago, in my book of shooting." The passage of the Toxophilus referred to, is as follows. "Whatsoever ye judge, this I am sure, that lutes, harps, barbitons, sambukes, and other instruments, every one which standeth by quick and fine fingering, be condemned of Aristotle, as not to be brought in and used among them, which study for learning and virtue. Much music marreth men's manners, saith Galen. Although some men will say that it doth not so, but rather recreateth and maketh quick a man's mind, yet methinks, by reason it doth, as honey doth to a man's stomach, which at the first receiveth it well; but afterward it maketh it unfit to abide any strong nourishing meat, or else any wholesome sharp and quick drink; and, even so in a manner, these instruments make a man's wit so soft and smooth, so tender and quaisy, that they be less able to brook strong and rough study. Wits be not sharpened, but rather made blunt, with such soft sweetness, even as good edges be blunted, which men whet upon soft chalk-stones."

These opinions require considerable limitation. Music is so high a delight to such as are really capable of enjoying it, that there is some danger of its incroaching too much upon the student's time, and it is frequently a passport to very undesirable company; but if these evils be avoided, its effects on the mind are extremely salutary and refreshing. Nothing calms the spirit more sweetly than sad music; nothing quickens cogitation like a lively air. But the truth was, that honest Roger had no ear, and like a true Englishman of an age when Kings were wrestlers, and Queens not only presided at tournaments, but " rained influence" upon bear-baitings, delighted rather in muscular exertion than in fine fingering. That the practice of music no way impairs the faculty of severe thought, is sufficiently evinced by the fact that Milton was a skilful musician, and that most of the German philosophers of the present day, who in mental industry excel the whole world, play on some instrument. Mathematical pursuits are so far from disqualifying men for business, that of all others they are most necessary to such as are intended for public life. A mere mathematician, is indeed often rude and unlicked enough; but this may partly be accounted for from the circumstance, that many more persons of plebeian origin attain eminence in the mathematics than in the classics, and being, like most mathematicians, very honest men, do not readily acquire the distinguishing manner of genteel society. For it is a general observation, that a facility of adopting manners is the talent of a knave. A pick-pocket looks, speaks, and behaves much more *like* a gentleman, than an honest tradesman does. It is only in the highest class that fine manners bespeak noble sentiments.

Ascham took his master's degree in 1544, when he was no more than one and twenty. His character as a tutor was already high, and several excellent scholars were among his pupils; particularly Mr. William Grindall, who was afterwards, by Sir John Cheek's recommendation, preceptor to the Princess Elizabeth. Though the Regius Professorship of Greek was not yet formally founded, yet Ascham read lectures on that language, and received a considerable stipend from the University. About this time he was involved in a most singular controversy, which although the subject be of no very general interest, is yet so character-istic of the times, that we shall briefly describe it. Sir John Cheek and Sir Thomas Smith had introduced some alterations into the pronuncia-tion of the Greek language, which had previously been even more barbarous than at present. Ascham at first opposed the inno-vation, and defended the established errors, in a disputation with Mr. Ponet, an ingenious youth, who was Fellow of Queen's College; but his mind was ever open to conviction on all subjects, great and small, and he had adopted the new and improved method, when a more formidable person than any yet engaged in the busi-ness thought fit to interfere in a truly despotic manner, giving thereby a sample of the temper, which he afterwards indulged so frightfully against innovations of a more important kind. This was the notorious Stephen Gardiner, then Chancellor of the University of Cambridge, who issued his peremptory prohibition of the new pronun-ciation, and after defining, with great strictness, the sound to be given to each letter, denounced the penalties for disobedience, suspension of degrees for graduates, and private whipping for undergraduates. Sir John Cheek, however, who was destined to yield to Gardiner in a con-cern of far higher moment, had the courage to defend his system; and the Bishop's attention was soon after diverted to other objects. As Gar-diner was no fool, but partook largely of the subtlety of that Being whom he so closely resembled in wickedness, we ought not to ascribe this strange proceeding to mere caprice, or wantonness of power. In fact, had he been a conscientious supporter of the ancient church, a honest upholder of established authority, he would have acted very wisely in forbidding change, even in the merest trifle; for whatever alteration, great or small, tended to impair the credit of tradition, and to accustom men to think and judge for themselves, was prejudicial to a Church that claims a traditional infallibility, and denies the right of private judgment. But it is not impossible that the mandate really proceeded from bluff King Harry himself, whose interest in literary questions was one redeeming point of his character, and whose most pardonable foible, or perhaps rather the foible of his age, was an itch to be legislating on all possible topics, from articles of faith to rudiments of grammar.

Ascham, in an epistle addressed to Hubert Languet, a continental scholar and statesman, declares his adherence to the new pronunciation, and defends the change with considerable humour. Among other absurdities of the exploded system, was that of giving the sound of the English V to the Greek B. Now Eustathius, asserts that the Greek word BH exactly resembled the bleating of a sheep, and therefore it is easy to determine how it is to be pronounced; unless, says Roger, the Greek sheep bleated differently from those of England, Italy, and Germany; " Jam utrum ulla ovis effert *ve* ut vos an *be* ut nos, judicetis. Anglæ scio omnes et Germanæ et Italæ pro nobis faciunt; sed fortasse Græcæ oves olim non *balabant* sed *vilabant*." The same argument would prove, that the Greek Eta should, after the Italian accent, be pronounced not as ee but as ay. From the manner in which Ascham speaks of the new pronunciation, it is manifest that the reform was at the date of his letter, (6th of March, 1553,) firmly established in England, while the continental nations still adhered to the old method, which was probably derived from the Constantinopolitans by whom the Greek language was revived in the West, as it nearly resembles that of the modern Greeks. Correctness of course is out of the question in either case; but that system is to be preferred which gives to each letter a distinct sound.

In the year, 1544, Ascham produced his " Toxophilus; the school or partitions of shooting, in two books," dedicated to King Henry VIII. then just setting out to invade France, where his predecessors Edward and Henry had conquered so gloriously with the bow. So well was the monarch pleased with the dedication, that he settled an annual pension on the author, at the recommendation of Sir William Paget,*

* Sir William, afterwards the first Lord Paget, of Beaudesert, in Staffordshire, the lineal ancestor of the present Marquis of Anglesea, was one of the most eminent diplomatists of his time; a firm but tolerant adherent to the ancient church; and a liberal patron of literature. His descent was humble. His family sprang from Staffordshire, but his father migrated to London, and obtained the office of Serjeant at Mace to the Corporation. William was born in 1506, educated at St. Paul's School, under the famed grammarian Lilly, and at Trinity Hall, Cambridge. His rise was owing in a great measure to the patronage of Gardiner, who sent him to complete his studies at the University of Paris. In 1530, when no more than twenty-four, he was sent into France to collect the opinions of the most distinguished Jurists of that kingdom upon Henry's proposed divorce. In 1537, he was employed as a secret envoy in Germany; in 1542, he was ambassador in France, knighted in 1543, and made one of the two principal Secretaries of State. In 1545, he negociated in concert with the Chancellor Wriothesly, and the Duke of Suffolk, the

which was discontinued after Henry's death, but renewed during pleasure by Edward VI. The Toxophilus did not wholly escape censure
from certain morose critics, who thought the subject inconsistent with
the gravity of a scholar; but against these cavils he effectually vindicated himself in the first book, wherein he shews the usefulness of bodily
exercise both to body and mind.

The peculiar beauty of Ascham's hand-writing first introduced him
to the court, where he had the honour of teaching Prince Edward, the
Princess Elizabeth, and the two sons of Brandon, Duke of Suffolk, the
use of the pen. He was also the University amanuensis, and wrote all
the letters which Cambridge addressed to the Kings and other people
of Quality; in which sort of correspondence, perspicuity and beauty of
penmanship are of great efficacy, and may chance to procure for a .
petition an early reading. All formal and official letters (at least where
the Church or the Universities were concerned) were then written in
Latin, and Ascham's Latin style was well fitted for actual business.
Avoiding the barbarisms and solecisms of the *Monks*, and conform-

terms of the marriage between Margaret, niece to King Henry VIII. and the Earl of
Lennox, (from which union the Lady Arabella Stuart derived her descent, and that
unhappy proximity to the Crown which consigned her to life-long captivity.) Soon
after, he was engaged in negociations with France, which, though attended with difficulty, were brought to a successful issue a few months before Henry's decease. Sir
William Paget was an executor of the King's will, and one of the council to his minor
successor. Though opposed to the ecclesiastical revolution, he was politically attached
to the Protector Somerset, by whom he was invested with the Garter, sent ambassador to
the Emperor, and advanced to the Peerage. Of course he did not wholly escape the
suspicions and indignities which fell on the whole Somerset party. In particular the
Dudley faction, with exceeding great littleness, divested him of his order, on the
ground of insufficiency of blood. But all his misfortunes passed away at the accession
of Mary, whose title he was among the first to assert. He was honourably re-elected
to the Garter, and employed in several negociations of great moment. It is not
improbable that to his influence with Gardiner, Ascham owed his security in the days
of persecution. Lord Paget retired from public life at the demise of Mary, and died
in 1563.

As a curious specimen of the style of an author with whom all our readers may not
be familiar, we shall present them with Lloyd's character of this eminent statesman,
the founder of a distinguished House :—

" His education was better than his birth, his knowledge higher than his education,
his parts above his knowledge, and his experience beyond his parts. A general learning furnished him for travel, and travel seasoned him for employment. *His master-
piece was an inward observation of other men, and an exact knowledge of himself.* His
address was with state, yet insinuating; his discourse free, but weighed; his apprehension quick, but stayed; his ready and present mind keeping its pauses of thoughts
and expressions even with the occasion and the emergency; neither was his carriage
more stiff and uncompliant than his soul." .

ing his sentences to the analogies of Roman authors, he nevertheless writes rather as a man who was accustomed to speak and think in Latin, whose words were the natural body and suggestion of his thoughts, than as one that having stocked his memory with the phraseology of some particular writers, constrained his thoughts to fit preexistent frames of diction. On the resignation of Sir John Cheek he was made public orator. Thus dividing his time between London and Cambridge, and his studies between his books and the world, he passed the four years from 1544 to 1548, at which latter period William Grindall died; and Ascham was summoned to attend on England's future Queen, to complete that structure of learning which his pupil had begun. It must be an affair of delicate management to teach Greek to a Princess; but Ascham had a love and a genius for teaching, and Elizabeth possessed in an extraordinary degree the facility of her sex in learning languages. She had then little or no expectation of reigning. Her situation was one of peculiar difficulty: she needed a spirit at once firm and yielding; and displayed in earliest youth a circumspection and self-controul in which her latter years were deficient. Ascham found her a most agreeable pupil; and the diligence, docility, modest affection, and self-respective deference of the royal maiden endeared an office which the shy scholar had not undertaken without fears and misgivings. His epistles to his friends are full of the Princess' commendations and his own satisfaction; and in his later works he refers to this part of his life with honest pride. In this happy strain he writes to John Sturmius, of Strasburg:—" If you wish to know how I am thriving at Court, you may assure yourself that I had never more blessed leisure in my college than now in the palace. The Lady Elizabeth and I are studying together, in the original Greek, the crown orations of Demosthenes and Æschines. She reads her lessons to me, and at one glance so completely comprehends, not only the idiom of the language and the sense of the orator, but the exact bearings of the cause, and the public acts, manners, and usages of the Athenian people, that you would marvel to behold her." In like temper he told Aylmer, afterwards Bishop of London, that he learned more of the Lady Elizabeth than she did of him. " I teach her words," said he, " and she teaches me things. I teach her the tongues to speak, and her modest and maidenly looks teach me works to do; for I think she is the best disposed of any in Europe." In several of his Latin epistles, and also in his "Schoolmaster," he explains and recommends his mode of instructing the Princess with evident exultation at his success. It was the same method of double translation pursued with such distinguished results in the tuition of the young sovereign, by Sir John Cheek, from

whom Ascham adopted it: and indeed, like many of the best discoveries, it seems so simple that we wonder how it ever could be missed,
and so excellent, that we know not why it is so little practised. It
had, indeed, been suggested by the younger Pliny, in an epistle to
Fuscus, and by Cicero, in his Dialogue de Oratore. "Pliny," saith
Roger, "expresses many good ways for order in study, but beginneth
with translation, and preferreth it to all the rest. But a better and
nearer example herein may be our noble Queen Elizabeth, who never
yet took Greek nor Latin Grammar in her hand after the first declining
of a noun and a verb; but only by this double translating of Demosthenes and Isocrates daily without missing, every forenoon, and likewise some part of Tully every afternoon, for the space of a year or two,
hath attained to such perfect understanding in both the tongues, and to
such a ready utterance in the Latin, and that with such a judgment,
as they be few in number in both Universities, or elsewhere in England,
that be in both tongues comparable to her Majesty." And so in an
epistle to Sturmius:—" It is almost incredible to how excellent
an understanding both of Greek and Latin I myself conducted our
sacred Lady Elizabeth by this same double translation, constantly and
in brief time delivered in writing." In the same letter he insists upon
the pupil making the translations with his or her own hand, proprio,
non alieno stylo, whence it may be concluded, that Elizabeth was her
own amanuensis on these occasions.

We may well allow a teacher to be a little rapturous about the
proficiency of a lady, a Queen, and his own pupil; but after all due
abatements, the testimony remains unshaken both to the talent of the
learner, and the efficiency of the system of instruction.

For two years the most perfect harmony subsisted between Elizabeth
and her preceptor. The intervals of study were occasionally *relieved*
with chess, at which Ascham is said to have been an adept. It is to be
hoped that he had too much prudence and gallantry to beat the Lady
oftener than was necessary to convince her that he *always* played his
best. True, the royal virgin was not then Queen, or even presumptive
heir; but no wise man would take the conceit out of a chess-player,
that stood within the hundredth degree of relationship to the throne.
Elizabeth was not the only distinguished female whose classical studies
were assisted by our author; he taught Latin to Anne, Countess of
Pembroke, to whom he addressed two letters in that language still
extant.

The court of the young Edward was filled with lovers of learning, in
whose society and patronage Ascham enjoyed himself fully, as Sir John
Cheek his old friend, Lord Paget, Sir William Cecil, and the Chancel-

lor Wriothesly. He had a share in the education of the two Brandons, whose premature and contemporaneous decease has been before alluded to, and he partook the favour of the youthful King, who honouring knowledge, and all its professors, must have especially esteemed it in the instructor of his *Lady Temper*, as the amiable boy used to call his favourite sister. It was at this period that he became acquainted with the lovely Jane Grey, a creature, whose memory should singly put to rout the vulgar prejudice against female erudition.

After two years passed in occupation and society so congenial, a mis-understanding took place between Roger and his charge, and, in a fit of mortification, he returned to his college, but soon repented of his impatience, and sought the mediation of the German reformer Martin Bucer, then just arrived in Britain. Bucer, however, did not think fit to interpose, as appears from a letter addressed to him by Ascham some time after, (January 7, 1551,) from Augsburgh, in which occurs a passage to this effect:—" You have not forgotten how, on your first coming to England, when you dwelt at Lambeth, while yet we were unknown to each other, I came and laid before you what usage I had received, not from my Lady Elizabeth, but from certain of her household. I then requested you by your letters to aid in restoring me to that favour from which I had been in some sort estranged, God knows by no fault of my own, but by the ill offices of others. Before my going abroad, I visited my illustrious Mistress; she received me most graciously, and yet more graciously reproached * me with leaving her in such a manner, and *neglecting to retrieve her good graces by any mediator.*" Bucer was in the ague, and, besides, thought Ascham in the wrong for taking umbrage at the young Lady's frowns, which after all he might be mistaken in attributing to any body, or any thing, but her own coquetry. He had too high an opinion of her to allow for her humours. Not but what all poor scholars who would thrive (and it is their only chance of thriving) by the tutorage of the great, must put up with a great deal of insolence from waiting gentlemen and waiting gentlewomen. If the tutor keep them at a distance, their hatred is dangerous, if he allow them any liberties, their impertinence is tyrannical. But neither the malice of underlings, nor his own impatience, did lasting injury to Ascham. Returning to his duties, as public Orator at Cambridge, he still retained his pension, and the confidence of the worthiest persons about court. His interest must have been very considerable if, as one † quaintly expresses it, " he hindered those who had *dined* on the church

* Multo humanius objurgavit. Ascham, academician as he was, knew something of woman. A woman's reproach is often the best sign of her favour.

† Lloyd's State Worthies.

from *supping* on the Universities;" but the sentence is too witty to be literally interpreted. He was certainly well thought of by Elizabeth, and of her he spoke with enthusiasm to his latest day, not without a pleasing consciousness of his own services in making her what she was. Thus, in the " Schoolmaster," his latest work, he makes her perfections a reproach to all her male subjects. " It is your shame, (I speak to you all, you young gentlemen of England,) that one maid should go beyond ye all in excellency of learning, and knowledge of divers tongues. Point out six of the best given gentlemen of this court, and all they together show not so much good will, bestow not so many hours daily, orderly, and constantly, for the increase of learning and knowledge, as doth the Queen's Majesty herself. Yea, I believe that besides her perfect readiness in Latin, Italian, French, and Spanish, she readeth here now at Windsor more Greek every day, than some prebendary of this church doth Latin in a whole week. Amongst all the benefits which God hath blessed me withal, next the knowledge of Christ's true religion, I count this the greatest, that it pleased God to call me to be one poor minister in setting forward these excellent gifts of learning."

In excuse, however, of the " six best given gentlemen," it should be stated, that the learning of languages is emphatically a female talent, bearing a much larger ratio to general ability in woman than in man. Yet who can but admire the indefatigable intellect of our renowned Queen, harassed in youth with peril and persecution, and burdened in early maturity with public cares, which could yet attain a proficiency in polite learning, such as few professional scholars have excelled. The bare titles of the works which she translated evince the variety of her philological attainments, and justify the praises of her eulogists.[*] When no more than eleven years of age she translated out of French verse into English prose, " The mirror, or glass, of the sinful soul," dedicated to Queen Catherine Parr, 1544. At twelve, she rendered out

---

[*] The praises of Elizabeth were not confined to her own subjects. Scaliger declared that she knew more than all the great men of her time. Serranus honoured her with the dedication of his Plato, in terms flattering enough, but only a learned Queen could be so flattered. Dedicators and panegyrists dabble much in prophecy; but it is not often that they prophecy truly. Serranus, however, was right for once, when he foretold the future fame of " good Queen Bess," and " Eliza's Golden-days." " Quemadmodum Salomonis vel Augusti felix imperium, notabile fuit ad designandam civilem felicitatem : ita et tuum, regina, illustre sit futurum, tuaque insula non amplius Albion sed Olbia et vere fortunata sit porro nuncupanda. Quidenim? In regno tuo vera illa regnat philosophia cujus vix ac ne vix quidem umbram vidit Plato." The large paper copy of Serranus's Plato, holds up its head magnificently at thirty guineas!!! Is there a man or a woman living that can read and understand Plato, and has thirty guineas to spare?

of English into Latin, French, and Italian, " Prayers or Meditations, by which the soul may be encouraged to bear with patience all the Miseries of Life, to despise the vain happiness of this World, and assiduously provide for eternal Felicity, collected out of prime writers by the most noble and religious Queen Catherine Parr," dedicated by the Princess Elizabeth to King Henry VIII." dated at Hatfield, in Hertfordshire, Dec. 30. Much about the same time she translated a treatise originally written by Marguerite of Navarre,* in the French language, and entitled the "Godly Meditation of the Inward Love of the Soul towards Christ the Lord," printed in the " Monument of Matrons, containing seven several Lamps of Virginity."† These were the works of the " tender and maidenly years " of her childhood. At a riper age she turned from Greek, into Latin, portions of Xenophon, Isocrates, and Euripides ; from Greek to English, Plutarch on Curiosity ; from Latin to English, Boethius, Sallust's Jugurthine War, and part of Horace's Art of Poetry. From Italian she translated certain sermons of Bernardine Ochine, an Italian Protestant divine. It is hard to say what assistance she may have had in these labours, nor can we speak of their merits from personal inspection : but if she produced any considerable part of them, they must evince extreme activity, and a laudable love of

---

* This once celebrated lady, the sister of Francis I., exhibited in her writings an interchange of the amorous and the devout, which was long common in the lives of her countrywomen. Her Heptameron, or collection of Tales, is said to copy the Decameron of Boccacio too closely in other matters besides its title ; while her Miroir de l'Ame pecheresse, Spiritual Songs, Sacred Dramas, and other compositions, are filled with agonies of penitence and extacies of divine love. Of the former, the following passage from Elizabeth's English may serve as a specimen, "Where is the Hell full of travail, pain, mischief and torment? Where is the pit of cursedness, out of which doth spring all desperation? Is there any hell so profound that is sufficient to punish the tenth part of my sins, which in number are so many, that the infinite swarm of them so shadoweth my darkened senses, that I cannot account them, neither yet well see them?" Her sacred and *profane* poems were promiscuously published by her valet de chambre, Jean de la Haye, in 1547, with the following quaint title :—" Les Marguerites de la Marguerite des Princesses," which can be translated into no language in which Marguerite does not happen to mean a pearl.

† The rare and curious Heptateuch bearing this seemingly contradictory title is described at considerable length in Dibdin's Library Companion. We are free to confess that our sole acquaintance with it is owing to that useful volume. We never hung over its fragrant pages, or reverendly touched its antique "kivers." It is a manual or Hortus siccus of prayers and meditations, many of them by Queens and other great ladies, as Catherine Parr, Mary, Elizabeth, Judith, Queen Esther, and Sappho.

literary employment. What pædagogue would not be proud of such a scholar ? *   But we must return to her preceptor.

In the summer of 1550, while Ascham was spending his vacation among his friends, and recruiting himself with his native air, a summons from his constant friend Sir John Cheek recalled him to court, in order to attend upon Sir Richard Morisine in his embassy to the Emperor Charles V. Such an appointment, which he probably owed to his skill and despatch in epistolary composition, was not to be declined. He set out forthwith, and on his journey to London paid that visit to Lady Jane Grey, of which it would be unpardonable to speak in other than his own language :—often has it been quoted before.

---

* The number of royal and noble authors is an agreeable trait in human nature. We are all of us, Tories as well as Whigs, disposed to judge most hardly and unjustly of crowned heads, and " hearts that lurk beneath a star," forgetting, that while the vices of the great are seen in the magnitude of their effects, their saner thoughts and kindlier affections are out of our sphere of vision. It is only in the world of intellect that it is easy to be at once great and good. Great actions are almost always bad actions ; but it by no means follows, that the doers of great actions are bad beyond the common limit of human peccability, or that they too have not their " little, daily, unremembered acts of love." The jewels of a court do not extinguish the light of Heaven. The busiest toilers in war and politics have their hours of repose when they feel themselves to be men, and many have sought the sympathy of their fellow creatures, by weaving their thoughts and feelings into curious webs of verse or prose ; a proof that they are not satisfied with the power which rank and place bestow. They long to converse with the souls of others, because they feel a soul alive within themselves. No aboriginally selfish man, unless for bread, would ever publish a book, though it must sorrowfully be acknowledged, that the collisions of authorship are apt to produce sad callosities in our feelings for others, and most morbid acuteness about ourselves. Unluckily, the royal authors have not generally ranked with the little band of virtuous kings. Yet we may set Alfred against Dionysius, and James I. of Scotland against Nero—Antoninus against King Jamie, who was no bad fellow after all : he saw through his own demonology, and owned his error, and had he lived a few years longer, would doubtless have unsaid his calumnies against tobacco. The house of Brunswick, at least since their transplantation, have not been at all poetical, seeing that the only metrical composition I have ever known to be attributed to a star of that constellation, was a not very decorous ditty, written, I believe, by Captain Morris, but impudently ascribed to our late lamented sovereign. It is, however, stated, that George the Fourth was an admirer of Wordsworth. As a friend to the monarchy, I wish I were sure of this. Upon better authority I have heard, that George the Third loved Spenser. Nichols suggested to Johnson a life of that poet, as an acceptable offering to royalty. I should really be glad to have good evidence of this, for it would put to flight and to shame the vulgar prejudice against the intellects of that honest and right-hearted Englishman, who wanted nothing but better advisers, and a more extensive knowledge of mankind, to have made his government as beneficial to his subjects as it was creditable to his own good purposes.

" Before I went into Germany I came to Brodegate, in Leicestershire, to take my leave of that noble lady, Jane Grey, to whom I was exceedingly much beholding. Her parents, the Duke and Duchess, with all the household gentlemen and gentlewomen, were hunting in the park. I found her in her chamber alone, reading Phædo Platonis in Greek, and that with as much delight as some gentlemen would read a merry tale of Boccace. After salutation, and duty done, with some other talk, I asked her why she would lose such pastime in the park? Smiling, she answered me, " I wist all their sport in the park is but a shadow of that pleasure I find in Plato. Alas, good folk, they never felt what true pleasure meant." " And how came you, madam," quoth I, " to this deep knowledge of pleasure? And what did chiefly allure you unto it, seeing not many women, and but very few men, have attained thereunto?" " I will tell you," quoth she, " and tell you a truth which perchance ye may marvel at. One of the greatest benefits God ever gave me, is, that he sent me so sharp and severe parents, and so gentle a schoolmaster. For when I am in presence either of father or mother, whether I speak, keep silence, sit, stand, or go, eat, drink, be merry or sad, be sewing, playing, dancing, or doing any thing else, I must do it as it were in such weight, number, and measure, even so perfectly, as God made the world, or else I am so sharply taunted, so cruelly threatened, yea, presently, sometimes with pinches, nips, and bobs, and other ways (which I will not name for the honour I bear them), so without measure misordered, that I think myself in hell, till time come that I must go to Mr. Elmer, who teacheth me so gently, so pleasantly, with such fair allurements to learning, that I think all the time nothing while I am with him. And when I am called from him I fall on weeping, because whatsoever I do else beside learning, is full of grief, trouble, fear, and whole misliking unto me. And thus my book hath been so much my pleasure, and bringeth daily more pleasure and more: that in respect of it, all other pleasures, in very deed, be but trifles and troubles unto me."

" I remember this talk gladly, both because it is worthy of memory, and because also it was the last talk I had, and the last time that ever I saw that noble and worthy lady."

Before leave-taking, Ascham obtained a promise of the Lady Jane to write to him in Greek, on condition that he should first write to her, as soon as he arrived in the Emperor's court.* His epistle is extant in

* These particulars we learn from a letter of Roger's to Sturmius, dated 14th December, 1550, in which he promises to shew Jane's epistle to the German scholar, when it should arrive. It appears too that the Lady was requested to correspond with Sturmius in Greek.

choice Latin. Alluding to the circumstances of their last interview, he declares her happier in her love of good books, than in her descent from Kings and Queens. No doubt he spoke sincerely; but he knew not then *how* truly. Her studious quietude of spirit was her indefeasible blessing, while her royal pedigree* was like an hereditary curse, afflicting her humility with unwilling greatness, and her innocence with unmerited distress.

When Jane Grey was surprised with Plato in her hand, a sober hope might have conjectured, that if ever there was a marriage made in Heaven, if ever earthly pair was predestined to bless each other and their country, such a couple were Jane Grey and her cousin Edward. Of one blood, and companionable age, their studies, talents, virtues, faith the same; each seemed a " fair divided excellence," to be perfected in holy union. He, the gentle offspring of a most ungentle sire; she the meek daughter of the haughtiest of women; both the elect exceptions of their races, as if the saintly Margaret of Lancaster, cutting off the intermediate line of Tudors, had entailed her nature on these her distant progeny. But it was not to be so. Their fortunes were never ordained to meet, but ever to run parallel. Each bore awhile the royal title, while others exercised the sovereign power. Both gave forced assent to deeds done in their name, which their hearts approved not. Both lived to see their kindred dragged, not guiltless, to the scaffold, though Jane was spared the agony of assenting to their execution. In fine, they both died young, but who can say that either died untimely? Rather be it thought, that they had done *their* work; they had fitted themselves for immortality: and as for the work of the world, what God purposes, God will do, using indifferently the agencies of good and evil, as of day and night, sunshine and storm. Nor be it supposed that He whose name is Merciful, was less merciful in calling Jane to himself by the swift stroke of an axe, than in conducting Edward homewards by the slow declivity of a consumption. This at least is certain, that she was favoured in the defeat of the party which usurped her name. For what was the death

* As pedigrees are not at every bodies finger's end, and are, indeed, the most troublesome part of modern history, it may be well to remind the reader, that Lady Jane Grey was the daughter of Frances Brandon, the daughter of Mary Queen Dowager of France, and sister of Henry VIII. by Charles Brandon, Duke of Suffolk. Her father was Henry Grey, Marquis of Dorset, descended from Elizabeth, Queen to Edward IV. by her former marriage, through her son, Thomas Grey, who married the King's niece. The father of Lady Jane was created Duke of Suffolk, on the failure of the male line of the Brandons. He had divorced his first Lady, the daughter of Fitzalan, Earl of Arundel, on the ground of barrenness, in order to marry Frances Brandon. Thus among the other conformities between the Lady Jane and Edward, it may be observed that both were children of divorced fathers.

she died, what had been the *life in death* of an inquisitorial dungeon, to what she must have undergone, if the wicked Dudleys had defloured her conscience? forcing her to things which, in her simplicity, she could not distinguish " whether she suffered or she did," but which would have left her, like Lucretia, impure in her own eyes, though stainless before the universal reason?

After that memorable leave-taking, which had been sorrowful indeed, could he have " looked into the seeds of time," Ascham proceeded to London, and in September set sail with the ambassador for Germany, where he continued three years, the busiest of his life; for besides his regular occupation as Secretary, his correspondence and intercourse with the most distinguished scholars, his active observations on the men whom he saw and the countries through which he passed, and the unavoidable expense of time in form and ceremony, he officiated as Greek tutor to the ambassador, to whom he read and expounded twice a day four days out of the week. In the morning he read and explained three or four (folio) pages of Herodotus, and in the afternoon, two-hundred and twelve or thirteen lines of Sophocles or Euripides. Thus, according to his oratorical biographer Grant, he got through, between the 12th of October, 1550, and the 12th August, 1551, all Herodotus, five plays of Sophocles, most of Euripides, and twenty-one orations of Demosthenes: a great deal for an ambassador to listen to. On the other two days he copied the letters of state sent to England, and at leisure moments entered his observations in his diary, and collected, if not arranged, the materials for his treatise called " A report and discourse of the affairs and state of Germany, and the Emperor Charles his court." * His urbanity, readiness, and general information, recommended him not less to Princes and Ministers, than his Greek, Latin, logic, and divinity, to John Sturmius and Jerome Wolfius. The courtiers thought it a pity he was not always attached to an embassy, and the learned regretted that he should ever leave the schools. Whatever he was doing seemed his *forte*, and so rife were his praises in every mouth, that he was in peril of the woe denounced against those whom " all men speak well off."

A few miscellaneous extracts from his English correspondence at this period, will not be an unpleasant relief to our narrative. These notices,

---

* The full title of this treatise is, " A report of discourse, written by Roger Ascham, of the affairs and state of Germany, of the Emperor Charles V. his court during certain years, while the said Roger was there, printed by John Day, Aldersgate-street." It is said to contain a clear indication of the causes that induced Charles V. to resign. Its form is that of a reply to a letter: written about 1552, but not published till 1570. We have read no part of it, but it is highly spoken of.

among many others, were addressed to Mr. John Raven, a Fellow of John's college. They confirm what we have said of Sir R. Morisyne's Greek studies.

"As I wrote in my last letter, 3rd Oct., we came to Mechlin; I told you at large both of the Abbey, with 1600 nuns, and also the Landgrave (of Hesse,) whom we saw prisoner. He is lusty, well favoured, something like Mr. Hebilthrout in the face; hasty, inconstant, and to get himself out of prison, would fight, if the Emperor would bid him, with Turk, French, England, God, and the Devil. The Emperor perceiving his busy head without constancy, handles him thereafter: his own Germano, as it is said, being well content that he is forthcoming.

"John Frederick is clear contrary; noble, courageous, constant, one in all fortunes desired of his friends, reverenced of his foes, favoured of his Emperor, loved of all. He hath been proffered of late, it is said, by the Emperor, that if he will subscribe to his proceedings, to go at large, to have all his dignities and honours again, and more too. His answer was from the first one, and is still that he will take the Emperor for his gracious sovereign lord; but to forsake God and his doctrine, he will never do, let the Emperor do with his body what he will."

"At Mechlin we saw a strange bird. The Emperor doth allow it 8d. a day. It is milk-white, greater than a swan, with a bill somewhat like a shovel, and having a throat well able to swallow, without grief or touch of crest, a white penny loaf of England, except your bread be bigger than your bread-master of St. John's is wont willingly to make it. The eyes are as red as fire, and, as they say, an hundred years old. It was wont, in Maximilian's days, to fly with him whithersoever he went."

"4th Octob. we went to Brussels, twelve miles. In the mid-way is a town called Vilfort, with as notable strong hold of the Emperor's in it. Traitors and condemned persons lie there. At the town's end is a notable strong place of execution, where worthy Will Tyndall was unworthily put to death. Ye cannot match Brussels in England, but with London.

"At afternoon, I went about the town. I came to the Friar Carmelites house, where Edward Billick was warden; not present there, but being then at Colen, in another house of his, I heard their even-song: after I desired to see the library. A friar was sent to me, and led me into it. There was not one good book but Lyra. The friar was learned, spoke Latin readily, entered into Greek, having a very good wit, and a greater desire to learning. He was gentle and honest; and being a Papist, and knowing me to be a Protestant, yet shewed me all gentleness, and would needs give me a new book in verse, titled De Rusticitate Morum."

" I have seen the Emperor twice, first sick in his privy-chamber, at our first coming. He looked somewhat like the parson of Epurstone. He had a gown on of black taffety, and a furred night-cap on his head, Dutch like, having a seam over the crown. I saw him also on St. Andrew's day, sitting at dinner at the feast of Golden Fleece ; he and Ferdinando both under one cloth of estate ; then the Prince of Spain ; all of one side, as Knights of the Garter do in England ; after orderly, Mr. Bussie, master of the horse, Duke d'Alva, a Spaniard, Dux Bavariæ, the Prince of Piedmont, the Count of Hardenburgh.

" I stood hard by the Emperor's table. He had four courses : he had sod beef very good, roast mutton, baked hare ; these of no service in England ; fed well of a capon. I have had a better from mine hostess Barnes many times in my chamber. He and Ferdinando eat together very handsomely, carving themselves where they list, without any curiosity."

" The Emperor drank the best that ever I saw; he had his head in the glass five times as long as any of us, and never drank less than a good quart at once of Rhenish wine. His chapel sung wonderful cunningly all the dinner-while."

" England need fear no outward enemies. The lusty lads verily be in England. I have seen on a Sunday more likely men walking in St. Paul's church than I ever yet saw in Augusta, where lieth an Emperor with a garrison, three kings, a queen, three Princes, a number of Dukes, &c. I study Greek apace, but no other tongue ; for I cannot. I trust to see England shortly, God willing. I am sorry that I hear no word from Ireland. Commendations to you all, because I would leave out none ; to Dr. Haddon, father Bucer, John Scarlett, mine hostess Barnes."

" If ye will know how I do, I think I shall forget all tongues but the Greek afore I come home. I have read to my Lord since I came to Augusta, whole Herodotus, five tragedies, three orations of Isocrates, seventeen orations of Demosthenes. For understanding of the Italian, I am meet well ; but surely I drink Dutch better than I speak Dutch. Tell Mr. D. Maden, I will drink with him now a carouse of wine ; and would to God he had a vessel of Rhenish wine, on condition that I paid 40s. for it ; and perchance when I come to Cambridge, I will so provide here, that every year I will have a little piece of Rhenish wine." (24.)

The Hockheim and Joannisberg, or whatever else was the prime vintage, when Rhine flowed from its fountain to the sea through the domains of the Emperor Charles, was peculiarly congenial to Roger's palate and soul, for in his next letter to Raven, written evidently with the smack on his lips, commences, " This Rhenish wine is so gentle a drink, that I cannot tell how to do when I come home." An orderly attachment to the blood of the grape is not unusual among great linguists. We have already mentioned Bentley's constancy to port. Adelung used to call his cellar his Bibliotheca selectissima.

But the studies, the diplomacy, and the conviviality of Ascham, were sorrowfully interrupted by the death of the young King, who had not only continued his pension, but appointed him his own Latin Secretary in his absence. Edward VI. died July 6, 1553, having just lived long enough to sign the will, which proved the death-warrant of Jane Grey. Ascham did not return till the few unhappy days of that Lady's nominal reign were passed, and she was a prisoner in the Tower at his arrival in September, from whence she would probably in time have been liberated with a free pardon, had it not been for the madness of her father, who, by joining in Wyat's insurrection when the wax on his pardon was hardly dry, may be justly called an accessory to his child's murder. When Ascham, after three years absence, again set foot on the English shore, he found England a sadly changed country: one royal patron dead, with dark suspicions hovering over his grave, for it was whispered that Edward's health declined from the hour that the Dudleys came about him : the friendship of Elizabeth not only unavailing, but dangerous : his college friends and fellow students either dead, or flying, or imprisoned, or holding their preferments and their very lives, by a most insecure tenure. Cheek, who had joined himself to the supporters of Lady Jane's title, was in prison. Bucer, who had come to England only to lay his bones, where they were not permitted to rest, was no more. The persecution, which was accelerated by Wyat's unsuccessful rising, was not yet begun, but was already lowering in the distance, and, as it peculiarly threatened the Universities, Roger was not only likely to be deprived of his Fellowship and support, but to undergo examinations and tests, which would have compelled him to put his conscience in the opposite scale to his interest and safety. He retired, however, to Cambridge, to wait the event, not expecting nor soliciting anything from the new court, and esteeming himself happy if he was overlooked. But he had friends whom he knew not of, and one, that considering his acquiescence in the Reformation, could scarcely be looked for. This was Stephen Gardiner, who, at the accession of Mary, had been delivered out of custody, restored to his see of Winchester, and made Chancellor. But his great supporter was Lord Paget, by whose influence with Gardiner, he was called to court, and appointed to the office of Latin Secretary, which he formerly held by the interest of Cecil, and which he declared that he would not exchange for any other in the Queen's gift. Of this appointment he gives a lively account to his constant correspondent Sturmius, particularly dwelling on the urbanity with which he was received by the Chancellor Bishop:—" Stephen, Bishop of Winchester, High Chancellor of England, hath treated me with the greatest courtesy and kindness, so that I cannot tell whether the Lord Paget, was more ready to commend me, or the Chancellor to honour and protect me. There have not been wanted those, who have done their best to stop the course of his benevolence towards me, on pretence of religion, but have profitted nothing. Therefore I am exceedingly bound to my Lord of Winchester's goodness, and gladly accept the obligation. Nor I alone, but many others have experienced his goodness."

" None are all evil." Let us not therefore suspect the sincerity, or the good sense of these grateful commendations, though bestowed on a name usually coupled with Bonner. Gardiner might take pleasure in doing kindnesses, which did not interfere with his schemes of vengeance and spiritual empire, though to promote those schemes he stuck at no degree of cruelty. More intensely wicked than Bonner, who was merely brutal, he was too wise to be more wicked than need was. He was learned himself, and inclined to promote all sorts of learning, which had no tendency to enlighten men on points whereon the interests of Church and State required that they should be kept in the dark. Ascham, whatever his religious sentiments might be, had always borne them discreetly, and had "won golden opinions of all sorts of men." Moreover he was capable of being eminently useful, for it would have been difficult to find another who with such qualifications for the secretariship, and such diligence in the discharge of its duties, had so little cupidity or ambition, or would be content with so humble a reward.

The office of Latin Secretary was then no sinecure. Almost immediately after the marriage of Philip and Mary, Ascham had to write seven and forty letters to as many foreign Princes, of whom the lowest in rank was a Cardinal. The elegance of his style, and his ready despatch were generally applauded. It is not easy to state what were the emoluments of the place ; but the pension which Ascham had enjoyed from Edward VI., was enlarged from ten to twenty pounds a year, and, at the special desire of the Queen, and of the Lord Chancellor, (who was also Chancellor of Cambridge University,) he retained his Fellowship of John's college, and his place of public Orator, when by strict statute he might have been deprived of them, till they were vacated by his marriage. The object of his choice was Mistress Margaret Howe, a lady of some fortune and good family, to whom he was united on the 1st of June, 1554. A letter from the " German Cicero," Sturmius, who corresponded with our author with all the warmth and frequency of school friendship, dated the 24th of the same month, jocosely reproaches him with omitting to communicate such an important piece of business. "But what is it I hear? Would you keep your engagement close, for fear I should send you a High-Dutch epithalamium? I am informed that your intended is neice to the wife of Mr. Walop, that was governor of Guisnes when I was at Calais. Ah! but she was an honest madam, a fair and comely dame! If it be so, that you are going to make her your spouse, or if you have any other in your eye, do let me know, and tell me when the day is to be, that if I cannot myself be present at the espousals, I may send Thalassius * to make my compliments to your love in my stead." Ascham replied,—" As for my wife, she is the picture of her aunt Walop, and all that John Sturmius could wish the wife of Roger Ascham to be."

In the enjoyment of honourable competence, congenial occupation, and domestic affection, we can hardly suppose that Ascham was quite at ease under the patronage of Queen Mary and Bishop Gardiner; for, however free from personal apprehension, he could not coldly contemplate the perils, torments, and executions of multitudes, among whom were some whom he loved, and doubtless many whom he had known.

The gentle creature whose praises he had so industriously divulged over Germany had fallen beneath the axe, testifying, by her latest acts, her attachment to the studies of her happy years.† Elizabeth, to whom he appears to have been really and warmly attached, continually assailed with plots and suspicions, was shifted about from one custody

* Thalassius was the Roman nuptial god, as Hymen was the Greek. A song was sung at weddings, in which " Io Thalasse" was perpetually repeated like a burden. Plutarch, who was very indifferently acquainted with Roman antiquities, and quite ignorant of the Oscan and Etruscan languages, which were to the Latin what the Anglo-Saxon is to the English, is sadly puzzled to explain this word:—no wonder, as he sought its derivation in Greek. If he must give it an Hellenic origin, would not Thalassa, the sea, whence Venus arose, and to which Homer gives the epithet of " many-sounding," which is, moreover, the cabalistic type of change, fickleness, and agitation, have furnished a ready etymon?

† Lady Jane Grey, or to speak more correctly, Lady Guildford Dudley (for she perished in her honey moon), wrote her last letter to her sister Catherine in the blank pages of her Greek Testament; and when she saw her bridegroom led to execution under her prison window, she wrote three several sentences in her tablets in as many languages. The first in Greek, to this effect:---If his slain body shall give testimony against me before men, his blessed soul shall render an eternal proof of my innocence before God. The second Latin:---The justice of men took away his body, but the divine mercy has preserved his spirit. The third English:---If my fault deserved punishment, my youth and my imprudence were worthy of excuse: God and posterity will shew me favour.

to another, obliged to veil her faith in equivocations and external compliances, which, if she had a christian heart, must have been exceedingly grievous to her conscience, and were, at all events, cruelly mortifying to her pride : for, to say no worse of it, any the least interference with the belief and worship of any human being, is the greatest possible insult to human nature. Ridley, an old college acquaintance, was committed to the flames, and most of his earlier connections in voluntary exile.

Some have wondered how he escaped question himself, as his intimacy with many of the chief Reformers, and his profession of the reformed doctrines, were well known. But a greater marvel has been made of this than the case warrants. He had never been a very active promoter of the Reformation ; he had no share in the spoils of the church. No Catholic could charge him with the severities of former reigns ; nor could Mary alledge that he attempted or even approved her exclusion from the throne, (there it is possible he was lucky in being abroad), nor had he, like Ridley, attempted to convert her. He had nothing which it was worth while to take from him : his virtues were such as would have made his persecution very odious, and yet not such as to be anywise formidable ; for he assumed no extraordinary sanctity or rigour. His talents were serviceable to his employers, and dangerous to nobody. If he did not enter zealously into the re-establishment of the ancient church, it does not appear that he opposed it by book or discourse; nor did he refuse, in the discharge of his office, to do what a zealous Protestant would not have done. Thus he translated into Latin the speech delivered by Cardinal Pole, on his first appearance in Parliament in the quality of Legate, which necessarily contained an assertion of the papal supremacy, and an imputation of heresy to the reformers. Ascham's translation was made by the Cardinal's express desire, to be sent to the Pope, and gained for the translator a degree of favour with that high-born ecclesiastic of which he was a little proud. We are far from accusing Roger of apostacy, or mean disguise : we only say, that there was no such stubbornness in his religion as wilfully to provoke martyrdom. With such patrons as Paget and Pole, he might easily be excused giving an opinion on the disputed points : his absence from mass might not be noticed ; and as long as his own devotions were free, he was not the man to censure the practice, or contradict the opinions, of his superiors. It is true, that Sir John Cheek was not so favourably treated : to him was offered the alternative of recantation or the stake. Let those who despise him for accepting the former, remember what old Fuller saith :—" The flames of Smithfield were hotter than the

pictures in the Book of Martyrs." *   Nor is every man favoured with
that perfect assurance of his own belief, as to feel justified in sacrificing
the life which he is *sure* God gave him, for opinions which he only
believes to be of God.   Yet perhaps Cheek suffered more from his own
conscience, than the burners could have made him endure.   He pined,
and pined, and never held up his head, or took any delight in his old
studies, but found that life itself may be bought too dear, and only
evaded the martyrdom of fire, to suffer the lingering martyrdom of a
broken heart.   But then, he had upheld the title of Jane Grey : he
had, as far as his power extended, disinherited and bastardized Mary,
which Ascham had not done.   There was the mighty difference.   The
real grounds of the Marian persecution were political, not religious.
Religion was only called in to smother the consciences of the persecutors, some of whom would have shrunk from the deadly acts of vengeance which they perpetrated, if they could not have contrived to
believe that they were vindicating the true church against soul-killing
heresy.   We say advisedly, *some;* for the prime movers in all persecutions have been men indifferent to all creeds, who have regarded
articles of faith as creatures of statutes, ordained to secure the permanence of *institutions*, and the security of *constituted authorities*.   Here
and there, a Bonner or a Jeffreys appears, in whom the lust of blood is

---

* Such at least is Fuller's meaning and illustration.   I am afraid I have not quoted
his words exactly, for to tell truth, I know not in which of his works to look for them.
But I recollect reading the sentiment in "Lamb's Selections," to which I owe my
first knowledge and constant love of Fuller, as of many other worthies.   Why are
not more gems from our early prose writers scattered over the country by the periodicals?   Selections are so far from preventing the study of the entire authors, that they
promote it.   Who could read the extracts which Lamb has given from Fuller,
without wishing to read more of the old Prebendary?   But great old books of the
great old authors are not in every body's reach; and though it is better to know
them thoroughly than to know them only here and there, yet it is a good work to give
a little to those who have neither time nor means to get more.   Let every book-
worm, when, in any fragrant, scarce old tome, he discovers a sentence, a story, an
illustration, that does his heart good, hasten to give it the widest circulation that
newspapers and magazines, penny and halfpenny, can afford.   Remember that

The worst avarice is that of sense.

Appropos to the pictures in the "Book of Martyrs."   In those embellishments of
that ghastly work which pourtray the sufferings of the primitive Christians under
the Roman Emperors, there is an anachronism which affords a singular display of
national antipathy.   The Roman tormenters are all in Spanish costume.   The
Inquisition and the Armada had identified the ideas of Spain and persecution.   Even
in the representation of St. Laurence's martyrdom on the gridiron, which is dated
A. D. 258, in the reign of the Emperor Valerian, a Spanish Bishop in his mitre
presides.

not a mere metaphor, but a physical appetite ; but they are as rare a phenomenon as the Siamese twins. But I doubt whether Christianity, however corrupted with error, ever urged one human being to oppress or destroy another. An erring Piety may *consent* to persecution ; but the promoters of persecution are Revenge, Ambition, Avarice, and the other bastards of the World, which the Church adopted when she married the World. It may be said, that among the victims in Mary's reign, there were many poor, insignificant individuals, that could be formidable to no government ; but if it were possible, at this distance of time, to investigate the history of such cases, we should find that there was some old quarrel, some malicious neighbour, some *Tony Fire-the-faggot* at the bottom of it. Besides, there is nothing provokes High-Church so much as that a poor man should presume to think for himself ; and the Church of Rome is THE High Church.

In fact, many more active and decided Protestants than Ascham were unmolested in the æra of burnings, and we doubt if negative Protestantism brought any to the stake. Any reason, religious or political, will serve a despotic government to destroy a suspected person ; but Gardiner had too much sense to burn a good subject only because he had doubts about the ubiquity, or was not quite convinced of the expediency, of *Duleia* to the Virgin, or *Hypo-duleia* to her image. In the black list of persecutors, depend upon it, there have been three atheists to one sincere bigot.

Dr. Johnson, who prefaced Bennet's edition of Ascham's works with a short memoir controverts the opinion, that either the innocence of his life, or the usefulness of his pen, was the cause of his security, in a paragraph which deserves to be quoted, as exhibiting the Doctor's skill in the art of seeming to mean much, and meaning little or nothing :—" But the truth is," says the great Cham, " that morality was never suffered to protect heresy in the days of persecution ; nor are we sure that Ascham was more clear from common failings than those that suffered more ; and whatever might be his abilities, they were not so necessary but Gardiner could easily have supplied his place with another secretary. Nothing is more vain than, at a distant time, to examine the motives of discrimination and partiality ; for the inquirer, having considered interest and policy, is obliged at last to omit more frequent and more active motives of human conduct,—caprice, accident, and private affection. At that time, if some were punished, many were forborne ; and of many, why should not Ascham happen to be one ? He seems to have been calm and prudent, and content with that peace which he was suffered to enjoy ; a mode of conduct that seldom fails to produce security."

If all the Protestants under Mary had expressed their protestation in sentences of such oracular no-meaning as the foregoing, they might have sat quietly in the chimney nook, and warmed their Christmas ale with the faggots that were wasted in burning them. But the very little sense that there is in the Doctor's multitude of words is not true. Rigidity of morals, formidable or conspicuous virtue, is so far from being a protection against persecution, that nothing provokes persecutors so much. But that sort of sociable goodness commonly called innocence, which consists in the absence of all qualities that can excite envy or fear, is the best security. Ascham, with all his genius and all his business-like talents, had a great deal of simplicity, a childishness, that admirably fitted him for an instructor of children. Witness his observing little in the foremost potentate of the age, but his resemblance to the parson of Epurstone, and his quaffing a quart of Rhenish at a gulp. Now even the staunch murderer will not kill a child if he can help it ; and something of the same sentiment protects all childish persons, and even idiots. Had Burke burked the learnedest Professor in Edinburgh, he would not have excited so much popular indignation as he did by murdering Daft Jamie.

After all, what proof is there that Ascham did offer any overt opposition to the Catholic doctrines or ceremonies in the time of peril ? and for whatever suspicion might adhere to his real opinion, a word from Cardinal Pole (who is honourably recorded as the advocate of mercy and moderation) would have been sufficient to screen a more obnoxious person from troublesome interrogatory. Pole was even intimate with Ascham, of which Roger does not omit to inform Sturmius :—" Reverendissimus Cardinalis Polus valde humanus est, et haud scio an quisquam Italus, eloquentiæ laude, cum eo comparari queat. Me utitur valde familiariter"—" The most Reverend Cardinal is the very pink of courtesy, and for eloquence, I know not if Italy ever produced his equal. He is hand and glove with me." The friendship of Pole must have been very serviceable to Ascham after the death of his patron Gardiner, who expired October 22, 1555. That he was a ruthless persecutor, was in a great degree the vice of his age: that he was an ambitious time-server, and wrote in defence of the supremacy claimed by Henry VIII. was his own peculiar fault, and goes a great way to deprive his cruelties of the allowance they might otherwise claim on the ground of a mistaken conscience. Those who delight in contemplating the agonies of an impenitent death-bed, may find a very satisfactory account of Gardiner's in the Book of Martyrs.

What might have been the consequence to England and to Ascham had Mary reigned much longer, is not very easy to conjecture, but she died too soon to accomplish her purpose, and five years too late for her own fame and happiness. Of death-beds there are very seldom well-authenticated accounts. Nothing in Fox's martyrology is so apocryphal as his tales of judgments upon the persecutors. We read, indeed, that Mary broke her heart for the loss of Calais, but it does not appear that she suspected any judgment in the matter. Cardinal Pole died a few hours after—a fortunate circumstance for himself and the country, for there is a rumour of designs among the Catholics to advance his claims to the throne, which were about as valid as Jane Grey's.

The accession of Elizabeth seemed to promise high preferment to her quondam preceptor; especially as the deprivation of so many ecclesiastics, who refused the oath of supremacy, made a great deal of room. And in truth he was not altogether neglected. He was continued in his office of Latin secretary, restored to his honorary dignity of Greek preceptor to the Queen, and, on the deprivation of George Palmer, LLD., was installed in the prebendary of Wetwang, in the cathedral church of York, on the 11th of March, 1599. He had the opportunity of frequent interviews with her Majesty, and had the favour to talk Greek and Latin, and play chess with her,—openings which a more artful and ambitious man might easily have improved. But the pride or modesty of Roger would not suffer him to ask any thing for himself or others. Indeed he used to boast of his backwardness in this particular, often averring in conversation, that during all the happy hours that he had enjoyed his Lady Sovereign's presence, he never opened his mouth to enrich himself or any that belonged to him; that to serve his mistress well was his best reward; that he had rather freely win her good opinion than be dressed out in her munificence. The Lord Treasurer, who was his friend and well-wisher, often admonished him to take less pains, and urge more requests. But Ascham was slow even to receive what was offered, and thoroughly content with his condition, which, though moderate, was never, as Anthony a Wood states broadly, and a hundred others have copied from him, miserably poor. He had always sufficient for the day, and was not one of those that lay up store for the morrow. He was extremely indignant when any one offered him presents to purchase his interest with the Queen, saying, that God had not given him the use of his tongue that it might be venal and subservient to his profit. Queen Elizabeth has been censured for scanty remuneration of her faithful servants; a fault seldom found with princes in these days, when Economy would fain starve Gratitude to death. Ascham has been cited as an instance of her parsimony. But it should be remembered that, in the beginning of her reign, neither she nor her kingdom were rich; and that her rigid economy did not always preserve her from financial embarrassments. Yet Grant assures us, that she did bestow many unsolicited bounties on her tutor. *Nihilominus tamen Regia Majestas multis eum et magnis beneficiis e suâ munificâ voluntate locupletavit.* This is saying a great deal, for little is got at court without asking for.

But we are told, by Wood, Lloyd, Camden, Fuller and others, that Roger was discreditably impoverished in his latter days, by his addiction to dice, and cock-fighting. Wood, who does not seem to have loved his memory, says, that though he had a considerable fortune with his wife, yet, notwithstanding, "that and his place, he lived and died not according to his condition, being given to dicing and cock-fighting." And Lloyd in his *State-Worthies*, asserts that "what he got by his ingenuity, he lost by his gaming, viz. at dice and cock-fighting." Fuller, who gives Ascham an honourable place amongst the Worthies of Yorkshire, says that in his youth, his recreation was the bow, but in his riper years, one less healthful and less innocent; to wit cock-fighting. Bishop Nicholson, in his English Historical Library, questions the authority of these allegations, but had he looked into "the Scholemaster" or Grant's oration, he would have found that they were correct, as far as regards our Author's partiality to the exhibitions of the feathered gladiators, for he himself announces his intention of publishing a treatise on the subject, as follows:—"But of all kinds of pastime fit for a gentleman, I will, *God-willing,* in fitter place, more at large declare fully in my book of the cock-pit, which I do write to satisfy some, I trust, with some reason, that be more curious in marking other men's doings than careful in mending their own faults, and some also, will busy themselves in marvelling and adding thereunto unfriendly talk, why I, a man of good years and of no ill place, I thank God and my friend, do make choice to spend so much time in writing of trifles, as the school of shooting, the cock-pit, &c." To the offence given by these pursuits, his eulogist pointedly alludes, in that funeral oration to which the Biographers of Ascham have been so largely indebted, "What should hinder Roger Ascham from having his honest diversions, from using his bow, or engaging in the *Alectryomachia?*" Hence it appears, but too clearly as many would say, that Roger was a cock-fighter. Had he been a contemporary of Hogarth, his features would have been preserved in that wonderful man's living representation of the cock-pit. It is also evident, that certain curious persons were scandalized at the propensity, not however, as tender-hearted persons unacquainted with ancient manners may suppose, on account of the inhumanity, or vulgarity, of the amusement, but because it was not deemed compatible with the severity of the scholastic character. Few, if any in the sixteenth century, condemned any sport because it involved the pain or destruction of animals, and none would call the pastime of monarchs *low*. At a more advanced æra, Isaac Walton—"surely not a man ungently made"—when, in describing the best method of stitching a frog's thigh to a pike-hook, he cautions you "*to use him as if you loved him*," never suspected that the time would come, when his instruction would expose him to a charge of cruelty, of which there were not a particle in his whole composition; or in Roger Ascham's either. Angling is, doubtless, much fitter recreation for a "contemplative man," besides being much cheaper for a poor man, than cock-fighting, but it is equally opposite to the Poet's rule which bids us

> " Never to blend our pleasure, or our pride
> With sorrow in the meanest thing that feels."

If animal suffering be computed, the sod is an altar of mercy compared to the chace, for the excitement of the combat is an instinctive pleasure to the pugnacious fowls, who, could they give an opinion on the subject, would infallibly prefer dying in glorious battle to having their necks ignominiously wrung for the spit, or enduring the miseries of superannuation. We do not deny that our author shewed in this particular a strange taste, but it is a taste we have ourselves known to exist in men of the kindest hearts, and most powerful minds. Are not the features of Lord Albemarle Bertie, in Hogarth's print above mentioned, indicative of benevolent simplicity?* Roger never lived to publish, or probably to compose, his apology for the cock-pit: but we know not whether it was in pursuance of his recommendation that a yearly cock-fight was till lately, a part of the annual routine of the northern free-schools. The master's perquisites are still called cock pennies.

We should by no means have wondered, if Ascham had dedicated his "cock-pit" to Queen Elizabeth; for that learned lady, at her famous visit to Kenilworth, was entertained with bear-baiting, and looked with much complacence on the "bloody cynarctomachy."

But in all this, what proof is there that Ascham was a Gamester? This seems to be a gratuitous assumption, suggested by the circumstance that he left his family ill provided for. But that is the case with scores of poor clergymen, who never rattled dice-box or polished spurs. His income was narrow—his wife's large fortune is only attested by Wood—he was neither importunate to get, nor provident to save—his purse and

---

* This nobleman, who is also represented as attending a pugilistic engagement, in the march to Finchley, was entirely blind; a circumstance which easily explains his partiality to scenes of noisy excitement.

house were always open to the distressed scholar, and whatever was his, was his friends' also. He delighted much in an epigram of Martial,

Extra fortunam est quicquid donatur amicis
Quas solas dederis, semper habebis opes.
The friendly boon from fate itself secures,
And what you give, shall be for ever yours.

This is not the way to grow rich. Roger Ascham was generous, and it may be, imprudent; but there is no just cause for supposing him viciously extravagant.

There is little more to relate of the last ten years of his life. Finding his health injured by night studies, he for a time discontinued them, and became an early riser; but towards the close of 1568 he sat up several nights successively in order to finish a poem addressed to the Queen on the new year. That new year he was never to see. Long subject to fever, and latterly to a lingering hectic, this over-exertion brought on a violent attack which his weakened constitution was unable to withstand. Sleep, which he had too long rejected, could not be persuaded to visit him again, though he was rocked in a cradle; all opiates failed, and in less than a week, exhausted nature gave way to the slumber, from which there is no waking on this side of the grave. He took to his bed on the 28th of December, and expired on the 30th of the same month, 1568, aged fifty-three. He was attended to the last by Dr. Alexander Nowel, Dean of St. Paul, who, on the ensuing fourth of January, preached his funeral sermon, in which he declares that he never knew man live more honestly nor die more christianly. As he had many friends, and no enemies, his death was a common sorrow, and Queen Elizabeth is reported to have said, that she had rather have thrown ten thousand pounds into the sea, than have lost her Ascham. And well might she say so, for whom had he left behind that loved her so truly, served her so disinterestedly, or bore such fair testimony to her name?

Ascham left three sons, Giles, Dudley, and Sturmius, (the last so named after his Strasburg correspondent,) of whom the eldest could not be more than twelve years of age; with his last breath he recommended the care of their education to their mother. It was partly with a view to the instruction of his own children, that he commenced the "Schole-master," the work by which he is most and best known, to which he did not live to set the last hand. He communicated the design and import of the book in a letter to Sturmius, in which he states, that not being able to leave his sons a large fortune, he was resolved to provide them with a preceptor, not one to be hired for a great sum of money, but marked out at home with a homely pen. In the same letter he gives his reasons for employing the English language, the capabilities of which he clearly perceived and candidly acknowledged, a high virtue for a man of that age, who perhaps could have written Latin to his own satisfaction much more easily than his native tongue. But though the benefit of his own offspring might be his ultimate object, the immediate occasion of the work was a conversation at Cecil's, at which Sir Richard Sackville expressed great indignation at the severities practiced at Eton and other great schools, so that boys actually ran away for fear of merciless flagellation. This led to the general subject of school discipline, and the defects in the then established modes of tuition. Ascham coinciding with the sentiments of the company, and proceeding to explain his own views of improvement, Sackville requested him to commit his opinions to paper, and the " Schole-master" was the result. It was not published till 1670, when it appeared with a dedication by his widow to Sir William Cecil, the great Lord Burleigh, in which she pathetically declares her destitute condition, and prays his protection for her orphan family. The appeal was not made in vain, for Cecil's interest procured her son Giles a Fellowship at John's College. He had been previously educated at Westminster, under Grant, his father's biographer, and he inherited, in a great degree, his father's skill in Latin epistolary composition.

Our limits will not allow us to extend our quotations from this work so far as we could wish, or fully to enter upon the merits of Ascham's plans for instructing youth in the languages, but we may quote a few passages, which throw light upon the author's good sense and good nature. To all violent coercion, and extreme punishment, he was decidedly opposed:—" I do agree," says he, " with all good school-masters in these points, to have children brought to good perfectness in learning, to all honesty in manners ; to have all faults rightly amended, and every vice severely corrected, but for the order and way that leadeth rightly to these points, we somewhat differ."

" Love is better than fear, gentleness than beating, to bring up a child rightly in learning."

" I do assure you there is no such whetstone to sharpen a good wit, and encourage a will to learning. as is praise."

These are expressions which must have galled the worthy wielders of the rod extremely. The charge of over harshness they could endure and glory in, but to be accused of ignorance, stupidity, and a false appreciation of talents, must have been truly provoking. Speaking of their clumsiness in Latin composition, he says:—" The scholar is commonly beat for the making, when the master were more worthy to be

2 т

beat for the mending, or rather marring, of the same; the master many times being as ignorant as the child what to say properly and fitly to the matter."

Are not masters, of a somewhat higher order, still sometimes apt to mistake precocious apprehensiveness for a firm promise, and natural tardiness for wilful sullenness, or unconquerable indocility? Let such consider well the voice of experience uttered by Roger Ascham :—

" This will I say, that even the wisest of your great beaters do as oft punish nature as they do correct faults. Yea many times the better nature is the sorer punished. For if one by quickness of wit take his lesson readily, another by hardness of wit taketh it not so speedily; the first is always commended, the other is commonly punished, when a wise school-master should rather discreetly consider the right disposition of both their natures, and not so much weigh what either of them is able to do, as what either of them is likely to do hereafter. For this I know, not only by reading of books in my study, but also by experience of life abroad in the world, that those which be commonly the wisest, the best learned, and best men also, when they be old, were never commonly the quickest of wit when they were young. Quick wits commonly be apt to take, unapt to keep. Some are more quick to enter speedily than able to pierce far, even like unto over sharp tools, whose edges be very soon turned. Moreover commonly men very quick of wit, be also very light of condition, and thereby very ready of disposition to be carried over quickly to any riot and unthriftiness when they be young, and therefore seldom either honest of life, or rich in living, when they be old. For quick in wit and light in manner, be either seldom troubled, or very soon weary, with carrying a very heavy purse. Quick wits be also, in most part of all their doings, overquick, hasty, rash, headie, and brainsick.   *   *   *   In youth they be ready scoffers, privy mockers, and ever over light and merry. In age, sore, testy, very waspish, and always over miserable, and yet few of them come to any great age, by reason of their misordered life when they were young; but a great deal fewer of them come to shew any great countenance, or bear any great authority abroad in the world, but either live obscurely, men know not how, or die obscurely, men mark not when. They be like trees, that shew forth fair blossoms and broad leaves in spring time, but bring forth small and not long lasting fruit in harvest time, and that only such as fall and rot before they be ripe, and so never or seldom come to any good at all." The life and death of a town wit could not be more succinctly described.

The following sentence is so beautifully expressed, and contains so just and religious a view of the divine economy at the conclusion, that we cannot forbear it, though it has been quoted often enough to be familiar, even to such as are no readers of black-letter :—

"The fault is in yourselves, ye noblemen's children, and therefore ye deserve the greater blame, that commonly the meaner men's children come to be the wisest counsellors and greatest doers in the weighty affairs of this realm.   And why? God will have it so of his providence, because ye will have it no otherwise by your negligence."   If negligence of study be meant, the censure is no longer applicable.   For the sons of the nobility labour as hard for academical distinctions as the youth to whom learning is to be instead of house and land.   All classes, (to whom instruction is attainable at all,) emulate each other in the race of intellect, and a book on any subject by a peasant, or a peer, is no longer so much as a nine-days wonder.   But in the application of their attainments to the purposes of worldly advancement, the plebeian has still the start, possessing also this inestimable advantage, that he can submit to much more, and make himself much more serviceable, without the loss of personal dignity.   Men, very highly descended, will sometimes do mean actions, but then they lose their self-esteem, and throw themselves away ; but let a man once be convinced that nothing *useful* (to himself or others) can be mean, and he needs nothing else but honest industry to raise him to the top of the tree.   Poor and proud must 'perish in his pride.' "

One extract more, and we must unwillingly take leave of Roger.   We have seen advertisements of quack schoolmasters (a race almost as numerous as the quacks in physic, and more mischievous by half), where, as a bonus to good guardians (for it can hardly be intended for parents), there is an "N. B. No vacations."   This is probably defended on the ground, that any interruption of studies is not only a loss of time, but unfits the mind for returning to its labours.   Some people were of that opinion in the sixteenth century, but not so was Ascham, who strengthens his own by others' sentiments :—" I heard a good husband at his book say, that to omit study some time of the year, made as much for the increase of learning, as to let the land lie fallow for some time maketh for the better increase of corn.   If the land be ploughed every year the corn cometh thin up,—so those which never leave poring on their books have oftentimes as thin invention as other poor men have."   Hear this, ye little boys, and when Christmas comes, sing a christmas carol to the memory of Roger Ascham, who was one of the truest and wisest friends you ever had,—the pupil of Sir John Cheek, the tutor of Queen Elizabeth—of whom Sir Richard Sackville * said, that he was the "scholar of the best master, and the master of the best scholar."

* Sir Richard Sackville, father to that famous Thomas Sackville who wrote the

The method of learning Latin (of course equally adapted to any other language) advised by Ascham consists chiefly in *double translation*. He would have the master construe and explain a given portion of an author to the pupil, till the words and arrangement were fixed in the memory ; then let the pupil be set apart, and, without prompter, write down the translation in English ; and after a sufficient interval, turn it back into Latin, on a separate piece of paper.   Then let the master compare the second translation with the original, and explain such differences of diction and idiom as may occur, referring to the grammar for the proper rules ; thus teaching the grammar in the concrete rather than in the abstract.   Whatever difficulties may attend the adoption of this system in public establishments, it is obviously most proper for private tuition and self instruction.

The "Schole-master" is the best known of all Ascham's works. Of the Toxophilus nothing more need be said, except that an admirable analysis of it, with copious extracts, may be found in the Retrospective Review, vol 1., p. 76   Of his "Report and Discourse of the Affairs and State of Germany," published after his death, in 1570, we have already spoken.   His Latin Epistles were collected and edited by his admirer, Dr. Grant, with a dedication to Queen Elizabeth, and that panegyrical oration to which we have so often referred.   An immense deal of information might be gleaned from these letters, as to the literary and political state of Europe at a most interesting juncture.   The mere names of Ascham's correspondents shew how much intercourse subsisted between scholars in those days.   Antony Wood attributes to our author a treatise against the Mass, but this is doubtful.

"Induction to the Mirror for Magistrates," perhaps the best poem produced between Chaucer and Spencer, was Chancellor of the Exchequer, and so famous for the wealth which he amassed, that he was anagrammatically called Fill-sack.   The family came in with William the Conqueror. Sir Richard Sackville died in 1566, and his loss was severely felt by Ascham, whose "Schole-master," says Dr. Johnson, "though begun with alacrity, in hopes of a considerable reward, was slowly and sorrowfully finished, in the gloom of disappointment, under the pressure of distress." The office of patron was for some generations hereditary in the house of Sackville. The praises bestowed upon Charles, Earl of Dorset, by grateful or hungry poets, would fill a large folio. Nor did they cease with his death. Prior's dedication to his son, is one of the most elegant panegyrics in the English language, and Pope's Epitaph, though very incorrect in expression, will make Dorset longer remembered than any of his own writings, though Dryden puts him on a level with Juvenal.

> Blest Peer ! his great forefather's every grace
> Reflecting and reflected in his race,
> While other Backhursts, other Dorsets shine,
> And poets, still, or patrons, deck the line.

Ascham was of a slender form and weak constitution, temperate in his general habits, and particularly averse to a fish diet, which in those fasting times was a considerable inconvenience. He was interred in the most private manner, in St. Sepulchre's. Buchanan wrote an epigram on his death, with which we shall conclude :—

> Aschamum extinctum patriæ, Graiæque Camœnæ
> Et Latiæ verâ cum pietate dolent.
> Principibus vixit carus, jucundus amicis
> Re modica, *in mores* dicere fama requit.

> The native Muses join with those of Greece
> And mighty Rome, in pious grief for Ascham,
> Whom Princes valued, and his friends beloved;
> With little wealth he lived, and spotless fame.

Some of our readers may feel a little curiosity to know who was the *Mr. Elmer* of whom Lady Jane speaks so affectionately. He will not be found under that name in any Biographical Dictionary with which we are acquainted. Yet he was a man of some note: he suffered persecution, and obtained the reputation of a persecutor. As it may not be unprofitable to contrast to the quiet unambitious life of Roger Ascham the perturbed career of one of his earliest friends, who made what would be called a better use of his opportunities, we shall set down a few notices of Mr. Elmer, referring those who wish to know more, to "Stype's Life of Bishop Aylmer," "Neal's History of the Puritans," and the other works from which we derive our knowledge of the ecclesiastical history of his times; warning them, however, against believing either party too confidently in any point where they could err without wilfully lying.

The name of this *little* great man is variously written Elmer, Aylmer, or according to his own signature, Ælmer. He was of a good old family, as his Saxon name indicates, a younger brother of the Aylmers, of Aylmer hall, Norfolk, born 1521, studied both at Oxford and Cambridge, as was then usual, at the cost of Henry Grey, Marquis of Dorset, and afterwards Duke of Suffolk. When he was well furnished with University learning, the Marquis made him tutor to his own daughters, of whom Jane was the eldest. Being a zealous Protestant, he instilled into his pupil the principles of the reformed religion: for a time he was the only preacher in Leicestershire. (Be it recollected, that not every curate, no, nor every rector, was then a preacher, or even a reader of lithographed MS. sermons, to supply which deficiency, the Homilies were put forth.) By the interest of his patrons he was made, in 1553, archdeacon of Stow; but, Mary succeeding, he at once confirmed his reputation and lost his archdeaconry, by disputing against the real presence in the convocation, commenced on the 16th October. He was one of six, who, in the midst of all the violences of that clerical assembly, challenged all comers to argue on all points of religion, and offered to maintain the Reformation against the world. But when the secular power interfered in the controversy, Ælmer withdrew beyond seas: the shortness of his stature providentially preserving his life. For the ship wherein he was embarked being suspected, and searched by the agents of persecution, he was concealed in a large wine vessel, which had a partition in the middle, so that while the bloodhounds were lapping wine from the one side the cask, Ælmer lay snug in the other.

This tale, which I relate on the authority of my special favourite, old Fuller, is needlessly questioned by some gnat-strainers, as if there were any miracle in the matter. Might not the wine cask be contrived on purpose to serve at such a crisis? Persecution sharpens men's wits to cunninger devices than that. However, Ælmer (for it is a point of conscience with me to spell good men's names as they chose to spell themselves) did escape, and took up his abode, first at Strasburgh, and afterwards at Zurich, and there in peace followed his studies, occasionally travelling to other cities, so that he visited most of the Universities of Italy and Germany, and had an offer from the Elector of Saxony, of the Hebrew Professorship at Jena. During his exile, he published (according to Stripe) Lady Jane Grey's letter to Harding, a chaplain of her father's, who had apostatized; assisted Fox in translating his Book of Martyrs into Latin; and made a version of Cranmer's vindication of the Book of the Sacrament against Gardiner, Bishop of Winchester. But his chief work was one which well became the preceptor of Lady Jane Grey. John Knox had just sounded his furious "First Blast against the monstrous Regiment," to which we have heretofore taken occasion to allude. Ælmer, moved, it may be, by recollection of that vernal flower of womanhood which himself had helped to rear, opposed the salique divinity of Knox, and maintained the rights of the sex, in a discourse entitled "An Harborowe for faithful and trewe Subjects, against the late blowne Blast concerning the Government of Women; wherein be confuted all suche reasons as a Straunger of late made in that behalfe. With a briefe Exhortation to Obedience." Printed at Strasburgh, 1559; dedicated to the Earl of Bedford, and to Lord Robert Dudley, Master of the Horse, afterwards the famous Leicester. The book was well-timed, appearing in the first year of Queen Elizabeth, and prepared the way for its author's return. The fact is, that in 1556 the reformers of Great Britain had every thing to dread from women; Queen Mary reigning in England, and Mary of Guise, in her daughter's name, exercising sovereign authority in Scotland. But when Ælmer's reply appeared, in 1559, the tables were turned. A woman was the hope of the Protestant cause, as opposed to papal supremacy, though to Reformation, in John Knox's view, she was the great and only obstacle. Ælmer's vindication of female sovereignty could not be unacceptable to Queen Elizabeth, nor his dedication, to her favourite. Perhaps neither of them were displeased with a passage which brought the author into a good deal of trouble, when time and experience, and a mitre, had shewn him reason to change his green opinion. "Come off, ye Bishops," saith the future prelate; "away with your superfluities, yield up your thousands, be content with hundreds, as they be in other reformed churches, where be as great learned men as you are. Let your portion be priestlike, not princelike. Let the Queen have the rest of your temporalities, and other lands, to maintain these wars, which you procured, and which your mistress left her embroiled in; and with the rest to build and found schools throughout the realm; that every parish church may have *his* preacher, every city *his* superintendant, to live honestly, and not pompously, which will never be, unless your lands be dispersed, and bestowed upon many, which now feed and fat but one. Remember, that Abimelech, when David in his banishment would have dined with him, kept such hospitality, that he had no bread in his house to give him but the shew bread. Where was all his superfluity, to keep up your pretended hospitality? For that is the cause that you allege why you must have thousands, as though you were commanded to keep hospitality with a thousand, rather than with a hundred." Surely Abimelech would have taken care to be better provided with bread for unexpected visitors, if he could have foreseen what a conclusion was to be drawn from the barrenness of his pantry. Never was a well-meaning Scripture more illegally subpœnaed to give evidence in an alien cause in all the annals of controversy ; not even when Herodias and her daughter are brought to prove the unlawfulness of dancing. But there is no limit to the absurdities into which wise men may fall, when they begin to rummage the Bible for precedents, instead of abiding by the commandments of their Saviour, and the doctrines of the Spirit. Barring this outrageous inference, the passage was not ill timed. The exhortation to give up the "rest of the temporalities" to the Queen, was no way disagreeable to Elizabeth, whose aim was to keep the clergy in subjection to herself; the reducing of the Bishops from thousands to hundreds, could not offend Bedford, who was rich in abbey-lands, nor Dudley, who had a greedy eye upon the residue of the widow Church's jointure : no wonder that they favoured the Puritans. As for what is said about schools and preacherships, and the new-fangled term Superintendant, the literal translation of the word usually represented by its curtailed descendant Bishop, that might serve well enough to give a popular colour to aristocratic rapine. The republican tendencies of Puritanism were then very imperfectly understood by the majority of the Puritans themselves.

When Dr. Ælmer was, in after times, reproached with these expressions, he never attempted to explain them away, as his biographer Strype has done, as if only *Popish* Bishops were meant, but honestly confessed that " when he was a child, he spake as a child," cum essem parvulus, loquebar cum parvulis, sapiebam ut parvulus," perhaps he might have said, still more honestly, " Cum essem pauperculus, loquebar cum pauperculis." Every poor young author should remember the possibility of his sometime being rich, and the impossibility of recalling his words. As well might the quick repenting murderer whistle to the bullet that is sped, or bid it go another way, as the writer that has published a popular sentiment attempt to retract or change its meaning. He that has once opened a fountain of truth, can never seal it up again. " It flows, and as it flows for ever shall flow on." There is another passage, in Ælmer's " Harborough," which defines the three estates of the English constitution so plainly, that we cannot resist extracting it :—" The Regiment of England is not a mere monarchy, as some for lack of consideration think; nor a mere oligarchy, nor democracy; but a rule mixt of all these; wherein each of these have, or should have, like authority. The image whereof, and not the image, but the thing indeed, is to be seen in the Parliament house; wherein you shall find these three estates, the King or Queen, which representeth the monarchy, the noblemen, which be the aristocracy, and the burgesses and knights, which be the democracy. The very same had Lacedæmonia, the noblest and best governed city that ever was," and here he goes on to describe the Spartan constitution, blunderingly enough; but Ælmer was never happy in finding precedents. But what follows is worthy notice :—" If the Parliament use their privileges, the King can ordain nothing without these. If he do, it is his fault in usurping it, and their folly in permitting it. Wherefore those that in King Henry's days would not grant him that proclamations should have the force of a statute, were good fathers of the country, and worthy commendation in defending their liberty." Such sentiments publicly avowed in a work professing the principles of civil obedience, and never formally recanted, did not prevent Ælmer from being made a Bishop. Yet Hume could say, that the first definition of the English constitution, according to our present ideas of it, was contained in a declaration issued under the name of Charles I. after his retreat to York in 1642; and that " this style, though the sense of it was implied in many institutions, no former King of England would have used, and no subject would have been permitted to use." We see that a subject did use it unpunished, and any King would have used it, if his interest had required him to shew that the government of England was *not* a pure *democracy*, that the King was an essential member of it, as well as the Lords and Commons. But no former monarch had been set to prove this in his own behalf, and it was not very likely that Kings and Queens would volunteer to set limits to their own authority. Hume sophistically confounds the theory with the practice of the former days. The Tudors were practically despotic enough, and so were the Plantagenets whenever they had the power; but the arbitrary maxims of the prerogative lawyers and court divines were new in the reign of Elizabeth. Be it recollected, that Ælmer's work was not an attack upon royal prerogative, but a defence of it.

Soon after the accession of Elizabeth, Ælmer returned to England, and was one of the eight divines appointed to dispute with as many Romanist Bishops, at West-minster. Of course his arguments were then as strong as in the convocation of 1553, they had been weak. In 1562 he obtained the Archdeaconry of Lincoln, and after several intermediate preferments, was finally advanced to the see of London, in 1576, from which time to his death he was continually engaged in quarrels, which did him little honour, but leave an impression that he was not only an intolerant and overbearing, but a captious, avaricious, and litigious man. He sued his predecessor, Edwin Sandys, for arrears and dilapidations, and was afterwards prosecuted before the privy council, for injuring the property of his diocese by cutting down wood, which exposed him not only to a severe censure from Burleigh, and a prohibition from the crown, but to an infamous pun upon his name, some would-be-witty Puritan saying, that he was no longer Elmar, but Mar-elm. Men seldom pun so vilely as when they are in a passion : and Bishop Ælmer was a severe prosecutor, not to say persecutor, both of the Catholic recusants and the Puritans, against whom his seve-rities were either too great or too little for sound policy, and at all events inconsistent with christian charity. His acts of discipline were rendered more obno. ious by his addiction to railing, and calling hard names. But there can be little satisfaction in dwelling on this part of his conduct, which was too much in the spirit of the times, and provoked such extreme opposition, that he was fairly worn out, and vainly requested to exchange his diocese of London for that of Ely. He died June 3d, 1594, and was buried at St. Paul's. He wrote nothing of any consequence, but his " Harborough," the rough treatment that work received from certain quarters dis-gusting him with the press; so that he declined to answer the Jesuit Campion's " Ten Reasons," though pressed to the task by the treasurer, Lord Burleigh. He composed, however, a short prayer, to be used in churches and private families, on occasion of the earthquake of 1580, and another, against the excessive rains of 1585. He was also a zealous and frequent preacher, and of so lively a strain, that whenever there was any bad news afloat, he was sure to be appointed to preach at court, and never failed to revive the Queen's spirits. Anthony Wood gives a choice specimen of one of these cordial discourses, preached, it would seem, when some alarm had arisen from astrological predictions, and possibly rumours were afloat of Elizabeth's proposed marriage. " Here is much talk of malum ab aquilone, and our prophets have prophecied that in exaltatione Lunae Leo jungetur Leaenae, and the astrono-mer tells us of a watery Trigon. But as long as Virgo is in that ascendant with us we need not fear of any thing. Deus nobiscum, quis contra nos ? " If such was the usual style of his discourses, we may rather wonder at the effect produced, when, upon one occasion, seeing his audience half asleep, he began to read a long text in

Hebrew, which presently set their drowsy eyes wide open, whereupon he turned their awakened attention to profit, by pointing out their absurdity in listening to Hebrew, of which they understood not a word, and neglecting English, which might make them wise unto salvation. The fanatics may claim the credit of banishing buffoonery from the church, as Tom Paine banished infidelity from the polite circles, by carrying it into pot houses.

Bishop Ælmer was doubtless a learned divine, though he has not thought fit to leave many proofs of his learning behind him. He was a great Hebraist, and a patron of Hebrew scholars, particularly of the celebrated Broughton, who first maintained the now approved exposition, that *Hell*, in the Apostle's Creed, means *Paradise*, a very comfortable doctrine for sinners. The word ought to be altered. Hades, the original term, like the Hebrew Scheol, means simply the place, or rather state, of separate spirits; but Hell, in modern English, has no such latitude of signification, therefore, though Hades may signify Paradise, Hell cannot; and though the creed is scriptural in Greek, it is unscriptural in the English translation. But Bishop Ælmer was not only learned, but brave; of mean stature, saith Anthony, but in his youth very valiant, which he forgot not in his old age. Of his valour in old age, Stripe, his panegyrical biographer, produces an instance which, for the credit of all parties concerned, we hope is fictitious:—Queen Elizabeth was once grievously tormented with the tooth ache, and though it was absolutely necessary, was yet afraid to have her tooth drawn : Bishop Ælmer being by, to encourage her Majesty, sat down in a chair (which no man could have done unbidden in Bessy's presence without a sound box on the ear), and calling the tooth drawer, Come, said he, though I am an old man, and have few teeth to spare, (he must have lost his *Dentes Sapientiæ*), draw me this; which was accordingly done, and then the Queen had her's drawn too. So goes the tale, which is a servile imitation of what is related about Nero's desiring somebody to set him an example of suicide. Another story is rather less improbable, but not quite so reputable, considering that St. Paul requires a Bishop to be " no striker."---1 Tim. iii. 3. One of his daughters was married to a swaggering parson called Squire, who made a very bad husband, not only neglecting and abusing his wife, but, with a baseness of which none but a cassocked profligate would have been capable, justifying himself by casting aspersions on her character. The Bishop, according to rumour, vindicated his daughter's honour effectually with a cudgel, or, as Martin Mar-Prelate styles it, "he went to buffets with his son-in-law for a bloody nose." We have no hesitation in rejecting this and similar anecdotes, which the enemies of Ælmer imposed upon the gaping admiration of his partisans. It is evident that he made himself extremely obnoxious to all dissidents, without gaining the general confidence of his brethren of the church. He had a violent temper, the common infirmity of short statures, and did not always preserve that dignity of language which became his age and station. The particular instances may be false, but still they testify to the general habit. His playing at bowls on the sabbath gave great offence to the stricter religionists, so that they gave ready credence to Martin Mar-Prelate when he asserted, that " the Bishop would cry rub, rub, rub, to his bowl, and when 'twas gone too far, ' the devil go with it,' and then," quoth Martin, "the Bishop would follow." That he *could* call names, the following passage, taken from a work in defence of the fair sex, will fully evince. "Women are of two sorts; some of them are wiser, better learned, discreter, and more constant, than a *number* of men. But another and a worse sort of them, and the *most part*, are fond, foolish, wanton flibbergibs, tattlers, triflers, wavering, witless, without counsel, feeble, careless, rash, proud, dainty, nice, tale-bearers, eves-droppers, rumour-raisers, evil-tongued, worse minded, and in every respect doltified with the dregs of the devil's dunghill." After all, let Ælmer live in the single commendation of Jane Grey, for he has won a better memorial by teaching one little girl Greek, than by shepherding the souls of the first city in the world.

As Alexander Nowell was a Lancashire worthy, not of sufficient importance to furnish a distinct article, we may as well give the few heads of his life in connection with that of Ascham, whose last hours he witnessed, and whose eulogy he pronounced from the pulpit.

Alexander Nowell was born at Read, in Lancashire, in 1511: was of Brazen-nose College, in Oxford, M.A. and Fellow, 1540. Kept a school in Westminster in the reign of Edward VI. Was returned for a Cornish borough in the first parliament of Mary, but declared "not duly elected," as being a Prebendary of Westminster, and therefore a member of the Lower House of Convocation. Whence it appears, that holy orders did not of themselves disqualify him for sitting in the House of Commons. When the persecution commenced he was marked out as a victim, but was saved by the contrivance of Mr. Francis Bowyer, afterwards Sheriff of London, A. D. 1577, and escaped beyond sea; to which service Fuller gratefully recurs in his dedication of the 2d section of the 8th book of his Church History, to Thomas, grandson of the aforesaid Francis Bowyer. Nowell was the first of the Protestant exiles that returned to hail the accession of Elizabeth, and was a prosperous man ever after. He took a rational view of the dispute between the High Church and the Puritans respecting vestments, affirming them to be *lawful*, but not expedient. He died in 1602, aged 90, the founder of the Free School at Middleton, in Lancashire, and a benefactor to the College of Brazen-nose and the School of St. Paul's.

JOHN FISHER, BISHOP OF ROCHESTER.

THE character of this good Prelate has been variously represented, his actions related with diversity of circumstance, and his death described by some as the reward of treason, by others as the testimony of martyrdom. Certainly he was a martyr to his own creed, no less by the voluntary mortifications of his whole life, than by the enforced sufferings of his latter end. Of himself, we shall speak the language of his friends rather than his revilers : his opinions we shall endeavour to explain, but shall neither condemn nor justify ; simply presuming, that of all errors the most venial is a disinterested adherence to the errors of antiquity, especially when worse novelties are proposed to be substituted.

John Fisher was born at Beverley, A. D. 1459. His father, a respectable merchant of that town, died before he or his brother orphan, Robert, could compute their loss ; yet left them not unprovided, for Fuller says he was a wealthy man, and that John's estate had a paternal bottom. His mother, a worthy and pious woman, though she took a second husband, did not neglect the children of the first, but committed them to the charge of a priest of the collegiate church of Beverley as soon as they were deemed capable of initiation into grammar learning. John Fisher shewing a great aptitude for study, it was determined to train him for the Church's service. Accordingly, in 1484, when he was about twenty-five, he was entered of Michael-house, then a rich foundation,* afterwards dissolved along with King's Hall, the best landed in Cambridge, by Henry VIII., in 1546, and its revenues swallowed up in his new foundation of Trinity College. From the unusually late age at which he commenced his University education, it is probable that his studies were interrupted by some secular occupation, of which we have not read. He proceeded Bachelor of Arts in 1488, and Master in 1491 ; was elected Fellow, served the office of Proctor in 1495, and in the same year, on the promotion of William de

* According to Fuller (History of the University of Cambridge, page 12, 1655), the yearly rents of Michael-house, at old and easy rates, amounted to £144 3s. 1d., a very large sum in those days.

Melton, heretofore his tutor, to the Chancellorship of the cathedral of York, was chosen head of his house. Having now devoted himself to the study of theology, he took orders, and became a distinguished divine, famous in all *acts* and *disputations*. He appeared to great advantage in the public exercises, when in 1501 he proceeded DD. Shortly after he was appointed Vice Chancellor, and held the office two years successively. It is said that about this time he assisted the studies of the young Prince Henry, afterwards Henry VIII., whose proficiency in scholastic divinity was such, that some thought his father intended to make him a churchman, had not his elder brother died. Had this intention taken effect, what more likely, than that he who proved the most formidable adversary of the Popedom, might have been Pope himself?

But it is more certain that the fame of Dr. Fisher reached the ears of Margaret of Lancaster, the mother of Henry the Seventh, and that by her solicitation he quitted Cambridge, to become her confessor almoner, and spiritual director. This preference he probably owed not so much to his skill in the application of Aristotle's logic to the doctrines of the Church of Rome, or even to his mastery over those casuistical subtleties which were the professional knowledge of a confessor, as to his fervent and indefatigable devotion, his ascetic mortifications, his frequent fasts and continual abstinence, his whips and hair shirts, his zeal for good works, and his eminence in that sort of charity which was then accounted most acceptable to Heaven. He became a member of the Lady Margaret's family, wherein he directed all things with the regularity, if not the severity, of a monastic establishment, when monasteries were really the abodes of prayer, penance, and contemplation. Never forgetting the interest of his University, and of religious learning, he encouraged her to those magnificent foundations by which she continues to be remembered ; not as she purposed, with prayers and masses, but in thanksgivings and college festivals. On the 8th of September, 1502, she instituted two perpetual lectures in divinity, one at Oxford, and the other at Cambridge. Fisher was the first Margaret's Professor at Cambridge.

From 1502 to 1504 we have nothing to record of him, though doubtless he did much good in that interval; but in 1504 he was suddenly, and it is said unexpectedly, called to the see of Rochester, upon the translation of Richard Fitz-James to the see of London. This promotion was naturally enough attributed to the Lady Margaret's influence with her son. It were well if Bishops had always been made on such good recommendation ; or rather, if the appointment to all church dignities were vested in persons of religious experience. But though Henry's dutiful observance of his mother was the best point in his character, she was always careful to conceal her power over him, whatever it might be, and never countenanced the Ultra-Lancastrians in their opinion, that he held the crown only by her sufferance; which was true as regarded any right to the crown he could claim by descent. She almost merged the parent in the subject, with a humility rather heroic than christian; for it was too conscious and deliberate to be the spontaneous issue of a soul renewed. Nor would it have accorded with Henry's policy to allow any of his acts to be traced to a woman, even if that woman were his mother. When, therefore, it was surmised in his presence that Fisher had to thank the Countess of Richmond for his Bishopric, he answered, "Indeed the modesty of the man, together with my mother's silence, spake in his behalf;" and denied that the Lady had ever opened her mouth on the subject, which was probably true, for Henry was too great a politician to volunteer a gratuitous falsehood. He knew her wish, and with true filial courtesy, made that his request which he might have magnified into a boon. His letter consulting his mother on the propriety of Fisher's advancement is extant, and commences as follows:—"Madam, and I thought I should not offend you, which I will never do wilfully, I am well minded to promote Master Fisher, your confessor, to a Bishopric; and I assure you, Madam, for no other cause, but for the great and singular virtue that I know and see in him, as well as in cunning and natural wisdom, and specially for his good and virtuous living and conversation. And by the promotion of such a man, I well know it should courage others to live virtuously, and to take such ways as he doth, which should be a good example to many others hereafter. Howbeit, without your pleasure known, I will not move him nor tempt him herein."

There is a respectful delicacy in this letter which does honour to the writer: nor was this consultation a mere matter of etiquette, since the advancement of Fisher tended to deprive the Lady of her chaplain and confessor. The style in which Margaret used to address her son is not so pleasing. An epistle of her's, apparently a strictly private communication respecting her own business, commences thus:—"My dearest and only desired joy in this world. With my most hearty loving blessings, and *humble* commendations, I pray our Lord to reward and thank your *Grace*, for that it hath pleased your *Highness* so kindly and lovingly to be content to write your letters of thanks to the French King for my great matter that hath been so long in suit, as Master Welby hath shewed me your *bounteous goodness* is pleased." This letter is subscribed—"At Calais town, this day of St. Anne, that I did bring into this world my good and gracious Prince, King, and only beloved son, by your *humble servant, beadswoman* and mother." Surely this preposterous reversal of the order of nature, wherein a mother abases herself before her own offspring, before the creature whom she herself had held " muling and puking " in her arms, is a satire upon monarchy.* But all have their infirmities. Margaret, with all her humiliations, and hair cloths, and washing of beggars' feet, was proud of having a King for her son, and delighted most to contemplate her son as a King.

Though Fisher was repeatedly offered wealthier dioceses, he always stuck fast to Rochester, then the poorest see in the kingdom, saying, " he would not forsake his poor little old wife, with whom he had lived so long." In order fully to enter into the spirit of this saying, it should be recollected, that those who advocate the celibacy of the clergy maintain, that St. Paul, when he says " a Bishop *should be the husband of one wife*," † meant that a Bishop should have no wife but his church.

Soon after his ordination as Bishop, Dr. Fisher was elected High Chancellor of Cambridge, an office which had previously been annual ; but the University, either finding the inconvenience of such frequent elections, and desirous to bestow an extraordinary honour on the favoured of their great benefactrix, decreed that the Bishop of Rochester be their High Chancellor for life ; and his successors have generally held the dignity on the same terms. The decree was not solemnly confirmed till 1514.

In 1505, the Lady Margaret founded Christ College, or rather restored and completed an imperfect foundation of Henry VI., known by the name of God's house, which the troubles of that Monarch prevented him from finishing. Margaret, ("accounting herself as of the Lancaster line, heir to all King Henry's Godly intentions"), ‡ executed this design, only altering the name from God's House to Christ College. King Henry the Seventh himself was present at the commencement of the work, and gratified the University by unwonted liberality. Fisher was appointed to superintend the building and ordering of the new college, and, that he might be the better accommodated with a lodging,

---

* Did Henry partake the Roman feeling of Coriolanus :---

My mother bows
As if Olympus to a mole-hill should
In supplication nod.----*Act 5. Scene 3.*

† 1st Timothy, iii. 2. : " A Bishop then must be blameless, the *husband of one wife.*" The Catholic interpretation of this text would be very admissible, if any other text required a Bishop to live single.

‡ Fuller.   Hist. of Cambridge.

he was chosen President of Queen's, on the death of Dr. Wilkinson ; this headship he thankfully accepted, and kept it a little more than three years. It is said that the fame and friendship of Fisher determined Erasmus to prefer Queen's College for the place of his studies at Cambridge, which he first visited in 1504 or 5. That Erasmus highly esteemed our Bishop is evident from many passages in his epistles, in which he ascribes the great improvement in the studies in Cambridge, (particularly in Greek,) to Fisher's exertions. The improvement must have been as great and rapid as that which has lately taken place in Oxford within the same space of time, and which is still proceeding to higher degrees of perfection :—" Almost thirty years ago," says he, " nothing else was handled or read, in the schools of Cambridge, but Alexander,* the Little Logicals, (as they call them,) and those old Dictates of Aristotle, and Questions of Scotus. In process of time there was an accession of good learning, the knowledge of Mathematics came in ; so many authors came in, whose names were anciently unknown—To wit, it hath flourished so much, that it may contend with the prime schools of this age, and hath such men therein, to whom if such be compared that were in the age before, they will seem rather shadows of divines, than divines." Epist. 10. B. 2. To this reform he alludes again, with a special commendation of Dr. Fisher :—" John, Bishop of Rochester, (a true man, a true Bishop, a true divine,) told me some three years since, that in Cambridge, (whereof he is perpetual Chancellor,) instead of sophistical querks, now sober, and sound disputations, are agitated amongst divines, whence men depart not only learneder but better."

In another place :—" England hath two famous Universities ; Cambridge and Oxford ; in both of these the Greek language is taught, but in Cambridge quietly, because John Fisher, Bishop of Rochester, sits governor of the school, not only for his learning's sake, but for his divine life. But when a certain young man at Oxford, not meanly learned, did happily enough profess the Greek tongue there, a barbarous Fellow, in a popular sermon, began to rail against the Greek tongue with great and heinous revilings." Book 6, Epistle 2. Again :—" By the wisdom of Thomas, Cardinal of York, the school of Oxford shall be adorned not only with all kinds of tongues and learning, but also with such

* He means Alexander Hales, the father of school philosophy in England, and the master of Thomas Aquinas, and Bonaventure, " whose livery in some sort the rest of the school-men may be said to wear." He was, like most of the teachers and preachers of his time, a Franciscan, and the first of that order who took a Doctor's degree. He was called the irrefragable Doctor, and Doctor Doctorum ; so great an honorer of the Virgin Mary, that he never denied those that sued in her name. Died 1245.

manners as become the best studies.   For the University of Cambridge
long ago, doth flourish with all ornaments, John, Bishop of Rochester,
being Chancellor thereof."

Thus though there was a great difference of temper, and, at that
time, no little variety of opinion, between the grave, ascetic Fisher, and
the liberal, cosmopolite Erasmus, yet there was between them the common tie of a love for the Greek language, wherein the one rejoiced in
his proficiency, and the other wished to make up for his deficiency.   At
the time that Fisher received his education, Greek was in a manner
unknown in England; or if understood by any, it was only by those
who had completed their studies in foreign Universities.   The first
teachers of that language had to contend with strong prejudices, and
the students were sometimes exposed to manual violence.   Greek was
an innovation, and liable to the same plausible and prudential objections
which apply to innovations in general; for every accession of knowledge
convicts antiquity of ignorance, and the security of establishments
requires that antiquity be deemed infallibly wise.   Whatever tempts a
young man to say " I am wiser than the aged," infringes upon discipline, and reverses order.   Old men are naturally averse to new studies,
and cannot be expected to yield a ready approbation to novelties, which
reduce them to the alternative of yielding their pre-eminence, or struggling for it with their juniors.   It was, therefore, a great generosity in
Fisher that he encouraged the new learning by his fostering influence;
and a wonderful proof of candour, industry, and good sense, that he, an
elderly man, and a Bishop, already engaged in many labours at an age
when most men think themselves entitled to rest, set himself to acquire
a very difficult kind of knowledge, and persevered till he had acquired
it.   Knight, in his life of Dean Colet, gives a pleasing account of the
Bishop's Greek studies, which we shall give verbatim:—" Dr. John
Fisher, reputed the best preacher, and the deepest divine in these
times, Head of Queen's College, in Cambridge, Chancellor of the University, Chaplain at Court, and Bishop of Rochester, was very sensible
of this imperfection, [the want of Greek,] which made him desirous to
learn Greek in his declining years, and for that purpose he wrote to
Erasmus to persuade William Latimer, an Englishman, (who from his
travels had brought home that language in perfection,) to be his
instructor in it.   Erasmus accordingly wrote to Latimer, and importuned him to it.   But he declined undertaking to teach the Bishop at
those years, alledging the long time it would take to make any proficiency, from the example of the greatest masters of it then in England,
Grocyn, Linacre, Tonstal, Pace, and More, and, to excuse himself,
advised that the Bishop should send for a master out of Italy."   Bishop

Fisher's want of Greek made him the greater patron and promoter of it in Cambridge; and his being Chancellor of that University made it more eminent than Oxford in that respect. Knowing, therefore, the abilities of Erasmus* this way, he invited him thither, and supported

* " About this time (1504) Erasmus came first to Cambridge, (coming and going for seven years together,) having his abode in Queen's College, where a study, on the top of the South-west tower, in the old court, still retaineth his name. Here his labour in mounting so many stairs, (done perchance on purpose to exercise his body and prevent corpulency,) was reconciled with a pleasant prospect round about him. He often complained of the college ale—*Cerevisia hujus Collegii mihi nullo modo placet.* (*Epist.* 16, *libri* 8,) as raw, small, and windy; whereby it appears, 1st. Ale in that age was the constant beverage of all colleges, before the innovation of beer, the child of hops, was brought into England : 2nd. Queen's College Cerevisia was not vis Cereris, but Ceres vitiata. In my time, when I was a member of that house, scholars continued Erasmus's complaint, whist the brewers, (having, it seems, prescription on their side for long time,) little amended it. The best was that Erasmus had his lagena or flagon of wine, (recruited weekly from his friends at London,) which he drank sometimes singly by itself, and sometimes encouraged his faint ale with the mixture thereof.

" He was public Greek Professor, and first read the grammar of Chrysoloras to a thin auditory, whose number increased when he began the grammar of Theodorus. Then took he, by grace freely granted unto him, the degree of Doctor in divinity, such his commendable modesty, though over deserving a Doctorship, to desire no more as yet, because the main of his studies were most resident on humanity. Here he wrote a small tract, *de conscribendis epistolis*, (*on epistolary composition*), set forth by Sibert, printer to the University. Some years after, he took upon him the Divinity Professor's place, (understand the Lady Margaret's,) invited thereunto, not by the salary, so small in itself, but with desire and hope to do good in the employment.

"If any find him complaining, *Hic, O Academiam nullus*, &c. *Here's an University indeed, wherein none can be found who will at any rate be hired to write but indifferently,* know this might tend much to his trouble, but sounds nothing to the disgrace of Cambridge. Indeed, in Dutch academies, many poor people make a mean livelihood by writing for others, though but liberal mechanics in their employment. No such mercenary hands in Cambridge, where every one wrote for himself, and if at any time for others, he did it gratis, as a courtesy for good will, no service for reward. But too tart and severe is Erasmus his censure of Cambridge townsmen. *Vulgus Cantabrigiense inhospitales Britannos antecedit qui cum summa rusticitate summam malitiam conjunxere.* "The Cambridge mob outdo the general inhospitality of Britons, uniting the greatest spitefulness with the greatest clownishness." Fuller's Hist. of Cambridge, page 88.

Had Erasmus visited the English Universities in the 19th instead of the 15th century, he would have found plenty of persons who could be hired not only to write but to compose indifferently, and who make a very comfortable livelihood thereby. But it is probable that, in Erasmus his time, *impositions* had not yet been substituted for corporal punishment by the conservators of academical discipline, and to be flogged by proxy, was the exclusive privilege of royal blood. The office of whipping boy still continued in the pupillage of Charles I., for Burnet mentions the person who held it. It was much coveted for the children of the poorer gentry, as the first step in the

him in professing Greek, which he himself had at last made himself
master of."

ladder of preferment.   It is a wonder that it is not continued as a *sinecure*.   Barnaby
Fitzpatrick was whipping boy, or, as Fuller, with more than his usual delicacy
expresses it, *proxy for correction*, to King Edward VI., which, considering the good
disposition and towardliness of that Prince, must have been a very easy office.   He
was afterwards employed as an emissary in France.

It is to be hoped that Erasmus has been wrongfully accused of spoiling his lagena
by adulterating it with the *Ceres vitiata* of Queen's college.   If he was guilty of such
an enormity, the kindness of his London friends was thrown away upon him.

Our readers will doubtless remember the distitch, (read with considerable variations):—

> Hops and Turkeys, Carp and Beer,
> Came into England, all in a year.

The precise year has not been mentioned, but it must have been after 1504, and
during the reign of Henry the Eighth, which was a great epoch in the annals of
schism and gastronomy.

Queen's college Ale no longer deserves the imputation cast upon it by the philologer of Rotterdam; but we are sorry to say that the commonalty of the University
towns are not much mended in their manners.   The hostility of Town and Gown still
continues.   Much of the rudeness, not to say brutality, of the natives in and around
these fountains of Christian knowledge, is to be ascribed to the vulgar contempt with
which they are treated by a certain part of the students.   If it be essential to gentility
to speak contemptuously of the *vulgus*, it were surely more decorous to call names in
Greek or Latin, (and the vituperative *copia verborum* of those learned languages is
peculiarly ample,) than in such bald English as *Clods, Snobs, &c.*

But what right had Erasmus to affix the character of inhospitality to the English
in general, cherished and honoured, as he was, by the highest in the English nation,
and made a Professor in an English University?   Yet the charge has been repeated
from generation to generation.   Perhaps it is true, that foreigners are subject to more
insults, *out of doors*, in England than elsewhere, but where do they find so much kindness within doors?   Where is there so sure a refuge for the distressed of all nations?
Hither come the proscribed of every sect in religion, and every grade of no religion,
and every party in politics; the monarch flies hither from the storm of revolution,
and hides his " grey discrowned head" in a palace, and the priest, when his function
has become a bie-word in his own land, finds here a welcome and a congregation.

> For sure, the blest, immortal Powers
> Have fixt a pillar in the desert sea,
> A steadfast column of security,
> Even this isle, this sea-fenced land of ours:
> Appointed by divine behest,
> A sea-mark for the wandering guest,
> A safety for the poor opprest,
> Here is a home for all that need,
> For every speech, and every creed.
> So it was, long time ago,
> May time for ever find it so.

The foundation of Christ College was completed in 1506, and the Bishop of Rochester was appointed Visitor for life by the statutes, in case of the demise of the foundress. No sooner was this great work finished, than the Lady Margaret projected another still more magnificent, and obtained the King's license for founding St. John's College; but before it could pass through all the necessary forms, King Henry VII died, at his favourite palace of Sheen, which he had named after his own youthful title, Richmond, April 22, 1509; and his venerable mother followed him on the 29th of the ensuing June, leaving it to her executors, of whom our Bishop was one, to continue and confirm her charities, and to execute her design of John's College, which was greater than any hitherto undertaken in either University; and now is only exceeded by her grandson's *opus magnum*, Trinity College. But the original foundation was much narrower than the present. Her funeral sermon was preached by her long-tried friend and spiritual physician. The view he gives of her character is a favourable specimen of the style of that age, and the only extract we can give from the Bishop's writings. It is as follows:—" She was bounteous and liberal to every person of her knowledge or acquaintance. Avarice and covetyse * she most hated, and sorrowed it full much in all persons, but

Imitated and amplified from Pindar's 8th Olympic, verse 33 to 38, Heyne's edition.

The original application is to Ægina, but why should not Ægina be considered as a type of England?

* Here the Bishop has been supposed to glance at the memory of Henry VII., whose "avarice and covetyse" were long a topic of reproach, though of late they have found palliators if not vindicators. The reflection was likely to be popular, and as Henry VII. was dead, and his successor of so different a turn, it might be made safely. One instance of his parsimony must have been very grievous to his good mother, who would gladly have had the Calendar graced with a royal saint of the line of Lancaster. There were serious thoughts of procuring the canonization of Henry VI., who in no condition of saintship fell much short of Edward the Confessor, and, in the article of sufferings, very far exceeding him. Application was made to Pope Alexander VI., but it is commonly asserted, that the fees demanded were so enormous, that his economical successor could not be prevailed on to disburse them; and so St. Henry of Lancaster was defrauded of his apotheosis. But we must abridge old Fuller's characteristic account of this matter, which doubtless vexed Bishop Fisher and all true English Bishops deeply for their country's honour:—

" The King had more than a month's mind (keeping seven years in that humour) to procure the Pope to canonize King Henry the Sixth for a saint. For English Saint-Kings, so frequent before the Conquest, were grown great dainties since that time. His canonizing would add much lustre to the line of Lancaster, which made his kinsman and immediate successor, King Henry the Seventh, so desirous thereof. Besides, well might he be a saint who had been a prophet. For when the wars of

specially in any that belonged unto her.   She was of singular easyness
to be spoken unto, and full certain answer she would make to all that

Lancaster and York first began, Henry the Sixth, *beholding this Henry the Seventh,
then a boy, playing in the court, said to the standers by, "See, this youth one day will
quietly enjoy what we at this time so much fight about."*   This made the King, with so
much importunity, to tender this his request to the Pope; a request the more reasonable, because it was well nigh forty years since the death of that Henry, so that *only
the skeletons of his virtues remained in men's memories,* the flesh and corruption of his
faults being quite forgotten.   Pope Alexander, instead of granting his request, acquainted him with the requisites belonging to the making of a saint.   First, that to
confer that honour was only in the power of the Pope.   Secondly, that saints were
not to be multiplied but on just motions, lest commonness should cause their contempt.   Thirdly, that his life must be exemplarily holy, by the testimony of credible
witnesses.   Fourthly, that such must attest the truth of real miracles wrought by him
after death.   Fifthly, that very great was the cost thereof, because all the chaunters,
choristers, bell-ringers (not the least clapper in the steeple wagging, unless money
were tied to the end of the rope), with all the officers of the Church of St. Peter,
together with the commissaries and notaries of the court, with all the officers of the
Pope's bedchamber, down to the very locksmiths, ought to have their several fees of
such canonization.   Adding, that the sum total would amount to fifteen hundred
ducats of gold.

Tantæ molis erat Romanum condere *Sanctum.*

Most of these requisites met in King Henry the Sixth in a competent measure.
First, the holiness of his life was confessed by all.   As for miracles, there was no want
of them, if *credible* persons might be believed.   Thomas Fuller, a very *honest* man,
living at Hammersmith, had a hard hap accidentally to light into the company of
one who had stolen cattle, with whom, though wholly innocent, he was taken,
arraigned, condemned, and executed.   When on the gallows, blessed King Henry
(loving justice when alive, and willing to preserve innocence after death) appeared
unto him, so ordering the matter, that the halter did not strangle him.   For, having
hung a whole hour, and taken down to be buried, he was found alive; for which
favour he repaired to the tomb of King Henry, at Chertsey (as he was bound to do
no less), and there presented his humble and hearty thanks to him for his deliverance.
The very same accident, *mutatis mutandis* of place and persons (with some addition
about the apparition of the Virgin Mary) happened to Richard Boyes, dwelling
within a mile of Bath, the story so like, all may believe them equally true.

Men variously conjecture why the Pope should in effect deny to canonize King
Henry VI.: a witty but tart reason is rendered by a noble pen,---because the Pope would
put a difference between a *saint* and an *innocent* (Lord Bacon's Hist. of Henry VII.):
more probable it is what another saith,---that, seeing King Henry held the crown by
a false title, the Pope could not with so good credit fasten a saintship upon his
memory.   But our great antiquary (Camden) resolveth all in the Pope's covetous-
ness, demanding more than thrifty King Henry VII. would allow; who at last
contented himself (by the Pope's leave hardly obtained) to remove the corpse from
Chertsey, in Surrey, where it was obscurely interred, to Windsor Chapel, a place of
greater reputation.   Thus is he, whom authors have observed twice crowned, twice
deposed, twice buried."---*Church History. Book IV.* 153.

The miracle attributed to King Henry is by no means uncommon in legendary

came unto her. Of marvellous gentleness she was unto all folks, but specially unto her own, whom she trusted, and loved right tenderly. Unkind she would not be unto no creature, nor forgetful of any kindness or service done to her before, which is no little part of very nobleness. She was not vengeable nor cruel, but ready enough to forget and to forgive injuries done unto her, at the least desire or motion made unto her for the same. Merciful also and piteous she was unto such as were grieved, and wrongfully troubled, and to them that were in poverty and sickness, or any other misery. She was of a singular wisdom, far passing the common rate of women. She was good in remembrance, and of holding memory; a ready wit she had also to conceive all things, albeit they were right dark. Right studious she was in books, which she had in great number, both in English, and in Latin, and in French; and for her exercise, and for the profit of others, she did translate divers matters of devotion out of the French into English.* In favour, in words, in gesture, in every demeanor of herself, so great nobleness did appear, that what she spake, or did, it marvellously became her. She had in a manner all that was prizeable in a woman, either in soul or body."

These are praises as suitable to our times as to those in which they

history. Mr. Southey has founded two tales on this sort of suspended animation, "The Pilgrim of Compostella," and "Roprecht the Robber." There is no occasion to impute wilful falsehood to all these narrations. The hangman might in some cases do his work so discreetly as to be accessory to the miracle. But resuscitation after hanging has often taken place; and in an age that ascribed every unusual phenomenon to the immediate interference of Divine agency, it would certainly be taken as a miraculous attestation of innocence by all; and by none more deeply than by an innocent sufferer. This was natural: it was good. But the Church always took care to appropriate the miracles to herself.

* Among the Lady Margaret's translations were "The Mirroure of Goulde for ye sinfulle Soule," from the "Speculum Aureum Peccatorum." "The fourth book of Thomas a Kempis, Of the Imitation and Followynge of our most merciful Saviour, CHRIST." Printed at the end of Dr. William Atkinson's translation of the other three books, in 1510. Both these she translated through the medium of French versions. She often lamented that she had not made herself mistress of Latin in her youth, though she was not so ignorant of that language but that she could use it in the service of charity. When she was at Cambridge, superintending her new foundation of Christ's College, a student, detected in some irregularity, was driven past her window to the academic whipping-post, on which she cried out *Lente, Lente,* as a Scotch lady would have rendered it, "*Canny,... canny, noo.*"

The Lady Margaret, at the desire and by the authority of her son, drew up the orders for great estates of ladies and noblewomen, for their precedence, &c., particularly at *funerals.*

were spoken.   But it is with virtues as it is with books; the true and
excellent are never long without just commendation, though the false,
and hollow, and affected, are often still more noisily celebrated for a
season.   There were other parts of the Bishop's discourse that have a
stronger savour of antiquity.   He parallels the Countess with Martha
in four respects.—1st, Nobility of person!!   2d, Discipline of her body.
3d, In ordering her soul to God.   4th, In hospitality and charity.—
Now, unless there be, as in all probability there is, a traditional history
of Martha, containing many particulars not recorded by the Evangelists,
it would puzzle a herald to prove her *nobility*, except it consisted in
her descent from Abraham, which made her akin to all the kings of
Israel and Judah.   Neither does it appear in scripture that she disciplined her body in the sense here meant.   As for the third and fourth
conformities, it is to be remarked, that in the only passage of the
Gospel wherein much is said about Martha, she is rather reproved for
not turning her soul to God, and for being too intent upon her hospitality.   But it had long been a common-place to represent Martha
and Mary as the types or symbols of the active and the contemplative
duties, and every good woman was compared to the one or the other.
    As all funeral panegyrics are in some degree biographical, Fisher
recounted the leading circumstances of Margaret's life, not forgetting to
magnify her high parentage, (which nevertheless laboured under the
imputation of an illegitimate origin,) and told his audience that she was
related, by birth or marriage, to thirty Kings and Queens, (it should
be recollected that she had three husbands, the first of whom was
grandson to a King of France.)   She was born in 1441, at Bletsho, in
Bedfordshire, where long after remained some of her needle-work, (the
eldest of all graphic arts, and most primitive of lady accomplishments,)
which James the First always asked to see when he came into that
neighbourhood.   She was the sole child and heiress of John Beaufort,
Duke of Somerset (grandson of John of Gaunt and Catherine Swinford),
by Margaret Beauchamp.   While yet very young, she was sought by
two distinguished suitors; the favourite Suffolk solicited her for his
son, and the King Henry VI. recommended his own half-brother, the
Earl of Richmond, son of Catherine of France, the Queen dowager, and
Owen Tudor, who traced his pedigree through Arthur and Uther Pendragon up to the Trojan Brutus; nor was this derivation from the first
possessors of Britain without its use in conciliating the people to the
line of Tudor.   It fulfilled several prophecies of Merlin, whom all that
portion of the community whose books were ballads, and whose histori-
ographers were the wandering minstrels, held for a great and veracious
seer.   It is related, and affirmed by the Bishop of Rochester, in his

sermon aforesaid, that the young maiden Margaret, being sorely perplexed between her two lovers, referred to an old lady, her usual confidante, who advised her to apply for direction to St. Nicholas, the tutelar saint of youth; and Margaret earnestly besought the saint in prayer to guide her choice according to the best purposes of Heaven; so it came to pass, one morning, she knew not whether she were sleeping or waking, a venerable man in the habit of a Bishop, (whom she conceived to be St. Nicholas himself,) tendered her Edmund Tudor as her husband. She related this vision to her parents; the supernatural warning was accepted, and she was married accordingly. Such is the story, and there is nothing in it incredible. Bishop Fisher believed it, or he would not have related it in the awful presence of death; no doubt he received it from Margaret herself; and would she have imposed a fiction on the man before whom she was wont to lay bare her soul in the dreadful secrecy of the confessional? Her funeral took place before it was become necessary " to prop a falling church with *venial* falsehood," and though the supposed miraculous interposition might be of use in sanctifying the Tudor dynasty, it was not at all indispensable to Henry VIII., who had an undisputed title from the House of York: and besides, Fisher lived and died to shew that he was not a man to belie his conscience for any king. But what we mainly rest upon is the probability of the story in itself. Margaret, though she was allowed no choice, might still have a preference between her suitors. Even the romantic pedigree of the Earl of Richmond, certainly royal on one side, (a descendant of St. Louis,) and connected on the other with so much of the poetry, then rife in baronial halls, might deeply affect her virgin imagination. Her sight was familiar with the images of the saints, her memory with their legends. She was used from infancy to make all her desires known in prayer, which *might* reach Heaven, though it went a round-about road. She would naturally dream of what her thoughts and feelings were engaged in, and what form would her dreams more naturally assume, than that of the most revered and striking objects to which her waking life had been accustomed? Even in this day, young ladies sometimes dream of their lovers, it may be in connection with a ball or a review, or any thing else that they have associated with them. Now all Margaret's thoughts were associated with saints and visions, and religious pageantry.*

Some may think this apparition an *innocent stratagem*, concerted by

---

* Should any be disposed to give another explanation, and hold that the prayer of pure lips was actually answered, I should neither ridicule nor contradict them. That the circumstances of the vision were accommodated to the habits of the beholder's imagination, is in strict analogy with undoubted revelation.

Margaret with her aged friend, to obtain the *Man of her Heart*. A
Lady of so much piety, and so much benevolence, could not have lived
all her life without falling in love. But we think she dared not have
trifled with St. Nicholas. However it was, Margaret was married to
Edmund of Hadnam; but short was his term of wedded bliss, for he
died in the second year of his nuptials, leaving his only son, the future
monarch of England, a fifteen months' infant. Though the Countess of
Richmond had two subsequent husbands, she never had another child,
and devoted to the offspring of the husband of her virginity as much of
her affections as she thought heaven could spare. Her second marriage
was with Sir Henry Stafford, second son of that Duke of Buckingham,
who has been dishonourably immortalized by Shakspeare, as the unconscientious ally of Duke Richard, and the selfish rebel against the King
Richard of his own making. Sir Henry died in 1482, soon enough to
escape participation in his father's double treasons. His widow married, before her weeds had lost the freshness of their sable tint, Thomas
Lord Stanley; it is said, under an implied condition that the marriage
was never to be consummated. Her husband, and alas, she also, played
a very treacherous part to Richard the Third, which the fullest belief
in his recorded atrocities cannot justify. Margaret held the train of
Richard's Queen, at his coronation, and continually supplicated him to
restore her son to his patrimony, and to allow him to marry one of the
daughters of Edward IV., while she was intriguing with her father-in-
law, Buckingham, and the Queen Dowager, to supplant Richard and
set her son on the throne. Her principal agent in these negociations
was Morton, Bishop of Ely. It is needless to say, that this conspiracy
failed, and its prime mover was very deservedly decapitated; for whoever was the rightful king, he was a most egregious traitor, "So much
for Buckingham." The Lady Margaret Stanley, whose machinations
were well known, was treated by the *tyrant* Richard far more gently
than her son treated the widow of Edward the Fourth. She was only
committed to the custody of her husband, whose defection at the battle
of Bosworth brought about the destruction of the last, it may be the
worst, of the Plantagenets. Stanley was made Earl of Derby, for what
the event of a battle might have made the blackest treason. Thomas
Lord Stanley, first Earl of Derby of the Stanley's, died in 1504, leaving
no issue by the Lady Margaret, who then, at the mature age of sixty-
four, after the death of her third husband, took a vow of celibacy, which
still remains among the archives of St. John's college. In some portraits
she is represented in the habit of a nun, but it does not appear that she
ever entered formally into any religious order.

Her charities were great and meritorious. If in some instances, they were not what the present age would call *judicious*, still they were such as her age approved ; and, in as much as she was an encourager of learning, it is evident that she looked to an age beyond her own. So large were her beneficences, that as Stow says, " they cannot be expressed in a small volume." She daily dispensed suitable relief to the poor and the distressed. She kept twelve poor persons constantly in her house, and having acquired that knowledge of practical surgery, which was then a regular part of the education of the high-born female; she frequently dressed the wounds of the indigent diseased with her own hands. She was born either too late or too soon ; had she lived in an earlier age, she would have found more to sympathize with that zeal which impelled her to declare, " that if the Princes of Christendom would lay aside their mutual quarrels, and combine in a crusade against the Turk, she would most willingly attend them, and be the laundress in their camp." Had she been born later, her excellent heart would have been regulated by a better instructed head, and she would have built the fabric of her religion and morality exclusively on " the foundation of the Apostles and Prophets." If she had lived in our days, perhaps she would not have committed the error recorded in Jortin's Life of Erasmus, in making the son of her third husband a Bishop, without being well certified that he was divinely called to the office. But here is the tale, judge of it as you please. "At this time (1496,) Erasmus refused a large pension, and larger promises, from a young illiterate Englishman, who was to be made a Bishop, and who wanted him for a preceptor. He would not, as he says, be so hindered from prosecuting his studies for all the wealth in the world. This youth, as Knight informs us, seems to have been James Stanley, son to the Earl of Derby, and son-in-law to Margaret, the King's mother, and afterwards made Bishop of Ely by her interest. *This* (says Knight) *surely was the worst thing she ever did,* and indeed, if it be the *Catholic*, it is not the *apostolic* mode of bestowing, and of obtaining, Bishoprics. However, it appears that the young gentleman, if ignorant, had a desire to learn something, and to qualify himself in some measure for the station in which he was to be placed." If Margaret never did any thing worse than this, she was a happy woman indeed. Bishoprics never can be obtained, or bestowed, in the apostolic method, till it shall please the Almighty to gift the rulers of the church with the miraculous discernment of the Apostles. As long as ever the church is in any degree connected with the property of the country, the superior offices in it must, and will be bestowed, on political considerations ; and what proof is there that young Stanley was less fit for a Bishop than any other person, whose name might have been drawn in the lottery? As an

Earl's son, he had at least a good chance of being a gentleman, which for a man who exercises a somewhat invidious superiority over gentlemen and scholars often his seniors, and it may be, in some respects, his betters, is no small recommendation. As long as patronage is permitted, it is natural and right that the patrons should patronize those whom they know best, and love best. No established church can bear any resemblance to the primitive church, which grew up in opposition to all establishments ; and prevailed over all the banded powers of earth and hell by " an invincible patience."   But considering the church in its political relations, as a mean of civilization, and an organ of the state, useful to sanctify civil obedience, it is specially desirable, in every country where an aristocracy exists, that a large, perhaps a major portion of the heads of the church, should be selected from the aristocracy. Even in a land of slaves it will always be found that the higher the rank of the slave-master, the better the condition of the slave. God save me, said a poor christian negro, from having Blackee for Massa. God save me, might the poor Vicar say, from a Bishop that has *tutored*, and *written*, and *preached* himself to a mitre. No doubt, it would be a very good thing, if the church were so constituted, that the best and most experienced ministers, could always be intrusted with the highest authority. But while the church is a member of the state, we must be thankful that its emoluments are so well distributed as they are, and that there are always so many liberal *gentlemen* on the Bench as to prevent the English clergy from degenerating into mere priests.

A single fact will at once justify and explain our meaning. Cardinal Pole was the descendant of kings ; a man devotedly attached to that Church, of which, had he lived longer, he probably might have been the chief ; yet he was an enemy to persecution. Gardiner and Bonner were both natural children of men not high enough to dignify their bastardy ; they derived their *respectability* solely from their rank in the church, and they were the cruellest of persecutors.

No panegyric can be more concise, pregnant, or proper, than Fuller's upon the Lady Margaret, which is almost equally applicable to Bishop Fisher, that she was " the exactest *pattern of the best devotion that those times afforded*, taxed with no personal faults, but *the errors of the age she lived in.*"   She was buried nearly a month after her departure, in the South isle of Henry VII's chapel, with all the pomp then usual, and had a sumptuous monument, with a gilt brass effigy, and an epitaph, for writing which Erasmus received twenty shillings of the University of Cambridge, a very scanty remuneration, even when all allowances are made for the high value of money. It is as follows :—

" Margaretæ Richmondiæ, septimi Henrici Matri, Octavi Aviae, quæ stipendia constituit tribus hoc coenobio Monachis, et Doctori Grammatices apud Winborn ; perque Angliam totam divini verbi præconi duobus item interpretibus litherarum sacrarum, alteri Oxonis Alteri Cantubrigiæ, ubi et collegia duo, Christo et Johanni discipulo ejus, struxit. Morilur An. Dom. 1509, tertio Kal. Jul."

" Sacred to the memory of Margaret, Countess of Richmond, mother of Henry VII. and grandmother of Henry VIII, who founded salaries for three Monks in this convent, for a grammar-school at Winburne, and a preacher of God's Word throughout England; as also for two divinity lecturers, the one at Oxford, and the other at Cambridge, in which last place she likewise built two colleges in honour of Christ and of his disciple St. John. She died in the year of our Lord 1509, June 29."

Thus far the life of Fisher had been a life of peace, piety, and usefulness : from the decease of his good mistress his troubles may be said to have begun. As one of the eight executors of the Lady Margaret's will, he undertook the weighty task of perfecting the foundation of John's College, in which he met with unexpected opposition :—" A generation of prowling, progging, projecting *promoters* (such verminlike Pharaoh's frogs will sometimes creep even into King's chambers), questioning the title of the land of the college, took from it at once four hundred pounds of yearly revenue."* This took place in the very commencement of the reign of Henry VIII. and was never redressed. But notwithstanding this unpropitious circumstance, the College was rapidly finished, and immediately crowded. That man must indeed have been highly favoured, who was allowed a study to himself ; and it is said that those who had private letters to write were obliged to cover the paper with their hands, to prevent their secrets being overlooked by the throng of chums.

In 1516 Bishop Fisher repaired to Cambridge, to open the new house of the Muses with due solemnity, and was commissioned to make statutes for its regulation. How mightily it grew and flourished we have already declared in the life of Ascham. It has always been a resort of students from the northern provinces, who, if less brilliant and mercurial than the children of the south, are not less eminent in *honours*, their slow and sound minds being peculiarly adapted for the patient toil of mathematics, in which branch of knowledge St. John's competes honourably with Trinity.

During the first years of Henry VIII. Bishop Fisher retained a large portion of favour. The Countess Margaret, on her death bed, commended the inexperience of her grandson to his pastoral care, and Henry, who was not born without good dispositions, though he outlived

* Fuller.

them all, respected him as a spiritual father. In 1512 he was appointed to represent the English Church at the Council of Lateran, but, for some forgotten cause, the appointment never took effect. Doubtless he was consulted by the young King in regard to the confirmation of his espousals to Catherine, his brother's widow, of which nothing but the ceremony had hitherto taken place. It is by no means true that Henry had no scruples respecting the lawfulness of that union, till his conscience was awakened by the charms of Anne Boleyn. Though no more than twelve years of age at his brother Arthur's death, he remonstrated strongly against the project of marrying him to a woman considerably his senior, of a very ordinary person, and a demure, spiritless reservedness of manner, which youth is ever apt to ascribe to a morose temper. But his father could not prevail upon himself to restore the 200,000 ducats which composed Catherine's portion. The Pope's dispensation was as potent to annul the rights of nature as the laws of Moses, and the contract was formally made. Still Henry might, when arrived at years of discretion, have refused to ratify an act in which he had never, in any true sense of the word, been a consenting party. It is even said that his father, on his death-bed, urged him to break off the contract. Warham, the Primate, certainly disapproved of it; but the majority of the council, and the Lady Margaret, who only just survived the solemnization of the nuptials, were of the contrary opinion. Whether Fisher approved of the marriage, we can only conjecture. Certainly he was strongly opposed to the divorce, and believed in the dispensing power of the see of Rome.

For some years the Bishop of Rochester took little part in public affairs. Pageantry, war, and negociation were the main occupations of the English court, and in the first and last, the clergy were as much busied as the laity. But Fisher had little taste for either. Ambition and vanity were as alien to his nature as they were predominant in Wolsey's. To the dangers which threatened the Church he could not be entirely blind. The opinions of Wickliffe, in spite of increasing persecution, were gaining ground. Henry VII., who, like his predecessor Henry IV., needed the sanction of the clergy to heal the defects of his title, had, in the latter part of his reign, enforced the laws against heresy with ruthless severity, and Henry VIII., though more secure on his throne, shewed no inclination to treat the Lollards with more lenity. Even those who saved their lives by recanting were forced to wear a representation of a faggot worked in thread on their left sleeves all the days of their lives, on pain of death. " And indeed, to poor people it was—*put it off, and be burned—keep it on, and be starved;* seeing none generally would set them to work that carried that badge."*

* Fuller.

Fisher had his share in these persecutions; for his faith was in every tittle the faith of his Church, to doubt or swerve from which he held the worst of crimes; and any compassion done or felt towards such revolters he held to be soul-murder. But when it is considered that the more enlightened mind of Sir Thomas More was persuaded to support the falling fabric by the rack, the scourge, and the stake, there can be little surprise that Fisher knew nothing of toleration. He was not ignorant of the needfulness of practical reforms in the church: he disapproved of exorbitant wealth or temporal power in the hands of the clergy: he abhorred licentious manners and lax opinions in the servants of the altar: but he would have all reforms brought about by the authority of the church alone, without any interference of lay power; and in doctrinal points he dared not so much as admit the possibility of error in the established creed. Meantime he did not forbear to reprove the wordly dispositions and inconsistent conduct of the priesthood both by his example and his discourses; of which latter the following speech, delivered in convocation,* is no unfavourable sample :—

" May it not seem displeasing to your Eminence and the rest of these grave and reverend fathers of the church, that I speak a few words, which I hope may not be out of season. I had thought that when so many learned men, as *substitutes*† for the clergy, had been drawn into this body, that some good matters should have been propounded for the benefit and good of the church; that the scandals that lie so heavy on her men, and the disease which takes such hold on those advantages, might have been hereby at once removed, and also remedied. Who hath made any the least proposition against the ambition of those men whose pride is so offensive, whilst their profession is humility? or against the incontinency of such as have vowed chastity? How are the goods of the church wasted? the lands, the tithes, and other oblations of the devout ancestors of the people (to the great scandal of their posterity) wasted in superfluous riotous expenses? How can we exhort our flocks to fly the pomps and vanities of this wicked world, when we that are Bishops set our minds on nothing more than that which we forbid? If we should teach according to our doing, how absurdly would our doctrines sound in the ears of those that should hear us? And if we teach one thing and do another, who shall believe our report? which would seem to them no otherwise, than if we should throw down with one hand what we build up with the other. We preach humility, sobriety, contempt of the world, and so forth, and the people perceive in the same men that preach this doctrine, pride and

* In the synod of the whole clergy assembled by Wolsey in his capacity of legate *a latere.*   † i. e. Representatives.

haughtiness of mind, excess of apparel, and a resignation of ourselves to all worldly pomps and vanities.   And what is this otherwise than to set the people at a stand, whether they shall follow the sight of their own eyes, or the belief of what they hear?   Excuse me, Reverend Fathers, seeing herein I blame no man more than I do myself; for sundry times, when I have settled myself to the care of my flock, to visit my diocese, to govern my church, to answer the enemies of Christ,* suddenly there hath come a message to me from the court, that I must attend such a triumph, or receive such an ambassador.   What have we to do with Princes' courts?   If we are in love with Majesty, where is a greater excellence than whom we serve?   If we are in love with stately buildings, are there higher roofs than our cathedrals?   If with apparel, is there a greater ornament than that of the clergy?   Or is there better company than a communion with the saints?   Truly, most Reverend Fathers, what this vanity in temporal things may work in you I know not; but sure I am, that in myself I find it a great impediment to devotion.   Wherefore I think it necessary (and high time it is) that we that are the heads should begin to give example to the inferior clergy as to these particulars, whereby we may all be the better conformable to the image of God.   For in this trade of life which we now lead, neither can there be likelihood of perpetuity in the same state and condition wherein we now stand, or safety to the clergy."

It may be remarked, that the ostentation of Wolsey, and the superiority which he claimed and asserted, even over the Archbishop of Canterbury, in his own province, was deeply offensive to the great body of his clerical brethren, who, though apparently included in Fisher's censure, would take care to apply it, in their minds, to the Cardinal alone.

The events between 1516, and 1529, are so vast, and so infinitely ramified, the great outlines are so universally known, and the detail so complex, and in many parts so obscure, that while such a sketch of them as could be reduced within our limits, could be nothing more than a bald recital of facts with which every schoolboy is acquainted, and dates easily ascertained from any table, a full and comprehensive survey would turn our memoir of Bishop Fisher into a civil and religious history of the world.   Nor would it be possible to treat the subject without entering into controversies, both on questions of opinion, and on matters of fact, quite alien to our purpose.   We shall confine ourselves chiefly to the part acted and suffered in the contest by our present subject.

Almost as soon as Luther appeared in the character of a Reformer,

* i. e. Persecute the Lollards and Lutherans.

Bishop Fisher entered the polemic field against him. It has even been asserted that the famous defence of the Seven Sacraments, which obtained for the King of England the title of " Defender of the Faith," was in a great measure his composition.* The Bishop certainly took upon himself to answer the answerers of his sovereign, little thinking how fell a foe that sovereign was ordained to prove to the system he was then upholding.

Though Fisher must have felt Wolsey's monopoly of the King's countenance very grievous, and, doubtless, groaned in spirit for the scandals and oppressions of the church, he offered little or no opposition to the court measures, and perhaps, had too entire a devotion to that pontifical power, which he esteemed the earthly dispenser of salvation, to dispute lightly with the Pope's legate, however surreptitiously his legatine office might have been obtained, or however indiscreetly exercised. It was not till the legality of the King's marriage began to be called in question, and the infallibility of the Vatican implicitly limited, that he became an obstacle at once to the King's passions and the Cardinal's purposes. Henry and Wolsey were alike bent on the repudiation of Catherine, who was now somewhat declined into the vale of years, with little hope of male issue. It is pretended that Wolsey's resentment against the Emperor Charles V., who had duped him with regard to the Papacy, was the fountain head of all those scruples, examinations, negociations, and protestations, which ended in the divorce between England and the church of Rome. The favourite intended to give his sovereign in marriage to the French King's sister, and the rupture with the Emperor likely to be occasioned by the slight put upon his aunt, would, in a manner, compel Henry to side with the French interest. However this might be, the majority of divines, casuists, and canonists, were agreed that the King's marriage

---

* " There is a tradition that King Henry's fool (though more truly to be termed by another name) coming into the court, and finding the King transported with an unusual joy, boldly asked him the cause thereof, to whom the King answered, it was because the Pope had honoured him with a style more eminent than any of his ancestors; " O good Harry, (quoth the fool,) let thou and I defend one another, and let the Faith alone to defend itself." Fuller's Church History. Book Vth.

Is the use of this title by the Protestant King's of England perfectly honest? It is not long since our sovereigns laid down the style of King's of France, and they did wisely; but of the two they had better have retained a memorial of the Fifth Harry's valour, than of the Eighth Harry's school divinity. Titles, ceremonial privileges, and armorial bearings, are only interesting or significant, in so far as they are historical. Let those then be maintained which are associated with the most glorious passages of history.

was unlawful, and the bull of Pope Julius II. invalid ; inasmuch as the alleged grounds for granting were not true. For in the preamble it was stated that the dispensation was granted at the special request of Prince Henry, who, at the *time* that the bull was obtained, had scarcely reached his twelfth year, and, as far as he had any will of his own, was strongly opposed to the bargain.

When, after many delays, it was at last decided by the Pope to send Campeggio as Wolsey's assessor, and that they, in the quality of commis- sioners for the Pope, should take cognizance of the cause pending between Henry and Catherine, Bishop Fisher, along with Nicholas West, Bishop of Ely, and Henry Standish, Bishop of St. Asaph, were appointed the Queen's advisers and counsel. Henry could have had no thought at that time, of disowning the Papal authority, for he appeared in person at the citation of the Pope's representatives, to answer their interrogatories.

" It was fashionable among the heathen," says old Fuller, " at the celebration of their centenary solemnities, which returned but once in a hundred years, to have a herald publickly to proclaim ' Come hither to behold what you never saw before, and are never likely to see again.'" But here happened such a spectacle, in a great room called the Parlia- ment chamber, in Blackfriars, as never before or after was seen in England, viz. King Henry summoned in his own land to appear before two judges, the one Wolsey, directly his subject by birth, the other his subject occasionally by his preferment, Campeggio being lately made Bishop of Salisbury. Summoned, he appeared personally, and the Queen did the like the first day, but afterwards both by their Doctors." As to be present on such a strange occasion would be no trivial incident in any man's life, and the part he bore in the proceedings was a most important one in Fisher's, we shall not scruple to extract largely from the account of this trial, given by Cavendish, the faithful servant and biographer of Wolsey, a contemporary, and probably an eye-witness, whose leaning, if any, was to the Queen's, which was also Fisher's side. It must be premised, that the trial commenced on the 31st of May, 1529.

" Then after some deliberation, his (Campeggio's) commission, under- stood, read, and perceived, it was by the council determined that the King and the Queen his wife, should be lodged at Bridewell,* and that

* The sending of the King and Queen to Bridewell seems ominous to modern ears, till they recollect (if ever they knew) that the Bridewell here meant was a magnificent house in Fleet-street, sometime the property of the extortioner Empson, but merged in the crown at his attainder, and given by the King to Wolsey. In the patent, dated 1510, an orchard and twelve gardens are enumerated as belonging to it. It stood

in the Black-Friars, a certain place should be appointed where the King and the Queen might most conveniently repair to the court, there to be erected and kept for the disputation and determination of the King's case, whereas these two legates sat in judgment as notable judges, before whom the King and Queen were duly cited and summoned to appear. Which was the strangest and newest sight, and device, that ever was heard or read in any history or chronicle in any region, that a King and Queen should be convented and constrained by process compellatory to appear in any court as common persons, within their own realm or dominion, to abide the judgment and decrees of their own subjects, having the royal diadem and the prerogatives thereof."

*   *   *   *   *

" If eyes be not blind men may see, if ears be not stopped they may hear, and if pity be not exiled they may lament, the sequel of this pernicious and inordinate carnal love. The plague whereof is not ceased, (although this love lasted but a while,) which our Lord quench, and take from us his indignation.

" Ye shall understand, that there was a court erected in the Black-Friars, in London, where these two Cardinals sat in judgment. Now will I set you out the manner and order of the court there. First, there was a court placed with tables, benches, and bars, like a consistory, a place judicial, for the judges to sit on. There was also a cloth of estate, under the which sat the King, and the Queen sat at some distance beneath the King : under the judges' feet sat the officers of the court. The chief scribe there was Dr. Stephens,* who was afterwards Bishop of Winchester : the apparitor was one Cooke, most commonly called Cooke of Winchester. Then sat there, within the said Court, directly before the King and the judges, the Archbishop of Canterbury, Doctor Warham, and all the other Bishops. Then at both ends, with a bar made for them, the counsellors on both sides. The Doctors for the King were Dr. Sampson, that was afterwards Bishop of Chichester, and Dr. Bell, who was afterwards Bishop of Worcester, with divers others.

---

upon the ground which is now occupied by Salisbury Square and Dorset-street, its gardens reaching to the river. In this Bridewell took place that interview between Queen Catherine and the two Cardinals, so beautifully dramatized by Shakespeare. Henry VIII. Act 3, Scene 1st.

* This was the Gardiner, " of undesirable celebrity," who in his younger days was usually called by his christian name, Stephen, or Stevens. He was the natural son of a Bishop, therefore he had but an equivocal title to a sirname.

It should be remembered, that the practitioners in the courts of civil and canon law were generally ecclesiastics before the Reformation.

"Now on the other side stood the counsel for the Queen; Dr. Fisher, Bishop of Rochester, and Dr. Standish, some time a Grey Friar, and then Bishop 'of St. Asaph, two notable clerks in Divinity; and *in especial the Bishop of Rochester*, a very godly man and a devout person, who after suffered death at Tower-Hill; the which was greatly lamented through all the foreign Universities of Christendom. There was also another ancient Doctor, called, as I remember, Doctor Ridley, a very small person in stature, but surely a great and an excellent clerk in Divinity.

"The court being thus furnished and ordered, the judges commanded the crier to proclaim silence: then was the judges' commission, which they had of the Pope, published and read openly, before all the audience there assembled. That done, the crier called the King by the name of 'King Henry of England, come into court,' &c. With that the King answered and said, 'Here, my Lords.' Then he called also the Queen, by the name of 'Catherine, Queen of England, come into court,' &c., who made no answer to the same, but rose up incontinent out of her chair, where as she sat, and because she could not come directly to the King for the distance which severed them, she took pain to go about unto the King, kneeling down at his feet in the sight of all the court and assembly, to whom she said, in effect, in broken English, as followeth :—*

"'Sir,' quoth she, 'I beseech you, for all the loves that have been

* "Here the Queen arose, and after her respects dealt to the Cardinals, in such manner as seemed neither uncivil to them, nor unsuiting to herself, uttered the following speech at the King's feet, in the English tongue, but with her Spanish tone, a clip whereof was so far from rendering it the less intelligible, that it sounded the more pretty and pleasant to the hearers thereof. *Yea, her very pronunciation pleaded for her with all ingenuous auditors, providing her some pity, as due to a foreigner far from her own country*".----*Fuller's Church History. Book V.*

The speech which Fuller puts into the Queen's mouth is essentially the same as that in Cavendish, from whom it was transferred into the Chronicles. Shakespeare has shown his good sense and good feeling by preserving it almost entire in his Henry VIII.

"Hall has given a different report of this speech of the Queen's, which he says was made in *French*, and translated by him, as well as he could, from notes taken by Campeggio's secretary. In his version she accuses Wolsey with being the first mover of her troubles, and reproaches him, in bitter terms, with pride and voluptuousness. Such harsh language could hardly deserve the praise '*modeste tamen eam locutam fuisse*' given by Campeggio.----*Note to Singer's edition of Cavendish's Life of Wolsey.*

Burnet, whose "cue" was not to excite compassion for Queen Catherine, denies the authenticity of the speech altogether. He affirms positively that the King did not appear personally, but by proxy; and that the Queen withdrew after reading a protest against the competency of the judges "And from this it is clear," says the

between us, and for the love of God, let me have justice and right; take of me some pity and compassion, for I am a poor woman and a stranger, born out of your dominions. I have no assured friend, and much less indifferent counsel, I flee to you as to the head of justice within this realm. Alas, Sir, wherein have I offended you, or what occasion of displeasure? Have I designed against your will and pleasure, intending, as I perceive, to put me from you? I take God and all the world to witness, that I have been to you a true, humble, and obedient wife, ever conformable to your will and pleasure, that never said or did any thing to the contrary thereof, being always well pleased and contented with all things in which you had any delight or dalliance, whether it were in little or in much, I never grudged in word or countenance, or shewed a visage or spark of discontentation. I loved all those whom ye loved, only for your sake, whether I had cause or no, and whether they were my friends or my enemies. This twenty years I have been your true wife, or more, and by me you have had divers children, although it hath pleased God to call them out of this world, which hath been no default in me. And when ye had me at the first, I take God to be my judge I was a true maid; and whether it be true or no, I put it to your conscience. If there be any just cause by the law that ye can allege against me, either of dishonesty or any other impediment, to banish and put me from you, I am well content to depart, to my great shame and dishonour; and if there be none, then here I most lowly beseech you, let me remain in my former estate, and receive justice at your hands. The King your father was, in the time of his reign, of such estimation throughout the world for his excellent

Bishop, "that the speeches that the historians have made for them are all plain falsities." It is easy to contradict the confident affirmation of the historian, upon the authority of a document published by himself in his records, p. 78. It is a letter from the King to his agents, where he says, "At which time both we and the Queen appeared in person, and they minding to proceed further in the cause, the Queen would no longer make her abode to hear what the judges would fully discern, but incontinently departed out of the court; wherefore she was thrice *preconnisate*, and called eftsoons to return and appear, which she refusing to do, was denounced by the judges, *contumax*, and a citation decerned for her appearance on Friday." Which is corroborated also by *Fox's Acts*, p. 958. Indeed the testimony for the personal appearance of the King before the Cardinals is surprisingly powerful, even though we did not go beyond Cavendish and the other ordinary historians. But in addition to these, Dr. Wordsworth has produced the authority of William Thomas, Clerk of the Council in the reign of Edward VI., who, in a professed apology for King Henry VIII. extant in MS. in the Lambeth and some other libraries, speaking of this affair, affirms, "that the Cardinal Campeggio caused the King, as a private party, in person to appear before him, and the Lady Catherine both."--*Singer*.

wisdom, that he was accounted and called of all men the second Solomon, and my father, Ferdinand, King of Spain, who was esteemed to be one of the wittiest Princes that reigned in Spain, many years before, were both wise and excellent Kings in wisdom and princely behaviour. It is not therefore to be doubted, but that they elected and gathered as wise counsellors about them as to their high discretions was thought meet. Also, as to me seemeth, there were in those days as wise and as well learned men, and men of as good judgment as be at present in both realms, who thought then the marriage betwixt you and me good and lawful. Surely it is a wonder unto me, that my marriage, after twenty years, should be thus called in question, with new invention against me, that never intended but honesty. Alas, Sir, I see I am wronged, having no indifferent counsel to speak for me, but such as are assigned me, with whose wisdom and learning I am not acquainted. Ye must consider, that they cannot be indifferent counsellors for my part which be your subjects, and taken out of your own council before, wherein they be made privy, and dare not, for your displeasure, disobey your will, being once made privy thereunto. Therefore I most humbly require you, in the way of charity, and for the love of God, who is a just judge, to spare me the extremity of this new court until I may be advertised what way and order my friends in Spain will advise me to take. And if ye will not extend to me so much indifferent favour, your pleasure then be fulfilled, and to God I commit my cause." Having thus spoken, she rose, courtesied to the King, and left the court, accompanied by Griffith, her steward, and though summoned a second time in due form, she refused to return, or in any way to acknowledge the jurisdiction of the court; nor could she ever after be induced to appear before it. Nevertheless, the trial or rather examination proceeded, the Queen being adjudged contumacious.

According to the author just quoted, the King next addressed himself to the judges and audience; commencing with a full acknowledgement of Catherine's freedom from all personal offence, and resting his cause solely on his conscientious scruples. "For as much," quoth he, " as the Queen be gone, I will in her absence declare unto you all my Lords here presently assembled, she hath been to me as true, as obedient, and as conformable a wife as I could, in my fancy, wish or desire. She hath all the virtuous qualities that ought to be in a woman of her dignity, or in any other of baser estate. Surely she is also a noble woman born, if nothing were in her, but only her conditions will well declare the same."

He then, after explaining the first suggestion, and progressive corroboration of his scruples, (to which he would not allow that any amorous considerations were accessory,) demanded of the assembled Prelates, and first of his own Confessor, Longland, Bishop of Lincoln, whether his present course were not taken with their advice and approbation, signified under their own seals." Whereupon, if we believe the biographer of Wolsey, a singular scene took place, in which Fisher displayed uncommon boldness of soul and bluntness of speech. The Archbishop of Canterbury obsequiously assented to the King's assertion. "That is the truth if it please your Highness ; I doubt not but all my brethren here present will affirm the same." "No sir, not I," quoth the Bishop of Rochester, "ye have not my consent thereto." No! ha! the !! quoth the King, "look here upon this ; is not this your hand and seal ?" and shewed him the instrument with seals. "No forsooth, sire," quoth the Bishop of Rochester, "it is not my hand nor seal." To that quoth the King to my Lord of Canterbury, "Sir, how say ye ? Is it not his hand and seal ?" "Yes, sir," quoth my Lord of Canterbury. "That is not so," quoth the Bishop of Rochester, "for indeed you were in hand with me to have both my hand and seal, as other of my Lords had already done ; but then I said to you, that I would never consent to no such act, for it were much against my conscience, nor my hand and seal should never be seen at no such instrument, God willing, with much more matter touching the same communication between us." "You say truth," quoth the *Bishop* of Canterbury, "such words ye said unto me ; but at the last ye were fully persuaded that I should for you subscribe your name, and put to a seal myself, and ye would allow the same," "All which words and matter," quoth the Bishop of Rochester, "under your correction my Lord, and supportation of this noble audience, there is no thing more untrue." "Well, well," quoth the king, "it shall make no matter, we will not stand with you in argument herein, for you are but one man." And with that the court was adjourned to the next day of session.

The next court day the Cardinals met again, but neither the King nor the Queen were present. The discussions, which are given at great length by some historians, respected chiefly the circumstances of the marriage between the Prince Arthur and the Lady Catherine, which was positively declared by the Queen and her counsel to have been a mere ceremony. The evidence of course was circumstantial, and the conclusion come to by the one side, seemingly very just, that it was impossible to know the truth : But this, though urged by his own party, did not satisfy Fisher.

"Yes," quoth the Bishop of Rochester, "*Ego nosco veritatem*, I know the truth." "How know you the truth," quoth my Lord Cardinal. "Forsooth, my Lord," quoth he, "*Ego sum professor veritatis*, I know that God is truth itself, nor he never spake but truth that saith, " whom God hath joined together, let no man put asunder, and forasmuch as this marriage was made and joined by God to a good intent, I say that I know, the which cannot be broken or loosed by the power of man upon no feigned occasion."   " So much do all faithful men know, quoth the Lord Cardinal, as well as you.   Yet this reason is not sufficient in this case, for the King's counsel doth alledge divers presumptions to prove the marriage not good at the beginning, *ergo*, say they, it was *not* joined by God at the beginning, and therefore it is not lawful; for God ordaineth nor joineth nothing without a just order.   Therefore it is not to be doubted but that these presumptions must be true, as it plainly appeareth; and nothing can be more true in case these allegations cannot be avoided; therefore to say that the matrimony was joined of God, ye must prove it further than by that text which ye have alledged for your matter; for ye must first avoid the presumptions."   " Then," quoth one Doctor Ridley, " it is a shame and a great dishonour to this honourable presence, that any such presumptions should be alledged in this open court, which be to all good and honest men most detestable to be rehearsed."   " What," quoth my Lord Cardinal, " *Domine Doctor, magis reverenter*."   " No, no, my Lord," quoth he " there belongeth no reverence to be given to these abominable presumptions; for an unreverend tale would be unreverently answered."   And there they left, and proceeded no farther at that time."

The exertions of Fisher in defence of the legality of the Queen's marriage, were not confined to these altercations, to which divorce causes have ever been disgracefully liable.   He addressed a letter to Wolsey in her favour, and presented to the legates a book entitled " De causa matrimonii Regis Angliæ."*   " The Case of the King of England's marriage."   But it was neither books nor legates that were to stop the course of Henry's will.   The separation of Britain from the Roman communion was decreed, and providence ordered that the passions of men should minister to the mighty end, that so the glory might be God's alone.

The investigation was protracted from sitting to sitting, and no real progress made, or intended to be made.   Henry, weary and impatient,

---

* " This work of Fisher's was long supposed to exist only in MS. but in the public auction of Don Jos Antonio Conde's library, a printed copy was purchased for Mr. Heber, which appears to have issued from the press of Alcala (Complutum) in Spain, the printer of which says, that the manuscript copy was given him by the Archbishop of Toledo.   It is probable that the Spanish agents in England contrived to obtain a copy, and sent it to the Emperor Charles V.   It would not have been permitted to issue from the press in England."---*Singer*.

at the suggestion, it is said, of the Earl of Wiltshire, father to Anne Boleyn, urged, and in a manner compelled the two Cardinals to repair to the Queen's apartments, * and persuade her by their politic and ghostly counsels, to avoid the scandal and mortification of the public trial, by surrendering the whole matter, with her own free consent, to the King's discretion.   This was, in effect, commanding her to resign her connubial rights and royal dignity, and to retire into a convent, or any other place, where she might be out of the way.   She remonstrated with much dignity, and shewed much unwillingness to trust the two churchmen, who pretended to advise her for the best.   She complained that she was " a simple woman, destitute and barren of friendship and counsel in a foreign region," and never could be brought to gratify the King by confessing herself to have lived for so many years in unholy matrimony.   Her reliance on her nephew, the Emperor, whose influence over the vacillating Pope Clement had alone prevented the disso_ lution of her marriage by Papal authority, emboldened her to avoid the snare, which was laid before her eyes.   To the Pope she had privily appealed, and the Imperial interest now preponderating at the Vatican, Campeggio received secret instructions, unknown, it is said, to Wolsey, to adjourn the court and advoke the cause to Rome.   The artful Italian spun out the trial till the 23rd of July, when there was a general expectation that the definitive sentence would be passed.

The King was seated in a gallery, where " he might both see and

* According to the narrative of his attendant, Wolsey was very indignant at being forced into this service; not the less probably, though Cavendish does not admit it, because he saw that Anne Boleyn was to reap the fruit of all his intrigues in first setting the divorce on foot, and then delaying its completion till his own schemes were perfected. The Earl of Wiltshire, therefore, was naturally the most unwelcome messenger that could have been despatched to him.

" To fulfil the King's pleasure my Lord said he was ready, and would prepare him to go thither out of hand," (he was in bed when the King's commands were brought him,) saying further to my Lord of Wiltshire, " Ye, and other my Lords of the council, which be near unto the King, are not a little to blame and misadvised to put any such phantasies into his head, whereby ye are the causes of great trouble to all the realm, and in the end get you but small thanks either of God or of the world," with many other vehement words and sentences that were like to ensue of this matter, which caused my Lord of Wiltshire to *water his eyes*, kneeling all this while by my Lord's bedside, and in conclusion departed."---*Singer's Cavendish, p.* 226.

It appears from the following passage, that George Cavendish himself attended his master, the Cardinal, on this visit, and was ear witness to the first part of the conference, which Shakspeare has versified. " And with that she took my Lord by the hand, and led him into her privy chamber, with the other Cardinal; where they were in long communication; *we*, in the other chamber, might sometime hear the Queen speak very loud, but what it was *we* could not understand."

hear all speak;" the whole proceedings were read over in Latin, and then the King's counsel prayed for judgment. But Campeggio absolutely refused to make any decision, before he had laid the whole matter before the Pope, and received his Holiness's orders, declaring " that he would damn his soul for no prince or potentate alive," and so adjourned the court, which never met again. The cause was in appearance removed to Rome, whither Campeggio soon returned ; and so ended the period of Fisher's official advocacy for Queen Catherine ; but he continued to the end of his life to maintain the justice of her cause.

The Parliament met Nov. 3, 1529. The Commons, who always looked upon the wealth of the clergy with invidious eyes, expecting, without much wisdom, to be gainers by its diminution, however that were brought about, zealously entered into the King's design of humbling the church of Rome. Violent censures were passed upon the vices of the ecclesiastics, the suppression of monasteries began to be rumoured, and no less than six bills were introduced " which at once gratified the present humour of the King, and the constant temper of the people," all tending to depress the sacerdotal order : 1st. Against the extortions of the ecclesiastical courts : 2nd. Against their exactions in mortuaries, &c. 3rd. Their worldly occupations, as tanning, grazing, &c. : 4th. Merchandize : 5th. Non-residence : 6th. Pluralities. Very much the same subjects of complaint that are reiterated to this day. Some of them were abuses which Fisher would gladly have seen the clergy reform in themselves ; but, he had so high a notion of the sanctity of priesthood, that he abhorred the attempts of the laity to resist priestly oppression. When the six bills were brought up to the House of Lords, he spoke in his place as follows :—

" My Lords, here are certain bills exhibited against the clergy, wherein there are complaints made against the viciousness, idleness, rapacity, and cruelty of the Bishops, Abbots, Priests, and their officials ; but, my Lords, are all idle, all vicious, all ravenous, or cruel Priests and Bishops ?   And for such as are so, are there no laws already provided against them ?   Is there any abuse that we do not seek to rectify ?   Or can there be such a rectification, as that there shall be no abuses ?   Or are not clergymen to rectify the abuses of the clergy ?   Or shall men find fault with other men's manners while they forget their own, and punish where they have no authority to correct ?   If we be not executive in our laws, let each man suffer for his delinquency ; or if we have not power, aid us with your assistance, and we shall give you thanks. But, my Lords, I hear that there is a motion made that the small monasteries shall be taken into the King's hands, which makes me fear that it is not so much the GOOD, as the GOODS of the church, that is looked after. Truly, my Lords, how this may sound in your ears, I cannot tell; but to me it appears no otherwise than as if our holy mother, the Church, were to become a bond-maid, and be new brought into servility and thraldom, and by little and little to be quite banished out of those dwelling places, which the piety and liberality of our forefathers, as most bountiful benefactors, have conferred upon her; otherwise, to what tendeth these portentous and curious petitions of the Commons? To no other intent or purpose, but to bring the clergy into contempt with the laity, that they may seize their patrimony. But, my Lords, beware of yourselves and your country; beware of your Holy mother the Catholic Church; the people are subject unto novelties, and Lutheranism spreads itself amongst us. Remember Germany and Bohemia, what miseries are befallen them already: and let our neighbours' houses that are now on fire teach us to beware of our own disasters. Wherefore, my Lords, I will tell you plainly what I think; that except ye resist manfully, by your authorities, this violent heap of mischiefs offered by the Commons, ye will see all obedience first drawn from the clergy, and secondly from yourselves. And if you search into the true causes of all these mischiefs which reign among them, you shall find that they all arise through *want of faith.*"

This speech, which was any thing but conciliatory, while it was highly applauded by those who abhorred or dreaded change, excited the alarm and indignation of the Reformers in both Houses, and was not calculated to remove from the King himself those unfavourable dispositions which the Bishop's conduct in the divorce business had occasioned. The Duke of Norfolk, who was nearly connected with Anne Boleyn, arose in his place and said, " My Lord of Rochester, many of these words might well have been spared; but it is often seen, that the greatest clerks are not always the wisest men." Fisher retorted, " My Lord, I do not remember any fools in my time that proved great clerks." But the Commons were particularly scandalized at the conclusion of this harangue, which plainly ascribed their enmity to the clergy to their unbelief in the Catholic doctrines. As soon as they were informed of this attack, they sent Sir Thomas Audley, their speaker, with thirty of their members, to complain before the King, to whom, as they shrewdly suspected, complaints against Bishop Fisher were far from unacceptable. The speaker, in the name of the Commons of England, set forth " how shameful and injurious it was that they, the chosen representatives of the English people, selected from among their countrymen for their wisdom, virtue, and good fame, should be taxed (and through them the Commons of all England) with infidelity and atheism." The King summoned the Bishop to his presence, and asked him, sternly, " Why he spake thus?" Fisher justified himself by saying, " that being in council, he spake his mind in defence of the Church, which he saw daily injured and oppressed by the common people, whose office it was not to judge of her manners, much less to reform them; and therefore he thought himself in conscience bound to defend her all he could." Henry, in his latter years, when he was utterly corrupted by the habit of despotism, would scarce have endured this plain speaking; but he had an old reverence for Fisher, which he had not yet quite shaken off, so he dismissed him with an admonition, " to use his words more temperately." But some explanation was necessary to appease the House of Commons, which Henry wished to keep in good humour, as the most legal and convenient instrument of his rapacity and of his vengeance. So the venerable Prelate was forced to the subterfuge, that it was the troubles of Bohemia, not the acts of the Commons, which he ascribed to want of faith; and this *explanation*, which the speech, as delivered down to us, will by no means admit, was conveyed to the House by Sir William Fitz-Williams, the Treasurer of the King's Household. Burnet says, that *" though the matter was passed over, they were not at all satisfied with it."* If they really hated the church, they could not have obtained a more satisfactory triumph than that of compelling a Bishop to prevaricate in his own defence. The speech was very injudicious and ill-timed. Nothing tends so much to precipitate revolution as imputing revolutionary purposes to all proposals of reform; and refusing what is justly claimed, because the concession may be followed by a further and unjust claim. And the people will always be more reasonably satisfied with a moderate reform, in which they themselves *appear* to co-operate, than with a much larger *boon*, the acceptance of which is an acknowledgment of subjection. But if only one man, in his zeal for established things, declare that there shall be no reform, he is *politically* answerable for whatever extremities may follow. Fisher, it is true, when he was addressing the clergy, insisted on the propriety of their reforming themselves, but he could not persuade the laity that the clergy ever would voluntarily reform abuses which it was their interest to perpetuate.

In the autumn of 1529 a side-blow was aimed at the Court of Rome, which, though its immediate intention was only to ruin Wolsey, tended to break the connection between the English clergy and the Pope, by making it penal. The Lords had drawn up forty-four articles of accusation against Wolsey, which passed through their House without

much opposition; but in the House of Commons, Thomas Cromwell *
defended his master's cause with so much spirit and argumentative
power, as to prove that it is not absolutely true, that " a favourite has
no friend." The object was to deprive the Cardinal of his wealth, his
great offence in the public eye, as his supposed double-dealing in
the matter of the divorce was his crime against the King, who was
not insensible that confiscation is generally popular with the many,
and the spoils of the mighty always acceptable to the mightier.
But the forty-four articles† were either so weak in themselves, or so

* "The case stood so, that there should begin shortly after All-Hallown-tide the
Parliament, and he (Master Cromwell) being within London, devised within himself
to be one of the burgesses of the Parliament, and chanced to meet with one Sir
Thomas Rush, Knight, a special friend of his, whose son was appointed to be one of
the burgesses of that Parliament, of whom he obtained his room, and by that means
put his foot into the Parliament House: then within two or three days after his entry
he came unto my Lord (Wolsey), at Esher, with a much pleasanter countenance than
he had at his departure, and meeting with me before he came to my Lord, said unto
me, " that he had once adventured to put his foot where he expected shortly to be
better regarded, or all were done."---*Cavendish's Wolsey, p.* 273.
So the friendly traffic in parliamentary seats, at which " our ancestors would have
started with indignation," was not unknown in the reign of Henry VIII. True there
is no mention of money given or received, but it is plain that no constituents were
consulted on the occasion.

† The character of Wolsey has been hardly dealt with; not too hardly, if we compare what he was with what a minister and ruler of Christ's people ought to be; but
comparing him with the class of clerical statesmen to which he belonged, he had so
many virtues, and has been even accused of so few and trivial offences, that surely his
memory might plead for less rigorous justice. He was a very bad clergyman, he was
not a good man, but he was not by any means a wicked politician. The atrocities
which blacken the reign of Henry VIII. did not begin till after, and did begin almost
immediately after, his disgrace and dismissal. He appears to have truly loved his
King; he was a kind, an affectionate master to his dependants, and was much
beloved by some who knew him well. The narrative of his life by his servant Cavendish, is one of the most delightfully affecting pieces of biography that we ever read.
For the gentleness with which it shadows, not conceals defects, and the warm light of
affection in which it brings out every semblance of goodness, it vies with Johnson's
Life of Savage; but over all, and through all, there is a deep gratitude, a veneration,
a religious loyalty, and a holy mourning for the departed, which is peculiarly its own.
Cavendish was a zealous Catholic, but not as such had he any cause to consecrate the
ashes of Wolsey, who certainly hurried the downfal of his church, by rendering its
wealth and power the objects of universal envy, and set the example of diverting the
monastic revenues to other purposes than those for which they were bequeathed. As
Fuller felicitously expresses it, " having of his own such a stock of preferment,
nothing but the poor man's *Ewe Lamb* would please him, so that being to found two
colleges, he seized on no fewer than forty small monasteries, turning their inhabitants
out of house and home, and converting their means principally to a college in Oxford.

ably rebutted, that the Commons, perhaps the King himself, were ashamed to proceed upon them.   However there was a *rusty sword*, (to

This alienation was confirmed by the present Pope Clement the Seventh, so that in some sort his Holiness may thank himself for the demolishing of Religious Houses in England.   For the first breach is greatest in effect; and Abbies having now lost their virginity, diverted by the Pope to other purposes, soon after lost their chastity, perverted by the King to ordinary uses."   If in addition to this, Wolsey really did instigate the divorce to bring about a French alliance, he did as much as the folly of man could do, towards bringing about the Reformation. But this his devoted servant would not believe.   Cavendish's account of the prosecution of his master, and of Wolsey's defence, is so clear and interesting, that we may be allowed to extract it, if it were only because Wolsey was an Archbishop of York.

"Then was there brought in a Bill of Articles into the Parliament House to have my Lord condemned of treason; against which bill Master Cromwell inveighed so discreetly, with such witty persuasions and deep reasons, that the same bill could there take no effect.   Then were his enemies compelled to indite him in a præmunire, and all was done only to the intent to entitle the King to all his goods and possessions, the which he had gathered together and purchased for his colleges in Oxford and Ipswich, and for the maintenance of the same, which was then a building in most sumptuous wise.   Wherein, when he was demanded by the judges which were sent to him purposely to examine him, what answer he would make to the same, he said, ' The King's Highness knoweth right well whether I have offended his Majesty and his laws or no, in using of my prerogative legatine, for the which ye have me indited.   Notwithstanding I have the King's license in my coffers, under his broad seal, for exercising and using the authority thereof, in the largest wise, within his Highness' dominions, the which remaineth now in the hands of my enemies.   Therefore, because I will not stand in trial or question with the King in his own cause, I am content here, of mine own frank will and mind, in your presence, to confess the offence in the inditement, and put myself wholly in the mercy and grace of the King, having no doubt in his godly disposition and charitable conscience, whom I know hath an high discretion to consider the truth, and my humble submission and obedience.   And although I might justly stand on the trial with him therein, yet am I content to submit myself to his clemency, and thus much ye may say unto him in my behalf, that I am intirely in his obedience, and do intend, God willing, to obey and fulfil all his princely pleasure in every thing that he will command me to do; whose will and pleasure I never yet disobeyed or repugned, but was always contented and glad to accomplish his desire and command before God, whom I ought most rather to have obeyed; the which negligence greatly reproveth me.   Notwithstanding, I most heartily require you to have me most humbly to his royal Majesty commended, for whom I do and will pray for the preservation of his royal person, long to reign in honour, prosperity, and quietness, and to have the victory over his mortal and cankered enemies."   And they took their leave of him and departed.----*Cavendish*, 274, 275, 276, 277.

If Wolsey was not the best of Chancellors, he well understood the duties of his office, as will appear from his speech made to the King's emissaries, who came to demand of him to surrender to the crown York Place, now White-Hall, an ancient appanage of his diocese :——

recur to a favourite expression of Bentley's, who was a Henry the Eighth in his way,) which served the purpose, and a deeper purpose too. This was the *statute* of *Provisors*, which made it criminal to procure any bull, or the appointment to any benefice, from the Pope, under the penalty of a *præmunire,** which was, (the very thing wanted) a forfeiture of all effects, real and personal to the King, and an outlawry, or exclusion from the King's protection. In a *præmunire* therefore he was indicted, chiefly on the ground that his obtaining and exercising the office of legate by virtue of a bull from Rome, came

"Master Shelley, I know the King of his own nature is of a royal stomach, and yet not willing more than justice shall lead him unto by the law. And therefore I counsel you and all other fathers of the law, and learned men of his council, to put no more into his head than the law may stand with good conscience; for when ye tell him, this is the law, it were well done ye should tell him also, that although *this* be the law, yet *this* is conscience; for law without conscience is not good to be given unto a King in counsel to use for a lawful right, but always to have a respect to conscience before the rigour of the law, for *laus est facere quod decet, non quod licet.* The King ought of his royal dignity and prerogative to mitigate the rigour of the law where conscience hath the most force; therefore in the royal place of equal justice he hath constituted a Chancellor, an officer to execute justice with clemency, where conscience is opposed by the rigour of the law. And therefore the Court of Chancery hath been heretofore commonly called the Court of Conscience; because it hath jurisdiction to command the high ministers of law to spare execution and judgment where conscience hath most effect. Therefore I say to you in this case, although you and other of your profession perceive by your learning that the King may, by an order of your laws, lawfully do that thing which ye demand of me; how say you, Master Shelley, may I do it with justice and conscience, to give that away from me and my successors which is none of mine? If this be law with conscience, shew me your opinion I pray you."

* A critic would certainly reckon this barbarous Latin word among those *quæ versu dicere non est*, which are incapable of naturalization in the kingdom of Parnassus; yet Shakespeare has introduced it into blank verse, a proof of the truly *historical* feeling in which historical plays were written and heard. He commits no such enormities in his *tragedies.*

> SUFFOLK—Lord Cardinal, the King's further pleasure is,
>   Because all those things you have done of late,
>   By your power legatine within this kingdom,
>   Fall into the compass of a *præmunire*,
>   That therefore such a writ be sued against you,
>   To forfeit all your goods, lands, tenements,
>   Castles, and whatsoever, and to be
>   Out of the King's protection. ACT 3, SCENE 2.

The same scene continues a tolerably ample enumeration of the principal charges against Wolsey.

The statute of Præmunire was passed A.D. 1393.

within the compass of the statute. It would have been no avail for
Wolsey to plead, that he had the King's express and written permission
to accept and exercise that office, and indeed, he had reason to be thankful that instead of an old law of præmunire, he was not included in a
new law of treason. The *statute of Provisor* was indeed a production
of the age of Richard II., but it had grown almost obsolete. Its
enforcement was therefore an ill omen from the Papal power in
England, for its provisions gave the King all the supremacy which any
King ought to claim, the supremacy over all property, and all temporal
power, however sanctified, in his own dominions. It forbad any subject
to withdraw his person or property from the common operation of the
land's law. It was a good act, and King Henry did well and wisely in
making it effective, for till his time it had little more than the declaration of a right in abeyance. But since his predecessors had suffered it
to sleep, and he himself had formally dispensed with its violation, even to
the extent of pleading before the Legate, in his own person, in his own
dominions, he should not have given any retrospective or punitive effect.
But Wolsey's destruction was determined, and with that the King was
for the present content ; but afterwards, his avarice increasing with his
years, he included the whole clergy and laity of England in a præmunire for their compliance with the legatine authority. The clergy were
fain to compromise the matter with one hundred and eighteen thousand
eight hundred and forty pounds, a sum more than equal to half a million of present money. The laity were held in suspense awhile, and their
supplications for indemnity haughtily answered ; but at last they had a
free pardon. All these were progressive steps towards the final breach
with Rome, and consequent ecclesiastical revolution ; but it does not
appear that any of the superior clergy opposed the condemnation of
Wolsey on such anti-papal grounds. They rejoiced in the fall of him
who had outshone and overawed them, and reckoned not how soon they
were themselves to be curtailed of their gettings,—not by the poor
Commons, against whom their invectives were levelled, but by that
monarchy and aristocracy with which it was their pride to vie. Fisher
had no affection for Wolsey, and was as short sighted as the generality
of narrow minded honest men. Besides he had already made himself
obnoxious both to King and people, and had no hopes of bettering the
church's prospects, or his own, by thrusting himself between " the lion
and his wrath."

The year 1530 was one of the most eventful years in the history of
the world, and a perilous year for Bishop Fisher. Twice was his life
attacked ; it is not very plain why. One Rouse, or Rose, who was
acquainted with the Bishop's cook, came into his kitchen, and while the

cook was gone to fetch him some drink, made use of his opportunity to mingle poison in the gruel that was preparing for the Bishop and his household. Probably it was a fast day; for the Bishop, fasting altogether, escaped; but of seventeen persons, who partook of the gruel, two died, and the rest were terribly disordered. We may suppose the crime of poisoning to have been frightfully common in England, since it was thought necessary, by an express act, to declare it high-treason, and to punish it by boiling alive, which horrible death was inflicted upon the miserable Rouse. If he thought to please the King by removing a thorn out of his side, he found himself mistaken. But it is more likely that he was a fanatic, whom Fisher's severity in enforcing the laws against heresy had driven mad. Excessive cruelty in punishment rarely answers its purpose, for we find that the example of boiling Rouse did not deter a woman servant from poisoning three families; She suffered the same penalty, which was abolished along with the rest of Henry the Eighth's new invented treasons. It is the chance of impunity; not the lenity of punishment that encourages crime. The Spanish inquisition was the only system of cruelty that perfectly answered its end; but this succeeded rather by destroying all confidence and security than by the terror of its ghastly tortures.

The other danger which threatened the Bishop proceeded from a cannon ball, which being shot from the other side of the Thames, pierced through his house at Lambeth-marsh, and only just missed his study. This might possibly be accidental, but Fisher suspected a design against his life, and retired to his see of Rochester.

The divorce cause, which, upon the Queen's appeal, had been *advoked* to Rome, still lingered on. The case had been divided into three and twenty heads, and a year was consumed in discussing the first, which had little relation to the main point, and was of a nature which had better not been discussed at all. Perhaps the suit was wilfully protracted, in hopes that the death of Catherine would end it in the most convenient manner; for she had many infirmities, and a breaking heart: but this prospect suited not the impatience of Henry. That he endured so long delay can only be ascribed to his reluctance to break with the see of Rome. But accident about this time introduced him to Cranmer, and all his scruples were quickly removed. In 1521 it was first proposed in Convocation to bestow on the King the title of Supreme Head of the Church. Fisher opposed the innovation, which to him appeared blasphemous, with all his might, and succeeded so far as to get a clause inserted to the effect, that the King was acknowledged Head of the Church, IN SO FAR AS IT IS LAWFUL BY THE LAW OF CHRIST, which was almost taking away with the one hand what was given by the other.   In this form, however, it passed the upper house of Convocation, nine Bishops and fifty-two Abbots and Priors voting in its favour.

If we are to believe the author of the Life of Bishop Fisher, published under the name of Bailey, but really composed by Hall, a bigotted Romanist, and seminary priest at Cambray, King Henry was mightily enraged at the introduction of this neutralizing ingredient into his title.   He sent for those whom he had employed to manage the business in the Convocation, and rated in the following kingly strain:—" Mother of God! you have played me a pretty prank: I thought to have made fools of them, and now you have so ordered the business that they are likely to make a fool of me, as they have done of you already,   Go unto them again, and let me have the business passed without any *quantums* or *tantums*.   I will have no *quantums* or *tantums* in the business, but let it be done."   But in truth, there is nothing in eastern fiction more unfounded than the reports of Princes' private conversations with which many so-called histories abound.   The poet may well be allowed to overhear the whispers of lovers, and the soliloquies of captives in their dungeons, but the historian should not usurp the same privilege.   This assumption of supremacy met with little opposition in the province of Canterbury, but York, encouraged by Archbishop Lee, held out long and honourably, and sent two letters to his Majesty, respectfully informing him of their reasons for denying the title he claimed.   The King, the evil of whose violent nature was not yet ripened, answered the northern Convocation in a mild and argumentative letter, probably composed, however, by Cranmer, in which " he disclaimed all design by fraud to surprise, or by force to captivate, their judgments, but only to convince them of the truth, and the equity of what he desired.   He declared the sense of "*Supreme Head of the Church*," (though offensive in the sound to ignorant ears) claiming nothing thereby more than what christian princes in the primitive times assumed to themselves in their own dominions, so that it seems he wrought so far on their affections, that at last they consented thereunto."

So says that stout Church and King man, Tom Fuller ; but we believe that the King's prerogative, after all, was more effective than his sophistry.   If nothing more be meant by the King's supremacy than his right to govern the persons and properties of *all* his subjects, this had been asserted over and over again by almost every monarch in Europe.   Even the royal right to the appointment of Bishops, &c., to the summoning convocations and synods, and the passing of regulative ordinances for the Church, was not altogether a new claim, though it had been stoutly resisted by the more zealous Church-men. And indeed, however expedient it may be in a secular point of view, that such power be vested in the crown, it is utterly without example in the primitive church, or even analogy in the Jewish theocracy. It is a moot point whether the Bishops who purchased of Constantine an establishment for Christianity, and a secular rank for themselves, were not traitors to the Church. The question should be argued on grounds of christian expediency. If, however, it be deemed necessary that the Church possess a fixed property, and that property be the foundation of political privileges, it seems inconsistent with public safety, that the civil government should suffer the disposal of such property to pass out of its own hands. But Henry, following the precedent of Constantino-politan Emperors, doubtless meant, by assuming the spiritual supremacy within his own dominions, to be lord of his subjects' faith as well as of their works, and to dispose of their creeds as well as of their properties; in fact, to be *Alterius orbis Papa*, the Pope of his own kingdom. Now of all possible tyrannies, this would have been the worst. No need to suppose a succession of Harry the Eigths. Such a power would have been fatal to all civil and intellectual freedom, even if possessed by Princes mild, intelligent, and pious as Charles the First. That no toleration would have been admitted or admissible, that every shade of opinion or mode of adoration that did not accord with the fancy of the reigning monarch would be subject to the penalties of treason; and, on the other hand, that every effort on behalf of civil liberty would be treated as schism or sacrilege, would not have been the worst conse-quence of the royal and national papacy. There would have been a new creed at least with every reign, perhaps with every year. The Church would have been impoverished and the clergy ruined by capri-cious changes in garments, which would be altered as frequently and as expensively as the uniforms of crack regiments. But worse than all, nobody who wished to be saved in the Church Royal would know what to believe, or how to pray. It is by no means impossible that the immortality of the soul might have been abolished, or purgatory esta-blished by royal proclamation, and royal proclamations would then have had the force of laws.

We think, therefore, that the clergy of Yorkshire and the other northern provinces acted commendably in delaying to transfer their spiritual allegiance; for as Henry still maintained the doctrines of the Church of Rome,—nay, even burned many for the disbelief of tenets grounded solely on the authority and tradition of that Church—tenets of which he could have no proof that did not rest on the infallibility of that Church, of which the papacy is the sealing stone. The mere act of separation from the Catholic body was on Henry's part an act of schism, however justifiable in those real reformers, who held conscientiously that the Popes had been, and continued to be, corrupters of christianity, and upholders of corruption.

But unfortunately for their own credit, the adherents of the ancient Church attempted to support their failing cause by means the most ill-judged and unjustifiable; and Bishop Fisher in his old age betrayed a degree of credulity, or rather gullibility, which the darkness of the time can hardly excuse. At the same time, we entirely acquit him of any participation in, or connivance at, the fraud. He was one of those good men who think the excellence of faith consists in believing readily and much. He was weak and grey-headed. He saw that Church which he esteemed the kingdom of heaven upon earth, and the Israel of God, in peril of being led away captive; and thought that if ever power divine displayed itself at time of need, that time was come.

> Nothing almost sees miracles,
> But miseries.

In the parish of Aldington, in Kent, there lived a young woman, named Elizabeth Barton, of mean birth and no education, who was subject to that sort of epileptic fits which the ignorance of mankind was wont to attribute either to possession or inspiration. When in these trances, she uttered wild incoherent speeches, which sometimes seemed to have relation to the passages of the times. Hereupon Masters, the priest of Adlington, hoping to draw much custom by means of this poor diseased creature, drew up an account of her ravings and prophecyings, and went to the Archbishop Warham, and wrought so successfully upon the aged prelate, that he received orders to attend the damsel carefully, and bring tidings of any new trances she might fall into. It is probable that the woman was not from the beginning an impostor; but rather affected with that sort of docile insanity which has proved in past times so serviceable to the cause of priestcraft. When she awoke out of her trances, she was utterly unconscious what she had been saying; but the crafty priest would not have the matter to stop so, but persuaded her to believe, or at least to profess herself inspired by the Holy Ghost. He afterwards induced her to counterfeit, or perhaps wilfully to produce, renewed trances, and to deal in visions and revelations. The affair at length made a considerable noise, and many came to see her; and Masters, in order to raise the reputation of an image of the Virgin that was in a chapel within his parish, by which he might expect to profit largely from the offerings of devotees and the concourse of pilgrims, chose for an associate in his imposture one Dr. Bocking, a canon of Christ Church, in Canterbury. By these means, the Holy Maid of Kent was instructed to say, in her trances, that the Virgin Mary had appeared to her in a vision, and revealed that she never should be relieved of her infirmity till she visited the image in question. She accordingly went in pilgrimage to the chapel, where, in the midst of a great concourse of people that were there assembled, she fell into a trance, poured forth extatic ejaculations, declaring that God had called her to a religious life, and appointed Bocking to be her ghostly father. She afterwards pretended to be recovered of all her distempers by the intercession of the Virgin, took the veil, saw visions, heard heavenly melodies, and passed with great numbers for a prophetess; in which belief it is probable that Archbishop Warham died, luckily for himself, before the imposture was exposed.

It does not appear that either the poor crazy woman or her sacerdotal keepers had originally any political designs. But as the divorce of Queen Catherine, and its unforeseen consequence, the rupture with Rome, approximated to a crisis, the prophetic powers of the Holy Maid took a more public turn, and ventured to prophecy destruction to the King himself. It is by no means impossible that the persecutions of Catherine really made a deep impression on her disordered imagination: for all women who have *ever* had a spark of goodness, feel that their whole sex is injured when one individual woman is wronged. She might think herself inspired to denounce the wrath of heaven against a tyrant. She might very easily be persuaded that she had a special dispensation for any measure of pious fraud. But her prompters more probably foresaw that there was but one way to save *their* Church and *their* trade, and aimed at nothing less than a general revolt against the innovating King. It may be remarked, that the inspirations of the Holy Maid did not take a treasonable aspect till after the death of Warham, and the promotion of Cranmer to the Primacy; nor were the Protestant inclinations of Anne Boleyn unsuspected.

Dealers in mock-miracle and false prophecy seldom display much imagination: for it is not to the imagination, or generous passions, but to the selfish hopes and fears of men, that they address themselves. But one of the Holy Maid's fabrications has at least the credit of bold invention. She asserted, that when the King was last at Calais, whilst he was at mass, she being invisibly present either in the body or out o. the body, saw an angel snatch the consecrated Host out of his hand, and give it to herself, whereupon she was instantaneously conveyed back to her monastery, no person being aware of her presence, absence, or removal. The drift of the story of course was, that Henry, by plain and infallible tokens, was rejected of God, and ought to be deprived of his kingly dignity. As the tale found ready credence with Catherine's party, and perhaps with Catherine herself, the nun or her directors grew yet bolder, and she ventured to announce, that if the King should persist in putting away his Queen, and take another wife, he would not be King seven months longer, but would die the death of a villain.

As Bocking and Masters appear to have been mere knaves, with little or no mixture of fanaticism, it did not suit their purpose that these denunciations should reach the King's ear till such time as matters were ripe for an explosion. Fisher, who had been at first attracted by the report of the woman's exceeding holiness, easily believed what he wished to be true, and was as easily persuaded to keep all secret. This is little to be wondered at ; for his intellect, never of the first order, was impaired by superstition, increasing with his years and troubles ; and not improbably, his excessive fastings, watchings, and meditations on the lives of saints and virgins, had prepared him for the contagion of religious madness. But it would be very difficult to account for Sir Thomas More's belief, not in the prophecies of the Maid of Kent, yet in her pretended sanctity. For More's eyes, naturally acute, had, in his youth, been purged and opened, and always continued open when he did not think it his duty to shut them. But though a lamentable, he was not a solitary, instance of a great man acquiescing in what he conceives salutary prejudices, till he loses the power of distinguishing between truth and falsehood. It is not certain, however, that the maiden ventured upon any express prophecies in the hearing of Sir Thomas ; but we are afraid that Bishop Fisher gave into her grossest delusions, and even believed in the authenticity of a letter written in golden characters, and purporting to be the blessed Virgin's autograph, though afterwards confessed to be the handy-work of a Canterbury monk called Hankherst. Fisher, however, refrained from promulgating the treasonable prophecies ; he only concealed them ; but others of the believers were less prudent : in particular, one Peto, preaching at the palace of Greenwich, was so far emboldened by the maiden's revelations, as to denounce heavy judgments against the King in his own royal presence, telling him, "that many lying prophets had deceived him, but he, as a true Micajah, warned him that the dogs should lick his blood as they had licked Ahab's." Extraordinary impudence sometimes passes with impunity where a less liberty would have been severely visited. No punishment was awarded to Peto ; only a Doctor was appointed to answer him the next Sunday. Dr. Curwen, such was his name, began his discourse in defence of the King's pro-

ceedings in a style seldom now to be heard from the pulpit, calling
Peto rebel, slanderer, dog, traitor, liar, and the like, till a friar, named
Elston, arose and told him, that he was one of the lying prophets, who
sought by adultery to establish the succession to the throne, and that
he would justify all that Peto had said. And the friar spake many
other things in a similar strain, and would not be silenced till the King
himself commanded him to hold his peace. Neither Elston nor Peto
suffered any other penalty than a reprimand before the privy council.

But the Holy Maid and her accomplices were not to escape so easily;
and, indeed, the obvious tendency of their proceedings to promote
rebellion, was what no monarch could have overlooked, with due regard
to the security of the state. But it also suited Henry's present purposes to expose an imposture, the detection of which not only brought
discredit on the opposers of his will, but cast suspicion upon the whole
series of monastic miracles and trances, and what was still more in
point, seriously impeached monastic holiness, and reconciled the people
to the confiscation of monastic property. Accordingly Elizabeth Barton,
together with Bocking, Masters, and other of their colleagues were
summoned before the star-chamber, and without torture, but perhaps
not without fear of torture, or hope of pardon, made a full confession of
the plot, not forgetting to mention their success in imposing upon
Fisher.

While the exposure of this affair was in progress, our Bishop received
a warning and counsel which he would have done prudently to follow.
Thomas Cromwell, then Secretary of State, sent Fisher's brother to
him, taking him severely to task for his credulity in believing, and yet
more for his negligence in not disclosing, prophecies so absurd and dangerous; but at the same time exhorting him to write to the King,
acknowledging his offence, and beg forgiveness, which he knew the
King would not refuse to one so old and infirm. It is not improbable
that Cromwell sent this message at Henry's suggestion. However that
might be, Fisher did not take his advice; but declining to apply to the
King, wrote back to Cromwell in his own justification, declaring that all
he had done was only to prove whether the Nun's revelations were
authentic or no. He confessed that he had conceived a high opinion of
her holiness, both from common fame, and from her devoting herself to
a religious life; from the report of her *ghostly father*, (Bocking,)
whom he esteemed a godly and learned divine, whose testimony was
corroborated by that of many other learned and virtuous priests; from
the high opinion the late Primate, Warham, entertained of her; but
above all, from the words of the prophet Amos, " that God will do
nothing without revealing it to his servants." That upon these grounds

he did not think himself justified in rejecting her mission without examination, but had conversed with her himself, and sent his chaplains to converse with her, and neither of them had discovered any falsehood in her. And as to his concealing what she had told him about the King, which was laid to his charge, he thought it needless for him to speak concerning it to the King, since she had said to him that she had told it to the King herself; and she had named no person who should kill the King, nor encouraged any to rise against him; but simply foretold the conditional judgments of Heaven. These arguments, it must be confessed, are none of the soundest, nor was he likely to better himself by declaring, in a communication, sure to pass under Henry's eye, that the harshness with which the King had spoken to him on former occasions made him fearful of offending by imparting the Nun's denunciations.

To this ill judged letter Cromwell replied at large, urging the Bishop not to rely on such insufficient reasons for his justification, but to seek forgiveness of the King while it was yet to be obtained, seeing that if brought to trial he would certainly be found guilty. But Fisher would make no submissions. Sir Thomas More, who had been involved in the same charge, succeeded in exculpating himself by a long explanatory epistle to the Secretary, a sufficient proof that his destruction was not yet determined on.

In 1534 a bill of attainder was introduced into Parliament, which imposed the penalties of treason on Elizabeth Barton, Bocking, Masters, Deering, (author of a book of the Holy Maid's revelations) Rich, Risby, and Gold, her associates, who all suffered at Tyburn; not receiving, or deserving, much compassion even from the most zealous members of the Catholic church. The female, however, was most to be pitied, and in her last confessions, laid the weight of her offences on her male associates, who had availed themselves of her ignorance and infirmity to debauch her soul and body.

In the same act of attainder, Fisher, with five others, among whom was Abel, Queen Catherine's confessor, was adjudged guilty of misprison of treason, in concealing those speeches of the Nun that related to the King; and he was condemned to forfeit all his goods and chattels, and to be imprisoned during his Majesty's pleasure. While the proceedings were pending, he addressed a letter* to the House of Lords,

---

* "It may please you to consider that I sought not for this woman's coming unto me, nor thought in her any manner of deceit. She was a person that by many probable and likely conjectures, I then reputed to be right honest, religious, and very good and virtuous. I verily supposed that such feigning and craft, compassing any guile or fraud, had been far from her; and what default was it in me so to think,

reiterating the reasons for his conduct which he had formerly given to Cromwell, a singular instance of infatuation.   But what is remarkable in the letter is, that he still seems to have retained some faith in the Holy Maid after the imposture was confessed and proved.   Such is the final perseverance of superstition.   Fisher was treated with what, in that age, must have been great lenity, even by the most unfavourable accounts, for, according to his Catholic biographer, Hall, he was discharged with a fine to the King of £300 ; but Bishop Burnet, who, though less a lover of Kings than most of his order, is an industrious vindicator of Henry VIII., says that he does " not find that the King proceeded against him upon this act, till by new provocations he drew a heavier storm of indignation upon himself."

But the provocation was certain to occur ; for in the same session of Parliament that attainted the Holy Maid, the secession of England from the Catholic communion was completed, and, while Fisher was condemned of one misprison of treason, another species of the same offence was invented as it were purposely to entrap his conscience. Henry's marriage with Catherine of Arragon had already been dissolved by Cranmer, and he was privately united to Ann Boleyn ; but now the Parliament solemnly declared the former marriage null and void, con-

---

when I had so many probable testimonies of her virtue?   1. The report, of the country which generally called her the HOLY MAID.   2. Her entrance into religion upon certain visions, which was commonly said she had.   3. For the good religion and learning that was thought to be in her ghostly father, (Dr. Bocking,) and in other virtuous and well-learned priests, that then testified of her business, as it was *commonly* reported.   Finally, my Lord of Canterbury, (Warham,) that then was both her ordinary, and a man reputed of high wisdom and learning, told me that she had many great visions.   And of him I learned greater things than ever I heard of the Nun herself.   But here twill be said she told me such words as were to the peril of the Prince and of the realm.   The words that she told me concerning the peril of the King's Highness were these : That she had her revelation from God that if the King went forth with the purpose that he intended, he should not be King seven months longer ; and she told me also, that she had been with the King, and shewed unto his Grace the same Revelation.   But whereas I never gave her any counsel to this matter, nor knew of any forging or feigning thereof, I trust in your great wisdoms that you will not think any default in me touching this point.   It will be said that I should have shewed the words to the King's Highness.   Verily if I had not thought undoubtedly that she had shewed the same words unto his Grace, my duty had been so to have done.   But when she herself, which pretended to have had this revelation from God, had shewed the same, I saw no necessity why I should renew it again to his Grace.   And not only her own saying thus persuaded me, but her Prioress's words confirmed the same, and their servants also reported unto my servants that she had been with the King.   And yet besides all this, I knew it not long after by some others, that so it was indeed."

firmed the latter, and entailed the crown upon the issue of Henry and Ann Boleyn. It was also adjudged misprison of treason to slander or do any thing to the derogation of the King's last marriage, and all persons whatsoever were enjoined to maintain and keep the provisions of the act so ordaining. And in pursuance of it, on the day of the prorogation, March 30, 1534, an oath was taken by both Houses, wherein they swore " to bear faith, truth, and obedience alone to the King's Majesty, and to the heirs of his body, of his most dear and entirely beloved lawful wife Queen Anne, begotten and to be begotten. And further to the heirs of the same Sovereign Lord, according to the limitation in the statute made for surety of his succession in the crown of this realm, mentioned and contained, and not to any other within this realm, nor foreign authority, nor potentate, &c. To this oath Fisher would never consent, yet he did not venture to oppose it in the House of Lords, but retired to his episcopal palace at Rochester.

But he was not allowed to remain there long. Not above four days were past when he received an instant summons to appear at Lambeth before Cranmer, now Archbishop of Canterbury, who, with other commissioners, were appointed to tender the oath of succession. He obeyed. The oath, in all its plenitude of verbiage, was presented to him ; he perused and meditated over it awhile, then requested time to consider of it. Five days were granted, which having elapsed, he again appeared before the commissioners, and told them that " He had perused the oath with as good deliberation as he could ; but, as they had framed it, he could not, with any safety to his own conscience, subscribe thereto, except they would give him leave to alter it in some particulars ; whereby his own conscience might be satisfied, as well as the King." To this the commissioners, with one consent, made answer, " That the King would allow no alterations, exceptions, or reservations, in the oaths," and Cranmer added, " You must answer directly, whether you will or will not subscribe." Then Fisher, seeing the worst, said decisively, " If you will needs have me answer directly, my answer is, that for as much as my own conscience cannot be satisfied I absolutely refuse the oaths." The commissioners had now but one course ; for the act adjudged that whosoever should decline to swear to all its provisions was, *ipso facto*, guilty of misprison of treason, and to be punished accordingly. On the 26th of April, 1584, the aged Bishop was incarcerated in the Tower, from whence he never came forth again but to trial and execution. Whatever might be the case with the King, the most eminent persons, both in the church and in the state, were evidently reluctant to proceed to extremities against a white-headed man with one foot in the grave, the fame of whose learning and piety was spread over Europe, whose very offence was calculated to procure him a worthy remembrance with the good of his own time, and of-succeeding ages, especially as Sir Thomas More was involved in the same conscientious delinquency. As there was no hope of persuading Henry to abate any article of the oath, great efforts were used to induce Fisher to take it unreservedly. Secretary Cromwell, who seems to have been his sincere well-wisher, urged him once more to write to the King, and at least explain the perfect loyalty of his sentiments, and his readiness to make any submission which his conscience did not prohibit. But Fisher could not bring himself to this measure, and declined any direct solicitation of his Sovereign, whose temper was such, he said, that it was impossible to address him without giving fresh umbrage. Several Prelates visited him in his confinement, if possible to argue away his scruples, and the Lord Chancellor Audley,* a subtle and complying politician, as honest as most politicians think necessary, with others of the Privy Council, tried their rhetoric and influence to the same end, but all without effect.

The main point at which the Bishop stuck was that clause of the succession act which declared the marriage between Henry and Catherine null and void from the commencement, as being contrary to the Levitical laws, and therefore unlawful, notwithstanding any dispensation whatever. This was indeed a virtual denial of the infallibility of the Church ; it was setting Scripture above the Church, and therein renouncing the great and peculiar tenet upon which rests the whole fabric of that Church which he held to be the Catholic and sole saving Church. Cromwell, who laboured in a manner creditable to his heart, to induce the Bishop to save himself, sent Lee, Bishop of Litchfield and Coventry, to argue this question with him ; and at length he agreed to a compromise, which might have satisfied any but a despot : " that he would swear to the succession, and never dispute more about the marriage, and he promised allegiance to the King ; but his conscience could not be convinced that the marriage was against the laws

* If Audley deserved the character given of him by Lloyd, (who is often accused of sacrificing truth to antithesis,) there can have been too little sympathy between him and Fisher to enable them to understand one another. " The King might very well trust him with his conscience when he trusted the King with his; owning no doctrine but what was established, ever judging the Church and State wiser than himself; rather escaping than refusing dangerous employments in which he must either displease his master or himself. He was tender, but not wilful, waving such employments dexterously, wherein he must offend his master dangerously." Such a conscience as this would be more serviceable than even no conscience at all. Audley was the founder of Magdalen College, Cambridge, and the second lay Chancellor, Sir Thomas More, whom he succeeded, being the first.

3 c

of God ;" and to the same modified acceptance of the oath, Sir Thomas More also agreed.

Cranmer was very desirous that this partial concession should be admitted, and foreseeing, as Burnet says, "the ill effects that would follow on contending so much with persons so highly esteemed over the world, and of such a temper that severity could bend them to nothing, did by an earnest letter to Cromwell, dated the 27th of April, move that what they offered might be accepted ; for if they once swore to the succession it would quiet the kingdom, for they once acknowledging it, all other persons would acquiesce and submit to their judgments." Cromwell probably did his best, but Henry had now "abandoned all remorse," and would have his own will to be law, conscience, and religion, to all his subjects, as he had made it to himself. He replied to the representations of Cromwell, and his fellow counsellors, with more than usual fury: " Mother of God ! both More and Fisher shall take the oath, or I will know why they should not ; and ye " (Cromwell and the counsellors,) " shall make them do it, or I will see better reasons why ye cannot." Such at least are the words recorded, and they are such as Henry was likely to have used. It is certain that he refused to accept any thing less of More or Fisher than an unconditional surrender of their scruples.

The Parliament, since we must give that name to the slavish assembly, whose shameless haste to legalize every issue of their master's passions, perhaps made him worse than he would have proved, had he formally possessed an absolute crown, met on the 3rd of November, 1534, and one of its first acts was to attaint Bishop Fisher for refusing the oath of succession, and to declare his Bishopric void from the 2nd of January following.

When all hopes of accommodation were lost, he was suffered to remain in his miserable durance, possibly in expectation that death would obsequiously come to spare his enemies the trouble and disgrace of murdering him. To his other calamities was now added the lowest poverty, for all his property was confiscated, and he was so infamously neglected by those who ought at least to have reverenced his age and his order, that it is only charity to think his brethren of the clergy were *forbidden* to relieve him. Dr. Lee did venture to represent to Cromwell that "his body could not bear the clothes on his back ; that he was well nigh going, and that he could not continue, unless the King were merciful to him." Yet more feelingly are his necessities expressed in a letter of his own to Cromwell, which we hope at least obtained him an enlarged allowance of food and raiment :—

" Furthermore I beseech you be good master unto me in my necessity. For I have neither shirt nor suit, nor yet other clothes that are necessary for me to wear, but that be ragged and rent too shamefully; notwithstanding I might easily suffer that, if they would keep my body warm. But my diet also, God knows how slender it is at many times. And now in my age, my stomach will not away but with a few kind of meats, which if I want, I decay forthwith, and fall into crases and diseases of my body, and cannot keep myself in health. And as our Lord knoweth, I have nothing left unto me for to provide any better, but as my brother of his own purse layeth out for me, to his own great hinderance. Wherefore, good master Secretary, eftsoons 1 beseech you to have some pity upon me, and let me have such things as are necessary for me in mine age, and especially for my health. And also that it may please you, by your high wisdom, to move the King's Highness to take me unto his gracious favour again, and to restore me to my liberty, out of this cold and painful imprisonment. Whereby ye shall bind me to be your poor bedesman for ever unto Almighty God, who ever have you in his protection and custody. Other twain things I must desire of you. That I may take some priest with me in the Tower, by the assignment of Master Lieutenant, against this holy time. That I may borrow some books, to say my devotions more effectually these holy days, for the comfort of my soul. This I beseech you to grant me of your charity. And for this our Lord God send you a merry Christmas and a comfortable to your heart's desire. At the Tower, the 22d day of December, your poor bedesman,

JOHN ROFF."

Thus, to borrow the quaint yet affecting language of Fuller, he " lived in durance, and so was likely to continue, till, in all probability, his soul should be freed from two prisons,—I mean that of his body and of the Tower. For his life could do the King no hurt, whose death might procure him hatred, as of one generally pitied for his age, honoured for his learning, admired for his holy conversation. Besides, it was not worth the while to take away his life, who was not only *mortalis*, as all men, and *mortificatus*, as all good men, but also *moriturus*, as all old men, being past seventy-six years of age."

But the fame of his fidelity and sufferings in the cause of his church had reached Rome, where Cardinal Farnese, a very different sort of Pope from the either-sided hesitating Clement, was recently elevated to the Tiara by the title of Paul III. Had Paul determined of malice prepense to procure for the papal cause the honour of Fisher's martyrdom as a set-off against the Protestant martyrs, he could scarcely have taken a more effectual method than by bestowing upon him an unseasonable honour, the acceptance of which might be construed into a

defiance to a King whose anger was death.   But as we are not among
those who hold that every Pope becomes, *ex-officio*, an incarnation of
the evil principle, we rather believe that Paul, in ignorance of the true
state of things in England, imagined that a Cardinal's hat would procure for the aged Prelate reverence, liberty, and security.   Be it as it
might, Fisher was created, on the 21st of May, 1535, Cardinal Priest
of St. Vitalis; most likely without his own knowledge or wish: though
it is highly improbable that he ever said, as Fuller reports,—" If
the Cardinal's hat were lying at my feet, I would not stoop to pick
it up."   He revered—nay, adored—*his* Church too much to speak
lightly of her dignities, and was above the hypocrisy of pretending to
despise what, if he did not covet, he religiously esteemed.

No sooner did Henry hear of this promotion, than he gave orders
that the hat should be stopped at Calais; and sent Cromwell to sift out
how far the Bishop was a privy or consenting party to his own elevation.
After some general conference, no doubt upon religious topics, the
artful secretary entered upon his real business.   " My Lord of Rochester," says he, " what would you say if the Pope were to send you a
Cardinal's hat, would you accept of it ? "   Fisher replied, " Sir, I know
myself to be so far unworthy of any such dignity, that I think of
nothing less ; but if any such thing should happen, assure yourself that
I should improve that favour to the best advantage I could in assisting
the Holy Catholic Church of Christ, and in that respect I should
receive it on my knees."   When Cromwell reported this manly avowal
to his master, Harry exclaimed, in " right royal rage,"—" Ha ! is he
yet so lusty ?   Then let the Pope send him a hat when he will; but
by God's mother, he shall wear it on his shoulders then, for I will
leave him never a head to set it on ! "   And thenceforth it was determined to cut off the poor remainder of the old man's days.

He must, however, be butchered according to law, and no act of his
had hitherto subjected him to capital punishment.   What then ?   The
Solicitor General, Rich, was either commissioned, or which is just as
likely, volunteered, to trepan him into *treason*.   A convenient statute
had not long before passed the two houses of Parliament, and of course
received the royal assent, by which it was made high treason " maliciously to wish or desire by words or writing, or to imagine, attempt,
or invent, any bodily harm to be done to the King, the Queen, or their
heirs apparent ; or to deprive any of them of the DIGNITY, STYLE, OR
NAME OF THEIR ROYAL ESTATES."   Now among the dignities and
names of the royal estates was that of SUPREME HEAD OF THE
CHURCH, and " upon this hint " the man of law proceeded.   He came
with a great face of importance and mystery, as if secretly despatched

by the King, for the quieting of the royal *conscience*, to consult upon the question of the supremacy. Well had it been for Fisher had he remembered the words of the Psalmist, "I will keep my tongue as it were with a bridle while the ungodly is in my sight:" but he was a man of infinite simplicity, and perhaps thought that even silence on this head was a denial of his Saviour, or at all events a treason against his Saviour's Church. He therefore answered to this effect :— " As to the business of the supremacy, I must needs tell his Majesty, as I have often told him heretofore, and would so tell him if I were to to die this present hour, that it is utterly unlawful ; and therefore I would not wish his Majesty to take any such title or power upon him as he loves his own soul."

It was enough. A commission was issued to the Lord Chancellor Audley, Brandon Duke of Suffolk, Clifford Earl of Cumberland, Thomas Boleyn Earl of Wiltshire, Mr. Secretary Cromwell, and eight of the Judges, to try John Fisher, *late* Bishop of Rochester, for high treason, upon the statute of 26th Henry VIII. The charge against him ran,—" That, in the twenty-seventh year of King Henry's reign, he, the said John Fisher, *late* Bishop of Rochester, had, in the Tower of London, falsely, maliciously, and traiterously spoken and divulged against his due allegiance, before several of the King's true subjects the following words in English :—*That the King our Sovereign Lord is not Supreme Head, on earth, of the Church of England."*

As Fisher had been already deprived of his episcopal functions for misprison of treason, he was not allowed a trial by his peers, but was tried by a common Middlesex jury * of twelve. The indictment was found on the 11th of June, but the poor old man was so sick and infirm, that even the inhumanity of that age shrunk from the shame of dragging him before the court. All his books and papers were seized, no doubt with a view to extract evidence from them. On the 17th he was so far recovered as to render it possible to carry him before the bar of the King's Bench. He wore a plain black cloth gown, without any episcopal vestment. Part of the way he proceeded through the streets on horse-back, but his strength failing, he was put into a boat, and conveyed to Westminster by water.

The trial of a doomed man is generally soon over. The jury knew that they were to find him guilty, and they condemned the Bishop

* It had been called in question whether *any* Bishop was entitled to a trial by his peers : first, because his peerage is not of blood, but official merely,—a weak argument, for the nobility is inherent in the see : secondly, because Bishops not being allowed to sit as judges in cases of life and death, he has no proper peers by whom he can be tried.

chiefly on the evidence of Rich, which they might very justly, though certainly not safely, have rejected : for the man who would treacherously obtain such evidence, may well be supposed capable of fabricating it. The Bishop, though he could not expect his objections to be allowed any weight, did protest against the villainy of Rich * in bold terms :—"I cannot but marvel to hear *you* come in and bear witness against me, knowing in what a secret manner you came to me." Then turning to the court,—"He told me that the King, for the better satisfaction of his own *conscience*, had sent unto me, in this secret manner, to know my full opinion in the matter, for the great affiance he had in me more than in any other: he told me that the King willed him to assure me, on his *honour*, and on the *word* of a *King!* that whatever I should say unto him, by this his secret messenger, I should abide no peril or danger for it, neither that any advantage should be taken against me for the same. Now, therefore, my Lords, seeing it pleased the King's Majesty to send to me thus secretly, under the pretence of plain and true meaning, to know my poor advice and opinion in these his great affairs, which I most gladly was, and ever will be, willing to send him : methinks it is very hard injustice to hear the messenger's accusation, and to allow the same as a sufficient testimony against me in matter of treason.

"I pray you, my Lords, consider moreover, that by all equity, justice, worldly honesty, and courteous dealing, I cannot, as the case standeth, be directly charged with treason, though I had spoken the words indeed, the same being not spoken *maliciously*, but in the way of advice and counsel, when it was requested of me by the King himself : and that favour the very words of the statute do give me, being made only against such as do *maliciously* gainsay the King's supremacy, and none other ; wherefore, although by rigour of law you may take occasion thus to condemn me, yet I hope you cannot find law except you add rigour to that law, to cast me down, which herein I hope I have not deserved."

The jury found him guilty, and the court sentenced him to die the death of a traitor in all its horrid particulars. The trial over, he was carried back to the Tower, haply with a lighter heart than when he was brought forth from thence ; for the hopeless possibility of an acquittal could have administered no comfort, while the certainty of undeserved

* This Rich rose from small beginnings to be Lord Chancellor and a Baron under Edward VI. He was the founder of a *noble* family, from which sprung Robert, Earl of Warwick, and Henry, Earl of Holland, his brother, distinguished for their frequent change of sides in the civil wars under Charles I. The direct line became extinct in 1759.

death gave resignation and repose, and a self-fulfilling hope on high. When arrived at the Tower, he turned to the officers who had attended him on his passage thence and back, and said cheerfully and court-eously, "My masters, I thank you for all the great labour and pains ye have taken with me this day. I am not able to give you any thing in recompense, for I have nothing left, and therefore, I pray you, accept in good part my hearty thanks."

Four days elapsed between the sentence and the execution, during which the King mitigated the mode of death into simple beheading. He employed the interval in fervent devotion, doubtless not omitting any rite approved by his creed, the use of which he could procure. The account of his last day on earth is given by Fuller from a Catholic writer, with so much simplicity, and such an air of reality, that we cannot alter it but for the worse, and shall therefore extract it entire.[*]

"After the Lieutenant of the Tower had received the writ for his execution, because it was then very late, and the prisoner asleep, he was loth to disease him from his rest. But in the morning, before five of the clock, he came to him in his chamber, in the bell tower, finding him yet asleep in his bed, and waking him, told him, 'He was come to him on a message from the King, to signify unto him that his pleasure was, that he should suffer death that forenoon.' 'Well! (quoth the Bishop) if this be your errand, you bring me no great news, for I have looked long for this message, and I most humbly thank his Majesty that it pleaseth him to rid me of all this worldly business. Yet let me by your patience sleep an hour or two, for I have slept very ill this night, not for any fear of death, I thank God, but by reason of my great infirmity and weakness.'

"'The King's pleasure is farther,' (said the Lieutenant) 'that you shall use as little speech as may be, especially of any thing touching his Majesty, whereby the people should have any cause to think of him or his proceedings otherwise than well.' 'For that,' (said he) 'you shall see me order myself as, by God's grace, neither the King nor any man else shall have occasion to mislike of my words.' With which answer the Lieutenant departed from him, and so the prisoner, falling again to rest, slept soundly two hours and more; and after he was awaked, called to his man to help him up. But first commanded him to take away his shirt of hair (which customably he wore) and to convey it privily out of the house; and instead thereof, to lay him forth a clean white shirt, and all the best apparel he had, as cleanly brushed as might be. And, as he was arraying himself, his man, seeing in him

---

* Fuller. Church History of Britain, Book V. Section 3. Copied from "Hall's (then) MS. Life of Bishop Fisher," afterwards published by Dr. Bailey.

more curiosity and care for the fine and cleanly wearing of his apparel that day than was wont, demanded of him, What this sudden change meant? saying, That his Lordship knew well enough that he must put off all again within two hours, and lose it. 'What of that?' said he, 'dost not thou mark that this is our marriage day, and that it behoveth us therefore to use more cleanliness for solemnity thereof?' About nine o'clock the Lieutenant came again, and finding him almost ready, said, 'He was now come for him.' Then said he to his man, 'Reach me my furred tippet to put about my neck.' 'Oh, my Lord!' said the Lieutenant, 'what need ye be so careful for your health for this little time, being, as yourself knows, not much above an hour?' 'I think no otherwise,' said he, 'but yet in the mean time I will keep myself as well as I can. For I tell you truth, though I have, I thank our Lord, a very good desire and willing mind to die at this present, and so trust of his infinite goodness and mercy he will continue it, yet will I not willingly hinder my health in the mean time one minute of an hour, but still prolong the same, as long as I can, by such reasonable ways and means as Almighty God hath provided for me.' And with that, taking a little book in his hand, which was a New Testament lying by him, he made a cross on his forehead, and went out of his prison door with the Lieutenant, being so weak that he was scant able to go down stairs; whereupon, at the stairs foot, he was taken up in a chair between two of the Lieutenant's men, and carried to the Tower gate, with a great number of weapons about him, to be delivered to the Sheriff of London for execution.

"And as they were come to the uttermost precinct of the liberties of the Tower, they rested there with him a space, till such time as one was sent before to know in what readiness the Sheriffs were to receive him. During which space he rose out of his chair, and standing on his feet, leaned his shoulder to the wall, and lifting his eyes towards heaven, he opened a little book in his hand, and said, 'O Lord! this is the last time that ever I shall open this little book; let some comfortable place now chance unto me, whereby I, thy poor servant, may glorify thee in this my last hour.' And with that, looking into the book, the first thing that came to his sight were these words:—*Haec est autem vita aeterna ut cognoscant te solum verum Deum, et quem misisti Jesum Christum. Ego te glorificavi super terram, opus consummavi quod dedisti mihi, &c.,** and with that he shut the book

---

* St. John xvii. 3. 4.—And this is life eternal, that they might know thee, the only true God, and Jesus Christ whom thou hast sent. I have glorified thee on the earth. I have finished the work which thou gavest me to do.

The Catholics generally quote Scripture in Latin, from the Vulgate.

together, and said, 'Here is even learning enough for me to my life's end.' And so the Sheriff being ready for him, he was taken up again among certain of the Sheriff's men, with a new and much greater company of weapons than was before, and carried to the scaffold on the *Tower-hill*, otherwise called *East-Smithfield*, himself praying all the way, and recording upon the words which he before had read.

"When he was come to the foot of the scaffold, they that carried him offered to help him up the stairs, but said he, 'Nay, masters, seeing I am come so far, let me alone and ye shall see me shift for myself well enough;' and so went up stairs without any help, so lively, that it was a marvel to them that before knew his debility and weakness. But as he was mounting the stairs, the south-east sun shone very brightly in his face, whereupon he said to himself these words, lifting up his hands: '*Accedite ad eum, et illuminamini, et facies vestrae non confundentur.** By that time he was upon the scaffold, it was about ten o'clock; where the executioner, being ready to do his office, kneeled down to him (as the fashion is), and asked his forgiveness. 'I forgive thee,' said he, 'with all my heart, and I trust thou shalt see me overcome this storm lustily.' Then were his gown and tippet taken from him, and he stood in his doublet and hose in sight of all the people, whereof there was no small number assembled to see the execution.

"Being upon the scaffold, he spoke to the people in effect as follows:

"'Christian people. I am come hither to die for the faith of Christ's holy Catholic Church, and I thank God, hitherto my stomach hath served me very well thereunto, so that yet I have not feared death; wherefore I desire you all to help and assist with your prayers, that at the very point and instant of death's stroke, I may in that very moment stand steadfast, without fainting in any one point of the Catholic faith, free from any fear. And I beseech Almighty God, of his infinite goodness, to save the King and this realm, and that it may please him to hold his holy hand over it, and send the King a good Council.'

"These words he spake with such a cheerful countenance, such a stout and constant courage, and such a reverend gravity, that he appeared to all men, not only void of fear, but also glad of death.

"After these few words by him uttered, he kneeled down on both his knees, and said certain prayers. Among which (as some reported), one was the hymn of *Te Deum laudamus*, to the end; and the psalm *In te Domine speravi*. Then came the executioner and bound a handkerchief about his eyes; and so the Bishop, lifting up his hands and

---

* Draw nigh unto him and be enlightened, and your faces shall not be cast down."

3 D

heart to heaven, said a few prayers, which were not long, but fervent and devout. Which being ended, he laid his head down over the midst of a little block, where the executioner, being ready with a sharp and heavy axe, cut asunder his slender neck at one blow, which bled so abundantly, that many (saith my author) wondered to see so much blood issue from so lean and slender a body; though in my judgment, they might rather have translated the *wonder* from his *leanness* to his *age*, it being otherwise a received tradition, that lean folks have the most blood in them.

"Thus died John Fisher, in the seventy-seventh year of his age, on the 22d of June, being St. Alban's day, the proto-martyr of England, and therefore with my author most remarkable. But surely no day in the Romish Calendar is such a skeleton, or so bare of sanctity, but (had his death happened thereon) a priest would pick a mystery out of it. He had a lank, long body, full six feet high, toward the end of his life very infirm, insomuch that he used to sit in a chair when he taught the people in his diocese.

"His corpse (if our author speaketh truth) was barbarously abused, no winding sheet being allowed it, which will hardly enter into my belief. For, suppose his *friends* durst not, his *foes* would not afford him a shroud, yet some *neuters*, betwixt both (no doubt), would have done it out of common civility. Besides, seeing the King vouchsafed him the Tower, a noble prison, and beheading, an honourable death, it is improbable he would deny him a necessary equipage for a plain and private burial. Wherefore, when Hall tells us, that 'the soldiers attending his execution could not get spades to make his grave therewith, but were fain with halberds (in the north side of the church of All Hallows, Barking,) to dig a hole wherein they cast his naked corpse;' I listen to the relation as inflamed by the reporter's passion. Be it here remembered, that Fisher, in his life-time, made himself a tomb on the north side of the chapel in St. John's College, intending there to be buried, but was therein disappointed. This Fisher was he who had a Cardinal's hat sent him, which (stopped at Calais) never came on his head; and a monument made for him, wherein his body was never deposited.

"Our author reporteth also, how Queen Ann Boleyn gave order that his head should be brought unto her (before it was set up on London bridge) that she might please herself at the sight thereof, and like another Herodias,* insult over the head of this John, her professed

---

* The tale is sufficiently confuted by its servile imitation of that of Herodias; though, as he that steals a sheep, even if he forget to obliterate the true master's

enemy. Nor was she content alone to revile his ghost with taunting terms, but out of spite, or sport, or both, struck her hand against the mouth of this dead head brought unto her; and it happened that one of Fisher's teeth, more prominent than the rest, struck into her hand, and not only pained her for the present, but made so deep an impression therein, that she carried the mark thereof to the grave. It seems this was contrary to the proverb, *Mortui non mordent*; but enough, yea too much, of such damnable falsehoods."

Thus was a faithful shepherd of Christ's flock destroyed. But he would not have lived many years longer. His work was done. He neither flung away his life madly, nor preserved it basely. He was a martyr, if not to the truth that is recorded in the authentic book of Heaven, yet to that copy of it which he thought authentic, which was written on his heart in the antique characters of authoritative age. Those who think him right, justly hold him a martyr to the Faith; and we who think him mistaken, must still allow him to have been the martyr of Honesty.

Bishop Fisher was a tall and robust man in his youth, but excessively emaciated in his later years. He practised fasting and watching even to supererogation, and was too prone to the opinion, that the reason requires to be mortified as well as the body. Most unjustly has he been accused of avarice, whereas he was a wise and liberal economist, desiring his brother Robert, who was his steward, that the revenues of his Bishopric might be regularly expended every year, but not exceeded; and whatever was beyond the frugal provision of his household went in alms. After his own slender meal (he took but one in the four and twenty hours), he would stand at a window, to see the poor fed at his gate, with a sort of vicarious voluptuousness. He was a man of more acquired learning than natural genius, and is said to have had the best library in England. His works are pretty numerous, but consist entirely of sermons and controversial treatises, mostly against the doctrines of Luther. One of them bears a very uncharitable title, " *Pro Damnatione Lutheri.*"

mark, makes a new nick in the ear, that he may claim it for his own; so the perverters and copiers of truth generally add some little circumstance, more or less cleverly imagined, for a *difference*, as the heralds say,—for instance, the tooth-mark in Anne Boleyn's hand. The wrath of the Catholic writers against poor Anne breaks out in still more improbable accusations than this. Not content to charge her with cruelty, treachery, and incontinence, they make her positively ugly,—blear-eyed, wry-necked, sallow-complexioned, like Envy personified. Yet these descriptions were printed and published at a time when many persons living must have seen and remembered Anne Boleyn. But writers who intend their works solely for the perusal of some particular sect or party, are never deterred from falsehood by the fear of contradiction.

The following may be regarded as a tolerably complete list of the Bishop's writings :—

1. A Sermon on Psalm 116, at the funeral of King Henry VII.

2. A Funeral Sermon at the *moneth mind* * of Margaret, Countess of Richmond. Printed by Wynkin de Worde, and republished in 1708, by Thomas Baker, DD., with a learned preface.

3. A Commentary on the seven penitential Psalms. Written at the desire of the Countess of Richmond. Printed at London, 1509, 4to., 1555, 8vo.

4. A Sermon on the Passion of our Saviour.

5. A Sermon concerning the Righteousness of the Pharisees.

6. The Method of arriving at the highest Perfection in Religion. These four last were translated into Latin by John Fenne.

7. A Sermon preached at London on the day in which the writings of Martin Luther were publicly burnt, on John xv. 26. Cambridge, 1521. Translated into Latin by John Pace.

8. Assertionum Martini Lutheri confutatio. *A confutation of Luther's assertions, in forty one articles.*

9. Defensio Assertionis Henrici VIII. de septem sacramentis contra Lutheri "Captivitatem Babylonicum." *A Defence of Henry VIII. his Apology for the seven Sacraments against Luther's "Babylonish Captivity."*

10. Epistola reponsoria, Epistolæ Lutheri. *An Epistle in Answer to Luther.*

12. Sacerdotii Defensio contra Lutherum. *Defence of the Priesthood against Luther.*

13. Pro Damnatione Lutheri. *For the condemnation of Luther.*

14. De veritate corporis et sanguinis Christi in Eucharistiâ. *Of the real presence of Christ's Body and Blood in the Eucharist.* Against Occolampadius.

15. De Unicâ Magdalen : contra Clichtoveum et Jac Fabrum Scapulensem. *That there was only one Mary Magdalen.* Did you ever hear of more?

16. Sanctum Petrum Romæ fuisse, contra Ulricum Velenum. *That St. Peter was at Rome,* against Ulric Veleno.

17. Several other small tracts:—On the Benefits of Prayer. The Necessity of Prayer. The Lord's Prayer. A Letter on Christian Charity, to Hermolaus Lectatius, Dean of Utrecht. A Treatise on Purgatory, &c.

Most of the forementioned pieces were published separately in England, and were printed collectively at Wurtzburg, in one volume folio, 1595.

Of his book on the King's marriage, printed at Alcala, we have already spoken. There is another tract of Fisher's on the same subject, in the collection of records at the end of Collier's Ecclesiastical History.

No doubt these works were many of them composed with intense thought, labour, and learning, after preparation of fervent prayer ; and yet, who is there living that has read a page of any of them, excepting the Lady Margaret's funeral sermon ? It is to the cruelty of his Sovereign that Fisher owes his ransom from oblivion.

---

* *i. e.* Month's mind. The funeral obsequies of the Countess were not performed till a month after her death. Here we see the origin of a proverbial saying, " to have a month's mind to a thing ; " but how the phrase came to be transferred from the *monthly anniversary* (Hibernice) of a person's death, to signify a strong desire, we are unable to explain.

THE REVEREND WILLIAM MASON.

So happy a life as Mason's, though exceedingly agreeable to think of, is neither easy to write, nor very entertaining when written. Even when such favoured mortals have chosen, like the excellent Lindley Murray, to be their own biographers, though their reflections and observations are most valuable, their actions exemplary, and their tranquillity and thankfulness truly edifying, more good people will be found to recommend their work than to peruse it. Yet Mason was not a man to be forgotten. He was the friend and biographer of Gray, and he was the most considerable Poet that Yorkshire has produced since Marvel.

As a man, as a poet, as a politician, and as a divine, he was highly *respectable*, and he that is thoroughly respectable, and nothing more, has the best possible chance of earthly happiness. A few squabbles with managers and critics, were all that he had to convince him that " man is born to mourn." He had the good fortune too to be born in one of those " vacant, interlunar" periods of literature, when a little poetic talent goes a great way : and in an age when a clergyman, if not negligent of his professional duties, was allowed to cultivate his talents in any innocent way he thought proper. His character was deservedly esteemed by many who were themselves estimable, and his genius is praised by some who themselves possessed more.

William Mason was born in 1725. His father, who was Vicar of St. Trinity-Hall, in the East Riding, superintended his early education himself, and instead of checking, kindly fostered his poetical tastes, for which judicious indulgence he made grateful acknowledgment in a poetical epistle, written in his 21st year. Unlike too many poets, he never had occasion to regret his early devotion to the Muses ; but then,

He left no calling for the idle trade,
No duty broke, no father disobey'd.

However little parents may approve of their offspring being bad poets, or however barren they may think the bays of the good ones, they will always do wisely to imitate the worthy father of Mason, and let

instinct have its course. To oppose, is certain to add the curse of disobedience to the calamities of poetry.

In 1742, young Mason was entered of St. John's College, Cambridge.
His tutor was Dr. Powell, a man of the same liberal sentiments as his
father, who, while he directed his pupil to the classic models of antiquity, did not dissuade him from cultivating English verse. Mason's
scholarship, though elegant and diffusive, was not of that accurate and
technical kind, which may strictly be called academical; but he passed
his time happily at Cambridge, with good books and good company,
studying rather for delight and public fame, than for college honours
and emoluments. It is too much the habit of tutors, and of those who
should give the tone to our Universities, to consider all study which has
not a direct reference to the tripos and class-paper, as mere mental dissipation: a prejudice which not only turns the young academician into a
school-boy, but converts the full grown academicians, who should form
the learned class, into common-place schoolmasters. The constant routine of tuition leaves the senior neither time nor spirits for fresh acquisitions of knowledge, and in consequence many, many men of high
attainments, whose continued residence in their colleges would be highly
beneficial both to themselves and to the community, are driven away
from absolute want of genial society and conversation. Few now choose
a college life, but such as are either tutors for subsistence, or decorous
loungers and temperate bonvivants; consequently the Universities have
lost a part of their salutary influence on the public mind, and are too
sharply opposed to current opinion to modify and moderate it as they
ought to do. Such, we fear, is the general case; but the exceptions
are many, honourable, and yearly on the increase; and there is great
hope that, ere long, specimens of every cast and size of intellect may
grow and flourish on the peaceful borders of Cam and Isis.

> Far from the madding crowd's ignoble strife.

The youthful character of Mason, as drawn by his early and constant
friend Gray, is at once amiable and amusing. He says, that " he was one
of much fancy, little judgment, and a good deal of modesty; a good well
meaning creature, but in simplicity a perfect child; he reads little or
nothing, writes abundance, and that with a design to make a fortune by it;
a little vain, but in so harmless a way, that it does not offend; a little
ambitious, but withal so ignorant of the world and its ways, that this
does not hurt him in one's opinion; so sincere and undisguised, that no
one with a spark of generosity would ever think of hurting him, he
lies so open to injury; but so indolent, that if he cannot overcome this
habit, all his good qualities will signify nothing at all." Very few of
these traits outlasted Mason's youth, and perhaps some of them never

existed but in Gray's good natured interpretation. To have more fancy than judgment, to be very modest, and a little (which means not a little) vain, are qualities common to every young man that is, or is to be, or sincerely wishes to be, a poet :* and a stripling, who came to college direct from his father's parsonage, might well be ignorant of the world. But his simplicity and unsuspicion, like his extravagant expectations, seem to have arisen solely from his ignorance of the world, and his indolence was probably more than half affected out of vanity ; for vain clever men cannot bear to be suspected of fagging.

Mason took his Batchelor's degree in 1745. Probably it was about this time that he composed, or at least began to compose, his Monody on the death of Pope, who died in the preceding year ; but it did not appear before 1747, when it was published by advice of Dr. Powell. As the work of an author of two and twenty, it is greatly commendable, and contains some really fine lines. But grief, if we may judge by the practice of poets, has a privilege above all other passions, love itself not excepted ; a plenary indulgence for all sins of nonsense. Elegies, Monodies, and Epicedia, have generally less meaning than any other compositions. Mr. Mason begins thus, in complicated imitation of the whole tribe of poetic mourners :—

> Sorrowing I catch the reed, and call the Muse,
> If yet a muse on Britain's plain abide ;
> Since rapt Musæus tuned his parting strain,
> With him they lived, with him perchance they died :
> For who e'er since their virgin charms espied,
> Or on the banks of Thames, or met their train
> Where Isis sparkles to the sunny ray ?
> Or have they deign'd to play
> Where Camus winds along his broidered vale,
> Feeding each blue-bell pale, and daisy pied
> That fling their fragrance round his rushy side.
>
> Yet ah, ye are not dead, Celestial Maids,
> Immortal as ye are, ye may not die,
> Nor is it meet ye fly these pensive glades,
> E'er round his laureate herse ye heave the sigh.
> Stay then awhile, O stay, ye fleeting fair,
> Revisit yet, nor hallow'd Hippocrene,
> Nor Thespia's grove ; till with harmonious teen,
> Ye sooth his shade, and slowly-dittied air.

* An ingenuous youth will always be modest in proportion as he is vain. For modesty and vanity are only different phænomena of one and the same disposition, viz. an extreme consciousness and apprehensiveness of being observed. In the well-constituted young mind, there is a perpetual struggle between the fear to offend, which is modesty, and the desire to please, which is vanity.

Such tribute pour'd, again ye may repair
To what loved haunt ye whilom did elect;
Whether Lycæus, or that mountain fair
*Trim Mænalus with piny verdure deck't.
But now it boots ye not in these to stray,
Or yet Cyllene's hoary shade to choose,
Or where mild Ladon's welling waters play,
Forego each vain excuse,
And haste to Thames's shores; for Thames shall join,
Our sad society, and passing mourn,
The tears fast trickling o'er his silver urn.
And when the Poet's widow'd grot he laves,
His reed crown'd locks shall shake, his head shall bow,
His tide no more in eddies blith shall rove,
But creep soft by with long drawn murmurs slow.
For oft the mighty Master rous'd his waves
With martial notes, or lull'd with strain of love :
He must not now in brisk meanders flow
Gamesome, and kiss the sadly-silent shore,
Without the loan of some poetic woe.

Say first, Sicilian Muse,
For, with thy sisters, thou didst weeping stand
In silent circle at the solemn scene,
When Death approach'd, and wav'd his ebon wand,
Say how each laurel droopt its with'ring green ?
How, in yon grot, each silver trickling spring
Wander'd the shelly channels all among;
While as the coral roof did softly ring
Responsive to their sweetly-doleful song.
Meanwhile all pale th'expiring Poet laid,
And sunk his awful head,
While vocal shadows pleasing dreams prolong;
For so, his sick'ning spirits to release,
They pour'd the balm of visionary peace.

Considered as a specimen of versification these lines have great merit, and prove that Mason had read and studied the elder English poets diligently and profitably. It was by no means so easy to compose such a copy of verses in 1744 as it would be at present, for the tunes of ancient song had " left the echo ;" so completely had the Popean couplet (itself, deny it who will, an admirable measure for many and excellent purposes) taken possession of the general ear, that it was not without effort, and a certain confusion of ideas, that ordinary readers could admit any other system of syllabic arrangement to be verse at all.

* Is not *trim* a strange epithet for a mountain ? We have *trim* gardens in Milton, properly ; but was the *piny* verdure of Mænalus wrought into topiary works, or regularly clipped by " old Adam's likeness ?"

At present the turns and phrases of the Italian school are rather more familiar than those of the French, and a man might compose a very tolerable cento, without ever looking at a poet at all, out of magazine articles and familiar letters.

There is some little originality in the plan of Mason's Musæus. Instead of heathen Gods, or rivers, or abstract qualities in masquerade, Pope, or Musæus, in the trance preceding his departure, is visited by the " vocal shadows" of Chaucer, Spenser, and Milton, each of whom confesses his own inferiority to the dying Swan, with no small extravagance. Vocal shadows ought not to flatter.

It would seem that these spirits of poets past came to convince Mr. Pope that he would have as little occasion for plain speaking in the world he was going to as in that he was leaving. Spenser is not happily characterized as " the blithest lad that ever piped on plain," for the prevailing hue of his poesy is melancholy tenderness. His " Faerie Queen" is the requiem of chivalry ; a cenotaph of stainless marble, into which he invokes the shades of virtues that never lived

" But in the vision of intense desire."

Spenser, in Mr. Mason's allegorical procession, is Colin Clout; Chaucer is Tityrus, and is masked " as a Palmer old," no very appropriate habit for a writer who satirized the religious orders with so much severity, and who had no high opinion of the moral effect of pilgrimages. The style and obsolete language of these two poets are skilfully taken off, though, after all, their speeches are more like Pope's burlesque imitations, than their own original strains. It is rather too bad to state that Una and Florimel are drooping before the superior charms of Belinda. No two poems on earth can be more unlike than the " Faerie Queen," and " The rape of the Lock." Una with her " milk white lamb" is the most unearthly efflux of pure imagination. Compared to her, Milton's Eve is a substantial woman. Belinda, on the other hand, is the exactest transcript of a drawing-room beauty, and every image with which she is attended is drawn from double-refined high life. The " Rape of the Lock" is to St. James's, what the " Beggar's Opera" is to Newgate, with the merit of more perfect consistency ; for there are certain strokes of true nature in Polly Peachum, which make you feel for her as a being out of her place. Belinda is altogether the fine lady : you find and wish for no more nature in her, than perspective in a china vase. But we are criticising Pope instead of Mason.

The most remarkable thing in the " Musæus" is that Pope is made to disclaim all praise but that of being the poet of virtue, and Virtue appears, *propriâ personâ*, to thank him in heroic couplets for his mighty services.

3 E

We have said more perhaps than necessary about this tuneful trifle, both because it was Mason's maiden poem, and therefore a mark whereby the progress of his mind may be computed, and because it really shews how nearly a young man may come to be a poet by mere dint of loving poetry, and indefatigably striving to attain it.

Such was the fashion of celebrating departed excellence in the early part of the eighteenth century. A great spirit is just departed from among us, and when the seemly silence of a recent grief may fitly be broken, some sad and solemn strains, not unmingled with deep and joyful hope, will haply break from the poets that survive ; but let there be no pastoral, no allegory, no heathenism : let us at least talk sense beside the grave. There is no man of twenty now living who *could* write half so well as Mason, that *would* not write much better on such an occasion. So much has been done in the last fifty years to reconcile poetry with reason. Mason did something himself, and even his Musæus is an improvement on the then established models.*

In 1747, Mason was chosen Fellow of Pembroke College, chiefly by the recommendation of Gray, who had removed thither from Peterhouse, whence he was driven by the noise and practical jokes of a set of young bloods, who thought his timidity and old-maidenly preciseness fair game. We wonder at such irreverend treatment of the author of the Elegy, yet it is not unlikely that Shakespeare was sometimes hissed and pelted on the stage. Mason, however, was not allowed 'to take possession of his fellowship without some difficulty, of which he himself spoke thus :—"I have had the honour, since I came here last, to be elected by the Fellows of Pembroke into their society ; but the Master,

---

* The "melodious tears" of our "Augustan age" are pleasantly ridiculed by Steel in that number of the Guardian which led to the quarrel between Pope and Phillips.

"In looking over some English pastorals a few days ago, I perused at least fifty lean flocks, and reckoned up a hundred left-handed ravens, besides blasted oaks, withering meadows, and weeping deities. Indeed, most of the occasional pastorals we have are built upon one and the same plan. A shepherd asks his fellow 'Why he is so pale? if his favourite sheep hath strayed? if his pipe be broken? or Phyllis unkind?' He answers, 'None of these misfortunes have befallen him, but one much greater, for Damon (or perhaps the god Pan) is dead.' This immediately causes the other to make complaints, and call upon the lofty pines and silver streams to join in the lamentation. While he goes on, his friend interrupts him, and tells him that Damon lives, and shews him a track of light in the skies to confirm it; then invites him to chestnuts and cheese. Upon this scheme most of the noble families in Great Britain have been comforted, nor can I meet with any right honourable shepherd that doth not die and live again, after the manner of the aforesaid Damon."---*Guardian*, No. 30. 1713.

who has the power of a negative, had made use of it on this occasion, because he will not have an *extraneus* when they have fit persons in their own college. The Fellows say they have a power from their statutes, *indifferenter eligere ex utraque academiâ*, and are going to try it with him at common law, or else get the King to appoint a visitor. If this turns out well, it will be a very lucky thing for me, and much better than a Platt, which I came hither with an intention to sit for: for they are reckoned the best Fellowships in the University." Whether the Master and Fellows of Pembroke did proceed to extremities or no, is matter of little consequence; but Mason was declared duly elected, after two years' suspense, in 1749, in which year also he took his Master's degree. It is possible that the Master of Pembroke might dislike Mason both for his poetry and for his politics. As to the former, sage gentlemen in office generally regard it as coldly as the great Lord Burleigh, and the philosophical Locke, who, in his tract on education, warns all young men against associating with poets, as being commonly found in company with gamesters. In politics, Mason was a Whig, perhaps more from a scholastic admiration of the antique republics, than from any experimental knowledge of the wants and capacities of English society. Of this he gave proof in his "Isis," a metrical attack upon the Jacobitism of Oxford, which had the honour of rousing Tom Warton to a reply, properly named the "Triumph of Isis," since Mason himself confessed it to be the better poem of the two. Neither of them won much glory in the contest; but the heart certainly goes along with Warton, who loved his *Alma Mater* for her venerable cloisters, her ancient trees, her shady walks, her cloudy traditions, her precious libraries, her potent loyalty, and mighty ale, and wrote in her defence with a generous anger too sincere to be thoroughly poetical.

Why do the Universities ever meddle with factious politics? In their corporate capacity they should never allude to any event later than the restoration. That was their triumph—the reward of their loyal sufferings, the resuscitation of the church. They ought to take it for granted, that all has gone on well since; as the happy couple of the fifth act, or third volume, are conceived to be still living happily— keeping their honey-moon to the end of time.

Warton and Mason never liked one another, which has been attributed by some to their poetical rivalry, and by others to the difference of their politics. But may it not more rationally and less discreditably be ascribed to the contrariety of their habits, and the antipathy of their tempers? Mason was a correct, precise, clerical gentleman, as much attached to the decorums of life, as to those of the drama! by

no means incapable of quiet sarcasm, but much above the vulgarity of
a joke :—the vanity which Gray could smile at in his boyhood, sobered
down into a prudent self-appreciation, that taught him to furbelow a
good deal of true dignity and self possession with a little of what, in
the other sex, would be called prudery. Warton was a good-natured sloven,
somewhat given to ale and tobacco, and not very select either as to the
company he drank and smoked with, or the jests with which he set
the table in a roar. It is recorded (and the tale would not have been
invented if it had not been characteristic) that Tom Warton was once
missing, when in his capacity of public orator, or poetry professor, we
are not sure which, he had to compose a Latin speech for some public
occasion. To save the trouble of going the round of his haunts, a happy
thought occurred, that he never could, whatever he was engaged in,
forbear following a drum and fife. A drum and fife therefore were
directed to proceed with their spirit-stirring music along the streets
of Oxford, and ere long, from a low-browed *hostel*, distinguished by a
swinging board, the Professor issued, with cutty pipe in mouth, greasy
gown, and dirty band, and began strutting after the martial music, to
the tune of "give the King his own again."

The anecdote is probably fabulous, but it would never have been
told of Mason. The difference of the men appears in the fact, that
Warton was always Tom, while Mason was never Billy. The natural
consequence of this discrepancy of manners would be, that neither
could feel himself at ease in the other's society. Mason would suspect
that his dignity was violated by the very negligence of Warton's dress,
and Warton would be annoyed with the propriety of Mason's behaviour.
He used to describe him as a " buckram man."

The " Isis" appeared in 1748, and does not seem to have offended
the Cantabs in general, for in the next year our author was requested
to compose an ode for the installation of the Duke of Newcastle as
Chancellor of the University of Cambridge. Gray thought the ode
" uncommonly well for such an occasion," a praise not to be acceded to
his own ode on the installation of the Duke of Grafton, which is a great
deal too good for the occasion. But Mason was so little pleased either
with his subject, or his treatment of it, that he had no pleasure in
recollection of the task, and omitted it in his works.*

---

* If this omission was meant to cast a slight upon the Duke or his memory, it was a
littleness unworthy of a poet, and at all events, it was disrespectful to the University
which had approved, and to the many noble Lords and learned Doctors (not to
mention Ladies) who had listened to it with patience, and rewarded it with applause.
But the Duke of Newcastle was not the Chancellor which Cambridge would have
freely chosen. He was neither remarkable for literary attainment in himself, nor for

Though so little eager to record his academical distinctions, he ever retained a grateful and affectionate remembrance of Cambridge, which he testified in an ode addressed to his liberal tutor, Dr. Powell.

The two or three years ensuing his admission to his Fellowship he spent between town and college, frequenting such society in each as were distinguished for their devotion to the fine arts and fine literature, continually exercising himself in composition, but so far from expecting to make a fortune by his poetry, that, according to his own assertion, he would have been happy if the profits of his pen procured him the purchase of an opera or concert ticket. Yet he had his ambition,—an

patronage of literature. His only claim, besides his rank, was his ministerial office, and his Hanoverian zeal; and Cambridge, in fixing upon him to support her highest honorary dignity, only meant to prove her readiness to oblige the administration in everything, and to testify her abhorrence of the imputed disaffection of Oxford, whose loyalty was supposed to be "far over sea." Oxford had been very severely treated lately; for two or three fresh men who had drunk the *Pretender's* health when they had better have drunk no more, instead of being left to the college discipline, had been taken into custody by a messenger of state, "and two of them being tried in the Court of King's Bench, and being found guilty, were condemned to walk through the courts of Westminster with a specification of their crime fixed to their foreheads; to pay a fine of five nobles each; to be imprisoned for two years, and find security for their good behaviour for the term of seven years after their enlargement." The cry of Jacobitism was loudly trumpeted against the whole community of Oxford. The address of the University to congratulate his Majesty upon the peace of Aix la Chapelle was contemptuously rejected; and a proposal similar to that made some two and thirty years before (vide Life of Bentley, p. 242), to subject their statutes to the inspection of the King's Council, was unwillingly relinquished, in deference to the opinions of the Court of King's Bench. Cambridge, meanwhile, had crept into favour with the ministry, and to make the most of that inestimable advantage, resolved to fill the vacancy occasioned by the death of the "proud Duke," (whose political conduct was such as gave him a right to be proud) in the most prudential manner. "The nation, in general," says Smollett, "seemed to think it would naturally devolve upon the Prince of Wales, as a compliment at all times due to that rank; but more especially to the then heir apparent, who had eminently distinguished himself by the virtues of a patriot and a prince. He had even pleased himself with the hope of receiving this mark of attachment from a seminary for which he entertained a particular regard. But the ruling members, seeing no immediate prospect of advantage in glorifying even a Prince, who was at variance with the ministry, wisely turned their eyes upon the illustrious character of the Duke of Newcastle, whom they elected without opposition, and installed with great magnificence; learning, poetry, and eloquence joining their efforts in celebrating the shining virtues and extraordinary talents of their new patron."

The conduct of the University on this occasion deserves no breath of censure. Where no interest but one's own is concerned, to be disinterested is a crying absurdity. As a body, the academicians were in duty bound to elect the most efficient protector: as individuals, they did right in choosing the most powerful patron.

ambition to reconcile the college and the town—to be at once the poet of the common-room and the green-room ; in short, to mediate between John Bull and Aristotle ; to produce an acting play on the ancient plan ; such a play as Sophocles or Euripides would produce if they were now in being.   The result was his Elfrida, published in 1752.

Elfrida is very, very far from a contemptible piece of workmanship : it is manifestly the production of a scholar and a gentleman, of an ardent lover of poetry, and platonic inamorato of abstract virtue : but impossible as it is to approve our conjecture by experiment, we do shrewdly suspect that it is nothing like what Sophocles or Euripides would have written had they risen from the dead in the plenitude, or, if you will, with only a tithe, of their powers, and an inspired mastery of the English language,* to exhibit to the eighteenth century the marvel of a modern ancient drama.   For his deviation from the exact model of the Athenian stage, he thus apologizes in a *letter to a friend*, prefixed to the first edition of his Elfrida.†   " Had I intended to give an exact copy of the ancient drama, your objections to the present poem would be unanswerable."   (What objections does not appear, but may easily be guessed.)   " I only meant to pursue the ancient method so far as it is probable a Greek poet, were he alive, would now do, in order to adapt himself to the genius of our times, and the character of our

---

* It would not have taken Euripides many months to acquire a style quite as English as Mason's. Mason cautiously avoided everything like English idioms in his serious works, and for the most part uses words, where he uses them correctly, in the most definable meaning. He has none of those *chromatic* shades and associations of sense which render a writer untranslateable. His Caractacus has been translated both into Greek and Italian, and I dare say lost not a drop in the transfusion.

† We do not exactly know who first introduced the practice of Poets criticising their own works, and anticipating objections in prologues, prefaces, letters to friends, &c. It does not appear to have been familiar to the Greeks, unless the *Parabasis* of the old comedy, wherein the poet addressed the audience through the chorus, may be supposed to have set the example. Terence, in his prologues, sometimes deprecates the anger of critics ; and Martial occasionally apologizes for his epigrams, and tells you what you have to expect,—a practice followed, if not imitated, by Chaucer, in the prologue to his "Miller's Tale." But the earliest example we remember in English (we by no means assert that it is the first) of an author formally pleading his own case in prose, is in the epistle dedicatory to Davenant's Gondibert. Dryden followed the fashion obliquely or directly in his various delightful prefaces. Sir Walter Scott (eheu !) has very ingeniously contradicted whatever cavils his tales might seem exposed to, in his introductory dialogues, epistles, and narratives. But Mr. Moore has in this sort outdone all competition ; for what can be said against "Lalla Rook," which Fadladeen has not uttered with the keenness and brilliance of a diamond !

tragedy. According to this notion, every thing was to be allowed to the present taste which nature and Aristotle could possibly dispense with; and nothing of intrigue or refinement admitted at which ancient judgment could reasonably take offence. Good sense, as well as antiquity, prescribed an adherence to the three great unities; these, therefore, were strictly observed. But, on the other hand, to follow the modern masters in those respects in which they had not so faultily deviated from their predecessors, a story was chosen in which the tender rather than the noble passions were predominant, and in which even love had the principal share. Characters, too, were drawn as nearly approaching to private ones as tragic dignity would permit, and affections raised more from the impulse of common humanity, than the distresses of royalty and the fate of kingdoms. Besides this, for the sake of natural embellishment, and to reconcile mere modern readers to that simplicity of fable in which I thought it necessary to copy the ancients, I contrived to lay the scene in an old romantic forest. For by this means I was enabled to enliven the poem by various touches of pastoral description; not affectedly brought in from the storehouse of a picturesque imagination, but necessarily resulting from the scenery of the place itself,—a beauty so extremely striking in the 'Comus' of Milton, and the 'As you like it' of Shakespeare; and of which the Greek Muse (though fond of rural imagery) has afforded few examples besides that admirable one in the Philoctetes of Sophocles. By this idea I could wish you to regulate your criticism. I need not, I think, observe to you, that these deviations from the practice of the ancients may be reasonably defended. For we are long since agreed, that where love does not degenerate into episodical * gallantry, but makes the foundation of the distress, it is, from the universality of its influence, a passion very proper for tragedy. And I have seen you too much moved at the representation of some of our best tragedies of private story, to believe you will condemn me for making the other deviation."

* I once thought that Lord Byron's

> "Man's love is of his life a thing apart:
> 'Tis woman's whole existence,"—

might have been suggested by this expression of Mason, but I am told the noble author was indebted to Madame de Stael.

Though "episodical gallantry" be not an unexceptionable phrase, the observation and the distinction is more just than any thing else in the letter. Love, at least in the drama, should never be introduced as an accessory. It should be the leading passion and source of interest, or it should be excluded as carefully from a tragedy as from a boarding school. What can be more miserably out of keeping than the love-scenes in Addison's "Cato," unless it be the underhand courtship of Edgar and Cordelia, foisted by Nahum Tate into King Lear?

We cannot forbear thinking that Mason had formed his idea of the Greek stage, more from the French critics and imitators, than from the Greek originals. That his acquaintance with Aristotle was drawn through the Gallic filter, may be regarded as certain. He talks of Sophocles, but he is thinking of Racine. He refers to Aristotle, but he relies on Boileau, Bossu, and Dacier. How thoroughly his taste had been gallicised, is proved by his eagerness, in his second auto-critical epistle, to quote the censure of Voltaire upon Shakespeare, and to dwell delighted upon the sobriety and chastity of Racine's Melpomene. Speaking of the common objections to the ancient form of drama, he says:—"The universal veneration which we pay to the name of Shakespeare, at the same time that it has improved our relish for the higher beauties of poetry, has undoubtedly been the ground-work of all this false criticism. That disregard which, in compliance merely with the taste of the times, he shewed of all the necessary rules of the drama, hath since been considered as a characteristic of his vast and original genius; and consequently set up as a model for succeeding writers. Hence M. Voltaire remarks very *justly*, "Que le merite de cet auteur a perdu le theatre Anglois. Le tems, qui seul fait la reputation des hommes, rend à la fin leurs defauts respectables.'*

"Yet notwithstanding the absurdity of this low superstition, the notion is so popular among Englishmen, that I fear it will never be entirely discredited, till a poet rises up among us with a genius as daring and elevated as Shakespeare's, and a judgment as chastised and sober as Racine's."

If Mason had simply asserted his right to introduce a new form of Drama, occupying a middle point between Shakespeare and Euripides, and protested against the "low superstition" (if any such existed) of

---

* "The merit of this author has ruined the English theatre. Time, which solely raises the reputation of men, at last makes their defects venerable."

Voltaire had too great an intellect not to perceive the mightiness of Shakespeare,—too much sense to deny it,—and not heart enough to acknowledge it. Vanity was his ruling principle, but not that happy vanity which makes a man's own imaginary merit his horizon, beyond which he can see nor conceive nothing. He was keenly alive to superior excellence: he both saw and hated. His aversion to Christianity arose from wounded pride: he could not brook a truth and a power above him which he had nothing to do in discovering. If he had really thought Christ an impostor, he would have praised him as he has done Mahomet. In just the same spirit he sets Ariosto above Homer, and animadverts on the perverseness of the English, who continued to worship Shakespeare when their language could boast of a Cato. He knew well enough that he could make a better tragedy than Cato at a week's notice; while to move in the orb of Shakespeare, he must have undergone a change in the inner man.

condemning all plays in which the Unities were observed, because Shakspeare has succeeded gloriously without them, he would have done well. The more shapes and moulds poetry is cast into, the better; and the more these moulds are varied, provided that each contain a principle of unity, a law of proportion in itself, the greater the gain. And it is certain that no dramatist will ever win a place, we say not at the side, but at the feet, either of Shakspeare or of the Athenian trio, who does not differ widely from each and all of those his great predecessors. Sweet is Shakspeare's praise to all that know and love him; but we would rather never hear his name mentioned, for good or evil, than have it muttered like a malignant spell, to stop the current of another's fame, or seal up the springs of hope and enterprise. We hate to hear Shakspeare praised by odious comparisons with Racine, or Schiller, or Goethe. Who blames the lily for not being a rose?

But Mason has fallen into an error in which far greater men than he have both preceded and followed him. Milton was not content to write blank verse, but he must decry rhyme; and Mason could not invite the public to be pleased with his endeavours, without trying to convince that unconvincible aggregate, that it ought not to have been pleased with its old favourites, and thus created an unnecessary prejudice against his own experiment. Even supposing a popular taste to be vicious, it can only be cured by calling into action a higher power, and exciting a sense of purer pleasure. This a writer may do by his works, but he will never do it by his arguments. You may argue a man or a people out of their admiration, out of their respect, out of their fear, out of their creed, but never out of their pleasure, faith, or love. " To count all former gain as loss," is a sacrifice which only Religion has a right to demand: for in poetry, if not in politics, it is easy to innovate without destroying. There is ground enough on Parnassus " to let upon a building lease," without razing either the ancient castles or the new crescents: no occasion even to disturb the temporary booths and bazaars till the fair is over.

There was nothing very new in Mason's attempt, either as regarded the unity, or more properly speaking, the unbroken continuity of action, or the introduction of the chorus. The plays of Robert Garnier, and other early French dramatists, make at least a pretence of adhering to the ancient models; and the dramas of Lord Brook, of the Earl of Stirling, and of Daniel, had moralizing choruses. Yet he speaks as if Milton's Samson Agonistes was the only English poem constructed according to antique regularity; and this, he contends, runs to an extreme of austerity, arising from the author's *just* contempt of his

3 F

contemporaries, whom he would not condescend to amuse or instruct. (Milton would never have condescended to *amuse* any age, and to instruct was not his vocation : his office was to exalt and purify : but this was no rule for Mr. Mason.)   " He had before given to his *unworthy* countrymen the noblest poem that genius, conducted by ancient art, could produce, and he had seen them receive it with disregard, perhaps with dislike.   Conscious therefore of his own dignity, and of their demerit, he looked to posterity only for his reward, and to posterity only directed his future labours.   Hence it was, perhaps, that he formed his SAMSON AGONISTES on a model more severe and simple than Athens herself would have demanded ; and took Æschylus for his master rather than Sophocles or Euripides ; intending by this conduct to put as great a distance as possible between himself and his contemporary writers ; and to make his work (as he himself said) *much different from what passed amongst them for the best.*   The success of the poem was accordingly what one would have expected.   The age it appeared in treated it with total neglect ; neither hath that posterity to which he appealed, and which has done justice to most of his other writings, as yet given to this excellent piece its full measure of popular and universal fame.   Perhaps in *your* closet, and that of a few more, who unaffectedly admire genuine nature, and ancient simplicity, the Agonistes may hold a distinguished rank.   Yet surely we cannot say (in Hamlet's phrase) ' that it pleases the million : it is still caviar to the general.'*

" Hence, I think, we may conclude, that unless one would be content with a very late and very learned posterity, Milton's conduct in this point should not be followed.   A writer of Tragedy must certainly adapt himself more to the public taste ; because the dramatic, of all poems, ought to be most generally relished and understood.   The lyric Muse addresses herself to the imagination of a reader ; the didactic to his judgment ; but the tragic strikes directly on his passions.   Few men have a strength of imagination capable of pursuing the flights of Pindar ; many have not a clearness of apprehension suited to the reasonings of Lucretius and Pope.   But every man has passions to be excited ; and every man feels them excited by Shakspeare.

" But though Tragedy be thus chiefly directed to the heart, it must be observed that it will seldom attain its end, without the concurrent approbation of the judgment.   And to procure this, the artificial con-

---

* Hamlet's phrase would have served Mr. Mason's purpose better if he had quoted correctly.   It is, in *our* Shakspeare, " The play, I remember, pleased *not* the million, it was Caviare to the General."   Whence we may deduce the important fact, that the immortal bard was himself fond of Caviare.

struction of the Fable goes a great way. In France, the excellence of their several poets is chiefly measured by this standard. And amongst our own writers, if you except Shakspeare, (who indeed ought, for his other virtues, to be exempt from common rules,) you will find that the most regular of their compositions are generally reckoned their chef d'œuvre, witness the All for Love of Dryden, the Venice Preserved of Otway, and the Jane Shore of Rowe."

In all this there is little more than a glimmering of Truth; but some of the remarks on Milton require examination. We are to suppose then, according to Mr. Mason, that Milton, being quite disgusted with the public for its neglect of " Paradise Lost," wrote " Samson Agonistes" to convince the said public how little he cared for it. That he made his drama as severe and unattractive as he possibly could, with an express and conscious design of differing, *toto cœlo*, from his contemporaries, as Jack, in the " Tale of a Tub," tears his jacket to tatters, that he may differ from Peter's laced coat. Now, though Milton must have been aware that his work *did* differ from those of his contemporaries, he doubtless fashioned it according to his own sense of fitness, neither following nor flying the path of the time. If Samson Agonistes be of a sterner character, and less accommodated to popular liking, than any of his earlier works, (and, indeed, its almost wintry bareness makes a singular contrast to the full blossom of Comus and Lycidas,) the change is to be attributed to his advancing years, and to that blindness, which cutting him off from all visual beauty, would make him more and more a dweller with abstract forms. The sympathy of blindness directed him to Samson as a subject. We cannot think the choice very happy, but having made it, and determined upon the most regular mould of drama, (which Mason thoroughly approves,) what greater variety of incident, or interest, could he have admitted without gross impropriety? It is needless to say that Samson Agonistes would not have been any more popular in Greece than in England, or that it is formed on a model more simple than Athens herself would have *demanded*. Athens did not *demand* severe and simple models. The Athenians, in the infancy of their stage, were *satisfied* with bald and naked representations of mythological stories, which carried the weight of religious association along with them; but it was only till they were accustomed to livelier excitements, more intricate plots, more complicated and contrasted passions, and more splendid decorations.

To suppose that Milton was annoyed or disappointed at the reception of Paradise Lost, is to do him gross injustice. He never expected that it would have a *great run*, or be bought up like a satire or a love song. He knew that it had to swim against the tide, against the associations of the many, and against the more inveterate prejudices of the critics. An epic in blank verse, produced at a time when the favourites of the Town were adopting heroic rhyme for tragedy; in which there was no epigram, no point, and next to no wit; which was far too solemn for the men of wit and pleasure, and as much too poetical for the severe religionists; a religious poem, which embodied the tenets of no sect; written moreover by a man abhorred by the ruling party, and little beloved by the nonconformists, at once a republican and an Arminian; was likely to attract few purchasers; the only wonder is, that it found so many.

Two large Editions, comprising at least 2,800* copies, were sold in

* It should be recollected that in Milton's time there were but three, or at most four classes of readers: The Religious, the Learned, and the Town; to which we may perhaps add such of the nobility and country gentlemen as bought books to furnish their libraries, who would, of course, be guided either by their chaplains, by their booksellers, or by the fashion. The religious, including the clergy of all denominations, the discreet part of the female sex, with the respectable heads of families, and substantial citizens, confined their reading pretty much to religious publications, admitting little poetry but what was purely didactic and devotional, and moreover, proceeded from their own church or sect. Fathers of families looked very jealously, and who that knows the character of the current poetry of that day will blame them,) at every work with a capital at the beginning of each line. The pious lady would consult her spiritual adviser upon the propriety of buying a new poem, and he would tell her, truly enough, that she might spend the money in a way more conducive to the glory of God. The clergy and the learned liked poetry of any sort in Greek or Latin; still it was rather heathenish, and besides they thought that all the good poetry that could be written, had been written; a new epic was as heretical as a new creed. The Town, comprising the " mob of gentlemen that wrote with ease," with all actors, booksellers, writers by trade, young genius's, and ladies gay, took their tone from the court, or bowed to the despotism of the French critics. And as for the country gentlemen, if religious, they were good customers to the sellers of polemical divinity, if otherwise, they carried down with them the new plays, pamphlets, and lampoons, to sleep beside the worthier inmates of their shelves, the old romances and chronicles; where perhaps a folio Shakspeare was treasured in honour of King Charles. Now to which of these classes could Milton look for a purchaser? Not to the religious, for he belonged to no church. The royalist clergy held him in conscientious abhorrence. Who could willingly believe that a good poem, and that too a christian poem, could be written by a wicked man? By a murderer, a parricide, a blasphemer! Would it not prove, if such a thing were possible, that poetry was an accursed art, *vinum Dæmonum*, (as a holy father called it,) the *Devil's dram*, execrable in proportion as it was excellent? Yet it is certain that the orthodox clergy did consider Milton as an exceeding wicked man, worse than a parricide, yea, a deicide; inasmuch as he justified regicide, and he who justifies an act, to all intents and purposes makes it his own, and regicide was, in the apprehension of many and sound divines, not only parricide, but the nearest approximation man could make to deicide; for if a Prince may be insulted in his ambassador, so might the supreme Prince be murdered in his Vicegerent. And the Catholics never more completely identified Christ and the Pope, than

little more than two years; no ordinary sale for a poem of such bulk at any time, and under any circumstances: but when the circumstances

the royalist clergy identified Christ and King Charles, even to the extent of paralleling the sufferings of the one with the mysterious agonies of the other. (There is some little difference between plain beheading and crucifying, but let that pass.) It would not be difficult to prove, from the 30th of January sermons, and other like productions, that we are guilty of no exaggeration; but the authorized service for "King Charles's Martyrdom" is quite enough. Had Paradise Lost been published as a posthumous work of Judas Iscariot, it would have met as kind a reception from the zealous Episcopalians, as it could hope for with the name of John Milton on the title page.

"But (says a great authority, from whom it is almost presumptuous to differ), if Milton's political opinions, and the way in which he expressed them, had made him many enemies, they must have also made him many friends." This is not necessary, nor is it according to the common course of things. Rancour and bitterness make no friends, "they love not poison that do poison need," and of the high abstract principles, the soaring speculations upon the possibilities of human nature, that justified Milton to himself, how few were apprehensive or participant? The party to which he belonged (if he could be said to belong to any party at all) were the very smallest fragment into which society was broken. A few classical republicans there might be, like Marvell, that understood and reverenced him, but they never were, and never can be many. The great mass of the nonconformists, both in religion and politics, were either too ignorant to appreciate a learned poem, or of too rigid minds to yield to imaginative impulses, or too constantly whirling in the vortex of faction, to give ear to a strain, which above all uninspired works, demands a Sabbath mind. The Learned are never a very large class. They might be free from the superstitions and prejudices of the vulgar and of the unlearned religionists; but they have little curiosity about the works of their contemporaries. If they read a modern book at all, it is for mere amusement, or to discover imitations, or to speculate on the decline of genius. No doubt there are exceptions, and among them many of the first purchasers of Paradise Lost were to be found. As to the Town and the country gentlemen, it would be waste of words to shew how little they could see in such a poem, and how glad they would be of any critical opinion which assured them it was not worth reading. Who then, it may be asked, were the readers or the buyers of Paradise Lost? They were the small number of Milton's friends, and the liberal lovers of true poetry, who are many, though not the many: young men, eager to admire, who found a new power created within them by the influences of that "mighty orb of song," and old men, that felt their youth restored in all its energy, but with none of its turbulence, by that divinest harmony,

> Of man, and angels, and the awful choir
> Of angels fallen, that yet remember Heaven,
> And the low bellowings of the nether void
> Melting at last to penitential peace
> And holy silence.

We are told how many editions Cowley went through. No wonder. Cowley was the cavalier poet, just as much as Tom Moore is the Whig poet. Every loyal man, that bought books at all, bought Cowley. Then he was the best writer of his school,

of that time are considered, we hesitate not to declare that it was
nothing less than extraordinary.   That amid so much political confusion, so much and manifold fanaticism, such general poverty of the
nation, and such dissoluteness of the literary class, there should yet
have remained so many strong, pure, and powerful minds to approve a
Paradise Lost, is an honourable recollection for England and for human
nature.   There is no instance of merit of so high an order making so
great a way, not only without adventitious aid, but against every
conceivable obstacle.   " Fit audience may I find, though few," was the
aspiration of the blind bard; and can it be dreamed, that having
obtained all that he asked, and more, he indulged a vain chagrin, and
debased his noble thoughts with the pettish pride of mortified vanity ?
Impossible !   Neither did he think of appealing to posterity from contemporary injustice.   He wrote no more for posterity than for his own
age ; but for the wisest and best of all generations, present and to
come :—for men whose imagination is an active power, to whom profound and prolonged thought is a " labour of love ; " who can find
strength and freedom in a rigid self-controul, a beauty in all truth,
and a moral truth in all beauty.

From the latter part of this epistle, it is obvious that Mason, though
he affects to disclaim it, did write his Elfrida with a wish, at least,
that it might be represented ; for there is no possible reason why a
poem in dialogue, interspersed with lyrics, having a beginning, middle,
and end, if written for the closet, should be more obsequious to public
taste than any other species of poetic composition.   A dramatist, if he
has no eye to the eclât and the profits of the play-house, may form his
plot according to his own fancy, and say, " Fit audience let me find,
though few." Albeit, no manager would ever respond Amen.   Tragedy,
considered as a poem, does not strike more directly at the passions than
ode, or elegy, or poetic narrative.   Like all other poetry that is worthy
of the name, it addresses the passions chiefly through the medium of
the imagination ; seldom, if ever, without calling either the imagination

which was the fashionable school, and in spite of all his conceits, there is a vein of
good-hearted common sense and shrewd observation, which must have endeared him
to those (a very numerous class) who like to see their own thoughts cleverly expressed
and curiously illustrated.   In this respect he was the forerunner of Pope ; but his
morality was much better than Pope's, and there was not a spark of ill nature about
him.   He is among the most amiable of poets.   We stare indeed to hear him called
sublime ; but it was by those who thought sublimity to consist in novel juxtaposition
of thoughts, and feats of intellectual agility.   Southey says, the metaphysical school
spoiled a great poet in Cowley.   This we doubt.   We do not think he could have
been greater than he is, and as he is we are very well content with him.   But what
an inordinate note !

or the thinking faculty into play. To address the passions directly and merely, is to decline farther and worse from the just measures of ancient art, than to annihilate time and space—overleap years, mountains and seas—twist half a dozen plots together like the plies of a cable, and keep them all agoing like the Indian jugglers' balls—blend comedy, tragedy, farce, pastoral, and ballet together—fill the stage with horses, elephants, and dromedaries—kill off your *dramatis personæ* till the scene is choked with carcases, and the living are not enough to shove aside the dead—or commit any other modern enormity against the Unities, the legitimate drama, Aristotle, and common sense.

There are three more of these letters, but we have quoted enough to shew the critical calibre of Mason's mind. The other letters are taken up with a defence of the chorus, in which he displays neither learning nor philosophy. He does not seem to remember (for he could scarcely be ignorant) that the chorus was not introduced into the drama by Greek judgment, but that the drama, *i. e.* the dialogue and action, was *superinduced* upon the chorus, which kept its place more by prescription than reason, becoming of less and less importance in the hands of every successive dramatist, till at length the choral odes came to have little or no connection with the subject of the play, and were even transferred, like the songs of our operas, from one play to another. The idea of making the chorus a running commentary on the piece, was of late origin. In the earliest and best tragedians, the chorus is always an active character, and its presence as well accounted for as circumstances admit. To employ it simply to fill up the intervals of time, to relieve attention without withdrawing it, to afford the actors an opportunity of loosening their buskins, shifting their robes, changing their masques,† and clearing their voices, was an afterthought.* A

---

* On the Athenian stage, one actor had frequently to represent several parts in the same piece, as we see done in scanty itinerant companies, where an exchange of wigs often effects a change of characters. Not more than four actors were generally engaged, exclusive of the chorus.

† " The chorus should be considered as one of the persons in the drama, should be a part of the whole, and a sharer in the action : not as in Euripides, but as in Sophocles. As for other poets, their choral songs have no more connection with their subject than with that of any other tragedy ; and hence they are now become detatched pieces, inserted at pleasure ; a practice first introduced by Agatho."— *Twining's Aristotle's Poetics, Part II., section* 21, *page* 158.

" It is curious to trace the gradual extinction of the chorus. At first, it was all ; then relieved by the intermixture of dialogue, but still *principal* ; then subordinate to the dialogue ; then digressive, and ill-connected with the piece ; then borrowed from *other pieces* at pleasure ; and so on to the fiddles and act-tunes, at which Dacier is so

noble use the great Athenians doubtless made of the chorus; yet it cannot be denied, that the drama is more completely dramatic, and so far, more simple and perfect without it. Of the difficulty of amalgamating the lyric and dramatic portions of a play, we need look for no further proof than appears in the gradual disconnection of the chorus and dialogue among the Greeks themselves. Mason's partiality for this portion of the antique arose from a secret consciousness of his own strength and his own weakness. For dramatic composition, he had neither genius nor skill: his conceptions of character were vague, he had little pathos, nor could he even distribute his speeches in such a manner as to bear the smallest resemblance to actual conversation. But he had considerable powers of description, personification, and amplification, and he delighted in moral common places, which he certainly utters with much dignity, and an air of great earnestness. The model which he would have best succeeded in imitating was "Comus." He had the good sense to perceive that no excellence of individual parts can atone for a want of unity in the whole: but he was not able to see of himself (and there was nobody then to shew him)

angry. The performers in the orchestra of a modern theatre are little, I believe, aware, that they occupy the place, and may consider themselves as the lineal descendants of, the ancient chorus. Orchestra was the name of that part of the ancient theatre which was appropriated to the chorus." (*Twining's note on the passage.*)

We know not any prose translation of any classic worthy to be compared with Twining's "Poetics," for elegance, correctness, and pure Anglicism. The notes are a treasure of classical information; and the two preliminary dissertations ("*On Poetry, considered as an imitative art*," and "*On the word Imitative, as applied to Music.*") are among the earliest specimens of philosophical criticism. Twining understood his author well, and has shown clearly how grossly, if not wilfully, the French interpreters have misunderstood him. It is to be regretted that he is not as bold in advancing his own clear view of Aristotle's purport, as in demolishing the flimsy comments of Bossu and Dacier. It was much that he dared to use his common sense and common eyes; but he might have discovered much more had he used the telescope of an imaginative philosophy; not that he wanted imagination or philosophy either, but he was afraid to trust them together.

About one third of Aristotle's treatise of Poetics is worthless,—so corrupt that it cannot be restored, and so trifling, that the loss is little to be lamented. But the rest is so admirable, that a commentator is always justified, whenever the meaning is doubtful, in supplying the highest sense which the connection authorizes, without being over delicate of the present text, which was patched together by ignorant transcribers from a mutilated copy. In the time of Sylla there was only one copy of the works of Aristotle known to exist, and that impaired by damp and worms. How near was a treasure lost to the world!

Twining was a great admirer, perhaps a personal friend, of Mason. Had his translation and commentary existed when the Elfrida was published, Mason would have altered many things in his epistles.

that a perfect unity may be attained, though the technical unities (which have no use or beauty except in so far as they produce *unity*) be disregarded. But Mason could not have done this, and therefore he was right in preserving a simplicity of plot, and a *bona-fide* continuity of action. He was right, also, in adopting that appendage of the ancient stage, which gave him an opportunity of shining in his own way, without too much encumbering the dialogue with description and reflection. To exemplify his plan for reconciling the ancients and moderns, he published, at a considerable interval of time, two serious dramatic poems, of very unequal merit, and it is pleasant to remark a decided improvement in the later production. "Elfrida" appeared in 1751, "Caractacus" in 1759, and Mason's genius grew wonderfully in those eight years.

His "Elfrida" labours under the disadvantage of an ill-chosen story: a story scarcely familiar or important enough for the foundation of a tragedy of an austerely simple construction, in the treatment of which he has departed so far from what at least passes for authentic history, as to produce an unpleasant jumble of fact and fiction. Elfrida is recorded only as an adultress and a murderess. Mason, in direct opposition to a sound precept of Aristotle, makes her a pattern of conjugal love and devoted widowhood. Nor are the manners of the time better preserved. But the sentiments of the poetry are pretty, and the tale is certainly a good deal prettier than it is in the History of England. The real Elfrida would have been a tempting subject for Euripides, who delighted to contemplate woman under the influence of strong and dark passions; but we like Mason the better for his inability to pourtray such a character, and approve his judgment in not attempting it.

Among the peculiar difficulties of dramatic composition, what is called the *opening of the plot* is one of the most formidable, and we know very few plays in which it has been skilfully surmounted. But this difficulty is materially augmented if the unities of place and of time are to be kept inviolate; for in that case, it is impossible to represent a series of actions from their commencement: the play must begin just before the crisis, and the auditor must be put in possession of the previous occurrences as soon as possible; for if they be left in obscurity till they are naturally developed by the incidents and passions of the action itself, half the play will pass over before any one knows what is going forward, or where is the scene, or who are the *dramatis personae.* In written or printed plays, to be sure, we may be informed of these particulars by lists of characters, stage directions, &c.; but no play can be regarded as a legitimate work of art, which would not be intelligible

3 G

in representation.   The ancient dramas, so long as the genuine Greek tragedy flourished, were, with few exceptions, taken from the store-house of mythology, which was familiar to every Greek from his child-hood, consequently the Athenian audiences were never at a loss to understand the subject of a new production.   But this, though it was a great convenience, did not exonerate the poet from his duty : he was not to take it for granted that his story was known, but was to make his plot unfold itself.   The chorus was of great use in this business, their odes consisting for the most part of references to the past, and forebodings of the future.   Prophecies and oracles to be fulfilled, old crimes to be expiated, mysterious circumstances to be cleared up, a fearful future involved in a fearful past, were the main ingredients of the choral strains, in which nothing is *told* ; every thing is assumed or hinted at, in accordance with the religious nature of Greek tragedy. But as some more straight-forward exposition was deemed necessary in many instances, Euripides, in particular, had recourse to the very inartificial expedient of a retrospective soliloquy, sometimes spoken by a ghost, in which the history was brought down to the point at which it was convenient that the scene should open.   This is but a clumsy device, but perhaps it is better than occupying the first act with tedious narrative, in which *Prologue plays dialogue with Dummy ;* and it avoids the worst of all *critical* faults, that of tediousness.   Such as it is, Mason has adopted it in his Elfrida, without an attempt to disguise its manifest absurdity.   Orgar, the father of the heroine, appears on the lawn before Athelwold's castle in Harewood Forest, and after a few lines, very prettily descriptive of the venerable wood, the orient sun, and the flower-besprinkled lawn, which give you to understand, like the Gun in Sheridan's Critic, that the time is early morning, begins to explain his own business to himself, setting forth as how his daughter has been three months married to Earl Athelwold, who has persuaded him, for some undiscovered reasons, to let the match remain a secret for " some little space ;" that Earl Athelwold has conveyed his bride by stealth to Harewood Castle, " enjoyed and left her," gone to court, and occasionally visited his wife in disguise, and in such a mysterious fashion, that the old man cannot tell what to think of it ; begins to suspect that Athelwold has another wife, and intends to lurk about in disguise of a pilgrim, in order to find out the real state of the case, vowing vengeance if his suspicions should turn out to be true.   His soliloquy is interrupted (just when it has said all that it has to say) by singing behind the scenes, which he rightly supposes to proceed from Elfrida's waiting maids, the companions of her solitude ; whereupon, not to interrupt their harmony, he gets behind a tree, resolving to address them "with some feigned tale," as soon as they have done their song. The chorus of waiting-maids enter singing a hymn to the Morning. A hymn to the Virgin, or to St. Nicholas, or any saint, would certainly have been more appropriate, but the lines are not amiss. Mason had a fine ear, and considerable knowledge of music, which enabled him to give the true lyric air to his choral odes:

> Hail to thy living light
> Ambrosial Morn! all hail thy roseate ray,
> That bids young Nature all her charms display
> In varied beauty bright.
> Away! ye goblins all
> Wont the bewilder'd traveller to daunt,
> Whose vagrant feet have traced your secret haunt
> Beside some lonely wall,
> Or shattered ruin of a moss-grown tower,
> Where, at pale midnight's stillest hour,
> *Through each rough chink* the solemn orb of night
> *Pours momentary gleams of trembling light.*
> Away, ye elves, away!
> Shrink at ambrosial morning's living ray;
> That living ray, whose power benign
> Unfolds the scene of glory to our eye,
> Where, throned in artless majesty,
> The cherub Beauty sits on Nature's rustic shrine.

Sweet verses, truly, and at least one beautiful image, though even this is falsified by the epithets. Moonshine is not momentary, except in a high wind, when the clouds are driven rapidly across the " solemn orb;" nor is it trembling, except when reflected on water, or bright leaves. But what a jumble of religions! The Saxon damsels are first of all ancient Persians, then superstitious Scandinavians; but when they talk of the "cherub Beauty sitting on Nature's rustic shrine," they are Christians, Platonists, modern Deists, and good Catholics all in a single verse. This is the consequence of a determination to bring as many pretty things together into a given space as possible. At the end of the song Orgar comes forward. The chorus are offended at him for listening. He makes a flattering apology: tells the ladies that he never passes "the night bird's favourite spray" without stopping to listen, and that they had voices as sweet as nightingales, with a great deal more science. The ladies are mollified: a long dialogue ensues, in which Orgar pretends to be a man of quality from the north, whose property has been laid waste by an invasion of the border Scots. With some difficulty he prevails on the virgins so far to deviate from their master's orders as to afford him a place of shelter and concealment. He withdraws, and Elfrida enters, bitterly complaining of her husband's want of punctuality (after all, he is not more than an hour after his time), and appears not over well pleased with her secluded state. The chorus moralizes, and gives advice in a strain which few ladies would endure in their waiting-women, and sings another ode, which begins very ornithologically about the turtle (dove), and the lark, and the linnet, and then goes on about the Goddess of Content. At the end of this ditty Athelwold enters, and the chorus, if they had any sense of delicacy or propriety, would have withdrawn. As it is, they stand still, very much in the way. So much for the rationality of a Drama on the ancient plan, founded upon the tender passions. But even if this absurdity had been avoided, matrimonial caresses and reproaches can rarely be exhibited without making both parties rather ridiculous. It is very well that such folly should exist, but the less display is made of it the better: it is peculiarly annoying to the hopeless celibate,* a large and increasing class, which, if the times do not improve, or rather, if the habits of society are not reformed, and the money price of respectability is not lowered, will go near to include the whole middle class of gentry. We have long thought it rather creditable to poets, or their wives, that there are so few poetical addresses to Hymen ;† for the happiness of the married pair neither requires nor admits of public sympathy. There must always be something defective in the moral feelings, or very unfortunate in the circumstances of a man who makes the public his confidante.

Elfrida has a natural longing for the court, which Athelwold endeavours to flatter her out of :—

* It is fearful to think how many rash and unhappy marriages are contracted in sheer despair of ever being able to marry with prudence! How many men, and, in the humbler classes, how many women, plunge into vice and dissipation from the same cause! No political change can remedy this evil, unless, along with free institutions, it introduces republican habits of thinking and feeling. But something would be done, if all hopes of patronage were cut off, and every man without patrimony saw plainly that he had no dependence but upon his own industry and frugality. The manner in which the revenue of England has been spent, has been ten times more grievous, and a thousand times more mischievous, than the taxation by which it is raised.

† To this observation there is one exception ; that is, when poets have addressed their wives in the decline of life, or after long marriage. Nothing can be more beautiful than some of Wordsworth's pieces of this kind. There is a pretty lively copy of verses by Samuel Bishop, master of Merchant Taylors' School, on presenting his wife with a knife after fourteen years' marriage, beginning,—

    A knife, my dear, cuts love they say;
    Mere modish love perhaps it may.

These are pleasant reading. But let all married poets beware of deluging the public with *treacle*.

Elfrida. Blame me not, my Lord,
If prying womanhood should prompt a wish
To learn the cause of this your strange commotion,
Which ever wakes, if I but drop one thought
Of quitting Harewood.
    Athel. Go to the clear surface
Of yon unruffled lake, and bending o'er it,
There read my answer.
    Elfrida. These are riddles, sir.
    Athel. No, for its glassy and reflecting surface
Will smile with charms too tempting for a palace.
    Elfrida. Does Athelwold distrust Elfrida's faith?
    Athel. No, but he much distrusts Elfrida's beauty.
    Elfrida. Away! you trifle.
    Athel. Never more in earnest;
I would not, for the throne that Edgar sits on,
That Edgar should behold it.

Here the plot begins to open. Athelwold, commissioned to woo Elfrida for the King, has taken her himself, and represented her to Edgar as a dowdy. Now, alarmed at the idea of his treachery being discovered, he cautions her earnestly against the amorous disposition of the young Monarch, and is proceeding with his monitory harangue when a messenger arrives with the unwelcome news, that the King is on the way to Harewood. Athelwold is dumbfoundered. The ensuing scene, in which he gives way to his horror and despair, is written with more dramatic power than Mason generally displays. Naturally enough, he requests the chorus to retire; but as the rules to which the author had bound himself cannot dispense with their presence,* he calls them back again, saying, that "concealment would be vain," and reminds them of their obligations to him, which they very prettily acknowledge. He then confesses the whole truth to Elfrida, and tells her that to his love she owes the loss of a crown:—

"But where's the tie, Elfrida, that may bind
Thy faith and love?"
    Elfrida. The strongest, sure, my Lord,
The golden nuptial tie. Try but its strength.

---

* The rules of the Greek stage did not absolutely forbid the temporary absence of the chorus, for there was an express word (*Metanastasis*) to designate their retirement. Dr. Blomfield thinks that the stage was occasionally left altogether vacant, and intervals of time similar to our between-acts interposed; but this is so awkward an expedient, that we cannot suspect the Athenians of having recourse to it.

We forgot to mention that gentlemen (we hope there are no such ladies) who dislike poetry had better skip this article, for it is only for his poetry that Mason's life is worth writing.

> *Athel.*   I must, perforce, this instant : know, Elfrida,
> Once on a day of high festivity,
> The youthful King, encircled with his nobles,
> Crown'd high the sparkling bowl; and much of love,
> Of beauty much, the sprightly converse ran :
> When, as it well might chance, the brisk Lord Ardulph
> Made gallant note of Orgar's peerless daughter,
> And in such phrase as might inflame a breast
> More cool than Edgar's.   Early on the morrow
> The impatient monarch gave me swift commission
> To view those charms of which Lord Ardulph's tongue
> Had given such warm description; to whose words,
> If my impartial eye gave full assent,
> I had his royal mandate on the instant
> To hail you Queen of England.

So far the truth of history is followed.   But now commences the deviation.   The actual Elfrida, deeply resenting the fraud which had given her a simple Thane instead of a royal lover, put on all her charms to captivate Edgar, and rejoiced in the ruin of the too fond Athelwold. Such at least is the narrative of the Monkish historians, who were never better pleased than when villifying woman, whose society they had superstitiously forsworn.   But the wickedness of Elfrida is too well authenticated to admit of rational doubt : the fame of her beauty has never raised her a vindicator, though the power of beauty oft times long outlasts its brief possession, witness the enamoured defenders of Mary Stuart, and of Anne Boleyn.   But Mason avails himself of a poet's liberty, and makes her reply.

> Stead of which
> You came, and hail'd me wife of Athelwold.
> Was this the tale I was so taught to fear?
> Was this the deed that known would make me fly
> Thy clasping arm, as 'twere the poisonous adder?
> No, let this tender fond embrace assure thee
> That thy Elfrida's love can never die;
> Or if it could, this animating touch,
> Would soon rewake it into life and rapture.

We are afraid that there are few, even of the best of women, who would not feel a momentary anger against the man whose passion had defrauded them of a diadem.   The love of rank is the besetting temptation of womanhood.   Elfrida, however, has not one misgiving, but first proposes to hide herself in her chamber, and robe Albina, (the principal of the chorus,) in her bridal vestments, and when afraid that this stratagem would be unavailing, as Ardulph accompanied the King, she declares that she will stain her complexion with berries, hang her head,

> Drawl out an idiot phrase, and do each act
> With even a rude and peasant awkwardness.

Athelwold expresses a degree of shame and contrition at the prospect
of meeting the King, which the occasion does not seem to warrant.
Any man, King, or other, who chooses a wife by other's reports, and
makes love by proxy, richly deserves to be cheated, and so Elfrida very
sensibly thinks.   This scene is, on the whole, very pleasing, but it is
obvious how terribly the chorus hangs on, the little they say being quite
superfluous.   Athelwold goes off, and Elfrida, after receiving her
attendants' compliments upon her virtue, which she declares is nothing
but love, follows him.   The chorus sing an ode to constancy, wherein,
not content with turning that abstract quality into a Goddess and a
heaven-born Queen, the Anglo-Saxon maidens talk of " Cynthia riding
on the brow of night."   But Shakspeare was never more negligent of
the proprieties of time and place than Mason has shewn himself in this
drama, which affects the praise of consummate art.

The concluding stanza, though sadly encumbered with epithets, contains a just and noble sentiment :—

> The soul which she inspires has power to climb
> To all the heights sublime
> Of virtue's towering hill.
> That hill at whose low foot, weak warbling strays
> The scanty stream of human praise,
> A shallow trickling rill.
> While on the summits hov'ring Angels shed
> From their blest pinions, the nectarious dews
> Of pure immortal fame : From these the Muse
> Oft steals some precious drops, and skilful blends
> With those the lower fountain lends :
> Then showers it all on some high-favoured head.

The next scene introduces Elfrida, striving to escape the importunity
of Orgar, whom she hardly recognizes through his disguise.   He discovers himself, sets no limits to his indignation against Athelwold, flies
into a passion with his daughter for calling him husband.

> Husband—'Sdeath what husband ?
> Is Athelwold thy husband ?   Sooner call
> The impeached thief true master of the booty
> He stole or murdered for.   Disdain the villain
> And help me to revenge thee.

The chorus moralizes on the unlawfulness of revenge in good set terms,
but this grave office sits very awkwardly upon young females.   Moral
truths, elicited by sudden feeling or conviction, even by virtuous scorn
and anger, are never more effective than when uttered by female lips ;
but to be watching for every occasion of giving advice, or reading a
lecture, as it is an odious propensity in any age or sex, so it is an
absolute outrage in a young woman.   Orgar, however, is not in a

humour to be schooled.   He drops more than a hint that Christian
ethics are not for him, a secret adherent to the creed of the Bards and
Druids.   And he insists upon it that Elfrida, so far from hiding or dis-
guising her beauty, shall call forth all her attractions :——

> Hear me, daughter,
> You went to search for flowers, to blot your charms
> With their dun hue.   Yes, thou shalt search for flowers,
> Yet shall they be the loveliest of the spring:
> Flowers, that entangling in thine auburn hair,
> Or blushing 'mid the whiteness of thy bosom,
> May, to the power of every native grace,
> Give double life, and lustre.   Haste my child,
> Array thyself in thy most gorgeous garb,
> And see each jewel, which my love procured thee,
> Dart its full radiance.   More than all, put on
> The nobler ornament of winning smiles
> And kind inviting glances.

Surely no *man of honour*, no haughty British chieftain, however his
better nature might be perverted by ambition or revenge, would or
could give such advice to a daughter.   It might fitly enough proceed
from a Circassian merchant, anxious to sell a she-slave to the best
advantage.   But when Orgar, impatient at Elfrida's repugnance,
charges her on her duty, and by what he calls " a father's just prerogative" to act the part of a wanton for the ruin of the man whom she
has sworn to love and honour, we turn away disgusted from such a treasonable libel on paternal authority.   The chorus, left alone, divide into
semi-choruses, and sing some irregular lines, in imitation of the ancient
monostrophes, in which the pen of fate, dipt in its deepest gall, is
employed, somewhat incongruously, to write mystic characters on a
wall.   This shews that the young ladies had read the Pantheon and
the book of Daniel.   The King and Athelwold enter.   The King commends his host's taste in architecture and the picturesque ; the beautiful
site of his castle, and its " goodly structure," its " turrets trim " " and
taper spires," (is not this mention of Gothic ornaments premature ?)
and its " choicest masonry :"——

> Each part
> Doth boast a separate grace; but ornament,
> Tho' here the richest, that the eye can note,
> Is used, not lavish'd : Art seems generous here,
> Yet not a prodigal.

And then the King pays his respects to the ladies of the chorus.   Athelwold is alarmed to see them in tears, and expresses his apprehensions in
an *aside*.   Edgar too is surprised and concerned at their mournful
taciturnity, and courteously hopes that no " discourteous treatment " is

the cause of their sorrow. They break silence to do justice to Athelwold, " the noblest, gentlest, best of masters," and are proceeding in his praises, when Orgar bursts in to make his complaints to Edgar, calls Athelwold traitor, and at last, after several interruptions, discloses how he has been tricked of his daughter, and the King of his bride. Edgar takes all very coolly, but is prevailed on to go and judge of Elfrida with his own eyes. Athelwold, forgetting the courtier, the host, and the husband, stands still, and asks the chorus twenty questions in a breath. " What said she when I left her? How came her father hither? How did she receive him? Did she marshal him to his deed of vengeance? The chorus exculpate Elfrida from the suspicion of disclosing the secret, and confess their own disobedience in concealing the unknown stranger, who proves to be Orgar, and who from his concealment has over-heard all. There is a loftiness in Athelwold's reply, by no means unfrequent in Mason's writings, which would excuse worse faults of construction and language than he is guilty of:—

> *Chorus.* This our disobedience
> We own—
>   *Athel.* Was my perdition. Yet 'tis well.
> I blame ye not; it was Heaven's justice, Virgins;
> This brought him hither; this annull'd your faith;
> I do not think you purpos'd my destruction,
> But yet you have destroy'd me. O, Elfrida!
> And art thou faithful? This my jealous eye
> Thought it had mark'd some speck of change upon thee;
> Thought it had found, what might have made thy loss,
> Somewhat within endurance. 'Tis not so;
> And this thy purity but serves t' augment
> The sum of my distractions. Meet me, Edgar,
> With thy raised sword; be merciful and sudden.

He departs; and the chorus recite an Ode upon Truth, which may be found in Enfield's Speaker. No one who reads it there would suppose that it ever was intended to form part of a drama, much less that it was chaunted by a company of young ladies, at a crisis of the utmost distress, when their master and mistress were in the jaws of ruin, partly too by their fault. There is no authority or precedent for such an absurdity in the works of the Greeks; nor can it be excused by that compliance with modern taste which is announced with so much ado, in the explanatory epistles. The verses must have been written for some other occasion, and were thrust in here because they were too good to be lost. They are, however, very indifferent, in a most tawdry style, and no way above the reach of any school-boy, who had read Akenside, and learned to tag verses.

After the Ode is finished Athelwold rushes in, bent upon self-murder, for Edgar has seen Elfrida, and Athelwold is banished. The chorus make a tolerable speech against suicide. Athelwold wavers. Elfrida enters, and Edgar follows. Elfrida pleads for her husband with considerable earnestness and dignity. Athelwold is all despair and contrition, talks of killing himself. Edgar is melted, and forgives him all freely, with a generosity very fine ; but not at all to be expected from a despot, who, a few minutes before, thought of falling foul on a woman, a wife, whom he perceives has given the heart, upon which he never had the slightest claim, to another. He goes off to chace the " nimble roebuck," bidding Athelwold follow, who, after one farewell, obeys. The detestable Orgar, (who has been standing by all the while without opening his mouth) now breaks out into a storm of reproaches, which are deprived of all verisimilitude by being clothed in pompous dignified language. Shakspeare understood human nature far better when he made old Capulet call poor little Juliet " tallow-face" and " green-sickness carrion ;" nor are the vituperative passages in Æschylus, Sophocles, or Euripides, a bit more polite. Rage is essentially vulgar, and never vulgarer, than when it proceeds from mortified pride, or disappointed ambition, or thwarted wilfulness. A baffled despot is the vulgarest of dirty wretches, no matter whether he be the despot of a nation vindicating its rights, or of a donkey sinking under its load.

Mason makes a poor attempt to dignify the villainy of Orgar. He, forsooth, is of ancient British line, and Athelwold's perfidy has prevented the British blood from being regalized. Accordingly, he resolves to wait his return, and give him " fair combat." He retires. A pretty dialogue ensues between Elfrida and the chorus, who are, however, a sort of Job's comforters, tormenting the poor lady with likelihoods of her husband dispatching himself. But he is destined to another end. Edwin, the representative of the *nuntius*, or messenger of the old drama, arrives to relate that Edgar, having drawn Athelwold into a retired part of the wood, and declared that, as a sovereign, he forgives his disloyalty, challenges him to combat, as man to man, and friend to friend, for Elfrida. Athelwold only makes a feint of defence, quickly falls, and dies smiling. Elfrida invokes all Heaven's vengeance upon Edgar, and gathers strength from intensity of sorrow. The dignity of *her* anger is true to the noblest nature. Orgar, hearing her lamentations, comes in. She falls at his feet, implores him to avenge her, and then suddenly recollects that he too was sworn against the life of Athelwold :

> Alas! I had forgot : had Edgar spar'd him,
> That sword to which my madness called for vengeance

> Ere long was meant to do the bloody deed,
> And make the murder parricide.

Orgar, not at all displeased at what has happened, tries to comfort her; but she will not be comforted, and withdraws with the principal virgin, Albina, the *coryphaeus* or spokeswoman of the chorus. Orgar goes to confer with the King, whom he now feels confident of getting for a son-in-law: charging the virgins, as soon as Elfrida's grief is a little quieted, to hint the King's praises till, "by practice won, she bear their fuller blazon." The semichorus resolve to say truth, and nothing but truth. Albina returns, and informs her companions that Elfrida has resolved on perpetual widowhood: and then Elfrida enters herself, and kneeling down, vows to build a convent on the spot where her husband fell, and to preserve "for aye, austerity, and single life:"

> Hear next, that Athelwold's sad widow swears
> Never to violate the holy vow
> She to his truth first plighted; swears to bear
> The sober singleness of widowhood
> To her cold grave.

The chorus pray that the vow may be enrolled "mid the dread records of eternity," and so the curtain drops.

An acute and elegant critic remarks, that this conclusion reminds the reader too much of the proverbial instability of widows' vows,

> Vows made in pain as violent and void.

But does not this feeling arise chiefly, if not solely, from the confusion between the Elfrida of history, and the Elfrida of the play?

As an accommodation of the ancient drama to modern habits and sympathies, "Elfrida" must be pronounced a decided failure. The Unities are indeed preserved; but at the expense of probability and common sense. The chorus, instead of forming a necessary and integral part of the drama, is a mere incumbrance on the action, and at best a *Divertissement* between the acts. But a worse, because a moral fault, is, the unnecessary degradation of the parental character in the person of Orgar. His mock-mendicity, and lying, and skulking, and eves-dropping, and tale-telling, effect no purpose that might not have been better brought about in other ways; and after the discovery of Athelwold's treachery, he is of no use at all, but a dead weight upon the scene.

We cannot help thinking that Mason *began* his "Elfrida" with an eye to the theatre; but finding the lyric parts, in which his strength lay, overgrow the dramatic, he abandoned that intention, and did not even offer it to a manager. When, however, he had acquired a name, which was likely to fill the house, the elder Colman most unjustifiably produced it at Covent-Garden, with his own or somebody else's alterations.

Mason was angry at this, no wonder ; and Colman threatened him with a chorus of Grecian washerwomen. Mason prudently let the matter drop. He had an irritable anxiety about his reputation, which made him a very unequal match for managers of iron nerve and brazen face ; and though he had undoubtedly the right on his side, Colman and the chorus of washerwomen would have had the laugh on theirs. In 1776, " Elfrida" appeared at Govent Garden with the author's own alterations. It was probably heard once or twice with respectful attention, and then heard no more. " Elfrida " would have sunk in oblivion if Mason had never written Caractacus.

Nearly eight years, " not idly nor unprofitably spent," intervened between the publication of Elfrida and that of Caractacus ; but it is convenient at once to finish our notices of Mason's dramatic career. His talent was of the improving kind ; and as he seems to have delighted in composition, he never let it rust for want of use. Accordingly, Caractacus, compared to Elfrida, is as the well-considered work of a man, to the rash adventure of a boy. Much of its superiority depends, however, upon the choice of the scene and of the story. The last of the Britons making his final stand in the hallowed seat of the Druidical religion, is an imposing and magnificent object, accordant to the spirit of that Grecian tragedy which Mason proposed as his model. The Druids possess the sacerdotal and mysterious character which properly pertains to a chorus ; and the awful scenery of Mona's Isle affords space for landscape painting, which, though sparingly indulged by the Greek tragedians, is by no means incompatible with the nature of the Attic drama.

The opening speech has been censured as too poetical,—a very false and idle censure ; for poetry cannot be too poetical. A sounder objection is, that it violates the moral probabilities of character. Aulus Didius is come on a wicked purpose, to be executed by the wickedest of means, by urging two British youths to betray, with blackest falsehood, the veteran defender of British liberty. We should be sorry for Nature, if such a man, at such a time, could have any perception of her beauties. A superstitious shuddering at her wild and awful shapes he might feel ; but coward superstition suggests only mean, and ugly, and loathsome images. A poet may—indeed he must—give voice to feelings that in real life are silent : he must develope the imperfect germs of thought, and give them form and outwardness. It is a senseless cavil to say, that such and such a character would not, in the given situation, speak the words that the poet attributes to him, or any thing like them. But still the words should express some meaning of the supposed speaker's mind or heart, though it should be a meaning that in reality would not be summoned to consciousness. Tarquin must not stay his "ravishing strides" to praise the moon for her chastity.* Had Aulus come to worship the old divinities of Mona, or had he been making a *tour in search of the picturesque*, the lines, which are quite Salvator Rosa, would have been perfectly appropriate :

> " Here, Romans, pause, and let the eye of wonder
> Gaze on the solemn scene; behold yon oak,
> How stern he frowns, and with his broad brown arms
> Chills the *pale* † plain beneath him : mark yon altar,
> The dark stream brawling round its rugged base,
> These cliffs, these yawning caverns, this wide circus,
> Skirted with unhewn stone : they awe the soul
> As if the very Genius of the place
> Himself appeared, and with terrific tread
> Stalk'd round his drear domain."

The following scene, between Aulus Didius and the sons of Cartismandua, Elidurus and Vellinus, supposed to be hostages, whose liberty is promised as the price of decoying Caractacus into the Roman power, is not deficient in dramatic vivacity. Ever since the *Babes* were led into the *Wood*, and perhaps long before, if ever two villains are set to one service, one of them turns out to be quite a good, honest, tender-hearted fellow ; while the other is an obdurate scoffer at his scruples. So as soon as Aulus Didius quits the Druidical circle, Elidurus and Vellinus ‡ fall to an altercation, the former determining

* What can be more beautiful than the scene between Lorenzo and Jessica, at the beginning of the fifth act of the Merchant of Venice ? but how utterly absurd would it have been, if even that single line—
  " How sweet the moonshine sleeps upon this bank ! "
had been put into the mouth of Shylock ? Yet an equal absurdity is perpetrated in Cibber's alteration of " Richard the Third," where the descriptive lines of the chorus of " Henry the Fifth " are put into the mouth of King Richard. Shakspeare, however, has himself neglected the propriety for which we are contending, in two instances. The beautifully-fanciful poetry uttered by Iachimo, in Imogen's chamber, could have no seed or root in the heart of such a ribald scoundrel. The other is a less glaring case, but still the flowery description of Cleopatra on the Cydnus does not proceed naturally from a rugged old soldier like Ænobarbus.

† *Pale* is one of Mason's *perpetual* epithets. The compound *pale-eyed* occurs some fifty times in the course of his lyrics ; and yet he never had the courtesy to pen a little note to explain what he means by it.

‡ From a letter of Gray's to Mason, it appears that these decoy-youths were not in the first sketch of the play, supposed to be the sons of Cartismandua, but nobodies, like the Nuntius of the ancient drama, or Shakspeare's still more anonymous " two gentlemen." This, with several others of Gray's letters, shews how long Caractacus was in writing, and how many alterations it underwent before it came before the public eye. Its date is Sept. 28, 1757. We shall transcribe the first paragraphs,

to "proceed no further in this business," while Vellinus will have it
that honour, duty to their mother (who is the prime promoter of the
treason), and religion, which will be undone if the Romans execute
their threat of destroying the sacred groves, oblige them to fulfil
their engagement.   And so they go off without coming to any agreement.   Then the chorus of Druids make their entrance, and divide
into responsive semi-chori.   There is something very antique and
mystical about their opening incantation.   The following lines read
almost like a translation from the Welsh or Runic:

> But tell me yet,
> From the grot of charms and spells
> Where our matron sister dwells,
> Brennus! has thy holy hand
> Safely brought the Druid wand,
> And the potent adder-stone,
> Gender'd fore the autumnal moon,
> When in undulating twine
> The foaming snakes prolific join;

together with a note of Mason's own; for the history and progress of Mason's works
is the most important history of his life.

"I have (as I desired Mr. Stonehewer to tell you) read over Caractacus twice, not
with pleasure only, but with emotion.   You may say what you will; but the contrivance, the manners, the interests, the passions, and the expression, go beyond your
Elfrida many, many leagues.   I even say (though you will think me a bad judge of
this), that the *world* will like it better.   I am struck with the chorus, who are not
there merely to sing and dance, but bear throughout a principal part in the action;
and have (beside the costume, which is excellent) as much a character of their own
as any other person.   I am charmed with their priestly pride and obstinacy, when,
after all is lost, they resolve to confront the Roman general, and spit in his face.
But now I am going to tell you what touches me most from the beginning.   The
first opening is very greatly improved: the curiosity of Didius is now a very natural
reason for dwelling on each particular of the scene before him; nor is the description
at all too long.   I am glad to find the two young men are Cartismandua's sons.
They interest me far more.   I love people of condition: they were men before that
nobody knew: one could not make a bow to them if one had met them at a public
place."---*Letter 27, Mason's edition.*

To which Mr. Mason subjoins:---"In the manuscript now before him, Mr. Gray
had only the first ode; the others were not then written; and although the dramatic
part was then brought to a conclusion, yet it was afterwards in many places altered.
He was mistaken with regard to the opinion the world would have about it.   That
world, which usually loves to be led in such matters, rather than form an opinion for
itself, was taught a different sentiment; and one of its leaders went so far as to
declare, that he never knew a second work fall so much below a first from the same
hand.   To oppose Mr. Gray's judgment to his, I must own, gives me some small
satisfaction; and to enjoy it, I am willing to risk that imputation of vanity which
will probably fall to my share for having published this letter."

> When they hiss, and when they bear
> Their wondrous egg aloof in air,
> Thence, before to earth it fall,
> The Druid in his hallowed pall
> Receives the prize,
> And instant flies,
> Follow'd by the envenom'd brood,
> Till he cross the chrystal flood.

Gray had courteously collected for his friend whatever records of the Druidical superstitions are to be found in the Greek and Roman writers, and Mason has made a skilful use of those scanty materials, with such additions from his own invention as seemed to harmonize with what was known of Celtic theology. He is also somewhat indebted to the Edda and other relics of Scandinavian fable. With the Druidical metaphysics, commemorated in the Welsh Triads, and songs of the bards, since brought to light by the industry of Cymrodorian scholars, he does not appear to have had much acquaintance. If these metaphysical doctrines were really couched in the Druids' mysteries, the Druids were very philosophical dreamers indeed.

The presence of the Druidical bards is well accounted for,—an important circumstance in the formation of a chorus. Caractacus is about to be admitted into the order, and initiated into their mystic rites. Abandoning all hope of successful resistance to the Roman invaders, he is resolved to lay aside his royalty, and

> To end his days in secrecy and peace,
> A Druid among Druids.

His approach is well described. He enters accompanied by his daughter Evelina, and apostrophizes the oaks in some very spirited and well-versified lines. The whole scene is good, but it is a question whether it would not be still better without Evelina. The delineation of female characters was not in Mason's province. He tries to make them tender, but he only makes them fond; and what is worse, he throws their expressions of fondness into the form of abstract propositions, clothed in language which not only *is* studied, but *appears* so. Evelina, in good sooth, talks more like a Roman *blue stocking* (a character that did exist) than like a British maiden. She is too sentimental for a heroine, and too sententious for a girl. There is a speech of Caractacus's which has been highly praised, and by a high authority, for its pathetic simplicity: perhaps Evelina's reply, in the same judgment, is simple and pathetic likewise. The principal Druid bids the King bethink himself

> If ought in this vain earth
> Still holds too firm a union with thy soul,
> Estranging it from peace?

> *Carac.* I had a Queen,
> Bear with my weakness Druid! this tough breast
> Must heave a sigh, for she is unrevenged,
> And can I taste true peace, she unrevenged?
> So chaste, so lov'd a Queen?   Ah Evelina!
> Hang not thus weeping on the feeble arm
> That could not save thy mother.
>   *Evelina.*   To hang thus
> Softens the pang of grief; and the sweet thought,
> That a fond father still supports his child,
> Sheds on my pensive mind such soothing balm,
> As doth the blessing of these pious seers,
> When most they wish our welfare.   Would to heaven,
> A daughter's presence could as much avail
> To ease her father's woes, as his doth mine.

The *meaning* of these lines is indeed pathetic, and it is probable that when the author first conceived the situation, he really felt for Caractacus and his daughter.   But it was his practice to write and re-write till his original conceptions were evaporated, and nothing but his own words remained upon his memory.   He was like a painter who, having taken a hasty sketch of a landscape on the spot, goes into his study and touches and re-touches till the little recollection of the original, which he retains, only serves to puzzle him, and his work at last has neither the Catholic truth of art, nor the individual reality of nature.

Mason, as we have seen, was a great stickler for the *Unities*, yet he violated the most essential unity of all—the unity of interest.   He attempted to combine interests which destroy one another.   Had " Caractacus" been composed according to the ideal of the ancient drama, Caractacus would have appeared simply as the impersonation of British liberty; and the predominant feeling should have been, that the fate of an individual involved the doom of a state.   And had Mason written for *himself* he would have preserved this singleness of purpose, and produced a single satisfactory impression.   But he thought it necessary to *condescend* to the popular weakness: to shew Caractacus as the man, the husband, the father, and thereby, he has introduced as great an inconsistency as could have been effected by the most tragi-comic alternation of mirth and tears.

There is something wild and grand in the address of the bards to Snowdon, and the spirits resident thereon.   A locality has seldom been made better use of in the drama:—

> Strike, ye Bards,
> Strike all your strings symphonious; wake a strain
> May penetrate, may purge, may purify,
> His yet unhallowed bosom;

Call ye hither
The airy tribe, that on yon mountain dwell
Ev'n on majestic Snowdon; they who never
Deign visit mortal men, save on some cause
Of highest import; but sublimely shrined *
On its hoar top in domes of chrystalline ice,
Hold converse with those spirits that possess
The skies' pure sapphire, nearest Heaven itself.

The ode which follows this invocation has been as highly praised as any thing that Mason has written. The opening lines are certainly sounding and harmonious; but like most odes of your *correcting* writers, far from correct. The third is absolutely ludicrous. Mona must have *fretted herself to fiddle strings:*—

Mona on Snowdon calls,
Hear, thou King of mountains, hear,
Hark she speaks from all her strings,
Hark, her loudest echo rings.
King of mountains, bend thine ear,
Send thy spirits, send them soon,
Now, when midnight and the moon
Meet upon thy front of snow,
See! their gold and ebon rod,
Where the sober sisters nod,†
And greet in whispers sage and slow.
Snowdon! mark, 'tis magic's hour;
Now the mutter'd spell has power;

* Above me are the Alps,
The palaces of Nature, whose vast walls,
Have pinnacled in clouds their snowy scalps,
And throned eternity in icy halls,
Of cold sublimity.'' CHILD HAROLD. CANT. I.

† Gray seems to have been much pleased with these lines. Speaking of the advantages and licences of subjects like Caractacus, drawn from a period of whose manners and opinions scarcely anything is known, he says, " They leave an unbounded liberty to pure imagination and fiction, (our favourite provinces,) where no critic can molest, or antiquary gainsay us: and yet (to please me) these fictions must have some affinity, some seeming connexion, with that little we really know of the character and customs of the people. For example, I never heard in my life that midnight and the moon were sisters; that they carried rods of ebony and gold, or met to whisper on the top of a mountain; but now I could lay my life that it is all true, and do not doubt it will be found so in some pantheon of the Druids, that is to be discovered in the library at Herculaneum."—LETTER 27.
I cannot think " sober sisters" by any means a happy epithet in the present state of the English language. Sober originally meant sound-minded, self-possessed; but at present it only implies the absence of ebriety.

Power to rend thy ribs of rock,
And burst thy base with thunder's shock.
But to thee no ruder spell
Shall Mona use, than those that dwell
In music's secret cells, and lie
Steep'd in the stream of harmony.

Snowdon has heard the strain,
Hark, amid the wondering grove
Other voices meet our ear,
Other harpings answer clear,
Pinions flutter, shadows move,
Busy murmurs hum around,
Rustling vestments brush the ground,
Round, and round, and round they go,
Through the twilight, through the shade,
Mount the oak's majestic head,
And gild the tufted mistleto.

This last image, pretty as it is, is far too pretty for the occasion. It would be well in a sportive fairy-tale; but the Druids, while invoking mysterious powers, in whose existence they had a real, not a poetical belief, could not be in a mood to observe such minute effects.

This choral ode, which poor as our literature then was in good lyric poetry, might well pass for a chef-d'oeuvre, is very skilfully broken off by the principal Druid announcing that "a sullen smoke involves the altar," that "the central oak doth quake," and that he hears the sound of profane steps. Vellinus and Elidurus have been detected in the "bottom of a shadowy dell holding earnest converse." They are dragged in by the attendant Druids. Their treacherous purpose of course could not be more than suspected; but the very presence of unconsecrated persons in the sacred island is a sacrilege. Elidurus is abashed, and on the point of stammering out a confession, when Vellinus snatches the words out of his mouth, and lies with tragic audacity. He pretends a commission from his mother, Cartismandua, Queen of the Brigantes, to invite Caractacus to her aid against the legions of Ostorius, the Roman general, who, though kept at bay "for three long moons," still hover round the frontiers,

Like falcons
They hang suspended, loth to quit their prey,
And yet afraid to seize it.

(a striking and appropriate image.) The whole speech is well written, and has skilfully adopted the sustained *rhetorical* style in which

Shakspeare* clothes the harangues of deceivers. Every period is evidently balanced and digested before hand; nothing trusted to the impulse of the moment. Caractacus, hearing his name mentioned, steps from behind the altar, and declares his readiness to shed his "last purple drop" for Britain. The chorus, not liking the bold look and nimble tongue of the young orator, censure his rashness: but Vellinus, to make sure of him, touches his tenderest point by telling him that his Queen Guideria is safe in Cartismandua's court, having been rescued by his (Vellinus's) valour. Caractacus is entrapped. The speech with which he welcomes the intelligence is really affecting, though it shews that the British hero was no physiognomist:—

> Let me clasp thee, youth,
> And thou shalt be my son; I had one, Stranger,
> Just of thy years; he look'd, like thee, right honest,
> And yet he fail'd me. Were it not for him,
> Who, as thou seest, ev'n at this hour of joy,
> Draws tears down mine old cheek, I were as blest
> As the great Gods.

and so he calls for his spear, bow, target, &c. The chorus check his impetuosity, reminding him of the unfavourable omens. He, like Hector, despises auguries, exclaiming:—

> No, by Heaven I feel,
> Beyond all omens, that within my breast,
> Which marshals me to conquest.

But the Druid asserts the superiority of the priesthood to the monarchy with a boldness worthy of Pope Gregory or Pope Boniface. Mador is the model of what a High-Church-man *ought* to be:—

> Thou art a King, a Sov'reign o'er frail man,
> I am a Druid, servant of the Gods,
> Such service is above such Sovereignty.

At some times, and from some persons, such sentiments as these, though spoken in the character of a Druid, would have exposed an author to peril. But Mason was then a known Whig, and the violence of Whig jealousy was blown over. Yet in a note he has thought proper to prove from Dion, Chrysostom, and Helmodus de Slavis, that this supreme authority of the priesthood over the civil power was an historical fact.

---

* As examples of this management, see Macbeth's speech in justification of himself for killing the grooms; the speeches of the King in Hamlet; Antony's Oration, where however there is a mixture of sincerity and fraud. An admirable instance of bold and eloquent pleading in a bad cause may be found in Webster's "Vittoria Corombona," extracted in Lamb's specimens of early Dramatic Writers, a work to which my obligations are only less than those I owe to his "Tales from Shakspeare."

After some farther conversation about patriotism, death and destiny, and the fiend oblivion,* the principal Druid, resolving to seek for the counsel of the Gods in sleep, desires the uninitiated to retire, and then addressed the bards in lines which have been much and justly admired for the vivid manner in which they picture sound, and describe the powers of music. Indeed, except the description of the nightingale's song, in the Odyssee, the lines on music in Milton's L'Allegro, and Crashaw's "Music's Duel," (taken from Strada's Prolusions) we do not remember any thing of the kind equal to these verses :

> Ye time-enobled seers, whose reverend brows
> Full eighty winters whiten ; you, ye bards,
> Leoline, Cadwall, Hoel, Cantaber,
> Attend upon our slumbers ; wondrous men,
> Ye whose skill'd fingers know how best to lead
> Through all the maze of sound, the wayward step
> Of Harmony, recalling oft, and oft
> Permitting her unbridled course to rush
> Through dissonance to concord, sweetest then,
> Even when expected harshest.

The first strophe and anti-strophe of the following chorus are so

---

* " The time will come, when Destiny and Death,
    Throned in a burning car, the thundering wheels,
    Arm'd with gigantic scythes of Adamant,
    Shall scour the field of life, and in the rear,
    The fiend Oblivion : kingdoms, empires, worlds,
    Melt in the general blaze : when lo ! from high,
    Andraste darting catches from the wreck,
    The roll of fame, claps her ascending plumes,
    And stamps on orient stars each patriot name,
    Round her eternal dome."

Is not this "Hercles vein?" Could Kidd or Marloe, Mahound and Termagant, or "bedlam Tamburlane" have out-heroded this ? Go by, Jeronymo. Yet not unlikely Mason thought it the very finest passage in the whole Drama. It was, however, written differently at first, and altered at Gray's suggestion. " The car of Destiny and Death is a very noble invention of the same class, and as far as that goes, is so fine, that it makes me more delicate than perhaps I should be about the close of it. Andraste sailing on the wings of Fame, that snatches the wreaths to hang them on her loftiest amaranth, though a clear and beautiful piece of *unknown* mythology, has too *Greek* an air to give me perfect satisfaction."

Second thoughts, in poetry, are seldom best, especially when those thoughts are not the poet's own. The original image is more agreeable and less monstrous than the one substituted. Strabo informs us, that the Druids foretold the final destruction of the world by fire.

beautiful, that we cannot forbear them, though we have already exceeded in quotation:

> Hail, thou harp of Phrygian fame !
> In years of yore that Camber bore
> From Troy's sepulchral flame.
> With ancient Brute, to Britain's shore.
> The mighty minstrel came:
> Sublime upon the burnish'd prow
> He bade thy manly modes to flow.
> Britain heard the descant bold ;
> She flung her white arms o'er the Sea,
> Proud in her bosom to enfold
> The freight of harmony.
> Mute till then was every plain,
> Save where the flood o'er mountains rude
> Tumbled his tide amain,
> And Echo, from the impending wood,
> Resounded the hoarse strain ;
> While from the north the sullen gale
> With hollow whistlings shook the vale ;
> Dismal notes, and answered soon
> By savage howl the heaths among,
> What time the wolf doth bay the trembling moon,
> And thin the bleating throng.

But Mason never long together keeps clear of personifications, which, if they were always striking, or beautiful, or singly appropriate, would be cumbersome, because there are too many of them for any but an expressly allegorical poem. But sometimes the personification is merely verbal,—a stale device to exalt the style,—and sometimes they produce an incongruity, being unsuited to the time, the speaker, or the occasion. The bard Mador talks far too like a modern poet, when he speaks of "Fancy the Fairy," and "Inspiration, bright ey'd Dame." The mention of these nonentities takes away from the credibility of the supernatural agencies, which the interest of the drama requires us *pro tempore* to admit to be real existences. Some verses in the sequel of this ode are exquisite, as

> Lo ! the sound of distant plumes
> Pants through the pathless desert of the air.

Some villainous, as

> Tis not the flight of *her*;
> Tis sleep, her dewy harbinger.

and worse if possible :

> I sing
> A sevenfold chime, and sweep and *swing*,
> To mix thy music with the spheres.

How could Gray suffer such enormities as these to pass? The description of Inspiration, when she comes, "with a pencil in her hand," is very indifferent.

While this chorus, which begins so well, is singing, the Druid seer goes to sleep, has very painful dreams, and at the end of it starts up in great terror, and utters an incoherent speech, which is timely interrupted by the entrance of Evelina, who, after pardon asked for her intrusion, declares her suspicions of the two Brigantine youths, and specially the elder, Vellinus. The Druids caution her to beware of rash judgment, with a just compliment to her sex:

> Say'st thou, virgin?
> Heed what thou say'st. Suspicion is a guest
> That, in the breast of man, of wrathful man,
> Too oft *his* * welcome finds; *yet seldom sure
> In that submissive calm that smooths the mind
> Of maiden innocence.*
>   *Evelina.* I know it well,
> Yet must I still distrust the elder stranger;
> For while he talks (and much the flatterer talks),
> His brother's silent carriage gives disproof
> Of all his boast; indeed, I mark'd it well;
> And as my father with the elder held
> Bold speech and warlike, as is still his wont
> When fir'd with hope of conquest, oft I saw
> A sigh unbidden heave the younger's breast,
> Half check'd as it was rais'd, sometimes methought
> His gentle eye would cast a glance on me,
> As if he pitied me; and then again
> Would fasten on my father, gazing there
> To veneration; then he'd sigh again,
> Look on the ground, and hang his modest head
> Most pensively.

This is beautifully true to nature.† Men are deceived in their

---

* This is one, but not an only instance in which Mason has injured and overclouded his phrase by unnecessary and imperfect personification. How much clearer and more flowing were this passage, were it written "too oft a welcome finds." As it is, we can hardly tell to what antecedent *his* refers,—whether to *suspicion* or to *man*.

† I trust I shall not be censured if I quote from an author whom it might not beseem *me* to praise; but the passage occurs in a piece not so well known as some others, and illustrates the principles I have endeavoured to explain:

> "And yet Sarolta, simple, inexperienced.
> Could see him as he was, and often warned me:
> Whence learned she this?—O, she was innocent!
> And to be innocent is Nature's wisdom!
> The fledge-dove knows the prowlers of the air.

judgments of others by a thousand causes : by their hopes, their ambition, their vanity, their antipathies, their likes and dislikes, their party feelings, their nationality, but above all, by their presumptuous reliance on the rationative understanding, their disregard of presentiments and unaccountable impressions, and their vain attempts to reduce every thing to rule and measure. Women, on the other hand, if they be very women, are seldom deceived, except by love, compassion, or religious sympathy,—by the latter too often deplorably ; but then it is not because their better angel neglects to give warning, but because they are persuaded to make a merit of disregarding his admonitions. The craftiest Iago cannot win the good opinion of a *true* woman, unless he approach her as a lover, an unfortunate, or a religious confidante. Be it, however, remembered, that this superior discernment in character is merely a female *instinct*, arising from a more delicate sensibility, a finer tact, a clearer intuition, and a natural abhorrence of every appearance of evil. It is a sense which only belongs to the innocent—quite distinct from the tact of experience. If, therefore, ladies without experience attempt to *judge*, to draw conclusions from premises, and give a reason for their sentiments, there is nothing in their sex to preserve them from error. But we must return to Caractacus, and show how thoroughly the notions of the Druids coincide with our own, though they have their way of accounting for it :

> The Gods, my brethren,
> Have waked these doubts in the untainted breast
> Of this mild maiden ; oft to female softness,
> Oft to the purity of virgin souls,
> Doth Heaven its voluntary light dispense,
> When victims bleed in vain.

On Evelina's intreaty, the chorus consent that she shall sift Elidurus, and, if possible, draw from him a disclosure of his brother's plots. But at this juncture Caractacus enters with the two Brigantian youths, eager to know the answer of the gods. The Druid informs him that it is unfavourable ; describes his horrible though undefined visions, and hints his suspicions. Vellinus interrupts him haughtily and rudely. The Druid sternly rebukes, and Caractacus apologizes for him. Through-

> Fear'd soon as seen, and flutters back to shelter ;
> And the young steed recoils upon its haunches
> The never-yet-seen adder's hiss first heard.
> O, surer than Suspicion's hundred eyes
> Is that fine sense, which, to the pure in heart,
> By mere oppugnancy of their own goodness,
> Reveals the approach of evil.
>   *S. T. Coleridge's "Zapolya," a Tragedy.*

out the scene, indeed throughout the play, he behaves with that unfaltering boldness, and exhibits that readiness of reply, which the ignorant are so apt to mistake for an evidence of pure intent and innocence,—a mistake which has acquitted many a thief, and not seldom condemned the guiltless.   At last it is decreed that one of the youths shall undergo the ordeal of the rocking stone, which will best be described in the Druid's own words : *

> Behold yon huge
> And unhewn sphere of solid adamant,
> Which poised by magic, rests its central weight
> On yonder pointed rock; firm as it seems,
> Such is its strange and virtuous property,
> It moves obsequious to the gentlest touch
> Of him whose breast is pure; but to a traitor,
> Though e'en a giant's prowess nerved his arm,
> It stands as fixt as Snowdon.

The brothers draw lots; the lot falls on Elidurus.   He fears, yet does not shun the trial, as hardly secure of his own guilt or innocence.

Caractacus and Vellinus are commanded to retire.   The chorus sing the "custom'd hymn," preparatory for the trial of the stone.   It is too much out of character.   Instead of invoking any real or accredited Power, it apostrophizes *Truth*, and gives that ideal personage some very extraordinary properties; at least if Truth is not the Spirit addressed it is by no means clear what is :—

> Thou Spirit pure, that spread'st unseen,
> Thy pinions o'er this ponderous sphere,
> And breathing through each rigid vein,
> Fill'st with stupendous life the marble mass,

(By the way, it was adamant a little while ago,)

> And bid'st it bow upon its base,
> When sovereign Truth is near.

altogether, this "custom'd hymn" is not equal in merit to the generality

---

* "This is meant to describe the rocking stone, of which there are still several to be seen in Wales, Cornwall, and Derbyshire.   They are universally supposed by antiquarians to be Druid monuments; and Mr. Toland thinks 'that the Druids made the people believe that they only could move them, and that by a miracle, by which they condemned or acquitted the accused, and often brought them to confess what could in no other way be extorted from them.'   It was this conjecture which gave the hint for this piece of machinery.   The reader may find a description of one of these rocking stones in Camden's Britannia, in his account of Pembrokeshire; and also several in Borlase's History of Cornwall."---*Note on the passage.*

Similar rocking stones have been discovered in America, and may serve to support the opinion of those who derive the aborigines of the western continent from British parentage.

of Mason's lyric effusions, and might well have been spared. Yet Elidurus says it came over his soul as doth the thunder:—

> While distant yet with unexpected burst,
> It threats the *trembling** ear.

and desire to be led to the trial, though cautioned that Death must be
the penalty of failure. Just as the Druid has pronounced " Thou must
die," Evelina enters and starts at the word, for she is very much interested in the tender-conscienced stripling. He is not less agitated, but
cries out " Lead to the Rock ;" yet the Druid affords him what he
seems to think cruel mercy—a private examination by the Princess.
The scene which follows contains a good situation, and sets the characters of Elidurus and of Evelina in a very pleasing light ; but Mason, in his passion for illustrations, purely Celtic, stumbles into the
profoundest *Bathos*, when he makes the young lady tell the young man
that on his brow the liberal hand of Heaven has pourtrayed truth as visible and bold as were the pictured suns that decked the brows of her
brave ancestors. What a simile !

The conference is prolonged through many speeches, in which however no business is done. Elidurus, though smitten at once with love
and with conscience, will not speak to betray his unworthy brother.
Evelina adjures—weeps—kneels :—

> Ah, see me kneel !
> I am of royal blood, not wont to kneel,
> Yet will I kneel to thee ; O save my father,
> Save a distressful maiden from the force
> Of barbarous men ! Be thou a brother to me,
> For mine alas ! ah !

As she utters these words her real brother enters. There is certainly
no physical impossibility in this. It is one of those coincidences which
" amid the infinite doings of the world," must some time or other have
occurred, as a pack of cards, if shuffled a billion times, would, according
to the doctrine of chances, sometimes produce a perfect sequence. Still
we should vehemently suspect the player in whose hand it occurred.
Gray calls this situation *superlative,* but it seems too melo-dramatic for
a regular and serious drama, and in the closet, produces no effect powerful enough to atone for its improbability. It is a proof, among many
others, that Mason had always a hankering after the stage. But the
dialogue that follows, the surprize and indignation of Arviragus at
finding his sister on her knees before a stranger youth, the severe

---

* Would not this epithet apply better to ears more moveable and muscular, as well
as more elongated, than the human usually are ?

inquiries of the Druid, the confident yet modest tone in which the son
of Caractacus explains his imputed flight and absence, and at once
announces the arrival of the Romans, and the treasonable design of the
young Brigantes, display an energy, a precipitation, an heroic pathos,
of which the later English tragedy has few instances to boast.   Not
less excellent is the conduct of Elidurus, who, after asking for "death,
sudden death," and being threatened with "lingering, piece-meal
death," still refuses to disclose his brother's infamy :—

> It is not fear,
> Druids, it is not fear that shakes me thus,
> The great Gods know it is not.   Ye can never—

This is true tragic language.   But when the Druids threaten him with
torture, and that, too, in terms which imply that it is to be inflicted
by their own sanctified hands, we cannot but think that the *terrible* is
purchased too dear.   Such a proceeding, though not perhaps at variance
with the traditional character of the Druids, who were as little tender
or scrupulous as other sacerdotal *castes*, with regard to the means by
which they maintained their authority, jars painfully with the almost
christian morality uttered by the bardic chorus and the coryphæus.   It,
however, serves its purpose : it elicits the stubborn honour and frater-
nal affection of Elidurus, who interests Arviragus and Evelina so much
in his favour, and gains so much upon the good graces of the chorus, that at last it is agreed that he shall be free, and his brother
hostage for his fidelity.   He wishes to rush forth and engage the
Romans, but this the chorus will not permit till he shall be duly
purified by priestly rites.   The speech in which this declaration is
made, is, though perhaps not meant to be, a master-piece of priestly
sophistry :—

> Hear us, Prince,
> Mona permits not that he fight her battles
> Till duly purified : For though his soul
> Took up unwittingly this deed of baseness,
> Yet is lustration meet.   Learn that in vice
> There is a noisome rankness, unperceived
> By gross corporeal sense, which so offends
> Heaven's pure divinities, as us the stench
> Of vapour wafted from sulphureous pool,
> Or pois'nous weed obscene.   Hence doth the man
> Who even converses with a villain, need
> As much purgation as the pallid wretch
> 'Scap'd from the walls where frowning Pestilence
> Spreads wide her livid banners.   For this cause,
> Ye priests, conduct the youth to yonder grove,
> And do the needful rites.

These sixteen lines, though probably introduced for no other purpose than to get Elidurus out of the way, do in effect comprise the whole art and mystery of priestcraft, as far as it can be practised in a civilized society: of priestcraft, distinguished on the one hand from the mere necromancy of savages, and on the other, from the christian ministry of an enlightened church. The great arcanum of the priest is to convince his subjects of the indispensable necessity of his own order and office. He is not content, by his instructions, to point out the way to righteousness,—by his example, to lead it,—by his admonition and discipline, to restrain those that would stray from it;—but he will have it that his passport is needful to gain admission at the end. He urges great and momentous truths, even the exceeding sinfulness of sin, its deadly and infectious quality, its offensiveness to the pure Divinity, as a quack doctor describes, often with fearful eloquence, (for knavery is more eloquent than honesty) the horrors of disease, and when the vivid picture is strongly stamped on the passive imagination, then he reckons upon a ready reception for his own panacea. Quacks in medicine, however, are generally content to sell their *nostrums*, and suffer their patients to take them in their own way, and at their own time ; but quacks in divinity make the efficacy of the catholicon depend chiefly upon the hand that administers it ;—the physic, according to them, is of no use without the physician. The Druid, in the play, speaks well and wisely of the rankness, the pollution of vice, and the contagion of evil communication ; only, with another Hieratical artifice, expressed in such metaphors as produces a confusion between fancy and conviction, a spiritualizing of the corporeal, and a corporealizing of the spiritual, which predisposes the mind to attribute spiritual effects to corporeal acts,—the very definition of superstition, and the condition of sacerdotal despotism. The power of rites and lustrations (whatever the Druidical lustrations consisted of) to remove the pollution spoken of, the Druid prudently leaves to be inferred.

The meeting of Caractacus and Arviragus follows. The first interview of a father with a son whom he has wrongfully suspected of flight and baseness, and of whose honour he is but now satisfied, is one of those *situations* in which no writer can help being pathetic. As little generally is said when such junctures take place in real life, at least till the first painful transport is passed, and as sighs, and tears suppressed, are not very easily printed, it is perhaps better, in plays meant to be read only, that these meetings should be described than represented. The speech with which Caractacus receives his son is a great deal too long and declamatory ; and it may be remarked, that the old warrior throughout is too fine a talker. Arviragus is brief,—so much the better. It transpires, that as soon as ever Evelina announced to her father the appearance of Arviragus, Vellinus fled to join the Romans. Some scenes follow, which, though well written, do not promote the catastrophe, and seem introduced only to present Evelina in the amiable light of a suppliant for Elidurus, whose life is forfeited by his brother's flight. She prevails. He is purified according to poetic rites :—

> Thrice do we sprinkle thee with day-break dew,
> Shook from the May-thorn blossom ; twice and thrice
> Touch we thy forehead with our holy wand;
> Now thou art fully purged. Now rise, restored
> To virtue and to us

Caractacus and Arviragus re-enter. The Druids pronounce their benediction, and present Caractacus with the " sword of old Bellinus," Trifingus, which sheds " portentous streams of scarlet light," and has slept for many an age within a consecrated oak. Their charge and adjuration is almost literally rendered from an old Greek writer, quoted by Selden in the Prolegomena to his treatise on the Syrian Gods. Mason has studded it with unnecessary epithets, yet it has an imposing magical effect :—

> By the *bright* circle of the *golden* sun,
> By the brief courses of the errant moon,
> By the dread potency of every star
> That studs the mystic zodiac's burning girth,
> By each and all of these supernal signs,
> We do adjure thee with this trusty blade
> To guard yon central oak, whose holiest stem
> Involves the spirit of high Taranis.

Then follow prayers and benedictions, and farewells. The scene would be capital, were there not too much of it. The words of the chorus—

> Now rise all ;
> And Heaven, that knows what most ye ought to ask,
> Grant all ye ought to have,

are worthy of a better religion than theirs. Yet they nearly resemble, if they were not suggested by, a dititch attributed to Homer.

The time, which commenced with the first glimpses of the moon, has now advanced to black midnight ; " the stars are faded." At this " dreadful hour " it is resolved to attack the invaders. The bards, for the sign of onset, sound the ancientest of all their rhymes :—

> The force of that high air
> Did Julius feel, when fired by it, our fathers
> First drove him recreant to his ships; and ill
> Had fared his second landing, but that Fate
> Silenced the master bard, who led the song.

The brave youths are directed to march in silence till they hear the blast of the sacred trumpet, then to make the onset—a singular piece of tactics—the moment of attack to be chosen by bards who had no opportunity of seeing how or where the enemy was posted. Evelina's adieu is affecting :—

> Brother,
> Let us embrace. Oh! thou much-honoured stranger,
> I charge thee fight by my dear brother's side,
> And shield him from the foe; for he is brave,
> And will, with bold and well-directed arm,
> Return thy succour.

Aviragus and Elidurus set forth for battle. Mador, the principal bard, falls into a transport, snatches his harp, and strikes the famous strain :—

> Hark! heard ye not yon footstep dread,
> That shook the earth with thundering tread?
> Twas DEATH :—in haste
> The warrior pass'd;
> High tower'd his helmed head,
> I mark'd his mail, I mark'd his shield,
> I 'spy'd the sparkling of his spear,
> I saw his giant arm the faulchion wield,
> Wide wav'd the bick'ring blade, and fired the angry air.

The idea of making death a martial and inspiring Deity, and putting into his mouth an exulting battle-hymn, is happy, novel, and in strict keeping with the recorded character of the northern nations, both Celtic and Teutonic, who thought natural dissolution, by disease or age, the worst disgrace, or cruelest calamity :

> Fear not now the fever's fire,
> Fear not now the death-bed groan,
> Pangs that torture, pains that tire,
> Bed-rid age, with feeble moan:
> These domestic terrors wait
> Hourly at my palace gate:
> And when o'er slothful realms my rod I wave,
> These on the tyrant King and coward slave,
> Rush with vindictive rage, and drag them to their grave.
> But ye my son's, in this high hour,
> Shall share the fulness of my power.
>   * ° * *
> Where creeps the nine-fold stream profound
> Her black inexorable round,
> And on the bank,
> To willow's dank,
> The shiv'ring ghosts are bound.
> Twelve thousand crescents all shall swell,
> To full-orb'd pride, and fading die,

> Ere they again in life's gay mansions dwell,
> Nor such the meed that crown's the sons of liberty.

> No my Britons! battle-slain,
> Rapture gilds your parting hour:
> I that all despotic reign,
> Claim but there a moment's power,
> Swiftly the soul of British flame,
> Animates some kindred frame,
> Swiftly to life and light exultant flies,
> Exults again in martial extacies,
> Again for freedom fights, again for freedom dies.

Caractacus, enraptured with the enthusiasm of the song, yearns after life renewed, longs to rush into the fray, that some " blessed shaft may rid him of the clog of cumbrous age." The Druid bids him observe the prosperous omen, the clear and amber-skirted clouds that rise from the altar. At the instant a Bard announces that the Romans are fled! His account of the engagement is spirited, expressed with an epic pomp and elevation borrowed from the narrative orations of the Heralds, and Messengers of the Greek Tragedy, with which Shakspeare, whether led by his own judgment, or by the custom of his contemporaries, has also coincided in adopting a diction unusually elaborate and ornate, when any thing is to be related.

There is one line of the Bard's tale which, if pronounced on the stage, would be very apt to disturb the gravity of a tragic scene, and " strain men's cheeks to idle merriment :"

> No sound was heard,
> Step felt, or sight descry'd : for safely hid,
> Beneath the purple pall of sacrifice,
> Did sleep our holy fire, nor saw the air,
> Till to that pass we came, where whilom BRUTE,
> Planted his five hoar altars.

This comes of the folly of clipping ancient or foreign names to make them look like English. Our language has no inflexions or analogies which require this practice, and indeed the general ruggedness of our orthoepy is agreeably relieved by the intermixture of the sounding appellatives of the southern nations. We are happy to see Dante, Petrarcha, Boccacio, Raffaello, restored to their natural proportions, and hope they will be shortly followed by Ovidius, Horatius, Livius, and others. Pray let us hear no more of Cicero's being *le meme que Marc Tulle.*

The sum of the Bard's information is, that the Romans, after a sharp and brief conflict, are driven to their ships, pursued by Arviragus and Elidurus, who,

> Like Twin-Lions,
> Did side by side engage.

Caractacus, like an old man, replies :—

> Thus my friend Ebrancus
> Ill-fated Prince! didst thou and I in youth
> Unite our valours.

Six Roman captives are led in, who afford the Rev. Mr. Mason an opportunity of paying a compliment to the cloth, rather, it must be confessed, at the expense of nature and probability. But throughout the play the Druids, though sufficiently Druidical in their costume, and their allusions, are very good Protestants in their moral principles, and barring the occasional flashes of fierceness which belong to the martial crisis, utter sentiments that would do no discredit to the clergy of any archdeaconry whatsoever. Generally speaking, this is unexceptionable. The real morals of a barbarous age, above all, of a barbarous priesthood, can never be exhibited, by authors of a more advanced period, with producing loathing or shuddering; because the morals and manners of civilization cannot be wholly excluded, nor can any power of writing bring the reader's imagination to the level of the time represented. Still, some regard should be had to consistency of character. We must not make an Indian warrior talk like a Quaker, nor the priest of an idolatrous worship discourse like a Paley or a Priestley. But Mason has made his Hero disagreeable, in order to bestow upon his chorus a virtue which becomes them less than any one else. Caractacus, addressing the captives, tells them, with a bombast circumstance, about the native rights " man claims from man," that they are not to be slaves, nor to be dragged behind the " scythed cars in arrogance of triumph." Neither were they, till the Britons had learned avarice of the Romans, to be bartered for gold ; but, what he concludes will be perfectly satisfactory, they are to be lifted to the Gods in the " radiant cloud" of sacrifice. He comforts them with the assurance that the Gods will either advance them to a better world or give them fresh bodies in this, and asks :—

> Does there breathe,
> A wretch so *pall'd* with the vain fear of death,
> Can call this cruelty : 'tis love, 'tis mercy ;
> And grant, ye Gods, if e'er I'm made a captive,
> I meet the like fair treatment from the foe,
> Whose stronger star quells mine.

Any child may see the impossibility of this tirade about " love and mercy" taking place in a land of human sacrifices. A cruel religion must engender a cruel morality. But this is not the worst. It would be naturally supposed that the captives would be lovingly and mercifully led off, to suffer combustion in a colossus of basket-work, unless Evelina or Arviragus should interpose in their favour. But no. The Druids are made to forbid and execrate the holiest *sacrament* of their own religion :—

> O think not King,
> That Mona shall be curst by these dire rites,
> Even from the youth of time yon holy altar,
> Has held the place thou seest: ages on ages,
> Have there one sacrifice, but never yet,
> Stream'd it with human gore: nor ever shall
> While we hold office here: 'tis true that Gaul,
> True too that Britain, by the Gauls mistaught,
> Have done such deeds of horror; deeds that shock'd
> Humanity, and call'd from angry Heaven,
> These curses on our country.
>				*Carac.* Can the Gods
> Behold a sight more grateful, than the flame,
> That blasts impiety?
>				*Chorus.* Admit they cannot:
> Need they the hand of man to light that flame?
> Have not those God's their lightning? Taranis,
> Doth he not wield the thunder?
>				*Carac.* Holy Druid,
> I stand rebuked. Will ye then pardon them?
>	*Chor.* We say not that. Vengeance shall have her course,
> But vengeance in her own peculiar garb,
> Not in the borrowed weeds of sage religion:
> They suit not her.

This conclusion reminds one rather awkwardly of the inquisition delivering over its victims " to the secular arm."

Altogether we think this scene intrusive and improper. It does not at all further the plot; it violates the truth of history; it represents Caractacus as a pitiful and superstitious sophist, and makes a *heathen* priesthood the opponents of bloody superstition.

The play now draws to a close. Evelina rushes in, trembling and alarmed. She has heard hostile footsteps in the grove. Caractacus tries to laugh away her fears; but she is positive that she saw sacrilegious brands. The grove is on fire. Caractacus mistakes the flames for the rising sun. Not so the Druids. They see plainly what is the matter, call again to arms, Caractacus runs out to defend the altars. The chorus scamper to and fro in consternation. Arviragus enters, leaning on the arm of Elidurus, mortally wounded. Dying scenes, tediously protracted, are the most disagreeable of all tragic expedients. If there be one rule of the French stage, which we could wish to be adopted on ours, it is that which banishes murder from the stage.

Mason, moreover, gives the agonies of death without the animation of a fight. The clash of swords always sounds well in a theatre; but dying groans and convulsions are dull to read, and either horrible or ridiculous to see acted.

It is difficult to guess our author's motive for keeping Arviragus so long in his misery; for all he has to say might be said in five lines, and just as well by Elidurus as by himself. It amounts to this;—that the flight of the Romans to the ships was a feint;—that only one half of the invaders had been discovered and repulsed by the Britons, while the other moiety, guided by Vellinus, had pursued an unobserved track, gained the pass, and were even now surrounding the sacred recess. Aviragus, having dissuaded Elidurus from suicide by recommending Evelina to his guardianship, expires, with a request that his remains may rest within the hallowed circle:—

> I fought to save these groves,
> And fruitless though I fought, some grateful oak,
> I trust, will spread its reverential gloom
> O'er my pale ashes.

Evelina first faints, and then talks wildly, in a way for which the Druids, had they resembled some *clerks* of the present day, would have read her a severe lecture:—

> Yes,
> Now he is dead; I felt his spirit go
> In a cold sigh, and, as it pass'd, methought
> It paused awhile, and trembled on my lips!
> Take me not from him: breathless as he is,
> He is my brother still, and if the Gods
> Do please to grace *him with some happier being,*
> *They ne'er can give to him a fonder sister.*

This sounds rather like a denial of omnipotence. The chorus, however, are too much engaged to animadvert upon it. Pressed as they are on every side,—the sacred oaks crackling in irreligious flames,—their monarch slain or captive,—their brethren scattered or massacred,—the holy circle on the point of bloody desecration, they nevertheless stand firm to raise their last dirge for their dying champion. There is something grand in this stern determination to do their duty so long as there is ground free to do it in; and the lines are noble in spirit, though rather rugged in their construction:—

> While yet a moment Freedom stays,
> That moment which outweighs
> Eternity's unmeasured hoards,
> Shall Mona's grateful bards employ
> To hymn their godlike hero to the sky.
> Ring out, ye mortal strings!

> Answer, thou heavenly harp instinct with spirit all,
> That o'er the jasper arch self-warbling *swings*
> Of blest Andraste's throne.

At this instant Aulus Didius and Romans enter. A fierce combat of words ensues between the Druids and the Roman general, who, having power and success on his side, naturally keeps his temper much the best. The Druids curse lustily and honestly, and Aulus responds in the general common-place falsehoods of civilized liberticides, that "they fight not to enslave, but humanize;" and points out in a friendly manner the great danger and impropriety of "aiding the foes of Cæsar." Mason excels in this sort of dialogue: he ennobles anger, and when, as in the present case, the anger is really noble, it glows and flashes magnificently through his gorgeous diction, like thunder bursting from cloudy masses,—

> Their torn skirts gilded by the sunken sun.

A bard enters, and says that Caractacus is captive, but yet not basely, nor easily :—

> Know, ere he yielded,
> Their bravest veterans bled. He, too, the spy,
> The base Brigantian prince, hath seal'd his fraud
> With death. Bursting through armed ranks that hemm'd
> The caitiff round, the bold Caractacus
> Seiz'd his false throat, and, as he gave him death,
> Indignant thundered, "*This is my last stroke—*
> *The stroke of Justice !*"

Then enters Caractacus, as captive, and there are some good speeches, taken from Tacitus, Suetonius, &c.; but though good, and well translated, they are as heavy as "more last thoughts" generally are. Caractacus, Evelina, and Elidurus are marched off the stage, ready and resigned for their voyage to Rome.

We are almost afraid that we have done Mason some injustice in this cursory review of his best known productions. But nothing could be further from our intention, than to reduce that just estimation which his energetic and cultivated talents have gained him. So far from it, we think Caractacus better, even as a tragedy, than any thing that was produced in Mason's time. It aims at a high mark. It addresses itself to the moral imagination: it recognizes a sympathy between the uneasy strivings of the soul of man, and the everlasting works of nature: it proves its author to have been a true poet in desire and object; and if, instead of a tragedy, he has given a serious poem in dialogue, let us not quarrel with a golden vase, if it should not exactly correspond with its description in the catalogue.

Caractacus was altered by the author, and produced at Covent Garden—with applause, as the Biographia Dramatica informs us—in 1776. We do not recollect what the alterations were, though we have seen the play, as performed, in Bell's " British Theatre," but we doubt not they were for the *worse*. Probably Mason would never have made them, had he not recollected the surreptitious mangling of " Elfrida." In the days of yore, when college halls were fitted up for theatres, and when the fairest ladies of the court of King Charles (the *first*, mind you,) did not disdain to take a part in the masques of Ben Jonson, Caractacus might have been acted as it should be ; but it is either too good, or not good enough, for an acting play on our common stages.

Besides " Elfrida " and " Caractacus," Mason produced two dramatic performances, of which the world and the critics have taken little notice, and which we can only slightly mention. The first, " Argentile and Curan," a legendary drama, taken from a story in Warner's " Albion's England," to be found in Percy's Relics, and in Campbell's Selections. It is truly a *Yorkshire tragedy*, the scene being " in and about the castle of Whitby, afterwards in the valley of Hakeness." In this, Mason has relinquished his allegiance to the Greeks and French, and imitated pretty closely the Elizabethan writers. Of the irregularity of the composition he seems to have been fully aware by his motto, from the prologue to Beaumont and Fletcher's " Captain : "—

> " This is nor comedy, nor tragedy, nor history."

No matter what it be if it be good of its kind, and that we really think it is. It does not contain many very fine *extractable* passages, but we have seldom read a play that carried us more pleasantly from beginning to end. It is interspersed with comic scenes in prose, wrought with considerable ingenuity into the texture of the piece, but too obviously imitated from Shakspeare. It is not comedy, but tragedy making herself quite at home. The story is briefly as follows : Adelbright, King of Deira, (the southern division of what was afterwards the united and heptarchic kingdom of Northumberland,) on the point of death, retires into the monastery of Whitby, leaving the regency, and the guardianship of his daughter Argentile to his brother Edel, King of Bernicia. The play commences with a dirge, sung by Monks and Nuns, and addressed to Hilda, the sainted Patroness of the Abbey and Kingdom. Adelbright, according to the fashion of early Saxon Monarchs, preparing for death, divests himself of royalty, and becomes a Monk ; but ere he quits the world for ever, implores his brother to bring about the marriage already negociated between his daughter Argentile, and the young heir of Denmark. Edel professes himself willing to rule over Bernicia and Deira, jointly with his niece and her young husband ; but as soon as Adelbright is out of the way, like the common uncle of tale and plays, sets about to frustrate the match, and defraud his niece of her inheritance : he plots with the Prior of Whitby (whom he gains over by promises of church preferment) to give out that Adelbright is already dead; and to cut off that aged monarch from all intelligence of what is going on without the convent. When the Danish ambassadors arrive, Edel breaks off the match abruptly, on a false pretence of Argentile's over youth and repugnance to marriage. Curan, the Danish Prince, and intended spouse of Argentile, who has accompanied the ambassadors incog, with a design to obtain a sight of the lady to whom he is to be united, and a pretty strong headed determination to break off the alliance himself, if the maiden prove homely, remains behind, in the disguise of a minstrel, gains admission to King Edel's court, attends him on a hawking party, and delighting the usurper alike with his music and his skill in field-sports, is at once advanced to the place of cup-bearer. Still farther pleased with his youthful beauty, and noble air, the tyrant resolves to make the supposed minstrel subservient to a vile purpose he has hatched of ridding himself of his niece Argentile, by inveighling her into a low marriage. He therefore proposes to Curan that he shall act the Prince of Denmark, and be introduced to the Princess in that character. This idea of making a man *play* himself is very felicitous. Curan, of course, readily closes with the proposal, and assures the King that he had been the Prince's companion in childhood, that in sport they sometimes changed dresses, and that their resemblance in mien and features was so striking, that they were frequently mistaken for each other. This promising scheme is, however, disappointed by the disappearance of Argentine, who with Osward, an old faithful courtier, and her confidante Editha, has fled through the forest. This intelligence is communicated by the head Falconer (who officiates in this play as clown) to the cup-bearer, who persuades him, instead of carrying his information to the King, to set off himself, accompanied by the said cup-bearer, in pursuit of the fugitives. Off they go. But happening soon to part company, the Falconer falls in with Oswald, rather inopportunely, for instead of arresting the revolted Lord, he gets his own hands tied behind his back, and so is turned loose. Caran, meanwhile, having lost his way, lies down on a bank and goes to sleep. Argentile, in search of Editha, who is disguised in male apparel, mistakes the slumbering youth for her friend, and speaks some fond words, at which he awakes, and falls in love at the instant. Argentile is not a little surprised, both at her own mistake and at his raptures. Several scenes of love-making follow, till at length Curan, yet ignorant of the quality of his flame, discovers his own; tells how he came with intent to woo the beauteous Princess Argentine, but he is now ready to relinquish her and all her dower of kingdoms for his lovely shepherdess. Argentile no doubt is in heaven, but still she tries his love, telling him that she cannot wed a Prince while she remains a humble shepherdess, and winds him to that pitch, that he consents for her sake to be a shepherd :—

> I here disclaim all royalty ; I'll live
> In this still valley, tend thy little flock,
> Sleep with thee in yon cot, and with thee press
> This perfumed bank.

This quite overcomes her coyness, and she consents to be his. Just at this happy moment, Oswald and Editha enter. Oswald is astonished to see Argentile " locked in a peasant's embrace ;" but all his quickly cleared up, for the Danes, headed by the son of Oswald, march in victorious, having vanquished and slain Edel. The Danish Lords recognize their Prince. Argentile appears in her own character. Adelbright comes to life again, having never been dead, and all ends happily. There is an underplot of the loves of Editha and Oswald's son, who, of course, are to be married also. In point of style, we think this the best of all Mason's works ; but the comic part is very dull. The play was written in the year 1766.

Of Sappho, a lyrical drama, meant to be set to music after the manner of Metastasio's operas ; and Pygmalion, a dramatic scene, translated from Rousseau, no particular account is necessary. It is time, indeed, to return to the events of Mr. Mason's life, which have been too long interrupted.

Towards the end of 1753, he had the affliction to lose his father. From a letter of condolence, written by Gray* on this occasion, it appears that the old gentleman had given his son reason to be dissatisfied with the arrangement of his affairs ; but what the particular ground of dissatisfaction was, we have not been able to discover. At the same time, and by the same infectious fever, Mason was deprived of Dr. Marma-

---

* " I know what it is to lose persons that ones eyes and heart have long been used to ; and I never desire to part with the remembrance of that loss, nor would wish you should. It is something that you have had a little time to acquaint yourself with the idea before hand ; and that your father suffered little pain, the only thing that makes death terrible. After I have said this, I cannot help expressing my surprize at the disposition he has made of his affairs. I must (if you will suffer me to say so) call it great weakness; and yet perhaps your affliction for him is heightened by that very weakness; for I know it is possible to feel an additional sorrow for the faults of those we have loved, even where the fault has been greatly injurious to ourselves."—LETTER 18.

Was it quite right of Mason to publish this letter? Certainly it is very provoking of him to publish it without informing the world what the weakness complained of was. It is dated December 26, 1753.

duke Pricket, a young physician, of his own age, with whom he had been brought up from infancy. Death of friends is a sorrow that must come to all who have any friends to love, saving that happy number who join the blessed band of innocents " ere sin can blight or sorrow fade," a sorrow which they feel most keenly whose lives are happiest. Mason, who lived long, must have had many to lament, nor was there any thing in his existence to teach him that an early death is often the truest blessing.

In 1754 he took orders. It is said that Warburton, on this occasion, advised him to give up the study of poetry, as inconsistent with his sacred profession. Such counsel did not come with any great force from a divine whose own clerical vocations had left him time to write notes to the "Dunciad," and to conjure a meaning into the " Essay on Man," which he knew well enough was not the meaning of its author. Mason sensibly took this admonition as words of course, like the common dehortation from fiddling, fox-hunting, and Pitt-dinner-frequenting, which is one of the common-places of a Bishop's charge.

The *trade* of authorship should never be pursued by a clergyman. One object of a church establishment is to exempt the ministers of the altar from following any trade for subsistence. But Mason never had been, and never was, an author for bread. The aim of all his writings was to dignify the poetic art: his object was noble, and if there may be some differences, with regard to the degree of success with which he accomplished it, there can be none with rational Christians, as to the perfect consistency of this design with the duties of a Christian minister.

Very soon after his entrance into the sacred profession, he was appointed chaplain to the Earl of Holderness, and by the Earl's influence, chaplain to the King. As one of the Earl's domestic chaplains, he attended that Nobleman in a foreign tour, in the course of which he met William Whitehead, then officiating as travelling tutor to Viscount Villiars, son of the Earl of Jersey, and Viscount Nureham, son of the Earl of Harcourt. They met at Hanover, in the course of the year 1755, and their friendship continued till death. Mason lived to be the biographer of Whitehead. Mason did not (why did he not?) publish an account of his travels; but soon after his return, in 1756, he received the living of Aston, in Yorkshire, in the vicarage of which he continued to reside, with short intermissions, till his death, and there he found an opportunity of realizing those speculations on landscape gardening, which he *poetized* in his English Garden. In the same year, 1756, he published four odes, of which we need only notice two, for as to the ode on Independency, (a mis-nomer for *independence,* for *independency* is what no parson of the Church of England ought to make an ode to,) it is generally agreed that Smollett's was better, and if so, no matter.

One of these odes " On the fate of Tyranny," is, as Mr. Mason tells us, a free paraphrase of part of the 11th chapter of Isaiah, where the Prophet, after he has foretold the destruction of Babylon, subjoins a song of triumph, which he supposes the Jews will sing when his prediction is fulfilled. " And it shall come to pass in the day that the Lord shall give thee rest from thy sorrow and from thy fear, and from the hard bondage wherein thou wast made to serve, that thou shalt take up this parable against the Kings of Babylon, and say, How hath the oppression ceased, &c. If any one would know what the sublimest poetry is, and how immortal, nay inspired poetry, may be spoiled by mortal mixtures, let him compare the 14th chapter of Isaiah and Mason's ode. And yet that ode is one of the best, perhaps the best, paraphrase of Scripture that ever was made.

To confirm our sentence we will give a few words which certainly do prove the advantage of a few words over many:

Isaiah. " How art thou fallen from Heaven O Lucifer, son of the Morning!" 12, 13, 14.

> *Mason.* " Oh Lucifer thou radiant star,
> Son of the morn; whose rosy car
> Flamed foremost in the van of day:
> How art thou fall'n, &c.

Ohe, jam satis est. Milton himself, who produced the greatest, aye, far the greatest work of the mere human mind, failed deplorably in the attempt to versify a psalm. In the ode to " an Æolus Harp," we look in vain for one line better or worse than another. It is a copy of verses and that is all.

These odes were ludicrously parodied by Colman and Lloyd, who treated with equal disrespect the Bard and other lyric compositions of Gray. Gray took this as he took most things—very quietly, but Mason seems to have been considerably annoyed. His style had certain peculiarities, which made it easy to take off, and there was a buckram solemnity, especially in his earlier works, and a degree of assumption, which always is sure to provoke ridicule. Gray's letter upon this publication of the travestied odes, and Masons remarks thereon, shew the character of the two poets in a strongly contrasted light:

" I have sent *Musæus* back as you desired me, scratched here and there, and with it also a bloody satire, written against no less persons than *you* and *I* by name. I concluded at first it was Mr. * * *, because he is your friend and my humble servant, but then I thought he knew the world too well to call us the favourite minions of taste and fashion, especially as to odes. For to them his ridicule is confined,—so it is not he, but Mr. Colman, nephew to Lady Bath, author of the Conoisseur, a member of one of the Inns of Court, and a particular acquaintance of Mr. Garrick. What have you done to him? for I hever heard his name before: he makes very tolerable fun with me where I understand him (which is not every where), but seems to be more angry with you. Lest people should not understand the humour of the thing (which, indeed, they must have our lyricisms at their finger ends to do), letters come out in Lloyd's Evening Post to them who and what it was that he meant, and says it is like to produce a great combustion in the literary world. So if you have any mind to *combustle* about it, well and good: for me, I am neither so literary nor so combustible. The Monthly Review, I see, just now, has much stuff about us on this occasion. It says *one* of us, at least, has always *borne* his faculties meekly. I leave you to guess which of us it is."

To which Mason subjoins the following note:—" Had Mr. Pope disregarded the sarcasms of the many writers that endeavoured to eclipse his poetical fame, as Mr. Gray here appears to have done, the world would not have been possessed of a Dunciad, but it would have been impressed with a more amiable idea of its author's temper." Mason afterwards proved that he wanted not abilities to have vindicated his muse by powerful satire, which is the only way for an aggrieved author to get the public to his side.

In the year 1757, the death of Cibber left the laureateship vacant, and it was offered to Gray, who politely declined it, though it was thought he would have been allowed to hold it as a sinecure. The Ministry apologized for not offering it to Mason, on the score that he was in orders; a false excuse, which he was willing enough to admit, having no ambition for the office. His politics, not his cloth, were the true ground of his inelegibility. A clergyman was surely as fit to write the praise of " sacred majesty" as a player; and in fact, Eusden, the predecessor of Cibber, was an honest Vicar. It was well for Mason's peace that he was not invested with this ill-paid and invidious honour. Ever since the Restoration, every successive Laureate has been the mark of scurrility. Davenant was the original hero of the Rehearsal; but when Dryden succeeded to the Bayes, he also inherited the ridicule from which death had delivered its first object. Dryden was no sooner stript of the laureate-ship himself, than he held it up to scorn in the person of Shadwell. The fatal example, shewn by King William or his ministry, of bestowing what ought to have been the highest poetical honour, upon mere party considerations, was more mischievous to the crown than superficial observers would readily conceive. It tended to bring all loyal poetry into disrepute. It stripped the kingly office of its poetic halo. Statesmen have perhaps yet to learn how much it is to have the imagination of the country on their side.

We may suppose that Mason was not displeased to see his friend Whitehead advanced to the honours of "the Butt and Bayes." In fact, the appointment was very judicious. The character of Whitehead was highly respectable, and he was at least a *respectable* poet.

Of the publication of Caractacus in 1759 we have already spoken. Nothing remarkable appears to have befallen our author till 1762, when he was preferred to the Canonry of York, the Prebend of Driffield, and the Precentorship of York Minster. He still, however, made Aston his principal residence,—somewhat, it seems, to the dissatisfaction of Gray, who, in a letter from which we have extracted pretty largely, says, " I do not like your improvements at Aston, it looks so like settling ; when I come I will set fire to it."

In 1764, Mason published a collection of his poems, with a dedicatory sonnet to the Earl of Holderness, including most of the poems he had hitherto produced, but omitting the Isis. If, however, he was content to have that juvenile indiscretion forgotten, he did not quite forget it himself, and apprehended consequences from its in-dwelling in the memory of others, against which he might modestly have felt himself secure. It is reported that, passing through Oxford late in the evening, he observed to his travelling companion, that he was glad it was dark ; and being interrogated why he was pleased at that circumstance, answered importantly, " Do not you remember my Isis ? "

In 1765, he married Miss Maria Sherman, of Hull, but few indeed were his days of nuptial happiness. Consumption, the bane of the young and beautiful, was lurking in Mrs. Mason's constitution, and began to shew unequivocal symptoms almost immediately after her marriage. During the short period of their union, her husband was incessantly employed in watching the vicissitudes of a malady which mocks despair with similitudes of hope ; and in less than twelve months from their nuptials, the lady expired at the Bristol hot-wells, whither she had been carried, not so much in real expectation of benefit, as that nothing for her recovery might be left undone. Mason bore his loss with the tenderness of a man and the resignation of a Christian.

Mrs. Mason lies buried in Bristol cathedral, and her husband has recorded her merits and his own loss, in an epitaph, of four elegaic stanzas. He also alludes to his bereavement, in the invocation of the first book of the " English Garden."

3 M

Nothing worthy of record took place in the few next succeeding years of Mason's existence. The death of Gray, in 1771, exhibited him in the new light of an editor and biographer. Gray had visited his friend, at Aston, in the summer of 1770, and even then his health was declined so much, that he expressed his determination to resign his professorship of modern history if he continued unable to execute its duties,—a sacrifice of income from which Mr. Mason, less scrupulous, endeavoured to dissuade him. But whatever might be his plans of exertion or retirement, they were rendered abortive by his death, which happened on the 31st of July, 1771. Mason did not receive the intelligence of this event (which, though not unexpected, was sudden at last) in time to see the remains of his friend interred. Gray died at Cambridge, yet he was buried beside his mother and aunt, in the church-yard of Stoke-Pogis, said to be the scene of his famous Elegy; but there is little in the Elegy whereby its locality can be ascertained. A monument was erected to his memory in Westminster Abbey, for which Mason wrote a short inscription, that does little honour either to Gray or to himself; for the praise it contains is both hacknied and inappropriate, and the turn of the verses trivial:—

> " No more the Grecian muse unrivall'd reigns;
> To Britain let the nations homage pay,
> She boasts a Homer's fire in Milton's strains,
> A Pindar's rapture in the lyre of Gray."

Gray bequeathed to Mason £500, with his books, MSS., &c. In the volume entitled "Memoirs of Gray," Mason has written no more than was just necessary to connect the letters of his subject. He had little to do, but that little is done judiciously: no letter is published which ought not to have been so, nothing is elucidated which had better been left in obscurity. Yet to Gray's literary fame he is hardly just; for many of the "remains" which have since appeared, set his learning, taste, and talent in a higher point of view than either his poems or his correspondence.

The next important work of our author's was his "English Garden," of which the first book appeared in 1772; the second, 1777; the third, in 1779; the fourth and last, in 1782. As this poem was the production of a powerful mind in its maturest vigour, as it had every advantage of delay and revision, and treats of a topic apparently capable of much descriptive embellishment, and with which the author was familiarly and practically acquainted, it is hard to suppose it wholly destitute of beauties, especially as it consists of 2423 lines of blank verse. We will not, therefore, say that it is the dullest poem we ever read, but it is assuredly one of the dullest we ever attempted to read. The most interesting passages are, the tribute to the memory of his wife, in the first book, and the remembrance of Gray, in the commencement of the third.

Mr. Mason's love of landscape gardening and of *simplicity* appeared in 1773, in a far more sprightly production, " *An heroic Epistle to Sir William Chambers.*" Sir William Chambers, a Scot by descent, but born in Sweden, having come to England in his infancy, had risen by good fortune, enterprise, talent, and the patronage of Lord Bute, from the supercargo of a Swedish vessel (in which he visited China) to the posts of Royal Architect and Surveyor-General of the Board of Works to his Majesty. In this capacity he was engaged in laying out the royal gardens at Kew, in which he shewed a striking disregard of Mr. Mason's ideas of the picturesque. In a work published about the same time, he expatiated on the wonders of Oriental gardening, as displayed in the imperial gardens of Yven Minn Yven, near Pekin, and more than implied a contempt for the simple natural-imitating system, and no great respect for nature herself. Mason, whose temper was by no means free from suspicion and jealousy, perhaps thought that his book was reflected upon in Sir William's, or he might think that to satirize the court architect was a good method of satirizing the court, to which his politics were strongly opposed. The method he adopted to ridicule the orientalist was simple and effectual. He just versified the most glaring paragraphs, and subjoined the original prose as a running commentary. One or two specimens must suffice :—

Sir William Chambers :

" Nature affords us but few materials to work with. Plants, water, and ground are her only productions ; and though both the forms and arrangements of these may be varied to an incredible degree, yet they have but few striking varieties, the rest being of the nature of changes rung upon bells, which, though in reality different, still produce the same uniform kind of gingling, the variation being too minute to be readily perceived. Art must therefore supply the scantiness of nature. Our larger works are only a repetition of the smaller ones, like the honest bachelor's feast, which consisted in nothing but a multiplication of his own dinner; three legs of mutton and turnips, three roasted geese, and three buttered apple-pies.—*Preface, page 7.*

Mr. Mason :

> For what is Nature? Ring her changes round,
> Her three flat notes are water, plants, and ground :
> Prolong the peel, yet spite of all your clatter,
> The tedious chime is still, earth, plants, and water.
> So when some John his dull invention racks
> To rival Boodle's dinners, or Almacks,

> Three uncouth legs of mutton shock our eyes,
> Three roasted geese, three buttered apple pies."

One passage is remarkable, as displaying the antipathy of Mason to the great Tory of the age, coupled with something bordering on disrespect to royalty itself. After designating the monarch

> Patron supreme of learning, taste, and wit,

he proceeds :—

> Does Envy doubt? Witness, ye chosen train,
> Who breathe the sweets of his Saturnian reign;
> Witness, ye Hills, ye *Johnsons*, Scots, Shebbeares,
> Hark to my call, for *some* of you have ears;
> Let David Hume, from the remotest north,
> In see-saw sceptic scruples hint his worth;
> David, who there supinely deigns to lie,
> The fattest hog of Epicurus' sty;
> Though drunk with Gallic wine and Gallic praise,
> David shall bless old England's halcyon days:
> The mighty Home, bemired in prose so long,
> Again shall stalk upon the stilts of song;
> While bold Mac Ossian, wont in ghosts to deal,
> Bids candid Smollett from his coffin steal;
> Bids Malloch quit his sweet Elysian rest,
> Sunk in his St. John's philosophic breast,
> And, like old Orpheus, make some strong effort
> To come from hell, and warble "Truth at court."

Surely the political prejudices of that man must have been pretty strong, who could mention Johnson along with Hill and Shebbeare.

This epistle, and several others published about the same time, appeared under the name of Malcolm Macgregor. By some they were attributed to Horace Walpole, and one writer says, "It is not improbable that Walpole furnished the venom, and that Mason spotted the snake." To Mason, however, they were confidently ascribed by his old rival Tom Warton, and his denial is a sort of *Waverley* confession.

Politics, in the latter part of his life, took up a very large portion of Mason's attention. He continued a staunch Whig during the whole period of the American war, defended the resistance of the revolted colonies, and inveighed boldly against the measures of government. He was a decided advocate for parliamentary reform, and a stirring member of the county reform associations. Being given to understand that his conduct was displeasing to the court, he resigned his chaplainship, and in 1788 composed a secular ode on the "glorious Revolution." But the word Revolution, almost immediately after, acquired a new and more terrible signification. Whether Mason ever looked with satisfaction on the proceedings of the French Revolution is uncertain; but he very soon followed the course of Burke, and after writing, talking, perhaps sometimes preaching, for the better part of a long life, to promote freedom and circumscribe prerogative, he discovered, all at once, that mankind had all along had quite as much liberty as was good for them, and that the so-called abuses, corruptions, and oppressions of society were so intrinsically wrought into its texture, that to attempt to pluck them out was to unravel the whole web of the community. In this new faith he composed a Palinodia, which, though written in 1794, was not printed till 1797, the last year of his life. It betrays no marks of senility. There is the same heat, earnestness, verbosity, and self-confidence that appear in his earliest compositions; the same redundancy of epithets, compound terms, and personifications; much which every poetic boy can admire, and little or nothing which any one, without getting by heart, would remember. Two stanzas will be a sufficient sample of this, the latest published work of our author:—

> And art thou mute? or does the fiend that strides
> Yon sulphurous tube, by tigers drawn,
> While seas of blood roll their increasing tides
> Beneath his wheels, while myriads groan,
> Does he with voice of thunder make reply,
> "I am the Genius of stern Liberty;
> Adore me as thy genuine choice;
> Know, where I hang with wreaths my sacred tree,
> Power undivided, just Equality,
> Are born at my creative voice!"

> Avaunt, abhorr'd Democracy!
> O for Ithuriel's spear!
> To shew to Party's jaundiced eye
> The fiend she most should fear;
> To turn her from the infernal sight,
> To where, array'd in robes of light,
> True Liberty, on seraph wing,
> Descends to shed that blessing rare,
> Of equal rights, an equal share
> To people, peers, and king.

In abjuring Democracy, Mason did not, like too many, become the enemy of humanity, or the advocate of men stealers, but continued, as a good citizen and a christian minister, to urge the abolition of the slave trade. The only sermon he ever published is in furtherance of this object.

Notwithstanding the disturbed state of the political world, the last days of Mason were spent in peace, and he enjoyed the reward of a life of temperance, healthful occupation, and calm piety. For some years before his death, he was in the habit of composing an anniversary

sonnet on his birth-day (the 23d of February). The following, perhaps
the last lines he ever wrote, commemorate the completion of his 72nd
year, A.D. 1797 :—

> Again the year on easy wheels has roll'd,
>   To bear me to the term of seventy-two;
>   Yet still my eyes can seize the distant blue
> Of yon wild Peak, and still my footsteps bold,
> Unprop'd by staff, support me to behold
>   How Nature, to her Maker's mandate true,
>   Calls Spring's impartial heralds to the view,
> The snow-drop pale, the crocus spik'd with gold;
>   And still (thank Heaven) if I not falsely deem,
> My lyre, yet vocal, freely can afford
>   Strains not discordant to each moral theme
> Fair Truth inspires, and aid me to record
>   (Best of poetic pains!) my faith supreme
> In thee, my God, my Saviour, and my Lord!

From this sonnet it might have been expected that the venerable
poet had years in store; and perhaps his life might have extended to
fourscore, but for one of those accidents which shew the peculiar insecurity of the tenure of an old man's life. In stepping out of a
carriage, he stumbled and occasioned a contusion on his leg, which
did not appear at first to be any thing serious, but being neglected
turned to a mortification, which proved fatal, in May, 1793. Previous to his death he had prepared a collection of his poems, in which
the " Isis " was suffered to resume its place.

Besides his skill in poetry and in gardening, he was a considerable
proficient in painting, and a respectable amateur in music. He translated Du Fresnoy's " Art of Painting " in early life, chiefly, as himself
declares, for his own instruction. This version was laid aside in an
unfinished state for many years, till being accidentally shown to Sir
Joshua Reynolds, he was so much pleased with it, that he desired it
might be completed, and enriched it with his annotations, which undoubtedly are the most valuable part of the joint performance. Mason
also wrote essays, historical and critical, on English church music.
As in gardening, so in music, he was the votary of simplicity; but the
simplicity he demands is too severe to be generally adopted, even in
congregational psalmody.

With the great poets in any department of poetry, Mason cannot be
numbered, yet for many years of his life he was England *greatest*
living Poet.

SIR RICHARD ARKWRIGHT.

So now, where Derwent guides his dusky floods,
Through vaulted mountains, and a night of woods,
The Nymph, *Gossypia*, treads the velvet sod,
And warms with rosy smiles the watery God,
His ponderous oars to slender spindles turns,
And pours o'er massy wheels his foamy urns;
With playful charms her hoary lover wins,
And wields his trident, while the monarch spins.
First, with nice eye emerging Naiads cull,
From leathery pods the vegetable wool;
With wiry teeth *revolving cards* release,
The tangled knots, and smooth the ravell'd fleece,
Next moves the *iron-hand* with fingers fine,
Combs the wide card, and forms the eternal line,
Slow, with soft lips, the *whirling can* acquires
The slender skeins, and wraps in rising spires,
With quickened pace, *successive rollers* move,
And these retain, and those extend the *rove*;
Then fly the spoles, the rapid axles glow,
And slowly circumvolves the labouring wheel below.

Darwin's " Loves of the Plants." Canto, 11, 85, 104.

" *Gossypium, the Cotton Plant.* On the river Derwent, near Matlock, in Derbyshire, SIR RICHARD ARKWRIGHT has erected his curious and magnificent machinery for spinning cotton, which had been in vain attempted by many ingenious men before him. The cotton wool is first picked from the pods and seeds by women. It is then carded by *cylindrical cards*, which move against each other with different velocities. It is taken from these by an *iron hand*, or *comb*, which has a motion similar to that of scratching, and takes the wool off the cards longitudinally in respect to the fibres or staple, producing a continued line loosely cohering called the *Rove* or *Roving*. This Rove yet very loosely twisted, is then received or drawn into a *whirling canister*, and is rolled by the contrifugal force in spiral lines within it, being yet too tender for the spindle. It is then passed between two *pairs* of *rollers ;* the second pair moving faster than the first, elongate the thread with greater rapidity than can be done by hand, and is then twisted on spoles, or bobbins.

The great fertility of the cotton plant, in these fine flexible threads, whilst those from flax, hemp, or from the bark of the Mulberry tree, require a previous putrefaction of the parenchy matous substance, and much mechanical labour, and afterwards bleaching, renders this plant of great importance to the world. And since SIR RICHARD ARKWRIGHT's ingenious machine has not only greatly abbreviated and simplified the labour and art of carding and spinning the cotton-wool, but performs both these circumstances better than can be performed by hand; it is probable that the cloth of this small reed may become the principal clothing of mankind."— *Darwin's note on the passage.*

> Now *Richard's* talents for the world were fit,
> He'd no small cunning, and he'd some small wit,
> * * * * *
> Long lost to us, at length our man we trace,
> *Sir Richard* Munday, died at Munday place. CRABBE.

Some are born great, some atchieve greatness.—SHAKSPEARE.

It may seem somewhat paradoxical if we declare an opinion that Arkwright, the penny-barber, who came to be a Knight-batchelor, and died worth double the revenue of a German principality, belonged to the class of men *born* great, rather than of those who *atchieve* greatness, and yet, if they be duly considered, there are good substantial reasons for that opinion. For he either did invent the machinery that made his fortune, or he did not,—therefore he was either a great mechanician or a great knave, and no man can be either the one or the other without certain powers, capacities, and Ideas, which are not acquirable, but must be intertwined by Nature herself with the thread of his destiny. It is no doubt easy, for any man that chooses, to be a *knave*; knave enough to ruin himself and his friends, knave enough to lose his character and his soul, but all this a man may do without being a *great* knave, without realizing a fortune of half a million. The common run of small knaves, like small poets, are wretchedly poor, living from hand to mouth upon their shifts or their verses, because they are not the knaves or the poets of nature, but of vanity or necessity. They play off their tricks and their sonnets on the spur of the moment, and are incapable of forming any scheme befitting "a creature of large discourse, looking before and after." But the *great* knave despises all the epigrams, and impromptus, and fugitive pieces of knavery. As the great poet speaks plain prose to his neighbours, writes a letter of business like a man of business, and can see a rose or a pretty milk-maid without committing rhyme or blank upon either, reserving and consolidating his powers for some great and permanent object, that will rather enoble his genius, than be enobled by it. So the truly great knave never throws knavery away; in all but the main point he is minutely honest, and only to be distinguished from the naturally honest man, by a greater anxiety about appearances. But in one thing the great knave differs from the great poet. The poet conceives great ideas of his own, and in the production and developement of those ideas his delight consists; he does not readily adopt the ideas of others, far less does he make any use of them. Now the leading faculty of the knave, and it is a faculty which none can acquire who is not born with it, is a quick apprehension of the *use* to be made of others' labours, others' thoughts, others' inventions. Not that this faculty compels a man to be a knave. We believe it to be possessed in a very great degree by many persons of the highest integrity. Still, if they had not been persons of *more* than average integrity, they would have run a hazard of being great knaves. Let us not be accused of Fatalism, as though we had said, that nature forces men to be knaves. She only gives the capabilities of being a *great* knave.

But on the former, more probable, and more agreeable supposition, that Arkwright was a mechanical inventor, then we fearlessly assert that he gave a proof of congenital endowment as decisive as if he had produced an Iliad. We rest nothing upon Arkwright's want of education, for all the classical and mathematical education in the world, with the most accurate study of mechanical powers, and long and minute observation of their practical operations, would not have enabled him to advance a step in the art. Indeed we doubt if many persons really comprehend the principal of the most ordinary mechanical contrivances, (as a roasting jack, or a squirrels cage.) The great multitude of operatives work by mere imitation and blind rule, bit by bit, each executing his portion, more or less neatly, according to his care, manual dexterity, and length of practice, but without ever thinking or asking to what purpose their handiwork is to serve, and in fact knowing little more of mechanics than an organ pipe does of music. Yet you will find, in the shop or factory, some three or four, without an atom more scholarship, and, it may be, with rather less general intellect than their mates, who know perfectly what they are about, and want nothing but mental industry, or in other words, a will to be first-rate engineers. So too, in the classes that do not labour, you will perceive in some an invincible propensity to mechanical inventions, while others, not only cannot execute, but cannot be taught, how the simplest processes are executed. This constructiveness is a distinct function, or organ, we had almost said, a peculiar sense, but what it is, or how it operates, we confess our inability to explain, or to imagine. We are utterly destitute of the organ.

In this case, as in others, where the pursuits of the subjects of our memoirs lie out of the sphere of our own knowledge, we shall borrow freely from those sources of intelligence which lie open to us. The following notice of SIR RICHARD ARKWRIGHT is taken, verbatim, from that admirable work, the Library of Entertaining Knowledge, and from one of its most delightful departments—that which illustrates the "Pursuit of knowledge under difficulties."

We are glad of this opportunity to express our gratitude to the author of these pleasant and profitable little volumes, and think we do him both honour and justice by giving his facts, in his words, better than if we should attempt to appropriate what is not our own, by a paraphrase.

Arkwright was born on the 23rd of December, 1732, at Preston, in Lancashire. His parents were very poor, and he was the youngest of a family of thirteen children; so that we may suppose the school education he received, if he ever was at school at all, was extremely limited. Indeed, but little learning would probably be deemed necessary for the profession to which he was bred,—that of a barber. This business he continued to follow till he was nearly thirty years of age; and this first period of his history is of course obscure enough. About the year 1760, however, or soon after, he gave up shaving, and commenced business as an itinerant dealer in hair, collecting the commodity by travelling up and down the country, and then, after he had dressed it, selling it again to the wig-makers, with whom he very soon acquired the character of keeping a better article than any of his rivals in the same trade. He had obtained possession, too, we are told, of a secret method of dyeing the hair, by which he doubtless contrived to augment his profits; and perhaps, in his accidental acquaintance with this little piece of chemistry, we may find the germ of that sensibility he soon began to manifest to the value of new and unpublished inventions in the arts, and of his passion for patent-rights and the pleasures of monopoly.

It would appear that his first effort in mechanics, as has happened in the case of many other ingenious men, was an attempt to discover the perpetual motion. It was in inquiring after a person to make him some wheels for a project of this kind, that in the latter part of the year 1767, he got acquainted with a clockmaker of the name of Kay, then residing at Warrington, with whom it is certain that he remained for a considerable time after closely connected. From this moment we may date his entrance upon a new career.

The manufacture of cotton cloths was introduced into this country only towards the end of the seventeenth century; although stuffs, improperly called Manchester cottons, had been fabricated nearly three centuries before, which, however, were made entirely of wool. It is generally thought that the first attempt at the manufacture of cotton goods in Europe did not take place till the end of the fifteenth century, when the art was introduced into Italy. Before this, the only cottons known had been imported from the East Indies.

The English cottons, for many years after the introduction of the manufacture, had only the weft of cotton ; the warp, or longitudinal threads of the cloth, being of linen. It was conceived to be impracticable to spin the cotton with a sufficiently hard twist to make it serviceable for this latter purpose. Although occasionally exported too in small quantities, the manufactured goods were chiefly consumed at home. It was not till about the year 1706 that any considerable demand for them arose abroad.

But about this time the exportation of cottons, both to the continent and to America, began to be carried on on a larger scale, and the manufacture of course received a corresponding impulse. The thread had hitherto been spun entirely, as it still continues to be in India, by the tedious process of the distaff and spindle, the spinner drawing out only a single thread at a time. But as the demand for the manufactured article continued to increase, a greater and greater scarcity of weft was experienced, till, at last, although there were 50,000 spindles constantly at work in Lancashire alone, each occupying an individual spinner, they were found quite insufficient to supply the quantity of thread required. The weavers generally, in those days, had the weft they used spun for them by the females of their family ; and now " those weavers," says Mr. Guest, in his History of the Cotton Manufacture, " whose families could not furnish the necessary supply of weft, had their spinning done by their neighbours, and were obliged to pay more for the spinning than the price allowed by their masters ; and even with this disadvantage, very few could procure weft enough to keep themselves constantly employed. It was no uncommon thing for a weaver to walk three or four miles in a morning, and call on five or six spinners, before he could collect weft to serve him for the remainder of the day ; and when he wished to weave a piece in a shorter time than usual, a new ribbon, or gown, was necessary to quicken the exertions of the spinner."

It was natural, in this state of things, that attempts should be made to contrive some method of spinning more effective than that which had hitherto been in use ; and, in fact, several ingenious individuals seem to have turned their attention to the subject. Long before this time, indeed, spinning by machinery had been thought of by more than one speculator. A Mr. Wyatt, of Litchfield, is stated to have actually invented an apparatus for that purpose so early as the year 1733, and to have had factories built and filled with his machines, both at Birmingham and Northampton. These undertakings, however, not being successful, the machines were allowed to perish, and no model or description of them was preserved.* There was also a Mr. Laurence

* See Essay on the Cotton Trade, by Mr. Kennedy, Manchester Memoirs, second series, vol. iii.

Earnshaw, of Mottram, in Cheshire, of whom "it is recorded," says Mr. Baines, in his History of Lancashire,* "that, in the year 1753, he invented a machine to spin and reel cotton at one operation, which he shewed to his neighbours, and then destroyed it, through the generous apprehension that he might deprive the poor of bread "—a mistake, but a benevolent one.

It was in the year 1767, as we have mentioned, that Arkwright became acquainted with Kay. In 1768 the two friends appeared together at Preston, and immediately began to occupy themselves busily in the erection of a machine for the spinning of cotton-thread, of which they had brought a model with them. They had prevailed upon a Mr. Smalley, who is described to have been a liquor merchant and painter of that place, to join them in their speculation ; and the room in which the machine was fixed was the parlour of the dwelling-house attached to the free grammar-school, the use of which Smalley had obtained from his friend, the schoolmaster. At this time Arkwright was so poor that, an election contest having taken place in the town, of which he was a burgess, it is asserted that his friends, or party, were obliged to subscribe to get him a decent suit of clothes before they could bring him into the poll-room.† As soon as the election was over, he and Kay left Preston, and, carrying with them their model, betook themselves to Nottingham, the apprehension of the hostility of the people of Lancashire to the attempt he was making to introduce spinning by machinery having, as Arkwright himself afterwards stated,‡ induced him to take this step. On arriving at Nottingham, he first made arrangements with Messrs. Wrights, the bankers, for obtaining the necessary supply of capital ; but they, after a short time, having declined to continue their advances, he took his model to Messrs. Need and Strutt, stocking weavers of that place, the latter of whom was a particularly ingenious man, and well qualified, from his scientific acquirements, of which he had possessed himself under many disadvantages, to judge of the adaptation of the new machinery to its proposed object. An inspection of it perfectly satisfied him of its great value ; and he and Mr. Need immediately agreed to enter into partnership with Arkwright, who accordingly, in 1769, took out a patent for the machine as its inventor. A spinning-mill, driven by horse power, was at the same time erected, and filled with the frames ; being, unless we include those erected many years before by Mr. Wyatt, the first work of the kind that had been known in this country.

* Vol. i. p. 115.

† Baines's History of Lancashire, vol. ii. p. 481.

‡ See his " Case," 1781.

In 1771 Arkwright and his partners established another mill at Cromford, in the parish of Wirksworth, in Derbyshire, the machinery in which was set in motion by a water-wheel; and in 1775 he took out a second patent, including some additions which he had made to his original apparatus.

In what we have hitherto related, we have carefully confined ourselves to facts which are universally acknowledged; but there are other points of the story that have been stated in very opposite ways, and have given rise to much doubt and dispute.

The machinery for which Arkwright took out his patents consisted of various parts, his second specification enumerating no fewer than ten different contrivances; but of these, the one that was by far of greatest importance, was a device for drawing out the cotton from a coarse to a finer and harder twisted thread, and so rendering it fit to be used for warp as well as weft.* This was most ingeniously managed by the application of a principle which had not yet been introduced in any other mechanical operation. The cotton was in the first place drawn off from the skewers on which it was fixed by one pair of rollers, which were made to move at a comparatively slow rate, and which formed it into threads of a first and coarser quality; † but at a little distance behind the first was placed a second pair of rollers, revolving three, four, or five times as fast, which took it up when it had passed through the others, the effect of which would be to reduce the thread to a degree of fineness so many times greater than that which it originally had. The first pair of rollers might be regarded as the feeders of the second, which could receive no more than the others sent to them; and that, again, could be no more than these others themselves took up from the skewers. As the second pair of rollers, therefore, revolved, we will say, five times for every one revolution of the first pair, or, which is the same thing, required for their consumption in a given time five times the length of thread that the first did, they could obviously only obtain so much length by drawing out the common portion of cotton into thread of five times the original fineness. Nothing could be more beautiful or more effective than this contrivance; which, with an addi-

* This was, in truth, the principal subject of Arkwright's first patent; and, accordingly, on the great trial (afterwards mentioned) which took place in June, 1785, his opponents accused him of endeavouring unfairly to prolong his first patent by means of his second.

† In Arkwright's apparatus, which was a combination of the carding and spinning machinery, this first part of the process was somewhat modified; but the principle of the two pairs of rollers, the one revolving faster than the other, which forms the peculiarity of the machine, was employed as here described.

tional provision for giving the proper twist to the thread, constitutes what is called the water-frame or throstle.*

Of this part of his machinery, Arkwright particularly claimed the invention as his own. He admitted, with regard to some of the other machines included in his patent, that he was rather their improver than their inventor; and the original spinning machine for coarse thread, commonly called the spinning-jenny, he frankly attributed in its first conception to a person of the name of Hargrave, who resided at Blackburn, and who, he said, having been driven out of Lancashire in consequence of his invention, had taken refuge in Nottingham; but, unable to bear up against a conspiracy formed to ruin him, had been at last obliged to relinquish the farther prosecution of his object, and died in obscurity and distress.

There were, however, other parties as well as Arkwright in these new machines, and who would not allow that any of them were of his invention. As to the principal of them, the water-frame, they alleged that it was in reality the invention of a poor reed-maker, of the name of Highs, or Hayes, and that Arkwright had obtained the knowledge of it from his old associate Kay, who had been employed by Highs to assist him in constructing a model of it a short time before Arkwright had sought his acquaintance. Many cotton-spinners, professing to believe this to be the true state of the case, actually used Arkwright's machinery in their factories, notwithstanding the patent by which he had attempted to protect it; and this invasion of his monopoly was carried to such an extent, that at last he found himself obliged to bring actions against no less than nine different parties.+

The first of these, in which a Colonel Mordaunt was defendant, was tried in the Court of King's Bench, in July, 1781. Upon this occasion, however, the question as to the originality of the inventions was

* So called from its having been originally moved by water power.

+ It is asserted, in the article on the cotton manufacture, in the Supplement to the Encyclopædia Britannica, and repeated in a paper on the same subject in the 91st number of the Edinburgh Review, that a trial took place upon the subject of Arkwright's first patent in the year 1772, on which occasion he obtained a verdict establishing its validity. This statement, however, for which no authority is given, appears to be altogether without foundation. No such trial is alluded to in the course of the proceedings in the Court of King's Bench in June and November, 1772, although both that of July, 1781, and that of February, 1785, are repeatedly mentioned; nor is it noticed, we believe, in any of the earliest accounts of Arkwright's machinery. Mr. Guest (who has written a history of the cotton manufacture, which is marked by a somewhat strong dislike to Arkwright) searched the records of the courts of King's Bench, Common Pleas, and Exchequer, for the year 1772, without finding any trace of it.

not mooted; the defence taken being the insufficiency of the specification on which the patent had been obtained; and upon that ground a verdict was given in favour of the defendant. On this result Arkwright abandoned the other eight actions he had raised; and instead of attempting any longer to maintain his patent in a court of law, published a pamphlet, containing what he called his "Case," with a view of inducing the legislature to interfere for his protection. It is proper we should here mention that, although the first of these actions in 1781, which decided the fate of the others, thus went off without the real merits of the case having been gone into, yet several of the defendants were prepared to dispute the claim of the patentee to the invention of the machines, and that both Highs and Kay had been summoned to give their evidence upon that point, and were actually in court during the trial of the action against Colonel Mordaunt, the former having been brought over from Ireland, where he was then residing, expressly for the occasion.

Arkwright submitted to the verdict that had been given against him for nearly four years; but at last, in February, 1785, he commenced a second action upon the subject, which was tried in the Court of Common Pleas; and, having brought forward several artists who declared that they could make the machines from the descriptions which he had given in his specification, he obtained a verdict which reinstated him in the enjoyment of his monopoly. Upon this, as on the former occasion, the only question submitted to the jury was that regarding the sufficiency of the specification; although it soon appeared that several of the parties interested were determined not to rest satisfied with a decision of the matter upon that ground alone.

Accordingly, in the month of June, in the same year, a *scire-facias*, an action which is nominally at the suit of the King, was brought against Arkwright in the Court of King's Bench to repeal the patent, in the trial of which the whole of the question was at last gone into. The principal evidence on which it was attempted to be shewn that the water-frame was not invented by Arkwright, was that of Highs, of Kay, and of Kay's wife, the substance of which was, that the double rollers had been originally contrived by Highs in the early part of the year 1767, while he was residing in the town of Leigh; that he had employed his neighbour and acquaintance Kay to make a model of a machine for him upon that principle; and that Kay, upon meeting with Arkwright a short time after, at Warrington, had been persuaded by him to communicate to him the secret of Highs's invention, on the understanding, as it would appear, that the two should make what they could of it, and share the advantages between them. The evidence of each of the witnesses corroborated, so far as the case admitted, that of the others ; Highs stated that he had been first informed of the manner in which Arkwright had got possession of his invention by Kay's wife, who, on her part, swore that she recollected her husband making models, first for Highs, and afterwards for Arkwright, although she could not speak with any distinctness to the nature of the machine ; while Kay himself acknowledged the treachery of which he had been guilty, and gave a particular account of the manner in which he said that Arkwright had contrived to obtain from him the secret of Highs's invention.   Highs also stated that, upon meeting with Arkwright in Manchester, some years after he had taken out his patent, he charged him with the source from which he had derived the machine ; to which Arkwright said nothing at first, but afterwards remarked that, if any person, having made a discovery, declined to prosecute it, he conceived any other had a right, after a certain time, to take it up and obtain a patent for it, if he chose.

This famous trial lasted from nine o'clock in the morning till half-past twelve at night, and excited the greatest interest, both among those more immediately concerned, and among the public generally. Among the witnesses examined were Mr. Cumming, the well-known watchmaker, Mr. Harrison, the son of the inventor of the marine chronometer, Dr. Darwin, and the since celebrated James Watt.   The result was a verdict again invalidating the patent ; which, on a motion being made for a new trial, the court refused to disturb.   Arkwright after this never took any further steps to vindicate his patent rights. On this account some writers have been disposed to maintain that he really had obtained the inventions in the manner that Highs and Kay alleged.   It is, however, to be remembered that it has been a common fate with those who have been fortunate enough to enrich themselves by their happy inventions to have attempts made to take from them the honour of those discoveries, of the profits of which it is found impossible to deprive them—and that it has seldom, in such cases, been difficult to find some hitherto unheard-of genius to set up his claim to the prior discovery of what, nevertheless, it would appear he scarcely knew the value of, after he had discovered it.   In this particular case the other party had a strong interest in setting aside Arkwright's pretensions if they could, and the circumstance of Kay having been connected with Highs before he was employed by him, afforded them a tempting foundation on which to erect what they, no doubt, considered a very convenient theory.   Then again, as for so much of their allegation as rested upon the evidence of this Kay, it was not entitled to command much attention, since it appeared both that he had some time before quarrelled with Arkwright, and that he must, even by his own account, have acted so perfidious a part in regard to his first friend Highs, as to deprive him of all claim to be believed in any thing he might now choose to assert. Highs's own evidence is undoubtedly what seems to bear strongest against Arkwright; but he, from very natural causes, might have been mistaken as to various points. He appears to have told his story in a very confused and ineffective way—much as if he either did not feel his ground to be very sure, or was not at all aware of the importance of the facts to which he was brought to speak. It is not impossible that, if he actually did invent the machine in question, Arkwright may have also hit upon the same idea about the same time; or may at least have been led to it merely by some vague rumour that had got abroad as to what Highs was about—not an unnatural supposition, when we reflect that his operations seem to have been a good deal talked of in the neighbourhood, and that the slightest hint of the principle of the water-frame would have sufficed to put an ingenious man like Arkwright in possession of the whole machine. And this after all gives us, perhaps, the most natural explanation of his conversation with Highs at Manchester. If he knew that he had really stolen his invention from that person in the manner stated in Kay's evidence, it is not likely that he would have been much disposed to meet him at all; whereas the interview appears to have been arranged by the intervention of a mutual acquaintance, who had in all probability obtained the consent of both parties to his bringing them together. His silence, when Highs charged him with having got possession of his invention, or rather merely noticed the circumstance (for the whole seems to have passed in quite an amicable manner), will depend for its interpretation very much upon the exact words used by Highs, which it is very possible he did not recollect perfectly when he gave his evidence in the Court of King's Bench twelve or thirteen years afterwards. Perhaps he said nothing about Kay at all; but merely remarked in general terms that he had been beforehand with Mr. Arkwright in thinking of the two pairs of rollers which formed so valuable a part of his patent machinery. This was an averment which for anything that Arkwright knew might be true, and which if incorrect he had at any rate no means of refuting;— so that nothing could be more natural than his remaining silent— although he would scarcely, one should think, have taken the thing quite so passively if he had been flatly charged with the base conduct afterwards imputed to him. The observation, again, he is said to have made a little while after, is perfectly consistent with this view of the case. He waves the question as to which of the two might have been first in possession of the idea; and contents himself with simply remarking that, however that might be, he conceived any one who had made a discovery which he thought might be turned to advantage was quite entitled to take it up and prosecute it by himself, even though another might also be in possession of it, if that other shewed no intention of stirring in the business. And to this remark Highs, by his own account, quietly assented, although it certainly would have been natural enough for him to have hinted, if he really had previously advanced the charge which on the trial he said he had done, that whatever a man might do with regard to an invention that was really his own, he could hardly have a right in any circumstances to steal those of other people, and take out a patent for them.

Whatever conclusion may be come to on the subject of Arkwright's claim to the invention of the machinery introduced by him into his spinning factories, it is incontestable that to him alone belongs the merit both of having combined its different parts with admirable ingenuity and judgment, and of having by his unwearied and invincible perseverance first brought it into actual use on anything like an extensive scale, and demonstrated its power and value. The several inventions which his patent embraced, whether they were his own or not, would probably but for him have perished with their authors; none of whom except himself had the determination and courage to face the multiplied fatigues and dangers that lay in the way of achieving a practical exemplification of what they had conceived in their minds, or to encounter any part of that opposition, incredulity, ridicule, of those disappointments, repulses, losses, and other discouragements, over all of which he at last so completely triumphed. When he set out on this career he was poor, friendless, and utterly unknown. We have already stated that, on his coming with Kay to Preston, he was almost in rags; and it may be added that when he and Kay made application immediately before this to a Mr. Atherton for some pecuniary assistance to enable them to prosecute their plans, Arkwright's appearance alone was enough to determine that gentleman to have nothing to do with the adventure. Can we have a more exciting example, then, of what a resolute heart may do in apparently the most hopeless circumstances? —of what ingenuity and perseverance together may overcome in the pursuit of what they are determined to attain? And this is the grand lesson which the history of Arkwright is fitted to teach us—to give ourselves wholly to one object, and never to despair of reaching it. Even after he had succeeded in forming his partnership with Messrs Need and Strutt, his success was far from being secured. For a long time the speculation was a hazardous and unprofitable one; and no little outlay of capital was required to carry it on. He tells us himself in his "Case," that it did not begin to pay till it had been persevered in for five years, and had swallowed up a capital of more than twelve thousand pounds. We cannot doubt that it required all Arkwright's dexterity and firmness to induce his partners to persevere with the experiment under this large expenditure and protracted disappointment. But it was the character of the man to devote his whole heart and faculties to whatever he engaged in. Even to the close of his life the management of his different factories was his only occupation, and even amusement. Although he had been from early life afflicted with severe asthma, he took scarcely any recreation—employing all his time either in superintending the daily concerns of these establishments—which were regulated upon a plan that itself indicated in its contriver no little ingenuity and reach of mind ;* or in adding such improvements to his machinery from time to time, as his experience and observation suggested. And thus it was, that from a poor barber he raised himself to what he eventually became—not merely to rank and great affluence—but to be the founder of a new branch of national industry, destined in a wonderfully short space of time to assume the very first place among the manufactures of his country."

Here, we regret to state, our guide deserts us. Having accomplished his purpose, and displayed the claims of Arkwright to the merit of an inventor, he forbears to depict him in the character of a wealthy man, increasing in honours as in years. But, in fact, the increase of the cotton trade was the increase of Arkwright's prosperity ; he saw and heard the sources of his riches on every side of his growing mansion, and having once tasted the pleasure of growing wealthy, adhered to it with commendable constancy. By pursuing his fortune, he acquired the praise which many purchase by the sacrifice of fortune, time, and ease—that of a public benefactor, and a friend to the poor. It has been said, that his frugality bordered on parsimony ; but we should not hastily conclude that he was discreditably penurious, or would have begrudged to spend when human kindness or Christian duty bade him loose his purse strings. Seeing him possessed of the revenues of a prince, the world expected him at least to adopt the style of a gentle-

---

* " The originality and comprehension of Sir Richard Arkwright's mind," says the writer of the article on the cotton manufacture, in the Supplement to the ' Encyclopædia Britannica,' " were perhaps marked by nothing more strongly than the judgment with which, although new to business, he conducted the great concerns his discoveries gave rise to, and the systematic order and arrangement which he introduced into every department of his extensive works. His plans of management, which must have been entirely his own, since no establishment of a similar nature then existed, were universally adopted by others; and after long experience they have not yet in any material point been altered or improved."

man; but the world is an unreasonable personage, and by no means so charitable in its judgments of the rich, as devout in its adoration of riches. For a man accustomed from infancy till middle age to a homely method of living, to adopt the sumptuous elegancies of artificial society, is to make himself thoroughly miserable. The expense is the least part of the annoyance. His bed, his meals, his garments, every piece of furniture in his mansion torments him, his servants agonize him, but his wife and daughters are worse than all. To say nothing of elegances or luxuries, the most essential comforts of genteel existence are nuisances to those who have grown up without them, e. g. frequent changes of linen, daily shaving, &c. Arkwright had no pretensions to the philosophic mind of Watt, or the tasteful genius and magnificent soul of Wedgwood; he did not value his discovery for the scientific power it displayed, nor did he make it subservient to the revival of the forms of antique beauty. He saw its utility, and that was enough.

In politics he does not seem to have taken an active part, at least he never aspired to a seat in parliament, which he might easily have commanded; but perhaps he thought it throwing money away. Yet on occasion of presenting an address, in the year 1786, he was knighted by the hand of George the Third. This is an expensive honour, which has been made rather too common; but it had the effect of giving the barber's wife precedence over all the untitled ladies in the county.

Sir Richard Arkwright died at his seat at Cromford, Derbyshire, August 3d, 1792. He left the bulk of his fortune between his son and daughter, his only surviving issue, but settled £500 a year on his widow, and remembered all his nieces and nephews in his will. He was buried at Matlock, but gave directions that his body should be removed to the chapel he had himself begun to build at Cromford as soon as it should be finished; and appointed, in his last testament, that his son should complete the structure, and settle £50 a year on the chaplain. This bequest proves that prosperity had not produced the same ungodly changes on Arkwright as on Pope's Sir Balaam. It could not be said of him,—

> What once he called a *blessing* now was *wit*,
> And God's good providence a *lucky hit*.

But why was not the fifty pounds made three hundred? The times are past when a country parson could be " passing rich with forty pounds a year," if indeed they ever existed, save when " every rood of ground maintained its man:" or to refer to a period somewhat nearer to historic existence, since forty pounds were equivalent to three hundred. Under the present aristocratic constitution of the church, three hundred a year is requisite to keep a married clergyman on a level with his brethren. These are not the days of "wonderful Robert Walker." A clergyman could not now marry a domestic without *losing caste*, nor could he employ his daughters in spinning, or his sons in the labours of the field, without staining his cloth in the public estimation. This, we apprehend, is no new state of things. The few clergymen who have eked out a small income by the labour of their families, and yet commanded the respect of their parishioners, have lived out of the world's eye, in remote mountain dales, where simple manners and christian equality having once grown, have long continued, like morning dew at noon in the centre of a forest. But clergymen, living in general society, were always obligated to be gentlemen, and though the expense of gentility has varied at different times, yet it has generally been so much as to be inconvenient to a poor parson with a large family (and poor parsons have generally large families), and less than three hundred a year. Less than this no beneficed clergyman ought to have, as long as any have more than five.

Wherever exorbitant wealth exists, whether in a church, a profession, a regiment, or a nation, there will be keenly-felt and discontented poverty, which will assume its most fearful form of lawless and infuriate want, if the customary circulation of wealth be impeded, or the number of the poor exceed the demands of the rich.

And here the question occurs, is Arkwright, and other such as he, who, by multiplying the powers of production, have so greatly increased the public and private wealth of Britain, to be considered as benefactors or not? Or, to state the question more strongly and more truly, was it in wrath or in mercy that mankind were led to the modern improvements in machinery? Should we merely take a survey of the present state of the country, especially as regards the labouring classes, we should be apt to denominate these inventions the self-inflicted scourge of avarice. They have indeed increased wealth, but they have tremendously increased poverty; not that willing poverty which weans the soul from earth, and fixes the desires on high; not that poverty which was heretofore to be found in mountain villages, in solitary dwellings mid-way up the bleak fell side, where one green speck, one garden plot, a hive of bees, and a few sheep would keep a family content; not that poverty which is the nurse of temperance and thoughtful piety;—but squalid, ever-murmuring poverty, cooped in mephitic dens and sunless alleys; hopeless, purposeless, wasteful in the midst of want; a poverty which dwarfs and disfeatures body and soul, makes the capacities and even the acquirements of intellect useless and pernicious, and multiplies a race of men without the virtues which beasts oft-times display,—without fidelity, gratitude, or natural affection.

The moral degradation of this caste may not be greater in England than elsewhere, but their physical sufferings are more constant than in the southern climates, and their tendency to increase much stronger than in the northern latitudes. But has machinery occasioned the existence or growth of this class? Certainly not,—for it has always existed since society assumed its present shape, and is to be found in countries like Spain and Naples, where pride and indolence are too powerful even for the desire of wealth to overcome.

But the artificial wealth which manufactures have assisted to generate, has generated or aggregated a factitious population, dependent for employment and subsistence on a state of things exceedingly and incalculably precarious, and seldom able to practice more than one department of a trade, in which labour is minutely divided; a population naturally improvident in prosperity and impatient in distress, whom the first interruption of trade converts to paupers, and whom a continuance of bad times is sure to fix in that permanent pauperism, from which there is no redemption. Times may mend, but man, once prostrate, never recovers his upright posture. Once a vagabond and always a vagabond. Once accustomed to eat the bread of idleness, the operative seldom takes pains to procure employment, and having been paid something for doing nothing, thinks ever after that he is paid too little for toil, and seizes every pretext to throw up his work again. Character has little influence on a man whom the world considers, and teaches to consider himself but as a portion of a mass. To be sensible of character Man must feel himself a responsible individual, and to individualize the human being, not only must the reflective powers be evoked and disciplined by education, but there must be property, or profession, or political privilege, or something equivalent, a certain sphere of freeagency, to make the man " revere himself as man," and respect the opinions of his fellow men. Now it is the tendency of wealth to increase the number of those who have no property but the strength or skill which they must sell to the highest bidder: who either by labour, or without labour, must live upon the property of others, and who, having no permanent mooring, are liable by every wind of circumstance, to slip their cables, and drift away with the idle sea-weed and the rotting wrecks of long-past tempests. Thus, to vary the metaphor, the sediment of the commonwealth is augmented with continual fresh depositions, till the stream of society is nigh choaked up, and our gallant vessels stranded on the flats and shallows,—without metaphor, so many of the people drop into the mob, that the mob is like to be too many for the people, and wealth itself to be swallowed up by the poverty itself has begotten.

But these evils do not rise directly from the machinery which expedites labour, but from the blind desire of accumulation, the passion for sudden wealth, which that machinery has helped to pamper, and which first the ambition and then the necessities of the state have fostered and flattered. The right use of machinery is to enable men to produce what is necessary and comfortable for the body, at the least possible expense of time, labour, care, thought, and capital, and so far to free every man of every nation from the worky-day business of the world, that the poorest, while he looks forward with assurance to his morrow's meal, may have some leisure for rational enjoyment, mental cultivation, meditation, and devotion ; that, whatever ranks, orders, honours, or dignities may subsist, and however the political functions of the commonweal may be distributed, there may be none who toil merely to eat, and eat to toil.   Then, and not till then, will Freedom be more than a name.

> The Earth has lent
> Her waters, Air her breezes; and the sail
> Of traffic glides with ceaseless interchange,
> Glistening along the low and woody dale,
> Or on the naked mountain's lofty side.
> Meanwhile, at social Industry's command,
> How quick, how vast an increase ! From the germ
> Of some poor hamlet, rapidly produced
> Here a large town, continuous and compact,
> Hiding the face of earth for leagues—and there,
> Where not an habitation stood before,
> The abodes of men irregularly massed
> Like trees in forests—spread through spacious tracts,
> O'er which the smoke of unremitting fires
> Hangs permanent, and plentiful as wreaths
> Of vapour glittering in the morning sun.
> And, wheresoe'er the traveller turns his steps,
> He sees the barren wilderness erased,
> Or disappearing; triumph that proclaims
> How much the mild directress of the plough
> Owes to alliance with these new-born arts !
> —Hence is the wide sea peopled,—and the shores
> Of Britain are resorted to by ships
> Freighted from every climate of the world
> With the world's choicest produce.   Hence that sum
> Of keels that rest within her crowded ports,
> Or ride at anchor in her sounds and bays;
> That animating spectacle of sails
> Which through her inland regions, to and fro
> Pass with the respirations of the tide,
> Perpetual, multitudinous! Finally,
> Hence a dread arm of floating Power, a voice

SIR RICHARD ARKWRIGHT.

Of Thunder, daunting those who would approach
With hostile purposes the blessed Isle,
Truth's consecrated residence, the seat
Impregnable, of Liberty and Peace.

  *   *   *   *   *

                 Yet I exult,
Casting reserve away, exult to see
An Intellectual mastery exercised
O'er the blind Elements; a purpose given,
A perseverance fed; almost a soul
Imparted—to brute Matter.   I rejoice,
Measuring the force of those gigantic powers,
Which by the thinking Mind have been compelled
To serve the Will of feeble-bodied Man.
For with the sense of admiration blends
The animating hope that time may come
When strengthened, yet not dazzled, by the might
Of this dominion over Nature gained,
Men of all lands shall exercise the same
In due proportion to their Country's need;
Learning, though late, that all true glory rests,
All praise, all safety, and all happiness,
Upon the Moral law.   Egyptian Thebes;
Tyre by the margin of the sounding waves;
Palmyra, central in the Desart, fell;
And the Arts died by which they had been raised.
—Call Archimedes from his buried Tomb
Upon the plain of vanished Syracuse,
And feelingly the Sage shall make report
How insecure, how baseless in itself,
Is that Philosophy, whose sway is framed
For mere material instruments :—how weak
Those Arts, and high Inventions, if unpropped
By Virtue.— He with sighs of pensive grief,
Amid his calm abstractions, would admit
That not the slender privilege is theirs
To save themselves from blank forgetfulness !

               WORDSWORTH'S EXCURSION.

Published May 1. 1810 by R.P. Dundas & Private 1810.

WILLIAM ROSCOE.

HITHERTO we have spoken of men whose lives were history,—flowers, or medicinal plants (for as yet we have encountered no weeds), preserved in a *Hortus-siccus*, to which we have done our best to restore the lively hue and appropriate aroma. We have now a more delicate task to perform. We speak of a man whose death is a recent sorrow; whose image lives in eyes that have wept for him. The caution and reserve, which honour and duty exact from the biographer of a living contemporary, are more especially required of him who essays to collect the scattered lineaments of one who no longer lives to confute or approve the portrait, which yet may give pain or pleasure to many, who compare the likeness with their own authentic memory.

I never saw Roscoe. I have heard much of him, both from the many who delighted in his praise, and from some who reluctantly assented to it. Unseen, yet not quite unknown of me, he performed his earthly pilgrimage, and went to his reward. If his life were not a theme of commendation,—if, however told, it were not a bright example and an argument of hope to all, who, amid whatever circumstances, are striving to develope the faculties which God has given them, for the glory of the Giver, and the benefit of his creatures,—if there were any thing to tell, or *any thing to leave untold*, which those who knew him best would rather have forgotten, his life would never have been written by me. I am not ignorant, that one who has an hereditary right to be his Biographer, is even now performing that office. With his filial labours I presume not to interfere. Let the son tell of his father what the son knows of the father. Roscoe, as a scholar, an author, a politician, and a philanthropist, is public: his praise, and if censure were due, his censure, is as much a public property as Westminster Abbey should be. With his more familiar privacy I meddle no otherwise, than as he who treats of fruits and flowers must necessarily say something of the soil in which they were grown, and the culture by which they were reared to perfection.

Among those men who have attained to literary eminence without the ordinary assistance from their elders, Roscoe was especially distinguished by the variety, and by the elegance of his acquirements. Most of the self-taught have been men of one talent and one idea—one exclusive passion for one sort of knowledge. Their bias has been much more frequently to the mathematics, physics, or mechanics, than to general literature. The poor classics of Scotland and Germany, such as Adams, Heyne, and Winkelman, are not fairly cases in point ; for though they underwent great toil and privation in obtaining tuition, they did obtain it, therefore were not self-taught. As little to the purpose are the instances of uneducated Poets. For we are not speaking of men who have displayed great genius with little culture, but of those who have cultivated their own powers without the customary aids.

With respect to the *uneducated* Poets, however, not many of them are any thing more than *nine-days'-wonders*. Some great man, or great lady, finds out that a peasant or menial can tag rhimes ; and having at once a most exaggerated notion of the difficulty of rhiming, and a most contemptuous estimate of the faculties of the *lower orders*, straightway gives information of a self-taught poet, whom patronage is to select for a victim.

But secondly : Far be it from us to deny that there have lived, and are living, true and great poets, who have not only been all but destitute of *tuition*, but have been very scantily furnished with book-learning. We do not, however, count Shakspeare in the number ; for he was manifestly a great and extensive reader, and got from books whatever could have been of any use to him ; his genius, his intuitive knowledge of human nature, concreted by wide and perspicacious observation of human life, his shaping and combining imagination, his electrical fancy, no book could supply. The world is still too much in the habit of confounding the absence of regular tuition, with positive ignorance ; though we do hope, that the preposterous folly of dignifying a little, a very little Latin, and very, very, very little Greek (forgotten long ago), with the exclusive name of learning, is far gone in the wane. Indeed there is more need to assert and vindicate the true value of Greek and Roman lore, than to level the by-gone pretensions of its professors. This age has a sad propensity to slay the slain, to fight with wrath and alarm against the carcase of extinct prejudices, because some two or three men of genius, and perhaps a score of blockheads, are striving to galvanize them to a posthumous vitality. Admitting, however, that Shakspeare could not, with the assistance of grammar and dictionary, construe an ode of Horace, (which is a pure and rather improbable assertion, for Latin was then taught far more generally than at present), he certainly was not unacquainted with the ancient authors,* most of which were translated early in Elizabeth's reign, rudely and incorrectly enough it may be, (there was little or no accurate scholarship in England before Bentley), but still so, that neither the feelings nor the thoughts were wanting. An *uneducated* man he was: his mind had never been disciplined, but it was completely armed and ammunitioned. Had he been educated, he would perhaps have avoided some few faults, but he would, in all probability, have fallen considerably short of his actual excellence,—not that his matter would have been less original (Milton, in the true sense of the word, is as complete an original as Shakspeare), but his manner would have been more restrained, more subdued, and therefore would have presented a less exact image of truth; for he was a man modest and gentle by nature, with little of Milton's mental hardihood. It was well for him and for mankind, that he did not know how widely he differed from his great predecessors.

But though we except Shakspeare from the list of *unlearned* authors, we admit that there have been, and are, men who, with no assistance from teachers, and little from books, have justly earned the name of Poets. But they are men with whom poetry is a passion, or a con-

---

* Dr. Farmer is supposed to have settled the question as to Shakspeare's learning by proving (as far as the matter is capable of proof), that he used the translated, not the original classics. As it is always delightful to trace the reading of great men, Dr. Farmer's work is as pleasing as it is ingenious and satisfactory. But the inference, that Shakspeare, *because* he read Seneca done into English, and Dr. Philemon Holland's translation of Amyot's translation of Plutarch, (the best by the way that has appeared, far better than Langhorne's,) had never learned *hic, hæc, hoc*, that his ignorance extended from *Alpha* to *Omega*, we reject without hesitation. Why might not Shakspeare, like a gentleman as he was, have learned Latin and forgotten it again? How many Eton scholars can read a page of Virgil, taken haphazard, with any degree of facility or pleasure at forty? Not more than could help to win a cricket match in their grand climacteric. Professional scholars, school-masters, &c. of course are excepted.

The question cannot be called uninteresting, for it regards Shakspeare; but it is of no sort of consequence.—*Small Latin and less Greek*, especially when forgotten, being for all purposes of wonder and astonishment, quite as good as none. Nor would it detract an atom from Shakspeare's fame, were he proved to have been a perfect Porson. But there are certain people who had rather look upon genius as something monstrous and magical, than as a healthy human power, effecting a noble end by intelligible means.

solation, and their excellence will be found to consist in short effusions of natural feeling, in descriptions of what they have actually seen or experienced, and in records of the manners, devotions, loves, and superstitions of those among whom they have been bred up. It is, moreover, doubtful how far extensive reading of any sort is beneficial to any but a very great Poet: that indiscriminate reading of vernacular poetry is prejudicial to poetic powers, there can be no doubt at all. Any but a surpassing genius, who has the "British Poets," or even the "Elegant Extracts," by heart, must either become a mere compiler, in despair of novelty, or must go out of his way, to avoid saying what has been said before. And here we perceive the true reason why the greatest poets generally appear in the early stages of literature; or if, like Wordsworth and Byron, they are products of a later age, they are yet the earliest great poets of their kind. Here, too, we find the main value of a skill in ancient or foreign languages, whereby the mind is enriched with thoughts which it is in a manner compelled to make its own.

But Roscoe's passion was knowledge in general, with a peculiar bias to the beautiful in art and nature. Perhaps it was in some measure owing to the universality of his studies, that he was never tempted to neglect or discard his professional duties; for had he devoted himself exclusively to any one study, it would most likely have gained so entire a dominion over his imagination, as to render business an insupportable distraction.

WILLIAM ROSCOE was born on the 8th of March, 1753. The house in which he first drew breath is standing still, but instead of a rural retirement, is now a tavern, in a crowded and almost central street of Liverpool, recording, by its name of Mount Pleasant, its former suburban rusticity. So mightily is the inundation of brick and mortar spreading, uniting village after village to the great centres of population, as the ocean "drinks up all the little rills:" overrunning fields, and parks, and gardens, which, like the political institutions of a decaying nation, bear names to testify what they have been, and are not.

The house in which Roscoe was born is now known as the "Old Bowling-green House," and is well represented in an engraving by Austin.

Mr. Roscoe's parents were persons in humble but respectable circumstances. Having lived together as domestics with a worthy old bachelor, they formed an attachment, and married with their master's approbation. By their own savings, and probably with the assistance of the same benevolent gentleman (who is said to have left the bulk of his property to the subject of this memoir), they were enabled to rent a few fields, and the house at Mount Pleasant, where their son William was born.

Though exempt from the evils of actual poverty, it cannot be supposed that the honest couple were able, or in the first instance desirous, to afford their child any thing above the commonest education. At six, he was sent to a day school kept by a Mr. Martin, and two years afterwards removed to the seminary of Mr. Sykes, then in considerable repute as a commercial academy. Young Roscoe was by no means remarkable for diligence or proficiency at these schools. The books then selected (if in truth there was any selection at all) for elementary instruction were little attractive, and Roscoe's mind was not one of those that are peculiarly delighted with the science of numbers. Yet as he was found qualified, at sixteen, for an attorney's office, we may conclude that he was a respectable penman, and discovered no inaptitude to figures. At twelve, he was taken from school at his own request, and from that period was mainly his own instructor. Reading, writing, arithmetic, and a little geometry, were then all his acquirements. Perhaps he had learned all that was taught in the usual routine of Mr. Sykes's establishment. If so, he displayed his early good sense in voluntarily withdrawing from it. Mutual instruction was not yet in vogue; and perhaps even at this time it may be proper to remind parents, especially those of humble rank in easy circumstances, that a day school is a very dangerous lounge for either boy or girl past childhood, whose time is not fully occupied in the business of that school. It is too much the practice to permit youth of both sexes to remain at school, not because they are doing any good there, but because their parents do not know what else to do with them. With regard to females of the higher class, this may not be objectionable: the intermediate state between pupilage and companionship in which young ladies continue with their schoolmistresses has its advantages; the articles of female education are so multifarious, that it can hardly ever be said to be completed. A ladies' boarding-school approaches to a domestic establishment; and wherever there is a *home*, a female need never be idle. But for the infinitely larger class, whose destiny is labour, and indeed, for males of all classes, a school becomes almost prejudicial as soon as it ceases to be necessary. The higher education of England will never be what it ought to be, till there is some institution for the youths who are too old for Eton or Harrow, and not old enough for Oxford or Cambridge. In the mean time, we think it the less evil, that they should go too early to the University, than that they should continue too long at the school.

From twelve to sixteen, young Roscoe continued under his father's

roof, employing his time partly in reading, and partly in assisting the labours of the farm.   He also paid frequent visits to a
porcelain manufactory in the neighbourhood, where he amused himself
with china-painting.   His reading was desultory, as that of a boy left
to himself always will be; but it could not be very miscellaneous, for
his command of books was extremely limited, and the few volumes to
which he had access, were rather such as chance threw in his way,
than what his unaided judgment would have recommended.   There
was, however, no lack of good matter among them.   His favourites
were Shakspeare (an odd volume most likely), Shenstone, the Spectator,
and the poems of Mrs. Katherine Philips.   Perhaps these were all the
books of a poetical or imaginative cast which his library afforded.   The
names may now seem oddly grouped; yet if the merit of a writer be
measured by the plaudits of contemporary pens, the fame of Mrs.
Katherine Philips,* alias "the matchless Orinda," would soar high

* Mrs. Katherine Philips, whose maiden name was Fowler, was born in London,
baptized on the 11th of January, 1631, at the church of St. Mary, Woolnoth;
educated at Hackney, by Mrs. Salmon, (thus early was Hackney the seat of the
educational Muse); married James Philips, Esq.; accompanied the Viscountess
Dungannon into Ireland; died in 1664; and was buried in the church of St. Bennet's,
Sherehog.   Cowley wrote an ode on her death, to which she probably owes whatever
little celebrity she may retain.   Her poems were published, without her consent, not
long before her death.   In 1667 appeared another and fuller edition of "Poems, by
the most deservedly-admired Mrs. Katherine Philips, the matchless Orinda;" and a
third, in 1678.   Whether any later has been called for we cannot say.   She translated
the Pompey, and four acts of the Horace of Corneille: the former was acted, and
honoured with a prologue by Lord Roscommon, an epilogue by Sir Edward Deering,
and a copy of commendatory verses by Lord Orrery, in which his Lordship not only
declares "the copy greater than the original," but asserts that

> "Rome too will grant, were our tongue to her known,
> Cæsar speaks better in't than in his own."

There is rather more sense and propriety in the panegyric which Sir Edward Deering
bestows in the epilogue :—

> "No nobler thoughts can tax
> These rhymes of blemish to the blushing sex;
> As chaste the lines, as harmless to the sense,
> As the first smiles of infant innocence."

She seems, indeed, to have been a woman of perfectly blameless life, though she
entered into a sort of Platonic correspondence with Sir Charles Cotterel, which produced a series of letters between Poliarchus and Orinda.   It is said by one of her
panegyrists, that she wrote her familiar letters with great facility, in a very fair hand,
and *perfect orthography*, then we may suppose a rare accomplishment.   As a specimen
of her poetry, we give her epitaph on her infant son Hector, buried in the church of
St. Bennet's, Sherehog.   It has been said, "Men laugh in a thousand ways, but all
weep alike."   See how a mother dropped her poetic tears in the seventeenth century :

above Addison himself, and poor Shakspeare and Shenstone must hide their diminished heads. There are few school-girls now who could not write better verses than her's; but then mediocrity was not so easy in the 17th century as in the 19th. We are disposed to hope that it will become so easy, that none will tolerate it, even in themselves.

If we might indulge a conjecture as to which among these was Roscoe's favourite, we should be tempted to fix upon Shenstone. Boys who have any thing of a poetical turn themselves, are often better pleased with verses which they think that they can imitate, than with those that defy emulation. No boy ever imagines himself a poet while he is reading Shakspeare or Milton. The thoughts, too obviously, are not his own. But Shenstone has much to charm, and nothing to overpower, the mind of boyhood. His pastoral imagery is pretty, and must have been new to Roscoe, though it was not to Shenstone. His versification is smooth and *imitable*; his sentiments, sometimes plaintively tender, and sometimes breathing disdain and defiance to the world, find a ready sympathy with those whose warmer feelings are just beginning to glow; and he has much of a temper with which all ages are ready to sympathize—namely, discontent.

The elegant memorialist, to whom this article is so largely indebted,

> " What on earth deserves our trust ?
> Youth and beauty both are dust:
> Long we gathering are, with pain,
> What one moment calls again.
> Seven years' childless marriage past,
> A son, a son, is born at last,
> So exactly limb'd, and fair,
> Full of good spirits, mein, and air,
> As a long life promised, .
> Yet in less than six weeks dead ;
> Too promising, too great a mind,
> In so small room to be confined;
> Therefore, as fit in heaven to dwell,
> He quickly broke the prison shell.
> So the subtle alchemist
> Can't with Hermes' seal resist
> The powerful spirit's subtler flight,
> But 'twill bid him long good night.
> And so the sun, if it arise
> Half so glorious as his eyes,
> Like this infant takes a shroud,
> Buried in a morning cloud."

Yet it is probable that the Poetess felt her loss as keenly as one who would have expressed herself with the most pathetic simplicity.

remarks upon this part of Roscoe's life : " It is curious to trace his attachment to botany and the fine arts to this early period.　The phæ-nomena of vegetation, and the cultivation of plants, appear to have made a deep impression on his youthful mind, and in the little culti-vator of his father's fields we can trace the embryo botanist, to whose ardent enthusiasm in after years we owe our botanic garden, *the world* the new arrangement of Scitamineæ, and the superb botanical publica-tion on the same beautiful order of plants.　The early essays in painting china-ware seem also to have first inspired him with a love of the fine arts, and drew him on to cultivate his taste in the arts of design, in which he not only displayed the knowledge of an intelligent amateur, but such practical proficiency as might have led to eminence, had his genius not been directed to other channels, as several slight but spirited etchings by his hand amply testify."*

All this is very agreeable to contemplate, and true it is, that the embryo botanist will often be found in the field and the garden, by the hedge-row, and in the thicket.　The embryo artist, if he cannot procure brush, or pencil, or crayon, will make "slight but spirited" sketches with chalk, or charcoal ; or carve fantastic heads on walking sticks.　But a fondness for plants by no means clearly *foretells* the botanist. All children are fond of flowers, (they would be little monsters if they were not) ; and all who possess any life of mind are curious to observe how plants grow, and feel wonder and delight when the peas begin to peep above the ground.　It is a pity that this happy curiosity is so seldom made an inlet to useful knowledge ; but it has no connection with scien-tific botany.　A child wishes to know the name of every thing it sees : this is nature ; but arrangement and classification are works of reason, of reason trained and informed by education. Again, we hardly ever knew a boy that had not a turn for the arts of design, if a passion for scratch-ing and daubing, for lake and gamboge, is to be called by that title. Some children, in their juvenile efforts, display a truth of eye and

* From a " Memoir of William Roscoe, Esq. by Dr. Thomas Stewart Traill, F.R.S.E. read before the Literary and Philosophical Society of Liverpool, in October 1831, communicated by the author to Dr. Jameson's ' Edinburgh New Philosophical Journal.'"

As Dr. Traill was the bosom friend and medical adviser of Mr. Roscoe in the latter years of his life, (the acquaintance commencing in 1806,) there can be as little doubt of the accuracy of his information, as of the warmth and sincerity of his attachment, and the justice of his admiration.　His memoir, though necessarily short, is perhaps the fullest that has yet appeared of its illustrious subject.　To this, and to the earlier notices of the Rev. Mr. Shepherd, a long and endeared intimate of Roscoe, we are chiefly indebted for the materials of our life of that excellent man.

obedience of hand of which others are quite destitute, yet the pictorial passion is equally strong in the latter. Still it must be granted that the painter, unlike the poet, *always* exhibits the bias of his talent in early life. You cannot, from the rapid improvement and enthusiastic devotion of the boy, securely prophecy the excellence of the future artist ; for some soon arrive at a certain degree of imitative skill, and then never advance a step further ; but it may safely be assumed that the man who, with any sort of opportunity, has not produced something of promise before his fifteenth year, will never be even a tolerable painter.

Nevertheless we cannot quite agree with Dr. Traill in referring Mr. Roscoe's intelligence as a connoisseur to his youthful love of china painting, though that certainly might contribute to give him a dexterity of hand, which, diligently cultivated, would have enabled him to execute as well as to judge. Youths, even of less stirring intellects than Roscoe, like to attempt every thing they see doing, and young eyes are almost sensually delighted with brilliant colours. Porcelain-painting is a gorgeous, an ingenious art, but it remained for Wedgewood to make it a fine, i. e. an intellectual art. Imitating the gaudy grotesques on china dishes was much more likely to spoil Roscoe's eye than to improve it. But Heaven had given Roscoe an inward sense of beauty, a yearning after the beautiful, which would have made him a botanist, had his father not possessed so much as a box of mignonette ; which would have led him to admire and criticise the productions of the pencil, the graver, and the chisel, had there been no china manufactory out of the Celestial Empire. We are not intending to charge Dr. Traill with the sophism, of which Dr. Johnson seems to have been guilty, of ascribing the original direction of genius to the accidents upon which it is earliest exercised. What *he says* is just, as it is pleasing ; it is against the false inferences of others that we are guarding. Of this stage of his existence Mr. Roscoe speaks thus in his earliest publication, the poem entitled " Mount Pleasant :"—

> " Freed from the cares that daily throng my breast,
> Again beneath my native shades I rest.
> *These shades, where lightly fled my youthful day,*
> *E're fancy bow'd to reason's boasted sway.*
> Untaught the toils of busier life to bear,
> The fools impertinence, the proud man's sneer,
> Sick of the world, to these retreats I fly,
> Devoid of art my early reed to try.
> To paint the prospects that around me rise,
> What time the cloudless sun descends the skies,
> Each latent beauty of the landscape trace,
> Fond of the charms that deck my native place.

Though Roscoe was doubtless storing his memory and maturing his powers in this interval of comparative leisure, it does not appear that he had yet formed any regular plan of study, or made a fixed distribution of his time.   To a mind of less energy, such early liberty might have been dangerous, and though nothing could have rendered Roscoe a mere idler, yet even he might have lost that self-controul without which industry is wasted, had he continued much longer the master of his own hours.   But at sixteen he became articled clerk to Mr. John Eyes, a respectable solicitor of Liverpool, and here, while he strictly performed the duties of the office, and acquired a measure of professional knowledge that led the way to competence and eminence, he commenced a course of self-education, the results of which appear in his biographies of the Medici.   Between the ages of sixteen and twenty he mastered the rudiments of Latin, with no other aid than that of a grammar and dictionary ; no trifling effort for one who previously knew no language but his own, and had never learned that grammatically. His studies, however, were not always solitary ; he read some of the best Latin authors, in company with William Clarke and Richard Lowndes, two young men of Liverpool, whose tastes were similar to his own ; but though a communication of knowledge can seldom be made without an accession, it does not appear that Clarke or Lowndes had been more regularly tutored, or had made any greater proficiency than Roscoe himself.   They were the comrades, not the leaders of his studies.

To Francis Holden, an able, but eccentric man, he ascribed his first inclination to the study of modern languages, and he was eager to acknowledge that by the advice and encouragement of this young friend he was led to apply himself assiduously to Italian reading.   Yet neither in the Italian nor the French tongue, both which he mastered during the term of his clerkship, had he any tutor.   Greek was a later acquisition.   A memorandum in a copy of Homer, yet in possession of his family, runs thus : " Finished the Odyssee the day I came to Allerton, March 18th, 1799.   W. R."   Can any thing evince his unconquerable mental industry more clearly than his entering upon the study of a language accounted so arduous as the Greek, after he had attained a considerable literary reputation without it ?   During the time of his apprenticeship, Mr. Roscoe formed an agreement with his friends Clarke, Lowndes, and Holden, to meet early in the morning, before the hours of business, to read some Latin author, and afterwards impart whatever observations might occur during the lesson.   The evening leisure was chiefly bestowed upon Italian.   Before his twentieth year he had perused, in the original, several of the Italian historians, and had already conceived a design to be the historian of Lorenzo de' Medici. Few are the men who persevere so nobly, and so successfully, in designs so early formed. Roscoe was not

> " A clerk foredoomed his father's soul to cross,
> Who penn'd a stanza when he should engross."

Yet, amid all his employments, he did find time to pen many a stanza: and many of his productions remain, full of fine feeling and beautiful fancy, though unfortunately disfigured with the inane phraseology which then passed for poetic diction. Several of his metrical pieces were addressed to a young lady, about his own age, of an ardently poetical genius, afterwards destined to become the mother of an eminent Poet. The admiration, for it does not appear to have been more, was mutual; and among the lady's manuscript poems are found the following laudatory and almost prophetic lines :—

> " But cease, my Muse, unequal to the task,
> Forbear the effort, and to nobler hands
> Resign the lyre.   Thee, Roscoe, every muse
> Uncall'd attends, and uninvoked inspires :
> In blooming shades and amaranthine bowers
> They weave the future garland for thy brow,
> And wait to crown thee with immortal fame.
> Thee Wisdom leads in all her flowery walks,
> Thee Genius fires, and moral beauty charms ;
> Be it thy task to touch the feeling heart,
> Correct its passions, and exalt its aims ;
> Teach pride to own, and owning, to obey
> Fair Virtue's dictates, and her sacred laws :
> To brighter worlds shew thou the glorious road,
> And be thy life as moral as thy song."

To this lady the descriptive poem of " Mount Pleasant " was originally inscribed, though, when it was published, the address was omitted. The poem was composed about 1772, when the author was not more than nineteen, though it was not published till 1777. Among juvenile productions it claims a very respectable rank : still, it is a *very* juvenile production, and as it probably received little after-revision, we think it more for Roscoe's honour to speak of it here, in connection with his youth, than to bring it into association with his riper years.

In the first-place, a word on the species of poetry to which it belongs, the loco-descriptive. Of all organized poems, the loco-descriptive has the most imperfect organization, and, unless it assume the shape of a journey, or series of descriptive sketches, the least natural progression. It may be any thing and every thing, and the parts may be arranged in any order that happens to occur. Hence, its tempting facility has made it a great favourite with many lovers of poetry, who resort to

poetical composition as an agreeable relaxation after business, or a
pleasant occupation of idle time—as commercial men, retired gentlemen,
and country clergymen.   In very few of these productions is the
description any thing more than the prelude to the reminiscences and
reflections, and in some, the locality merely supplies a title.   They
are no more local or descriptive than Cicero's " Tusculan Questions,"
or Horne Tooke's "Diversions of Purley."   Even where the Poet
attempts to vie with the landscape painter, his description must be in
a great measure vague and general, or it is not intelligible.   He does
best when he communicates to the reader the feeling which the scene
is calculated to inspire ; whether it be of beauty, richness, grandeur,
vastness, or of quiet seclusion.   He may, indeed, enumerate the objects
supposed to be in sight ; he may tell you their shape and colour, and
furnish them with a suite of similes ; but, after all, language cannot
paint, for it can only present things separately, and in succession,
which in nature appear simultaneously, and derive their principal
charm from their copresence and coinherence.   Painting imitates coex-
istence in space ; poetry, like music, expresses succession in time.
This may be one reason why the greater number of these poems are
about hills, where the gradual ascent produces a succession of prospects,
and supplies the want of action.   But in the best of them the objects
are not pourtrayed as they occur to the eye, but as they rise upon the
memory, or connect themselves with the feelings.   In fine, we cannot
consider the merely loco-descriptive poem as a legitimate work of art.
Yet it is pleasing, easily written, and as easily read ; for it demands
little care in the author, and little thought in the reader.

   Young poets are apt to have very exaggerated opinions of the powers
of verse to confer immortality.   After the lines on Mount Pleasant,
which we have already quoted, Roscoe proceeds thus :

> The shades of Grongar bloom secure of fame ;
> Edge-hill to Jago owes its lasting fame.
> When Windsor forest's loveliest scenes decay,
> Still shall they live in Pope's unrivall'd lay.
> Led on by hope an equal theme I choose,
> O, might the subject boast an equal Muse!
> Then should her name, the force of time defy,
> When sunk in ruin, Liverpool shall lie.

   Really we should have thought that Edge-hill owed its fame quite as
much to its being the scene of the first pitched battle in the civil wars,
the place where the gallant Earl of Carnarvon died in defence of
royalty, as to its giving name to some indifferent blank verse by one
Rev. Mr. Jago, who owes his own admission among the poets, chiefly to

the friendship of Shenstone. Jerusalem is not the more secure of fame, because it was the subject of a Seatonian prize-poem.

The real theme of "Mount Pleasant" is not Mount Pleasant, but Liverpool; or rather the commerce of Liverpool, and the money-getting propensities of her inhabitants, her new-born taste for the fine arts, her public institutions, and public spirit, with incidental reflections on commerce in general, and the slave trade in particular, which compose by far the most interesting portion of the poem. In dilating on the wrongs of the African, the style rises to an indignant fervour which is something better than poetical. That a young and hitherto undistinguished clerk should have ventured so boldly to denounce the traffic to which Liverpool attributed much of her prosperity, indicated no small moral courage. The voice of humanity was then as the voice of one crying in the wilderness; and so far from swelling the universal concert of a nation, was in danger of being drowned amid the hootings of an angry contempt. We are all too apt to undervalue common truths, as if they were common-place truisms, not thankfully acknowledging the blessing, that the most precious truths are become common-places, interwoven into the texture of thought, and involved in the very logic of speech. But these truths were not always common-places: time has been when the best of them were regarded as romance, or paradox, or heresy, or jargon—when the wise shook their heads at them, the fools made mouths at them, when many honestly opposed them, because they held them subversive of elder truth, and too many wickedly hated them, because they felt and feared them to be true.

While we admire the poetic enthusiasm of young Roscoe, and revere the pious indignation of Cowper, let us not uncharitably condemn, or intolerantly excommunicate from our esteem, all those who regarded their opinions with suspicion, or even with anger. St. Paul was once as bitter an enemy of Christianity as Alexander the coppersmith. The task of the true philanthropist, the genuine reformer, the enlightened iconoclast, would be easy to the heart, whatever toil and fortitude it might require, if they were opposed by none but the very foolish, or the very wicked. But they have also to endure the censure of the timid good; they cannot always avoid the praise and co-operation of the evil. They must learn to bear cold and reproachful looks from those whom they cannot, should not love the less for reproach or coldness. They run the risk of being classed with those, who are eager to commit sacrilege under pretence of cleansing the temple—who would overthrow the tables of the money-changers, in order to have a scramble for the money. They must encounter fightings from without and from within : they will painfully discover the difference between a dream of sensibility, and a labour of benevolence ; and they may have to labour through a long life without effecting any tangible good ; may wander for years in the desert, and never behold the promised land, even in a Pisgah-view—save with the eye of faith ; or having done much, find that all is yet to do.   If the days of persecution are past, the rack at rest, the wheel of torture revolve no more, and the fires of Smithfield be quenched for ever, the world has engines still to assault the man that goes about to mend it—calumny, false praise, bribery, poverty, witcheries of love, and sundering of loves ; but worse than the world, and stronger far, is the bosom fiend Despair.

The days are indeed gone by, when the mere announcement of a theory, or abstract position, true or false, was attended with any considerable peril to purse or person.   The widest diversities of creed hardly produce an interruption of social intercourse, provided that each speculator is content to enjoy and defend his own fancy, without intermeddling by advice or censure, with the conduct of the rest.   If any do this, he will be excluded, not as a heathen man and a publican, but as a bore.   It is a truly ridiculous instance of vanity, when a modern paradox-monger boasts of his courage and disinterestedness, talks of defying martyrdom, and refusing unoffered bribes, and quotes Galileo and Luther, in proof of his right to think as he pleases.   But the case is otherwise with practical truths even now ; for practical truths are duties, which, whoever acknowledges, is called upon to act or to abstain.   The announcement of these is attended with many heart-burnings even now, it often incurs the forfeiture of patronage, it is frequently treated with contemptuous pity, and sometimes brings down the charge of ingratitude, of all others the most grievous to a good mind.   But when Roscoe first raised his voice against slavery, and satirized the commercial spirit of his townsmen, the public were far from being as tolerant as they are at present.   The State opposed to him, the Church at best dubious, (with many glorious exceptions among its individual members), the Multitude decidedly hostile, and easily infuriated.   There was, therefore, some courage in avowing his sentiments, even in rhime ; at least as much as would be required to write a serious defence of slavery in heroic couplets at the present epoch.   We say a *serious defence,* for there is something sacred in scurrility, and ever has been.   Aristophanes was applauded for burlesquing the Gods, in the same Athens where Socrates was murdered for arguing against the absurdities of popular superstition.   Yet it must be allowed, that " Mount Pleasant " was published before the French revolution had stamped the brand of Jacobinism on every struggle for emancipation. Roscoe lived to do greater things in behalf of the Negro than writing verses, in seasons, when the cause had far more deadly enemies.

The lines introductory to the noble burst of feeling on which we have descanted, are a very good sample of what was then accounted the best versification and diction. Goldsmith, rather than Pope, had been Roscoe's model, or rather, his ear had been unconsciously influenced more by the former than by the latter. After describing the growing bulk, thronged population, and busy noises of Liverpool, and reproving " the sons of wealth" for adding " gold to gold," he thus proceeds :—

> " Far as the eye can trace the prospect round,
> The splendid tracks of opulence are found,
> Yet scarce an hundred annual rounds have run,
> Since first the fabric of this power began;
> His noble waves, inglorious, Mersey roll'd,
> Nor felt those waves by labouring art controul'd ;
> Along his side a few small cots were spread,
> His finny brood their humble tenants fed ;
> At opening dawn with fraudful nets supplied,
> The paddling skiff would brave his spacious tide,
> Ply round the shores, nor tempt the dangerous main,
> But seek ere night the friendly port again.
>
> Now o'er the wondering world, her name resounds,
> From northern climes, to India's distant bounds ;
> Where-e'er his shores the broad Atlantic laves;
> Where-e'er the Baltic rolls his wintry waves ;
> Where-e'er the honour'd flood extends his tide,
> That clasps Sicilia like a favour'd bride,
> Whose waves in ages past so oft have bore
> The storm of battle on the Punic shore,
> Have wash'd the banks of Græcia's learned bowers,
> And view'd at distance Rome's imperial towers.
> In every clime her prosperous fleets are known,
> She makes the wealth of every clime her own ;
> Greenland for her its bulky whale resigns,
> And temperate Gallia rears her generous vines ;
> Midst warm Iberia citron orchards blow,
> And the ripe fruitage bends the labouring bough ;
> The Occident a richer tribute yields,
> Far different produce swells their cultur'd fields ;
> Hence the strong cordial that inflames the brain,
> The honey'd sweetness of the juicy cane,
> The vegetative fleece, the azure dye,
> And every product of a warmer sky.

There Afric's swarthy sons their toils repeat,
Beneath the fervors of the noontide heat;
Torn from each joy that crown'd their native soil,
No sweet reflections mitigate their toil;
From morn to eve, by rigorous hands opprest,
Dull fly their hours of every hope unblest:
Till broke with labour, helpless and forlorn,
From their weak grasp the lingering morsel torn,
The reed-built hovel's friendly shade denied,
The jest of folly and the scorn of pride,
Drooping beneath meridian suns they lie,
Lift the faint head, and bend the imploring eye;
Till death in kindness from the tortur'd breast
Calls the free spirit to the realms of rest.

Shame on mankind, but shame to Britons most,
Who all the sweets of liberty can boast;
Yet deaf to every human claim, deny
The sweets to others which themselves enjoy,
Life's bitter draught with harsher bitter fill,
Blast every joy, and add to every ill;
The trembling limbs with galling iron bind,
Nor loose the heavier bondage of the mind.
Yet whence these horrors, this inhuman rage,
That brands with blackest infamy the age?
Is it our varied interests disagree,
And Britain sinks if Afric's sons be free?
No—Hence a few superfluous stores we claim,
That tempt our avarice, but increase our shame.
The sickly palate touch with more delight,
Or swell the senseless riot of the night.

Blest were the days ere foreign climes were known,
Our wants contracted, and our wealth our own;
When Health could crown, and Innocence endear
The temperate meal, that cost no eye a tear;
Our drink the beverage of the chrystal flood,
Not madly purchased by a brother's blood—
Ere the wide spreading ills of trade began,
Or luxury trampled on the rights of man.

When Commerce, yet an infant, rais'd her head,
'Twas mutual want her growing empire spread,
Those mutual wants a distant realm supplied,
And like advantage every clime enjoy'd.
Distrustless then of every treacherous view,
An open welcome met the stranger crew;
And whilst the whitening fleet approach'd to land
The wondering natives hail'd them from the strand;

> Fearless to meet, amidst the flow of soul,
> The lurking dagger, or the poison'd bowl.
> Now, more destructive than a blighting storm,
> A bloated monster, Commerce rears her form;
> Throws the meek olive from her daring hand,
> Grasps the red sword, and whirls the flaming brand.
> True to no faith, by no restraints controul'd,
> By guilt made cautious, and by avarice bold—
> Can this be she, who promis'd once to bind
> In leagues of strictest amity, mankind?
> This fiend, whose breath inflames the spark of strife,
> And pays with trivial toys the price of life?"

It is easy to see on what part of this effusion Mr. Roscoe would ever look back with self-congratulation, and what his riper judgment taught him to laugh at. He would soon discover that the slave-trade was not protected by the inveterate devotion of the English to rum and sugar, but by the powerful *vested interests* engaged in its support, by a false idea of national prosperity, and by the latent apprehensions that the right of men to freedom, admitted in one instance, would prove too much, and disturb that order which, Mr. Pope tells us, is " Heaven's first Law." His view of the rise and progress of commerce, her lovely infancy, and progressive depravation, is not strictly historical. Slave-trades, of one kind or other, are among the most ancient of commercial dealings: indeed, almost the earliest trading transaction of which we are informed, is the sale of Joseph to the Ishmaelites by his brethren. Instead of venting his ire against his own generation for *continuing* the slave-trade, Roscoe might have expressed thankfulness that he lived at a time when its enormity began to be acknowledged, and should have remembered that the vague reverence for the past which his diatribe tended to inculcate, was the strong hold of those who sought to perpetuate that traffic in which their forefathers saw no more sin than our Druidical predecessors in roasting a man in an osier colossus. As far as the annals of commerce have come down to us, it would seem to have become gradually more humane, as it grew more extensive.

Willing to propitiate his townsmen after rebuking them, the poet dwells with glowing satisfaction on the literary and scientific tastes of Liverpool, the improvement of its architecture, (under which heads we are sorry to find a sneer at the Gothic style,) encouragement of the fine arts, &c. above all the public and private virtues of its inhabitants. But we can only afford one more quotation, which shews a fine eye and considerable descriptive power.

> " Far to the right where Mersey duteous pours,
> To the broad main his tributary stores,

Ting'd with the radiance of the golden beam,
Sparkle the quivering waves; and midst the gleam,
In different hues, as sweeps the changeful ray,
Pacific fleets their guiltless pomp display;
Fair to the sight, they spread the floating sail,
Catch the light breeze, and skim before the gale,
Till lessening gradual on the stretching view,
Obscure they mingle in the distant blue,
Where in soft tints the sky with ocean blends,
And on the weaken'd sight, the long, long prospect ends."

" Mount Pleasant" certainly does not promise a *great* poet, but it clearly evinces a mind sufficiently poetical to enjoy and appreciate whatever of poetry is in books, in pictures, in nature, and in the heart of man. The elegance, and innate gentility of Roscoe's mind is very conspicuous in his selection of words and phrases, and has possibly led him to exclude the *operative* words of the language too strictly from his composition. He was afraid of calling things by their right names. His phraseology, where plain statement is required, reminds one of the silken tackle of Cleopatra's galley. Yet though his words are sometimes too fine for their business, they always do some work, only it is not precisely the work they are fittest for. He has few superfluous epithets, and hardly one empty line. Perhaps his Italian studies had given him a distaste for the homeliness of his native tongue; but indeed it was not the fashion in 1770, for poets to write English. Percy's ballads set some to mimic the antique turns of phrase, but Cowper was the first, after Churchill, who ventured to versify the English of his own day.

In 1772, a small society was formed in Liverpool " for the encouragement of designing, drawing, and painting," of which Mr. Roscoe was the prime promoter and most active member, while it continued in existence; but its date was short, its dissolution being hastened by the loss of an influential member who went to reside in Germany. Before this short-lived institute Mr. Roscoe recited an ode, which introduced him to the public as a lyric poet. A few copies were printed for private distribution in 1774, which had the fortune to win the approbation of the " Monthly Review," whereby the author was tempted to annex it to his publication of " Mount Pleasant," in 1777. Though not without strong indications of the writer's juvenility, and a savour of the taste of the times, this ode indisputably proves that Roscoe had already acquired one of the highest accomplishments of the poet, the art of expressing abstract thought poetically. If there be some partiality in the preference given to the silent muse over her vocal sisters, it might be deemed a compliment due to the occasion.

Copies of verses called odes have always been numerous, and were particularly so in the latter half of the last century. Yet there are almost as many good epics as good odes. We confine the observation solely to the sublime, the heroic, and the philosophical ode; for in the lighter effusions of the lyric muse, in the playful and the tender, many have attained to great beauty and sweetness. But there is nothing in common between an excellent ode and a plaintive or cheerful song, except the assumption, that the movement of both is promoted and modified by musical sound.

Lyric poetry is a vague and somewhat deceptive phrase. If it be defined as that species of metrical composition which *admits* a musical accompaniment, it is too general. The epic and dramatic poems of Greece, and all the early poetry of the world would then come under the denomination. If only that poetry be called lyric which *requires* a musical accompaniment, the definition is as much too narrow. For some of the finest odes are so far from requiring music for their full effect, that their effect would be marred by any music that we can conceive. Fancy Wordsworth's "Ode on the Intimations of Immortality," sung by the sweetest voice to the sweetest and fittest conceivable music? The absurdity of fiddling "Paradise Lost," and dancing "Paradise Regained," would be nothing to it. In truth the song, the only mode of composition to which music is now successfully united, has a very limited range of subjects indeed.

A song must be *short*. What devotee of music or poetry so devoted, who could bear to hear "Chevy chase," *to a dismal psalm tune?* Nothing sets the patience of our ancestors in a more conspicuous point of view, than the immeasurable lengths of narrative, and dreary monotony of thrumming instruments, which they not only endured, but enjoyed. The habit of silent reading is the bane of literary patience, at least as far as narrative is concerned. A man used to glance his eye over a page, and see at once the striking incidents which it contains, could never be brought to relish a story drawled to recitative. No inference is to be drawn from the success of certain selections from Scott's or Byron's narrative poems, set to music, and "sung with unbounded applause." Sweet music is always sweet, though it accompany words in an unknown tongue; its power is unquestionably increased, when associated with words so familiar as to bring a train of images and feelings along with them, and yet allow the meaning to be, as it were, diffused by the melody. A music which should be strictly subordinate to sense, would, to our ears, vitiated, an austere critic might say, by the complex attraction of modern strains, be a great deal more unsatisfactory than no music at all; as the *Vin ordinaire* and other continental thin potations, to an English palate, are absolutely weaker than water.

Now music, as all but those who have no music in their souls well know, is capable of expressing and evoking any simple emotion ; it may imitate the rapid succession or dazzling alternation of feeling, or dying away to silence, may symbolize the fading of passion into pensiveness. It may also, to a certain degree, express action, as action consists in motion ; but beyond this it cannot go. It cannot narrate, describe, or reason. It is of little assistance to the understanding, and though it may stimulate, it cannot inform the imagination. True, words may supply all these deficiencies, and true, there is no narrative, description, reasoning, or imagination, that is truly poetical, but what involves or engenders a pleasurable feeling, nor any feeling of which some modification of numerous sounds is not a conductor. But nevertheless, those compositions will be found best accommodated to musical expression, for which music supplies a natural and universal language, and such are love, grief, and devotion ; because in all these the feeling suggests the thought, and not the thought or imagery the feeling. A song however is not an ode ; it is only one, and not a high species of lyric composition. If there be any thing that generally distinguishes the genuine lyrist, it is the nature of his connections and transitions, which do not arise from the necessities of his theme, far less from the arbitrary turns of his convenience, but are determined by the flux and reflux, the under currents and eddies of the poetic passion, of that sense of power and joy which the poet feels in the exercise of his art for its own sake ; a passion easily mimicked, but not often real, even in those who possess every other requisite of pure poetry. Roscoe, in his ode on painting, has shewn no small portion of this true lyric element, and would have exhibited yet more, had he not been seduced into the didactic line of criticism.

After some animated stanzas on the removal of the arts from Greece and Italy to England, and a lively enumeration of the functions of Poetry and poetic Music, he gives a loose to his enthusiasm at the first appearance of Painting, which he considers to be the youngest Muse, and inheritor of all her elder sister's estates.

> " Next came the power in whom conjoined,
> Their differing excellence is shewn ;
> Yet sweetly blended, and combined
> With charms peculiarly her own.
> Beneath the great Creator's eye,
> 'Twas she with azure spread the sky ;
> And when creation first had birth,
> In happiest hues array'd the earth,

Still varying in each varied scene,
Bedeck'd the smiling meads with green,
Blush'd in the flower, and ting'd the fruit,
More lovely still as more minute:
O'er every part the veil of beauty cast,
In heav'nly colours bright, thro' numerous years to last."

" Her's is the glowing bold design,
The just and lessening perspective,
The beauties of the waving line,
And all the pencil's power can give."

" Majestic, nervous, bold and strong,
Let Angelo with Milton vie.
Opposed to Waller's amorous song
His art let wanton Titian try.
Let great Romano's free design
Centend with Dryden's pompous line :
And chaste Corregio's graceful air,
With Pope's unblemish'd page compare.
Lorraine may rival Thomson's name,
And Hogarth equal Butler's fame;
For still, where'er the aspiring muse
Her wide unbounded flight pursues,
Her sister soars on kindred wings sublime,
And gives her favourite names to grace the rolls of time."

The attempt to prove the equi-potency of poetry and painting by bracketing the poets and painters in couplets, after the manner of Plutarch's parallels, was somewhat rash, even in a Pindarique, and is not very successfully executed. The painters have cause to complain of injustice. Surely, if a wide and permanent fame, approved by those whose kindred excellence makes their judgment the constituent of true fame, be a criterion of merit, on which those, who want the skill or opportunity to judge for themselves, may safely rely, there can be no fair comparison between Titian as a painter, and Waller as a poet. Titian did not paint epigrams. If a pictorial correlative must be found for Waller, let him pair off with Monsieur Petitot, the famous minia-turist in enamel, who compressed the charms of many a court beauty into the dimension of a bracelet, which the fair original might wear unobtrusively upon her slender wrist. But besides the egregious inequality of the mighty Venetian and the English courtier, Waller's real merit consisted in certain elegances of thought and polite turns of phrase, for which the pencil offers no equivalent. " Chaste Cor-regio's graceful air" could never convey the strong thought and stittetto-like sarcasm of Pope, as Pope on the other hand neither conveyed images of chaste and simple beauty, nor suggested feelings analogous thereto. Hogarth has no other resemblance to Butler, than the ludicrous character of his subjects, and the power with which he instils serious meaning into mean and ridiculous images. But in the manner and spirit by which he effected this, he had more of Juvenal than of Butler. Michelangelo was certainly worthy to be paralleled with Milton. If he was inferior, the superiority was not in the men, but in their arts ; and no one, who is not either a painter, a connoisseur, or a young poet, reciting an ode before a " Society for the encouragement of the Arts" would maintain that lines and colours can embody as many, or as noble thoughts as can be communicated by words. The world of the eye is a great, a beautiful, a glorious world ; but it is only one part of the world of mind.

There is great ingenuity, and some truth in the following lines, which explain how painting compensates for the peculiar effects of music :—

> " When just degrees of shade and light,
> Contend in sweetest harmony,
> Then bursts upon the raptured sight
> The silent music of the eye.
> Bold, as the bases deeper sound,
> We trace the well-imagined ground,
> Next in the varying scenes behind,
> The sweet, melodious tenor find,
> And, as the softening notes decay,
> The distant prospect fades away ;
> Their aid if mingling colours give,
> To bid the mimic landscape live,
> The visual concert breaks upon the eyes,
> With every different charm which music's hand supplies.

This, in plain English, means that the pleasure derived from music, like that derived from colouring, depends upon just and varied proportions. Some virtuosos have carried the matter much further, and that too in sober prose, assigning a colour to every note in the gamut. A sound analogy may be stretched till it cracks.

But it is high time to make an end of our notices of Roscoe's juvenile poetry. Poetry was never more to him than a relaxation ; a moral, a manly, and an elegant relaxation he made it ; but to have become a *great* poet, he must have made it a serious business, and devoted to its cultivation a larger portion of his energies, if not of his time, than his vocation and duty allowed.

Soon after the expiration of his articles of clerkship, Mr. Roscoe became the partner of Mr. Aspinall, and commenced business as an attorney, a profession he never heartily liked, but which, in his hands, was the useful means of honorable competence. His disinclination to his calling never relaxed his attention to professional engagements ; nor did the variety of his intellectual pursuits prevent his attaining considerable eminence in a line of practice, which required not only regular industry, but much technical knowledge, and no small concentration of mind. Though he early formed a resolution to retire as soon as he had realized a sufficiency, he waited prudently till that period arrived, and it was not till 1796, in the forty-fourth year of his age, after the splendid success of his " Lorenzo *the* Magnificent" had spread his name over Europe, that he withdrew from the toils of the desk. In the latter part of his professional career he was in partnership with Mr. Joshua Lane. His business must indeed have been both extensive and lucrative, to enable him to escape from its trammels so soon with a competent fortune, and unspotted reputation. It is greatly to the credit of Liverpool, that its merchants continued to employ and confide in a literary man of business, proving themselves superior to the vulgar prejudice, that a man of any occupation must be ruining himself and all who were concerned with him, if his mind, heart, and soul are not absorbed in the worky-day means of his livelihood ; a prejudice which authors have contributed very much to cherish, not only by gross neglect of their positive duties, but by avowedly ascribing that neglect to their refined studies.

In the year 1781, Mr. Roscoe found his circumstances such as enabled him to marry the object of his affections, and he was united to Jane, second daughter of Mr. William Griffies, a respectable tradesman of his native town. From the terms in which Dr. Traill speaks of this union, we conjecture that it was the result of a long engagement, the consummation of which was deferred by prudence, a more usual companion of true love, than either the worldly or the romantic conceive. The patience of a well-grounded attachment was rewarded with long domestic felicity. Seven sons and three daughters were the fruit of the marriage, and they have been sons and daughters to make a good father happy. All except one daughter survived their parent, and more than one of them is eminently distinguished in polite literature.

Neither business nor domestic cares abstracted him from the accumulation of knowledge and the cultivation of taste. We have already mentioned that he conceived in very early life an ambition, which ripened to purpose, of becoming the historian of the Medici. Besides the attractions of the name to every lover of the arts and of learning, there may have been something in the " Princely Merchant" peculiarly delightful to an inhabitant of Liverpool. It proved at least that commerce is not inconsistent with art or with philosophy; it inspired a hope that the wealth which successful traffic was storing up might one day be employed in filling the streets and squares with temples and palaces, in calling forth the genius of sculpture and painting, in aiding the researches of science, and collecting the treasures of learning; and perhaps no history speaks more in favour of true freedom than that of the Florentine family, who were more than monarchs, while they were content to be citizens, but became exiles, or dependent tyrants, when they could no longer brook equality. Though many years elapsed before this great work of Roscoe's life was finished, many perhaps, before a page was written as it now appears, yet the immense variety of laborious reading which the "Lorenzo" and the "Leo" display, evince that the purpose never slumbered, that in the brief vacations of a busy existence, he was indefatigably collecting materials which his more perfect leisure was to cast into form.

Yet was he not so devoted to his "opus magnum," but his pen was ever ready when occasion called for its use. His political pamphlets were numerous, and though there may be diversities of opinion respecting the wisdom of his views, there is none as to the urbanity and temperance with which he advanced them. Many of his productions of this kind were anonymous, but he never wrote what he wished to deny. In the year 1787, he appeared as the champion of justice in the great cause of the abolition of the slave-trade, to promote which he put forth two tracts: the first, entitled "Original view of the African slave-trade, demonstrating its injustice and impolicy, with hints towards a bill for its abolition." The second was of a more controversial character. The Rev. Raymond Harris, a Roman Catholic clergyman, had published a pamphlet called "Scriptural researches on the licitness of the slave-trade," containing, we presume, the same plausible arguments which are repeated in the same interest to this day, to the perfect satisfaction of slavery-loving consciences; arguments occasionally adorned with an imposing display of Greek and Hebrew type. (We have seen a passage of the Talmud, in the original language, quoted in a news paper.) It must be admitted that if slavery be a spirit never to be cast out but by a text commanding him to come out by his Greek or Hebrew name, he may possess the body of society till it be dissolved at the general doom. If the slave-traders and slave-buyers are proof against the spirit, they may safely defy the letter. But yet they would do wisely to rely solely upon the negative, as the worthy ordinary of Newgate, in his last interview with Jonathan Wild, defended his preference of punch on the ground that nothing was said against it in Scripture. When they appeal to the Bible for a positive justification of slavery, they ought to enquire whether anything similar to modern colonial slavery existed when the Bible was written. Mere bond-service, or territorial vassalage, whether better or worse, were not the same thing. Now the preceptive part of Scripture is only so far prophetic, as all general truths necessarily provide for a number of unseen contingencies: the sacred penmen did not prohibit what those to whom their writings were primarily addressed did not, or could not practice, but left the case to be determined by reason and analogy. To vindicate slavery on Christian grounds, it would be necessary to prove that it is a state in which a Christian, judging wisely of his own and his offspring's welfare, would gladly consent to be. We know not whether the Rev. Raymond Harris proved this; but his performance so well satisfied the then common council of Liverpool, that they voted him £200 of the public money: and his reasonings were so convincing that two dissenting protestant ministers followed on the same side. We believe that no minister of religion, catholic, orthodox, or dissenter, would now hold up the Book of Revelation to the scorn of the infidel by representing it in as odious colours as the maddest infidel dare.

Mr. Roscoe stepped forward in defence of Christianity with an essay entitled "Scriptural refutation of a Pamphlet lately published by the Rev. Raymond Harris, &c.," on the Christian principle that "all men are equal in the sight of God," and the great law of our Saviour, "Therefore, all things whatsoever ye would that men should do to you, do ye even so to them." He also, in the same year, published his "Wrongs of Africa," a poem in two parts, the profits of which were at the disposal of the committee then formed for promoting the abolition of the slave trade.

About the same time, he succeeded in forming a new society for the encouragement of art in Liverpool. To the "Liverpool Academy for the encouragement of the Fine Arts," Mr Roscoe delivered a series of lectures on the progress and vicissitudes of taste, which he appears once to have designed to publish, but which yet remain in manuscript.

During these years of his life, he was engaged in the formation of a library, in an excellent collection of etchings and engravings by and from the old masters, and in literary correspondence with many of the first contemporary artists, amateurs, and literati, particularly with Mr. Strutt, the author of the "Dictionary of Engravers." The letters of Strutt acknowledge the receipt of various important disquisitions on the history of engraving from Mr. Roscoe, which are supposed to be incorporated in the preliminary essays to his Dictionary.

Engravings and sketches were at all times a favourite object of Mr. Roscoe's pursuit. An engraving bears somewhat the same relation

3 s

to a picture, that a play read does to a play acted. It does justice to the intellect of the artist, but not to the power, splendour, and magnificence of the art. No picture, the effect of which is wholly lost in a good engraving, can afford a real intellectual gratification, or deserve to rank with the works of dignified art. It is a motionless *spectacle*, a painted melo-drama, but neither tragedy, comedy, history, nor good broad farce. Engraving cannot, indeed, bewitch the eye with colour, but it can give the most delicate gradations, combinations, and interchanges of light and shade. The pleasure of colour is more in the sense than in the mind—the utmost skill in mere colouring only makes the painter a rival, if he be not rather a humble imitator of the velvet manufacturer. Engraving, too, partakes of the ubiquity and reproductive power of printing. It enables many, who can never visit the Vatican, to satisfy themselves that the fame of Raphael and of Buonarotti is not a vain sound; and it will bear testimony to their glories, if the works of their hands be doomed to perish like those of Apelles. Engraving, in fine, puts the enjoyment of art within the compass of moderate incomes, and fills up little room in a moderate mansion; therefore it brings art within the range of popular sympathy.

Roscoe was a true lover of books and prints, and continually added to his store, as often as business called him to London. As his habits were temperate, simple, and unostentatious, his library and his collection were his main sources of expense. Yet he purchased for use, not for shew or curiosity: he was superior to that petty pride of property, which values the mere possession of a thing which few beside possess. If he had a good thing that was a rarity, he perhaps preserved it the more tenderly, because its loss could be less easily repaired; but his good nature regretted that any good thing should be rare.

Latterly, he began to look out for original drawings of the great masters, which often unfold the artist's mind more than the most finished productions. They may be compared to a great man's private minutes.

In 1788 he took part in the celebration of the centenary of the Revolution, and composed an ode, which was recited at the Liverpool meeting on that occasion. It was probably as good as Mason's, but these things may generally be forgotten as soon as they are forgotten, without any mighty loss to their author's reputation. A change of dynasty, at the distance of a century, is not old enough to be modified by the abstract imagination, and yet too long passed to create a real and passionate interest. It is neither an idea nor a reality, but the *caput mortuum* of a fact. Besides, King William was the most prosaic of liberators.

In 1789, after years of previous preparation, he began to compose and arrange his notices of Lorenzo de' Medici. We might almost wonder that he did not find or make time to visit Italy, and tread the ground on which his hero walked in life. But fortunately for him, his early friend William Clarke, at that very time, had fixed his residence at Fiesole, in the immediate neighbourhood of Florence, and supplied him with the information which his own engagements did not permit him to seek. Of the assistance derived from this old companion of his studies, he speaks thus:—

"An intimate friend, with whom I had been for many years united in studies and affection, had paid a visit to Italy, and fixed his winter residence at Florence. I well knew that I had only to request his assistance, in order to obtain whatever information he had an opportunity of procuring, upon the very spot which was to be the scene of my intended history. My inquiries were particularly directed to the Laurentian and Ricardi libraries, which I was convinced would afford much original and important information. It would be unjust merely to say that my friend afforded me the assistance I required: he went far beyond even the hopes I had formed,—and his return to his native country was, if possible, rendered still more grateful to me, by the materials which he had collected for my use."

The friendly researches of Mr. Clarke discovered many poetical pieces of Lorenzo de' Medici, which were either supposed to be lost, or not known to have existed. From these Mr. Roscoe has given copious extracts in the body of his work, and several appear in his appendix that had never been printed in their native land. And he conferred a benefit on all merchants, all politicians, and all poets by so doing. For they prove, that neither commerce nor politics destroy the vigour of imagination, or make callous the poetic sensibilities; and prove, too, that the imagination may be exercised and beautified, the finest susceptibilities may be kept alive, without impairing the practical judgment and executive powers,—without unfitting a man for the world. In the faculties which the great Creator has bestowed upon his creatures, there is no envy, no grudging, no monopoly: one pines not because another flourishes: if any be emaciated, it is not because another is fed, but because itself is starved. Shakspeare himself displayed the abilities of a ruler. Was he not a manager? and in that capacity had he not jarring interests to reconcile, factions to pacify or subdue, finances to arrange, and a capricious public to satisfy? His worldly avocations were as little poetical as those of any man on change.

The French Revolution broke out in 1789. The downfall of the

Bastile, "with all its horrid towers," echoed throughout Europe, and
one voice of gratulation was heard above all the bodings of the fearful,
the grumblings of the dull, the coward outcries of the selfish, and the
sighs of the better few, that, while they abhorred oppression, and
coveted not privilege, yet knew in their hearts "that the wrath of man
worketh not the righteousness of God." It could not be but that
Roscoe, loving liberty as he loved the human race, with a soul cheerful
as day-light, and hopeful as spring, should join the joyful chorus.   To
see a monarch, descended from a long line of sensual despots, co-operate
with a nation, long idolatrous of despotism, in realizing a perfect freedom upon earth—a freedom embodied in laws and institutions, which
should be the limbs, organs, and senses of the moral will—whose vital
heat was universal love, was too great, too glorious, too new a spectacle
to give him time for doubt or question.   The black and portentous
shadow which the past ever throws on the future, fell beyond his
sphere of vision.   Whatever of pain or violence attended the nativity
of the deliverance, pain, which he deserved to suffer who would not
gladly suffer for such a cause, and violence most justifiable, if vengeance
ever could be justifiable, seemed no more than the constant law of
nature, which sets a price on every good, as the birth pangs of happiness, or the dying struggles of tyranny.

> "Oh! Times
> In which the meagre, stale, forbidding ways
> Of custom, law, and statute took at once
> The attraction of a country in romance,
> When Reason seem'd the most to assert her rights
> When most intent on making of herself
> A prime enchantress—to assist the work
> Which then was going forward in her name.
> Not favoured spots alone, but the whole earth
> The beauty wore of promise, that which sets
> The budding rose above the rose full blown.
> What temper at the prospect did not wake
> To happiness unthought of? The inert
> Were roused, and lively natures rapt away!
> Those who had fed their childhood upon dreams,
> The playfellows of fancy, who had made
> All powers of swiftness, subtlety, and strength
> Their ministers—who in lordly wise had stirred,
> And dealt with whatsoever they found there,
> As if they had within some lurking right
> To wield it :— they too, who of gentle mood,
> Had watch'd all gentle motions, and to those
> Had fitted their own thoughts, schemers more mild,
> And in the regions of their peaceful selves.

> Now was it that both found, the meek and lofty,
> Did both find helpers to their hearts' desire,
> And stuff at hand, plastic as they could wish,—
> Were called upon to exercise their skill,
> Not in Utopia—subterraneous fields—
> Or some secreted island—Heaven knows where,
> But in the very world, which is the world
> Of all of us—the place where in the end
> We find our happiness, or not at all.—WORDSWORTH.

So a great spirit describes his own emotions at the first heavings of that great convulsion, the gladness of his own young hopes—hopes which he was not quick to relinquish, when many years of bloodshed had passed over them. Roscoe never disowned his at all; but acknowledging that there was, from the beginning, an evil element in the revolution, continued to ascribe the temporary predominance of that evil to the hostility which the established powers of Europe had shewn to the good. Time doubtless abated much of the greatness of his expectations, and though he lived to hear of the three days of 1830, he would hardly, had his pulse been as strong, and his heart as light, at the one period as the other, have sung a strain so blithe as his

> " O'er the vine-covered hills and gay vallies of France."

or his,

> " Unfold Father time, thy long records unfold,"

which were produced in 1789, and recited at a meeting assembled to celebrate the emancipation of France. But the stream of his hopes, though it flowed with a weaker current, never changed its direction. It was to renovation and progression, not to restoration, or immobility, that he looked for the increase of human happiness. At the same time, there is no evidence that at any time he adopted levelling opinions, or wished to release mankind from any portion of the moral law acknowledged for ages. It is needless to say, that he was clear of all participation, in wish or will, with the massacres and executions of the Jacobins, and with the ambitious wars of their successors. If he erred, he erred in judgment, not in heart, and chiefly erred in attributing too much of the French atrocities to foreign interference, and too little to the national irreligion, which grew, and was growing, long before the revolution, and which made the revolution what it was, instead of what it ought to have been. Ill can he determine the rights of man, who denies the immortality of man, from which all rights, as well as duties, flow. He that would make earth likest Paradise must make it a mirror reflecting Heaven.* Perhaps Roscoe erred also in thinking

* It is absurd to speak of irreligion as an *immediate* effect of political changes.

peace practicable after it had ceased to be so.   But we must return to our narrative.

In the first years of the revolution, and long after, Mr. Roscoe held much epistolary correspondence with the late Marquis of Lansdowne, and other whig leaders, on the subject of parliamentary reform, a cause he had much at heart.   It is said that this correspondence proves that it was no " bit by bit" reform that the noble whigs of those days advocated.

But the times were growing unfavourable to reforms of all sorts. French affairs took a murderous aspect.   Alarm spread far and wide. The court, the church, the great body of the aristocracy, the elder and sager portion of the middle orders, the rustic population in general, and in many places the town populace, combined against the new opinions, which, like most opinions tending to change, were very miscellaneously supported by the noblest and the basest minds ; by those who deemed too highly of the dignity of human nature, and by those who quarrelled with every thing that distinguishes man from beast, by those who could not think, and by those who could do nothing but think ; by the most imaginative poets and the most absolute prosemen ; by the most ascetic and the most sensual ; by souls whose faith was the most spiritual, and by creatures whose materialism was most atheistic.   It is true, there was no agreement of doctrine among this motley tribe, nor did they coalesce, or attempt to coalesce, for any definite purpose : but they did agree in one thing, that the social system was not as good as it might be, and for this they were indiscriminately subjected to the ban of the church and state, and of the loyal and orthodox in all orders.   And as the heathen slandered the Catholic Church with all the insanities and abominations of all the heretics that usurped the Christian name ; so, under the common name Jacobin, every supposed favourer of French freedom was charged with every dogma that any Jacobin could hold.   The *sans culottes* were reproached with metaphysics, and the metaphysicians with having no breeches. The abolition of the slave-trade was coupled with the equal division of property ; and men were accused of craving for wholesale butchery, who condemned all homicide, even in self-defence.

Though there is reason to think that the really ill-disposed Jacobins, who hoped or wished for an English revolution, were not at that time

No man who ever truly believed in his Maker and Redeemer, would cease to believe, though throne and altar were to perish together.   A revolution which destroys the means of religious education, will ultimately produce irreligion, but this must be a work of time.   And surely the Church, if it fall, must fall for want of Religion, not Religion for want of the Church.

numerous, and that those who took any measures to promote it were fewer still, yet they were quite noisy, boastful, profligate, and ferocious enough to strike a panic into the well-meaning, and induce the better sort to approve of strong measures, to which in cooler times they would have been opposed. Their fears, though not their affections, confounded the philosophers and the blackguards; the reformers, who wished to remove the causes of revolution, and the anarchists, who loved destruction for its own sake. They did not, perhaps, account them equally bad, but they felt them equally dreadful. Every arrival from France brought intelligence of new horrors. The daring energy of Pitt, and the eloquent denunciations of Burke, gathered the friends of social order together under their banners, and there was nothing which the English nation would not have surrendered, had the statesmen been as wicked as their enemies have represented them. Never, since Charles the Second, had England been in such danger of enslaving itself by excess of loyalty.

The friends of liberty among the educated orders thought it right to counteract this excess, by a free declaration of their opinions. Accordingly, in 1792, when the town of Liverpool prepared an address of thanks for Mr. Pitt's proclamation against sedition, Mr. Roscoe and his friends succeeded in carrying a counter-petition. The mob rose the next day, broke into the place where it lay for signature, and tore it to pieces! Verily, John Bull is much changed in the course of forty years, whether for the worse or the better. It does not appear that Mr. Roscoe was in danger of personal violence, or that Liverpool imitated the outrages of Birmingham. But Roscoe was a townsman, and a layman; Priestley a stranger, and a dissenting minister. Now the English mob, when they assault any party or community, always select the clergy of that party for peculiar ill-usage. There is nothing political or religious in this; it is a mere antipathy, like that of a turkey-cock to scarlet—aggravated, it must be allowed, by ballads and caricatures. The moment a man, however poor or ignorant, begins to be of any religion, he ceases to be one of the mob.

Mob passions are not absolutely confined to the living aggregations in the streets. Party spirit ran so high in Liverpool at this time, that a small literary society, of which Mr. Roscoe, Dr. Currie, Mr. Shepherd, and others were members, found it necessary to dissolve, lest the purpose of their meeting should be misrepresented to the government.

When the Anti-jacobin war broke out, its commencement was followed by numerous bankruptcies, and commercial distress. Mr. Roscoe, wishing to deduce good from evil, attempted, by investigating

the causes, and magnifying the evils of this distress, to dispose the
nation, especially the monied part of it, without whose assistance the
war could not be carried on, to more pacific counsels.   With this
intent, he published, in 1793, an anonymous pamphlet, entitled,
" Thoughts on the Causes of the present Failures." It is short (the
fourth edition, which we have before us, contains thirty pages), written
with much perspicuity and amenity, but rather less vigour and earnest_
ness than might have been expected from the author on such a topic.
In truth, it is throughout an *argumentum ad hominem*, or which in
England is the same thing, *ad crumenam*, designed to demonstrate the
commercial impolicy of a contest which the author reprobated on far
higher grounds.   With this view, he enters upon an explanation of the
system of paper credit, accommodation, and bills of exchange, which he
deems essential to the commercial life of England,—and shews how
that credit is necessarily affected by war, whereby the fictitious, or
more properly ideal, capital perished along with the confidence which
it really represented.   Of the justice or injustice of the war he says
not a word.   He only hints at the absurdity of stopping the circulation
of the body politic, on account of the shutting of the Scheldt, which he
must have known was not the real cause of the war.   Throughout he
preserves the utmost sang_froid.   Not an angry, hardly a pathetic
expression escapes him.   He alludes to the slave_trade, but instead of
inveighing against its wickedness, simply mentions that " the trade to
Africa has been carried on for a few years past, with an avidity natur_
ally arising in the minds of mercantile men, from the apprehensions
that it would not long be permitted to continue ; " and states a fact, of
which we certainly were previously ignorant, that the bills of exchange
with which the planters paid for the slaves, were drawn at a longer date
than most others, sometimes payable at the end of three years.   The
reason is, however, sufficiently obvious: slave labour must take so long
to be converted into money.   But what is more remarkable, is the
evidence, that Roscoe would have signed a petition for peace, even if
it had emanated from the slaveholders.   One of the ablest and most
interesting passages is that in which, having pronounced that " war is
the cause of our calamities, and peace is the only cure," and glanced at
the little we had done for the cause in which we were embarked at so
much loss and hazard, he points out the needlessness of the conflict,
and the circumstances which rendered it peculiarly ruinous.

    " Let us, however, forget what is past, and regard with a steady eye
our present situation.   Driven within the limits of their own country,
and probably on the brink of a civil war, the French are no longer
formidable, and the object for which Great Britain engaged in the

war is now accomplished.   To proceed further would be to defeat the
end which the minister professed to have in view, and to destroy, not
to preserve, the balance of power in Europe.

" It is not difficult to foresee an objection on the part of those who
are reluctant to acknowledge the truths here attempted to be inforced.
If our misfortunes, say they, are occasioned by the war, whence comes
it, that the same events have not taken place under the same circumstances on former occasions ?   The short answer to this, is a denial of
the truth of the proposition contained in the question.   Have we
so soon forgotten the disasters occasioned by our contest with America ?
The depreciation of landed property, the fall of the public funds, and
the innumerable inconveniences attendant on the destruction of credit ?
The evils which this country then experienced, and those which we
now so intensely feel, are similar in their nature, and different only in
degree ; our present sufferings being augmented by many causes, some
of them perhaps imaginary, but not on that account less aggravating.
The enormous extent of our commerce, whilst it increased the probability of the explosion, rendered the consequences of it, when it once
took place, more general.   Again, it was presumed that the war was
not, as on former occasions, to be carried on in distant parts of the
globe, for ascertaining the boundaries of a desert, or determining the
right to a barren island : * but was supposed to be commenced by an
enraged and powerful enemy, and to be waged at our own doors, for
the purpose of depriving us of whatever we held dear and sacred.
Even at the first onset, we were witness to a vigorous attack on the
territories of an ally, with whom we stand closely connected in our
commercial transactions.   In addition to these considerations, no artifices were spared by the advocates for a war, to impress on the minds
of their countrymen at large, an idea that many of their countrymen—
men of rank, of talents, and of influence—were attached to the cause
of our adversaries.   Insurrections were alluded to that never had exist-

---

* The allusion here is to the renewal of war in 1756, on account of the boundary
lines of Canada and Nova-Scotia, and to the dispute of the Falkland Islands, in 1770,
which, however, passed over without fighting.   Petty reasons enough for war, if they
had been the real reasons, or if war could have been averted by surrendering the
points in dispute.   But the fact is, that neither Nova-Scotia, nor the Falkland
Islands, nor the Scheldt (though that river seems destined to gain as warlike a name
as Rubicon), nor Malta, were the real causes or objects of war.   Commercial supremacy and continental influence were the white elephants for which we shed our
blood and treasure.   Philosophically examined, the disputes of mankind will
generally be found to be less silly, and more wicked, than is generally supposed.
When Young called Satan a dunce, he was a dunce himself.

ence, and plots were denounced, that finished where they began—in the fertile brain of the informer.   Such are the peculiarities that distinguish this war from those in which Britain had before been engaged, and it would be astonishing indeed, if exertions so industriously made, and so pointedly calculated to destroy all confidence amongst us, political, moral, and commercial, should totally have failed of effect."

On the whole, it is doubtful whether this well-meant pamphlet was, or was not calculated to be very effective.   Men—many men at least—are easily seduced through their purses; but it is not through their purses that they are soonest tamed.   It is the advice of Machiavelli, never to make war on a nation in the hope of exhausting its finances. In like manner, never expect that commercial losses, or the dread of poverty, will induce a nation to submit to peace.   It may be, that many persons—it may be that Mr. Roscoe himself—looked with secret satisfaction at the increasing list of bankrupts in those disastrous years; that they shook their heads incredulously when they were told that markets were *looking up*; and watched the fall of the funds as wistfully as a farmer, whose crops are perishing of drought, would observe the fall of the mercury.   Not that they did not love their country, but because they hoped that failures and losses would starve out the military fever, and stop a contest, for the success whereof they could not conscientiously pray.   But whatever vices wealth may bring, it is not by poverty, or the apprehension of poverty, that they are to be cured.   As well might you expect to cure a populace of drinking by lowering their wages.   Children may steal or famish, wife turn beggar or prostitute, pot and pan, saw and hammer, go to the pawnbroker's: as long as a penny can be raised, the drunkard will have his drop; nor will his own hunger and nakedness, his bleared eye and palsied hand, nor his shame and remorse work his reformation.

War is the drunkenness of states, and when once they are debauched with its poison, they will have it, let it cost what it may.   Credit may perish, specie fly the country or hide its head, rent and tithe become, like Demogorgon, a horrible name without a substance, the manufacturers be as idle as their rusting machinery, yet noisy as it was when in full employment, the bankrupt merchant vainly seek a book-keeper's place, the labourers roam about in grim hungry bands, demanding charity with curses, the paupers breed a pestilence, and die of their own multitude (but they are very hard to kill), and the middle order disappear, or be represented by a few tottering old bachelors, a few angular-visaged spinsters,

> "In thread-bare finery, fifty fashions old,"

and an indefinite number of news-writers, pamphleteers, and victory-puffers, who write *gentleman* after their names, because the law has never recognized their occupation. Nobility itself may begin to find that all is not as it used to be. Still, the sinews of war will be found so long as a tax or a loan can be wrenched from the people. Every little victory renews the national vanity, and every discomfiture revives the national resentment.* The losing gamester plays on to retrieve his loss.

Mr. Roscoe probably did not foresee (or rather it was not to his purpose to foresee) that the very paper credit which he esteemed as the locomotive faculty of trade, would increase many-fold during the war which appeared to destroy it; would become the main support of that war, and, in the opinion of many, its greatest evil.

The following reflections furnish matter for thought at the present æra :——

" To enter into an enquiry at the present day, into the advantages or disadvantages which any country derives from an extensive foreign trade, would be to no purpose. Probably in the result of such a question it might appear, that there is a certain limit, beyond which commerce ceases to be lucrative, and increases the risque without increasing the profit. But a train of events, of which it would be useless to point out the causes, have brought us into a situation in which that commerce, whether abstractedly desirable or not, is become indispensable to us. Those who condemn the enterprising spirit of our merchants, the immense extent of credit, and the consequent circulation of paper, would do well to consider, that a sum not less than £17,000,000 is, even during the continuance of peace, annually to be raised in this country for what are called the exigencies of the state ; a sum not raised without some difficulty, even during the most flourishing periods of our commerce. However desirous we may be to tread back our steps from the dangerous eminence to which we have unawares attained, and to regain once more the safer track that winds through the forsaken valley, we find ourselves surrounded on every side by precipices that forbid our retreat. The diminution of our commerce will occasion a diminution in the revenue, which must be

* This we believe is hardly an exaggerated statement of the condition of France in the latter years of the succession war. If we refer to elder times, it is a very faint picture of the state of Scotland in the reign of David the Second, or of France during the wars of the Edwards and Henrys. Nor was England, though free from a foreign invader, free from sufferings that severely punished her persevering injustice. Yet the statesmen who put a stop to these horrors, were then held up to popular hatred as traitors.

supplied from other sources, and it is not difficult to foresee what those sources are. Hence, perhaps it is eventually not less the interest of the landed than of the trading part of the community, to support a system which, however introduced, is not only become essential to our prosperity, but to our existence ; and heartily to concur in the common cause ; if not till we conquer the difficulties that surround us, at least till we can effect a safe and honourable retreat.

"It is not uncommon to find those who have been the loudest in extolling the riches, security, and happiness of the nation, attempting to console themselves under the pressure of misfortunes which they cannot but feel, by attributing the present calamity to the improper extension of paper credit: according to their idea, the present is only the subsiding of a tumour which had already increased beyond all bounds, by which the body politic was soon to be restored to a better state of health.   But may we be permitted to ask these political optimists, what then was the origin and support of that unexampled series of prosperity which it seems this nation has of late years enjoyed ? Without the assistance of paper credit, can it be pretended that the manufactures of Great Britain could have been circulated to foreign parts, or the produce of foreign countries have been imported into Great Britain, even to one fifth of the extent that has actually taken place?   Or would the minister have been enabled to exult monthly and weekly over the amount of his revenue?   Either this felicity was visionary and ideal, or, being real and substantial, has been incautiously undermined and overthrown."

In another part of the pamphlet, Mr. Roscoe is rather severe upon the Bank of England, for contracting their discounts, when it would have been so much more public-spirited to have extended them, and instead of "shewing the example of confidence," "leading the way of pusillanimity."   We have heard and read the same complaint over and over again, but on its justice we are not moneyed enough ourselves to decide.   Public bodies hold a trust which hardly permits them to be generous, if by generosity be meant a sacrifice of their corporate interest for the benefit of others ; and if generosity do not mean this, it is a word without meaning, or at best, only a kind of speculative self-interest.   If chartered companies aggrandize themselves at the expense of the community, or withhold from the state assistance which it may justly claim, the national government, not the company's directors, are to blame.   Still, even upon self-interested principles, there can be no worse policy than over-caution.

Though the style of this pamphlet is easy, unaffected, and purely English, and the matter in the main sensible, it is only in a very few passages that we discover an indication of the powers which two years afterwards appeared in the "Life of Lorenzo de' Medici." This delightful work was published in the winter of 1795, printed by John M'Creery of Liverpool, and met with a reception that amply rewarded the author for his long, but pleasant labour. It was almost immediately translated into the principal European languages : it was hailed with delight by the Italians, compliments showered in from all quarters, and Mr. Roscoe was installed among classical historians.

Perhaps the most valuable, certainly the most pleasing, part of the book, is the information it affords on the revival of ancient, and the growth of modern Italian literature, together with the origin and progress of Italian art. We scarcely remember a work in which, with so few excrescences, there is so much incidental and collateral knowledge displayed,—so many little facts, so many traits of manners, so much that is not to be found elsewhere, which you would not expect to find there, where, notwithstanding, it is strictly relevant, and in its place. The singular characters, wonderful industry, and everlasting quarrels of the early scholars, who, if their mutual reports of each other are to be trusted, must have been the vilest set of miscreants that ever existed, compose a pleasant underplot; and the well-blended virtues and talents of Lorenzo himself, always great and always amiable, whether in public or in private, constitute a green spot in the waste of history, which certainly has every advantage of contrast with the dark mazes of Italian policy he was compelled to thrid. Roscoe has been accused of flattering his hero ; but if the portrait be not altogether ideal, never since our English Alfred has any state been guided by a man so good and so all-accomplished. But alas ! the transactions of Florence, even during his life, and yet more the calamities which followed his decease, do but confirm the lesson which the Antonines had taught before, how insufficient are the excellencies of an individual, though vested with sovereign power, to remedy the radical evils of a bad constitution.

The fame and profit derived from this publication finally determined Mr. Roscoe to relinquish his business as a solicitor. At one time, he had thoughts of being called to the bar, and actually entered himself of Grey's Inn. But in this intention he did not persevere. He had already formed the design of continuing the history of the Medici through the pontificate of Leo X. ; and having now acquired what to his moderate desires and elegant habits was an easy fortune, he hoped to divide his time between studious retirement, congenial society, and the promotion of such public objects as he deemed most worthy and desirable.

In 1796, he produced a pamphlet with a title which to some may seem portentous, if not profane,—" *Exposure of the Fallacies of Mr. Burke.*"

In 1797, in a visit to London of some continuance, he made the acquaintance and acquired the friendship of Mr. Fox, Mr., now Lord Grey, and several other persons of note in politics and literature, among whom was Dr. Moore, author of " Zeluco," whose familiarity with Italian manners, so vividly painted in his " Sketches of Manners," must have made his society both pleasant and profitable to our author. In the same year, Mr. Roscoe translated the " Balia " of Tansillo, a sportive poem of that sort which peculiarly suits the genius of the Italian language, though it has of late been transplanted, and has flourished in our " bleak Septemtrion blasts." Still, English humour is not Italian humour ; and English playfulness, if not tightly reined in, is very apt to degenerate into *horse-play* We have not seen either the original of Tansillo, nor Mr. Roscoe's version ; but we are sure that Roscoe would never forget the gentleman in his mirth, or translate what had better never have been written.

The year 1798 saw the institution of the Liverpool Athenæum, first projected by Dr. Rutter, but to the establishment of which Mr. Roscoe mainly contributed, and continued, to the end of his life, to take a warm interest in its welfare.

Finding his time at Liverpool too much interrupted by visits and invitations, he resolved to retire into the country, thinking a rural retreat favourable to his mental and bodily health, and to the gratification of that love of nature, and passion for agricultural pursuits, which began in his boyhood. With this view, he purchased half the estate of Allerton, from the trustees of Mrs. Hardman, and became, in the best sense of the word, a country gentleman. His pleasant anticipations from this change are happily expressed in a comic letter to Fuseli the painter. It is much to be regretted that he was ever induced to depart from this rational scheme of happiness and usefulness, and to launch into the world again. But yet the alteration of his course redounded to his honour; for it arose neither from restlessness, infirmity of purpose, avarice, nor ambition, but was a sacrifice of his own leisure and wishes, for the benefit of his friends.

About 1800, a period of general calamity and threatened famine, the affairs of Messrs. J. and W. Clarke, bankers, fell into considerable disorder. Mr. Roscoe was requested to lend his professional aid to their arrangement, and in conducting this business he was brought in contact with Sir Benjamin Hammet, banker, of London, a man who knew the power of money, and whose uneasy assumption of dignity, under the honours of knighthood, was the theme of much small wit. Sir Benjamin was so much struck with Mr. Roscoe's adroitness in unravelling the perplexed accounts of the embarrassed concern, that he insisted on that gentleman's becoming a partner of the bank, and threat- ened to make it bankrupt in case of refusal. Perhaps Sir Benjamin had an eye to Mr. Roscoe's property, as well as to his skill, but at all events, as he held acceptances to the amount of £200,000, he was able to put his threat in execution, and Mr. Roscoe reluctantly consented to avert it, having previously satisfied himself of Messrs. Clarke's ability to meet all demands, if proper time were given. Thenceforth he devoted the hours of business to attendance at the bank, and the hours of relaxation to the studies necessary to perfect his " Leo."

In 1802, he succeeded in establishing a Botanic Garden at Liver- pool, which, under the superintendence of its able curator, Mr. John Shepherd, has prospered exceedingly, to the great advantage of botanical science.

His interest in politics never slumbered. In the same year, 1802, he put forth a pamphlet " *On the Relative Situation of France and England.*" His earnest endeavours for peace exposed him for many years of his life to considerable obloquy, and made some good men, who loved and esteemed him, esteem his judgment the less. He certainly, like Cicero, was disposed to think the worst peace better than the best war; and knowing that the government could not long carry on the war if the people firmly demanded peace, and that the people were stimulated to battle chiefly by their indignation against the atrocities, and by their alarm at the ambition, of the enemy, he naturally sought to soften the national animosity, by palliating the conduct of the French, and representing the danger of the conflict as greater than the danger of a compromise. Perhaps he did not sufficiently observe how com- pletely the war changed its character and object in its progress; but continued to contemplate it as an interference with the right of the French to constitute their own government, long after all thought of such interference had been abandoned.

The year 1805 brought forth the " *Life and Pontificate of Leo X.*" in four volumes quarto. This Roscoe esteemed his great work, but it was by no means so favourably received in England as its predecessor. The partiality which had found a ready sympathy when directed to the Florentine merchant, was harshly censured when it devolved on the more questionable character of his son ; and it was argued, that no patronage of art, or liberality to genius, should have been allowed to expiate the many offences of the dissolute free-thinking Pope, whose sale of indulgences aroused the wrath of Luther. Yet harder measure was dealt to Roscoe's alleged palliation of the crimes of Alexander VI. and his family, nor was he supposed to have done justice to the virtues of Luther. It is impossible to examine these objections in this place, but as far as regards Pope Alexander and his daughter,[*] we may observe, that there is a considerable difference between palliating crimes, and doubting whether they had ever been committed ; that to believe in monstrous wickedness, on insufficient evidence, indicates any thing but a healthy moral sense ; and that Roscoe had probably consulted more authorities, and weighed them more carefully, than any of his reviewers. As for Luther, he was not a man after Roscoe's own heart : there was little sympathy between them. Luther, though above his time, was still a man of his time, and it was not, even in the sunny realms of art and poesy, an age of soft speaking. Roscoe would have made as bad a reformer as Erasmus. These objections fell not unawares on our author. He had both anticipated and provided against them in his preface. His occasional deviations from received opinions of persons and things, he defends with spirit, eloquence, and a just sense of an historian's duty.

"With respect to the execution of the following work, I cannot but be well aware, that many circumstances and characters will be found represented in a light somewhat different from that in which they have generally been viewed, and that I may probably be accused of having suffered myself to be induced by the force of prejudice, or the affectation of novelty, to remove what have hitherto been considered as the land-marks of history. To imputations of this kind I feel the most perfect indifference. Truth alone has been my guide, and whenever she has steadily diffused her light, I have endeavoured to delineate the

---

[*] Lucretia, daughter of Pope Alexander VI. and Vanozza, sister to Cæsar Borgia. The charges against this lady are comprised in the following *epitaph*, written by an author whom she survived twenty years, which we shall give without translation :

> Hic jacet in tumulo Lucretia nomine, sed re
> Thais. Alexandri filia, sponsa, nurus.
>
> PONTANUS.

Sannazarius also thus addresses her :

> Ergo te semper cupiet, Lucretia, Sextus.
> O Fatum diri numinis, hic pater est !

a conceit, which hinging on an equivoque between Sextus Tarquinius and Alexander Sextus, *i. e.* the Sixth, is impossible as it is unworthy to be translated.

Mr. Roscoe, in a dissertation subjoined to the first volume of his "Leo," has elaborately, and in our opinion convincingly, exposed the no-evidence on which accusations so abhorrent have been repeated from age to age. Like all men of good hearts and innocent lives, he was averse to admit the existence of monstrous depravity in any, most of all in woman.

objects in their real form and colour. History is the record of the experience of mankind in their most important concerns. If it be impossible for human sagacity to estimate the consequences of a false-hood in private life, it is equally impossible to estimate the consequences of a false or partial representation of the events of former times. The conduct of the present is regulated by the experience of the past.

*　　*　　*　　*　　*　　*

If those in high authority be better informed than others, it is from this source that their information must be drawn ; and to pollute it is, therefore, to poison the only channel through which we can derive that knowledge, which, if it can be obtained pure and unadulterated, cannot fail in time to purify the intellect, expand the powers, and improve the condition of the human race.

" As in speaking of the natural world, there are some persons who are disposed to attribute its creation to chance, so, in speaking of the moral world, there are some who are inclined to refer the events and fluctua-tions in human affairs to accident, and are satisfied with accounting for them from the common course of things, or the spirit of the times. But as *chance* and *accident,* if they have any meaning whatever, can only mean the operation of causes not hitherto fully investigated, or distinctly understood, so *the spirit of the times* is only another phrase for causes and circumstances which have not hitherto been sufficiently explained. It is the province of the historian to trace and to discover these causes ; and it is only in proportion as he accomplishes this object, that his labours are of any utility. An assent to the former opinion may indeed gratify our indolence, but it is only from the latter method that we can expect to acquire true knowledge, or to be able to apply to future conduct the information derived from past events."

Some of the attacks of the censors were of a truly *nibbling* character. Yet these also he had foreseen, and hoped to crush them in the egg. He was found fault with for spelling Italian names as they were spelt in Italy, not as they had come to England in a Frenchified or Latinized form. This he ably justifies.

" The practice which I have heretofore adopted of designating the Scholars of Italy by their national appellations, has given rise to some animadversions, in answer to which I must beg to remark, that whoever is conversant with history, must frequently have observed the difficulties which arise from the wanton alterations in the names both of persons and of places, by authors of different countries, and particularly by the French, who, without scruple, accommodate every thing to the genius of their own language. Hence the names of all the eminent men of Greece, of Rome, or of Italy, are melted down, and appear again in such a form as in all probability would not have been recognized by their proper owners ; Dionysius if *Denys ;* Titus Livius, *Tite Live ;* * Horatius, *Horace ;* Petrarca, *Petrarque,* and Pico of Mirandola, *Pic de Mirandole.* As the literature which this country derived from Italy was first obtained through the medium of the French, our early authors followed them in this respect, and thereby sanctioned those innovations which the nature of our language did not require. It is still more to be regretted that we are not uniform even in our abuse. The name of *Horace* is familar to the English reader, but if he were told of the *three Horaces,* he would probably be at a loss to discover the persons meant, the authors of our country having generally given them the appellation of the *Horatii.* In the instance of such names as were familiar to our early literature, we adopt with the French the abbreviated appellation ; but in latter times we usually employ proper national distinctions, and instead of *Arioste,* or *Metastase,* we write without hesitation, *Ariosto, Metastasio.* This inconsistency is more sensibly felt, when the abbreviated appellation of one scholar is contrasted with the national distinction of another, as when a letter is addressed by *Petrarch* to *Coluccio Salutati,* or by *Politian* to *Hermolao Barbaro,* or *Baccio Ugolini.* For the sake of uniformity it is surely desirable that every writer should conform as much as possible to some general rule, which can only be found by a reference of every proper name to the standard of its proper country. This method would not only avoid the incongruities before mentioned, but would be productive of positive advantages, as it would in general point out the nation of the person spoken of, without the necessity of further indication. Thus in mentioning one of the Monarchs of France, who makes a conspicuous figure in the ensuing pages, I have not denominated him *Lodovico XII.* with the Italians, nor *Lewis XII.* with the English, but *Louis XII.* the name which he himself recognized. And thus I have also restored to a celebrated Scottish General, in the service of the same Monarch, his proper title of d' Aubigny, instead of that of Obigni, usually given him by the historians of Italy."

It seems hard that a man should have to apologize for doing right, especially where the right is so obvious as in this case. It is surely an advantage in the English language, that it can give the natives of every country their right names, without violating its own idiom ; an advantage which should not be given up in compliment to our French

---

* The English have used poor Titus Livius shamefully. Not content with taking away his *good name,* and giving him a very indifferent one (*Livy*) in its stead, they have suffered an impudent pretender to usurp his just titles. Thus while the ancient Patavinian is shrunk to *Livy,* a modern Italian who recorded in Latin the wars of Henry V. always figures, in a reference or quotation, as *Titus Livius.*

neighbours. The only exception to Mr. Roscoe's, is in the case of scholars like *Erasmus, Secundus,* &c. who are only known to the world through the medium of their Latin compositions, or such as *Melancthon* and *Oecolampadius,* who have, of their own free choice, exchanged or hellenized their patrimonian designations. With respect to the Italian names, euphony no less than propriety demands that they be restored to their natural proportions.

Another rather more plausible topic of animadversion, was the frequency of poetic quotations in the pages of a history. When quotations are introduced merely for their own sake, at some slight suggestion, or, as one might say, *appropos,* they are impertinent enough, but passages of contemporary writers, which either throw light upon facts, or indicate the feelings with which those facts were regarded, are never irrelevant, but tend especially to confirm and realize narrative. Let our author once more speak for himself.*

"There is one peculiarity in the following work, which it is probable may be considered as a radical defect; I allude to the frequent introduction of quotations and passages from the poets of the times, occasionally interspersed through the narrative, or inserted in the notes. To some it may appear that the seriousness of history is thus impertinently broken in upon, whilst others may suppose, that not only its gravity, but its authenticity is impeached by these citations, and may be inclined to consider this work as one of those productions in which truth and fiction are blended together, for the purpose of amusing and misleading the reader. To such imputations I plead not guilty. That I have at times introduced quotations from the works of the poets, in proof of historical facts, I confess ; nor, when they proceed from contemporary authority, do I perceive that their being in verse invalidates their credit. In this light, I have frequently cited the *Decennale* of Machiavelli, and the *Vergier d Honneur* of Audri de la Vigne, which are, in fact, little more than versified annals of the events of the times ; but in general, I have not adduced such extracts as evidences of facts, but for a purpose wholly different. To those who are pleased in tracing the emotions and passions of the human mind in all ages, nothing can be more gratifying than to be informed of the mode of thinking of the public at large, at interesting periods and in important situations. Whilst war and desolation stalk over a country, or whilst a nation is struggling for its liberties or its existence, the opinions of men of genius, ability, and learning, who have been agitated with all the hopes and

* And for *us* too, for we are aware that our own pages are very full of inverted commas.

fears to which such events have given rise, and have frequently acted a personal and important part in them, are the best and most instructive comment. By such means, we seem to become contemporaries with those whose history we peruse, and to acquire an intimate knowledge, not only of the facts themselves, but of the judgment formed upon such facts by those who were most deeply interested in them. Nor is it a slight advantage in a work which professes to treat on the literature of the times, that the public events, and the works of the eminent scholars and writers of that period, thus become a natural comment, and serve on many occasions to explain and to illustrate each other."

But it is quite impossible that in a work so extensive as the " *Leo*," written by a man whose hours of study were those which other men consider their hours of justifiable idleness, dependent in some measure upon contingencies for the books which he required, and a stranger to the country whose history he was writing, should not contain some errors more serious than poetical quotations or innovations in orthography.   The mistakes which Mr. Roscoe's English reviewers had not learning enough to detect, exposed him to the keen revisal of Sismondi, who not sympathizing with his admiration of the Medici family, and possessing an unlimited command of books and languages, animadverted on some parts of Mr. Roscoe's writings with an asperity which gave him more concern than any of the ignorant criticisms which emanated from English prejudice.   To these animadversions he replied in his " *Illustrations of the life of Lorenzo de Medici.*"   It is pleasant to record that this literary controversy did not prevent a friendly intercourse between Roscoe and Sismondi, when the latter visited England.

The next important event in Roscoe's life was his election into the short Parliament, which abolished the slave-trade.   As he partook the blessing of this great act of justice, it was no great hardship for him to participate in the unpopularity which national disappointment threw upon the short-lived ministry, which first adulation and afterwards irony denominated " All the Talents."   But it is woeful to think that the best act of that ministry was the most unpopular, and that the influence of the slave-traders at the gin-shops prevented Mr. Roscoe's re-election in 1807.   After the dissolution of Parliament he returned to his constituents, and a number of well-affected gentlemen went out to meet and to conduct him into the town which he had faithfully represented.   But an infuriated multitude opposed the entrance of his cortége, in Castle-street, and he found it necessary to withdraw from the contest, which was carried on against him by personal violence.   Should we not be thankful to Heaven, that in little more than twenty years, so great an improvement has taken place in public feeling, that all the rum in

Jamaica could not raise a mob in favour of slavery? It must not be omitted that the part taken by Mr. Roscoe, in the discussions on the Catholic question, furnished a convenient handle to his enemies, and perhaps alienated a few of his friends.

They who remember the dismissal of the whig ministry of 1807, the " no Popery" riots, and the enthusiastic burst of applause which attended the King's decided opposition to the Catholic claims, will perhaps form no high estimate of the stability of public opinion. The truth is the people were disappointed—they thought themselves cheated. They had been led to expect a great diminution of taxes—they experienced a large increase of their burdens. While the majority hoped for a decisive and vigorous prosecution of the war, and a respectable minority promised themselves that at least a sincere effort would be made for peace ; both parties were disgusted by negociations meant only for delay, and expeditions of which the failure was as probable as the success would have been insignificant.

Never, during the whole course of the revolutionary war, were the hopes of the English so little, or their weariness so great, as in the period intervening between the battle of Friedland and the French invasion of Spain. As the enemy had confessedly abandoned, or indefinitely postponed the threatened invasion of Britain, the high-wrought resolution, which had steeled every British nerve, the martial enthusiasm which almost craved the contest with the eagerness of anticipated victory, began to relax and to cool. It seemed that England had done all that Providence allotted for her own safety and honour ; she had annihilated the naval force of France, her trade and colonial dominion ; she had secured her own shores, and the empire of the sea. On the land she could attempt nothing, for there was no spot whereon to fix her engines. The Pitt plan of subsidizing, in which the wise never had any confidence, had now proved its inefficiency to the most sanguine. All saw the folly of putting their trust in continental princes. The world beheld the spectacle of two mighty nations at deadly enmity, armed and ready for the fight, each with an arm uplifted, yet prevented by enchantment from striking a blow.

Mr. Roscoe judiciously thought this a favourable juncture for pacific counsels ; and between 1807 and 1808, produced two pamphlets, one entitled, " *Considerations on the Causes, Objects, and Consequences of the present War, and on the expediency, or the danger of Peace with France.*" The second, " *Remarks on the Proposals made to Great Britain for opening negociations with France in the year* 1807." The following passage, near the beginning of the earlier pamphlet, may serve at least to record the general feeling of despondency which the rising of the Peninsula war soon to change into an extacy of hope : *

"Hitherto, indeed, we have contended with our enemies for prizes of great value. States and empires have been the objects of dispute, and as far as we have been interested in them, have been lost. But we have as yet struggled only for the possessions of our allies. · At the present moment we are called upon for a higher stake. *If the war is to be continued,* it is now no longer matter of exaggeration to assert, that the sovereign of these realms is to contend for his crown ; the people for their liberties and rights ; for the soil in which their forefathers lie intombed. Against this stake, what is the prize we can hope to obtain from the enemy ? The bare honour of having defended *ourselves with success ;* for in any hopes of our being able to make an impression on the dominions of France, the wildest advocates of the war will now scarcely indulge themselves. Thus we follow up a losing game. Holland, Switzerland, Germany, Sardinia, Italy, Prussia, Turkey, Denmark, and Russia, are not only lost to us as allies, but have thrown their weight into the opposite scale. With the assistance of these powers we have been completely disappointed in all our views. Is it then advisable that we should play the last desperate game, and exhibit ourselves to the world as the last object, with an adversary against whom we have been so far from gaining any substantial advantages, that the utmost efforts we have been able to make, have hitherto served to open to him an opportunity for still greater success."

Mr. Roscoe proceeds to shew that all the pretexts which had been successively advanced to justify the commencement, the renewal, and continuance of the war, had been successively abandoned. The infection of French principles, the restoration of the Bourbons, the inability of the revolutionary governments " to maintain the accustomed relations of peace and amity," the necessity of continuing hostilities till we had obtained indemnity for the past and security for the future, were no longer (in 1807) the alleged obstacles to a pacification. In adverting " to the short experimental truce of Amiens," he labours hard to throw the blame of its infraction on the war-party in England, on the French emigrants, and the French counter-revolutionary papers, published in London ; and on " another, and still more formidable party, consisting of the innumerable bands of journalists and hireling writers, who feed upon the credulity, and fatten upon the calamities of a nation ; men who flourish most in the midst of tumult ; to whom the disasters of

---

* The Pamphlet went through eight editions, but we transcribe from the fifth, dated February, 1808.

the country are as valuable as her triumphs ; a destructive battle as a rich triumph, and a new war as a freehold estate." In treating this part of his subject, our author falls upon expressions less favourable to the press than the general liberality of his opinions would lead us to expect. He has anticipated the arguments so frequently urged by Tory writers, against the impunity given to all attacks on foreign governments emanating from writers in this country,* and seems to blame the ministry of 1801 for not taking such decisive measures as Talleyrand suggested, to put a stop to those animadversions which the Premier Consul complained of so bitterly. Yet such could not surely have been Roscoe's meaning. He would not have purchased even peace by stifling the public voice of England, far less by the extrusion of the unfortunate exile from her shores.

But he was intent to prove that the peace might have been adjusted, confirmed, and preserved,—and that the resumption of hostilities was mainly to be attributed to exasperated passions and national antipathies, inflamed by prejudiced and interested individuals. Peace was an object so dear to Roscoe's heart, that he was willing to recommend it by a little special pleading ; and having persuaded himself that the French ruler really desired peace (which no ruler, legitimate or usurper, whose power is built on military glory does or can) he thought he was promoting conciliatory dispositions, when endeavouring to convince his unconvincible countrymen, that nothing but their own ill tongues and perverse humours prevented their deadly foe becoming their best and truest friend.

To the " 'impediments' as to the evacuation of Egypt and Malta

---

* "To foreign states, that which a country does, or that which it permits to be done by its subjects, is the same. With our internal regulations they can have no concern ; but they have a right to expect from us that respect for their institutions which we claim for our own. To encroach upon the freedom of the press will never be the act of any real friend to the interests of mankind; but to restrain its licentiousness is not to encroach upon, but to preserve that freedom. If it be in the power of every venal demagogue, or wild enthusiast, to throw out, unrestrained, the most unjust and offensive aspersions against the rulers and governments of other states, a cause of hostility will never be far to seek. In fact, nations, as they are composed of, so they feel like individuals, and the general sentiment differs from the particular one, only in being more permanent and more intense."---*Considerations, page* 26.

The same doctrine, almost in the same words, has been preached against the English vituperators of the restored Bourbons, of Ferdinand, of Miguel, and of the Emperor Nicholas.

It may appear to some persons a great triumph to find a liberal admitting that the licentiousness of the press requires to be curbed. It is indeed a "consummation devoutly to be wished." The man who shall invent a method of preserving liberty, and yet preclude the possibility of license, will deserve to be canonized.

by the English troops, and the evacuation of Holland by the French," he alludes very slightly, as matters admitting an easy settlement ; the invasion of Switzerland, and the inhospitable aggressions on English commerce, he passes wholly without observation.   It is true, that none of these, nor all of them, were either the real or the justifying causes of the war, but they have been supposed sufficient proofs of that reckless ambition and irreconcilable hatred, which rendered amity impossible, and an armistice perilous.

Having taken a rapid review of the events from the rupture of 1803, till the battle of Austerlitz, he adverts to the death of Mr. Pitt, and draws a character of that statesman, rather distinguished for the mildness of its phraseology, and an air of gentlemanly candour, than for any strong or vivid traits of portraiture.   Such *candid* pictures, as they never much resemble the original, so they satisfy neither his admirers nor their opponents.   After some handsome compliments to Mr. Pitt's talents, and regret that such accomplishments as his should be rendered mischievous instead of beneficial, by the predominance of a single passion, " inherited from his father," (whether a passion for power simply, or a passion for war, or a passion for popularity, any of which he might have inherited from his father, we are not certified), our author proceeds thus :—" Unfortunately, the system of education of Mr. Pitt was in politics, that which Lord Chesterfield's is in private life.   It was founded on too narrow a basis, and aimed too directly at its object.   A cultivated mind, and a humane disposition, will render their possessor truly polite ; sound principles and a real love of mankind, truly patriotic ; but without these neither the patriotism nor the politeness are any thing more than a whited sepulchre.   The system was however successful, the young orator began his career in a manner the best calculated to display his powers.   As he spoke the hopes of freedom revived ; corruption shrunk from his glance, and the nation hailed him as her deliverer ; but no sooner was the prize within his grasp than he seized it with an eagerness, and retained it with a tenacity, which all the efforts of his opponents could neither impede nor relax.   Having thus obtained the supreme power, the talents which had acquired it were employed with equal success to preserve it.   The correction of abuses, the removal of peculation and corruption, the reform of the representation, the extension of civil and religious liberty, were now no longer the objects in view, or were only recalled at stated periods to shew with what dexterity the minister could blast his promise without breaking his faith.   Well schooled in all the routine and arcana of office, an adept in the science of finance and taxation, Mr. Pitt's great accomplishment was a thorough knowledge of the *artificial* and complex machine of government ; and his great defect a total insensibility to the feelings of mankind, and an utter ignorance of the leading principles of human nature."*

---

* There is a position involved, and as it were diffused, in these latter sentences, which Roscoe had done well to announce more distinctly, and in which his ample knowledge would have been well employed to illustrate and enforce; for it is of more importance than the peace, or the battle of Austerlitz, or Mr. Pitt himself will ever be again. The position is simply this—*A mere apprenticeship is not good education.*

Whatever system of tuition is solely adapted to enable the pupil to play a certain part in the world's drama, whether for his own earthly advantage, or for that of any other man, or community of men, is a mere apprenticeship. It matters not whether the part be high or low, the hero or the fool.

A *good education*, on the other hand, looks primarily to the right formation of the Man in man, and its final cause is the well being of the pupil, as he is a moral, responsible, and immortal being.

But, because to every man there is appointed a certain ministry and service, a path prescribed of duty, a work to perform, and a race to run, an office in the economy of Providence, a good education always provides a good apprenticeship; for usefulness is a necessary property of goodness.

The moral culture of man, and so much of intellectual culture as is conducive thereto, is essential to education. Whatever of intellectual culture is beyond this, should be regarded as pertaining to apprenticeship, and should be apportioned to the demands of the vocation for which that apprenticeship is designed to qualify.

A man whose education is without apprenticeship, will be useless; a man whose education is all apprenticeship, will be bad, and therefore pernicious, and the more pernicious in proportion as his function is high, noble, or influential.

Most of the systems of tuition provided for the subordinate classes have been defective; as aiming either solely to qualify the pupil for his station, or to give him a chance and hope of rising above that station: either to make the man a mere labourer, or to turn the labourer into a gentleman,—the discipline and improvement of the man being too often postponed or omitted. The tuition of the higher castes is equally defective, when it forms gentlemen to be mere gentlemen; where it refers the primary duties to the rank, and not to universal obligation. Secondly, when it inculcates the acquirement of mental or personal accomplishments as ultimate ends, without reference either to practical utility, or to self-edification. Thirdly, when all apprenticeship is omitted, or an apprenticeship given wholly alien from the peculiar, individual, and functionary duties, as *e. g.* when a scion of nobility is crammed with the arbitrary technicals of professional scholarship, or wastes his time in learning to do for himself, what his steward, his game-keeper, or his chaplain could do better for him. Fourthly, when the whole education is rendered subservient to the apprenticeship. This is, perhaps, the commonest fault of all, especially with that unfortunate class, whose education is to be their portion, and means of advancement. It bears a creditable semblance of steadiness and industry, it wins the applause of parents and tutors, it makes shining and rising young men, and sometimes Judges, Chancellors, Ambassadors, and Ministers of State. But it does not make good men, or wise men either. Even if it leave the heart uninjured, it keeps the mind unnaturally ignorant; for viewing all things in an artificial relation to one object, it sees, and therefore

Our author does not scruple to attribute both the horrors of the French revolution, and the subsequent successes of the French arms, to the misadventurous attacks upon French liberty, of which he accounts Mr. Pitt the *primum mobile*. It is our business to record, not to confute or approve, Mr. Roscoe's sentiments. He shall utter them in his own words :—

" To what circumstance is it to be ascribed that a people so restless in their disposition, so changeful in their views, should have been united together through all the variations of their government, and have acted in all their external relations with one heart and as one man ? To what but the continued pressure of external force ? To the successive combinations formed under the auspices of Mr. Pitt, to compel them to submission. That France has suffered in the contest, that her best blood has flowed on the scaffold, that the luminaries of science have been extinguished, and the brightest gems of the human intellect trampled under foot ; that jealousy, ambition, cruelty, and revenge, have acted their dreadful parts in awful succession, and have produced a scene of calamity unexampled in history, is but too true ; but such was the price that France was compelled by Europe to pay for her independence on foreign powers, and in this view the purchase was after all cheaply made. The principle which carried that nation through all her difficulties, was the determination of the people to rally round the

knows, nothing in its true relations to man, and to the universe. The more their knowledge, the greater their errors. The greater their command of facts, the more perilously false their inferences. They may, indeed, be wise in their own craft, but they are pitiful blunderers when they step beyond it. Be it recollected, that we are not speaking of that devotion of time to a professional study, which may be a duty, but of that perversion of self-government, which makes the profession all in all.

Mr. Roscoe seems to accuse the Lord Chatham of making his son's education a mere apprenticeship to the art and mystery of statesmanship, and so teaching him to look upon his fellow creatures only as things to be governed ; as Chesterfield certainly trained his offspring to regard men and women alike as creatures to be pleased, courted, flattered, and despised. The truth of the allegation, as far as concerns Chatham, we neither affirm nor deny. A general truth is not invalidated by an incidental misapplication. We agree with the admirers of Pitt, that he had a strong and sincere passion for the public good in the abstract ; that he understood the true nature of that public good, which is good to each and to all, and *is* all in every part, we doubt exceedingly. In that knowledge of human nature which is acquired by observation and outward experience, he could hardly be deficient, for he was hacknied in the ways of men, and knew how to bend them to his purposes ;—in that knowledge of man, which consists in the intelligent sympathy of a good heart, instructed by kind affections and hourly charities, by pain that begets patience, by solemn or cheerful influences of happiness, by solitary musing, by self-examination, prayer, and faith, he had hardly time to be a proficient.

existing government, *whatever that government might be*, and to join in repelling with one hand, and one voice, the common enemy. To this they have sacrificed their ease, their property, their friends, their families, their lives, with a prodigality, which excites at the same time horror and admiration."

From the tone and passion of this eloquent effusion, we might almost have imagined that the author was exhorting his countrymen to perseverance in a deadly contest by French example, than breathing counsels of meekness and conciliation. If the exemption of a people from foreign interference be so necessary a blessing, that no horrors, no bloodshed, no anarchy, no tyranny should be declined to secure it, what could war, even a war entailed from generation to generation, like that of the Jews and Philistines, or of the Spaniards and Moors, bring with it that England ought not to endure rather than hold her peace, wealth, and happiness dependent upon the forbearance of a haughty foe? Mr. Roscoe, however, intended no such inference; his sole purpose was, to shew that France was grown formidable in consequence of the measures taken to crush her—that the confederacy of states and princes had awakened that intense spirit of nationality which neither disasters without, nor disorders within, can ever extinguish in the heart of a Frenchman, who, however excellent, or however depraved, is a Frenchman still, as long as he is anything.

Mr. Roscoe appears to have had more than a political attachment to Mr. Fox—a warm personal affection, and a lasting regret. This amiable feeling may account for the somewhat extravagant, if not invidious praise, he accords to his departed friend for rejecting, with indignation, a proposal made by some hungry fellow to shoot Bonaparte from a house at Passy. In all probability the man was a spy, ready to serve or shoot any king, emperor, or private gentleman whatever, for a consideration. But surely it was no remarkable virtue in Mr. Fox to decline the offer. Did Mr. Roscoe imagine that Mr. Pitt, or any other minister, would have closed with it? But, says our author, " the political opponents of Mr. Fox ought to have felt rightly on such a subject. They ought to have known that it was no effort to his great and generous mind to reject the proposals of an avowed assassin. It is not on this account that he is intitled to our applause; but it is because he had the virtue and the courage to bring forwards into public life, and to exemplify in the most striking manner, one of the most important maxims of morality —*that it is never expedient to do evil in the hope of producing an eventual good.*" What eventual good could Mr. Fox have expected from engaging his country in the ill-concerted conspiracy of a low bravo?. What personal wrong had he to forgive Bonaparte? On the very improbable supposition that this precious scheme had been put into execution, what could Mr. Fox expect for himself or for his country, by a participation in it? What for himself but disgrace and impeachment? What for his country, but a massacre of all the English in the French prisons, of all suspected royalists throughout France? Mr. Fox acted as he ought to have done, and is entitled to our approbation, but not to the rapturous panegyric of Mr. Roscoe.

We are not forgetful that the old question concerning the lawfulness of tyrannicide was very frequently mooted both in conversation and in print, with an express reference to the case of Bonaparte. Something of the kind had probably passed in our author's hearing. But no person, whose opinions were worth confuting, ever imagined that Englishmen ought to take the punishment of a French tyrant into their own hands, or that *they* ought to regard Bonaparte otherwise than as the chief of a hostile state, under the protection of the law of nations.*

---

* In a vigorously-written but very vituperative " Review " of Mr. Roscoe's pamphlet, this whole story of Mr. Fox's interview with the Frenchman is treated with ridicule, and a more than implied aspersion on Mr. Fox's veracity. "The truth is," says the reviewer, " that nine tenths of the political world believe that the incident alluded to was either a plot of Talleyrand's, or, I am sorry to add, a fabrication of Mr. Fox's. On the former supposition, he became the dupe of a political scoundrel; in the latter case, his enemies may say that he himself was something worse than a dupe."

Mr. Roscoe was not often in a passion—at least he did not print his choler; but on this occasion his wrath was certainly roused, and he vindicated the memory of his friend with a manly indignation. In the postscript to the pamphlet to which we have already alluded, he thus satisfactorily refutes the allegation of the anonymous reviewer:—

"Perhaps there never was an instance of a more gross and unfounded calumny, than in a recent attempt to asperse the memory, and impeach the veracity of the late Mr. Fox, by insinuating that the proposal made to him respecting the assassination of the French ruler, as related by him in his letter to M. Talleyrand, was a story fabricated by himself for the purpose of bringing on a negociation with France. The more immediate friends of Mr. Fox have disdained to take any public notice of the false assertions and scandalous imputations to which I allude, and I can scarcely suppose that any of my readers require any further evidence than what is contained in Mr. Fox's letter, of a fact, with regard to which his character and veracity are opposed to the malicious and wanton accusations which have been made against him. But that no possible doubt may hereafter remain as to this transaction, and for the entire refutation of these slanders, I think it incumbent upon me to state, from indisputable authority, that there exists evidence in documents at the alien office, of the arrival at Gravesend of the person named and described in Mr. Fox's letter; of his application from that place for an audience with Mr. Fox; of his private interview with that gentleman at his house in Arlington-Street; of Mr. Fox's order, in the first instance, to send the Frenchman out of the kingdom, and of his subsequent revocation of that order, in consequence of which, the intended assassin was detained in custody six weeks, and was then embarked at Harwich, on board a

The disclosure of this plot produced some very polite correspondence between Mr. Fox and M. Talleyrand, in which the latter conveyed the thanks of his master to the British minister, with an assurance, that " he recognized in the conduct of Mr. Fox those principles of honour and virtue by which he had ever been actuated, and which had already given a new character to the war." Affairs were quickly put in train for a negociation, of the progress of which, and its ultimate failure, Mr. Roscoe gives a particular, and at this time, rather tedious account. It may furnish a subject of speculation for future historians whether Napoleon, on this or any other occasion, sincerely desired peace with England, and what effect the longer life of Fox might have had on the policy of this country. Mr. Roscoe's main object is to prove that the French were disposed to pacific measures, that the treaty was broken off in consequence of the determination of the English ministry to make no peace in which Russia was not included, and that at the time when he was writing, (1808,) no obstacle could exist to the renewal of nego_ ciations, inasmuch as Russia was no longer our ally, but our enemy. He speaks with severe reprobation of the attack upon Copenhagen, and seems to have regarded the ministry, by which it was undertaken, with something more than political dislike. The shortest, but most impor_ tant part of the pamphlet, relates to the dangers of continuing the war, the madness of contemplating interminable hostilities, and the great advantages to be derived from a secure peace.

As he could not suppose that his arguments would obtain so much as a hearing from the government, his intentions in this publication must have been, first, to vindicate his political connections; secondly, to assuage the antigallican animosity, which he justly considered to be the fuel and bellows of the war: and thirdly, to produce an overwhelming army of petitions for peace. For this last, and only practical purpose, we cannot think his arguments very well chosen. Should a prudent

vessel bound for Husum. When to these particulars it is added, that the person who accompanied the Frenchman to the interview with Mr. Fox, and who acted under his directions in the measures for sending him out of the kingdom, was Mr. Brooke, who yet holds the same situation in the alien office as he did under the administration of Mr. Fox, I trust it will be wholly unnecessary for me to state any thing further in vindication of that distinguished character, against so malignant and foul a charge,"

The author of that charge has given the lie direct to Mr. Roscoe in every page of his review, and Roscoe was never moved to an angry reply till he found the memory of Fox insulted. We cannot help thinking that the *bravo on the tramp* must either have been a spy of Talleyrand's, or a man very little acquainted with English politics; otherwise Mr. Fox would have been the last man in Europe, Bonaparte himself excepted, to whom he would have disclosed a design on the person of the French Emperor.

adviser, in order to dissuade a fiery and exasperated youth from a duel, tell him with a tremulous voice, that his adversary was never known to miss his man, the peace-maker would perhaps succeed if he had to deal with a coward, ambitious of the honours of bloodless conflict, but in any other case, he would only make him the more resolute to meet a foe who might attribute any explanation to fear.   There was, in the English people at large, an eager desire to measure swords with the conqueror of the continent.   They thought, and rightly thought, that the more formidable the foe, the greater danger of trusting him. There is one argument which might, perhaps, have been applied with some success in 1807, but it was not in Roscoe's generous nature to use it.   Had he insinuated that the dread of Napoleon was a vain panic; that in peace or war the French could do nothing to hurt us ; that the ministry were husbanding the war, which a vigorous conduct might bring to a glorious conclusion, for their own purposes, for the patronage which it placed at their disposal, the taxes it furnished a pretext for exacting, the force it enabled them to levy, nominally against the enemy, but really against the people : or that the whole scheme was an understood arrangement between the treasury and the loan-jobber, it is very probable that a ferment might have been excited which would have compelled the government either to make peace on any terms, or to risk the whole strength of the country on some single effort, the defeat of which would have rendered the continuance of the war impossible. Assertions of a very similar character were plentifully scattered by the disaffected in the reign of Queen Anne, and succeeded in producing the disgrace of Marlborough, the change of administration, and the peace of Utrecht ; and there were periods in the late war, when they might have been made with quite enough of plausibility for popular credence.   But Roscoe had not the heart to do evil that good might come of it.   Neither were his talents at all calculated to excite the passions and jealousies of a nation.   He was not a *good hater ;* and (it is to his praise that we say it) he was not a good polemic.   There is a languid ease in his style by no means suited to produce temporary effect. There are no stings in his sentences.

Very shortly after his "Considerations," he published "Remarks on the Proposals made to Great Britain for opening Negotiations for Peace, in 1807."   The purpose of this pamphlet, which, though ably written, has now lost great part of its interest, is to convict the British Ministry of insincere conduct towards the allies, who offered their mediation to adjust the differences between France and England.   Nothing can be dryer, or to any but a diplomatist, more obscure than the history of an abortive negotiation.   To this treatise Mr. Roscoe prefixed a preface of thirty-one pages, from which we extract a single passage, wherein he apologizes for his severity upon English, and his lenity towards French errors appear.

" Can it be allowable, it may be asked, that any person shall point out the errors or the faults of his own country, and its rulers, and pass over without still greater reprobation the misconduct of other nations with which she is at enmity ; the crimes of whose people and of whose government are of the deepest die ? The answer is, that it is allowable, and for this very reason, that our country has a claim upon our services which a foreign country has not. The one bears a near resemblance to the self-examination, without which the sense of morals in individual characters would soon be lost, the other is the admonishing of a stranger of whose motives we can only imperfectly judge, and for whose conduct we are not accountable. But it may be said, that virtue and vice admit of degrees, and that however we may ourselves have erred, it may be proper to shew the guilt of other nations has far exceeded our own. To what purpose ? Will the crimes of others be an apology for ours ? and is it desirable that we should diminish the sense of our own misconduct by comparing it with the more enormous offences of others. This however is the fashion of the present day."

Not many months after the appearance of this appeal, the rising of the Spaniards gave a new aspect to the war, and rendered every wisper of peace so dissonant to the British ear, that for a while there seemed to be but one mind in the nation. And even in the darkest intervals of that protracted contest, when Spain seemed to despair of herself, and many denounced the Spaniards as unworthy of another drop of British blood, those who hoped least for the cause, would hardly think of peace with the faithless invader. We are not aware that Mr. Roscoe commented on the war in any subsequent publications. He never ceased to think peace desirable, or to express his opinion to that effect in public or private ; but he must have known that till Spain was evacuated, or entirely subdued, no ministry could dare to sheath the sword, which according to the faith of thousands was drawn in a holy warfare.

We have now said quite enough of Mr. Roscoe's endeavours to allay the military fervour of his countrymen. Disliking the war at first, because he conceived it to be a war against liberty, and then disliking it as a war without hope, he perhaps saw little to congratulate in its conclusion, except the cessation of bloodshed. Possibly he might have gained more disciples, had he maintained the utter unlawfulness of war in the abstract ; or restricted its lawfulness to the case of actual invasion. Certain it is, that on few points did so many good men differ with him, as in his specific objection to the war against Bonaparte.

Politics never ruffled the serenity of Mr. Roscoe's mind, or blunted his taste for those studies which were its natural element. Of his devotion to botany, we have already had occasion to speak. Being a science requiring a minute investigation of forms, displaying in the clearest light, how nature loves beauty for its own sake, and moreover dependent upon the pencil for much of its material, it seems naturally associated with a love of the fine arts. In 1809 our author presented to the Linnœan Society a paper on the Scitamineæ, a singular and important class of plants, few or none of which are natives of Europe, (though some of them, as ginger, by no means strangers to European palates.) The structure of the Scitamineæ being peculiar, and opportunities of seeing the plants in their natural state not common, neither Linnæus, nor any of the French or German botanists had been able to distinguish or arrange them in a satisfactory method. This feat, the difficulty and merit of which only scientific botanists can appreciate, Mr. Roscoe is allowed to have performed, and was rewarded, as botanists are wont to reward whom they delight to honour, by giving his name to the new scitaminean genus, *Roscoea*, of which only one species is known to exist, a purple flower, discovered by Dr. Buchanan in Upper Nepaul.

It is doubtless pleasant to be remembered in connection with the lovely productions of nature, but the Linnæan names will never do for poetry, though some of those which Linnæus himself invented are fanciful and well sounding. *

In 1810, Roscoe addressed to the present Lord Chancellor a letter on parliamentary reform, which has recently been re-published.

At the general election in 1812, he was proposed, without his own consent or knowledge, as a candidate for Leicester, and polled a respectable minority. In the same year, he indulged his pen in a sarcastic review of Mr. Canning's Liverpool election speeches, which some zealous partizan had published in a well-sized volume. Such productions should be suffered to pass away with the election head-aches.

In 1814, Mr. Roscoe paid a long and pleasant visit to a man united to him by accordant politics and sympathetic love of agriculture, the venerable Coke of Norfolk. The farm and the library of Holkham were almost equal sources of gratification. The magnificent collection made by Lord Leicester, uncle to Mr. Coke, is peculiarly rich in Italian

---

* Mr. Roscoe's paper on the Scitamineæ is to be found in the 8th vol. of the Transactions of the Linnæan Society, p. 330.

By far the greater number of this genus are aromatic plants. The name Scitamineæ is from the Latin scitamentum, an artificial or *knowing* piece of cookery; any thing spicy and relishing.

literature. There Roscoe saw, touched, explored, and enjoyed six hundred MSS. volumes of ecclesiastical annals, and Italian civil history. Here he discovered, in thrice-hallowed penmanship, one of the lost volumes of Leonardo Da Vinci's Treatise on Mechanics, and the long deplored and precious tome in which Raffaello, at the request of the Roman Pontiff, had made pen sketches of the remains of Rome, illustrated by short descriptions in his own hand writing. The manuscripts had been little attended to for many years; they were in confusion and disorder, but so much the better; Roscoe must have had as great delight in arranging them as in arranging the Scitamineæ, but alas! some of them were injured by damp and time—a sad proof of the perishable nature of earthly things, and of the base ingratitude of mankind. But in Roscoe they had a friend who could arrest the hand of time, and make amends for the ingratitude of men. The whole MS. collection were confined to Mr. Roscoe's care, who put them into the hands of that eminent binder, the late Mr. John Jones,* (of

* We must honestly confess we have no other acquaintance with this eminent Bibliopegist, than what we derive from the honourable mention of him, in Dr. Traill's memoir. His high merits, however, in *clothing the naked*, forbid us to pass him by, when we have an opportunity of recording his services. It is no reason for not doing a man justice, that we never had the honour of his personal intimacy.

A word or two on the useful and elegant art to which Mr. John Jones owes his celebrity. Books, no less than their authors, are liable to get ragged, and to experience that neglect and contempt which generally follows the outward and visible signs of poverty. We do therefore most heartily commend the man, who bestows on a tattered and shivering volume, such decent and comely apparel, as may protect it from the insults of the vulgar, and the more cutting slights of the fair. But if it be a rare book, "the lone survivor of a numerous race," the one of its family that has escaped the trunk-makers and pastry-cooks, we would counsel a little extravagance in arraying it. Let no book perish, unless it be such an one as it is your duty to throw into the fire. There is no such thing as a worthless book, though there are some far worse than worthless; no book which is not worth preserving, if its existence may be tolerated; as there are some men whom it may be proper to hang, but none who should be suffered to starve. To *reprint* books that do not rise to a certain pitch of worth, is foolish. It benefits nobody so much as it injures the possessors of the original copies. It is like a new coinage of Queen Anne's farthings. That any thing is in being, is a presumptive reason that it should remain in being, but not that it should be multiplied.

The binding of a book should always suit its complexion. Pages, venerably yellow, should not be cased in military morocco, but in sober brown Russia. Glossy hot pressed paper looks best in vellum. We have sometimes seen a collection of old whitey-brown black letter ballads, &c. so gorgeously tricked out, that they remind us of the pious liberality of the Catholics, who dress in silk and gold the images of saints, part of whose saintship consisted in wearing rags and hair-cloth. The costume of a volume should also be in keeping with its subject, and with the character of its author. How

Liverpool,) who, by great industry and skill, succeeded in restoring crumpled vellum to its original smoothness, and in pasting torn leaves with wonderful neatness, and who bound the whole collection in a durable and elegant manner. An ancient and admirable copy of the Hebrew Pentateuch, believed to be more than a thousand years old, written in a beautiful hand on deer skins, forming a roll thirty-eight feet in length, was mounted by the same ingenious artist on rollers, ornamented with silver bells, under the direction of an ingenious Rabbi who believed the MS. to be an eastern transcript of great antiquity."

A catalogue of these invaluable manuscripts was drawn up by Mr. Roscoe, and Mr. Madan of the British Museum, extending to four or five thick folios, enriched with engraved fac-similes and illuminated ornaments. To the genuine Bibliomaniac, this catalogue must be a treasure indeed, but is a luxury within the reach of few. Mr. Roscoe continued to work at it till within a few months of his death.

It is painful to turn from such a scene of happiness as Holkham Library, with Roscoe rummaging its riches, to record how misfortune overtook the good man in his "chair-days" when he might have counted on the reward of a life of industry in a quiet old age. Various commercial calamities which we are unable to particularize, brought a pressure on the bank in which he was a partner, and obliged it to stop payment, in 1815. Mr. Roscoe struggled with his difficulties for four years, "entertaining throughout, the most sanguine hopes of being able finally to discharge all their engagements, as the joint property of the partners was valued, at the time of suspension of payment, at considerably more than the amount of their debts. The depreciation, however, of that property, combined with other circumstances over which Mr. Roscoe had no controul, prevented the accomplishment of his most earnest wishes, and in 1820 he became a bankrupt." *

During this four years' struggle, he alienated those treasures of art and learning which it had been the pride and pleasure of his life to gather together. Books, prints, drawings, pictures, all went, rather to testify his honour, than to satisfy his creditors. Yet his feelings were not aggravated either by the world's reproach or his own. Those who lost by his losses never questioned his integrity ; and he never

---

absurd to see the works of William Pen, in flaming scarlet, and George Fox's Journal in Bishop's purple! Theology should be solemnly gorgeous. History should be ornamented after the antique or gothic fashion. Works of science, as plain as is consistent with dignity. Poetry, *simplex munditiis.*

* Dr. Traill's Memoir.

complained, or had cause to complain, of any superfluous rigour from the persons to whom he was indebted. It was a common misfortune, which was to be divided as equally as possible.

Nothing can better display the composure or the vigour of his mind, under these trials, than the beautiful sonnet with which he took leave of his library:—

> As one who, destined from his friends to part,
> Regrets their loss, yet hopes again erewhile
> To share their converse and enjoy ther smile,
> And tempers, as he may, affliction's dart—
> Thus, lov'd associates! chiefs of elder art!
> Teachers of wisdom, who could once beguile
> My tedious hours, and brighten every toil,
> I now resign you, nor with fainting heart:
> For, pass a few short years, or days, or hours,
> And happier seasons may their dawn unfold,
> And all your sacred fellowships restore;
> When, freed from earth, unlimited its powers,
> Mind shall with mind direct communion hold,
> And kindred spirits meet, to part no more.

His books, consisting of more than two thousand works, produced no less a sum than £5150; the prints, £1886; the drawings, £750; the pictures, £3239: total, £11,025.

A selection of books, to the value of £600, was purchased by his friends at the sale, and presented for his acceptance; but this offer he thought proper to decline, and the books were deposited in the Athenæum, where they occupy a distinct compartment by themselves. A few of his pictures, to the amount of £50, were also bought in, and given to the Liverpool Royal Institution, an establishment of which Dr. Traill was the original suggester, and in which Mr. Roscoe had taken a lively interest. The sale took place in 1816.

In the course of that year, his labours and anxiety in winding up his affairs were so intense, as seriously to endanger his health; and upon one occasion he was attacked with a slight loss of memory at the bank, but a short interval of repose soon restored his faculties.

When the inevitable termination of his difficulties in bankruptcy delivered him from the trouble of an ever-lessening hope, he returned to his studies with his wonted calm assiduity, not vainly repining after worldly goods, on which he never set more than a due value. Whatever he had lost, he had not lost his friends; and he had soon to experience a proof of their continued regard, alike honourable to him and to themselves. We will relate this circumstance in the words of the memorialist who bore so large a part in it:

"It would be unjust to omit, that the misfortunes of our distinguished fellow-citizen called forth the warm sympathy of his numerous friends, and prompted them to take steps for securing him against their immediate consequences.   It is more necessary to state this, because many unjust imputations have been vented against the inhabitants of Liverpool, on account of their supposed neglect of Mr. Roscoe in his adversity.   There was considerable delicacy necessary in the steps which were taken to testify their esteem and attachment.   Mr. Roscoe had a noble and independent mind.   He had steadily refused the proffered gift of a valuable selection from his library, even after it had been for that purpose bought by his friends at the sale ; and those who had the pleasure of being intimate with him, well knew how necessary it would be to keep him in ignorance of what was intended, until it was accomplished.   During a second visit which he made to Holkham, a private fund was quickly subscribed among his friends, for the purchase of an annuity on the lives of Mr. and Mrs. Roscoe.   The delicate task of communicating what was done, devolved on me ; and in the correspondence which ensued between us, the example of his friend Charles James Fox, under similar circumstances, was successfully urged to reconcile his mind to receive this spontaneous homage to his talents and his worth, from sincerely attached friends."

Thus rescued from all apprehension of wanting the comforts which old age requires, Mr. Roscoe passed the remainder of his life in much tranquility ; and the works that he executed, at that advanced period, were neither few nor trifling.   But for a mind like his, stored with much and various knowledge, and long inured to composition, to produce a book was no more than healthy exercise.   The track of literature which he pursued requiring rather taste, judgment, and research, than strong effort and violent excitement, was smooth and easy to his declining years.   He never was an ambitious writer, never aimed at saying striking things, or constructing sentences which should seem to mean a great deal in a narrow space.   His powers were not dependent on the flow of youthful spirits, on mercurial agility of thought, or fiery animation of feeling ; neither did his studies demand that long-continued, abstract attention and introversion, which, as it is the latest faculty that man achieves, so is it the first to suffer by bodily decay.

In 1822, he published "*Illustrations of the Life of Lorenzo de' Medici,*" in which he defends his former works from the criticisms of Sismondi : and about the same time, a "*Memoir of Richard Roberts,*" a self-taught linguist, no less distinguished for the dirtiness of his person, than for the number of languages which he could read.   A very curious work might be written on men of a single talent. Nothing goes farther to prove the organic theory of the phrenologists, than the wonderful facility in acquiring languages occasionally exhibited by beings not far removed from fatuity. Perhaps the secret consists in preserving an infantile passiveness of mind, or more properly, in never outgrowing that condition of intellect in which children learn to speak. The profits of Mr. Roscoe's memoir were given to poor Roberts, who had hardly sense enough to take care of himself, and used to carry his polyglot library, as wanderers of more worldly wisdom, in better begging days, did their hoarded gold and silver—between his rags and his body.

In the year 1824, Mr. Roscoe appeared as the editor and biographer of Pope, an office which he executed with his wonted ability, and with the zeal of a disciple. Had Pope been his own bosom friend, he could not have dilated his virtues more fondly, or touched his failings with greater tenderness. In the court of fame Roscoe was always counsel for the panel, and has pleaded in mitigation of sentence for some very desperate reputations, such as Pope Alexander VI., Lucretia Borgia, and Bonaparte. It must therefore have been a delightful employment to him to vindicate the memory of a poet whose style of excellence was highly congenial to his sympathies, whose literary merit he thought unjustly depreciated, and whose moral character had been most ungently handled. Pope owes small thanks to his former biographers: Johnson, to whom he must needs have appeared the greatest of poets, (for of any higher order of poetry than that in which Pope is greatest, Johnson seems to have had no conception,) had so little respect for him as a man, that he exerted more than his usual industry in collecting anecdotes to render him odious and contemptible. But Johnson appears to have written the lives of the poets with no other view but to convince the world that they were no more than "indifferent children of the earth."*

* " Throughout the whole of those lives there appears an assumption of superiority in the biographer over the subject of his labours, which diminishes the idea of their talents, and leaves an unfavourable impression of their moral character. It could only be from the representations of Johnson that so amiable a man as Cowper could thus close his remarks on reading the Lives of the British Poets. 'After all it is a melancholy observation which it is impossible not to make, after having run through this series of poetical lives, that where there were such shining talents, there was so little virtue. These luminaries of our country seem to have been kindled into a brighter blaze than others, only that their spots might be more noticed; so much can nature do for our intellectual part, and so little for our moral. What vanity, what petulance in Pope! how painfully sensible of censure, and yet how restless in provocation! To what mean artifices could Addison stoop, in hopes of injuring the reputation of his friend! Savage! how sordidly vicious! and the more condemned

By later writers, Pope has been yet more unfavourably depicted. Some
have taken upon them the functions of the *Devil's Advocate*, whose place
was, whenever a saint was to be made, to shew cause why he should not
be canonized. It would, we think, have been very easy to assign to
Pope his proper rank among poets, so as to restore the highest seats to
their original and legitimate possessors, without repeating every aspersion which his satire provoked in an age of calumny. But Mr. Roscoe
has propitiated his manes by a bloodless offering of milk and honey;
and though he has not removed all unfavourable impressions as to Pope's
temper and disposition, he has boldly met, and triumphantly overthrown,
the more serious charges against his veracity, integrity, and moral
worth.

The circumstances of Pope's life which have given rise to most

for the pains that are taken to palliate his vices! offensive as they appear through a
veil, how would they disgust without one. What a sycophant to the public taste was
Dryden! sinning against his feelings, lewd in his writings, though chaste in his conversation. I know not but one might search these eight volumes with a candle, as
the prophet says, to find a MAN and not find ONE, unless, perhaps, ARBUTHNOT were
he.' Can this have been said in the country of Shakspeare, of Spenser, of Sidney,
and of Milton? of Donne, of Corbet, of Hall, of Marvel, and of Cowley? of Roscommon, of Garth, of Congreve, of Parnelle, of Rowe, and of Gay? of Thomson, of
Lyttleton, and of Young? of Shenstone, of Akenside, of Collins, of Goldsmith, of
Mason, and of Gray?

> Unspotted names! and, memorable long,
> If there before, in virtue, or in song!

The lustre of which, as well as of many others that might be adduced, can never be
obscured, either by the most morbid malignity, or the darkest fanaticism."—*Roscoe's
Preface to the Life of Pope.*

The general drift of this passage is undoubtedly just, yet it may be doubted
whether, if Roscoe himself had written the lives of all those worthies he has here
named, (and some of the greatest are not included in Johnson's series,) he would have
brought Cowper to a more favourable conclusion. Had Johnson been as affectionate
to the reputation of all his subjects as he has proved himself to that of Savage, he
could not, with any regard to truth, have exhibited such MEN as Cowper longed for.
He might indeed have exhibited their virtues in a much stronger light, but there must
still have been enough of the old leaven to justify Cowper in saying "*so much can
nature do for our intellectual part, and so little for our moral.*" The great mistake seems
to be, first in expecting that a poet, as such, should be superior to human littleness,
and then in exaggerating his actual defects through the spleen of disappointment.
The world ignorantly expects that a great man shall be great even in his faults; but
this expectation is not borne out by experience; and if it were just, a great poet is not
ex-officio a great man. Of all our poets, we know none but Sir Philip Sidney and
Milton, who had, or made any, pretence to be *great men.* The faults of poets are
often more akin to those of ill-educated women than to those of great men. Yet it
would be hard to prove that the poets, as a body, have been less virtuous than any
class of citizens, who were not officially obliged to be professors of virtue.

animadversion, are 1st. his quarrel with Addison ; 2nd. his equivocal gallantry with Lady Wortley Montague, and his subsequent gross attacks upon her ; 3rd. his clandestine satire upon the Duke of Chandos, under the character of Timon, aggravated by the subterfuges by which he evaded the Duke's indignation ; 4th. his circuitous plot to get his letters published, and throw the onus of the publication on others ; 5th. his printing the character of Atossa, after receiving money to suppress it ; 6th. his connection with Martha Blount. For the last mentioned lady, Mr. Roscoe is a determined champion. Indeed he displays more warmth than the occasion justifies. In the name of honour, conscience, and humanity, what right has the *world*, the *public*, *posterity*, or whatever else a knot of busy individuals may think proper to call themselves, to institute an inquistorial examination into the *feelings* with which a valetudinarian regarded a female to whose society and attentions he was indebted for making his life endurable, and perhaps mankind are indebted for some of the noblest works which make him the object of their prurient curiosity. Before such self-appointed coroners, it was unworthy of Roscoe to give evidence. We must not omit to mention, however, that he completely exculpates Miss Blount from the charge of cold and unfeeling behaviour to Pope in his last moments. We are not sure, however, that " it was not till our own days that an attempt has been made to defame the memory of an elegant and accomplished woman, who passed through life honoured and respected." Defamation was quite as much the vice of Pope's age as of ours, though perhaps the poison was not then so rapidly and extensively diffused as by the machinery of the modern press. The truth is, that it was not till our age that such *liaisons* as that supposed to exist between Pope and his female friend were judged by the rigid rule of morals. The slanderers of no age are particularly eager to ascribe vices which that age will not think the worse of a man for having. In Pope's time it was necessary to impute extravagant follies, or horrid vices ; now slight imperfections will serve the turn as well. That we are more moral than our forefathers it were presumptuous to say ; but we certainly fix the standard of social morality much higher.

But it is very different with regard to those charges, which, if true, must convict Pope of gross ingratitude, duplicity, and malignity, in the discharge of his public office as a Poet. Here the world is the legitimate judge of his fame, and owes a satisfaction to the memory of those whom he is supposed to have injured. Here his advocate pleads before a competent tribunal, and rests his defence not on vain surmises and hypotheses, but on fair induction and comparison of evidence. We cannot help thinking that Mr. Roscoe's habits of business, and particularly his legal occupations, greatly assisted him in that most important part of an historian's duty, the adducing of documentary evidence. Two thirds of the grounds on which the later biographers of Pope have built their most unfavourable inferences, is cut away from under them by a careful revision of dates. Now a merchant always looks at the date of a paper, an author seldom or never. It will, however, sometimes occur to a historian, as to a judge, that he has to choose between conflicting testimonies, without any other guide than the general credibility and character of the witnesses, and in these cases the simple denial of an accused party, unsupported by circumstantial evidence, goes for nothing in a court of law. But not so in the courts of conscience and of history. Indeed where the question concerns motives and meanings, the bare affirmation of an honest man ought to weigh against the suspicions and asseverations, and hearsay reports of a thousand others. Upon these principles Mr. Roscoe has conducted his defence of Pope, which is not a shewy piece of special pleading, such as might suit any case however flagrant, but the honest endeavour of a good man to arrive at the truth.

The charge which perhaps lays heaviest upon Pope's reputation, is that of having suborned some person or persons to carry his letters to Curl, in order to gain a pretext for publishing them himself. Johnson has taken the most unfavourable view of this transaction, and yet spoken of it with an indifference not very consistent with his duty as *first moralist*. If his representation of it be true, Pope was a scoundrel. But Mr. Roscoe has satisfactorily shewn, that, unless credit be given to the self-contradictory evidence of Curl, a man who had no character to lose, there is not a shadow of proof that Pope was privy to this dirty business, though he might probably enough be anything but sorry that it was as it was. The case is made out with peculiar clearness and legal acumen; but for the details, we must refer to the " Life " itself, which ought to be, and we hope soon will be, published separately from the bulky edition of Pope's writings to which it is prefixed, though that too is worthy a place in the libraries of such as can afford expensive luxuries.

The characters of Atticus and of Atossa, and the description of Timon's villa, are perhaps the finest pieces of satire in the English language; and it would be most grievous to think that Pope was a villain, when he was enriching our literature so bountifully. As to the first, he had a perfect right to compose it, if he thought it true, and to publish it, unless he had promised the contrary, which is not asserted. Whether it be, or be not, a true portrait of Addison, is now of as little consequence, as whether Justice Shallow be a correct resemblance of Sir Thomas Lucy. The character is true—its prototype is to be found in every generation : happy will it be when the picture has no living original.

The Atossa is by no means so perfect. It is, in the true sense of the word, *personal* ; for though the separate features may be found in nature every day, yet they have no necessary coherence or inter-dependence. If you were not told that there *had been* such a woman, you could find no reason in general nature that there *should be* such a one. Atticus is a hundred men, but Atossa must always be Sarah Duchess of Marlborough. This is the test that distinguishes legiti-mate satire from lampooning, a Hogarth from a caricaturist, a Fielding* from a *fashionable novelist.* The question should be, not, Is the picture taken from individual life? but, Does its effect require that the individual likeness be recognized?

Yet there is one line in this character which is worth a volume of morality, and explains all the misanthropy, and no small part of the suicide in the world :—

" Sick of herself, for very selfishness."

notwithstanding which line, Pope would have been a much better man if he had never written the character at all. For his virulent person-ality, for the rancorous and unprovoked hatred which he cherished against that high-minded woman and her illustrious spouse, his gene-rous advocate offers no apology ; but for the story of his taking money to suppress the verses, Mr. Roscoe has proved that it rests on no sufficient foundation. This point had been cleared up before, in an excellent article of the " Quarterly Review."

As to the supposed breach of hospitality committed in the description of Timon's gardens, &c., there is not much in it after all. There is no indication of a *malus animus* ; and Pope, as Mr. Roscoe says, ought to be believed when he declared, that the passage had no *specific* appli-cation to Canons. It is a false taste of magnificence, a cumbrous and ungenial hospitality—not any individual Duke—that is held up to ridicule. Gratitude for a wearisome dinner could never fairly require of Pope to suppress his animadversions on " trees cut to statues," and such like enormities, because they happened to be found at Canons.

* We mention Fielding rather than a later great name, because in Sir Walter's works there is no character, that could possibly be meant for any living individual, which the original might not be proud to acknowledge. Sir Walter has shewn that there is no natural or necessary connection between laughter and scorn; that all the pleasure to be derived from a perception of the ludicrous, may be combined with perfect love and veneration of the being at whom you smile. Fielding *could* do this, but he has done it too seldom.

3 z

If the Curate dine now and then with the Squire, are all the Squire's vices to be left out of the litany? There is no fouler accusation than that of ingratitude, and yet there is none which is scattered so much at random.

We cannot say that Mr. Roscoe has been equally successful in treating of Pope's conduct to Lady Wortley Montague. It says little indeed for her Ladyship's conscience, that she should suppose a piece of gross ribaldry applied to her; and still less for her prudence, that she should openly resent an allusion which a delicate lady of our times would not be supposed to understand. But Pope's denial, which Mr. Roscoe takes seriously, appears to us to be malignantly ironical; this, indeed, is not the only occasion whereon Roscoe betrays a simplicity, which, taken in concert with his high intellectual powers, evinces no less genius than virtue.

All things considered, he has certainly left the character of Pope much clearer than he found it. It is plain enough, that the faults of that little man were in a great measure owing to his infirmities; while his virtues, and they were not few nor small, were his own. It is needless to say, that Roscoe was not of those who maintain that Pope is no Poet. He calls him the most *harmonious, correct,* and *popular* of English Poets, and we shall not argue the point here. Undoubtedly he was the best writer in his line. He could not have been Milton: and is it not better to have a Milton and a Pope, than two Miltons? or, which is likelier to befal, a *great* Milton and a *little* Milton?

In the year 1824, Mr. Roscoe was chosen "A Royal Associate of the Royal Society of Literature," an institution, of which the best design (and a truly excellent one) was, to give £100 a year each to ten literary gentlemen of mature age and narrow means. They were selected impartially, without regard to party, and were only required to produce and read an occasional essay, by way of quit rent. This association was broken up at the decease of King George IV., no funds having been provided for its continuance. May the poor, and *the poor in spirit,* be the better for the saving. Perhaps it is best as it is. Literary men now must understand, that they have nothing but their own industry and frugality to depend upon, and have no temptation to turn aside from the direct path of truth. Augustus and Louis XIV. did not benefit literature half so much by their liberality, as they disgraced it by the adulation with which that liberality was solicited and re-paid.

In the year following his appointment, Mr. Roscoe received the gold medal of the society, value 50 guineas, for his merits as an historian.

Two great works, of very unequal importance indeed, remain to be spoken of, which occupied the declining years of Roscoe's life, and sufficiently proved at once the versatility of his talents, and the perfection in which he retained them to the last.

The one was a series of plates and descriptions, illustrative of his adopted family, the Scitamineæ. This was printed at Liverpool, and is said to be "the most splendid work that every issued from a provincial press." We confess we never saw any part of it; nor should we be able to judge of its scientific merits if we had; but the most uninformed may understand that it was no trifling honour, for a man divided between many studies, and distracted by many cares, to gain a lasting fame in a walk of investigation, which men of considerable renown have thought a sufficient employment for their undivided powers. The plates were many of them from his own drawings, but the greater part from those of two ladies, his daughter-in-law Mrs. Edward Roscoe, and Miss R. Miller. In the execution of this design, he found great benefit from that botanic garden, which he had himself so great a share in establishing. What reception the work met with is testified by the fact, that before the second number was published, there was a call for more of the first than had originally been struck off.

The other, and greater labour, led his observation into a far less pleasing class of subjects, and called him to consider the most painful and perhaps the most difficult problem in civil polity, that of criminal jurisprudence, which engaged the last serious thoughts he devoted to earth.

We have more than once adverted to his political writings, and have not scrupled to declare our conviction that they shew him to have been a better man than a pamphleteer. Neither his heart nor his head seem suited to the trade. But when a great question of moral policy was to be argued; when the reason of man was to be reconciled with his noblest feelings, mercy to be identified with justice, and humanity with wisdom; there was a call as apt as meet for the ripest fruits of Roscoe's powers, and he obeyed it promptly and joyfully.

In 1819, he published his "*Observations on penal Jurisprudence, and the reformation of Criminals; with an Appendix, containing the latest Reports of the State-Prisons, or Penitentiaries of Philadelphia, New-York, and Massachusets, and other Documents.*" As the subject has been so frequently reconsidered since that time, and so many recruits have been continually added to the once little band of the champions of justice, much of what Roscoe advanced as neglected truth, will already appear as stale truism. We have discovered little in the treatise which he was the first to utter; but he has put the arguments against excessive punishment in a peculiarly concise and tangible form, and has expressed his conviction that reformation is the sole legitimate end of punishment, and moral improvement the only effective mean of reformation, with an outpouring of the heart, a meek solemnity, which cannot fail to make the most positive supporters of "things as they are," confess that there is a view of the subject neither absurd nor unchristian, very different from that which themselves have taken. The first head he considers is, "*the motives and ends of punishment.*" And here we cannot help noticing a remarkable omission. Mr. Roscoe seems to take it for granted, that the ends of all penal enactments have been either vindictive, or preventive, or corrective; either intended for satisfaction to the offended parties, or to prevent the repetition of the offence by terror and example, or to amend the criminal by suffering. But he does not recollect, that men in past ages considered the punishment of the guilty as an atonement, an expiation, a sacrifice, an indefeasible duty, the neglect of which involved the whole community in the guilt of the individual offender; that this supposed duty had no reference to the angry feelings of the injured persons, far less to general consequences, and least of all to any contingent benefit of the criminal, but to an everlasting law of retribution, of which the municipal law was only the exponent and instrument. The feeling on which this doctrine is founded, had probably never been cherished in Roscoe's bosom; nor was the doctrine often formally broached in his hearing, except, it may be, in reference to the eternal dealings of Divine Justice, which his good sense must have shewn him could be no authority for the dealings of sinful man with his fellow sinners. Still he might have found traces of the prevalence of such a doctrine, in scripture and in history; he might have found it in Shakspeare, in the rites and laws of honour, and in the feelings of the multitude. We are very, very far from assenting to the doctrine. It is, we conceive, a fearfully false inference from an awful truth; an inference recognized neither by Reason nor by Christianity. That the *crime* of each contains the *sin* of all, admonishes all to repent, proves to all the necessity of *some* Expiation, we do most firmly believe; but not that the sufferings or the death of the guilty can deliver either himself or the avenger from guiltiness. The blood of a murderer can no more atone for the murder, than it can resuscitate the murdered.

But without entering into further discussion of this doctrine of penal atonement, which, false as we esteem it, should never be confounded with the animal passion of revenge, it is sufficient to remark, that it is of considerable historical importance, in accounting for the ferocity of certain codes. The principle of sacrificing lives at the altar of expediency, and multiplying punishments for the security of property, is a heresy of later origin, founded in nothing but cowardice and selfishness. Roscoe is perfectly right in rejecting anger as a right motive to punishment; and it is a wonder that any rational being should assert that it is so. Indeed, one object in the appointment of fixed laws and official judges, is to exclude the influence of anger. If not, every man ought to be judge in his own cause, for who else can tell how much vengeance the stomach of his anger may require? If it be said, that, according to the terms of the social contract, each individual resigns his right of revenge to the state, which is bound to see that he does not lose by the surrender, we reply that neither Reason nor Religion acknowledge any such right. If acts of retaliation be ever justifiable, it is not on the principle of vengeance, but of self-defence.

Mr. Roscoe's second head is *" On punishment by way of example,"* under which he treats the sophistries of Paley with no more respect than they deserve. The following passage is so admirable that we can not forbear it :—"Example can only be legitimately obtained through the medium of justice; but as there is no rule to determine what degree of punishment is necessary to be inflicted in order to deter others from crimes, legislators have in all ages been induced to carry punishments to their utmost possible extent, so as to make examples still more horrible and striking; and thus this idea of the prevention of crimes by the severity of punishment, when carried to such a degree, has been a principal cause of the calamities of the human race, and has rendered the world a constant theatre of injustice and bloodshed.

"But whilst severe punishments are ineffectually resorted to, for the purpose of securing society from injury, they seem to deteriorate and degrade the public character, and to weaken, in the people at large, those dispositions which ought to be cherished with the greatest care. Nor is it the lower classes alone whose moral feelings are corrupted, and whose sensibilities are destroyed, by the establishment of systems of severity and terror. As the contest increases between obstinacy and crime on the one hand, and resentment and cruelty on the other, a similar effect is produced on every rank of society, all of whom become, by degrees, prepared to inflict, to suffer, or to witness every extreme of violence. The result of the destructive maxim, that mankind are to be kept in awe by terror alone, then becomes apparent, and desolation and death stalk through the city at noon-day. Such were the times when Henry VIII. sat upon the throne of England, employed in devising the most plausible pretexts, and the most horrible modes of destroying his people, whilst the Judges and Peers of the land became the ready instruments of his most cruel measures. The number of executions in his reign is stated to have been seventy-two thousand persons, being

efforts that have been made for this purpose, with the immense task that yet remains unaccomplished, we cannot flatter ourselves with having made any extraordinary progress. We seem as yet to have had but an imperfect glance of the true principles upon which a virtuous education is founded, and to have allowed a scanty and partial cultivation of the intellect to supersede the more important cultivation of the heart. The further this kind of instruction is carried, the more doubtful is its expediency, if the affections and feelings have not had an equal share of attention, as it places a weapon in the hands of youth; without directing them in the use of it. To suppose that talents and virtue are inseparably united, is to close our eyes against daily experience ; yet we neglect to avail ourselves of those tender years in which the deepest impressions are made, to form the character for the benefit of society, and to cultivate those seeds of social affection which nature has implanted in every human bosom. By a just retribution for our folly, it costs us more to punish crimes than it would to prevent them. Independent of all that the community suffers by plunder and depredation, in frequent bloodshed, and continual annoyance, it is harrassed a second time in bringing the offenders to justice ; and it may safely be asserted, that the amount it expends for this purpose, more than doubles the spoliation sustained. Perhaps a day may yet arrive, when it may be thought worth while to consider whether the great and annually increasing amount expended in bringing criminals to justice, would not be better devoted to the inculcation, on the minds and temper of youth, of such principles and dispositions as might prevent the perpetration of those crimes which it is now employed to punish."

Thus far Roscoe speaks like himself ; but when he advises legislators to appeal to the sense of honour and of shame, and to substitute disgraceful for painful penalties, we are inclined to demur. Honour and shame are feelings bestowed by nature for wise ends : their extinction marks the last hopeless stage of depravity ; but, like all other passions, they are good only so far as they are natural and necessary. They should never be artificially excited, or diverted from their instinctive course,—far less should they be enthroned in the seat of reason. But above all (and which is more to our present question), shame should never be made a punishment, nor should punishment be rendered unnecessarily shameful. If the punishment be capital, can it be right to distract the thoughts of the vilest malefactor, by withdrawing them from his own state to the opinions of curious or unfeeling gazers ? Is it right to desecrate the awfulness of death, by associations of gratuitous ignominy? Surely a day of execution should be a day of mourning and general humiliation ; but the correlative passion of shame is scorn, which makes Man proud, and what is worst of all, proud of others' disgrace, which he ought to consider his own. If, on the other hand, the punishment be not capital, the infliction of ignominy almost precludes the chance of reformation. It exiles the poor victim from all social sympathies; it begets either deadly resentment, or utter shamelessness; it induces, nay compels, a wretch, to whom solitude must needs be unindurable, to herd with those whose glory is in their shame. Rather let the code of Draco be executed by Rhadamanthus, and every offence be visited with the avenging sword, than condemn that man to live, whom the law has made a bye-word, and a plague-spot.

In the ensuing parts of his work, Mr. Roscoe considers the subject of capital and secondary punishments minutely. The infliction of death he appears to disapprove *in toto*, and appeals to the good success attending its abolition by the Grand Duke of Tuscany, in 1786. Whatever may be the tendency of individual opinions on the lawfulness or expediency of taking life for life, it is highly unadvisable to moot the point in the present state of public feeling. Such discussions could only retard that mitigation at which the advocates of humanity are aiming, by weakening their most *taking* argument; viz., the apparent injustice of subjecting unequal crimes to equal penalties.

The consideration of *punishments of inferior degree* led him to speak of penitentiaries. We cannot follow him through his various details on this head, which occupy the most considerable part of his volume, and a long appendix. He was clearly of opinion that a prison might be rendered a school of reformation. But while he contends for the necessity of seclusion and strict superintendence, he deprecates all extreme harshness, and particularly disapproves of solitary confinement.

Some remarks on the penitentiary system in the United States, repeated and reinforced in subsequent pamphlets, engaged Mr. Roscoe in a controversy with several writers of that republic, which commenced in 1825, and was only finished with his last exertions in this world. His intense application to this labour perhaps tended to shorten his days. But it was a cause to which he begrudged not the remains of his strength. It was a point where he was happy to say,—

Hic cæstus artemque repono.
My work is done: I here resign the pen,
And all my skill to plead the cause of men.

He had the comfort to hear that his arguments had not been vainly wafted over the Atlantic; that a milder plan had been adopted in the treatment of those unhappy beings, whom it was his hope, and struggle, and prayer to restore to the condition of useful citizens, and

4 A

the higher dignity of good men. Dr. Traill mentions having heard him declare, not long before his departure, "that no literary distinction had ever afforded him half the gratification he received from the reflection on the part he had taken in this great question; and he expressed his satisfaction, that he now might be permitted to think that he had not lived altogether in vain."

He was then fast approaching the period when such reflections are most of all precious. In the winter of 1827, in consequence of intense application to his work on Penitentiaries, to which he was urged by the approaching departure of a vessel for America, he was attacked with paralysis of the muscles of the tongue and mouth. His friend and physician Dr. Traill was immediately called; the patient was freely bled, on which he recovered his speech, and the introduction of a seton into his neck removed the paralytic affection of his mouth. Intense study was forbidden, and after an interval of perfect relaxation from his literary occupations, he recovered sufficiently to be able to complete his botanical work and the catalogue of Mr. Coke's library, and to correct for the press his latest tracts on prison discipline. It was a great satisfaction to find his intellect quite entire; and it remained so to within an hour of his death.*

For some time he had entertained a design of translating, in concert with Dr. Traill, Lanzi's "History of Italian Painting," a work which his own increasing years, and the various avocations of his associate, induced him to relinquish; with the less regret, as it devolved upon his son to execute the task, to his own and his father's honour.

The last public works of Mr. Roscoe were, a letter congratulating the Lord Chancellor Brougham on his elevation to the woolsack; and an earnest solicitation to La Fayette, on the arrest of Polignac and the other Carlist Ministers, urging him, by the utmost exertion of his authority and influence, not to let the triumph of the "three days" be stained by bloody and vindictive executions. So accordant were all the acts of Roscoe's life and pen.

Though he was now incapable of sustaining the excitement of promiscuous society, in the bosom of his family, and with a few old and valued friends, he still enjoyed an innocent cheerfulness. Death approached, not unforeseen, yet gently—rather announced by increasing weakness, than by actual pain. He looked calmly on the passage he had so soon to make. Not many days before his last, he was heard to declare, "that he thanked the Almighty for having permitted him to pass a life of much happiness, which, though somewhat checkered with vicissitudes, had been on the whole one of much enjoyment; and

* Dr. Traill's Memoir.

he trusted that he would be enabled to resign it cheerfully whenever it pleased God to call him."

That call was made on the 30th of June, 1831, when a fit of influenza ended the life of Roscoe.

His many friends, and many more who would gladly have been his friends, will look impatiently for the publication of his correspondence, and the more perfect picture of his mind and habits, the more minute narrative of his transactions, which may be expected from Mr. Henry Roscoe. Meanwhile, we trust we have done him no injustice, and have gratified our own feelings, by thus publicly testifying our respect to his memory.

From a general survey of what Roscoe was, did, and wrote, his character seems happily expressed in the words of Tacitus; "*Bonum virum facile credas, magnum libenter.*" The goodness of his heart appears in every page of his writings, and was in all his ways; but to discover the extraordinary powers of his intellect, and the noble energy of his will, it is necessary to consider the variety of his accomplishments, and the perseverant efforts of his long life for the benefit of his kind. His brightest literary praise is unquestionably that of a biographer and historian; but it was a far higher glory, that he was a grey-headed friend of freedom. The Romans went forth from their city, when threatened with a siege, to thank the Consul who fled from Cannæ, because he had not despaired of the republic. How should that man be honoured, who, after the disappointment of a hundred hopes, after a hundred vicissitudes of good and ill, *never despaired of human nature?*

P. S. We are aware that Mr. Roscoe wrote many things in periodicals, &c., of which we have given no account. Among the rest, a poem on the *progress of engraving.* But we cannot forbear to mention "*Butterflies Ball,*" which, though published merely as a child's book, has the true spirit of Faery poesy, and reminds one of the best things in Herrick.

CAPTAIN JAMES COOK.

It is by no means easy to do justice to this great and good man, or to distinguish amid the acts and accidents of his life, what was personal from what was adventitious; what was truly admirable from what was only extraordinary. Any child will wonder when shewn the picture of a man who has sailed round the world; but this wonder past, an inconsiderate or uninformed mind might enquire, what did Cook that might not have been done by hundreds? To circumnavigate the planet, even twice or thrice, could not, in the eighteenth century, make a Columbus or a Magelhaens, any more than a trip from the Archipelago to the Black Sea would make an Argonaut. To the unique greatness of him, who, in the faith of science, first sought a westward passage to the East, Cook had no claim; and in wild adventures, marvellous sights, appalling privations, hair-breadth-scapes, and terrific daring; in the romantic, the imaginative, the poetical, his voyages, though by no means barren, are certainly far exceeded by those of earlier discoverers. Whether any landsman, however scientific, can fairly appreciate the merit of Cook as a navigator and an improver of navigation, is extremely doubtful; certainly, words cannot convey the peculiar nature or aspect of his difficulties, and therefore must give a very inadequate apprehension of his skill in surmounting them. Our nautical readers will excuse our brevity and imperfection, and if need be, our probable errors in technicals. Nor is it possible, in a popular work, to explain to the uninitiate the extent of his benefits to geography, astronomy, and magnetism; how much he contributed to elucidate the sympathetic laws which bind the universe together, or what he added to our knowledge of the animal and vegetable productions of the earth.

But the moral greatness of Cook, his perfection of self-command, the power whereby he impressed inferior minds with the feeling of his mental superiority in emergencies, where nothing but such an impression could have maintained obedience, his considerate and manly humanity, his pastoral anxiety for all entrusted to his charge, his industrious zeal for the good of men so far removed from European sympathies and associations, that many would hardly have acknowledged them for fellow-creatures, the strength of his intellect in conceiving and comprehending great ends, his adroitness in adapting, his perseverance in applying means conducive to those ends; all, in short, which constitute the *man*, apart from the *science* and the *profession*, may be rendered intelligible to all; and to these points we shall direct our principal attention.

James Cook was born on the 27th of October, 1728. His father was an agricultural labourer, or farm-servant, who migrated from his native Northumberland, to the northern district of Yorkshire, called Cleveland. In the small village of Marton, in the North-Riding, midway between Gisbrough and Stockton-upon-Tees, the circumnavigator was born in a clay-biggin, which his fame has not protected from demolition. His mother's christian name was Grace, and he was one of nine children. No wonder if his first years were familiar with poverty and privation. Yet his parents, who seem to have been good in a class where goodness is not rare, contrived, even from the pittance of a labourer's wages, to set apart a few pence weekly, to procure for their offspring such instruction as the village dame could supply. Notwithstanding the obscurity of Cook's childhood, the name of his spectacled tutoress has been preserved from oblivion. It was Dame Walker. Whether the future navigator was distinguished by a rapid progress in A B C, we have not ascertained; but judging by analogy, we should rather conjecture the reverse. The men, who ultimately do their instructers most credit, are frequently those who give them most trouble; and strong masculine minds, whose characteristic is austere good sense, and that rigid self-controul which qualifies alike to obey and to command, seldom acquire the elements of any knowledge rapidly. A truly great man generally has the reputation of a dull boy. It is not recorded whether dame Walker discovered the germs of genius in young Cook, or whether he displayed, in childhood, that inquisitive spirit which afterwards conducted him round the globe. If he did, it is probable that his enquiries procured him more whipping than information; for there is nothing that teachers of the old school dislike more in a pupil than asking questions, especially if they chance to be questions out of the scope of the said teachers' knowledge.

The village dame, a character so useful in fact, so delightful to contemplation, and so beautifully described by Shenstone, is fast disappearing from society. Compared to the speed and efficiency of modern plans of education, their methods of instruction were as the toil of the distaff and spindle to the operation of the spinning jenny. It would be idle to regret a change which may produce much good, and which the present condition of the community in a manner necessitates; yet it is not without a strong feeling of interest that we regard the few survivors of this venerable sisterhood, and we cannot bear to see their little charges, their joy and their pride, taken from under their care. It is a common-place argument against improvements in education, that the new systems will never produce greater or better men than have grown up under the old ones. Persons who pursue this line of reasoning, may possibly point to the fame of Cook, in order to vindicate the sufficiency of dames' schools for popular education. But it is extremely unjust and delusive to calculate either the merit of individual teachers, or the value of establishments and systems by the number or eminence of the great men reared under them. For not to mention that all great men are, in some sort, *self* educated, the methods and circumstances most favourable to the maturing and exercise of great faculties, whether moral or intellectual, are by no means the most favourable to average hearts and minds. The most saintly virtue is often produced in the most dissolute ages, and appears in persons whose youth has been beset by temptation and ill-example. But that master, that university, that system is to be preferred, which produces the *best mediocrity*, and whose pupils are most generally *respectable*.

When little Cook had attained his eighth year, his father, who bore an excellent character for industry, frugality, and integrity, obtained the humble but confidential situation of hind, or agricultural superintendent of the farm of Airy Holme, near Great Ayton, belonging to Thomas Skottowe, Esq. Hither the good man removed with his family. James was sent, at Mr. Skottowe's expense, to a day school in the neighbourhood, where he was taught writing, and the fundamental rules of arithmetic—sufficient learning to qualify him for the situation of a shopkeeper, which is often the highest mark of rural ambition. There is something very tempting, especially to a mother, in the name of profits ; and tender parents of low condition are desirous of procuring in-door employments for their offspring. Before he was full thirteen years old, James was apprenticed to a haberdasher, at Staiths, near Whitby, then a considerable fishing town. The daily sight of vessels, and the conversation of seamen, soon discovered to his young mind that the sea was his vocation : he quarrelled with the shop, obtained his discharge, leaped over the counter, and bound himself for seven years to John and Henry Walker, of Whitby, two worthy brothers, of the society of friends, who were extensively engaged in the coal trade, and joint owners of the ship Free-Love, on board of which Mr. Cook spent the greater part of his marine apprenticeship ; and when that was expired, he continued to serve as a common sailor in the coasting trade, which, although it may furnish little to gratify either a wild passion for adventure, or the more laudable thirst for various knowledge, affords toil and hardship, peril and experience, in daily abundance. At length he was raised to the station of mate in one of John Walker's vessels. This is a favourable testimony to his general conduct, though it does not appear that the superiority of his mind was observed by his employers, or that any presentiment of his high destination had dawned upon himself. He was learning the practical detail of his profession, and perhaps meditating, through the long hours of the night-watch, on the scientific principles and possible improvements of navigation. During these years, it is probable that he never launched far from the British shores. The Newcastle coal trade, in which he was principally engaged, has long been " the nursery of British seamen," or rather a sort of government *preserve*, an unfailing resource, whenever the ocean is to be made the area of plunder, and the high-way of death.

In the spring of 1755, when certain disputes respecting the boundaries of the French and English settlements in North America, left undecided at the clumsy negociations of Aix-la-Chapelle, had produced aggressions which were supposed to render war "just and necessary," a hot press of sailors took place in all the principal ports of the kingdom. Cook's vessel was then lying in the Thames, and as he had little chance of escape or concealment, and perhaps secretly longed for a wider sphere of activity than the home commerce supplied, he resolved to prevent the indignity of impressment, by volunteering into the royal navy. He went to a rendezvous at Wapping, and entered with an officer of the Eagle man-of-war, a ship of sixty guns, then commanded by Captain Hamer. When Captain (afterwards Admiral Sir Hugh) Palliser was appointed to the Eagle, in October, 1755, he found James Cook already distinguished as an able and meritorious seaman, exact and adroit in the performance of his duty, and bearing marks of more intelligence than the duties of a fore-mast man called into exercise. All the officers concurred in testifying to his merits, and Captain Palliser gave him as much countenance and encouragement as the necessarily aristocratic discipline of the navy permits a commander to bestow upon a common man. Nor were his deserts unknown or neglected in his native province, for Mr. Osbaldeston, M. P. for Scarborough, wrote to the Captain, informing him that several neighbouring gentlemen had much interested themselves in behalf of one Cook, whom he understood to be a sailor on board the Eagle, and whom it was thought desirable to raise to a more advantageous station. Mr. Osbaldeston requested to know in what manner he might best conduce to the young man's promotion. Captain Palliser, in reply, admitted the justice of Cook's claims, and as the rules of the service did not allow him to be raised to a commission, suggested the propriety of procuring him a Master's warrant. The exertions of his friends were prompt and persevering, for no less than three such warrants were procured within five days. First for the Grampus sloop, which was found to be already furnished with a Master; secondly, to the Garland, which had sailed just a day before; and thirdly, to the Mercury, to which last he was actually appointed, May 15th, 1759. Though little is recorded of his proceedings in the four years intervening between 1755 and 1759, there can be no doubt that he employed himself in pursuits very different from the ordinary routine of a common sailor's life; and that his talents and proficiency were tried, proved, and appreciated by his superiors, since we shall soon see him recommended to a service requiring great science, experienced intrepidity, and that cool readiness of resource, which no difficulty finds unprovided.

The destination of the Mercury was to North America, where she joined the squadron under Admiral Sir Charles Saunders, then lying in the river St. Lawrence, to co-operate with the land forces under General Wolfe, in the famous siege of Quebec. When Wolfe was meditating his attack on the French camp at Montmorenci and Beauport, it was judged necessary that the soundings of the river, between the Isle of Orleans and the north shore should be accurately taken, in order that the Admiral might lay his ships so as to cover the approach of the army to the hostile posts. To this service Cook was specially recommended by Captain Palliser; and though it is doubted whether he had ever taken a pencil in his hand before, such was his natural sagacity, that he executed his difficult task in the most complete manner, and produced a chart which was long the model and authority of all others. As the tract of water to be explored was commanded by the enemy's shot, the work was altogether performed by night. Yet could it not escape observation. A number of canoes and Indians were collected in a wood by the water side, which, launching forth under favour of the darkness, were very near surprising our navigator, and cutting short his destined career. Unprovided with force or means for resistance, and unable to conjecture the number of the assailants, who came upon him before he was aware, he had nothing but to run for it, and get under shelter of the English hospital on Orleans Isle. So close was he pressed, that some of the Indians entered at the stern of his boat while he leaped out at the bow.

After the capture of Quebec, Mr. Cook was appointed, by a warrant from Lord Colvill, master of the Northumberland, which was laid up for the winter at Halifax, Nova Scotia, where his Lordship had the command of a squadron as Commodore. During this winter, Mr. Cook became first acquainted with Euclid, and with the more advanced theorems of astronomy. It is a peculiar advantage of the exact sciences that they may be acquired from a few books, and without any tuition. For practical purposes they are perhaps better thus acquired, than by the regular modes.

Cook was present, in September, 1762, at the recapture of Newfoundland, was employed in surveying the coasts and harbours, and obtained the signal approbation of Colonel Amherst and Captain Graves. At the close of the same year he returned to England; and on the 21st of December, married, at Barking, in Essex, Miss Elizabeth Batts, an amiable woman, who deserved and attained his full affection and confidence; but the state of a sailor's wife is for the most part a wedded widowhood.

Early in 1763, Captain Graves was sent out a second time as Governor of Newfoundland, and Mr. Cook again accompanied him as surveyor. Some difficulty was experienced in carrying the provisions of the recent treaty of Paris into execution, and some consequent delay obstructed Cook in his operations, which were, however, satisfactorily brought to a close, and he returned to England at the end of the season, but did not long continue there. Sir Hugh Palliser, his earliest patron, was now appointed Governor and Commodore of Newfoundland and Labradore, and Cook was desired to attend him in the same capacity of surveyor in which he had served Captain Graves. The charts of the North American shore and islands were at that time extremely defective, and no one was deemed more proper to remedy the deficiency, than he who had already begun the examination so successfully. In this employment, and in exploring the interior of Newfoundland, Cook was engaged at intervals, from 1764 to 1767, when he once more returned to England.

Had Cook's achievements been confined to the services we have thus briefly mentioned, he would yet deserve a respectable place among those sagacious and laborious minds who have acquired much knowledge under circumstances that might well excuse ignorance, and have turned their self-gained knowledge to practical account, in emergencies where more thorough erudition might easily have found itself at a loss. And yet there are many men who can go thus far—nay, to whose probable advance it might be rash to set a limit—who do unaccountably stop short, or retrograde, being either too well contented with themselves, or too ill contented with their reward, or lacking an external motive, example, or necessity. Had our present subject, for instance, realized a moderate independence a little while after his marriage, and retired to some cheap provincial town, who can say whether he would have been any wise distinguished from the ordinary race of half-pay subs, pursers, and sailing masters, so frequent in good neighbourhoods and sea-bathing villages? living barometers, morning loungers, and evening backgammon players; among whom there is doubtless much power of thought and of action, if they had any thing worth doing or thinking about?

Cook was destined to nobler labours. Those who most confidently reject the astrological hypothesis, may nevertheless admit that Cook's great actions were dependent upon planetary influence. The astronomers of Europe having determined by their calculations that a transit of Venus over the sun's disk would take place in the year 1769, and that the best point for observing this phenomenon, so important to science, would be found among the islands of the South·Sea, were naturally urgent for the assistance of their governments, to accomplish the observation required. In England, the affair was warmly taken up by the Royal Society, a body whose zeal and services in the promotion of knowledge, ought to put to shame the scurrilous abuse with which the society has been assailed, by satirists and buffoons, from Butler to Wolcot. A long memorial was addressed to his Majesty, dated February 15th, 1768, setting forth the great importance of the object, the attention paid to it by other states, and the proper means for its attainment. His Majesty, at the instance of the Earl of Shelburne (afterwards Marquis of Lansdowne), signified his pleasure to the commissioners of the Admiralty, that a convenient vessel be equipped to convey such astronomers and other men of science as the Royal Society should select, to the South Seas; and on the 3d of April, Mr. Stephens, Secretary to the Admiralty, announced to the Society, that a bark had been taken up for that purpose. The management of the expedition was originally intended for Mr. Alexander Dalrymple, F. R. S., a scientific amateur, who had made astronomy and geography the particular subjects of his investigation. But here a difficulty arose. Mr. Dalrymple, well knowing the impossibility of securing the obedience of a crew without the full authority of a naval commander, or of preserving discipline in a vessel not subject to martial law, requested a brevet commission as Captain, such as had been granted to Halley the astronomer, in his famous voyages to discover the variation of the compass. To this arrangement, Sir Edward Hawke, then at the head of the naval department, could not be brought to consent, alleging that his conscience did not suffer him to entrust any ship of his Majesty's to a man not regularly bred to the sea. And in this objection, which has been censured as a professional punctilio, it is extremely probable that

Sir Edward was in the right; for Halley's commission was little respected by his men, who ventured to dispute its validity. To maintain order in a ship or an army, or even in a school, something more is required than a legal commission,—a moral authority founded on prescription and association, and above all, a feeling among subordinate commanders, that their own honour, dignity and rank, require them to support the superior. As neither the admiral nor the philosopher would recede from their resolution, and Sir Edward declared that he would sooner cut off his own right hand than he would affix it to an irregular commission, the Society had no alternative, but either to abandon the project, in which the national credit as well as the interests of science was deeply concerned, or to look out for another conductor. In this emergency, Mr. Secretary Stephens, a man who must have possessed some extraordinary qualifications, for he retained his office in those changeable times under many successive administrations, directed the attention of the board to Mr. Cook. Sir Hugh Palliser, Cook's constant friend, readily vouched for his competency. Such recommendation was not likely to be disregarded, and the Lords of the Admiralty appointed Cook to command the expedition, with the rank of a Lieutenant in the royal navy, his commission bearing date the 25th of May, 1768.

The next thing was to select a vessel fit for the purposes of the voyage. Sir Hugh Palliser and Lieutenant Cook examined a number of ships then lying in the river, and at length pitched upon one of 370 tons burden, which they modestly and appropriately christened the Endeavour. Before the preparations were completed, Captain Wallis returned from his voyage round the world, and specially recommended the island which he had discovered, or re-discovered, and named, in honour of his Sovereign and Patron, King George's Isle, (since called by the native term Otaheite,) as the best station for observing the transit of Venus. Thither, therefore, the Admiralty directed Cook to steer. Mr. Green was appointed chief astronomer, Mr. (afterwards Sir Joseph) Banks, and Dr. Solander, accompanied the expedition as naturalists and students of life and manners. The complement of the Endeavour was eighty-four persons, exclusive of the commander; and she was victualled for eighteen months, carried ten carriage and twelve swivel guns, and was amply stored with ammunition and all other necessaries. Lieutenant Cook went on board on the 27th of May, sailed down the river the 30th of July, anchored in Plymouth Sound August 13th, waited for a fair wind to the 26th of that month, arrived in Finchiæle Road, in the island of Madeira, September 13th. The beauties and delights of Madeira, " the purple waves," the vineyards and orangeries, the restorative atmosphere, and the luxuriant hospitality of natives and denizens, have been celebrated again and again, never more passionately than by the author of " Six Months in the West Indies." Lieutenant Cook and his crew were received with the usual welcome, not only from the English, among whom Dr. Thomas Heberden deserved the thanks of all botanists for the assistance he rendered to Mr. Banks and Dr. Solander, in exploring the vegetable varieties of that fertile land, (Who would not be a botanist in a wilderness of nameless flowers?) but also from the Fathers of the Franciscan convent, who displayed a liberal interest in the object of the expedition, little accordant with the sloth, ignorance, and bigotry, which some of the tars had been used to associate with the garb of a friar. The visitors were also permitted to converse with a convent of nuns. What an incident in the lives of those poor recluses ! The ladies had heard that there were philosophers in the company, and having very indistinct notions of the limits of philosophic intelligence, asked with amusing simplicity, many questions which the philosophers were quite unable to answer ; as when it would thunder, whether there was a spring of fresh water to be found in the convent, &c. ; questions to which the oracular sages of old would easily have returned responses certain to save their own credit. And indeed it well might astonish the nuns, that men who were sailing to the farthest extremity of the ocean, in the certainty of seeing a particular appearance of the heavenly bodies on a particular day, should nevertheless be ignorant of the intentions of the weather.*

Having laid in a fresh stock of beef, water, and wine, the Endeavour weighed anchor from Madeira on the 18th of September, and proceeded across the Atlantic. In the run between Madeira and Rio Janeiro, on the night of the 29th October, the monotony of " blank ocean and mere sky " was interrupted by the strange appearance of a sea on fire. Sometimes quick successive flashes, sometimes a multitude of luminous

---

* It is probable, that the progress of discovery may in time enable philosophers to satisfy the curiosity of nuns on these questions. Even now, there are men whose surmises are grounded on experiment, who believe that the presence of hidden springs or metals may be detected by magnetic or galvanic effluvia, thus approving old Roger Bacon's "hazel rod of divination." The science of Meteorology is yet in its infancy ; but we can see no reason why it should not be so perfected, as to enable the proficient to calculate the changes of the atmosphere with an approximation to certainty. Wherever the Almighty acts through his handmaid Nature, he doubtless acts by discoverable laws. As those laws are more or less simple, they are more or less easily discovered. When many causes are at work together, mutually modifying and counteracting each other, it becomes proportionably difficult to calculate the mean result of the whole. But, though arduous, not impossible or unlawful. It is not in respect of natural forces, that *our God is a God that hideth himself.*

points illuminated the waves around the vessel, seeming to increase with the agitation of the waters. This phenomenon arises from luminous animals, chiefly of the genus Medusæ. Our voyagers ascertained this by experiment, but it had been suspected, if not proved, by former naturalists. The appearance, though most frequent between the tropics, is by no means unknown either in the Mediterranean, or in our own seas; but in those teeming latitudes, which almost favour the fanciful hypothesis, that all matter has some time been animated, the multitude of sea insects is so great, as to cover vast tracks of water with their light. Sir Joseph Banks (for why should not he, like Augustus and Charlemagne, be allowed to anticipate his title?) threw the casting net, and captured a hitherto nondescript species of Medusa, more splendent than any before noticed, which he called *pellucens*. When brought aboard, it emitted a strong white light, like heated metal. Along with this living gelatine he caught crabs of three different species, altogether new, each of which gave as much light as the glow-worm, though not above one third of the size. Doubtless Sir Joseph was a happy man that night, and continued, to the end of his long, happy, and virtuous life, to observe the 29th of October among his high days and holydays.

On the 13th of November the Endeavour arrived at Rio Janeiro, whither the commander had directed his course, as some articles of provision began to run short, anticipating the like favourable reception from the Portuguese authorities as he had experienced at Madeira. Herein, however, he was disappointed. The Viceroy would not believe, because he did not comprehend, the purpose of the expedition. When assured that its object was to observe a transit of Venus over the Sun, he could make nothing of it, but that it was expected to see the North Star pass through the South Pole, and he had the worse opinion of the English designs which were covered with such an incomprehensible pretext. Travellers, in exploring the ancient buildings of eastern lands, are exposed to perilous interruption from the natives, who insist upon it that they are hunting for hid treasures; and the representative of his Portuguese Majesty at Rio Janeiro might have heard that it was not to observe the stars that Englishmen used to traverse the ocean. Cook had need of his peculiar discretion and command of temper, in dealing with this ignorant, important personage, and never came to a thorough understanding with him at all. Water and other necessaries could not be refused, but when towing down the bay on the fifth of December (it being a dead calm), our navigators were startled by two shots from the fort of Santa Cruz, which commands the entrance of the harbour. Cook immediately dropped anchor, and sent to demand the reason of this insult. The governor of the Fortress answered that he could not allow the vessel to pass without the Viceroy's order. The Viceroy being questioned, asserted that he had issued the order several days before, but through some unaccountable negligence it had never been transmitted. It was not worth while to disbelieve this.

On the 7th of December the Endeavour was once more under way, and pursuing her voyage entered the Straits of Le Maire, January 7th, 1769, and the next day anchored in the bay of Good Success, on the coast of Terra del Fuego. This island is perhaps the most wretched spot that ever was a permanent habitation of men; and if human misery be produced by the total absence at once of physical accommodation and mental cultivation, of enjoyment and of hope, the inhabitants of Terra del Fuego might be fairly pronounced miserable. Nature has done little for them, and yet they have scarcely been urged to do any thing for themselves. Their hovels, composed of sticks and dry grass, afford no protection against the weather. The scanty bits of seal skin which serve them for garments, supply neither warmth nor decency. Indeed, decency, cleanliness and comfort, appear to be equally strangers to their wishes. They have no incitement to action beyond the craving for food, in search of which they paddle about in their canoes, or wander shivering about the dreary wastes that surround them. If they have any notion of a public blessing, it must be when the sea throws some huge carcase ashore, which may perhaps excite as great a sensation in Terra del Fuego, as a rich wreck would once have done on the coast of Cornwall. Cooking utensils they have none; nor any semblance of furniture; yet they would accept nothing but a few beads. They had probably no idea of any condition different from their own. Nature, denying them all beside, gave them apathy, the best possible substitute for content. Yet their squalid figures indicated habitual bodily distress, and the few words which made up their language had a whining tone, and were spoken with a shiver, such as we observe in beggar children, but probably unaccompanied with any positive consciousness of pain.*

While the Endeavour lay in the bay of Good Success, Sir Joseph Banks, Dr. Solander, Mr. Green, Mr. Monkhouse the surgeon, and others of the scientific party, were very near perishing of cold on a botanical excursion up a mountain in Terra del Fuego. Two black attendants actually died. It should be recollected, that January is the midsum-

---

* From the recent voyage of Captain Foster (the gallant Officer unfortunately drowned in the Chagre, just as he was bringing the scientific labours of his expedition to a happy close), it appears that the natives of Terra del Fuego are very little advanced since 1769. The march of mind, in the neighbourhood of Strait le Maire and Cape Horn, must be a *dead march*.

mer of the Southern Hemisphere. But the brief summer of Lapland cheers not the dwellers of the extreme south.

On the 26th of January, our voyagers left Cape Horn behind them, and on the 11th of April came in sight of Otaheite. In this interval they discovered several small islands, which were named Lagoon, Thrumb Cap, Bow Island, the Groups, Bird Island, and Chain Island. Most of these appeared to he inhabited, and the verdant palm groves rising above the waste of waters, were delightfully refreshing to eyes which for months had seen no earth but the desolate heights of Terra del Fuego. On the 13th the Endeavour anchored in Port-Royal-bay, Otaheite.

As their stay in this island was not likely to be short, and much depended on keeping up a good understanding with the natives, the first measure of Lieutenant Cook was to set forth certain rules and regulations, according to which the communication between his crew and the islanders was to be conducted. His orders were to this effect :—

1st. To endeavour, by every fair means, to cultivate a friendship with the natives, and to treat them with all imaginable humanity.

2d. A proper person or persons will be appointed to trade with the natives for all manner of fruits, provisions, and other productions of the earth ; and no officer, or seaman, or other person belonging to the ship, excepting such as are so appointed, shall trade, or offer to trade, for any sort of provisions, fruit, or other productions of the earth, unless they have leave so to do.

3d. Every person employed on shore, on any duty whatsoever, shall strictly attend to the same ; and if by any neglect he lose any of his arms or working tools, or suffer them to be stolen, the full value thereof will be charged against his pay, according to the custom of the navy in such cases, and he shall receive such further punishment as the nature of the case may deserve.

4th. The same punishment shall be inflicted on any person who is found to embezzle, trade, or offer to trade with any part of the ship's stores, of what nature soever.

5th. No sort of iron, or any thing made of iron, or any sort of cloth, or other useful and necessary articles to be given in exchange for any thing but provision.   J. Cook.

There are few spots of earth so remote, so recently discovered, and so little connected with the politics of Europe, of which so much has been talked and written, as of the isle of Otaheite. Sensual philosophists have extolled it as the very garden of delight and liberty—the paradise of Mahomet on earth—the floating island of Camoens come to an anchor ; and stern religionists have referred to its Areois, its infanticides, its bloody sacrifices, as irrefragable proofs of the innate depravity of human nature.   In later times, it has acquired a more honourable celebrity from the labours of the missionaries, whose smallest praise it is to have given more accurate accounts of the human natural history of barbarians than had ever been received before.   Could a description of this cele— brated island and its inhabitants form a proper part of any biography, it would not be of Cook's, for he was not the discoverer of Otaheite. According to some assertions, it had been visited as early as 1606, by Quiros.   But however this might be, the.fame of disclosing its existence to modern Europe belongs to Captain Wallis, whose vessel, the Dolphin, struck on one of the coral reefs that beset and fortify the coasts of the Polynesian Isles, and which, if no comet or conflagration interrupt the generation of insect architects in their labour, may at last form a new continent in the Pacific.   In the year following, Bougain ville, the first French circumnavigator, visited the Cyprus of the South Seas, and had not long departed, when our voyagers arrived.   Thus the natives had become sufficiently acquainted with the European aspect to feel no panic at a new arrival, and when the Endeavour anchored in Matarai bay, she was presently surrounded with canoes, offering cocoa-nuts, bread-fruit, and other refreshments for barter.   A friendly intercourse was soon established ; and the commander having issued the rules aforesaid, for the regulation of commerce, turned his attention to the grand object of his mission.

The first consideration was, to fix on the best point from whence to take the observation, then to provide means of taking it in security. Having explored the coast for some distance westward, and found no harbour more convenient than that in which the Endeavour lay, he went ashore, accompanied by Sir Joseph Banks, Dr. Solander, Mr. Green, and a party of marines and sailors, to pitch on a site for the observatory.   A piece of ground was selected, commanded by the guns of the ship, and remote from any native habitation.   Here it was resolved to erect a small fort, and to deposit the astronomical instruments. While the space was marking out, the natives, in straggling troops, began to gather round, but unarmed, and without any shew of animosity or of fear.   Mr. Cook, well knowing that a little salutary awe, timely impressed, might prevent the necessity of violence, signified that none should pass the line of demarkation, except Owhaw, (a native who had particularly attached himself to the English during Wallis's visit, and was inclined to renew his acquaintance,) and a single chieftain.   These two approached accordingly, and they were given to understand by signs, that the ground was merely wanted to sleep upon for a night or two, and that no violation of person or property would be attempted.

Whether this dumb communication proved intelligible or not, the work was allowed to proceed without interruption, the natives looking quietly on like children. The trench was drawn, and a tent erected, in which the scientific gentlemen placed their apparatus under a guard, and then, along with Mr. Cook, went on an excursion up the country. We can imagine Sir Joseph and Dr. Solander almost as happy as this state of probation permits frail man to be. The trees, and the flowers, and the butterflies, the green and fragrant earth, all teeming and scaturient with new species. At every step a discovery. If to feel the firm land under foot, to behold grass and trees once more, after months' confinement on ship board, where men, and most of all unemployed men, are doomed to feel from day to day—

> How like a cloud on the weary eye
> Lay the sky and the sea, and the sea and the sky.

If this be ecstacy even to an ignoramus, who has not an idea or an object to diversify the simplicity of pleasurable feeling, what must it be to a natural philosopher in a new discovered country!

Cool-headed readers at home, when they peruse the high-flown descriptions in old voyages, of fortunate islands, groves of perfume and melody, birds and flowers rivalling the rain-bow, women fair and kind as sea-born Cytherea, and a life of perpetual "dance and minstrelsy," should always take the *voyage* into consideration: especially when female charms are the topic of panegyric. Even the philosophers, Banks and Solander, no doubt were delighted to see a woman again, thought the gay Otaheitan dancing girls very pretty, and tatooing a very agreeable fashion. But it is a moot point whether any Otaheitan, any Indian beauty, would pass muster at an English fair or merry-night, even putting complexion out of the question. We mean as to beauty of feature, for in beauty of form, it is probable, that savages in a genial climate, where simple food is plentiful, and spirituous liquors have not become common, excel the average of a civilized people. But this need not be, if civilized nations made use of the knowledge that is given them. Bad or scanty food, premature and unwholesome labour, and the vices which oppression engenders and avarice encourages, dwarf and deform multitudes in our cities, and not in our cities *alone,* while the bodies, like the minds of the affluent classes are too often perverted by bad education. It must be added, that the rarity of mis-shapen or decrepit objects in savage tribes, arises as much from their crimes and miseries, as from any other cause. The old and diseased are suffered (or more humanely assisted) to perish ; the weakly infant is strangled at the birth, or dies of neglect and hardship—only the healthy and vigorous arrive at maturity. But these reflections

4 c

would not occur to a stranger just landed, and we conclude that to the philosophers, all things appeared *coleur de rose*.

Perhaps Mr. Cook's meditations were not of such unmingled bliss. He might have fears of what might breed in his absence, and unfortunately those fears were not altogether without cause. Almost as soon as his back was turned, one of the Otaheitans, (who were still assembled about the tent,) watched his opportunity to seize the sentry's musquet, and make off with it. Though repeatedly summoned, he shewed no disposition to give it up, and his countrymen were rather inclined to protect him than otherwise. This so far provoked the young midshipman who commanded the guard, that he gave the word to fire, and a volley was discharged among the multitude, who immediately fled in great terror and confusion. As it was observed that the thief did not fall, he was pursued and shot dead. This the tars probably thought no more than justice, (as in England it would have been law,) and good sport into the bargain, but the Lieutenant on his return, testified the utmost concern and displeasure, and reprimanded the young midshipman in a style that, we hope, he profited by. Thenceforth, orders were issued and enforced, that for no pillage or depredation should a shot be fired on any native. Yet it was some time before confidence was restored; even Owhaw kept aloof. But at last, by the good offices and skilful management of Mr. Cook and Sir Joseph, the fears of the islanders were appeased, and they began to bring their plantains, cocoa-nuts, and bread-fruit, again to the fort. It may be remarked, that in all dealings between our countrymen and the Otaheitans, Sir Joseph was the principal mediator: he managed all the traffic, he made acquaintance with many of the chieftains, he traversed the country in all directions, he was a spectator, sometimes an actor in the religious, festal, and funeral ceremonies. The universal passion for knowledge, and not less comprehensive benevolence of that excellent man, led him occasionally into situations bordering on the ludicrous, but they qualified him admirably to obtain the good will of a people, who by all accounts, seem to have been shrewd children with full-grown passions.

The small regard to the rights of property which the Otaheitans share in common with the south-sea islanders in general, (we might add, with all nations that have not been long *educated* by legal institutions—for the world are too little aware how much honesty is an artificial and conventional virtue,) had very near rendered the main purpose of the voyage abortive. Cook and the scientific gentlemen having gone upon an expedition into the interior, and not returned to the tent, (which was left unoccupied) till the next morning, found the great astronomical quadrant missing. The first supicion fell on the ship's crew: strict search was made in vain, and it became evident that the treasure had been purloined by Otaheitan hands. In this emergency, Sir Joseph volunteered his services, and by a series of well conceived manœuvres, not only discovered the place of its concealment, but obtained its restoration without a contest. All went on fair and friendly, and when the fort came to be thrown up, the islanders zealously assisted in carrying earth, piles, &c. So scrupulous was Cook, that he would not permit a stake to be cut in the woods, but what was purchased and paid for. When the guns were mounted, the natives were much disturbed. Some rumour or tradition of European rapine might have reached the isle of Ocean; for what land or sea have not Europeans stained with blood? But by the never-failing intervention of Sir Joseph, and the good offices of a chief called Tootahah, all apprehensions were dispelled. About the same time, Lieutenant Cook signalised his justice by a piece of necessary severity, which set the Otaheitan character in a very amiable light. The butcher of the Endeavour had violently assaulted a woman, who refused to exchange her hatchet for a nail. He had forcibly taken the hatchet, and threatened to cut the poor female's throat. The charge being fairly made out in the presence of Sir Joseph Banks, an information was laid before the commander. It was determined to make an example of the butcher. Several of the natives were invited on board to witness his punishment. They looked on in silence while he was tied to the rigging, but when the first lash was given, they began to intercede for the offender with most pathetic beseechings, and when the flagellation proceeded in spite of their intercession, they testified their sympathy with tears and lamentations. The ignorant savages were quite unacquainted with the use of the cat-o'-nine-tails. There would be small reason, however, to declaim against the cat on the score of humanity, if it never was employed but in cases like that of the butcher of the Endeavour.

On the 14th of May, which was Sunday, Divine service was performed at the fort, and Mr. Banks, at the suggestion of the commander, brought Tubonrai Tomaide, a native chieftain, and his wife Tomio, in hopes that their questions might open the door for some religious instructions. But the time for conversions was not yet. Neither to Captain Cook nor to Sir Joseph Banks was the glory assigned to turn the Heathen into the way of truth. Tubonrai and Tomio behaved very well, imitating Sir Joseph, who sat between them, most sedulously kneeling when he knelt, and standing when he stood: they seemed to be aware that they were engaged in some serious business, for they imperatively called on the people without the fort to be silent, but when all was over they asked no questions and would listen to no explanations.

Tubonrai Tomaide had hitherto shewed a respect to property, very unusual among his countrymen, but on the 15th the temptation of a basket of nails was too strong for his virtue. It was left in a corner of Mr. Banks's tent, to which the chief had always access. It was irresistible. Five nails were missing, and one of them inadvertently peeped out beneath the chieftain's garment. Had Tubonrai possessed the spirit of the Spartan boy, he would have preferred hiding the nails in his flesh to having them found upon him : but an Otaheitan is not a Spartan, so Tubonrai confessed the theft, but was very unwilling to make restitution. Restitution, however, was insisted on and promised, but never performed. No rough means were resorted to ; Tubonrai took his departure to Epasse, (his province or government,) and did not appear at the fort till the 25th, when he was received with a coldness and reserve which seemed to give him pain, but did not make him bring back the nails. The good heart of Sir Joseph was much wounded by this dereliction of the only Otaheitan whom he had suspected of honesty. Tubonrai had, on a former occasion, been accused unjustly of stealing a knife, and resented the imputation in a manner that shewed him not altogether insensible to its disgracefulness. So, at least, our voyagers, or Dr. Hawkesworth for them, interpreted his tears, (for the tears of an Otaheitan are as fluent as a spoiled child's or an ancient hero's,) but we think it probable, that if his sense was at all aggrieved at the accusation, it was not on the score of dishonesty, but of ingratitude and dishonour. Moralists are apt to consider honour as an acquired notion ; honesty, or an equitable regard to the *meum* and *tuum* as cóeval with the earliest dawn of human reason. But we believe the reverse to be the case, as any one who closely observes the habits of children, or of uncultivated men, may easily perceive. It requires a high degree of moral education to make men understand the sacredness of property, abstractedly considered as such. Few school-boys feel any compunction at robbing an orchard, especially if it be their master's. Piracy and robbery were long the honoured employ-ment of heroes. But school-boys and pirates always have acknowledged, if not observed, a bond amongst themselves, and can always understand the obligation of a kindness conferred or received.

On the 27th, Sir Joseph Banks suffered a much more serious inconvenience from the Otaheitan ignorance or disregard of the eighth commandment than the loss of the nails, which moreover furnished that wicked wag Peter Pindar with what he doubtless regarded as fair game. Oberea, a stately middle-aged lady, whom Captain Wallis, erroneously, as it appeared, had taken for the Queen of the island, with her attendants, male and female, including her paramour Obadee, and her high priest and prime minister Tupia, paid a visit to Tootahah, at the same time that our voyagers were honouring him with a visitation, to procure the delivery of certain hogs, which had been promised and paid for. As the assemblage on this occasion was unusually great, there occurred an accident, that often results from royal visits in more civilized communities, a scarcity of sleeping accommodations. Sir Joseph, says Dr. Hawkesworth, in the name of Captain Cook, thought himself fortunate in being offered a place in Oberea's canoe, (the canoes of the Otaheitans are often seventy feet long, but had Oberea's been less, it would have occasioned no scandal,) and wishing his friends a very good night took his leave. "He went to rest early, according to the custom of the country, and taking off his clothes, as was his constant practice, the nights being hot, Oberea kindly insisted upon taking them into her own custody, for otherwise, she said, they would certainly be stolen. Mr. Banks having such a safeguard, resigned himself to sleep with all imaginable tranquillity, but awakening about eleven o'clock, and wanting to get up, he searched for his clothes where he had seen them deposited by Oberea when he lay down to sleep, and soon perceived that they were missing. He immediately awakened Oberea, who starting up, and hearing his complaint, ordered lights, and prepared in great haste to recover what he had lost : Tootahah himself slept in the next canoe, and being soon alarmed, he came to them and set out with Oberea in search of the thief ; Mr. Banks was not in a condition to go with them, for of his apparel scarce any thing was left him *but his breeches ;* his coat and his waistcoat, with his pistols, powder-horn, and many other things that were in his pockets, being gone. In about half an hour his two noble friends returned, but without having obtained any intelligence of his clothes or of the thief. At first he began to be alarmed ; his musquet had not indeed been taken away, but he had neglected to load it ; where I and Dr. Solander had disposed of ourselves he did not know, and therefore whatever might happen, he could not have recourse to us for assistance. He thought it best, however, to express neither fear nor suspicion of those about him ; and giving his musquet to Tupia, who had been waked in the confusion and stood by him, with a charge not to suffer it to be stolen, he betook himself again to rest, declaring himself perfectly satisfied with the pains that Tootahah and Oberea had taken to recover his things, though they had not been successful. As it cannot be supposed that in such a situation he slept very sound, he soon after heard music, and saw lights at a little distance on shore. This was a concert or assembly, which they call a *Helou*, a common name for every public exhibition, and as it would necessarily bring many people together, and there was a chance of my being among them with his other friends, he rose and made the best of his way towards it ; he was soon led by the lights and the sound to the place where I lay with the other three gentlemen of our party, and easily distinguishing us from the rest, he made up to us more than half naked, and told his melancholy story. We gave him such comfort as the unfortunate generally give to each other, by telling him that we were fellow sufferers. I shewed that I myself was without stockings, they having been stolen from under my head, though I was certain I had never been asleep, and each of my associates convinced him, by his appearance, that he had lost a jacket. We determined, however, to hear out the concert, however deficient in point of dress ; it consisted of four flutes, three drums, and several voices ; when this entertainment, which lasted about an hour, was over, we retired again to our places of rest, having agreed that nothing could be done towards the recovery of our things till the morning.

"We rose at day-break (Sunday 28th), according to the custom of the country. The first man that Mr. Banks saw was Tupia, faithfully guarding his musquet ; and soon after Oberea brought him some of her country clothes as a succedaneum for his own, so that when he came to us he made a most motley appearance, half Indian and half English. Our party soon got together, except Dr. Solander, whose quarters we did not know, and who had not joined in the concert ; in a short time Tootahah made his appearance, and we pressed him to recover our clothes ; but neither he nor Oberea could be persuaded to take any measure for that purpose, so that we began to suspect that they had been parties in the theft. About eight o'clock we were joined by Dr. Solander, who had fallen into honester hands, at a house about a mile distant and had lost nothing." *

As our unfortunate adventurers were returning to the boat, they had the consolation (if such it was) of seeing the wonderful dexterity of the Otaheitans in swimming amid a tremendous surf. The inhabitants of

---

* Hawkesworth's Voyages. *Vol. 2d, page* 132.—Dr. Hawkesworth, by making the commanders whose adventures he narrates, speak in the first person, has certainly made his book a great deal prettier reading than it would have been if he had appeared himself as the historian ; but still, after all that has or can be said in defence of this method, it converts history into historical romance, and makes the Doctor, instead of the veracious recorder of important facts, no better than a poor imitator of De Foe.

tropical climates, who live in the vicinity of waters, are almost amphibious, and both sexes are alike aquatic. When the missionary vessel, commanded by Captain Wilson, in 1797, arrived off the Marquesas, the pious brethren were shocked by the appearance of two females in a state of nudity, who swam round the vessel for half an hour together, though the night was dark and tempestuous, crying in a plaintive tone, "*waheine, waheine,*" signifying woman, or we are women; a cry which had never failed to gain admission to an European vessel before.

As the day of the transit was now at hand, Mr. Cook, in pursuance of a suggestion of Lord Morton, sent out two parties provided with the requisite instruments; the one to Eimeo, an island to the westward of Otaheite, and the other to a station on the shore, to the east of the observatory, with a view to compare the different observations, and ward as far as possible, against the chance of failure. All was now in readiness; the astronomers on the tip-toe of expectation, watching now the sky, now the chronometer, and then the barometer. The pleasures of science, however pure and salutary, are liable to disappointment as well as those of more questionable character. A cloud might have rendered futile a south-sea voyage. The men of knowledge slept not a wink on the night of the 2d of June. But the sun of the third arose without a speck, and the passage of Venus over his disk was seen plainly through its whole duration, which, according to Mr. Green, was from 25 minutes 42 seconds past 9 A.M. to 32 minutes 10 seconds past 3 P.M. The latitude of the observatory was found to be 17° 29′ 15″ south, and the longitude 149° 32′ 30″ west of Greenwich.* But there

---

* According to Mr. Green—

	H.	M.	S.	
The first external conduct, or first appearance of Venus upon the sun was	9	25	42	Morning.
The first internal contact, or total immersion, was ..	9	44	4	
The second internal contact, or beginning of the emersion, ...	3	14	8	Afternoon.
The second external contact, or total emersion, ...	3	32	10	

Our scientific readers may find a full account of the transit in the sixty-first volume of "Philosophical Transactions," where we would advise our unscientific readers not to look for it, for we can say by experience, that it is neither entertaining nor instructive to persons endued, like ourselves, with a plentiful lack of mathematics, to the diligent study of which excellent branch of knowledge we seriously and earnestly exhort our younger friends. There is no reason why the rudiments of geometry should not be taught to every child as soon as it can read, and it is of great consequence that the dry and troublesome initiation should take place while the authority of masters can over-rule whatever obstacles the idleness or volatility of the pupil may present. No person ever neglects mathematics without bitterly repenting it, as we can testify to our sorrow. However little you learn, if it be well learned, it is a great deal better than none. Whereas, any proficiency in Greek or Latin short of that

was some little diversity in the different observations, owing to a halo around the body of the planet, supposed to be its atmosphere, which very much disturbed the times of contact, particularly the internal ones, i. e. the points when the planet was completely immersed in the sun, and when it began to emerge. From this celestial phenomenon, the ground on which the observatory stood was christened Point Venus; though possibly it might have deserved the appellation on other accounts.

This was the astronomers' day of happiness; the reward of all their pains, privations, shiverings, scorchings, salt diet, tossing to and fro, sea-sickness, and incarceration on ship board, which, in the opinion of Dr. Johnson, only differs from imprisonment in the county gaol by being much more disagreeable.

While the officers and *savants* were absorbed in observation and calculation, some of the ship's crew broke into one of the store rooms,

which enables to read and understand an author with vernacular fluency, and without the intervention of English, is of no use at all; any further than the practice of construing may give a command of language, very dearly purchased by the confusion which a superficial knowledge of derivations introduces into our apprehension of the primary meaning and collateral application of words. That a *good* classical scholar will understand his native tongue better than a man of only one language is more than probable, but the classic smatterer will be found to think more vaguely, and express his thoughts less precisely, than the mere English scholar of the same calibre of intellect. Sensible women, who have small French and no Latin, commonly express themselves both *viva voce*, and on paper, much better than their husbands and brothers, because they say the words which their thoughts bring along with them, whereas men used to construe, are always construing their thoughts into a diction as alien and unnatural as if they actually thought in one language and spoke in another. To the female, language is the body of thought; to the half taught male, the drapery. When we consider that in nothing has the discipline of intellect so strong a bearing on the moral being, as in what regards the just appreciation of words, we cannot think this a matter of light importance. Far be it from us to favour any system of education which would consign the beautiful works of antiquity to neglect and oblivion; but for those whose school days must necessarily be few, we very much doubt the expediency of giving any of that precious time to grammars and lexicons, unless the mind be of a very fanciful or poetical turn, or possess the peculiar faculty of a linguist. Latin and Greek should always make a part of the erudition of an idle gentleman, and of a professional scholar, but may well be dispensed with by the great and valuable class, who are destined to the active employments of life.

For the satisfaction of the few, who are unfortunate enough to be even more ignorant of astronomy than ourselves, we may take the liberty to state that the transit, or passage of a planet over the sun's disk, is an unfrequent phænomenon, only incident to the *inferior* planets (those revolving between the earth and the sun), and of great importance in determining the distances of the heavenly bodies from the sun, from the earth, and from each other.

and stole a quantity of spike nails. This was a very serious disaster, for the improvident distribution of the booty among the islanders tended to bring down the value of iron, the staple commodity. One of the thieves was detected, but, though punished with two dozen lashes, he refused to inform against his accomplices.

Sunday the 4th of June was, in strictness of speech, the King's birth day, but the celebration was deferred till the 5th, in order that all the parties might unite in the festivities at Point Venus. Events, trivial as this, are not without interest, when they carry the thoughts and feelings of man half across the globe. Narratives of voyages never are dull books, though they may sometimes have been written by very dull men. Their tedious minuteness is often their greatest charm. We are always interested to know what an Englishman was doing at half past ten at night on the Pacific Ocean. Several native chieftains were present at the commemoration, who drank the King's health under the name of Kihiargo, the nearest approximation their organs could make to King George. It was extremely amusing to hear the metamorphoses which these islanders, whose own language, soft, liquid, and melodious, was easily mastered even by the common seamen of the Endeavour, effected upon the crabbed, consonant-crowded names of their visitors. The commander was *Toote*, Mr. Hicks, *Hete* (a manifest improvement); *Boba* was Mr. Robert Molineux, the sailing master, for Molineux was quite unapproachable ; Mr. Gore was *Toaro ;* Dr. Solander, *Toruno ;* Mr. Banks, *Tapank ;* Mr. Parkinson, *Patini ;* Mr. Green, *Eteree*, and Mr. Petersgill, *Petrodero*. It is manifest how much the northern roughness of our appellatives is softened by Otaheitan Italianization. A skilful linguist might have derived many useful hints and agreeable speculations as to the formation of languages from this pretty miscalling.

Soon after the transit, our voyagers had an oppportunity of witnessing an Otaheitan funeral. In few matters have savage, not to say civilized nations, betrayed greater absurdities than in funeral rites ; and yet, the respect almost universally paid to the remains of mortality has been held, and not unwisely, a symptom of a stirring instinct and foreboding of immortality. The Otaheitan custom seems admirably calculated to bring on a pestilence ; yet, before their commerce with Europeans, it is said that epidemic disease was unknown among these islanders. Previous to interment the bodies are exposed in a shed, and not removed till all the flesh is putrified away ; then the bones are buried. In so warm a climate the decomposition must go on rapidly. Along with the body, which is laid out under a canoe awning, covered with fine cloth, some articles of food are placed, as an offering to the

4 D

gods, though, as they do not believe that the gods eat, this offering must be considered as merely ceremonial. Like the ancient Greeks and Orientals, the Otaheitans signalize their grief by wounding their bodies, which is performed with a shark's tooth. Fragments of cloth, stained with blood and tears are thrown upon the body. The relatives of the deceased occupy, for some time, a habitation near the place of sepulture, and the chief mourner another.*

* The following account of an Otaheitan funeral is taken from the "Family Library," vol. 25. It refers to the period of which we are writing, and admirably illustrates the two points of character we so much love and commend in Sir Joseph, his passion for observation, and his catholic spirit of accommodation, undaunted by "the world's dread laugh."

"An old woman having died, Mr. Banks, whose pursuit was knowledge of every kind, and who, to gain it, made himself one of the people, requested he might attend the ceremony, and witness all the mysteries of the solemnity of depositing the body in the Morai or burying place. The request was complied with, but on no other condition than his taking a part in it. This was just what was wished. In the evening he repaired to the house, where he was received by the daughter of the deceased and several others, amongst whom was a boy about fourteen years of age. One of the chiefs of the district was the principal mourner, wearing a fantastical dress.

Mr. Banks was stripped entirely of his European dress, and a small piece of cloth was tied round his middle. His face and body were then smeared with charcoal and water, as low as to the shoulders, till they were as black as those of a negro. The same operation was performed on the rest, among whom were some women, who were reduced to a state as near nakedness as himself—the boy was blacked all over; after which the procession set forward, the chief mourner having mumbled something like a prayer over the body.

It is the custom of the Indians to fly from these processions with the utmost precipitation. On the present occasion, several large parties of the natives were put to flight; all the houses were deserted, and not a single Otaheitan was to be seen. The body being deposited on a stage erected for it, the mourners were dismissed to wash themselves in the river, and to resume their customary dresses, and customary gaiety."

There is at least a consistency in blacking the body for mourning, where the body is tatooed for ornament. To the latter operation Sir Joseph Banks never submitted, though we doubt not he would have endured it, if his so doing would have elucidated any point of the history of nature or of man; especially as the Otaheitans seldom tatoo the face.

A man who makes the pursuit and enlargement of knowledge his main earthly object, should stop at nothing but crime to obtain it. Such a man was Sir Joseph Banks, and no duty, inherited or assumed, forbad the indulgence of his passion. But there are many situations in which it is, in the present state of society, a moral obligation to refrain from whatever has a tendency to the ridiculous. It would have been by no means proper for Captain Cook to have appeared at the funeral in Otaheitan mourning. It would neither have suited the dignity of his office, nor the gravity of his character. In fact, there are some people that may be laughed at, and not the less respected, and others who may not. In order to ascertain which genus you belong to yourself, you have only to consider whether there is any thing in your

On the 12th of June, some of the islanders came to complain that two of the seamen had stolen their bows and arrows, and some strings of plaited hair. The charge was investigated, and brought home; the offenders were punished with two dozen lashes. It is not mentioned whether the Otaheitans betrayed the same sensibility on this as on a former occasion.

Their bows and arrows are merely used for sport, or for killing birds. In battle they use only slings and javelins. Tubourai Tamaide could send a shaft more than the sixth part of a mile. He shot kneeling, and dropped his bow as soon as the arrow was discharged. Sir Joseph Banks in his morning walk met some Otaheitan minstrels, who poured forth extempore strains, mostly in praise of their English visitors, accompanied by the music of two flutes and three drums. The drummers were the improvisatori.

The filching disposition of the Otaheitans increasing with impunity, Mr. Cook resolved if possible to check it by some decisive step. He had strictly prohibited his men from firing on any pretext at the natives, as he justly thought that he had no right to act after the English law, in a country where no such law had been promulgated. It seemed the best expedient to retaliate by seizing certain canoes laden with fish. Twenty canoes and their freight were detained, and notice was given, that unless the stolen articles were restored, the canoes would be burned; a threat which there was no intention of putting in force. A list of the lost and stolen was made out, consisting of a coal-rake, the sentry's musquet, Sir Joseph's pistols, a sword, and a water cask. The Otaheitans thought to compound the matter, by bringing back the rake only, and begged hard to have their canoes released, as the fish was spoiling. But Mr. Cook insisted on the original condition. This firmness however did not produce its usual effects, and he was obliged at last to give up the canoes without recovering the lost property.

About the same time a deadly offence was committed by an officer of the Endeavour, who had gone ashore to get ballast for the ship, and

personal or official character which any one with whom you are likely to come in contact wishes to despise. Now, if you exercise an authority founded on that vague kind of fear which is the common substitute for respect, you may be pretty sure that you have. If your duty or vocation oblige you to exercise sway over coarse, boisterous, uncultivated minds—over men of strong passions and little sensibility—over proud men, or conceited boys, be sure that you have those who would hold you in contempt if they dare. Or if your virtue wears a severe aspect, and requires to be well known before it can be loved, depend upon it that the world is weary of reverencing you, and will shout triumph when you furnish it with a *reasonable* pretext for holding you up to scorn.

not finding any stones adapted for the purpose, began to demolish a Morai or sepulchral pile. The islanders violently opposed this proceeding, and sent a messenger to the fort, signifying that no such profanation would be permitted. Sir Joseph, as usual, was the peace-maker. The petty officer must have been a blockhead.

On another occasion Mr. Monkhouse, the surgeon, pulling a flower from a tree in a sepulchral enclosure, received a violent blow on the back of the head from one whose forefathers slept beneath the violated shade. He grappled the assaulter, but two other natives came and rescued him. Most nations, however ignorant, pay some respect to the depositaries of the dead, nor has any refinement of philosophy been able to argue the feeling away.

On the 19th, while the canoes were still detained, Oberea and her train arrived at the fort. She blushed not to request a night's lodging in Sir Joseph's tent; but his loss was too recent for even his gallantry to forget, so the lady was obliged to spend the hours of repose in her canoe. She had spirit and sensibility enough to feel this rebuke very severely, and the next morning she returned to the fort, and put herself, her canoe, and all that it contained into the power of the stranger. A hog and a dog were the price of reconciliation; and now, for the first time, Captain Cook and his friends tasted dog's flesh. Tupia, the priest, after the manner of the ancient Popæ, was both butcher and cook; but his method of extinguishing life by holding his hands over the animal's nose and mouth, took a full quarter of an hour; and his mode of baking the dog with hot stones, in a hole dug in the ground, was very tedious; but the dog made an excellent dish. The esculent dogs are fed entirely upon yams, cocoa-nuts, and other vegetables. All meat and fish is cooked in the same way; but hogs and dogs are the only quadrupeds eaten, and the poultry is very indifferent.

On the 21st the fort was visited by Oamo, the husband of Oberea, from whom she was separated by mutual consent, and they lived as amicably as any other neighbours; with him came the heir apparent, a minor, under the guardianship of Toothah, who exercised command in his name. Oberea and her attendants made their obeisance, by uncovering themselves from the waist upward. By a most singular law of succession, the child succeeds to its father's authority and title as soon as it is born, the father continuing to administer government as regent; but in this case the claims of Oamo were superseded in favour of Tootahah, who had distinguished himself as a warrior. The young prince was betrothed to his sister, an Egyptian fashion; though she was sixteen and he no more than seven. Neither of these young people were permitted to enter the tent. They were the children of Oamo and Oberea.

On the 26th of June, Mr. Cook with Dr. Solander, Mr. Banks, and a communicative Otaheitan called Tituboalo, set out to make a circuit of the island, and discovered that it consists of two peninsulas united by a neck of swampy ground, about two miles across, over which the islanders use to carry their canoes, as the Greeks in the Peloponesian war transported their triremes over the isthmus of Corinth. By their guide, Tituboalo, they were informed that each peninsula has its own king, (though the whole island was formerly under one head). The sovereigns are independent, but the ruler of Opoureonu, the north-western peninsula, claimed a sort of homage from him of Tiarraboo or Otaheite Nui, the eastern moiety of the isle. Our voyagers were introduced to Waheatua, the king of Tiarraboo, who was seated at ease under a canoe awning, no inelegant or unfitting canopy of state in a country where marine had far outstripped civil architecture. They also visited their friend Tootahah, and other chieftains, and were exceedingly well received every where. Hospitality, and something like politeness to strangers, are amiable qualities that cling to man in a lower state of moral culture than any others; they seem to precede or survive the maternal affection itself. Hospitality and revenge are the highest moral obligations of savage ethics. The gods of Homer, though not remarkable for their care of morals, except where their personalities were concerned, as in case of perjury and sacrilege, broken vows and neglected sacrifice; nevertheless avenged the poor and the stranger.* In civilized communities, strangers are generally objects of caution and mistrust. To the barbarian, the new-comer must be either a guest or an enemy.†

The most remarkable objects which our voyagers beheld in this excursion have relation to death. The one was a semicircular board, to which were appended fifteen human jaws, fresh, and with all the teeth entire. No account could be obtained of this ghastly exhibition; but it might easily have been conjectured that these jaws were trophies, like the scalps of the North American Indians, the bones with which the Ashantees ornament their drums, or the bleeding heads which the Huns fastened to their horses' necks. Was it in a milder spirit that the

---

* See Odyssee, B. xi. 207; xiv. 57; ix. 270.

† I remember to have heard a lady who had spent much time among the North American Indians, describe the opinions of one of the nations as to a future state to this effect:——The way to their paradise lies over a bridge of a hair's breadth, like the Alsirat of the Moslems; over this narrow passage those only can go in safety who can produce the scalps of their enemies, and from whose door the stranger was not turned away.

heroes of Morat piled up the skulls of the Burgundians, and affixed thereto that memorable inscription—" A. D. 1476, Charles the Bold, Duke of Burgundy, unjustly invading Switzerland, left this monument."

The other was the grand Morai or Mausoleum of Oberea. There is scarcely a cape or promontory in the whole circuit of the isle, on which one of these sepulchral edifices is not to be seen ; but the royal sepulchre was far more magnificent than the others. Had the Otaheitans been a Christian, or any wise a religious people, we might laud their piety in dedicating their only solid architecture to the departed. As it is, there is a whimsical contrast between the slight sheds which suffice for their living bodies, and the massy piles they prepare for their lifeless relics. An Otaheitan house, if it deserve that appellation, is merely a pointed roof, thatched with palm or banana leaves, and supported by three rows of posts, about nine feet high in the centre, while the eaves reach to within two feet of the ground. It is open on all sides ; no wattling fills the inter-columniations. The floor is uniformly covered with soft hay, on which the family sleep by night and recline by day ; the master and his wife in the middle, the unmarried females on one side, and the young batchelors on the other. If European delicacy be shocked at this, be it recollected that not so much separation obtains in many a hovel, rustic and urban, Cornish and Irish, that owns the sway of the "Defender of the Faith." In these levelling days, too, some may take offence at another regulation ; the Toutoos, or domestics, are not allowed to sleep under the thatch at all, unless it rains very hard, and then they *may* just creep under the eaves. But there is no great difference in Otaheite whether you sleep under a shed or under a tree, except for the honour of the thing, far less than there is between the scullion's attic in a great English house, and the hovels which serve the really servile part of our population for chamber, kitchen, parlour, and all, to say nothing of the multitudes who seldom pass the night under a roof, except when they are in prison.

But although these dormitories* (for they are nothing else) may seem to contribute little to the comfort, and not at all to the privacy of the Otaheitans, they must add greatly to the beauty and interest of the

---

* Besides these pervious homestalls, which serve the bulk of the population, there are another sort of tabernacles, appropriated to the chiefs ; moveable pavilions, formed of trellis-work, closely covered with cocoa-nut leaves. They are, like the sheds of the commonalty, seldom used except in the hours of repose ; but the chieftain and his wife are privileged to lie by themselves.

There are also public buildings, large enough to accomodate the whole population of a district, at times of general assembly, some of them as much as 200 feet long, and 50 feet high in the centre.

prospect. They are almost invariably erected in the woods, and only just enough space is cleared for them to prevent the thatch from being injured by the drippings of the trees; so that the inmates have but to step from their own—door we cannot call it—into the delightful groves of bread-fruit and cocoa-nut trees, from which they derive at once shade, provision and clothing. So that the reproach of Horace against the Romans of his time, that the useful olive and fig tree were supplanted by the umbrageous barrenness of the plane, is inapplicable to Otaheitan arboriculture. These groves are free from underwood, and every where intersected by the paths leading from one habitation to another. There are few effects of human neighbourhood more beautiful than the net-work of tracks in a peopled sylvan region.

Such are the abodes of the living Otaheitans, quickly set up, and readily abandoned. Our voyagers found some districts sprinkled thickly with the remains of deserted dwellings. But in the repositaries of their dead, they affect a permanence, and exhibit some skill in architecture. The Morais are erected on points and headlands, in the most conspicuous situations. The main ambition of an Otaheitan, is to have a respectable Morai, as a son of Erin sets his heart upon a numerous and jovial attendance at his funeral.* The bodies are first left to putrefy under

---

* Of all people the Otaheitans are the most aristocratical, for they carry their aristocracy beyond the grave. They believe in no hell, but in an upper and lower heaven, distinguished by different degrees of happiness, apportioned, not according to merit, but to rank. The heaven of the chiefs is *Tavirua l' erai*; the limbo of the Plebeians is *Liahoboo*. But it were well if the spirit of caste appeared in no more practical form. If a patrician female bear a child to a man of inferior condition, the offspring of the misalliance is never allowed to live. Yet this regulation no more prevents such connections, than the insuperable disgrace attached to *colour* in the slave-states of America prevents the breeding of mulattoes. Wherever a degraded caste exists, a gross profligacy of manners will be found to prevail.

When the missionaries first arrived at Otaheite, in 1797, Iddeah, wife of Pomarre, had a child by her *Cicisbeo*, a Toutoo or Plebeian. The brethren vainly strove to save its life. Iddeah declared that she would abide by *the customs of her ancestors!*

If some of the issues of savage aristocracy are loathsome and revolting, others are exquisitely ridiculous. An Otaheitan chieftan is fed by his attendants, like a baby, because it does not comport with his dignity to feed himself.

When it is deemed necessary to propitiate the divinity with a human sacrifice, the victim is always chosen from the lowest class. He is not apprized of the honour intended him, but secretly assassinated. This selection is not without parallel in ancient history. When the Massilians were afflicted with any pestilence, or public calamity, they took the most miserable wretch they could lay hold of, decked him with garlands, and offered him as a plenary satisfaction to the divine wrath. These idolaters must have thought their deities more gluttons than epicures in blood, since they gave them the vilest they could find.

In speaking of Otaheite, though we speak in the present tense, we would be under-a shed, called Tápowow, and then the bones are buried in the Morai, which is a sort of pavement, with a pyramid of stone on one side. The description and dimensions of Oberea's, or the royal Morai of Opoureonu, are thus given in the narrative of Cook's first voyage. "It is a pile of stone raised pyramidically on an oblong base or square, 267 feet long, and 87 feet wide. On each side is a flight of steps; those at the sides being broader than those at the ends, so that it terminates not in a square of the same figure as the base, but in a ridge, like the roof of a house. There were eleven of these steps to one of these Morais, each of which was four feet high; so that the height of the pile was forty-four feet; each step was formed of one course of white coral stone, which was neatly squared and polished; the rest of the mass, for there was no hollow within, consisted of round pebbles, which, from the regularity of their figures, seemed to have been wrought. The foundation was of rock-stones, which were also squared. In the middle of the top stood an image of a bird, carved in wood, and near it a broken one of a fish, carved in stone. The whole of this pyramid made one side of a spacious area or square, 360 feet by 354, which was walled in with stone, and paved with flat stones through its whole extent. About a hundred yards to the west of this building was another paved area or court, in which were several small stages raised on wooden pillars, about seven feet high, which are called by the Indians Eatuahs or Whattuas, and seem to be a kind of altars, as upon these are placed provisions of all kinds, as offerings to their gods."

Thus it appears that the Morai is at once church and church-yard, which might incline us to an opinion, that the spirits of the dead were the objects of Otaheitan worship. This, however, our voyagers did not discover to be the case. There are male and female Morais—and others, probably those of the inferior classes, which are common to both sexes. There are also male and female deities—worshipped by males and females respectively. Every individual is supposed to have a guardian power, of appropriate sex; as among the Romans, every man had his Genius, and every woman her Juno. The priestly office is always performed by men, but some officiate for their own sex, and others for the women. The Otaheitans do however acknowledge one supreme deity. The practice of human sacrifice was not fully ascertained during Cook's visit, though strong evidence of it appeared in

stood to speak of the times when it first became known to Europe. Great changes have been wrought since, and good men have done wonders to eradicate both the vices which were indigenous to the island, and those which Europeans had superadded to the original stock.

the skulls exposed on the Morais. Our voyagers, in this trip, not only gained correct knowledge of the dimensions of Otaheite, and the bays, harbours, and indentations of the coast, but became well acquainted with the general aspect of the country. The centre rises in ridges of mountains, visible at the distance of sixty miles, ragged and craggy, yet clothed with vegetation to the very top; the trees, and tree-like herbs, hang from every steep, shoot up in every fissure, and stretch over every ravine; numerous rivulets, and some streams of respectable breadth and depth, descend from these hills to water and fertilize the flat land which girdles the isle, as it were, with a garland of fruits and flowers, and here are the reefs and the gardens of the natives. A little plot suffices for each; for the banana, which, with the bread-fruit, and cocoa nuts, forms their staple of food, produces a large quantity of sustenance in a small space.* No species of grain seems to have been known in Otaheite at the date of Cook's arrival. Cultivation, therefore, where it existed, would scarcely vary the picture. There was nothing that could be called a town, or even a village; and the habitations, lurking among the trees, would not affect the prospect much more than the sheds erected by wood-cutters or charcoal burners in an English woodland, which, though they address themselves very pleasantly to the feelings, make little impression on the eye. The Morais and the canoes alone remind the sailor who coasts the shores of this gay island of human handiwork. The latter were very numerous, gliding along the waters, or drawn out upon the beach. The large double war canoes, with their high curving prows, and the passage canoes, with their shady awnings, had a picturesque and classical effect. On the 1st of July, the Lieutenant and his scientific companions returned to the fort.

This excursion had not quite satiated the curiosity of Sir Joseph. On the 3rd of June he set out again, with some Indian guides to trace a river to its source, and ascertain how far its banks were inhabited.

---

* "A spot of a little more than a thousand square feet will contain from thirty to forty Banana plants. A cluster of Bananas, produced on a single plant, often contains from one hundred and sixty to one hundred and eighty fruits, and weighs from seventy to eighty pounds. But reckoning the weight of a cluster only at forty pounds, such a plantation would produce more than four thousand pounds of nutritive substance. M. Humboldt calculates, that as thirty-three pounds of wheat, and ninety-nine pounds of potatoes, require the same space as that in which 4000lbs. of Bananas are grown, the produce of Bananas is consequently to that of wheat as 133, and to that of potatoes as 44." *Library of Entertaining Knowledge.*

Linnæus has been particularly complimentary to the Banana, naming it Musæ paradisaica, either from Mouza, a native term for the plant, or in honour of Antonius Musa, the favourite physician of Augustus.

4 E

Having past a house, which he was told was the last they should see, where they were hospitably entertained with cocoa nuts, they continued to follow the course of the stream, which led them a wild and rugged way, often passing under vaults of native rock. "The way up the rocks was truly dreadful, the sides nearly perpendicular, and in some places one hundred feet high; they were also rendered exceedingly slippery by the water of innumerable springs, which issued from the fissures on their surface; yet up these precipices a way was to be traced by a succession of long pieces of the bark of the *Hybiscus Tiliaceus*, which served as a rope for the climber to take hold of, and assisted him in scrambling from one ledge to another, though upon these ledges there was footing only for an Indian or a goat. One of these ropes was nearly thirty feet in length." From examination of these rocks, Sir Joseph formed an opinion that Otaheite, like Madeira, is of volcanic formation.

On the 4th, he benevolently employed himself in planting a variety of seeds, water-melons, oranges, limes, lemons, &c. Whether any of the stock survive, to testify the good man's kind intent, or any recollection of his beneficence abide in the minds of the natives, we are not informed; but in Otaheite, as in other places, the remembrance of evil seems to outlast that of good, for its inhabitants exactly chronicle the importation of European maladies, and will tell what particular ships brought the small-pox, the measles, and the avenging pest, which Europe derived from the isles on the opposite side of the American continent.

Our voyagers were now preparing for their departure, when a greater embarrassment occurred than had befallen them since their arrival. Webb and Gibson, two young marines, absconded on the night of the 8th of July, and were not missed till next morning. The Commander, who readily guessed the cause of their absence, waited a day or two for their return, but seeing and hearing nothing of them, he began to enquire of the natives where they were concealed; and was informed that they had fled to the mountains, where it would be impossible to find them. It was plain enough that their purpose of remaining behind was favoured by the people among whom they wished to naturalize themselves, but Cook, though he might feel some compunction in tearing them from the objects of their affections, could not suffer the example of desertion to be set with impunity, or he might soon have been left without hands to navigate the vessel. In this emergency, he had recourse to a harsh proceeding; but such as the laws, even of civilized nations, have generally justified. He seized on Tubourai Tamaide, Tomio, and Oberea, all of whom were in the fort at the time.

and made it known that they would not be dismissed till the marines were delivered up. Tootahah was also taken, with the rest, aboard the Endeavour. The poor creatures, especially the women, wept bitterly, when forced into the boat. This measure did not produce the intended result. The party who were sent to fetch back the deserters, did not return. At nine o'clock on the 10th, Webb, and several of the islanders, arrived at the fort with intelligence that Gibson, together with the petty officer and the corporal of marines, who were sent after him, would be detained till Tootahah was discharged from custody. The tables were now turned—but Cook had gone too far to retreat. He despatched Mr. Hicks in the long boat, with orders to rescue the prisoners by fair means or force, and exhorted Tootahah, at his personal peril, to use his influence in bringing about an amicable arrangement. Tootahah's missives soon brought the negotiation to a favourable issue. The fugitives returned, and the hostages were set at liberty. The two Englishmen had actually formed matrimonial connections with Otaheitan girls, purposed to make the island their country, and, in all probability, to adopt all the customs of its inhabitants.

On the 13th July, the Endeavour weighed anchor. At an early hour, the ship was crowded with chieftains, and surrounded by canoes. When she got under way, the superiors took leave, "with a decent and silent sorrow," the multitude with loud and emulous lamentation. It was not merely a parting of strangers from strangers. Tupia, the high-priest of Otaheite, and sometime minister of Oberea, accompanied the British as Pilot and Interpreter, and took with him a native boy, about thirteen years old. He bade adieu to his countrymen with pathetic dignity, and as a last memorial, sent a shirt to Tootahah's favourite paramour; then went with Sir Joseph to the mast-head, and continued waving as long as the canoes were in sight.

The period of our voyagers' sojourn in Otaheite was three months, during which they had acquired a more extensive knowledge of its surface, products, and inhabitants, than many persons, after a long life, possess of the district within a mile of their dwellings. One natural effect of their tarrying was to raise the market. At their first arrival, provisions were to be obtained in abundance for beads; after a little while, nothing would pass current but nails, and before their departure, hogs and poultry were only to be had for hatchets.

At Tupia's suggestion, Cook directed his course northward, for Tethuroa, an island situate about eight leagues N. W. of Point Venus, and visible from the hills of Otaheite. It was found to be small and low, without fixed inhabitants, but occasionally used by the Otaheitans for a fishing station. On the 14th, they passed by Eimeo and Tapomanao. The 15th was hazy, and little way made. Tupia displayed his priestly craft by praying for a wind to his god Tane, and constantly boasted of the efficacy of his prayers, which he secured by never praying till he perceived the breeze on the water.

On the morning of the 16th the Endeavour made the N. W. point of Huaheine. Canoes soon appeared ; shy at first, but grew bolder when they saw Tupia on deck. The king and queen of Huaheine, with some persuasion, were induced to come aboard. After their astonishment was a little abated, they grew quite familiar, and so gracious, that his Majesty of Huaheine proposed to the king of the ship an exchange of names, the highest mark of amity among the potentates of the South Sea, as an exchange of armour among Homeric warriors, or of orders among European princes. Of course the offer was embraced ; and King Oree was Cookee, and Captain Cook was Oree, in all subsequent interviews.

The people of Huaheine speak the language of Otaheite, and resemble the Otaheitans in all particulars, except that, according to Tupia, they would not steal ; but this national distinction they were not careful to preserve. The Endeavour anchored in Owharree bay, a commodious harbour on the west side of the island. Captain Cook, *alias* Oree, King Cookee, Sir Joseph Banks, Dr. Solander, and others, went on shore. Tupia performed some priestly ceremonies, and an exchange of presents was made in behalf of the *Eatuas,* or gods of the respective parties, which was equivalent to the ratification of a treaty. No European ship had previously touched at Huaheine. In order to establish his claim as discoverer, Cook presented King Cookee with a piece of pewter, on which was inscribed, "His Britannic Majesty's ship Endeavour, Lieutenant Cook commander, 16th July, 1769." With this testimonial his Huahienian Majesty promised never to part.

In this island Sir Joseph Banks observed a curious ark or coffer, which, as he was informed by Tupia's boy, was called *Ewharree wo Eatua,* the house of God. No information could be obtained respecting its uses ; but it reminded the philosopher of the ark of the covenant, and he reverently abstained from looking into it. Similar coffers were afterwards seen in other islands.

The natives of Huaheine are less timid than the Otaheitans, at least they shewed less alarm at the explosion of powder : but they are still more indolent, and excessively tedious in trading. Though so near to Otaheite, this island was at least a month forwarder in vegetation. Sir Joseph discovered few new plants, but several nondescript insects, and a remarkable variety of scorpion. He could not persuade any of the natives to climb the hills with him. They declared that the fatigue would kill them. The stay of our voyagers at Huaheine was only three days.

The next island visited was Ulietea, which, according to the information of Tupia, had been recently subdued by the Bolabolans. As soon as the Endeavour hove in sight, two canoes put forth, in each of which was a woman and a pig. The ladies were complimented with a spike nail apiece, and some beads, and were highly gratified with the acquisition. On landing, Tupia went over the same ceremonies as at Huaheine, and Cook took possession of the island in the name of the King of England, by planting the British flag, a ceremony not much wiser than Tupia's, as Cook doubtless felt, but which his commission made it unseemly for him to omit.

The most noticeable things in Ulietea were, 1st, A Morai, not pyramidal, as those at Otaheite, but square, and covered at the top with carved planks: at a little distance was an altar or Ewhatta, on which lay the last oblation—a hog of eighty pounds weight, roasted whole. 2nd, Four or five arks like that at Huaheine. Sir Joseph, unable to restrain his love of knowledge any longer, attempted to peep into them, which gave extreme offence. 3rd, A long house, wherein, besides several rolls of cloth, and other consecrated articles, was the model of a canoe, ornamented with eight human jaws, the trophies of recent battle. 4th, A tree of the Banian kind; a congeries of stems of vast bulk and circumference.

Hazy weather and foul winds till the 24th, when the Endeavour encountered imminent danger of striking against a reef, but providentially passed along a smooth ledge of coral, without damage. There are many of these walls of coral in the South Seas, as perpendicular as a house side.

Passing several small islands, on the 27th the Endeavour made Otahah, the usual residence of the conquering King of Bolabola, whose very name was enough to agitate Tupia with terror. The scientific party went on shore, procured three hogs and some plantains, the latter peculiarly acceptable as a substitute for bread; the rather as the ship's biscuit was all alive with animalculæ, of so pungent a taste, that they blistered the tongue like cantharides. Otahah is, in comparison with others in the same group, a thinly peopled isle; but the population are evidently of the same race. They flocked round the ship, offering provisions for barter. When informed by Tupia of the rank of the strangers, they made obeisance by stripping to the waist as in the presence of their own sovereigns.

On the 29th our voyagers arrived under the Peak of Bolabola, a high, rugged, and inaccessible cliff, beneath which it was impossible to land. It took till twelve o'clock at night to weather it. At eight next morning, they spied a small isle, called Maurua—i. e. the isle of Birds, surrounded by coral reefs and destitute of harbours, but inhabited, and bearing the same produce as the neighbouring isles. They did not attempt to anchor here, but on Sunday 30th, put into a harbour on the west side of Ulietea, in order to stop a leak and take in fresh ballast. In entering the port they met with some nautical difficulties, not easily comprehensible by landsmen.* The natives of Ulietea appear to be civil, well-disposed people, and not being spoiled by the habit of European traffic, parted with their hogs and poultry at reasonable rates. Sir Joseph and Dr. Solander spent a day ashore, very pleasantly; every body seemed to fear and respect them, placing in them at the same time the greatest confidence, behaving as if conscious that they possessed the power of doing mischief without any propensity to make use of it.† Their respect, however, must have been somewhat troublesome, for if any dirt or moisture happened to be in the way, the Ulieteans strove which of them should carry the gentlemen over on their backs. The manner of receiving the visitors at the principal habitations was somewhat different from what had been observed elsewhere. The people who followed them while they were on their way, rushed forward as soon as they came to a house, and went in before them, leaving a lane for

---

* "As the wind was right against us, we *plied off* one of the harbours, and about three o'clock in the afternoon of the 1st of August we came to an anchor in the entrance of the channel leading into it, in fourteen fathom water, being prevented from *working in* by a strong tide setting outwards. We then *carried out the kedge anchor* in order *to warp into* the harbour; but when this was done, we could not *trip the lower anchor* with all the purchase we could make; we were, therefore, obliged to lie still all night, and in the morning, when the tide turned, the ship going over the anchor, it *tripped of itself*, and we warped the ship into a proper birth with ease and moored in twenty eight fathom, with a sandy bottom." *Hawkesworth, vol. 2, page 62.* This Dr. Hawkesworth thought was sustaining the character of the mariner, just as a farce-writer makes an apothecary's diction of cataplasms, emulsions, and carminatives, and a sailor's of sea-terms, oaths, love, and loyalty. The doctor has indeed thought it necessary to apologise for his tedious detail of marine technicals, and shelters himself under the authority of Pamela. Unintelligible as this sort of language must be to many, it is by no means objectionable in the journal of a real sailor, nor is it improper in a fictitious auto-biography, like Robinson Crusoe, but it is surely unseasonable in a work composed by a professional writer, on a subject that needs not the *adscitious* recommendation of adroit mimicry.

† Whether this remark was Captain Cook's or Sir Joseph Banks', or was introduced by the compiler *suo periculo*, it is just and philosophic. Respect always includes fear, but it also includes esteem—an awe of superior power, combined with a confidence in rectitude of intention. There may be fear without respect, but no respect without fear.

them to pass. When they entered they found those who had preceded them ranged on each side of a long mat, which was spread upon the ground, and at the further end of which sat the family. The children were pretty, well-dressed, and well-behaved, although, like spoiled children in the Old World, they manifestly expected presents as soon as they saw visitors. As they were *pretty* children,* the presents were freely given and prettily received. One girl of six years old, evidently a little lady of consequence, stretched out her hand as the philosophers approached, and accepted the beads which they offered as gracefully *as any European princess.*

These presents propitiated the islanders wonderfully; they were intent upon nothing but how to entertain the strangers, not aware how easily they were entertained. In one place they had an opportunity of seeing a dance performed by one man, who put upon his head a large cylindrical piece of wicker work, about four feet long and eight inches in diameter, faced with feathers placed perpendicularly, with the tops bending forwards, and edged round with shark's teeth, and the tail feathers of tropic birds; when he had put on this head-dress, he began to dance, moving slowly, and often turning his head, so as that the top of his high wicker cap, described a circle, and sometimes throwing it so near the faces of the spectators as to make them start back; this was held among them as a very good joke, and never failed to produce a peal of laughter, especially when it was played off on one of the strangers.

On the 3d, our voyagers were spectators of another dance, executed by two women and six men, accompanied by three drums. The females had their heads dressed in a novel and elegant style; the coiffeure consisting of long plaits of braided hair wound many times round their heads, and ornamented with tastefully disposed flowers of the Cape Jessamine. The Ulietean dancers and musicians performed gratuitously, whereas the stroller ministrels of Otaheite were as craving as the finest singers in Europe. One of the girls had three pearls in her ear, which Sir Joseph Banks was vainly desirous of purchasing. Between the

---

* Sir Joseph, like all philosophers in whom much genius is combined with much simplicity, seems to have been more open to the influence of beauty than certain soi-disant *philosophers* (we scorn to degrade the English term) whose philosophy consists of equal portions of dulness, grossness, and malignity, would altogether approve. We like him the better therefore; only he should not have forgotten his gallantry so far as to let any lady discover from his behaviour, that she was not beautiful. On one occasion, he gave very serious offence to a Chieftain's wife, who was disposed to be gracious, by lavishing all his attentions on her pretty hand-maiden.

dances the men performed a sort of "play extempore," which was not very intelligible to the English ; yet here they might see the drama in its infancy. Just such exhibitions suggested the first idea of tragedy and of comedy in Greece. Another drama, which the gentlemen saw, was regularly divided into four acts. What a pity there were not five, that the critics might have proved the precept of Horace to be grounded in universal nature ! ! !

Soon after the King of Bolabola arrived in Ulietea, from the terror that seemed to attach to his name, the English naturally expected to see a fine specimen of barbaric heroism, but he proved a feeble old man, half-blind, and particularly stupid. He received the deputation without any of the usual ceremonies, and scarcely could understand whether hogs or women would be acceptable to his visitors. He treated them however with sufficient respect, and of course did not insult his Britannic Majesty by refusing the presents of his representatives. His name was Opoony, he reigned over three Islands, Bolabola, Ulietea, and Otahab, and must have been a very potent prince. The retention of sovereignty by an imbecile old man is an extraordinary circumstance in savage polity. In Otaheite, the son, as soon as born, nominally succeeds to his father's estate and office. The father becomes trustee for his son till the son's majority, and then becomes the subject and dependant on his own offspring. Such an unnatural arrangement has doubtless its effect in producing the slight esteem of marriage, and yet more fearful frequency of infanticide, which make that beautiful island a foul speck on the ocean. " Bearer of children," is an Otaheitan expression of contempt, used to designate such women, as from weak compassion to their babes renounce the privileged and Nicolaitan community of the Areoi, for the drudging existence of a wife and mother.*

*It is no rare phænomenon among the tribes of earth to find social institutions, and mechanic arts considerably advanced where the moral education has never begun; or which is more probable, has perished from neglect. The reverence of age, and the parental affection, the foci of the orbit in which all human virtue revolves, are sure to be thrust out of their place, where a moral religion is not the sun of the system. The Otaheitans were in many respects a civilized people at the period of their discovery; they had even a highly artificial construction of society, they had established orders, and a law of property ; they had kings, nobles, priests, poets, musicians; they had much natural amiability and considerable docility of intellect—yet they hardly recognised a distinction of right and wrong.

Wherever old age is held in reverence, we may conclude that the tradition of patriarchal morals, however obscured, is not utterly lost. But in all savage communities, the condition of the infirm must be deplorable, and it is not difficult to account for the custom so common among the barbarians of the ancient world, of dispatching the wretched creatures that could no longer defend or cater for themselves. Take away

Though it does not appear that Ulietea was ever united in government with either division of Otaheite ,yet Tupia previous to the Bolabolan conquest had possessed an estate in the former Island, the loss of which he bitterly resented.

The six Islands, Ulietea, Otahah, Bolabola, Huaheine, Tubai, and Maurua, constitute the group called by Cook, the "Society Islands." There are slight diversities of dress and character among them, and probably peculiarities of idiom and pronunciation, yet upon the whole, they do not appear to differ more than the contiguous counties of England; and the communication between them, by means of canoes, is more constant and easy than that between Britain and her neighbour Islands was a century ago. Compared to our Northern Seas, the Pacific Ocean deserves the name which Magalhaens bestowed on it in 1521 ; and to a people who can swim as soon as they can walk, the great waters are nothing dreadful. The length of the voyages undertaken by these Islanders in their canoes, appears wonderful, and clearly does away with the difficulty which some sceptical speculators have made concerning the original peopling of spots remote from the ancient continent. Tupia assured Captain Cook that he had visited Islands to the west, which it took twelve days to arrive at in a *Páhie*,* though the Páhie went much quicker than the Ship; but that in returning thence to Otaheite his company had been thirty days.

Declining to land on Bolabola, the approach whereto was dangerously beset with coral reefs, the Endeavour got under way on the 9th. of August. The purpose of the commander was now to ascertain or disprove the existence of the *Terra Australis Incognita*, which had been so positively assumed by Geographers, that ardent projectors had begun to lay plans for the colonization and conquest of this golden region of the south, and calculated the boundless profits of its trade. Various points of land seen by former navigators had been described as portions of the unknown continent, and probably Cook had little doubt of its reality.

As they were sailing out of harbour, Tupia earnestly requested that a shot might be fired in the direction of Bolabola, an Island for which he had a special antipathy, arising partly from the loss of his property in

---

the belief of immortality in connection with moral accountability, and man's life is cheap as beasts's. On his own principles, Marat was perfectly humane and just, when he proposed to secure the liberty of France by striking off 300,000 heads ; and surely if the dead rise not, the practice which has but lately become obsolete among the Battahs of Sumatra, of eating their relatives when they are past work, is as unobjectionable when applied to a biped as to an ox, and far more merciful than suffering them to die so slowly that none call it murder.

• The Pahie and the Tramah, are different species of canoes, the former the most useful for long trips, the latter for fishing and fighting.

Ulietea.   His wish was complied with, though Bolabola was seven leagues off.

On the 13th, about noon, land was seen to the south-east, which proved the Isle of Oheteroha.   From the natives of this place our voyagers experienced more decided hostility than from any they had hitherto met with, and could obtain no supply of provisions.   As they had furnished themselves with a considerable number of living hogs and poultry, at more hospitable stations, they hoped to fare well on the waves, but the hogs would eat nothing they had to give them, and the poultry perished of disease in the head.

Few incidents worthy of note took place in the passage between Oheteroa, and New Zealand.   On the 25th the voyagers celebrated the anniversary of their leaving England, by cutting a Cheshire cheese and tapping a barrel of porter, which proved very good.   On the 30th a comet appeared—when Tupia observed it, he cried out in consternation that as soon as the Bolabolans should see it they would massacre the people of Ulietea, who were doubtless even then flying to the mountains.   Was astrological prediction a part of his priestly function?   or was this the sincere surmise of his terrors?

On the 27th of September, a seal asleep on the surface of the water, and several bunches of sea-weed, announced the neighbourhood of land; next day, more sea-weed—on the 29th a bird resembling a snipe, with a short bill, which they hoped was a land bird—on the 1st October, birds in plenty, and another seal asleep on the water.   They now began to look eagerly for terra-firma.   A bird, or a piece of wood—anything is an incident in a sea voyage.   On Friday October 6th, land was seen from the mast head—On the 7th it fell calm, and when a breeze sprung up in the afternoon, the land was still distant seven or eight leagues.   As more distinctly seen it appeared the more extensive; with four or five ridges of hills, each rising above the other, and over all a chain of mountains that seemed to be of enormous height.   The general opinion was that this was the Terra Australis Incognita.   As the vessel approached the shore, one object after another grew upon the sight.   They saw the hills clothed with wood, the valleys sprinkled with tall trees! then huts, small but neat; and on a small peninsula, a high and regular paling, enclosing the whole top of a hill, which one of the crew insisted upon it must be a park for deer.   Canoes were gliding across a bay which run far in land, and by and by, a considerable collection of people were seen gathered on the beach.   About four, P. M. the ship anchored on the north-west side of the creek, in ten fathoms water.   The sides of the bay are white cliffs.   Did they not remind the roamers of dear England?   The middle low land with towering tiers of hills in the distance.

In the evening of Sunday the 8th of October, 1769, Lieutenant

Cook, Banks, Solander, and a party of men went ashore, as they vainly deemed on the long sought southern continent. But ill omens met them at the very threshold of their hopes, and it was destined that their arrival should be signalized with immediate bloodshed. A party of natives were seen on the west side of the bay. Cook and his company made for them, but as soon as their approach was perceived, the Indians all ran away. Their flight, however was no effect of timidity, for presently there rushed from the wood four men armed with lances, and evidently with bloody intentions. The coxswain of the pinnace twice fired over their heads, but as they continued brandishing their javelins, and one of them was in the act of darting, the coxswain fired with ball, and shot him dead. By this time Cook and his party, who had been unaware of the attack till they heard the shots, came up, and found the body lying lifeless, the ball having pierced the heart. The deceased was of middle stature, a dark brown complexion, curiously tatooed, his hair fastened in a knot at the top of his head; his dress composed of a cloth different from any they had seen before, but corresponding exactly with the description in the voyages of the Dutch navigator, Tasman, which perhaps first suggested the probability that this was the land which he had discovered, and called, first, Staten Land, and afterwards New Zealand. They then returned to the ship, and as their boat rowed off, heard the natives in loud and earnest discourse, as if debating on what had happened and what was to be done.

As the Coxswain's firing was merely an act of self-defence, and these people were not to be repelled by the smoke and noise of musquetry, he was not censured for the proceeding. A similar occurrence, but without the same apology had not prevented the most friendly intercourse at Otaheite, and Cook resolved to omit nothing that might procure the good will of the nation to whom he was so unexpected and unwelcome a visitor; but he was never able to come to any agreement with them, though Tupia, who soon found, to the great satisfaction of his English friends, that his language was almost the same as that of the natives, performed the part of a skilful negociator, assuring them that the strangers wanted nothing but provisions and water, and would give iron, the use of which he endeavoured to explain. Their aversion was not to be overcome; they did indeed consent to trade, but nothing that was offered appeared to them of any value. Beads they slighted, and of iron they did not see the utility. In this difficulty, Cook thought the best plan would be to entice some of the natives on board, that by kind usage and accustoming them to the sight of European articles, he might promote a treaty of commerce. This scheme was not successful, and produced the most culpable act in which the great navigator was engaged. On Monday the 9th, he had set out with three boats to make a circuit of the bay in search of fresh water. He saw two canoes coming in from sea, one under sail, and the other worked with paddles. He endeavoured to intercept one of them, which contained four men and three boys, before it got to land. In this he failed, for their paddles outrun the boat. Tupia called to them, but they would not stop. A musquet was fired over their heads, which provoked instead of terrifying them. They ceased paddling and begun to strip, clothes like theirs being an incumbrance in battle, and when the boat came up attacked it so lustily with their paddles, staves, and pikes, that the crew were forced to fire in their own defence, and the four men were killed. The three boys then leaped into the water, but were taken and forced into the boat in spite of their resistance. At first the poor youths were overwhelmed with grief and consternation, expecting nothing but instant death. But as soon as they were convinced that their lives were safe, their terror was converted to an ecstacy of joy and gratitude. They sang, danced, and eat voraciously, particularly of salt pork, which was peculiarly agreeable to their palates, possibly from the alleged resemblance of swine's to human flesh. Inordinate devouring is common to all islanders of the pacific, perhaps to savage tribes in general, whose stomachs possess an elasticity which enables them to endure degrees of inanition and of repletion incredible to an European gastronome. The utmost civic achievements in the turtle way fall far short of a Kamscadale's excesses in whale blubber. After an enormous supper, the three young Indians retired to rest. When left alone, their melancholy returned, and they were heard to moan and sigh deeply, but by the enlivening assurances of Tupia, whom they regarded, if not quite as a countryman, yet as a creature of the same species as themselves, they recovered their spirits in the morning, did abundant justice to breakfast, and favoured the company with a song. "The tune," says Cook, "was slow and solemn, like our psalm tunes, containing many notes and semitones." They were then dressed and adorned with bracelets, anklets, and necklaces, which gave them the utmost delight. When first told that they were to be set ashore, they expressed great satisfaction, but, being shewn the place where it was proposed to land them, their courage sunk within them, and they earnestly implored not to be left there, "because," said they, "that district belonged to their enemies, who would kill and eat them." This the English took at first for the exaggeration of terror, for they had not yet ascertained the existence of cannibalism among this people. Their fears were once more dispelled, when, on going ashore with their commander and a boat's crew, one of them espied his uncle among a group of Indians on the beach. Still they were unwilling to be left, changed their minds several times, and when the boat finally rowed away, earnestly entreated to be taken on board. Had Cook devoted his youth to the classics instead of the coal trade, he might have been reminded of the fair captives in Greek and Roman story, who looked on a separation from their captors as a renewal of their captivity.

Of this abduction and the bloodshed attending it, Cook, through his secretary, Dr. Hawkesworth, speaks thus—"I am conscious that the feelings of every reader of humanity will censure me for having fired upon these unhappy people, and it is impossible that on a calm review, I should approve it myself. They certainly did not deserve death for not choosing to confide in my promises, or not consenting to come on board my boat, even if they had apprehended no danger, but the nature of my service required that I should obtain a knowledge of their country, which I could no otherwise effect then by forcing my way into it in a hostile manner, or gaining admission through the confidence and good will of the people. I had already tried the power of presents without effect, and I was now prompted, by my desire to avoid further hostilities, to get some of them on board, as the only method left of convincing them that we intended them no harm, and had it in our power to contribute to their gratification and convenience. Thus far my intentions certainly were not criminal, and though in the contest, which I had no reason to expect, our victory might have been complete without so great an expense of life, yet in such situations, when the command to fire has been once given, no man can restrain its excess, or prescribe its effect."

Failing in all endeavours to procure supplies where he then was, Cook bestowed the name of *Poverty Bay* on the scene of his disaster, and next morning weighed anchor. The kind treatment of the boys had not been wholly thrown away, for when, in the afternoon, the ship lay becalmed off the new-named Bay of Poverty, several islanders came on board, manifested friendly dispositions, and invited the commander to return to his old station. But he resolved to pursue his discoveries, and sailed away southward, in hopes of obtaining better anchorage than he had yet seen. While the ship was hauling round the south end of a small island, which Lieutenant Cook, delighted it may be, with any thing in nature that wore an European aspect, named the isle of Portland, from its very great resemblance to Portland in the British Chanel, she fell suddenly into shoal water. The natives observing that the working of the vessel was less regular than usual, and the crew apparently at a loss, conceived a project to turn her distress to their own advantage. The white cliffs were peopled with a dusky multitude, moving to and fro in busy deliberation, and presently five canoes, full of armed warriors put out, with shouting and brandishing of lances. But a four pounder fired wide, so that the ball was seen leaping along the water, effectually cowed them. They rose up, and shouted, stood awhile in consideration, betook them to their paddles, and made a precipitate retreat. The 14th of October again threatened hostilities. Just as the pinnace and long boat were hoisted out to search for fresh water, five canoes, manned with between eighty and ninety New Zealanders quitted the shore, with the usual warlike demonstrations. To avoid extremities, Tupia was directed to explain to them, the destructive nature of the thunder with which the ship was armed, and though the savages seemed to give little credit to his statements, the four pounder, fired wide as before, and loaded with grape shot, overcame their incredulity, and sent them away paddling with all their might. By Tupia's persuasion, the people of one canoe, so far laid aside their fears as to come aboard the Endeavour, and receive presents. On the 15th, a trading transaction took place, which proved that civilization is not necessary to make men knaves. In a large armed canoe, which came boldly along side the ship, was a man, who had over his back a black skin, like that of a bear. Cook, wishing to know from what animal it had been taken offered him a piece of red baize in exchange for it. The bargain seemed to give great satisfaction. The man held out the skin as if willing to receive the baize, but when he had got the cloth in his possession, he began to wrap it up with the utmost nonchalance, showing no intention whatever of parting with his furry mantle, and so the canoe pulled off, none of its crew paying any regard to the British demands for restitution.

Cook was too prudent to revenge this piece of primitive swindling, which probably gained its perpetrator as much applause in New Zealand as the best managed roguery ever received in the oldest country ; but soon.after an act of violence was attempted, which although precedented by his own example in Poverty-bay, was not to be passed over so easily. During some traffic for provisions, Tayeto, Tupias' boy, was placed with others on the ship's side to receive the fish which the New Zealanders were to deliver ; some of the men in the canoe that then lay alongside the Endeavour, watching their opportunity caught hold of the child, and began to make off with him, while two of their number held him forcibly down in the forepart of the canoe. Nothing could be done but to order the Marines who were under arms on deck to fire ; though they purposely fired wide to avoid the chance of hitting Tayeto, yet one man dropped, and in the confusion the boy got loose and leaped into the water, a canoe pulled round to re-capture him, and did not desist till some

i

musquets and a great gun had been fired. The poor little Otaheitan gained the ship unhurt. The point off which this incident took place was forthwith named Cape Kidnappers.

October 18. The Endeavour lay abreast of a peninsula, called Ter-kake, within Portland isle. Two native chiefs were so taken with the English, or their presents that they insisted on remaining aboard all night, to which Lieutenant Cook somewhat hesitatingly consented, but the frank, open countenance of one of them disarmed his suspicions. Next morning, when set ashore, they expressed their surprise at finding themselves so far from their own habitations.

Monday, October 23. Endeavour laying in Tegadoo-bay. Cook went ashore to examine the watering-place, and found every thing to his wishes. The boat landed in the cove without the least surf; wood and water were plentiful, and the people well disposed.

Tuesday 24th. Mr. Gore, with a guard, was sent to superintend the cutting of wood, and the filling of water. On this day, Sir Joseph and Dr. Solander landed and enjoyed the sight of several natural curiosities, among the rest of "a rock perforated through its whole substance, so as to form a rude but stupendous arch or cavern opening directly to the sea; this aperture was seventy-five feet long, twenty-seven broad, and five and forty feet high, commanding a view of the bay, and the hills on the other side." Tegadoo-bay was found by observation to be in latitude 38° 22′ 24″ south. Having sailed in a southern direction as far as Cape Tur-ragain in latitude 40° 34′ our voyagers turned to the north. On the 28th October they were in Toluga bay. The scientific gentlemen went ashore on a small island at the entrance of the bay, where they observed the largest canoe they had yet seen; her length being sixty-eight feet and a half, her breadth five feet, and her height three feet six. They also saw a house of unusually large dimensions, but unfinished. Dr. Solander, among other trifles purchased a top of the natives, exactly resembling that European toy to which Virgil did not disdain to compare a queen. The sellers made signs that it was to be set in motion by whipping.

At day break, on the 1st November, lying in a bay which Lieutenant Cook named after his faithful officer Hicks, the Endeavour was surrounded by no less than forty canoes, followed by others from a different quarter, and manned by as impudent thieves as are commonly to be met with, taking what was offered as the price of their commodities, making no return, and laughing triumphantly at their own cleverness. One fellow in particular displayed a valour and coolness which it is hard not to admire even in an unbarefaced pilferer. Some linen hanging over the ship's side to dry, he calmly untied it and put it into his bundle, then dropping astern with his canoe he laughed heartily. A musquet fired

over his head did not put a stop to his mirth, and though a second musquet charged with small shot struck him on the back, he minded it no
more than a jack-tar would do, the stroke of a rattan, but persevered in
packing up his booty. All the canoes dropped astern, and set up a song
of defiance. Cook was loth to hurt these bold *free-traders*, whose offence
certainly did not deserve death, by the universal law of reason, yet it was
necessary to shew that the English were not to be robbed and insulted
with impunity. To have suffered this bravado to become a national
boast and precedent, would have super-induced the necessity of wholesale slaughter, or obliged the Endeavour to quit the shores of New Zealand without accomplishing one object worthy of her destination. To
convince the savages that their security arose, not from the impotence,
but from the forbearance of the civilized, the four-pounder was fired in
such a direction that the shot only just missed the canoes, whizzing,
and making ducks and drakes along the waves. This put the rowers
upon their speed, and effectually quashed their exultation. The same
method was occasionally resorted to in subsequent emergencies, and
sometimes seconded by a discharge of small shot, by which some peculiarly insolent personages were slightly peppered; but the case of these condign sufferers excited little apprehension and no compassion in their comrades, any farther than to render them rather more circumspect in their
attempts at imposition.

Continuing their course to the north west, after nearing the islet of
Mowtohora, and narrowly escaping some very dangerous rocks, our voyagers fixed on a convenient bay, defended by an island which they christened the Mayor, (probably in honour of Lord Mayor's Day,) to observe
the approaching transit of Mercury.

On the 9th of November, being Lord Mayor's Day, Lieutenant Cook,
Mr. Green, Sir Joseph Banks, Dr. Solander, and others, equipped with
the requisite instruments, went ashore to make the observations which
was performed by Mr. Green alone, the commander meanwhile taking
the sun's altitude; the weather which had been hazy in the early part
of the day, cleared up in time to allow the transit, and its attendant
phænomenon to be accurately observed. By taking the mean of several
observations it was ascertained that Mercury Bay, lies in south latitude 36° 47', west longitude 184° 4'.

It seemed to have been appointed by destiny that the value of Cook
should ever and anon be testified by some fatal accident in his absence.
While he was engaged in the astronomical business on shore, an affray
took place between his crew and the natives, on the usual ground of
fraudulently dealing and defiance, in which Gore, the officer in command, shot one man dead. Had the great navigator been on board, a
few small shot would have answered every good purpose, that could be

intended by the murderous bullet. Yet Gore probably had no greater love of bloodshed than belongs to every sportsman; he felt that the honour of the British flag was to be vindicated from foreign insult, and did not reflect that a savage, like an idiot or a maniac, is incapable of insulting.

Several days were spent in exploring the vicinity of Mercury Bay, the accommodations of which Cook was desirous of noting down for the benefit of future navigators. Not the least of these was an excellent supply of oysters, no way inferior to those of Colchester, whose fame was rife in imperial Rome, and worthy of comparison with the more recently celebrated Powldoodies. From these testacious dainties, the river which disembogues itself into Mercury Bay, received the name of Oyster River. Thus Astronomy and Gastronomy contributed to form a nomenclature at the Antipodes.* Another stream enters the bay, which from the quantity of mangroves growing in it, was named Mangrove River. Both the rivers brought down much iron sand, a sure indication that the metal exists in the island, though the natives were quite ignorant of its use, and could not readily comprehend its value. Unlike the Otaheitans, who would hardly trade for any thing but iron, the New Zealanders preferred cloth, beads, or indeed the merest trifles.

On the 15th November, the Endeavour sailed out of Mercury Bay, but not before the names of the ship and its commander, with the date of the year and month, were carved on a tree at the watering place. Men ever like to leave records of their existence. How many of us have scribbled our insignificant names, where they had less chance of being recognized than those of Cook and his comrades of being read, though in a land where letters were unknown! The usual ceremony of taking possession by hoisting the British flag in the king's name, which does not typify half so kindly a feeling, was not omitted, though the right of discovery, the only right which England could pretend, was clearly anticipated by Tasman, for the Dutch republic.

In the range from Mercury Bay, a threatened attack of the natives afforded Tupia an opportunity of displaying his eloquence and readiness of mind in a very creditable manner. Indeed, the Otaheitan priest possessed abilities which needed nothing but cultivation and a fair field to have set him on a par with the most famous diplomatic cardinals of European history: and then, to his praise, be it spoken

"Peace was *his* dear delight, not Fleury's more."

On the 18th several canoes put forth from different points, but evidently with a common purpose of hostility. Two of them, in which

* New Zealand is very near the Antipodes of London.

there might be as many as sixty men, as soon as they came within hearing, set up the war-hoop, and advanced in fighting attitude. Seeing little notice taken of them, they commenced throwing stones, then fell back, then advanced again, studiously provoking a contest. Tupia, of his own accord, without hint or command, began to expostulate and warn them of their peril, saying that the English had weapons against which theirs were utterly unavailing, and which would destroy them all in an instant. The undismayed islanders retorted, "Set a foot on shore, and we will kill you every one." Tupia rejoined—"Well, but why molest us while we keep the sea? We do not wish to fight, and shall not go ashore, but the sea is no more yours than the ship." These arguments, though they surprised the English by their reasonableness, had no effect on the New Zealanders, but a musquet ball passing clean through one of the canoes sent them ashore in a hurry.

The next station where the Endeavour rested was the Bay of Islands, into which flows a river, called by our voyagers, the Thames. Here the botanists examined some very lofty trees, similar to those which they had seen in Poverty Bay, but not near enough to ascertain their dimensions or species. One was nineteen feet, eight inches in girth, at six feet from the ground, and Cook, taking its altitude with a quadrant, found it eighty-nine feet in height, and as it tapered very little, he computed that it must contain at least three hundred and fifty-six feet of solid timber, straight as a mast, for which, however, it was too heavy, unless, as the ship-carpenter suggested, like the pitch-pine, it might be lightened by tapping.

So little comprehensible was the humanity of Cook to the mere men of action whom he was set over, that they seemed to delight in making up, during his absence, for the forbearance enforced upon them when under his eye. On the 22nd, while he was engaged on shore, Hicks thought proper to inflict the novel discipline of a round dozen on a young Zealander, who had laid hands on a half-minute glass. His countrymen on deck vainly attempted his rescue; Sir Joseph and Tupia interceded in vain; canoes crowded round the vessel, but dared not shew fight; and when the criminal was untied and delivered up, he received a second bastinado from an old man, supposed to be his father, who probably was more enraged at the disgrace incurred to his family and tribe, than indignant at the theft. This piece of subaltern authority produced a great alienation on the part of the natives, and next day, Cook and the gentlemen with him were surrounded in a small island where they had landed by an armed multitude, which exposed them to great peril, but, by the excellent management of the commander, they were dispersed without bloodshed. On the same day Mr. Cook made three of his own crew feel the cat-o'-nine-tails. These honest Englishmen, who were so ready to avenge the violation of property, had broken into the native plantations, and violently taken up the roots* with which they were stocked, maintaining, in the teeth of their captain, that English christians had a right to plunder savages.

On the 5th of December, the Endeavour was in imminent danger of being wrecked while getting out of the Bay of Islands. She weighed anchor about four in the morning, but owing to the light breeze and frequent calms, made little way till in the afternoon, the tide or current setting strong, she drove so fast towards land, that before any measures could be taken for her security, she was within a cable's length of the breakers. The pinnace was hoisted out to take the ship in tow, the men exerted themselves to the utmost, a breeze sprang up off the land, and our navigators rejoiced in their supposed deliverance. So near were they dashing on shore, that Tupia, who knew nothing of the peril which would have been none to *Ivamah* or *Pahie*, kept up a conversation with the people on the beach, whose voices were distinctly audible, in spite of the breakers. About an hour afterwards, the man in the chains cried out "seventeen fathom" at the instant the ship was striking. So uneven, and if the term be allowable, mountainous is the sea's bottom in those parts. The rock being to the windward the ship providentially came off undamaged, and sailed away gallantly.

On the 9th of December, the Endeavour being becalmed in DOUBTLESS BAY, the unavoidable delay was turned to profit by useful enquiries among the natives, from whom by Tupia's good interpretation, our navigator learned that at the distance of three days' row of a canoe, was a point called Moore Whennua, at which the land would take a short

* The potatoe, properly so called, was unknown to the New Zealanders till Cook's second voyage, but they cultivated several species of roots, and the neatness of their plantations, considering their very clumsy gardening tools, was remarkable. Their staple food was a sort of fern root, which grows without culture all over the country; but they planted the sweet potatoe, (called in their language coomera) cocos or eddas, (a plant well known both in the East and West Indies,) some gourds, &c. Grain of any kind they were utterly unacquainted with, and when wheat was first sown amongst them, dug it up, expecting to find the edible part at the root, like potatoes.

Mr. Banks saw some of their plantations where the ground was as well broken down and tilled as even as in the gardens of the most curious persons among us. The sweet potatoes were placed in small hills, some ranged in rows, some in quincunx, all laid by a line with the greatest regularity. The cocos were planted upon flat land, and the gourds were set in small hollows, much as in England. These plantations were of different extent, from one or two acres to ten. *Cook's First Voyage, II,* p. 113.

We have been informed, that the potatoe mentioned by Falstaff, in the Merry Wives of Windsor, as contributing to "the tempest of provocation" upon which the commentators have been so diffuse, was the sweet potatoe or *coomera*, and not our potatoe. It is but just to vindicate that useful vegetable from false accusations.

turn to the south, and thenceforth extend no farther to the west. This point was concluded to be Tasman's Cape Maria Van Diemen, so named by the Dutch discoverer, after the daughter of the Batavian Governor, the lady whose beloved image haunted him in all his wanderings over the deep. "Finding the people disposed to be communicative, Mr. Cook questioned them whether they knew of any country besides their own, they told him that they had seen no other, but that some of their ancestors had reported that there was a land to the north-west, of great compass," called Ulimaroa, where the inhabitants eat Bobrik. Now Bobrik is the word used in Otaheite and the neighbouring islands for a hog, an animal which was at that time unknown in New Zealand. This little word therefore gave a perfect confirmation of the tradition.

On the 13th of December our voyagers came in sight of Cape Maria Van Diemen. About Christmas, the Midsummer of the southern hemisphere, they were assailed by so tremendous a gale of wind, that had they not had good sea-room, it is questionable whether one would have returned to tell their tale. They were five weeks in getting fifty

The Endeavour was not the only European vessel beating about the shores of New Zealand in that tremendous gale. On the very same day (Dec. 12) that Cook left Doubtless Bay behind him, a French vessel, the Saint Jean Baptiste, under the command of M. de Surville, came in sight of the same part of New Zealand. De Surville had sailed from India, in consequence of a report that the English had discovered an island, seven hundred leagues to the west of Peru, abounding in the precious metals, and inhabited by Jews. The inlet which Cook had called Doubtless, he named LAURISTON Bay, in honour of the French Governor of India. He was most hospitably received by the natives, and by the natural address of a Frenchman, won their confidence and affection to a degree which the English could never attain. He suffered very severely by the Christmas storm; a boat containing the invalids of his crew, after the utmost peril of perishing, got into a small creek, which received the name *Refuge Cove.* The sick men were treated with all possible kindness by Naginoui, the chieftain of the adjoining village; they remained in his care, and fed upon his bounty (for which he would accept of no remuneration) till the storm was blown over. Such is the charm of French manners! but mark the sequel; De Surville on some suspicion that a boat of his had been stolen, enticed Naginoui on board the *Saint Jean Baptiste*, (why are holy names thus desecrated?) and forcibly took him away as a captive, and not content with this, ordered the village where his invalids had been tended and cherished, to be burned to the ground—he must have been a very civilised villain. Poor Naginoui died of a broken heart off Juan Fernandez. Singular enough that two Europeans, of two nations, and of such opposite characters, without any actual communication, should arrive at the same point of an unknown land, in the same month. It is not at all singular that the worse of the two was the better received; it only shews that New Zealand is composed of the same stuff as the rest of the Planet. This story, it observed, is taken from the *French* narrative of the Abbé Rochon. We do not tell it to disparage the French character; if the best read man in France, and the best read man in England were pitted against each other, each to relate a villainy committed on the high seas by his opponent's countrymen, and he that had first

leagues... On the 14th of January, they put into a harbour in QUEEN CHARLOTTE's SOUND, where it was proposed to careen and repair the ship, and take in supplies of wood and water. Good water was plenty, and for wood the country was one vast forest. In this station they first obtained proof that cannibalism was actually practised in New Zealand. Having one day gone ashore for provisions, they found a family engaged in cook-victuals after their fashion. The body of a dog was buried in their oven, and many provision baskets stood near it. "Having cast our eyes," says Cook, "carelessly into one of these as we passed by it, we saw two bones pretty cleanly picked, which did not seem to be the bones of a dog, and which upon a nearer examination, we discovered to be those of a human body. As we could have no doubt but the bones were human, neither could we have any doubt that the flesh which covered them had been eaten. They were found in a provision basket, the flesh that remained appeared manifestly to have been dressed by fire, and, in the gristles at the end, were the marks of the teeth which gnawed them. To put an end however to conjecture, we directed Tupia to ask what bones they were; and the Indians without the least hesitation, answered 'they were the bones of a man.' They were then asked what had become of the flesh, and they replied that they had eaten it; 'why did you not eat the flesh of the woman whose body we saw floating on the water?' 'because,' said they, 'she died of disease; besides, she was our relation, and we only eat the flesh of our enemies who are killed in battle.' One of us asked if they had any human bones with the flesh remaining upon them, and upon their answering that all had been eaten, we affected to disbelieve that the bones were human, and said that they were the bones of a dog; upon which one of the Indians with some eagerness took hold of his own fore-arm, and thrusting it towards me, said, that the bone which Mr. Banks held in his hand had belonged to that part of the human body; at the same time to convince us that the flesh had been eaten, he took hold of his own arm with his teeth and made show of eating; he also bit and gnawed the bone which Mr. Banks had taken, drawing it through his mouth, and shewing by signs that it had afforded a delicious repast."

played out his hand should forfeit, the game would hardly be decided in one year. But the tale is of some use to better study than the fostering of national antipathies. Some writers, blessed with short memories or plentiful ignorance, ascribe all the real and imaginary crimes of the French in modern times to the Revolution, and thence take occasion to condemn all efforts of all nations in behalf of liberty. Now M. de Surville visited New Zealand some years before the Revolution, and yet was as cruel, as treacherous, and as ungrateful, as if he had sailed with the tricolour at his mast head. The demoralization which made the Revolution what it was, grew up under the monarchy.

Voyagers and travellers of all kinds that have seen mankind in many shapes have generally "supped full of horrors," and learn to look as calmly on the moral aberrations of the species, as a physiologist considers the ghastly appearances of morbid anatomy; rather feeling power, and therein delight, from the extension of their knowledge, than dejection from the infirmity of their nature : yet we can scarcely imagine that the philosophers did not dream of cannibals; perhaps—nothing indeed more likely, that they were turned cannibals themselves, possessed with an unclean spirit that compelled them all loathing to gnaw and gnash at the festering bones of some living corpse, that all the while glared at them with its supernatural unmoving eyes. If their dreams were such, how pleased must have been their waking in the early morn by the sweetest melody of little birds that ever " broke the silence of the seas." The ship lay about a quarter of a mile from shore, and the distance and intervening waters made the music more harmonious. It was a throng of notes, from countless warblers singing as it were in emulation, and the sound was "like small bells exquisitely turned." Such bells, as in the voluptuous fancies of the east, ring the welcome of the blessed into paradise. These birds begin to sing about two hours after midnight, and continue their song till sunrise ; what fairy land of love and music might not a youthful poet have anticipated, who had heard these songsters while floating on the dark blue waters to an unknown isle. Unfortunately our navigators could not forget that they sang to cannibals—no matter, they sung for their own delight and their Maker's glory, and will sing when every child in that long savage region is taught to lisp its Maker's praise.

The Endeavour had now nearly circumnavigated the more northerly of the two islands which go by the common name of New Zealand. Queen Charlotte's Sound, in which she was lying, is in the north-eastern coast of the southern island, called by the natives Tavai-poenamoo. Cook was not yet aware of the strait which separates these islands, but his observation from a hill on the shore of Queen Charlotte's sound, determined him to search for the passage. The bay he found to be of great extent, indented with smaller coves and harbours in every direction; the country for the most part an impenetrable forest. On one excursion Mr. Cook and his friends fell in with a single man fishing in a canoe, at whom they wondered, because he did not seem to wonder at them ; but this was nothing unnatural; wonder is not the emotion of contented ignorance—it denotes the first quickening of the love of knowledge. Savages have in general as little curiosity as the utterly uneducated portion of civilized communities. He who never troubled himself to account for any thing, will not have his attention arrested by what he is unable to explain. When the comparing power is altogether inert, as in savages, idiots, and new-born babies, or suspended as in dreams, nothing appears extraordinary. The fisherman proved to be well disposed enough, and readily drew up his net to have it examined. The natives in the neighbourhood of Queen Charlotte's Sound, appeared to be a good-natured, intelligent race, ready to barter their fish for nails; whether they perceived, by a natural quickness of parts, the uses to which iron may be put, (which are obvious and easily shewn) or had become acquainted with its utility, by some means of which no record remains. There is indeed reason to conjecture, that some European vessel had fallen on the New Zealand coast, between the period of Tasman's, and that of Cook's visit, probably not long before the latter, and that the crew had been entirely cut off. Cook, desirous to ascertain if any memory of Tasman lingered among the savages, directed Tupia to enquire of an old man, whether he had ever seen such a ship as the Endeavour before; the old man replied in the negative, but said that a small vessel with four men in it had come from Ulimaroa, the land to the north, and that all the men were killed. It will be recollected that the people in the vicinity of Cape Maria Van Dieman spoke of their ancestors having been at a land to the north, called Ulimaroa. Capthin Cruise who was in New Zealand for ten months in 1820, heard a very similar tale from an aged native, who said that a boat's crew, who had gone ashore to trade for provisions, had been massacred by his own countrymen; yet of this crew, or the vessel they belonged to, no account had been received in Europe. The further enquiries of Captain Cook, in 1772 and 1774, still confirmed him in the opinion that some Europeans had perished in New Zealand, between 1642 and 1769.

While the Endeavour lay in Queen Charlotte's Sound, Mr. Cook, by repeated observations, satisfied himself that the inlet of the seas, which he had partially explored, was a strait, and the country to the north (called by the natives, Eaheinomauwe) an island, and resolved to make the passage. Previous to sailing, he erected two piles of stones, on separate eminences, in which he concealed bullets, shot, coins, and other articles of European manufacture, to convince whatever European might arrive in those parts, that the honours of discovery were anticipated. Not neglecting to take possession in the king's name, with the usual formalities, which, by an odd coincidence, was done on the 30th of January, and having christened the harbour Queen Charlotte's Sound, he prepared to depart, but was detained for some time by bad weather. The violent wind and rain on the 31st put to silence those sweet little birds whose nightly serenade had never before been intermitted. . On the 5th February, 1770. the Endeavour got under sail, but the wind failing, came again to an anchor.   To turn this delay to some account, Sir Joseph and Dr. Solander went on shore to see if any gleanings of natural knowledge remained, and in the course of their excursion, fell in with the most delightful family they had yet found in New Zealand ; so pleasant, so affable, so unsuspecting, so communicative, that it was quite heart-breaking not to have made their acquaintance before.   On the 6th February, Lieutenant cleared the sound, and stood away for the East. In passing the strait, which justly bears the name of its discoverer, the Endeavour was in great peril of shipwreck from the violence of the ebb-tide driving her upon the rocks in the narrow between Cape Tiera-witte on the north and Cape Koamoroo to the south.   Having escaped this, and surmounted some other difficulties, Mr. Cook established the insularity of Eaheinomauwe beyond contradiction ; and then proceeding southward from Cape Turnagain, he circumnavigated the southern divi-sion of New Zealand, (called Poenamoo) to the great advantage of geography and his own immortal honour, but without meeting any adventure which need detain our narrative.   We must not, however, forget to mention, that Mr. Cook and the whole ship's company were on one occasion seriously alarmed for the safety of our friend, Sir Joseph, who, intent on the pursuit of strange birds, had rowed away out of the reach of prompt assistance, when four canoes and fifty-seven men, were seen to put forth, apparently with evil designs against the philosopher. Signals were made to apprize him of his situation, but the position of the sun prevented his seeing them.   However, his boat was soon observed in motion, and he got safe on board before the people in the canoes, who gazed at the ship from a distance with a sort of stupid irresolute astonishment, took any notice of him.   We may be sure he was heartily welcomed, for he was a man whose good nature made him as dear to the tars, who doubtless had many a laugh at his scientific enthusiasm, as to the philosophic commander, who appreciated and sympathised with that passion for natural knowledge, which led him to forego the English comforts of a plentiful fortune, and undergo the dangers and privations of a voyage of discovery.   From the mixture of wonder and timidity exhibited by the natives on this occasion, Mr. Cook denominated the land whence they had put off the LOOKERS-ON.   An island further to the south, about five leagues from shore, received the name of BANKS' Isle. It is not the only spot in the Pacific that preserves the memory of the adventurous philosopher.

The circuit of Tavai Poenamoo commenced on the 9th of February, and was completed on the 27th of March, when the Endeavour anchored in Admiralty Bay, having surveyed the whole coast of New Zealand with an accuracy which had left little for subsequent navigators to do.

So perfect is Cook's chart that M. Crozet declared there were few parts of the coast of France so accurately laid down. The ingenuity of a discoverer is often severely tasked in the invention of names, and much of individual or national character appears in the nomenclature of new-discovered countries. The Spaniards and Portuguese, who mingle their religion with every thing, with their common salutations, their loves, their wars, their very crimes, have filled sea and land with their saints and holy times, thick as the sky with heathen deities and mythological monsters. The English, who did not commence discoverers till they were Protestants, have had either too little affection or too much reverence for Divine things to bestow sacred names on earth or water. Any little circumstance attending the discovery, any fancied resemblance to what they had left at home, serves them to give a name, and these failing, their own names, or the king's, or queen's, or the ministers', or lords' of the admiralty will serve the turn. It is a pity that our sir-names are the ruggedest part of our language, as any one who will cast his eye over a map of the United States may be convinced. Luckily, Cook's earliest patron was Palliser, and really, Cape Palliser would not disgrace a sonnet. But Hicks, and Banks, and Brett, and Hawke, and Saunders, absolutely make us regret the polysyllabic native nomenclature which they supplant, though Taoneroa, Shukehanga, Taranake, Wangaroog, Moore-whenuua, and Tierawitte are a great deal too long for the shortness of English breath and human life. Seriously, it is always good to preserve native appellations when they can be ascertained, and this seems to have been Cook's general practice. When new names are to be given, they should be either descriptive or historical. No man will ever be remembered for having his name affixed to a rock or a river, who would not be remembered without it. The calling of newly erected or discovered places after towns or rivers in the old world is very objectionable, as tending to confusion, though it arises from a natural feeling; a feeling which perhaps influenced Cook, when he marked out the banks of the Thames as the most eligible situation in New Zealand for a European settlement.

Though the coasts of the two islands were satisfactorily surveyed, and the connection of New Zealand with a Southern continent disproved during Cook's first visit, little was observed of the interior. The utmost diligence of the naturalists left them imperfectly acquainted with its natural productions. They saw no land quadrupeds but dogs and rats, and even these are supposed not to be indigenous. They heard, indeed, of great lizards, or alligators,* but never met with any. The

* According to Captain Cruise, the New Zealanders believe that the Atua, or destroying Daemon enters the body of the dying in the shape of a lizard, to devour

4 H

paucity of quadrupeds in all the South-sea islands is a strong presumption that the isles are of comparatively recent formation; raised from the depths of ocean by the agency of volcanic fire, or gradually constructed by the slow architecture of the coral insects, haply commenced at the beginning of time.* The prevalence of a mutually intelligible language proves indisputably that one race of men have peopled all the new-made spots that sprinkle the Pacific, and the radical identity of that language with the Malay, demonstrates that the population came, perhaps at no remote period, from the East. The cultivated vegetables, the bread fruit, the cocoa tree, the banana, the plantain, the sweet potatoe, point to the same quarter, and probably the hogs and poultry of the Society islands, and the dogs of New Zealand accompanied the first settlers in their migration.

Seals are common on the New Zealand shores. Of insects few were discovered, but birds are very numerous, and for the most part of peculiar species. The most interesting are a kind of mocking bird, and the little nocturnal songsters of which we have already spoken. There are also many sorts of wild ducks, sea gulls, wood pigeons, rails, parrots, and paroquets. Before they had experienced the fatal powers of fire-arms, these birds had no fear of man, but would perch on the muzzle of a musquet. Now they fly away at the sight of an European, or a native armed with a gun (for the bow is unknown in New Zealand.) Who will say that birds are without understanding, or improgressive, seeing they are capable of experience?

Dr. Solander observed about four hundred species of plants, most of them new. The timber trees are majestically straight and tall, and furnish almost the only articles of commerce which New Zealand has hitherto supplied. There is a kind of flax, a beautiful plant, the fibre of which the women work into the cloth which composes their dresses. This business is performed by the hand alone, upon pegs, in a mode similar to lace-making. Sir Joseph Banks had the honour of discovering a new sort of spinach,—the *Tevagonia expansa*—which lasts all summer. Its cultivation has succeeded in England.+

his entrails. The animal is held in the utmost horror, and is said to make great havoc among children. But it does not appear that any European has seen it. May not its existence in New Zealand be altogether problematical, and the superstition connected with it traditionary from the first oriental settlers? Do not the lions and serpents of early gothic fable, in like manner testify the oriental derivation of the Scandinavians?

* See Montgomery's "Pelican Island" for a beautiful illustration of this Hypothesis.

+ Whoever is curious to be further informed concerning New Zealand and its inhabitants, and has not time, means, or inclination to consult many and bulky books,

It was now to be considered which way the ship should steer. The commander's wish was to return by Cape Horn, in order to ascertain the existence or non-existence of the long-expected southern continent, the expectation whereof was already much abridged. But the state of the vessel, and the season of the year, dissuaded the enterprise, which Cook was destined one day to perform. After some deliberation it was resolved to steer westward, for the east coast of New Holland, and then track that coast to its northern extremity, and so return to England by the East Indies. On Saturday the 31st of March, 1770, our commander sailed from Cape Farewell,* so named to commemorate his adieu to New Zealand, around which he had now spent six months. New Holland came in sight on the 19th of April, and on the 28th of that month the ship anchored in a large inlet, which, from the richness and novelty of the surrounding vegetation, was afterwards called Botany Bay, and the Botanists, Banks, and Solander, gave their names to the two promontories that form its entrance. Botany Bay was doomed, however, to associations quite alien from the calm industry of botanical researches.

In the afternoon the boats were manned. Cook and his friends, with Tupia, made for a point whereon they had observed some sable human beings assembled, who, as they showed no sign of alarm at the approach of the ship, were not expected to make any opposition to their landing. This surmise proved false. As the British pulled up, most of the natives ran away; but two men, bearing lances ten feet long, advanced into the

---

may be satisfied with a perusal of " The New Zealanders," one of the pleasantest volumes in that rightly-named series, " The Library of Entertaining Knowledge." We know not of any work that within so comprehensible a compass, exhibits so true and vivid a picture of man in the state just above savage life. The New Zealander is a perverted rather than a degraded creature : he sometimes shocks, but he does not disgust; therefore he may safely be trusted with the youthful imagination. The little book which we recommend is written in a truly philosophic spirit. Clear alike from the jacobinical paradox and misrepresentation which hold up the so-called state of nature as the proper state of man, and from the weak-stomached and nervous irascibility which regards the poor tatooed cannibal as an irredeemable monster, fit only for slavery or extirpation, the intelligent author teaches an important lesson of self-knowledge, thankfulness, and beneficence. Of self-knowledge—for what the New Zealander appears, every man by nature is; of thankfulness, for the civilization which we inherit, and the light in which we live; of beneficence, by making us acquainted with beings of like passions and like capabilities as ourselves, to whom it rests with us to impart the blessings which we enjoy, and the faith in which we hope to be blessed eternally. Who is the compiler of this excellent book?

* Cape Farewell is the north-eastern extremity of Tavai Poenamoo. There is another Cape Farewell, named, no doubt, from a similar circumstance, at the southern point of Greenland, and eastern entrance to Davis' Straits.

water, to forbid the invaders' ingress, brandishing their weapons, and uttering harsh sounds unintelligible to Tupia. Two against forty, they seemed resolute to preserve their father-land from the pollution of a foreign foot. Cook, who could not but admire their courage, (which, after all, was not more extraordinary than that of the New Zealand birds, before they learned the power of fire-arms), ordered his boat to lay on her oars, and parlied with them by signs, threw them nails, and such like trifles, with which they seemed pleased, and then endeavoured to make them understand that he wanted water, and that he had no design to injure them. They waved their hands : this was interpreted as an invitation to proceed, and the boat put into shore ; the two war-riors bade defiance ; a musquet was fired between them ; the younger of the two started back, dropping a bundle of lances, but instantly recovered, and both stood their ground, and began to throw stones ; some small shot was discharged at them, which struck the elder on the legs, whereupon he ran to a house some hundred yards distant. Cook and his party landed, hoping the contest was over ; but presently the New Hollander returned with a shield or target. He and his comrade each darted a lance among the boat's crew, but without effect ; and on the firing of a third musquet, another lance was thrown, and then both fled. Cook and his companions advanced towards the huts, in one of which they found some children left alone. Into this they threw beads, ribbons, bits of cloth, and other like articles, which they hoped would propitiate the good will of the parents ; but on revisiting the hut next morning, they found the articles untouched. This experiment was repeated several times, increasing the value of the bait at each trial, but still the New Hollanders would not bite, and all attempts to establish a communication with them were unavailing.

Though the first landing had been so desperately disputed, the natives made no further shew of fight, but quitted their habitations, and fled up the country. If by chance any of them came in sight, they hid themselves in the woods when they saw the strangers, as regardless of all invitations to parley as rabbits in a warren. Little, therefore, could be learned of their habits, during the week that the Endeavour was moored in Botany Bay, but enough to shew that they were in the lowest grade of human existence.

Much more agreeable objects of contemplation were found in the trees, and flowers, and birds — the latter exceedingly numerous, and of splendid plumage. Loriquets, cockatoos, and parrots, green, red, blue, and glossy black, flew in coveys of a score together. Tupia, who was now become an excellent marksman, made great havoc among them, the feathers appearing to him a valuable prize. While engaged in a shooting excursion, he once met with nine of the natives, who scoured away precipitately at the sight of his gun. This terror of fire-arms is not instinctive either in men or animals; nor will a slight peppering of small shot give much uneasiness to a savage, who, for mourning, or embellishment, or distinction, is accustomed to mangle himself more painfully. The people had doubtless observed the destructive effect of English weapons upon birds.

One of the advantages which induced Cook to recommend Botany Bay as the site of a British settlement, might be the plentiful supply of oysters. Among other inhabitants of the waters in this vicinity, our voyagers caught large sting-rays—a fish cognate to the Torpedo, but without its electric properties, with whose jagged barb several tribes are used to point their weapons. Circe is described as arming her son with a dart headed in this manner. Very marvellous properties were formerly attributed to this sting, which might arise from confounding the animal bearing it with the Torpedo.

During the period of the Endeavour's lying in Botany Bay, Cook caused the English colours to be displayed every day on shore, and took care that the ship's name, and the date of the year, should be inscribed on one of the trees near to the watering place. This formality of taking possession in the King's name, in most instances meant only to assert the right of discovery, in this case proved a true omen. Botany Bay, though not at present the seat of a British Colony, has become in common parlance the English name of Australia.

Our voyagers sailed out of Botany Bay on Sunday, the 6th of May, and continued to track the coast northward. The navigation was rendered particularly tedious by the shoals which jut out suddenly from the shore, and the sharp coral rocks which rise in an abrupt pyramid from the bottom; by the irregularity of tides and currents, and by other causes—embarrassing under any circumstances, but especially so to the first vessel that braved the unknown perils of the voyage.* Yet Cook conducted his charge in safety for an extent of

---

* The length to which this article unavoidably extends forbids us to dwell upon the discoveries made in the passage between Botany Bay and Trinity Bay; nor were they of any great consequence except in a geographical point of view. Cook explored and named a number of bays, creeks, and headlands; but notwithstanding the general accuracy of his observations, many of the natural harbours and inlets which have since been discovered, escaped his notice in consequence of the manner in which the rocky heads and sandy downs on the coast overlap one another; among the rest Port Jackson, the Gyaros of Britain. Repeatedly he went ashore to take in provisions, wood, and water, to observe the natural productions of the country, and to make vain advances to the inhabitants, who, if by any chance they were visible, scampered

two and twenty degrees of latitude, or more than a thousand and three hundred geographical miles, before any serious accident occurred. But on the 10th of June, as he was steering from a bay to which he had given the name of TRINITY Bay, about 16° south latitude, on a fine moonlight night, in cheerful expectation of reaching the land discovered by Quiros in the early part of the seventeenth century; while the navigators were at supper, they suddenly found themselves in shoal water; the man in the chains called twelve, ten, and eight fathom in the compass of a few minutes. Every man was ordered to his station, and every thing was ready to put about and come to an anchor, when the next cast of the lead meeting with deep water, it was concluded that the vessel had gone over the tail of the shoal. The water deepened to twenty-one fathom, perfect tranquillity took the place of alarm, and the gentlemen whose duty did not require them to be watchers, went contentedly to bed. This was between nine and ten o'clock. About eleven, the water shoaled at once from twenty to seventeen fathom, and before the lead could be cast again the ship struck, and remained immovable, except so far as she was rocked by the breakers. In a minute every soul was on deck, and each might read his own terror in the other's countenance. The roughest sailors were tamed—not an oath was heard—the awe of a death bed was upon all.

The ship had been lifted over a ledge of rock, and stuck in a groove or hollow, of so cavernous a structure, that in some places there might be four or five fathom of water, and in others not so many feet. To add to her distress, the sheathing boards and false keel were riven off

away as soon as they saw the white men approach. Tupia seemed to feel his own superiority to these poor wretches, " Taata Enos," as he called them, with great complacency.

The naturalists were more successful in their researches among the animal and vegetable tribes. In one place they shot a bird like a Bustard, which proved such excellent eating, that it was thought worthy to give name to Bustard Bay, in 24° 4' south latitude. A little to the north of Cape Capricorn, Sir Joseph Banks caught two crabs of a novel species; one whose joints and claws were adorned with an exquisite ultra-marine blue, while its under surface was of a delicate semi-transparent white, giving its crustaceous armour altogether the appearance of fine porcelain; the other more slightly tinged with azure, and marked on the back with three brown spots. But these crabs are not good to eat. Still further to the north, they found the fields and trees covered with millions of butterflies, which absolutely thickened the air. Near the same part they discovered the leaping fish, which is about the size of a minnow, and from the strength and elasticity of its pectoral fins, jumps along the ground as nimbly as a frog.

It is pleasant to see strange animals in a menagerie, to see rare plants in a botanic garden; but what must it be to set the first scientific eyes upon them in their native haunts? Naturalists are the happiest of philosophers.

her bottom by the jagged points of the coral, and were seen floating about in the moonshine—every moment was making way for the waves to swallow up all the lives in her. The sole trust was in lightening her of whatever could be spared; and it was some comfort, that as the tide of ebb ran out, she began to settle, and was no longer beaten so violently from side to side. In extremity of peril, a little chance is a great hope, and one danger the less, a great deliverance. All hands set to work with alacrity—almost with cheerfulness—some plying the pumps, some heaving overboard guns, ballast, casks, staves, oil jars, decayed stores, all that was heavy and not indispensable. While they were thus employed, the morning of the 11th of June dawned upon them, and displayed the full prospect of their danger.

Providentially the wind fell, and early in the morning it was a dead calm. If it had blown hard, their destruction had been inevitable. High water was expected at eleven, and all was prepared to heave off the vessel if she should float; but when the day tide came, it fell so far short of that of night, that though the ship had been lightened nearly fifty ton, she did not float by a foot and a half. She had not yet admitted much water, but as the tide fell it rushed in so fast that she could hardly be kept free by the incessant working of two pumps. The most vigorous exertions were made to prepare for the tide at midnight, though it was too probable, from the gaining leak, and crazy state of the vessel, that she would go to pieces as soon as the rock ceased to support her—and then as it was impossible for the boats to save all, and subordination must be at an end, a frightful contest for preference would ensue, in which all might perish. The shore was eight leagues distant, and no island intervened to which they might be speedily conveyed, and thence by turns to the main land.

Amid these sad forebodings, Cook never relaxed a fibre of his diligence, determined to omit no point of his duty, though none should know whether he lived or was dead—nor was there a murmur or breach of discipline in his crew. As the critical moment approached, he ordered the capstan and windlace to be manned with as many hands as could be spared from the pumps—the ship floated about twenty minutes past ten—the grand effort was made—and she was heaved into deep water. It was no small encouragement to find that she did not now leak faster than when on the rock. Still, the leak gained on the pumps, and there were nine feet ten inches of water in the hold—there was no intermission of labour. Three pumps were kept incessantly going (the fourth was out of order), and thus the water was held at bay. Four and twenty hours the men persevered in this toil, harassed in mind and body, with little hopes of final success. At length their spirits began to flag: none of them could work at the pump above five or six minutes together, after which they threw themselves, totally exhausted on the deck, though a stream of water three or four inches deep was running over it from the pumps.   Another party relieved them at their labour, and having wrought their turn, flung themselves in like manner on the streaming deck: the former started up and to the pumps again.   Meanwhile, an accident seemed to prove all their efforts fruitless.   The planking which lines a ship's bottom is called the ceiling, between which and the outside planking there is a space of about eighteen inches. · From the ceiling only the man who had hitherto attended the well had taken the depth of the water, and had given the measure accordingly.   But upon his being relieved, the person who took his place gave the depth from the outside planking, which struck a general panic, as if the water had gained eighteen inches in a couple of minutes.   But the mistake was soon corrected, and every heart felt as if a great weight was lifted off it, and finding their condition not quite so bad as it appeared a moment ago, the poor sailors cheered up as if there had never been any real danger at all.   They tugged at the pumps with renewed energy, and by eight o'clock in the morning, found the water got under considerably.   They now began to talk confidently of taking the ship into some harbour.   The fore-top-mast and fore-yard were replaced, and there being a breeze at sea, the Endeavour was once more under sail by eleven A. M.   These hopes might yet have been frustrated, but for a suggestion of Mr. Monkhouse (a midshipman—not the surgeon), which was to fasten to the bottom of the vessel a spare sail, lined with wool and oakum, and covered with sheep's dung and other filth.   This process, which is called fothering, succeeded so far in stopping the leaks, that by the labour of one pump the ship was kept clear of water. The joy of the crew was proportionate to their recent distress.   To commemorate this dreadful trial, the point of land in sight was called Cape TRIBULATION.

On the 14th, a small harbour was discovered, excellently adapted for the purpose of refitting ; but it was not till the 17th, after considerable difficulty, that the ship was got in.

Mr. Cook bestowed the warmest commendation on his crew, and all on board, for their conduct under this peril.   Every one appeared to have the perfect possession of his mind, and every one exerted himself to the uttermost with a quiet perseverance, equally distant from the tumultuous violence of terror and the gloomy inactivity of despair.   Such is the power of a great man to inspire confidence in the hour of danger, and preserve obedience even when the great leveller death threatens to make all equal.

To complete the history of this wonderful preservation, we must not omit a circumstance which could not be discovered till the ship was laid down to be repaired. It then appeared that one of her holes, which was sufficient alone to have sunk her, was in a great measure filled up by a fragment of the rock upon which she had struck. Thus the cause of her danger had contributed to her safety.

But, though the immediate peril of death was escaped, the situation of our voyagers was still very distressing. The scurvy had made its appearance with very formidable symptoms. Tupia suffered dreadfully; and Mr. Green, the Astronomer, was daily wearing away. When the commander came to survey the country around the harbour, it presented the most comfortless aspect, the high grounds stony and barren, the low lands overrun with mangroves, among which the salt water flows at every tide. A boat dispatched to procure some fish for the invalids, returned without success. Tupia was more fortunate; he was an excellent angler, and living on what he caught, soon recovered his health. But Mr. Green continued to linger. Sir Joseph, on the 19th of June, making an excursion inland, found the country to consist of sand-hills. There were huts, which appeared to have been recently deserted, but no inhabitants to be seen. Large flights of crows and pigeons crossed him in his walk, from which an old Roman would have drawn a favourable or unfavourable omen, according as their flight was in a lucky or unlucky direction. Sir Joseph shot several of the pigeons, which were of a new and extremely beautiful kind; but the crows never came within the range of his fowling piece. On the twenty second, the ship's bottom was examined, and found to be considerably damaged. On the same day some of the people, who had been sent to shoot pigeons for the sick, returned with an account of an animal as large as a greyhound, of a mouse colour, which bounded along with amazing agility, springing from its hind legs. This was the Kangaroo. During the refitting of the ship, Sir Joseph was very near losing his fine collection of botanical specimens, gathered with so much care and delight, on so many untrodden hills, and in so many unrifled vallies. He had stored them in a part of the vessel where the process of repair exposed them to great danger of perishing. They were, however, preserved. On the 29th of June, Mr. Cook, in conjunction with Mr. Green, observed an immersion of Jupiter's first satellite, whereby they concluded the longitude of the place to be 214° 42′ 30″ west. There is a feeling in every thing, even in the longitude. How must the poor sick astronomer have felt the immensity of his distance from his native land on this inhospitable shore, that had nothing in common with England but the sun and stars!

By the use of such herbs as the part produced, and a fish diet, the crew began to recover their health, and Mr. Cook was anxious to proceed on his voyage. But when he mounted a hill and looked out upon the sea, the difficulties of his position pressed hard upon his thoughts. Innumerable sand banks and shoals lay in every direction along the coast, some extending as far as he could see with his glass, and others but just rising above the water. The master was sent out with a boat to seek a passage between these shoals, and in the course of his search found cockles left by the tide on a coral rock, so large, that one of them was an ample meal for two men. He reported that he had discovered a passage, but the commander, not choosing to rely on his report, after some days spent in refitting the vessel and exploring the country, sent him out again. He now expressed an opinion that the passage was not practicable; but the trip was not without benefit, for on the same rock, where the cockles were found, he fell in with excellent turtle, and though he had no better instrument than a boat hook, he captured three. It was the general opinion of the experienced part of the company, that the turtle, caught fresh on the coast of Australia, was very superior to that served up in London, after the fatigues of a west India voyage; but the state of their appetites ought to be taken into the account. At length the natives, who had hitherto kept aloof, began to make their appearance. On the 10th of July, four of them appeared in a canoe, busily employed in striking fish. Cook, who was now convinced that the more they were courted to an interview the more shy and perverse they proved, resolved to let them quite alone. This plan succeeded. After some conversation by signs, they came along side the ship, and carried on the dumb conference for some time with apparent cordiality; but when invited to come on board and partake of a repast, they took alarm, and pulled away. They were of average stature, slender limbed, their colour a dark chocolate, their hair black, but not woolly; their features not absolutely frightful. They possessed great flexibility of voice and quickness of ear; catching and mimicking several English words exactly. This parrot-like faculty is remarkable in the aborigines of New South Wales: those in the neighbourhood of the British settlements can take off every governor and every notorious character that has sought the retirement of Sidney-Cove. Next day the same party appeared again, accompanied by a man whom they called Yaparrico. He was probably a chief, being distinguished by the bone of a bird thrust through his nostrils, an ornament only once observed at New Zealand, but extremely general in New Holland.

On the 19th our voyagers were in danger of suffering severely by the vengeance of these savages. A party of them had been persuaded to visit the ship, and were particularly desirous to help themselves to the turtle which lay on deck. Frustrated in this object, they made for land in high dudgeon, and seeing a fire which had been lighted to heat the pitch-kettle, they seized a burning brand, and set the long dry grass, that overspread the ground, in a blaze. A tent of Sir Joseph's was in imminent danger of perishing, and whatever of the smith's forge would burn was consumed. Not content with this summary revenge, they proceeded to set fire to another spot, where the fishing nets and a quantity of linen were exposed to dry. A few shots drove them away for the present, but soon greater numbers began to assemble and a general attack was threatened; but by the temper and conduct of Cook and his associates, the peace was preserved. The flames were communicated to the wood, and spread so rapidly, that for miles the country appeared as one conflagration; and when in the evening the commander made an excursion in the boat, he saw the distant hills mapped out in many coloured fire.

After several unsuccessful attempts to discover a clear passage to the northward, the Endeavour got under way on the 4th of August, but only to encounter fresh difficulties and perils. The reefs and shoals stretched in every direction, and in one instance the ship was even nearer destruction than ever before. But we must be brief. Suffice it to say, that on the 17th of August, they arrived at an isle off the north-east extremity of New Holland, from whence Mr. Cook made such observations as convinced him that New Holland and New Guinea are separate islands, and he resolved to demonstrate this fact by sailing through the channel which divides them. This isle he called Possession Isle, from the ceremony of taking possession, in the king's right, of the whole eastern coast, by the name of New South Wales.

From the coast of New South Wales our commander steered on the 23rd August for the coast of New Guinea, of which he came in sight on the 3rd of September. The strait, which divides these islands he called Endeavour Strait, supposing that he was himself the first European who had discovered it. But as it has since been ascertained that it was known to the Spanish navigator Torres, as early as 1606, the honour of giving it a name has been restored to the prior claimant, and it is now called Torres Strait.

On the 3d of September, the pinnace was hoisted, and Cook, Banks, Solander, with their attendants, and a boat's crew, twelve persons in all, well armed, went on shore. As soon as they came ashore, they discovered the prints of human feet in the sand, which shewed that the natives could be at no great distance. They proceeded cautiously, lest their retreat to the boat should be intercepted. Skirting the margin of a noble forest they observed cocoa nut trees (a fruit not found in New Holland) but could not reach the fruit, which tempted them in a very tantalizing manner. They had not advanced above a quarter of a mile, when three naked savages rushed out of the wood, with a hideous shout. One of them darted something out of his hand, which flashed like gunpowder, but without any report. The other two discharged arrows. A volley from the musquets put them to flight without wounding them. Cook had no inclination to urge hostilities, nor time to penetrate a country of which he was not the discoverer. The party therefore returned to the ship. When they were aboard, the natives crowded in numbers to the beach. Their appearance resembled that of the New Hollanders, to whom they are nearly related. They are supposed to be an African race, though not quite so black as the Guinea negroes. Yet they are generally called negroes in the old voyages, and from this similarity most likely the island was named New Guinea. In the native language one tribe are called Papoos, whence their county is sometimes denominated Papua. They are somewhat more advanced in arts than the New Hollanders, at least in the arts of aggression, which they may have learned from the Malays who frequent the coasts. Their method of darting fire puzzled the English, and some persisted that they must possess silent fire-arms.

Cook resolved to lose no time on this coast, but sail with all despatch to the westward, a determination very pleasing to the majority of the crew, though some were desirous to go on shore and cut down the cocoa nut trees, but this was a violation of property the Commander would not permit.

Pursuing their course to the north-west, having left Timor and Timorlaut behind, on the 16th of September, about ten at night, our navigators perceived a phenomenon in the heavens, similar to the Aurora Borealis, but with many marks of difference. It was a dull, reddish light, which reached twenty degrees above the horizon, and comprehended from eight to ten points of the compass. Through, and out of the general phosphorescence, there shot rays of brighter light, which came and went, without any of the tremulous vibration characteristic of the Aurora Borealis. This phenomenon occurred somewhere near the islands of Rotte and Seman. On the following morning, an island was seen, bearing west-south-west, which, from the imperfection of the charts was at first supposed to be a new discovery. As the ship neared the north coast, the eyes of her inmates were refreshed with the sight of palm-groves, houses, and flocks of sheep. A landing was resolved on; and the island proved to be the Dutch settlement of Savu. Provisions were the great object of request, and after some little stupidity on the part of the Dutch resident, Mr. Cook succeeded in obtaining nine buffaloes, six sheep, three hogs, thirty dozen of fowls, many dozens of eggs, some cocoa-nuts, a little garlic, and some hundred gallons of palm syrup. In making their bargains, the English were much assisted by an aged native, who had great influence with the king of the island. They had the honour of an interview with his majesty, who entertained them with a banquet, though the royal etiquette did not permit him to partake of his own hospitality. Savu is a beautiful island, gently elevated—the slopes of the hills covered with rich verdure, and lofty trees—the cultivation general and amply repaid—the inhabitants, though of Malay origin, mild, virtuous, amenable to laws, constant in their connections, clean, and even delicate in their habits. Such, at least, was the representation of Mynheer Lange, the Dutch Governor.

On the 1st of October, our Navigators came in sight of Java. On the 2d, they fell in with two Dutch vessels, the first European ships they had met to the East of Cape Horn. The Commander sent Hicks on board one of them, to enquire for news from England, and brought back intelligence that Captain Carteret had been at Batavia two years before. On the morning of the 5th, a Dutch officer in a *Proa* came along side the Endeavour with a printed paper in bad English, of which he had duplicates in several other languages. It contained a variety of questions, few of which Mr. Cook thought proper to answer. On the 9th, he stood in for Batavia road, where he found the Harcourt East Indiaman, two private English traders, and a number of Dutch ships. Before our voyagers were allowed to land, several troublesome formalities were to be gone through, and Mr. Cook had to apologize to the Governor for not saluting, which ceremony, from the state of his ordnance, he thought better omitted.

On the 10th, there occurred a violent storm of thunder and lightning, during which the mast of one of the Dutch East Indiamen was split, and carried away by the deck, and the main-top mast and top-gallant mast were shivered to pieces. The stroke was probably directed by an iron spike at the top-gallant-mast head. The Endeavour, which lay close beside the damaged vessel, owed her safety to the conducting chain, which glowed like a line of fire.

As the necessary repairs of the vessel were likely to take some time, our voyagers engaged a temporary residence at Batavia, but the state of their health obliged them soon to remove into the country. When Tupia first landed in Batavia, the only city he had ever seen, the variety of objects delighted him above measure. Having heard that all nations appeared there in their national costume, he requested leave to array himself after the fashion of Otaheite. Otaheitan cloth was procured from the ship, and he finished his equipments with great expedition. But his happiness was not of long duration. The boy Tayeto sickened and died; and Tupia, who loved him as a parent, survived him but a few days.

The pestilential climate wrought its dire effect on the crew of the Endeavour. Only one man, an old sail maker, who was drunk every day while the ship remained at Batavia, wholly escaped the epidemic. To aggravate the calamity, Monkhouse, the surgeon, fell the first sacrifice. Sir Joseph Banks and Dr. Solander recovered with difficulty, and perhaps owed their lives to two Malay women, whom they purchased for nurses. Cook was himself attacked, and of the whole company, but ten were for some time upon duty. Only seven, however, including the surgeon, Tupia, Tayeto, Mr. Green's servant, and three seamen died. The repair of the ship was necessarily retarded by the sickness of the crew; but the Dutch ship-wrights performed their business much to Cook's satisfaction, and he declared, that there is not a marine yard in the world where a ship can be laid with more convenience, safety, and despatch, or repaired with greater diligence and skill.

On the 24th of December, when all was in order for sailing, and Mr. Cook had taken leave of the Dutch authorities, a new accident occurred to delay his departure. A seaman who had run away from one of the Dutch ships in the road, entered on board the Endeavour, and was reclaimed as a subject of Holland. Mr. Cook, who was then on shore, ordered him to be given up if he proved to be a Dutchman; but Lieutenant Hicks, who was the officer in command, refused to surrender him, alledging that he was a subject of Great Britain, born in Ireland. This conduct of Hicks' received his superior's approbation; and indisputable proofs being brought that the man was a British subject, it was resolved to keep him at all events. This firmness had due effect, and no more was heard of the matter.

Cook was now bound on a homeward course. He sailed from Batavia on the 27th December. On the 5th of January, 1771, he anchored under Prince of Wales's Island, to take in wood and water, and to procure refreshments for the sick. He had an interview with the king of that island, but could not agree with his majesty upon the price of turtle, which article was procured of the natives in rather a contraband manner. The sovereign, however, seems to have been convinced after a while, that free trade is the only preventive of smuggling; grew perfectly gracious, and promoted commerce to the utmost of his power. The palace of this potentate was situate in the middle of a rice field, and when he admitted the English to an audience, he was engaged in cooking his own supper.

The remainder of this voyage is a melancholy tale of death and suffering. The ship was nothing better than a hospital. In the course of six weeks, three and twenty corpses were plunged into the waves; among the rest, Mr. Green the astronomer, a native of Yorkshire, a man of much science, and active mind. He perished on the 29th of January. His constitution, impaired by hardship and the scurvy, was unable to resist the miasmata of Batavia, and he quitted that place only to drop his remains into the ocean, instead of leaving them in a strange land.

Among the deaths on the passage we may particularize the old drunken sail-maker, who perhaps was at last killed by the means to which he owed a temporary respite.

On Friday, the 15th of March, the Endeavour arrived at the Cape of Good Hope, where she lay till the 14th of April. On the 29th she crossed her first meridian, having circumnavigated the globe from east to west, in consequence of which a day was lost in the reckoning. On the 1st of May she touched at St. Helena. The treatment of the slaves on that island excited our voyager's indignation, and was so severely handled by Dr. Hawkesworth, that Captain Cook, in his own account of his second voyage, thought it just or prudent to soften the statements considerably.

On the 23d of May died Lieutenant Hicks, and was committed, with the usual ceremonies, to the waves. He seems to have been a brave and diligent officer, better fitted for the common routine of obedience than for emergencies, in which it is necessary to think, as well as act with celerity.

On the 10th of June, Cook came in sight of the Lizard. On the 11th he ran up the Channel; on the afternoon of the 12th he landed at Deal; and thus ended Cooks first voyage round the world.

There can be no doubt that our navigator met with a warm domestic welcome; but of the small portion of life which Cook spent at home little record remains. His home scenes presented no materials for scandalous history; and his public acts were so momentous, that there was no time for curiosity to invade his fire side. The public honours conferred on scientific discovery in this country have never been shewy or affecting: Newton, indeed, was knighted, and Davy was raised to a baronetcy; but is there one noble family that can refer to science for its patent? We mention not this for complaint or censure. Perhaps titles would now be more respected were they considered as the tokens of mental superiority; but after all, it is well that the philosophic genius should be undisturbed by ambition.   Anson was made a peer, not for contributing to our knowledge of the planet we live on, but for taking treasure from the Spaniards, which poorly repaid the expenses of his expedition.   Cook was promoted to be a Commander in his Majesty's navy, by commission bearing date the 29th of August, 1771.   With this advance, his sense of his own deserts was hardly satisfied: he wished to be a post captain, but the rules of the service forbad it.

Several meagre and surreptitious accounts of his voyage appeared before the authorized narrative of Dr. Hawkesworth, which was constructed from Captain Cook's and Sir Joseph Banks' papers.   It would have been better, if both Cook and Sir Joseph had put their observations into shape themselves; but Cook was not allowed time to make books.   Though his first voyage had considerably abated the hopes of a southern continent,—proved that neither New Zealand nor New Holland adjoined to such continent, and shewed the fallacy of much of the hypothetical reasoning upon which its existence had been assumed, the question was not yet set at rest.   There was still space enough in the unknown ocean for the *Terra incognita.*   Lord Sandwich, now at the head of the Admiralty, laudably resolved to memorialize his administration by deciding what more the South concealed, and Cook was the man to execute his purpose, in which the King himself is said to have been warmly interested.   To give every chance of secure success to the undertaking, two vessels were engaged, both built at Whitby by the builder of the Endeavour, and constructed nearly on the same plan.   They were called the Resolution and the Adventure; of the former Captain Cook was appointed commander,— of the latter, Captain Tobias Furneaux.   The Resolution was of 462 tons burthen; her complement, including officers and seamen, 112: the Adventure, 336 tons; her complement, 81.   In the equipment of these ships nothing was neglected that could contribute to the comfort and success of the expedition.   Lord Sandwich, who executed his high office *con amore,* visited them from time to time, to assure himself that all things were provided to the satisfaction of the commanders.   Every suggestion of Cook's experience was attended to; the Navy and Victualling Boards co-operated heartily in furnishing the best of stores and provisions, with such extraordinary allowances as the nature of the enterprize required.   The sufferings of the Endeavour's company from scurvy taught the propriety of an ample supply of antiscorbutics; such as malt, sour-crout, salted cabbage, portable soup, saloup, mustard, marmalade of carrots, inspissated wort, and beer.   Able men in various branches of science were appointed to attend the expedition.   William

Hodges embarked as landscape painter, John Reinhold Forster and his son as naturalists, William Wales and William Bayley as astronomers; all liberally furnished with apparatus. A sum was granted to defray the expense of zoological, botanical, and mineralogical collections. It is thus that a state should promote science and patronize learning.

The mathematical and astronomical instruments were supplied by the Board of Longitude, particularly four time pieces, three by Arnold and one by Kendal on Harrison's principles.

Preparations so multifarious necessarily took up a considerable time. Captain Cook received his commission on the 28th of November, 1771, but the ship did not sail from Deptford till the 9th April, 1772, nor leave the Long Reach till the 10th May following. In plying down the river, it was found necessary to put into Sheerness, to make some alterations in her upper works : Lord Sandwich and Sir Hugh Palliser went down to see that the work was done effectually. On the 3d of July, Captain Cook joined the Adventure in Plymouth Sound, where he received a farewell visit from Lord Sandwich, and his instructions, which comprehended the most enlarged plan of discovery then known in the history of navigation. He was instructed to " circumnavigate the globe in such high southern latitudes, making such traverses, from time to time, into every corner of the Pacific Ocean not before examined, as might finally resolve the much agitated question as to the existence of a southern continent in any part of the southern hemisphere to which access could be had by the efforts of the boldest and most skilful navigators." *

On the 13th July, 1772, Cook commenced his second voyage : on the 29th anchored in Funchiale Road : sailed again, August 1st : finding water run short, put into Porto Praya, in St. Jago, Cape de Verde Isles, on the 10th. After surveying and delineating the harbour of Porto Praya, which was not usually visited by British ships at that time, he proceeded southward. Violent rains descended on the 20th, " not in drops, but in streams," the wind at the same time rough and changeable, so that there was hardly a dry rag in the ship. The Commander had recourse to various means suggested by Sir Hugh Palliser to dry and ventilate his vessel, and preserve the crew from the ill effects of their drenching ; which precautions succeeded so well, that there was not one sick person aboard the Resolution.

On the 8th of September he crossed the line in longitude 8° west. On the 11th October observed a partial eclipse of the moon, at 6h.

* Life of Cook, by Kippis, in the Biographia Britannica. It must be obvious how much we are indebted to this excellent compendium of the larger works respecting our discoverer.

24m. 12° by Kendal's chronometer. Though previous to his quitting England it was foreboded by many that his course would be delayed by long and frequent calms in the neighbourhood of the line, he was favoured with a brisk south-west wind in the very latitudes where the calms had been predicted; nor was he exposed to any of the tornadoes which are so much spoken of by other navigators. A partial experience may mislead as well as a fanciful theory.

On the 29th, near the Cape of Good Hope, between nine and ten at night, the whole sea, within the visible horizon, was kindled with a white light, similar to that which had been observed in the former voyage between Madeira and Rio Janeiro, which Sir Joseph Banks and Dr. Solander ascertained to proceed from marine insects. Mr. Forster was inclined to dispute the certainty of this explanation, but having examined a few buckets of the sea-water, he abandoned his scepticism.* Next day the Resolution and Adventure anchored in Table-bay. The discoverers were courteously received by Baron Plettenberg, the Dutch Governor of the Cape of Good Hope, who informed them that two French ships, from Mauritius, about eight months before, had met with land in 48° south, along which they sailed forty miles, till they came to a bay, into which they were about to enter, when they were driven off and separated by a hard gale of wind. The Baron also informed Captain Cook that two other French ships of discovery, bound for the South Pacific Ocean, had touched at the Cape in May last. These were the ships of the unfortunate Marion, of whom we shall

---

* This illumination of the sea is by no means uniform in its aspects: sometimes it appears in repeated flashes and scintillations, sometimes as a diffused quiescent light; sometimes pale white, as if the sea were powdered with snow, and occasionally of a straw colour. These variations may arise from the various species, the differing multitudes, the comparative magnitude or minuteness of the phosphoric animalculæ; or may be influenced by the state of the atmosphere, temperature of the sea, tides, currents, or other causes.

The luminous appearance is not always on the surface. The Pyresoma Atlanticum, discovered by Peron, appears under the water like a red-hot bullet, and on the surface like a cylinder of heated iron.

Every species of marine illumination, whether scintillating or diffused, is commonly ascribed to the presence of phosphorescent animation; generally consisting of various tribes of Medusæ or Molusca, naked, gelatinous substances, with numerous arms and tentacula, presenting a fanciful resemblance of the Gorgon's snaky-locks, whence the Linnæan name Medusa. Strange, that nature should so burlesque human belief, as to bestow that luminous *glory* which surrounds the head of the saint, on the lowest of organized creatures.

Professor Mayer supposed that the sea imbibed the solar light, and gave it out again. We would advise the poets to adopt this theory, for they cannot make any thing of the Molusca.

have to speak in the sequel. Captain Cook was delayed at the Cape longer than he intended, by the difficulty of collecting all the stores necessary to face the icy seas. He had both the vessels caulked and and painted ; and on the 22d November, with crews in perfect health, and ships in as good condition as when he quitted England, he steered in search of the southern continent.

To provide against the coming cold, the Captain ordered slops to be distributed to such as wanted them, and gave each man the dreadnought jacket and trowsers allowed by the Admiralty. These benevolent precautions were not premature. Violent storms of wind, hail, and rain continuing with short intervals from the end of November till the sixth of December, and sometimes disabling the ships from carrying sails, drove the expedition so far from their destined track, as to leave no immediate hope of reaching Cape Circumcision, a point laid down by former navigators, for which they had been steering. In these tempests the principal part of the live stock perished ; and so intense was the transition from heat to cold, that it was judged necessary to support the radical heat with an occasional dram, in addition to the regular allowance of spirits. On the 10th December ice-islands began to appear. Such was the haziness of the weather, that Captain Cook did not see one of these immense masses of congelation right ahead of him till he was within a mile of it, though ordinarily their glimmer announces them afar off. The Captain judged it to be fifty feet in height, and half a mile in circuit, flat-topped and perpendicular-sided : others were of far greater altitude and dimension ; yet so tempestuous was the ocean, that the breakers "curled their monstrous heads" over the tallest ice-berghs, and drove and jostled their unwieldy bulks with fearful rapidity. Such floating towers, in hazy weather, required wary sailing. December 14th, the vessels were stopped by an immense field of low flat ice, to which no end could be seen, east, west, or south. The frozen plain was diversified with mountains of ice, which some on board mistook for land. Cook himself for a while indulged a hope ; but it was soon dispelled by closer observation. Still, as it had generally been held that floating ice is always generated in bays and rivers, the expectation of a continent did not utterly fail, although if it had existed in such a frigid region, it is hard to conjecture how it could have been available for commerce or colonization. From the 14th to the 18th, our voyagers were detained among the field ice ; and when they got loose, their only alternative was to thrid their way among the ice islands, a course perilous enough, yet preferable to getting entangled in the fissures of the field. As the land, if any, must have lain behind the ice, the object was to find in what direction it was situate ; Captain Cook, having run for thirty leagues westward along the edge of the ice, without meeting any open passage, determined to go thirty or forty leagues to the east, and then try for the south. If in this route no land nor other impediment occurred, his design was to stretch behind the ice, and thus bring the matter to a decision.

It was now Christmas-day, and should have been the height of summer; yet, though the thermometer was not much below the freezing point, it was colder than any English Christmas. The crew complained bitterly. To protect them against the chill, foggy atmosphere, the Captain had the sleeves of their jackets lengthened with baize, and gave each sailor a cap of the same stuff, lined with canvas. These habiliments proved some defence against the weather; but that old scourge the scurvy began to appear, to check which, fresh wort, prepared from the malt provided for that purpose, was given daily with good effect.

December 29th. It became evident that the ice-fields adjoined no land. The Captain resolved to run as far west as the meridian assigned to Cape Circumcision. But when, by the nearest calculations, assisted by an observation of the moon, which shewed her face on Friday, 1st January, 1773, for the first time since our voyagers left the Cape of Good Hope, they were under the longitude of that Cape, from all appearances Captain Cook concluded that the French navigator had mistaken ice for land, and abandoned the search in that quarter.

The early part of this year was spent among shoals and hills of ice, which compensated in some measure for the peril and toil which they occasioned by furnishing a constant supply of fresh water. The annals of a sea voyage can seldom be made intelligible, much less interesting, to any but those who are experimentally acquainted with the "art and practical part" of navigation, the various humours and aspects of sea and sky, the hopes and disappointments of the mariner, who strains his eyes for land in vain. A few circumstances, however, may suit the general reader. These southern seas are not utterly deserted by the animal world. Penguins, Albatrosses, and other birds of storm, were often seen perched on the floating ice, at an unknown distance from land. By Sunday, the 17th January, the expedition reached latitude 67° 15' south, and then were stopped by the ice, which stretched away interminably southward.

Seeing no chance of getting round the ice at present, Captain Cook spent some time in looking for the land, of which he had heard at the Cape, as discovered by the French. To multiply the chances of meeting with it, he spread the vessels abreast, four miles asunder. On the 1st of February, he approximated to the meridian of Mauritius, being in south latitude 48°, 30', east longitude 58°, 7', where, according to report, the French discovery should have lain, but no land appeared. Captain Furneaux indeed, conceived great hopes from a large float of sea or rock weed, accompanied by a detachment of the birds called Divers. A slight difference of opinion arose between the commanders, as to the direction in which land was to be expected. Cook, who attended to every reasonable suggestion, proved to be in the right. A remarkable phænomenon was observed about this time ; the variation of the compass was greatest when the sun was on the larboard, and least when on the starboard.

February 8th. Misty weather. No reply to signals by the Adventure. It was suspected that a separation of the vessels had taken place. After waiting two days, during which guns were kept discharging, and signal fires displayed, no doubt of the fact remained, and the Resolution was obliged to proceed alone. She met with penguins, petrels, and other fowl, which, though they ceased to excite hopes of a shore, were cheerful objects on the dim dreary cold ocean.*

* " I observed a wild duck swimming on the waves—a single solitary wild duck. It is not easy to conceive how interesting a thing it looked in that round objectless desert of waters. I had associated such a feeling of immensity with the ocean, that I felt greatly disappointed, when I was out of sight of all land, at the narrowness, and nearness as it were, of the circle of the horizon. So little are images capable of satisfying the obscure feelings connected with words."—S. T. Coleridge's " Friend" Satyrane's Letters.

The word Petrel is a diminative from Peter : Peterellus, quasi Peterkin, little Peter: so called from treading the water with its long-lark-like legs, adroitly evading the rise of the waves, and keeping its wings dry.

This companionable little bird often attends a ship for leagues and leagues in the roughest weather—thence called the stormy Petrel, Procellaria Pelagica a name which the sailors probably think of ill omen, for they give their little friends the subriquet of " Mother Cary's Chickens."

The multitude of sea-birds that throng the southern oceans, perform a very important part in the economy of nature. As soon as the coral insects have brought their work to the level of the sea's surface, their business is at an end: then the marine birds assembling in numbers on the reefs to lay their eggs, make deposits which in a short time turn to fertile soil, ready to receive whatever seeds the winds or waves may bring, and anon the stately palm grove rises self-sown, where a few years before nothing was seen but a warning ripple on the water. Thus, even at this time, new lands are growing up by the agency of living creatures; the inferior tribes are preparing abodes for man, and the same hidden reef on which the forefathers were wrecked, may become the verdant habitation of posterity.

The numbers of the birds destined to this great work correspond with its magnitude. Captain Flinders, no light tongued exaggerator, speaks thus of what he saw

February 17. Betwixt midnight and three o'clock in the morning, lights were seen similar to the Aurora Borealis. The officers on watch observed the shifting and changing of these lights for three hours together ; they had no certain direction, but appeared in different points at different times, shooting forth spiral rays, or glowing in circular rings of brilliance, and sometimes pervading the whole atmosphere with a soft illumination. The same appearance recurred on the 20th with increased lustre, first discovering itself in the east, but afterwards filling all the sky. Where is not nature capable of producing beauty ? Captain Cook notes this as the first Aurora Australis that had come to his knowledge. The phænomena, therefore, must have differed considerably from the lights observed in his former voyage, on the passage between New Guinea and Batavia.

February 23rd. The ship surrounded with ice, storm and darkness. The wind drove the ice-islands one against another, causing them to split with a noise of thunder. The detached pieces, multiplying around the vessel, increased her danger. Abandoning the design he had once entertained of again crossing the Antarctic Circle, Captain Cook stood for the north. The weather still continued stormy and intensely cold, and the ice-wrecks strewed the main. As they grew familiar they became less terrible, without being less dangerous, and the voyagers not only found profit in the fresh water, which the ice supplied, but amusement, in observing the caverns and grottoes wrought in the chrystal by the dashing billows. After several traverses and some deliberation, it was finally determined to stand away for New Zealand, where there was a probability of finding the Adventure, and an opportunity of refreshing the crew and recruiting the provision.

We have already remarked that a seeming trifle may be a great incident in a sea voyage. Captain Cook has not disdained to record— then why should we omit to mention ? that a sow was safely delivered of a fine litter, one morning, to the general joy of the ship's company ;

---

near Van Diemen's land. " There was a stream (of sooty Petrels) of from fifty to eighty yards in depth, and of three hundred yards or more in breadth ; the birds were not scattered, but flying as compactly as a free movement of their wings seemed to allow, and during a *full hour and a half,* this stream of Petrels continued to pass without interruption, at a rate little inferior to the swiftness of the pigeon. Taking the stream to have been fifty yards deep, and three hundred in breadth, and that it moved at a rate of thirty miles an hour, and allowing nine cubic yards of space to each bird, the number would amount to *one hundred and fifty one million five hundred thousand.* The burrows required to lodge this quantity of birds would be 75,750,000 ; and allowing a square yard to each burrow, they would cover something more than 18½ geographic square miles of ground."—*Flinder's Introduction, p.* 170.

but notwithstanding the utmost care and tenderness used to preserve the little strangers alive, the whole "nine farrow" perished of cold before evening. Yet, so effectual were the preventives administered, and the fumigation and cleanliness enforced aboard the resolution, that after months' of freezing and salt diet, there was but one man sick of the scurvy when the ship arrived at New Zealand, which took place on the 26th of March. Captain Cook put into Dusky Bay, at the south west extremity of Tavai Poenamoo, having been at sea one hundred and seventeen days, during which he had sailed 3660 leagues, without once coming in sight of land.

Since the departure of Cook, in 1769, New Zealand had been visited by another European expedition, and the cruelties of De Surville had been terribly expiated by his less guilty countrymen. We have already mentioned that two French discovery ships had called at the Cape of Good Hope a little before Captain Cook put in at that settlement. These were, the Marquis de Castries, under the command of M. Duclesmeur, and the Mascarin, commanded by M. Marion du Fresne. Their objects were, in a great measure, similar to those of Captain Cook ; only, in addition to the hopeless quest of the Terra Australis Incognita, they were to look for the rumoured island of gold—an avaricious dream of which English speculation was innocent. They were also to restore to his native island Aoutourou, an Otaheitan, whom Bougainville had carried with him to Europe. Poor Aoutourou however caught the small pox, and died at Madagascar. Marion directed his course southward from Mauritius, touched at the isles which now bear the names of Marion and of Crozet, his lieutenant, arrived off New Zealand in March, 1772, and after sailing about for some time, came to an anchor in the Bay of Islands. The natives at first received them not only peaceably, but affectionately. In the words of Crozet (to whom we owe the narrative of this calamitous voyage), "they treated them with every shew of friendship for thirty-three days, in the intention of eating them on the thirty-fourth." Whether the massacre had really been premeditated all this time, or was the effect of some sudden change of humour, it is impossible to tell. But certainly the kindness of the New Zealanders had all the effect of the best planned treachery, for it utterly disarmed the French of all caution. Crozet alone thought it necessary to keep an eye on their movements. On the 10th of June, Marion and sixteen others went ashore. Their prolonged absence at length occasioned alarm. Night came and they returned not. They had all been surprised and butchered. A similar fate attended eleven out of a boat's crew of twelve, who went ashore the next morning. When Crozet went ashore to seek for the remains of his countrymen, he found nothing but fragments gnawn and scorched. The French had nothing to do but to avenge their companions, and this they did terribly.

Whether the inhabitants of Dusky Bay, where Cook anchored, had any knowledge of what had taken place in the Bay of Islands (or as it was named by Marion's survivors, the Bay of Treachery), is doubtful. They were, however, shy at first, and averse to communication; few in number, and more barbarous than the natives of the northern island. The Captain spent some time in exploring Dusky Bay, which, notwithstanding its gloomy appellation, furnished good anchorage, a fine stream of fresh water, fish and fowl in abundance, and wood without stint. Among the vegetable productions was a tree resembling the American spruce, from the branches and leaves of which our voyagers brewed a very refreshing liquor. The cove in which the ship lay was christened Pickersgill Harbour, in honour of the Lieutenant by whom it was discovered: another cove in the bay was englished Duck Cove, from the slaughter of fourteen ducks which took place thereat. In Duck Cove, Cook fell in with a party of natives, whose fears he so far pacified, as to engage them in a long but rather unintelligible conversation. A woman, in particular, displayed a delightful volubility of tongue, talking strenuously, without minding that not one word in a hundred was understood. She also favoured the Captain with a dance, not deficient in agility. What a pleasant creature would this girl have been with a good education!

By degrees, the T'avai Poenamooites became quite familiar, even venturing on board. It was observed that the chieftains seemed to mistake the young and fair officers and seamen for females; a very easy mistake for a dusky people to make. We need not wonder if the Turks suspected Lord Byron of being a lady in disguise. To ascertain the nature of their musical perceptions, Captain Cook caused the bagpipes and fife to play, and the drum to beat. The drum excited much attention; it was a novelty which the New Zealander might hope to imitate. A sort of drum is common in Otaheite and the neighbouring islands, but the New Zealanders, though they had flutes, had no instruments of percussion.

There are some symbols which have been so universally adopted, that we are almost inclined to imagine a real and natural fitness between the sign and the thing signified. Such is the presentation of a green branch in token of peace. Who does not remember the pacific olive, derived by many from the olive leaf, which told that the waters of the deluge were abated? A palm branch, the ancient emblem of victory, in the South Sea, typifies concord; and when a New Zealand chief, approached the vessel with a green bough in his hand, and made a circuit, performing certain ceremonies of lustration, he meant to ratify a treaty of friendship and alliance. The inhabitants of Dusky Bay were fully aware of the value of iron, and would trade for nothing but spike-nails or hatchets.

Captain Cook left his five remaining geese at a retired spot, which he named Goose Cove, in hopes that they would escape notice long enough to multiply and become of permanent benefit to the people, or to such Europeans as might visit the island in future. With the same benevolent intentions he sowed several kinds of garden seeds. The coasts abounded in seals, many of which were taken by the English, to whom their skins furnished rigging, their fat oil, and their flesh food.

The whole interior of Tavai Poenamoo appeared to be a mass of dark craggy mountains, while the shores were covered with timber, much of which was valuable for nautical purposes: but fruit trees there were none. During great part of the time that the Resolution lay in Dusky Bay, the rain was heavy and incessant; but the crew, fortified by vigorous health, and the care of their good commander, suffered no serious detriment. Their main annoyance arose from the multitude of small black sand-flies. Unquestionably the insect tribes detract more from human comfort than any other portion of animated nature. Well might Beelzebub be the lord of flies.

Captain Cook left Dusky Bay on the 11th May, and sailed northward in search of the Adventure. On the 17th, the wind suddenly fell, the sky was obscured by dense clouds, and soon after six water spouts were seen, four of which rose and spent themselves between the ship and the land; the fifth was at a considerable distance on the other side of the vessel; and the sixth, the progressive motion of which was not in a straight, but in a crooked line, passed within fifty yards of the stem of the Resolution, without doing any injury. The Captain was so absorbed in observation of the phænomenon, that he neglected to prove by experiment whether the firing of a gun will dissipate these meteors.

May 18th. Coming in sight of Queen Charlotte's Sound, our voyagers had the satisfaction of meeting once more with Captain Furneaux. Since the separation in the Indian Ocean, the Adventure had explored the southern shores of Van Diemen's Land, and formed a decided opinion (since proved to be erroneous), that there was no strait between that country and New Holland, but a very deep bay. The Adventure had arrived in Queen Charlotte's Bay on the 7th, and the interval between her arrival and that of the Resolution had afforded such strong instances of the anthropophagous habits of the New Zealanders, that Furneaux called a particular inlet Cannibal Bay.

Commodiously anchored in Ship Cove, the two commanders tarried till the 7th of June, employed in exploring the vicinity, refreshing the crews, and labouring for the benefit of the natives, by planting turnips, carrots, parsnips, and potatoes, which took to the soil extremely well. Captain Cook set ashore a ram and a ewe, which died almost immediately, probably from eating poisonous herbage. Captain Furneaux left a pair of goats, animals much better adapted to run wild and increase in a new country than sheep, which have been time out of mind the helpless dependents on human care. The intercourse of our voyagers with the natives was of the most friendly description; but it was remarkable, that of all that appeared, not one recognized, or was recognized by, Captain Cook. No doubt the former occupants of the district had either emigrated or been expelled, and their successors were few and scattered. Many habitations were deserted and in ruins.

On the 4th of June the King's birth-day was kept with due solemnity, and the loyalty of the tars was stimulated with a double allowance of grog.' On the 7th the ships sailed for Otaheite, resolving to continue the examination of the southern seas next season. Both crews were then healthy; but before they had been two months at sea, alarming symptoms of scurvy appeared on board the Adventure, while the Resolution had not more than three men on the sick list. This difference may partly be accounted for from the circumstance, that Cook's men, induced by the authority and example of their commander, had been diligent in collecting esculent vegetables on the shores of Queen Charlotte's Bay, such as wild celery and scurvy-grass, which, mixed up with the peas and wheat in their portable soup, counteracted the ill effects of dry and salt provisions; while the Adventure's men either knew not where to look for the herbs, or could not be persuaded to use them. There is an antipathy, intimately connected with superstition, which makes even well-educated stomachs averse to the adoption of a new diet; and Cook himself had some difficulty in making the common sailors, or even the officers, boil the celery, &c. in their messes. An Englishman, in health, thinks there is something *spoony* in providing against contingent sickness. But by perseverance, and experience, these absurd scruples were completely overcome, so that whenever the ships put in the men set about looking for the wholesome plants of their own accord.

Captain Cook retraced the tracks of Carteret and Bougainville, with a view to correct or confirm their latitudes and longitudes, some of which, Carteret's in particular, were far from accurate. He failed of meeting with

Pitcairn's island, afterwards so famous for the retreat of the mutineers of the Bounty; but passed by a number of flat, low, island reefs, which Bougainville had not improperly designated "The dangerous Archipelago." Four of them were named by Cook, Resolution Island, Doubtful Island, Furneaux Island, and Adventure Island. The smoothness of the sea in those parts evinced the neighbourhood of a multitude of these coral banks, in different stages of progress, which made navigation very perilous, particularly in the night; but neither vessel met with any accident.

Early in the morning of the 15th August, the ships came in sight of Maiteea, or Osnaburgh Island, a discovery of Captain Wallis'. Soon after Cook acquainted Furneaux that it was his intention to put into Oaitapiha bay, near the south east end of Otaheite, to procure refreshments before he went down to Matavai. The approach of the vessels to Otaheite was attended with considerable danger from the reefs and currents. The Resolution had a narrow escape, but was brought off safe by the promptitude of Cook's assistance. During the time that the English were in this critical situation, many of the Otaheitans were either on board or paddling around in the canoes, but they testified neither joy, grief, fear, nor surprise, when the ships were knocking against the acute ridges of coral, and went away in the evening quite unconcerned. Though most of them knew Cook again, and some made particular enquiries after their old friend Sir Joseph, and other gentlemen of the Endeavour, no one said a word about Tupia, and they were alike indifferent to the fate of Aoutourou. In all this there was nothing extraordinary. Neither Tupia nor Aoutourou might be any thing to any of them; but Sir Joseph Banks was a great prince, from whom they had received many presents.

August 17th. The Resolution and Adventure anchored in Oaitapiha bay. Canoes, bringing cocoa nuts, bananas, yams, plantains, and other roots and fruits, thronged around them, and the usual barter for nails and beads commenced. Sundry persons, assuming the dignity of chiefs, received shirts and hatchets, on condition of bringing hogs and poultry, which, however, they never did bring; and when next day Captain Cook wished to bargain for some of the hogs which were about the houses, he was informed that they belonged to the *Earee de hi* (King) Waheatua, who had not yet made his appearance, nor indeed any other person really exercising the authority of a chief. Travellers, in older countries than Otaheite, have often been deluded by the pretensions of *soi disant* nobility, and sometimes, it may be suspected, have reported the tricks and affectations of sharpers as the manners of people of rank. Travellers, especially when they happen to be possessed with a passion for high life, always represent the company into which they happen to be thrown as the *elite* of the country they visit, and hence very false notions get abroad of the depravity and vulgarity of foreigners. Any body, who will read a tour in England, written by a Frenchman, or even by a German, will perceive the source of these errors, too rashly attributed to wilful falsehood and malice. Dr. Clarke* has a wonderful story of a Russian *nobleman* stealing a hat, and converting it into a jockey cap. And Captain Cook detected a pretended *Earee* in the act of theft. He ordered the privileged pilferer, with all his followers, out of the ship, and to convince him of the danger of his proceedings, fired two musquets over his head as he was retreating, at which he was so terrified that he leaped out of his canoe and swam to shore. The Captain sent a boat to seize the canoe; this being the only method of gaining restitution. The people on shore pelted the boat with stones; but the Captain, putting off in another boat himself, and causing a great gun to be fired with ball, cleared the beach without bloodshed. In a few hours peace was restored, and the canoes were given up to the first who came to claim them.

In the evening of this day, some enquiries were made after Tupia. When told that he died a natural death, the enquirers expressed neither suspicion nor concern, and Captain Cook thought they would have taken it very quietly had his death been ascribed to violent means.

Since the Endeavour quitted Otaheite, great changes had taken place. The two kingdoms into which that island is divided had been at war. Tootahah, Tubourai Tamaide, and many others who had made acquaintance with the English in their former visit, had fallen in battle. Otoo was now the reigning prince of the larger division, and peace had been renewed.

---

* "A hat had been stolen from our apartments; the servants positively asserted, that some young noblemen, who had been more lavish of their friendship and company than we desired, had gained access to the chambers in our absence and had carried off the hat, with some other moveables of even less value. The fact was inconceivable, and we gave no credit to it. A few days after, being upon an excursion to the convent of New Jerusalem, 45 versts north of Moscow, some noblemen, to whom our intention was made known the preceding evening at the *Societe de Noblesse*, overtook us on horseback. One of the party, mounted on an English racer, and habited like a New-market jockey, rode up to the side of the carriage; but his horse being somewhat unruly, he lost his seat, and a gust of wind blew off his cap. My companion immediately descended, and ran to recover it for its owner; but what was his astonishment to perceive his own name, and the name of his hatter, on the lining. It was no other than the identical hat stolen by one of them from our lodgings, now metamorphosed as a cap, although under its altered shape it might not have been recognised but for the accident here mentioned."—*Clarke's Travels in Russia.*

The events which occurred while our voyagers lay in Oaitapiha harbour were of little moment. A few petty frauds, and more attempts at frauds, on the part of the natives, were the most conspicuous. On the 23rd, Captain Cook had an interview with Waheatua, the ruler of Tiaraboo, who, at the period of the last voyage, was a minor, and called Tearee; but now, having succeeded to his father's authority, he had assumed his father's name. The result of this royal audience was a plentiful supply of pork.

On the 24th, the Adventure's people being in a great measure recovered, the ships put to sea, and arrived the next evening in Matavai Bay. Before they came to anchor the decks were crowded with the Captain's old acquaintance, and the meeting was to all appearance a joyful one. King Otoo and his attendants remained on shore, where a great multitude were gathered around him. Our Commander visited him on the 25th at Oparree. He was a tall personable man, but of weak mind and timid nature. When invited to come on board the ship, he confessed that he was afraid of the guns. Returning to the Bay of Matavai, the Captain found the tents and observatories set on the same ground from which the transit had been observed in 1769. The sick were landed, in number twenty from the Adventure, and one from the Resolution, and a guard of marines set over them, under the command of Lieutenant Edgecumbe, the same, we presume, who gave name to Mount Edgecumbe in New Zealand, and Edgecumbe Bay in New South Wales.

August 27th. Otoo was at last prevailed on to visit the Captain. He came attended with a numerous train, and brought with him a hog, fruits, and Otaheitan cloth, for which he received suitable presents. When Cook went ashore he was met by a venerable lady, the mother of the late Tootahah, who caught him by the hand, and exclaimed with a flood of tears, *Tootahah Tiyo no Tootee matty Tootahah*—anglice, "Tootahah, Cook's friend is dead Tootahah." The Captain was much affected by this effusion of maternal tenderness, and would have mingled his tears with hers, if the suspicious Otoo had not hastily broken short the interview. Some days after, he obtained permission to see the poor woman again, when he gave her an axe, and some other articles.

With one slight exception, when some liberties taken by the sailors with the Otaheitan females occasioned a scuffle, and a cry of murder, the intercourse between the islanders and their visitors was of the most amicable kind. Lieutenant Pickersgill made an excursion up the country, during which he saw the celebrated Oberea. Time and misfortune had lain heavy upon her: her mature comeliness was gone, her power and state were passed away: she looked both old and poor. Captain Cook, in his narrative of this voyage, gallantly steps forward to vindicate the virtue of the Otaheitan ladies.

On the 2nd of September the vessels arrived at Huaheine, and anchored in Owharre harbour. The two commanders were received by the natives with great cordiality, and trade was commenced on the most amicable terms. Hogs and poultry, which had been difficult to obtain at Otaheite, were plentiful in Huaheine, an important consideration to a crew whose health required fresh provision. Cook, together with Furneaux and Forster, paid a visit to Oree, the chief of the island. Oree was so keenly affected by meeting with his old friend, that he embraced him with tears. We have already remarked that barbarians are generally lachrymose, though capable of sustaining great bodily pain.

A stoic of the woods, a man without a tear,

is a very unusual character among savages. The aged Oree appears to have been the most amiable personage in the South Sea, and a sincere friend to the English, as he shewed on a very trying occasion. On the 4th, when Captain Cook went to the trading place, he was informed that one of the natives had behaved with great insolence. The man was standing equipped in his war habit, with a club in each hand. Cook, however, soon quelled his spirit, taking the clubs from him, and breaking them before his eyes. Meanwhile, Mr. Sparrman (the Swedish traveller), having unguardedly gone ashore to botanize, was assaulted by two men, who deprived him of every thing but his trowsers, gave him a severe beating with his own hanger, and then made off. Another of the natives brought a piece of cloth to cover him, and conducted him to the trading place. As soon as the people there assembled saw him in this plight, they fled in great consternation. Captain Cook assured them that the innocent should be unmolested, and went to complain of the outrage to Oree, whose grief and indignation were inexpressible. He wept aloud, and harangued his subjects earnestly, reproaching them with their perfidy and ingratitude. He then took a minute account of the things which Sparrman had been robbed of, and having promised to use his utmost efforts to procure their restitution, desired to go into the Captain's boat. The natives, fearful for the safety of their prince, protested against this confidence: they wept, intreated, and even attempted to pull him out of the boat, but all in vain. Even the remonstrances of Captain Cook were unavailing. Oree's sister alone approved of his going. The boat put off in search of the robbers. Restitution was at length made, and peace restored. Cook justly observed, that another chief may never be found, who would act like Oree. Before the ships left Huaheine, Captain Cook took an affectionate leave of his friend, and in addition to the inscribed plate which he left on the former voyage, gave him another small piece of copper, lettered thus: "Anchored here his Britannic Majesty's ships, the Resolution and Adventure. September, 1773." These plates, with some medals, were put into a bag, and Oree promised never to part with them, but to produce them whenever a European ship arrived in Huaheine. On the 7th September the ships sailed. From Huaheine Captain Furneaux carried Omai, a young native, whose visit to England was the subject of much conversation.

The vessels called at Ulietea, where nothing occurred worthy of record. On the 17th they sailed westward; on the 23d discovered land, which was named Harvey's Island. On the 1st of October they reached the isle called Middleburg by Tasman, but in the native language Eaoowe. The inhabitants were of the most friendly and pacific disposition; not so much as a stick was seen in their hands. Their language is nearly the same as that of the Society Islands, so that Omai conversed with them without difficulty. Eaoowe is a most beautiful spot, and is rendered delightful by the good nature and innate courtesy of the natives. So generous were the islanders, that they appeared more desirous of giving than of receiving, and threw whole bales of cloth into the boats, without waiting for any return. The chief or king was called Tioony. He had several interviews with the British Commanders, and behaved in the most amicable manner. Captain Cook presented him with a choice collection of garden seeds.

From Eaoowe our navigators sailed to Tongataboo (the Amsterdam of Tasman). This is a beautiful island, and highly cultivated: not a foot of ground is wasted. The inhabitants were friendly and peaceable, but a little addicted to theft. Instead of provisions, they brought nothing but cloth, matting, &c., for which the sailors were improvident enough to barter their clothes, a traffic the Captain found it necessary to prohibit. When the people found that nothing but eatables were saleable, they furnished them in abundance. Even a few old rags were sufficient to purchase a fowl or a pig. Captain Cook had an interview with the King, who preserved a stupid and inflexible gravity, very different from the energetic gaiety of his subjects. Such is dignity at Tongataboo. Captain Cook called the group to which Eaoowe and Tongataboo belong, the Friendly Islands. Like most of the isles of the Pacific, they are guarded by coral reefs, which makes them of dangerous access; but by breaking the force of the waves, render the harbours very secure. Forster discovered several new plants. Hogs and poultry were the only domestic animals. The inhabitants were considered by some of our voyagers to be a handsomer race than the Otaheitans, but with this opinion Cook did not coincide. But he does ample justice to the pleasantness of their manners. The women, in particular, he describes as the merriest creatures he had ever seen; and provided any one seemed pleased with their company, they would continue for hours chattering by his side, quite regardless whether they were understood or not. Yet they were not destitute of modesty—at least, they had tact enough to "assume a virtue, if they had it not." It may be remarked, that Cook gives a more favourable picture of the female morality, even of Otaheite, than former or subsequent visitors have confirmed. Perhaps he let the ladies understand that chastity was in his eyes their greatest ornament: and neither savage nor civilised impudence could stand his eye and his frown.

A very singular fashion prevailed in these islands. Almost all the people had one or both of their little fingers amputated. A similar practice is found among the women of New South Wales.

October the 7th. From Tongataboo Captain Cook sailed for Queen Charlotte's Sound, where he designed to take in wood and water, and make preparations for pursuing his discoveries in the south. Having passed the island of Pilstart, discovered by Tasman, he came in sight of New Zealand on the 21st, and anchored at the distance of eight or ten leagues from Table Cape.

It was the boast of the circumnavigator Malespini, that he had done no harm during his voyage. Cook was not satisfied with such negative self-congratulation. It was his ambition to be remembered for good. Wisely conceiving, that to promote agriculture was to promote civilization, and that to increase the comforts of barbarians is to raise them in the social scale, he had provided himself at the Cape with a great variety of garden seeds, and with as many domestic animals as the ship could conveniently carry, which he distributed among the islands where he called. These presents were not very rapturously received; and though he sometimes obtained promises that the animals should be allowed to multiply, there was little dependence on the stability of such resolutions.

The weather about this time became very unfavourable, and it was not till the 3d of September that the Resolution anchored in Ship Cove, Queen Charlotte's Sound. During this tempest the Adventure was separated from her companion vessel, and was not seen nor heard of during the sequel of the voyage.

There was no remarkable incident during Captain Cook's sojourn in New Zealand. He was chiefly employed in repairing the ship, drying the provisions, &c. There was some fear of the biscuit falling short, much of it being damaged, and four thousand two hundred and ninety-two pounds unfit for use. This was a loss which New Zealand could not supply. Fern root would, in an Englishman's opinion, be a very bad substitute for bread. Even while fresh vegetables can be procured, few persons, especially of the laborious classes, can endure to be stinted of farinaceous food: but the case of a ship's crew on the barren ocean, reduced to eat salt beef without biscuit, is perhaps as bad as any thing short of actual famine.

The benevolent efforts of Cook, in the former part of his voyage, had not been attended with any striking effect. Most of the animals were destroyed, and the gardens suffered to run wild. Yet he was not weary of well-doing. At the bottom of the West Bay he ordered to be landed, as privately as possible, three sows, one boar, two cocks, and two hens. To the people in the neighbourhood of Ship Cove he gave a boar, two cocks, two hens, and a young sow. The two goats which he left on a prior visit had been destroyed by a bloody-minded native of the name of Goliah; just as any strange animals which should be discovered loose in England would be. Captain Cook replaced them with two others, the last he had remaining; but, as if it were forbidden by destiny that New Zealand should be a land of goats, the buck went mad, and drowned himself in the sea.

Our Commander was under the necessity of punishing several of his men very severely for the robbery of a New Zealand hut, in which were deposited the gifts received by some chiefs from the English. The New Zealanders, prone as they were to pilfer, had a sufficient horror of theft when they were themselves the sufferers by it; and Cook would never allow retaliation to be a plea for violating their property.

The cannibalism of the New Zealanders was particularly offensive to Oedidee, a youth of Bolabola, whom Cook had brought from Ulietea as an interpreter. On beholding the gnawn and mangled remains of human carcases, he was struck motionless with horror; and when roused at last from his stupefaction, he burst into tears, wept and exclaimed by turns, telling the New Zealanders that they were vile men, and that he would be their friend no longer. Yet Oedidee had probably beheld human sacrifices, if not without pain, without a doubt of their propriety. May not all cannibalism have grown out of human sacrifice, and have been originally an idolatrous rite, though it afterwards became a gluttonous gratification?

The change of diet, good water, and plenty of vegetables, preserved and restored the health of the crew, so that there was not now a sick or scorbutic person on board. Though the Resolution had now to pursue her voyage alone, neither the commander nor the sailors were

4 M

disheartened. Summer was now smiling on November, the month so celebrated in the northern hemisphere for fog and hypochondria. The prosperous gales called on our navigators to launch once more in search of the Terra incognita. Captain Cook wrote a memorandum, containing such information as might be serviceable to Furneaux if he put into the Sound, and deposited it in a bottle, which he hid under a tree in the garden, in such a manner as to insure its being found by the Adventure, or any other European vessel that might chance to arrive. This done, he weighed anchor on the 26th of November, and steered south, inclining to the east. A few days after, according to their reckoning, they crossed the antipodes of London. The first ice island appeared on the 12th of December. The floating ice now became very troublesome, notwithstanding which, the ship arrived without injury in latitude 69° 31' south, the highest she had yet reached. From thence she declined to the north east. Christmas Day found the navigators in the midst of hundreds of ice shoals. This was the second Christmas they had passed amid the antarctic cold ; but the weather was much clearer and lighter than in the former year, a circumstance of hope and safety.

On the 5th of January, 1774, the ship was near the 50th degree of south latitude ; but two sick persons on board. But there were no signs of land. Captain Cook made a tack to the south, and attained the 71st degree on the 30th of January. To have gone forward would have been to encounter certain peril, and probable destruction, without an adequate chance of benefit ; for it was clear, that if any land lay in that quarter, it must be covered with everlasting ice, and destitute of human, animal, or vegetable life. Cook would fain have proved how far it was possible to go ; but his prudence overmastered his ambition, and he steered northward.

It was now sufficiently demonstrated that no southern continent was accessible in the Pacific. But there was still room for considerable islands in the unexplored tracks of that ocean, and Cook never left a work half done. He arranged his plans of discovery as follows.—First, to seek for the land said to have been seen in the 17th century by Juan Fernandez, about latitude 38°. This failing, to direct his course for Davis's Land, or Easter Island, the exact situation of which was undetermined, though no doubt was entertained of its existence. Then, getting within the tropic, to make for Otaheite, where it was necessary for him to look for the Adventure. He purposed likewise to run as far west as the Tierra Austral del Espiritu santo of Quiros, marked in old maps, as the true Terra Australis. Thence to steer south and east between the latitudes of 50 and 60, and if possible to reach the Cape of Good Hope by the ensuing November, when he should have the summer before him to explore the Southern Atlantic. When this extensive plan was communicated to the officers and company of the Resolution, they testified the utmost alacrity to go through with its execution, though it was to detain them from their native land another year. Cook had the talent of inspiring all whom he commanded with his own spirit of discovery.

In pursuing the northward route, it soon became evident, that the rumoured discovery of Juan Fernandez could be nothing but a very small island. The further search after it was relinquished, but Easter Island was still an object of pursuit. About this time Captain Cook was confined to his hammock by a severe attack of bilious colic. The management of the ship devolved on Mr. Cooper, the second in command, who executed his important charge much to his own credit, and his superior's satisfaction. The Captain's recovery was expedited by the skill and attention of Mr. Patten the surgeon; but when he became convalescent, his stomach required fresh meat, and none was to be had, for he had parted with all the live-stock at New Zealand. A favourite dog of Mr. Forster's fell a sacrifice to his returning appetite; and however European tastes may be prejudiced against such viands, our commander found it both wholesome and palatable. It appears from the work of Hippocrates on diet that dogs' flesh was occasionally eaten in Greece. On the 11th of March, our voyagers came in sight of Easter Island, or Davis's Land, which proved a barren uninteresting spot, remarkable for little except some gigantic statues. The natives were found to be as good natured and as dishonest as any of their neighbours. The Resolution next steered for the Marquesas. The Captain, on the passage, had a slight return of his disorder, but it soon passed away. On the 6th and 7th of April four islands came in view, which were known to be those discovered by Quiros in 1595, and by him named Christina, Magdalena, Dominico, and St. Pedro. Another of the same fraternity, which Cook was the first European to visit, was named Hood's Isle, after the young man who caught the first sight of it from the mast-head. The ship came to anchor in Madre de Dios, or Resolution Bay, in St. Christina. The natives were such audacious thieves, that it was found necessary to terrify them by discharges of musquetry; and contrary to the express injunction of Cook, one man, who had attempted to steal an iron stanchion from the gangway, was shot dead. This catastrophe neither put a stop to traffic, nor prevented depredation: yams, plantains, bread-fruit, cocoa-nuts, fowls, and pigs, were procured for awhile on reasonable terms, till the market was ruined by the imprudence of a youth, who gave for a pig a quantity of red feathers which he had brought from Tongataboo. It was impossible to continue trading at such extravagant rates; so the Captain, having taken in wood and water, and ascertained the precise situation of the Marquesas, sailed away rather sooner than he intended. The inhabitants of these isles are said to be the handsomest in the South Sea; but they are evidently of the common race. Oedidee conversed with them without difficulty.

In his way to Otaheite, Cook fell in with some small low islets, connected by coral reefs. One of them, on which Lieutenant Cooper went ashore, was called Tiookea, inhabited by a stout athletic people, of a very dark hue and fierce disposition, who subsist chiefly by fishing, and as the sign of their profession, have the figure of a fish tatooed on their bodies. This island had previously been visited by Captain Byron. Having passed by St. George's Islands—another discovery of Byron—and Palliser's Isles, a group which had escaped the notice of former navigators, the Resolution proceeded through a sea dangerously strewed with coral reefs, in various stages of their progress, to Otaheite, where they arrived on the 22d of April, and anchored in Matavia Bay, principally for the purpose of enabling Mr. Wales to ascertain the error of the chronometers by the known longitude; but finding provisions abundant, and the people well-disposed, the Captain was induced to protract his stay, in order to make some necessary repairs in the ship, which had unavoidably suffered in the high latitudes.

The stock in trade was now very low, so that, had it not been for the red parrots' feathers, which pleased the Otaheitans mightily, it might have been difficult to carry on commerce. A friendly and dignified interchange of royal visits took place between Captain Cook and the Otaheitan potentates, who entertained their visitors with the exhibition of a grand naval review. The marine force of the island must have been very formidable, since no less than one hundred and sixty large double canoes, well equipped, manned, and armed, and attended by one hundred and seventy small craft, intended for transports and victuallers, all gay with flags and streamers, manœuvred in sight of the English, who may have been reminded, both by contrast and resemblance, of the mighty armaments in their own ports. The fighting canoes were managed altogether by paddles; the smaller vessels had a mast and sail, with a sort of house or canopy in the middle. It was conjectured that there might be 7760 men in the whole fleet.

But with all this formidable force, Otoo was obliged to succumb to the commander of a single English vessel, who took it upon him to execute justice on one of King Otoo's subjects, in consequence of an attempted theft of a water cask. The thief was caught in the act, sent on board, and put in irons. Otoo demanded or requested his release, but Cook declared, that as he constantly respected the property of the Otaheitans, and punished stealing in his own people, it was not just that the depredations of the islanders should be encouraged by impunity. He knew that Otoo would not punish the culprit, so he determined to do it himself, which he justified on the principle, that it was indispensable, for the preservation of the Otaheitans themselves, that the system of robbery should be checked by a severe example, as otherwise it would be impossible to protect them from being shot to death. The Captain resisted the intreaties even of the King's sister, and only pledged himself that the man's life should be spared. Otoo discontinued his opposition. The criminal was brought to shore under a guard, and tied to a post. The crowd were warned to keep their distance, and the prisoner received two dozen of lashes in the presence of all. Notwithstanding the timidity imputed to the Otaheitans in general, the man sustained his punishment with great firmness:—perhaps it was not dealt with as much sincerity as if an English offender had been the subject. It is certainly a questionable point how far such an exertion of authority by an alien is reconcilable with the European law of nations; but,

Where Law can do no right,
Let it lawful be, that Law bar no wrong.

The Otaheitan chieftains were not altogether insensible to the national disgrace. Towtah harangued the people on the necessity of avoiding such punishments in future, by reforming their manners. Neither the speech nor the cat-o'-nine-tails produced any lasting amendment. A night or two after the discipline, the sentry allowed his musquet to be stolen. The fear of Cook's resentment made all the neighbourhood quit their habitations; but it was not without great difficulty, and repeated application, that the musquet was restored. When once the acquisitive and secretive propensities of man have gained by indulgence the strength of instinct, neither fear nor shame will make the pilferer honest, though they may make him miserable. Nor will the habit be corrected by change of circumstance, alteration of laws, or improvement of condition. There must be a change of nature—a new creature.

The bread fruits of Otaheite were very useful as a succedaneum for biscuit, which it was highly necessary to economize. Provisions of all kinds were uncommonly plentiful, and the people had overcome their reserve in parting with their stores. The Otaheitans, unlike the New Zealanders, had a correct appreciation of the value of domestic animals. Two goats left by Captain Furneaux in the former part of the voyage had become great favourites, and were in a fair way to multiply. The people of the Society Islands had a passion for cats, a quadruped quite new to them ; and Captain Cook distributed more than twenty at Otaheite alone. Sheep did not take kindly to the climate or herbage, but died almost as soon as they were set ashore.

It will be remembered, that during our commander's first voyage, he was joined by an Irish sailor, who was accused of deserting from the Dutch service. This man now belonged to the Resolution, and was one of the gunner's mates. Being a poor homeless creature, it is not wonderful that he should think of adopting Otaheite for his country. He was detected in the act of swimming to shore. The example of desertion could not be tolerated ; but had he asked the commander's consent to his remaining, it probably would not have been refused.

Cook next paid a visit to his friend Oree, at Huaheine. The old chief was as friendly as ever ; but the natives exhibited such a disposition to plunder, that it was thought expedient to overawe them with a solemn progress through the island, at the head of forty-eight men. The temerity of these islanders was partly ascribed to certain indifferent shots, who, in their shooting parties, had let the ignorant learn that fire-arms are not fatal in every hand. During their abode in Huaheine, the English gentlemen were spectators of a dramatic piece, in which their own characters were pretty freely represented. The subject of this entertainment was the adventures of an Otaheitan girl, who was supposed to have left her parents to follow the strangers. Now there was present a female who was partly in this predicament, having taken a passage in the ship down to Ulitea. She was almost as violently affected by the play as the King in Hamlet, particularly at the conclusion, which represented her reception on returning to her friends. So powerful is Huahenian dramatic satire. Perhaps some persons may think the stage of Huaheine, from this sample, more moral than that of Drury Lane or of Covent Garden, where the comedy generally concludes with the triumph of the runaway lovers. When Captain Cook bade adieu to Huaheine, as he supposed for the last time, and told Oree that they should meet no more, the venerable chieftain wept bitterly, and said, " Let your sons come, and we will treat them well."

Equally affecting was the parting with Oreo, the chief of Ulietea, where the vessel next touched. When Oreo could not obtain of Cook a promise to return, he requested above all things to know the name of his burial place. Cook answered without hesitation Stepney, the place of his residence in London : but when the same question was put to Forster, he replied, that it was impossible a man who used the sea should know where he was to be buried. Those who have imagined a prophetic import in the casual words of men, might almost fancy a reproof and a prediction in Forster's answer, sadly fulfilled in Cook's untimely fate and distant grave.

As Cook had then no expectation of ever revisiting the Society Islands, and knew not when another British ship might find its way thither, Oedidee could not make up his mind to accompany his new friends further. Yet he was very loath to part. When the ship sailed away, "he burst into tears, and then sunk back into his canoe." He was a youth of amiable dispositions, but almost wholly ignorant, even of the customs, manners, and religion of his own countrymen.

June 5th. Our voyagers left Ulietea next day; saw Howe Island, a mere reef. On the 16th discovered Palmerston Island: both these were uninhabited. On the 20th land appeared, which manifestly was an abode of man; but of men, as it proved, so ferocious and intractable, that their country received the title of Savage Island. All endeavours to bring them to parley failed: they rushed on with the fury of bulls, hurling their darts, undismayed by the sight or report of musquetry. One javelin passed close over Cook's shoulder: at the instant, his impulse was naturally to shoot, but his piece missed fire, which he afterwards considered as a providential escape from blood-guiltiness.

Quitting this inhospitable shore in haste, the Resolution steered for the south west, and after passing several small islands, arrived on the 26th at Anamocka, the Rotterdam of Tasman. As soon as the vessel was at anchor, the natives brought down their provisions, consisting chiefly of yams and shaddocks, which they were ready to barter for trifles. As usual, they gave a great deal of trouble by their thievish propensity, taking things which could not be spared. To procure restitution, it was resolved to make a formal invasion. All the marines were sent ashore, and drawn up, full armed, and in military array. Some resistance was offered, and one of the islanders was wounded with small shot. Peace being restored, the Captain endeavoured to make amends to the sufferer by a present, and had his wounds dressed by the surgeon.

Anamocka, or Rotterdam, is of a triangular shape, each side extending between three and four miles There is nothing very peculiar in its productions or population, which closely resemble those of Tongataboo; but the land is less fertile, and the cultivation far more imperfect. Like others in the same group, it is surrounded by innumerable small islands, which might not unaptly be compared to suckers around a parent tree. Cook learned the names of about twenty, lying between north-west and north-east, two of which are of remarkable height, and one was supposed to be a volcano.

Pursuing their course to the west, our navigators passed and named

Turtle Island. On the 16th of July, high land was seen bearing south
west, which was rightly concluded to be that which Quiros had mistaken for a southern continent, and named Tierra Australis del Espiritu
Santo, and which Bougainville, discovering the supposed continent to
be no more than a cluster of isles, now named the Great Cyclades.
The first of this group which the Captain visited was Mallicollo. As
usual, he invited the natives to a friendly commerce; but the pugnacity
of an individual, who was repelled as he was stepping into the boat,
had nearly been attended with fatal consequences. He was armed with
a bow, which he offered to draw first against the boat keeper, and when
his countrymen stopped him, aimed a shaft at Captain Cook. Two
discharges of small shot were necessary to make him retreat; and when
he dropped his bow and paddled off, arrows began to shower from
another quarter, but a great gun fired with ball put the archers to rout
without bloodshed. An hour or two after, the English landed from
the boats in the face of four or five hundred people assembled on the
shore, all armed with bows, but they offered no opposition. Cook and
a chieftain mutually exchanged palm branches, in ratification of peace.
Permission to cut wood was asked and granted in dumb show, for the
language of Mallicollo is not apparently connected with the dialects of
Otaheite, New Zealand, or the Friendly Islands. All went on quietly
thenceforth, but very little business could be transacted, because the
people of Mallicollo set no value on any thing which the strangers had
to offer. Whatever bargains they did make they scrupulously fulfilled.
Even when the Resolution was under way, and they might easily, by
dropping astern in their canoes, have evaded their engagements, they
pressed about the ship to deliver the articles that had been purchased.
One man followed the vessel a good way, and did not come up with her
till the thing he had been paid for was forgotten; and though several
of the crew offered to purchase it, he insisted on giving it to the right
owner. Only one attempt at theft was made, and then restitution was
obtained without trouble. This honest people are the ugliest beings
that our navigators had met with; black, stunted, woolly-headed, flat-
faced, and monkey-visaged. They had never seen a dog, and were
highly delighted with a male and female of that species which Cook
left on the island. Setting sail on the 23d of July, our navigators
passed by several small islands, to which names were given, either as
memorials of friendship, or compliments to greatness; thus, Shepherd's
Isles were called after the Plumian Professor of Astronomy at Cambridge, a learned intimate of the Captain's. Montagu, Hinchinbrook,
and Sandwich isles, record the parties in power at the period of their
discovery. A tall obelisk of rock, the inaccessible haunt of numerous

sea-birds, obtained the designation of the *Monument.* All these spots of earth were uninhabited, though the appearance of Sandwich Island promised fertility.

The next place at which the ships called was Erromango, where they hoped to obtain supplies. The inhabitants crowded to the beach with the most friendly indications—intending to tempt our voyagers ashore and then butcher them. This design, however, was detected by the vigilance of Cook, and a skirmish ensued, in which several of the treacherous barbarians fell, and pretended to be dead, but when they thought themselves unobserved, scrambled away. The scene of this transaction was properly designated Traitor's Head.

Tanna was the next stage. The inhabitants here at first shewed open hostility, but Cook, by the report of the great guns, contrived to terrify, without injuring them, and they became civil enough. They were suspected of being cannibals, because they asked whether the English were so—rather a dubious ground : at any rate, they cannot plead necessity for eating their species, since Tanna is a fertile spot, abounding in bread-fruits, cocoa-nuts, hogs, and poultry. The language of the aborigines was peculiar ; at least Mr. Forster, a speculative linguist, pronounced it to be different from all that had been heard before : but there were in the island many settlers from Erronan, who had introduced a dialect of the Malay, or common Polynesian tongue. The people of Tanna are of middle stature, slender and nimble, averse to labour, but very expert in the use of their weapons ; in so much, that they convinced the astronomer Wales of Homer's authenticity :—" I must confess," says he, " I have often been led to think the feats which Homer represents his heroes as performing with their spears, a little too much of the marvellous to be admitted into an heroic poem : I mean when confined within the strait stays of Aristotle. Nay, even so great an advocate for him as Mr. Pope admits them to be surprizing. But since I have seen what these people can do with their wooden spears, and them badly pointed, and not of a hard nature, I have not the least exception to any one passage in that great poet on that account. But if I see fewer exceptions, I can find infinitely more beauties in him, as he has, I think, scarcely an action, circumstance, or description of any kind whatever relating to a spear, which I have not seen and recognized among these people ; as their whirling motion and whistling noise when they fly ; their quivering motion as they stick in the ground when they fall ; their meditating their aim when they are going to throw ; and their shaking them in their hand as they go."

Tanna is a volcanic formation, and a volcano was in considerable activity when Cook was there in 1774, making a dreadful noise, and

4 N

sending forth sometimes smoke, sometimes flame, and sometimes great stones. Between the explosions there would elapse an interval of two or three minutes. At the foot of this volcano were several hot springs, and in its sides were fissures, whence issued sulphurous and mephitic vapour. Cook sent out an exploring party to examine this natural curiosity completely; but they met with so many obstacles, partly arising from the suspicions of the natives, for which Cook generously and philosophically apologizes, that they returned without accomplishing their purpose. They ascertained, however, that the crater is not on the ridge, but on the side of the mountain, and that the explosions are most violent after long continued rains.

The necessary business of taking in wood and water, neither of which had been procured at Erromango, detained our voyagers for some time at Tanna. The natives became quite reconciled to their visitors, and allowed them to wander about and shoot in the woods without the slightest molestation. Cook, with all his vigilance, could not always prevent his people from abusing the power which fire-arms bestow. On one occasion, when a few little naked boys had pelted with pebbles the men employed in cutting wood, the petty officers on duty fired, and though the Captain severely reprimanded them for their unfeeling hastiness, another sentry killed a native with even less provocation, in the commander's sight.

The Resolution sailed from Tanna on the 1st of September: on the 4th came in sight of an Island, the native appellation of which our navigators could never learn. Captain Cook called it New Caledonia. They remained here for some time, carrying on a very amicable commerce with the natives, and particularly with the chief Teabooma, to whom the Captain presented a dog and bitch, and a young boar and sow. The first were received with ecstacy, but when the pigs were sent, the chief was from home, and his attendants accepted them with a good deal of ceremonious hesitation.

The New Caledonians Cook conjectured to be a mingled race, between the people of Tanna and of the Friendly Isles, or of New Zealand. Forster could trace no analogy in their language to that of any other tribe; but the geneologies and affinities of unknown and unwritten languages are not to be determined in a fortnight. The New Caledonians are stout, active, and well made, their hair black and curly, not woolly, their beards thick and crisp: like the people of Erromango, they besmear their bodies with divers coloured pigments. Their only habiliment is a wrapper of bark or platted leaves. Their huts are something like bee-hives, composed of sticks wattled with reeds, thatched and carpeted with dry grass. With regard to the arts and conveniences of life, they seem to hold a middle place between the Australian savages and the almost civilized Otaheitans; but in the development of the moral sense they are perhaps farther advanced than either. Captain Cook pays a high compliment to the chastity of the New Caledonian females.

On the 13th of September the Resolution sailed with a design to examine the coast of New Caledonia, but such were the perils of the circuit, that the commander felt it his duty, considering the state of the vessel, and the long voyage yet before him, to leave the survey in some measure incomplete. Yet he ascertained that New Caledonia was, next to New Zealand, the largest country in the South Pacific, and that it furnishes excellent timber of the spruce pine species, well adapted for masts and spars. This discovery was valuable, for except New Zealand, he had not found an island in the South Sea where a ship could supply herself with a mast or yard, let her necessity be what it might. The first opportunity of examining these serviceable trees, the distant appearance of which had given rise to sundry conjectures, was on a small islet to the south-east, which received the appropriate designation of Isle of Pines. Another little plot of earth, presenting many new species of plants, was entitled Botany Isle, which is rather too hard upon Botany Bay. Captain Cook, like most Englishmen, betrayed a poverty in the invention of names.

Leaving the coast of New Caledonia, the Captain steered south-east, and discovered Norfolk Island; so named in honour of the noble family of Howard. It was then, and we believe is now, uninhabited, though a British colony for some years were settled or imprisoned there. It is lofty ground, abundant in fine forest trees, especially the *Auracaria excelsa*, or Norfolk pine. The New Zealand flax grows there luxuriantly, and the British settlers, in 1793, sent for two New Zealanders to instruct them in the method of spinning and weaving it. Unfortunately, flax-dressing in New Zealand is exclusively a female employment: the two persons carried to Norfolk Isle were both males; the one a warrior and the other a priest—and could give as little information on the clothing manufacture of their country, as could be expected from the military or clergy of Europe on the arcana of lady-like accomplishment.

From Norfolk Isle the Resolution made for New Zealand, and anchored in Ship Cove, Queen Charlotte's Sound, on the 18th of October. Little of moment occurred during this fourth visit of our commander to Poenamoo. At his first arrival he found the country deserted, and the gardens which he had planted run wild. On looking for the bottle which he had hidden when he last took leave, he found a memorandum, signifying that Furneaux had found it, but no information concerning the subsequent fate of the Adventure. No inhabitants appeared till the 24th, and then they were shy and timid at first, but when they found that it was Cook who had arrived, "joy took the place of fear, those who had taken refuge in the woods hurried forth, leaping and shouting for ecstacy, and embracing their old acquaintances with tears of delight." There was more in their former terrors and sudden joy than Cook at that time understood. He could not but be pleased with what appeared a genuine effusion of gratitude from an overflowing heart. Yet the mysterious answers or determined ignorance of the New Zealanders whenever the Adventure was alluded to, might have awakened the suspicions of a less cautious man. The truth, which he never knew till his return to England, was this—Furneaux, who had parted company with our subject during the storms of October, 1773, arrived in Ship Cove in the beginning of December, and found the bottle and directions which his consort had left. He waited some time to refit, lay in water, &c., and was ready to sail on the 17th. Intending to weigh anchor the next morning, he sent off one of the midshipmen with a boat's crew to gather a few wild greens, the use of which his men had learned duly to appreciate. Evening came, and the boat did not return according to orders, at which Captain Furneaux was probably irate; but when morning came, and still no boat, he became alarmed, and hoisting out the launch, sent Mr. (afterwards Admiral) Burney, with another boat's crew and ten marines, in search of the missing. The fact soon appeared. The party had been surprised, massacred, and eaten. The Adventure quitted New Zealand without imitating the fearful retaliation inflicted by the French on the murderers of Marion; but when an European ship was seen in the Cove, the first impression of the natives would naturally be, that it was come to avenge the massacre. But when they found it was not Furneaux, but Cook, whom they rightly supposed to know nothing of what had taken place, they felt his presence like a great deliverance, and expressed their joy with their usual vehemence. But it was a joy which most people have felt in some degree at some time or other. Who has not grasped with sincere delight the hand of a lounger to whom he was quite indifferent, simply because the rap at the door had raised the apprehension of some feared or hated visitation; a dun, a borrower, the bearer of a challenge, or a good adviser?

Whatever intercourse took place between Cook and the natives was answerable to this fair beginning. A chief called Pedero invested the British commander with the staff of honour, the Marshal's baton of New Zealand, and Cook dressed Pedero in an old suit of clothes, in which he felt his consequence wonderfully enlarged. The Captain, unwearied in his endeavours to stock the island with animals, which might be useful alike to the native population, and to such Europeans as might visit or settle in this remote region, sent ashore another boar and sow. Swine are so prolific, and so easily accommodate themselves to circumstances, that a single pair, escaping for a few years in a thinly peopled country, would multiply beyond the facilities of extirpation. Nothing was seen of the poultry left on former occasions except an egg, which appeared to be new laid.

The ship being now repaired, the crew refreshed, and the astronomical observations satisfactorily performed, Captain Cook sailed from New Zealand on the 10th of November, to resume his search for the southern continent. As it is well known that the only result of this arduous, painful, protracted, but worthy and scientific pursuit, was, that there is no habitable continent to be discovered; and as freezing narratives are rather dull till they reach the point of horror, we shall not accompany our navigator any longer in his sailings to and fro among the ice. We must, however, omit his spending his Christmas in Christmas Sound, on the west coast of Tierra del Fuego. Christmas, in an English imagination, is inseparably associated with cold weather and good cheer. In Tierra del Fuego it can only support the former part of its character. A more desolate place than Christmas Sound cannot be. Yet doubtless the wanderers drank " a health to them that's far away," as many a British fire-side drank to them. Their harbour, dreary as it was, furnished geese for their Christmas dinner, and fuel to roast it. Nor are the rocks of Tierra del Fuego without their beauty. They furnished occupation for the botanists: plants, elegant or curious in conformation, rich in hue, and fragrant of odour (as mountain plants generally are) peeped out of the crannies. But the human creatures were the same ugly, half-starved, helpless generation that dwindled beside the Bay of Success. Bougainville called them Pecheras, and Cook pronounced them the most wretched beings he had ever beheld.

New Year's Day, 1775, was spent in New Year's harbour, a port in Staten Land. Some small islands in its vicinity were named New Year's Isles. Here our voyagers observed a harmony between the animal tribes, not unworthy of brief notice. The sea coast is occupied by the sea lions; the white bears possess the shore; the shags are posted on the highest cliffs; the penguins fix their quarters where there is the most easy communication with the sea; other birds retire to remoter places; but all occasionally mingle together, like poultry in a farm yard. Eagles and vultures are seen perched on the same crag with shags, and the weaker shew no fear of the stronger.　The island is thronged with life, and the living prey upon the dead.

Proceeding from Staten Land, Captain Cook discovered Willis's Island, Bird's Isle, and South Georgia,—the last a land of 70 degrees compass, of which, worthless as it was, he took possession in the King's name.　At first our navigators hailed this icy waste, where no vegetation existed but a coarse tufted grass, wild burnet, and the moss on the rocks; where not a tree was to be seen, nor a shrub big enough to make a tooth-pick; and where no animal food could be obtained but the flesh of seals and penguins, to which bullock's liver is an Apician delicacy,— as the long sought continent of golden dreams.　A quaint honour to the warm-hearted old King, to affix his name to the planet most remote from the sun, and to the spot of earth least in favour with the same genial luminary.

Leaving South Georgia (after ascertaining it to be an island by sailing round it in a fog), our voyagers proceeded on their dreary adventures, and on the 31st of January fell in with an elevated coast, the most southern land that had yet been discoverd, and thence named Southern Thule, no comfortable place to be wrecked on, of which the Resolution was in no small danger, from the great western swell setting in right for the shore.　Cape Bristol, Cape Montagu, Saunder's Isle, Candlemas Isles, and Sandwich's Land, were discovered by the 6th of February.　The opinion of Cook was now decided, that there is a tract of land near the pole, which is the source of the ice spread over the Southern Ocean, and that it extended farthest north where the ice appeared farthest north; that is, towards the Atlantic or Indian Ocean.　But such land must lie chiefly within the antarctic circle, and be for ever inaccessible.　Cook, no boaster, fearlessly asserted that no man could venture further south, in seas beset with ice and fog, than he had done, without more than a risk of destruction.　He therefore wisely turned his thoughts to England, and steered northward.　Having formed this determination, he demanded of the officers and petty officers, in pursuance of his instructions, the log books and journals they had kept, and enjoined them never to divulge where or how far they had been, until authorized by the Lords of the Admiralty.　If he expected this order to be obeyed, and that, too, when his commissioned authority should cease, he shewed less than his usual knowledge of human nature. In the passage to the Cape of Good Hope, he met first a Dutch, and then a British East-Indiaman; the former commanded by Captain Bosch, and the latter by Captain Broadly.　Bosch offered our navigators sugar, arrack, and whatever else he had to spare, and Broadly gave them tea, fresh provisions, and news, which, though none of the newest (for he was returning from China), must still have been new to them.   From these vessels Cook was informed of what had befallen the Adventure after the separation.   On the 22d of March he anchored in Table Bay.   During the time that elapsed from his leaving the Cape of Good Hope to his return to it again, he had sailed no less than 20,000 leagues, nearly three times the equatorial circumference of the globe.   While at the Cape he met with Crozet, whom he describes as a man of abilities, possessed of the true spirit of discovery.

The remainder of the homeward voyage was over familiar ground, and needs no description.   Captain Cook left the Cape on the 27th of April, reached St. Helena on the 15th of May, Fernando Norhonha on the 9th of June, Fayal in the Azores on the 14th of July, Spithead on the 30th, when he landed at Portsmouth, having been absent from Britain three years and eighteen days, during which, amid all vicissitudes and hardships, he lost but four men.   And thus ended Cook's second voyage.   Its geographical results, though important, were chiefly negative, and therefore not of that kind on which imagination dwells delighted.   He had destroyed a vision of fancy, and instead of augmenting the map with new Indies, had reduced islands to fog banks and ice shoals, and continents to inconsiderable islets and reefs of coral. He had discovered, in short, that a fifth continent was as little to be hoped for as a fifth sense.   The voyage had doubtless been beneficial to navigation, to nautical astronomy, to botany, and to science in general ; it had enlarged the natural history of man a little ; but its happiest and fairest achievement was to shew how life and health may be preserved for years on the ocean, and how barbarians may be awed without cruelty, and conciliated without delusion.

It must have been no small satisfaction to Cook, that no change had taken place in the Admiralty Department during his absence : that the same Lords who employed his services were to dispense his reward. Lord Sandwich lost no time in recommending him to the Sovereign, and his remuneration was not delayed.   On the 9th of August he was made a Post Captain, and three days after a Captain in Greenwich Hospital, a situation of dignified repose, which he had fairly earned, and in which he might honourably have sat down for the remainder of his days.   His society was sought alike by the wealthy and the learned.

About the close of 1775 he was proposed a candidate for admission into the Royal Society, elected on the 29th of February, 1776, and admitted on the 7th of March, on which occasion was read a paper, addressed by Captain Cook to Sir John Pringle, President of the Royal Society, and author of a well known work on the diseases of the army, containing " An account of the method he had taken to preserve the health of the crew of his Majesty's ship the Resolution, during her voyage round the world," to which the President and Council of the Society decreed the Copley gold medal, with a handsome panegyric from the President, which Cook was not present to hear; nor did he ever receive the medal into his own hands, for before the day appointed for delivering it, he had set sail on his last expedition. It was given to Mrs. Cook, to whom it soon became a sad memorial of the departed.

The many objections raised against Dr. Hawkesworth's official compound had proved the folly of employing professed *Literateurs* to *distil, rectify,* and *flavour* the unadulterated observations of competent eye-witnesses. Cook was himself the narrator of his second voyage, and proved himself more than equal to the task. His style is just what it should be—like his meaning—thoroughly English, clear, and manly,—the less authorlike the better. George Forster also published an account of the voyage, which, whatever the Admiralty might say or think, he had a perfect right to do. The more accounts of any transaction proceed from eye-witnesses the better for the interests of truth. The astronomers Wales and Bayley produced a book, chiefly scientific, but interspersed with general observations.

Cook was now expected and intitled to rest, but neither his own spirit nor the spirit of the times would permit him to do so. Though the question of a southern continent was decided for all practical purposes, there was another great geographical problem which continued to agitate the public mind—that of the possibility of the passage to India by the north seas. Lord Sandwich was meditating an expedition for this purpose, and wished to have Captain Cook's opinion as to the manner in which it should be conducted, and the person to whom it should be intrusted. A great dinner was held at his Lordship's, at which the Circumnavigator, Sir Hugh Palliser, and other people of distinction were present. The north passage of course was the topic. The grandeur and importance of the project were eloquently magnified, —it was to consummate the system of discovery which Cook had all but finished. The Captain's imagination was fired: at last he leapt up and said, "I will do it!" This was just what was wished, perhaps not more than was expected, but what no one had ventured to propose.

On the 10th of February, 1776, Captain Cook received his commission. Two vessels were appointed to the service, the Resolution, commanded by Cook in person, and the Discovery, commanded by Captain Clerke, a meritorious officer, who had sailed with the circumnavigator in former voyages. The usual plan was to be reversed: instead of seeking a north west passage from the Atlantic to the Pacific, the expedition was to sail to the northern parts of the Pacific, explore the north west coast of America, and search for a passage to the East. An act to amend an act was passed in 1776, declaring, "That if any ship belonging to any of his Majesty's subjects, or to his Majesty, shall find out, and sail through, any passage by sea, between the Atlantic and Pacific Oceans, in any direction or parallel of the northern hemisphere to the north of the 52nd degree of northern latitude, the owners of such ships, if belonging to any of his Majesty's subjects, or the commander, officers and seamen of such ship belonging to his Majesty, shall receive, as a reward for such discovery, the sum of £20,000."

The ships were furnished with every thing that could contribute either to the accomplishment of their main design, the general advancement of science, the health of the crew, or the furtherance of Cook's beneficent projects with regard to the inhabitants of newly discovered lands.

Cook sailed out of Plymouth Sound on the 12th of July, taking with him Omai, who left England with a mixture of pleasure and regret. He had been a great Lion, and was painted by Sir Joshua Reynolds in the costume of his native country. Captain Clerke was detained for some time longer. The Resolution, having touched at Teneriffe and Porto Praya, anchored in Table Bay on the 18th of October. The Discovery joined on the 10th of November, and the two ships sailed southward on the 30th. On the 12th of December land was seen, which proved to be a group of islands, two of which, in honour of their French discoverers, were named Marion and Crozet's Isles. Two, of larger size, were called Prince Edward's Isles. After exploring the coast of Kerguelen's Land, a miserable country, which, if it had wanted a name, might fitly be called the Land of Desolation, the navigators made for Van Diemen's Land, and anchored in Adventure Bay on the 26th of January, 1777. They saw more of the inhabitants than any preceding visitors; found them savages of the lowest scale, but peaceable, neither doing nor apprehending evil. Omai, prouder of his superiority than a man longer acquainted with the advantages of civilization, laughed at their clumsiness in hitting a mark with their spears, and terrified them so much by the discharge of a musket, that they all ran away, and there was some difficulty in renewing their confidence. Cook left some swine in this island, but thought there was no chance that sheep or cattle would be allowed to increase. Though the females were any thing but beautiful, some gentlemen of the Discovery attempted to seduce them, at which the men were very indignant. Cook also speaks with great disapprobation of such profligate gallantry. It may seem somewhat remarkable for a ship's crew to go ashore to make hay, and yet this was one purpose of our voyager's tarrying in Van Diemen's Land. The numerous live stock which it was proposed to distribute among the South Sea islands were running short of provender. The grass proved coarse and scanty, but it was better than none.

The ships sailed again on the 30th of January, and on the 12th of February arrived at the old station in Queen Charlotte's Sound. And now the New Zealanders, seeing Omai on board, and concluding that the murder of Captain Furneaux's men must have come to Cook's knowledge, instead of the joy which succeeded their apprehensions on the last visit, displayed nothing but sullen mistrust, and for some time no kindness, no promises, could induce them to approach the vessels. At length Cook succeeded in convincing them that revenge was not the object of his return, and they became as familiar as ever. If, however, he refrained from shedding blood for blood, it was not for want of counsel to the contrary. "If," says the Captain, "I had followed the advice of all our pretended friends, I might have extirpated the whole race ; for the people of each hamlet or village by turns applied to me to destroy the other." In particular, there was a chief named Kahoora, the leader in the massacre, whom his countrymen were continually pointing out as a proper object of vengeance, in which they were strongly seconded by Omai. Kahoora almost won the Captain's admiration by confiding himself to his honour. He came to the ship in his canoe. "This was the third time," says Cook, "that he had visited us, without betraying the smallest appearance of fear. I was ashore when he now arrived, but had got on board just as he was going away. Omai, who had returned with me, presently pointed him out, and solicited me to shoot him. Not satisfied with this, he addressed himself to Kahoora, threatening to be his executioner if ever he presumed to visit us again. The New Zealander paid so little regard to his threats, that he returned the next morning with his whole family, men, women, and children, to the number of twenty and upwards. Omai was the first who acquainted me with his being alongside the ship, and desired to know if he should ask him to come aboard. I told him he might, and accordingly he introduced the chief into the cabin, saying, 'There is Kahoora, kill him.' But as if he had forgot his former threats, or were afraid that I should call upon him to perform them, he immediately retired. In a short time, however, he returned, and seeing the chief unhurt, he expostulated with me very earnestly, saying, 'Why do you not kill him ? You tell me if a man kill another in England that he is hanged for it. This man has killed ten, and yet you will not kill him, though many of his countrymen desire it, and it would be very good.' Omai's arguments, though specious enough, having no weight with me, I desired him to ask the chief why he killed Captain Furneaux's people? At this question Kahoora folded his arms, hung down his head, and looked like one caught in a trap; and I firmly believe that he expected instant death. But no sooner was he assured of his safety than he became cheerful. He did not, however, seem willing to give me an answer to the question that had been put to him, till I had again and again repeated my promise that he should not be hurt. Then he ventured to tell us, ' that one of his countrymen, having brought a stone hatchet to barter, the man to whom it was offered took it, and would neither return it nor give any thing for it; on which the owner of it snatched up the bread as an equivalent, and then the quarrel began.' " *

As no English eye-witnesses survived to tell the real circumstances of the massacre, it was impossible to know the truth or falsehood of Kahoora's story. All the New Zealanders, however, even those who desired Kahoora's death, and who had no personal concern in the butchery, declared that it was the unpremeditated consequence of a casual disagreement; and Kahoora's mode of accounting for it was as likely as any. He might very easily have invented a much greater provocation.

Though Captain Cook declined all measures of revenge, he wisely took much greater precautions in his dealings with the barbarians than he deemed necessary on former visits. A guard of ten marines constantly attended the party on shore, the workmen were well armed, and whenever a boat was sent out it was furnished with means of defence, and intrusted to officers well acquainted with the natives and their ways. The disaster of Furneaux's men gave the English sailors so thorough a hatred of the New Zealanders, that they would not even approach their women, a circumstance very agreeable to the commander, who, though he could not altogether prevent illicit intercourse, always discouraged it; and ably combats the assertion, that such transient connections are a security among savages. He maintains that they betray more men than they save,—" And how," he pertinently asks, " how should it be otherwise? what else can be expected, since all their views are selfish, without the least mixture of regard or attachment?" No quarrel occurred during this, the fifth and last visit of our commander to New Zealand. The people supplied the crew with plenty of fish, for notwithstanding the apparent imperfection of their hooks, they were much more successful, both with net and line, than the English. Cook made presents as usual to the chiefs; two goats

* Cook's Last Voyage, vol. i. 134.

and a kid to one, two pigs to another. He did think of leaving some sheep, a bull, and two heifers at Queen Charlotte's Sound, but finding no chief able and willing to protect animals which could not be concealed, he relinquished his purpose. He was informed that one chief, called Tiratou, had a cow, and many cocks and hens. So he had hopes that his endeavours for the benefit of this singular and improvable race would be finally crowned with success. Though the vegetables be had introduced had been neglected, they had sown and multiplied themselves, and the potatoes were meliorated by the change of soil.

Preparing to quit New Zealand for the last time, Captain Cook was persuaded by Omai to take with him two native youths. The father of the one dismissed him with indifference, and even stripped him of the little clothing he had; but the mother of the other took leave with all the marks of maternal affection. The Captain, before he would assent to their going, took care to make them understand that they were never to return.

On the 27th of February the Resolution and Discovery finally got clear of New Zealand. The poor boys were woefully sea-sick, and repented of their roving when it was too late. After calling at several islands,* the names of which we need not particularize, without obtaining many refreshments, our voyagers arrived at Annamooka on the 1st of May. Here provisions were abundant enough, but the thievishness of the inhabitants was very annoying. They cared not for a slight peppering of small shot, and as for corporal punishment, you might as well lash an oak tree. Their tattooed skins seemed absolutely insensible of pain. Captain Clerke hit on a mode of punishment, which was not altogether without effect, and may be worth the consideration of the revisers of the penal code. This was, to shave the heads of the offenders and let them go.

From Annamooka the ships proceeded to Hadpaee, where they met with a friendly reception from the inhabitants, and from Earoupa the chief. There was a reciprocation of presents, civilities, and solemnities: on the parts of the natives were displayed single combats with clubs, wrestling and boxing matches, female combatants, male dancers,

---

* At one of these islands, Wateeoo by name, some of the inhabitants who came on board the Resolution were terrified and astonished at the sight of the cows and horses, but testified no alarm or surprise at the goats or sheep, which they said they knew to be birds. In the same island Omai met with three of his own countrymen, though Wateeoo (situate in 20° 1' south latitude) is more than 200 leagues from any of the Society Isles. Twelve persons, of whom the three were survivors, had embarked in a canoe, to pass from Otaheite to Ulietea, and by stress of storms had been driven thus far south. Eight perished by fatigue and famine on the way.

nocturnal concerts, and balls. The English treated in return by a review of the marines, and an exhibition of fire-works. Cook afterwards explored the coast of Hapaee, Lefooga, and the neighbouring islands. On the return to Annamooka, May 31st, the Resolution was very near running full against a low sandy isle, surrounded with breakers. "Such hazardous situations," as the Captain says, "are the unavoidable companions of the man who goes upon a voyage of discovery." The accuracy with which Cook observed and noted down whatever might be of service to succeeding navigators, has materially diminished the dangers of the seas.

The Friendly Islands, in which group are included Anamooka, Tongataboo, Hapaee, Eaoowe, Lefooga, and others of less note, constituted a united kingdom; and Captain Cook met at Happaee with Poulaho, the reigning monarch, by whom he was invited to Tongataboo, whither, after touching again at Annamooka, the two commanders sailed, and had another hair-breadth escape on the passage. At Tongataboo, where Cook arrived on the 10th of June, our voyagers were hospitably received and industriously amused by the King, but sorely plundered by the commonalty, whose larcenies were the more irritating from the overt impudence with which they were perpetrated. It required all Cook's authority to hinder the sentinels from firing. On the 19th was a grand distribution of live stock. To King Poulaho was given a bull and a cow, and three goats; to Feenou, a chief of consequence, and an acquaintance of some standing, a horse and mare; to Mareewagee, a Cape ram and two ewes; besides which he left in the island four pigs, a pair of rabbits, and a buck and doe. In bestowing these gifts, the Captain perhaps regretted that there were no laws for preserving game in Tonga.

From Tonga our voyagers sailed to Eaoowe, where they met with some old friends,—for to a seaman in a far country every known face is an old friend. Captain Cook was one day served with a dish of turnips, the produce of seed sown by himself during his former voyage; and he was so pleased with the success of his beneficence, that he enriched the chief's plantation with melons and a pine-apple. The agriculture of the Friendly Islands was the best in Polynesia, and therefore the natives appreciated duly the value of cultivated vegetables. Our commander spent two or three months in this archipelago, and formed a very favourable opinion of the native character; abating that thievish instinct, which is only to be controuled by long subjection to law, and can never be eradicated but by the influences of a divine religion, (for whoever loves the world is a thief in his heart); and few will differ from Cook when he says, that "great allowances should be made for the foibles of the poor natives of the Pacific Ocean, whose minds are overpowered with the glare of objects equally new to them as they were captivating." He also acquits them of dishonesty in their dealings with each other.

. The Resolution and Discovery quitted Tongataboo on the 17th of July. An eclipse of the moon was observed on the night between the 20th and 21st. On the 8th of August appeared the isle of Tubooai on which, though invited by the inhabitants, our navigators did not land, but proceeded to Otaheite, where they arrived on the 12th. Omai at first was coldly received : he was of low condition, and no one cared to recognize him ; but the meeting between the traveller and his sister was affectionate in a high degree. His aunt also came, and washed his feet with her tears. Since Cook was in Otaheite last, two Spanish vessels had twice anchored in Oaita-piha Bay, and left animals in the country. Before a house which the Spaniards had occupied they had erected a wooden cross, on the transverse part of which was inscribed, " Christus vincit :" on the perpendicular, " Carolus III. imperat, 1774." On the other side of the post Captain Cook inscribed, "Georgius tertius rex. Annis. 1767, 1769, 1773, 1774, et 1777." Thus commemorating the visit of Captain Wallis and his own. The Spaniards were well spoken of by the Otaheitans.

A great instance of Cook's influence over his crew occurred about this time. As the voyage was inevitably to be protracted a year longer than was expected, and might be long delayed in frigid regions, where spirituous potations were really necessary, he persuaded the sailors to give up their allowance of grog (except on Saturday nights) so long as they were in a land of cocoa nuts, the liquor of which is so nutricious and refreshing. To this the whole company assented without a murmur, and the example was followed on board the Discovery.

It is a happy circumstance when generosity is convenient. Cook, in Otaheite, disposed of the greater part of his live cargo in gifts to the chieftains, whereby he did a good action, and lightened the vessels of very troublesome passengers. It was no cheap or easy effort of charity to carry cattle and provender half over the globe, to benefit an almost unknown race.

. A war was pending between Otaheite and Eimeo, and Cook was earnestly requested to take a part in it by the Otaheitans. But he steadily and conscientiously preserved neutrality, much to his own credit, and the Otaheitans' disappointment. Towtah, who commanded the expedition against Eimeo, was worsted, and obliged to submit to a disgraceful accommodation. On his return, he attributed his failure entirely to the want of proper support, and threatened, that as soon as the English were gone, he would join the people of Tiaraboo, and attack his sovereign Otoo at Oparre or Matavai. Captain Cook then publicly declared, that if any such combination were formed he would assist the King to the utmost of his power. This declaration had the desired effect, and Towtah continued quiet, instead of becoming the Otaheitan Coriolanus.

While remaining in Otaheite, our navigators witnessed a human sacrifice. The victim was stabbed unawares, and after a time exposed on the Morai. Though but one offering is ever made at a time, these sacrifices must have been pretty often repeated, for forty-nine fresh skulls appeared on the sacrificial pile. The victims selected were generally low fellows, who stroll about without fixed habitation or employment. A pretty effective vagrant law!

On the 14th of September, Captains Cook and Clerke mounted on horseback, and took a ride round the plain of Matavai. The surprise and admiration of the natives was as great as if they had seen centaurs in earnest—perhaps greater.

We must not omit that our commander was freed from a rheumatic attack about this time, by a process very similar to shampooing, in which the operators were Otoo's mother, his three sisters, and eight other women. The Otaheitan name for the operation is *Romee*. Before his departure, Otoo begged his acceptance of a large canoe, as a present to the *Earee Rahie no Pretrani; i. e.* King of Britain. Cook was pleased with the thought, which arose from no suggestion of his, but from Otoo's spontaneous feeling. But the canoe was too large to be taken on board.

On the 30th, our voyagers left Otaheite, and continued for some time cruising among the neighbouring isles; but we must pass over all that took place in these excursions, and only briefly mention that Omai was finally left at Huaheine, where a spot of ground was assigned him, a small cabin built, and his garden stocked with pine-apples, shaddocks, vines, and the seeds of several European vegetables.

On the 8th of December our voyagers sailed from Bolabola. They were lucky enough to find an uninhabited Christmas island, abounding with turtle for the Christmas dinner. On the 28th, an eclipse of the sun. On the 31st, after planting some cocoa nuts and melons, a bottle was left, with a paper denoting that the Resolution and Discovery had been at that spot on the last day of 1777.

For the events of 1778, the discovery of the Sandwich Islands, the exploring the north west coast of America, the ascertaining the vicinity of the Asiatic and American continents, we must refer to the published voyages of Cook. All that we can say, is, that they sustained his reputation to the utmost, and add to the regret with which every good mind must regard the catastrophe we proceed briefly to describe.

After proceeding as far north as was practicable in the advanced season, with the strongest hopes of finally accomplishing the object of the voyage, Captain Cook steered southward, with a design of wintering among the Sandwich Islands, and returning to Kamskatka the following spring. It was on the 30th of November that he discovered the fatal Owhyhee. Seven weeks elapsed in sailing round and examining its coasts, and in all this time the inhabitants shewed no symptom of hostility or suspicion. Not even the people of Otaheite had trusted themselves to English honour with such perfect confidence. On the 17th he anchored in Karakatooa Bay, where occurred the fatal quarrel in which he perished. A chieftain of rank was shot by the crew of an English boat, and in revenge, the Captain was attacked on all sides. His men strove in vain to assist him—he was stabbed in the back, and fell.

His life is his character and his panegyric. It ceased abruptly, but it will never be forgotten.*

* There is one circumstance connected with Cook's last voyage so honourable to human nature, that it must not be omitted. England was then at war with France. But the French King, considering the purely pacific and benevolent purpose for which Cook had braved the sea, ordered that the Resolution and Discovery should be treated as neutral vessels. Franklin, who was then Ambassador in France from the Congress, recommended that the United States should issue similar orders, but it does not appear that Congress attended to the suggestion.

WILLIAM CONGREVE.

YORKSHIRE claims but little in this fortunate wit, and her claim to that little has been litigated. His family was of Staffordshire, his education was in Ireland; he led a town life, and acquired a town celebrity. Yorkshire could only boast the place of his nativity—the hedge-sparrow's nest wherein the cuckoo was hatched—and this modest pretension has been controverted by the *isle of wits*, for so might the country of Swift, Farquhar, Sheridan and Moore be rightly denominated, rather than the *isle of saints*, seeing that for the Irish saints the *Acta Sanctorum* itself will not vouch, while the Irish wits need no vouchers. We have ourselves heard it vehemently asserted, that all the writers of the *middle* * *comedy* were Irishmen, of course including

* The terms old, middle, and new, applied to the dynasties of Greek Comedy, may with little violence be transferred to the English stage. It must, however, be remarked, that of the two latter races, each originated in the life-time of its predecessor. The old or poetical comedy, composed of a mixture of blank verse and prose, often with a strong infusion of pathetic interest, and very frequently interspersed with songs, dances, &c., flourished under Elizabeth and James. Fine specimens of it are found in Fletcher and Massinger, but perhaps the very finest in Shakspeare's Twelfth Night, and As You Like It. It has been revived or imitated by Tobin, in his Honey-Moon. The second, or middle style, was first perfected by Ben Jonson, though chronology would rather class him with the writers of the old comedy. But he seems to have been the earliest dramatist who, in a regular composition, relied for effect entirely on the representation of contemporary life and manners. The middle comedy became predominant after the Restoration, and numbers many writers of unequal merit; the last were Cumberland and Sheridan. It has many minor varieties, of which the most considerable are the moralizing genteel comedy, introduced by Cibber, and the Spanish intriguing comedy, of which the principal writers have been female. The new comedy, of which the principal masters are Colman, Morton, Reynolds, Dibdin, Diamond, &c., has been denominated sentimental, or by a French expression, *comedie larmoyant*, crying comedy, an apparent contradiction. It is, in truth, the comic correlative to Lillo's tragedy. Much as it is reviled by the critics, something very like it is occasionally to be found in old Heywood, the prose Shakspeare. Perhaps its just distinction is the *democratic* comedy, for the virtuous characters are almost always operatives, or shopkeepers, or small farmers. However inferior it may be to the middle or legitimate comedy as a work of art, and still more to the poetic comedy as

Congreve in the number.   It is true, that he called himself an Englishman, and expressly mentioned Bardsea, in Yorkshire, as his birth-
place ; but then a man may be mistaken as to the place he was born
in, or he may be ashamed of it.   Dr. Johnson's judgment in this matter
is a singular instance of that leaning against the subjects of his biography, of which he is justly accused by Mr. Roscoe.—" It was said by
himself," observes the Doctor, " that he owed his nativity to England,
and by every body else, that he was born in Ireland.   Southerne mentioned him with sharp censure, as a man that meanly disowned his
native country.   To doubt whether a man of eminence has told the
truth about his own birth, is in appearance to be very deficient in candour ; yet nobody can live long without knowing that falsehoods of
convenience or vanity, falsehoods from which no evil immediately visible
ensues except the general degradation of human testimony, are very
lightly uttered, and when once uttered are sullenly supported.   Boileau,
who desired to be thought a rigorous and steady moralist, having told a
petty lie to Louis XIV., continued it afterwards by false dates, thinking
himself obliged in honour, says his admirer, to maintain what, when
he said it, was so well received."

It is a pity that the Doctor, who, like Boileau, aimed at the character
of "a steady and rigorous moralist," did not reflect that sophistry is
first cousin, only once removed, to lying, and that an uncharitable piece
of special pleading, intended to injure the reputation of the illustrious
dead, is not a *very white* lie.   Congreve, whatever his faults might be,
was not a fool ; nor was his convenience or vanity at all concerned in
proving himself a Yorkshireman rather than an Irishman.   To be born
in Ireland was never disreputable, and to be born in Yorkshire is an
honour too common to be worth contending for.   Were there decisive
evidence that Congreve was wrong as to the fact, it had been candid to
suppose him mistaken, which the son of an officer in a marching regiment might easily be, about the year and place of his nativity.   But
there is decisive evidence that he was right,—to wit, the parish register
of Bardsea, and the matriculation book * of Trinity College, Dublin.

a birth of imagination, we cannot think it deserves all the vituperation that has been
heaped upon it.   Its worst defect is, that it does not represent the actual manners of
any class,—its characters are unreal without being imaginative.   Still, a composition
which excites laughter mixed with kindliness can never be worthless, for kindness is
always worth something, and laughter is always good when it does not proceed from
scorn.

* The notice of Congreve's matriculation, in the College Register, is as follows :
" 1685, die quinto Aprilis horâ diei pomeridianâ Gulielmus Congreve Pensionarius
filius Gulielmi Congreve Generosi de Youghaliâ annos natus 16 natus apud Bardse-

An extract from the former runs thus :—"William, the sonne of Mr. William Congreve, of Bardsey Grange, baptized February 10th, (1669)." In the notice of his matriculation at Trinity College, Dublin, he is expressly described as born at Bardsea, in Yorkshire. Now surely it is no advantage in Dublin College to be an Englishman. This important circumstance, therefore, we may consider as set at rest, and Congreve is fairly intitled to a place among the Yorkshire Worthies.

William Congreve, then, was descended from an ancient and respectable family, long settled in Staffordshire, whose armorial bearings figure in the margin of Dr. Plot's map, prefixed to his Natural History of that County. He was the only surviving son of William Congreve, Esq., second son of Richard Congreve, Esq., of Congreve and Stratton. His mother was a near relation of Sir John Lewis of Bardsea, and at Bardsey Grange he first drew breath. His birth-day is not precisely known, but it must have been towards the close of 1669, or commencement of 1670 ; for on the 16th of February, 1669-70, he was baptized. In his infancy he was carried into Ireland with his father, who was then in the army, but afterwards became manager of part of the large estate of the noble family of Burlington, which fixed his residence in the sister island. This sufficiently accounts for Southerne, who may have seen Congreve in Ireland a mere child, asserting so positively that he "meanly disowned his country." Young Congreve's early education was at the great school of Kilkenny, and his first poetical essay, an elegy on his master's magpie. In due time he was removed to Trinity College, Dublin, then flourishing under the tutorage of Dr. St. George

gram in Comitatu Eboracensi educatus Kilkenniæ, sub *ferulá* Doctoris Hinton, Tutor, St. George Ash."

" 1685. On the fifth day of April, at one o'clock in the afternoon, William Congreve, *Pensioner*, son of William Congreve, gentleman, of Youghal, aged sixteen, born at Bardsea, in the county of York, educated at Kilkenny, under the rod of Dr. Hinton. Tutor, St. George Ashe."

It may be observed, that his age in 1685 (sixteen) tallies with the Bardsea register, which fixes his birth somewhere about 1669. Yet the inscription on his monument states his age at fifty-six at the time of his death (January 29th, 1728-9), which would bring down his birth to 1771 or 1772. A year at least must be detracted from the marvel of his first plays.

N. B. A Pensioner at Cambridge and Dublin Universities (for the term is unknown at Oxford), implies a person *paying* for the benefit of the College, and receiving no *pension*.

Observe the phrase *sub ferulá* : a rod or ferule was then supposed as indispensable to an instructor as a nominative case to a verb. In a school lately established not a hundred miles from Leeds, the masters are bound by their engagement never to inflict corporal punishment. What would Orbilius, Busby, Boyeyer, Parr, and Holofernes say to this ?

WILLIAM CONGREVE.

Ash, where he acquired a larger portion of Greek and Latin than was then necessary for a fine gentleman. Whether in compliance with established custom, or with a view to profession, he was afterwards entered of the Middle Temple, and lived in chambers for some years, but probably paid no more attention to law than the critical Templar of the Spectator's club.

While little more than seventeen, he composed a novel, entitled, "Incognita, or Love and Duty Reconciled." It was dedicated, under the assumed name of Cleophil, to Mrs. Catherine Leveson. We are unable to determine who this lady might be, nor have we ever seen the novel itself. Could we procure it, we would not, like Johnson, *rather praise it than read it.* The following extract from the preface may shew, however, how Congreve could write at seventeen, and how early he turned his thoughts to dramatic construction.

"Since all *traditions* must indisputably give place to the drama, and since there is no possibility of giving that life to the writing or repetition of a story which it has in the action, I resolve in another beauty to imitate dramatic writing, namely, in the design, contexture, and result of the plot. I have not observed it before in a novel. Some I have seen begin with an unexpected accident, which has been the only surprizing part of the story,—cause enough to make the sequel look flat, tedious, and insipid; for it is but reasonable for the reader to expect, if not to rise, at least to keep upon a level in the entertainment; for so he may be kept on in hopes that at some time or other it may mend; but the other is such a baulk to a man,—it is carrying him up stairs to shew him the dining room, and after, forcing him to make a meal in the kitchen. This I have not only endeavoured to avoid, but also have used a method for the contrary purpose. The design of this novel is obvious, after the first meeting of Aurelian and Hippolyto with Incognita and Leonora; the difficulty is in bringing it to pass, maugre all apparent obstacles, within the compass of two days. How many probable casualties intervene in opposition to the main design, viz., of marrying two couples so oddly engaged in an intricate amour, I leave to the reader at his leisure to consider; as also, whether every obstacle does not, in the progress of the story, act as subservient to that purpose, which at first it seems to oppose. In a comedy this would be called the unity of action; here it may pretend to no more than an unity of contrivance. The scene is continued in Florence from the commencement of the amour, and the time from first to last is but three days. If there be any thing more in particular resembling the copy which I imitate, as the curious reader will soon perceive, I leave it to shew itself, being very well satisfied how much more proper it had been for him to find out this of himself, than for me to possess him with an opinion of something extraordinary in an essay, begun and finished in the idler hours of a fortnight's time; for I can only esteem that a laborious idleness, that is parent to so inconsiderable a birth."

The thought of confining a novel to the *unities* was something original. But French criticism was then the rage: Dryden, too wise to fetter himself in practice, had given a popularity to its principles by his discussions; and Congreve, a precocious mind, might hope to gain a laurel by applying the French rules to a species of composition never before made amenable to them; as if one should make tea or brew small beer in chemical nomenclature.

But the idea has nothing but novelty to recommend it. It may be laid down with as much certainty in literature as in politics, that all restriction is evil, *per se*, and can only be recommended or justified by a clear necessity, or a manifest benefit. The continuity and precipitation which a limited time or an immovable scene bestow, are of some value in the drama, and at any rate prevent the awkwardness of an interrupted action; but in a prose narrative the good cannot be obtained, while the restraint and inconvenience remain. We are told, that the story of "Incognita" is unnatural. How can it be otherwise, when two pair of lovers are to carry through their wooing and wedding, in spite of all the obstacles necessary to constitute a plot and an intrigue, in two days? But, besides unnaturally forcing the development of events, this confined construction forbids that natural development and growth of character which is the main charm of a good novel, in which the influence of every event upon the hearts and minds of the agents and *patients* should be distinctly, yet not obtrusively marked; and even the effect of time on passions and humours should not be unnoted.

We know not the precise æra at which Incognita was published; but it was not long before Congreve turned his efforts to that quarter in which alone he was destined to excel. He has himself told us, in his reply to Jeremy Collier, that to divert the tedium of convalescence from a severe illness, he began to compose a comedy. The result of his lucubrations was "The Old Bachelor."

At that time it was usual for authors to assemble in taverns and coffee-houses, and many a manuscript was discussed over the bottle. Every one must remember how Pope in his childhood was carried to the coffee-house where Dryden usually presided, and beheld the veteran in his arm chair, which in winter held a prescriptive place by the fire side. This *popination* (as a quaint old writer terms it) rendered the seniors of literature much more accessible to young aspirants than the domestic habits of the present race, with all their hospitality, permit them to be. Congreve, a templar, and almost a boy, had already heard and partaken the conversation of Dryden, Wycherly, Southerne, and other poets and critics, and frequenters of the theatre, so that he had the benefit of experience, by anticipation, in a line of writing which has been supposed to require more experience than any other. When the "Old Bachelor" was shewn to Dryden, he pronounced that "Such a first play he had never seen." Something, however, was yet wanting to ensure its success, for he added, "It was a pity, seeing the author was ignorant of stage and town, that he should miscarry for want of a little assistance. The stuff was rich indeed, only the fashionable cut was wanting." According to Southerne, it was near miscarrying from another cause:—"When he brought it to the players, he read it so wretchedly ill that they were on the point of rejecting it, till one of them good-naturedly took it out of his hands, and read it." The players must, however, have expected great things from him; for Thomas Davenant, then manager of Drury Lane, gave him what is called the privilege of the house half a year before his play came on the stage, a favour at that time unparalleled. Having undergone a revision from Dryden, Southerne, and Manwairing, the "Old Bachelor" was produced in 1693, before a crowded and splendid audience, and met with triumphant success. The prologue intended to have been spoken was written by Lord Falkland. The play, when printed, was prefaced with three copies of commendatory verses, by Southerne, Marsh, and Higgins. The pride or modesty of a modern writer would revolt at the ancient custom of publishing these flattering testimonials in the vestibule of his own book, where, after all, they could not answer the place of an advertisement. Flattery, wherever she may now abide, no longer rules despotic in first pages.*

The exhibition of the "Old Bachelor" was hailed as a new æra in theatric history. The praise which it fairly earned by its intrinsic merit was aggravated by respect to the author's youth. The critics were glad to display their generosity by applauding, and their candour by forgiving: the play-going public gave their usual hearty welcome to

* Congreve dedicated the Old Bachelor to the Lord Clifford of Lanesborough, son to the Lord Burlington. The allusion to the connection between the families is neat. "My Lord, it is with great pleasure I lay hold on this first occasion which the accidents of my life have given me of writing to your Lordship; for since, at the same time, I write to all the world, it will be the means of publishing what I would have every body know,—the respect and duty which I owe and pay to you. I have so much inclination to be your's, that I need no other engagement, but the particular ties by which I am bound both to your Lordship and family, have put it out of my power to make you any compliment, since all offers of myself will amount to no more than an honest acknowledgment, and only shew a willingness in me to be grateful."

a new comer : reader and auditor alike were amazed at the stripling whose maiden essay achieved what so many laborious brains had been toiling for the last half century to produce—perpetual excitement and incessant splendour. But this "gay comedy" brought down rewards more comfortable than the cold approbation of the few, more lasting than the manual plaudits of the many, and far more lucrative than the casual profits of an author's night. Charles Montague, afterwards Earl of Halifax, who owed his own advancement partly to a worthless jeu' d' esprit,* written in concert with Prior, in which he meanly and

---

* The Court and Country Mouse, a very flat imitation of the Rehearsal, meant to ridicule Dryden's Hind and Panther, not of course sparing his conversion to the creed of the abdicated monarch. It may be found in the State Poems, but it is not worth looking for. We are sorry that Prior, for whom we have a sneaking affection, should have had any thing to do with it. The manifest absurdity and incongruity of Dryden's allegory must have been obvious to Dryden himself; but perhaps he thought absurdity as necessary for a superstitious King, as obscenity for a polluted stage. Montague seems to have delighted in kicking at the Ex-Laureate. In one of the few copies of indifferent couplets which give him a place among the Poets (!!!) of Great Britain, occur the following lines, in which there is but too much truth,—but it is not truth which a generous mind would have cast in the teeth of a great man, oppressed with years and misfortunes :—

> " Dryden has numbers, but he wants a heart.
> *   *   *   *   *
> Now sentenced, by a penance too severe,
> For playing once the fool, to persevere."

That Dryden, as a Poet, wants heart (whatever he may have done as a man), his warmest admirers (and we are among them) can hardly deny; but this was not Montague's meaning. In the couplet, he hints that Dryden would gladly have returned to the Church of England if his double apostacy would have been acceptable. But this is an uncharitable surmise. He might not be, in the highest sense of the word, sincere in his reunion to the Church of Rome : but there is no reason in the world to assume that he was an absolute and deliberate impostor. Much more likely he was as sincere a Catholic as ever he had been a Christian,—as sincere as the bulk of professing Christians in any sect or denomination. His good sense convinced him that religion was *good*; but whether it was true or not, he very probably neither knew nor cared. Most likely he thought it a particularly good thing for the *common people*; and of course, therefore, concluded that form of religion to be best which is most potent over the many, and gives most power to the pastors. Now this is undoubtedly the Catholic. Any one who will read the preface to Dryden's Religio Laici, written while he was still a professing Protestant, will perceive that he had already adopted principles, of which the *expediency* of *Popery* was a necessary consequence.

The arguments which the Church of Rome has to advance are neither few nor easily answered. The communion of that Church offers many spiritual advantages and facilities to a man declining in years, who could not look back on his past course with much satisfaction, and who had all the work of religion yet to do. That the time of his conversion coincided with his apparent interest, might account for his

stupidly insulted the grey hairs of Dryden, had lately been invested
with the Chancellorship of the Exchequer, and as the gravity of that
office was not strictly compatible with the profession of a wit, he took
upon him the character of Mecænas,—a very expensive honour, when
it was expected of a patron to pay handsomely for every dedication that
was offered him.   Dorset, who preceded Montague as Mecænas, must
have been considerably out of pocket at the year's end on this score
alone, though some part of the onus fell on Nell Gwynne,* the Duchess
of Portsmouth, and Mary of Este.   But Montague having the fingering of the public money, and succeeding to the management of a
government in which interest was to supply the place of terror, and
influence to heal the breaches of prerogative, hit on a more economical
method of securing the adulation of prosemen and versemen than paying them for dedications.   Louis XIV. had pensioned poets, and was
supposed to have laid out the money at good interest ; but Louis was
an absolute sovereign, and had no Parliament to overhaul his accounts.
To have put a Poet into any post of responsibility was too hazardous.
It is assuredly better to pay men for doing nothing, than for spoiling
work.   But most conveniently it happened, that there were a large
stock of places, which had outlasted the occasions for which they were
invented.   There were Boards, which were furnished with a double
set of members,—one for use, which, like the vocal pipes in the body of
an organ, were kept out of sight, i. e. the clerks, deputies, &c., and
another, like the pipes in the front of an organ, displayed to public view
with all advantages of gilding.   Thus, without expense to himself,
additional expense to the country, or risk of exposure by appointing an
incompetent person to an office of trust, Montague was enabled to make
Congreve a Commissioner for licensing hackney coaches, to give him a
place in the pipe office, and shortly after another in the customs, worth
six hundred a year, and all for writing a single comedy.   Never, is

insincerity, were it proved ; and can it prove it while it is doubtful ?   No established
law of nature or reason forbids that a man's convictions shall coincide with his interests.   In truth, while man remains in the state of nature, the probabilities and
plausibilities, which are all that he can know of religion, are so equally poised, that
the scales might hang for ever in equilibrium, if the volition were not exerted to make
the one or other preponderate ; and the volition is always determined by the habit,
interest, or passion, if it be not modified and subjected by Divine influence.

* One of Mrs. Behn's plays is appropriately dedicated to this mother of nobles, who
had so much kind-heartedness as to remind one pitifully of the title of Ford's tragedy.
Otway dedicated his " Venice Preserved " to the Duchess of Portsmouth ; and Dryden
his abominable parody upon Paradise Lost, to Mary of Este, the beautiful and unfortunate Queen of James II., to whom certain of the patriots of eighty-eight, not content with depriving her of a crown, denied the holier honours of maternity.

England at least, was author rewarded so rapidly—seldom so highly. The money value of wit had risen mightily at court, since poor Butler was allowed to linger out a life of poverty. Even Dryden had little more than the Laureate's paltry hundred. Perhaps the Whigs wished to make the *amende honourable* to the Muses for their ejection of Dryden, by extraordinary liberality to Congreve.

The days of William were not the days of economical reform. It does not appear that this accumulation of places on a lucky theatrical adventurer excited any discontent, except, it may be, among some of the stricter sort, who deemed the Poet's meed the wages of vanity. We will not speculate on the reception that the sinecurist's next play would have met from the gallery in these days, or how the political economists would have approved so extravagant a bounty upon *unproductive labour*. Meanwhile, there is nothing moves the indignation of certain persons more than the evil eye which the poor, and not only the poor, are taught to cast on the gratuities of the Treasury. Few of these have lately descended upon authors, but those few have not escaped severe animadversion in the Extraordinary Black Book, and similar publications, wherein, as usual, the reflections are ever more bitter against the receivers than against the givers. Hireling and slave are the civilest phrases which any writer may expect who accepts a boon from the rulers of his country.

These feelings, however, are but natural to a period of financial embarrassment and general distress. A poor woman might very excusably complain of her husband, if he spent his wages upon poems, or play-books, or picture-books, while she and her children were wanting bread. But suppose this state of things passed away, the question would still remain;—In what measure, and by what method, should literature and the fine arts be fostered by the state? We might extend the enquiry further, and ask,—"Are the higher objects of the human intellect legitimate objects of civil government?" And,—"Should the achievements of intellect, simply as such, and without reference to any increase of wealth, or safety, or convenience to be derived from them, be rewarded or honoured by the community in its corporate capacity, or be left to the care of the people in their individual capacities?"

We purposely waive all discussion of these questions on grounds of public economy. We shall not enter into argument with the Utilitarians, as to what abstract science, or fine literature, or fine art, *are worth*, or what use they are of, or whether we might not do very well without them. We will, for the present, take it for granted, that the faculties of pure reason, imagination, and taste, ought to be perfected as

much as possible; that philosophy and poetry, truth and beauty, are
noble ends of human nature. We will assume—nay, assert—that every
man, rich or poor, is, or may be, the better for whatever exalts the
imagination, or humanizes the heart: in a short sentence of plain prose,
that public money would be well and wisely expended in the promotion
of literature, and of fine literature, if the disbursement were really for
the benefit of literature or its professors. But " there's the rub."

It is held by some, whose sentence is not lightly to be set aside, that
were it not for the support and sustenance of the state (which is and
must be represented by the government for the time being); were it
not for endowments, salaries, honours, privileges, determined by positive
laws, and involved in the very constitution of property, all studies
would cease but those which are subservient to the needs and appetites
of the body, or gratify the whim, humour, passion, or fashion of the
moment; all poetry become a dead letter, philosophy a forgotten
dream, religion a ghost untimely severed from the body,

And unawares Morality expire.

In short, that men would love, esteem, or venerate nothing beyond that
which they had in common with beasts, if there were not an imputed
dignity, an artificial system, to uphold the Man in Man.

This is a fearful denunciation, a woeful prospect,—but how far is it
borne out by facts? That mankind in general are too apt to forget the
interests of the soul, is a sad and awful truth; but it is a tendency
which no worldly power, no worldly wealth, no human bounty can
counteract. It is as impossible to bribe, as to persecute men into caring
for their souls. It can never be any man's worldly interest to be
unworldly. But, it may be answered, if endowments and establishments cannot avert the decay of piety, they may oppose the advances
of ignorance. They may make knowledge honourable, and secure
leisure for study. They may, which is more than all, disengage a
portion of the public heart from the passions and pursuits of the day,
and procure respect for accomplishments and acquisitions whose value
is to the mind. They may induce some, who would else be content to
stop at the needful, to aim at the perfect. And in this, there is certainly some truth. It is a work of long time, to interest the multitude,
the great vulgar or the small, in any thing that is not of the earth,
earthy; and yet how few would undergo the toil of intellectual exertion,
of deep research, of patient investigation, of painful thought, if they
knew not of any to appreciate their labours, to sympathise with their
perplexities of doubt, their joys of discovery? Or suppose that a few
have studied solely for their own delight, without a wish to communicate, the world has been none the better for their lucubrations. In

those rude and stormy periods, when war is the only occupation, and the chace or the banquet the only relaxations of the noble and the free,—while the laborious classes, brutalized by oppression, are too ignorant to desire knowledge, and the whole atmosphere of society too inclement for peaceful contemplation, or tender fancy,—whatever of learning or of art may subsist, would infallibly perish, if left to make its own way in the world. To ensure mutual aid, protection, and sympathy, the learned must separate themselves from the many, and be united under common regulations; they must form for themselves a corporate constitution, an *imperium in imperio*; they will need a strong arm to preserve their "pensive citadels" from violence; and, as their labours have yet acquired no saleable value, they must be dependent either upon alms, too often obtained by imposing on credulity, or on bequests and donations from the rich and great.

Here we may behold the origin and necessity of colleges, academies, and the like foundations, by means of which a learned class arose in the very heart of mediæval darkness,—instructors and counsellors were raised up, by whom a taste for knowledge was communicated to the higher gentry,—the value of learning was impressed upon the minds of the charitable, who were thus incited to provide the means of gratuitous instruction for the poor. The more information was diffused, the higher and purer was the respect paid it. The scholar and the philosopher obtained reverence as such from high and low, and were no longer obliged to be priests, conjurers, or astrologers.

We admit, therefore, that up to a certain point, an established order of learned men is absolutely necessary for the conservation of literature and the prevention of barbarism; and that this order can only be preserved by the power of the state, or by the superstitious reverence of the people,—that is, while the people remain so ignorant as to be incapable of conceiving the true value of knowledge, or till knowledge is so far perfected as to demonstrate its own value by its practical results.

But, after a certain point, there needs no adventitious advantages to conciliate regard to the perfections and achievements of intellect. The danger is, that they will be too much prized, too much desired, too much sought for. Already there are many who expect from human knowledge the work of Divine Grace. Science has made man master of matter; it has enabled him to calculate the revolutions of nature, to multiply his own powers beyond all that was dreamed of spell or talisman: and now it is confidently prophecied that another science is to remove all the moral and political evils of the planet; that by analysing the passions, we shall learn to govern them; and that, when the science of education is grown of age, virtue will be taught as easily as arithmetic, and comprehended as readily as geometry—with the aid of wooden diagrams. Let us not be deceived. "Leviathan is not so tamed." The tree of knowledge is not the tree of life.

These Utopian theories are of little consequence, any further than as they divert the mind from the true way to moral happiness. The almost universal desire for intellectual distinction is a fever that rather needs sedatives than stimulants; but it is an evil which, if left to itself, will remedy itself: when ordinary acquirements cease to be a distinction in any class, not more will attain to that eminence which may entitle them to look above their inherited station, than the demands of society will provide for. The rest will continue to study at leisure hours for their own improvement and delight, but without the ambitious yearnings which make homely duties irksome, the lazy conceit which calls honest industry vile drudgery, the inordinate hopes which, whether starved or surfeited, perish miserably, and leave behind them vanity, and vexation of spirit. There is no further need, then, for any interference of the state to keep learning in countenance, or to confer respect on genius. There is one way, however, in which the public money may sometimes be wisely expended for the promotion of knowledge or of art. This is, by furnishing employment to scholars and artists in works of public utility. We take the word utility in its widest sense, and hold all truth and all beauty to be useful. Expeditions fitted out for the extension of science are an honour to the liberal government which plans, and to the brave men who conduct them. Researches in natural history, mineralogy, botany, &c. especially if carried on in distant countries, are attended both with peril and expense. A wise government will not grudge any reasonable sum to secure and indemnify such of its subjects as devote their talents to pursuits so beneficial. The same may be said of chemistry, medicine, anatomy, &c. Nor will a judicious economist think that money mispent, which enables a man, tried and proved to be equal to the task, to execute any great work, the size or subject of which forbids a remunerating sale; or which necessarily takes up a long time in execution, or is too expensive for an author's purse to undertake :—such, for example, as a collection of ancient historical documents; a complete edition of the scarce and early poets; or a great etymological dictionary, which should include a progressive history of the language.

In like manner may the painter, the sculptor, and the architect be fostered and honoured by public employment, and labour to adorn their country. Genius of this kind requires more assistance from wealth than any other. But let the works for which the public are to pay be strictly of a public nature. Let them be accessible to all who can appreciate or enjoy them. Let the picture and the statue serve to exalt and purify the general imagination, not to pamper the odious pride of exclusive possession. By retrenching the waste of the nation's substance in tasteless pageantry, which has lost what meaning it ever had, England may become as much the country of art as of poetry, and a reproach be wiped away from the Reformation.

But whatever assistance the state may afford to literature or the arts, should always be given as a consideration for *work done*. No man should be pensioned or placed for the mere possession of genius or learning.

We are not ignorant that many persons advocate the position, that it were well for the community that the learned, strictly so called, should be maintained as an order in the state, on revenues set apart and consecrated to that purpose; and that poets more ennobled their skill, when they sung for monarchs, statesmen, noble dames, and barons bold, than now, when their fortunes, if not their fame, are dependent on the sale of their productions, or the speculative liberality of a Bibliopole. Even now there are many, who think that so-called *sinecures* might be rendered most beneficial, in giving leisure to intellect; so that the genius and the scholar, free from worldly toil and anxiety, may labour for glory and posterity, and repay their country's bounty with deathless honour. The advantages of " learned leisure " to the church establishment have been asserted with Paley's plausibility and Southey's upright zeal; and might not " learned leisure," wit in easy circumstances, imagination with a moderate independence, be serviceable to the state also? Shall there be no cushions, where unconsecrated heads may slumber *pro bono publico*?

This, it must be confessed, sounds well; but if the actual history of modern authorship were honestly written, we should discover that the expectation of patronage has ruined more geniuses, both in purse and character, than the liberality of patrons has ever benefitted. We shall not here inquire into the probability of the patronage being wisely bestowed, but it may just be observed, that those writers who have looked for support to the great, have been by no means conspicuous for the morality, or even for the decency, of their productions. But patronage should never be accorded to the presumptive evidences of genius, or even to the *promise* of excellence. The bounty, whether of kings, or of commonwealths, or of nobles, honours itself and its object, when it is bestowed on the veteran scholar, or grey-headed poet,—when it provides peace, comfort, and competence to venerable age. But it should be given unsought. No encouragement should be afforded to vain youth, who, by a servile display of flashy fantasies, and a presumptuous rivalry of well-bred vices, endeavour to insinuate themselves, canker like, into the opening blossoms of nobility ; nor should the more prudent advances of the middle-aged be suffered to outstep the bounds of modesty.

Although we cannot reckon the profusion of sinecures which rewarded the production of the "Old Bachelor" as one of the happiest signs of the times of Halifax, it was utterly unjust in Swift, Pope, and the other Tory wits, to represent that minister as regardless of the claims of genius, and only liberal to party virulence.   Yet the Dean, in one of his minor poems, literally holds up Congreve as having been long neglected, and half-starved.——

> "Thus Congreve spent, in writing plays,
> And one poor office, half his days ;
> While Montagu, who claimed the station
> To be Mæcenas of the nation,
> For poets open table kept,
> But ne'er considered where they slept ;
> Himself, as rich as fifty Jews,
> Was easy, tho' they wanted shoes ;
> And crazy Congreve scarce could spare
> A shilling to discharge his chair,
> Till prudence taught him to appeal
> From Pæan's fire to party zeal :
> Not owing to his happy vein
> The fortunes of his latter scene ;
> Took proper principles to thrive,
> And so might any dunce alive."

In this last line the Dean is deplorably in the wrong.   Dunces never thrive but in the way of honesty.   Had not Congreve been a splendid wit, he would not have been worth purchase.   We cannot conjecture why he calls Congreve crazy.   There is no madness is his writings,— neither the *fine madness* of poetry, nor the rant and fury of a disordered brain: and in his private conduct, whatever virtue he might want, he possessed an ample store of prudence.   With so little of truth or reason could the man write, who, of all his contemporaries, *might* have been the greatest philosopher.

Congreve's next play was the "Double Dealer," * produced in 1694.

* In the preface to this comedy are some observations, so just, and of so extensive an application, that they will be worth their room at the bottom of the page :—

"That which looks most like an objection, does not relate in particular to this play, but to all, or most, that ever have been written; that is, soliloquy; therefore I will answer it, not only for my own sake, but to save others the trouble to whom hereafter it may be objected. I grant, that for a man to talk to himself appears absurd and unnatural, and indeed it is so in most cases; but the circumstances

It seldom happens that a second work is received with an increase of applause. There is, independent of envy, a very strong tendency to suspect writers of falling below themselves. Homer himself has been accused of betraying senility in the Odyssee; and the more subdued interest necessarily arising from the plan and subject of Paradise Regained, has been ascribed, with little justice, to the increasing years of Milton. The Double Dealer, though the performance was honoured with the presence of Queen Mary, met with some opposition on the stage, and a good deal of severe criticism in the closet. Congreve had little difficulty in parrying the individual objections: of such criticism as was then current he was a dexterous master, and as he wrote with great care and forethought according to his own ideal of perfection, he probably anticipated every censure in his mind before it was uttered. But those who read his works in these days will be rather surprised to find him assuming the part of a censor and a moralist, and telling the *ladies* that he aims at their reformation and improvement. "There is one thing," says he, "at which I am more concerned, than all the false criticisms that are made upon me; and that is, *some* of the ladies are offended. I am heartily sorry for it, for I declare I would rather disoblige all the critics in the world than one of the fair sex. They are concerned that I have represented some women vicious and affected. How can I help it? It is the business of a comic poet to paint the vices and follies of human kind; and there are but two sexes, male and female, men and women, that have a title to humanity; and if I leave one half of them out, the work will be imperfect. I should be very glad of an opportunity to make my compliments to those ladies who are offended. But they can no more expect it in a comedy, than to be

which may attend the occasion make great alterations. It oftentimes happens to a man to have designs which confine him to himself, and in their nature cannot admit of a confident. Such, for certain, is all villainy; and other less mischievous intentions may be very improper to be communicated to a second person. In such a case the audience must observe whether the person upon the stage takes any notice of them at all or no; for if he supposes any one to be by when he talks to himself, it is monstrous and ridiculous in the last degree; nay, not only in this case, but in any part of a play, if there be expressed any knowledge of an audience, it is insufferable. But otherwise, when a man, in soliloquizing, reasons with himself, and *pros* and *cons*, and weighs all his designs, we ought not to imagine that this man either talks to us, or to himself; he is only thinking, and thinking such matter as it were inexcusable folly in him to speak. But because we are concealed spectators of the plot in agitation, and the poet finds it necessary to let us know the whole mystery of his contrivance, he is willing to inform us of this person's thoughts, and to that end is forced to make use of the expedient of speech, no other or better way being yet invented for the communication of thought."

tickled by a surgeon when he's letting them blood. Those who are virtuous or discreet should not be offended; for such characters as these distinguish them, and make their virtues more shining and observed; and they who are of the other kind may nevertheless pass for such, by seeming not to be displeased or touched with the satire in this comedy. Thus they have also wrongfully accused me of doing them a prejudice, when I have in reality done them a service."

This is the common plea of satirists, but it is at best an afterthought. We are far from deeming the satirists among the most malicious of mankind: they are, at worst, splenetic, but for the most part rather vain than ill-natured. But it is much easier to shine in depicting a moral than an immoral character; and of all characters, the truly virtuous female is the most difficult to draw satisfactorily in a dramatic poem. It is easy enough to describe, for it is not unfrequently seen; it is very easy for a poet to praise, for he has little to do but to collect all the fine and savoury comparisons which Europe, Asia, Africa, and America, botany, mineralogy, zoology, and metaphysics supply, and attach them to a sylph-like figure, with black or auburn locks, as the case may require. But when the woman is to speak and act, when she is to shed the perfume of her goodness spontaneously, and shine by her own light, and yet not overstep the reserved duties of her sex—there is a task beneath which human genius is in danger of breaking down. We really cannot recal to memory a single dramatic female whom we should recommend for a wife, or for an example. Shakspeare's women are many of them exceedingly lovely, but from the small discretion he seems to have used in the choice of his stories, what they *do* is not always in unison with what they *are*. Their words and feelings are their nature; their actions are their destiny. The common run of tragedy queens are very unamiable; so much so, indeed, that it is pleasant to reflect that they have no resemblance to nature or reality. Comic females are much more entertaining; but with the exception of one or two specimens of prudent perfection, generally introduced, like Lady Grace, for the sake of contrast, and a few pieces of sentimental simplicity, such as Cicely Homespun, they are almost universally distinguished by a readiness of falsehood, a spirit of intrigue, and stratagem, which must make them very dangerous inmates or companions. Yet it would be next to impossible to write a comedy from which this sort of underplay was exiled. The choice seems to be, whether the interest shall turn mainly upon the bad characters, and the better sort of persons throughout be dupes and victims, consigned to happiness at last by some wonderful accident or discovery (the plan generally pursued by Fielding in his novels), or whether, as in Congreve, all shall play a game of delusion, at which all the *dramatis personæ* are playing, in which the best player is the winner. There is a strong tendency in the human mind to exult in the success of stratagem. There must, indeed, be some excuse invented for cheating; but love, revenge, self-defence, or the mere pleasure of witty contrivances, will answer the purpose very well with an audience, who are always glad to give their moral judgment a holyday.

But though the heroine of a comedy can hardly be a good example to her sex, there is no necessity that she should be an offensive insult to it. Her faults should be such as a good woman might feel it possible for herself to have committed,—such as a moderate degree of self-delusion might pass off for virtues. The ladies were quite right in resenting the exhibition of Lady Touchwood. An innocent heart would require much and sad experience to convince it of the possibility of such a being. There are degrees of wickedness too bad to laugh at, however they may be mingled with folly, affectation, or absurdity.

Towards the close of 1694 Queen Mary died. Few Queens have made fewer personal enemies, and perhaps few have been more sincerely regretted. But were we to judge of the quality of the national affliction by the sable flights of lugubrious verse that were devoted to the good Queen's memory, we should say that the English nation were the worst actors of royal woe in the world. Congreve committed a pastoral among the rest,—perhaps not the worst copy of verses produced on the occasion.* It must be a very indifferent *Keen* that is not better than any of them. Such drivel might make the Muses join in the hyperbolical prayer of Flatman, that " Kings should never die."

Congreve's next play was " Love for Love," produced in 1695. A new play, acted on a new stage, has every advantage which novelty can

---

* Those who would form a comparative estimate of the national genius, as it was exerted on similar occasions at the close of the 17th, and at the commencement of the 18th century, may be amused by comparing the numerous tributes to the late Princess Charlotte, with the compositions that appeared on the decease of Queen Mary. The comparison will certainly shew favourably for the present race of poets. They at least speak seriously, on a serious subject—like men who felt the holiness of death. But we are not to conclude that men do not feel at all, because they choose to express their feelings in a whimsical masquerade. Grief, no less than mirth, has its fashions. Its outward signs are variable and arbitrary as mourning colours. In criticising funereal poetry it should be recollected, that the main purpose of a monument, whether of verse or of marble, is not to express the sorrow of the survivors, but to preserve the memory of the deceased. No one imagines, no one is asked to believe, that the poet, when he is composing his monody or elegy for Prince or Princess, is struggling with a sense of actual bereavement—that he is shedding painful tears.

confer. Congreve advanced the higher claim of a service to an old favourite of the public. Betterton, who has left behind him a permanence of fame which some have denied that the actor can achieve, having reason to complain of his treatment by managers, was about to open a new theatre in Lincoln's Inn Fields. "Love for Love" was the first play acted on this stage. Its success was considerable, and it continued to be acted at intervals longer than any other of its author's comedies. But its charm as an acting play is gone; and perhaps it owed its occasional representation more to its containing those never-failing characters, a positive overbearing father, and a jack tar, than either to its wit or its licentiousness. It is said that Congreve, while engaged in composing this piece, paid a six weeks' visit to Portsmouth, in order to study sea manners from the life. Yet it has been objected, that the marine phraseology is not very accurate; and certainly, the character is so wide from the warm-hearted, gallant sailor of the modern stage, as to appear almost like a libel on the favourite profession. "Love for Love" is dedicated to Charles, Earl of Dorset and Middlesex, Lord Chamberlain of the King's Household, &c. One of Congreve's biographers commends this as containing "*no fulsome adulation.*" Pray what call you this?—"Whoever is King, is also the father of his country; and as nobody can dispute your Lordship's monarchy in poetry, so all that are concerned ought to acknowledge your universal patronage." If this was meant to be believed, it was adulatory enough. But before we charge the authors of past days with universal sycophancy, we should duly consider, not merely what their words mean, but what sense they were intended to convey. The language of compliment was the only dialect in which a peer and a commoner could converse. The dedication was itself a real and sincere compliment; for it implied either gratitude for bounty, or a confidence in generosity. But the terms in which it was couched were merely conventional: to vary and adopt the topics of panegyric was a harmless exercise of ingenuity. Compliments, in ages past, were paid to sex or rank; in ours, they are directed to the person. Compliment, however, is not necessarily flattery. It is, at worst, but a foolish fashion, a misuse of words.

The experience of ages had not then convinced the poets that a battle fought last week is by no means a happy subject for a pindaric. The capture of Namur by Louis XIV. had been magnified by all the bards of Paris. The same fortress was unfortunate enough to give occasion to another volley of odes when recaptured by King William. Congreve's contribution was a series of irregular stanzas; a species of versification to which Cowley and his imitators had given a temporary eclat, confirmed and heightened by the success of Alexander's Feast. Congreve afterwards condemned these lawless measures; and, according to Johnson, had the merit of teaching the world, "that Pindar's odes were regular," a discovery which, we venture to affirm, an English ear, unassisted by eyes and fingers, would never have made. There seems to be no sufficient reason why a long ode should not occasionally vary its movement, if there be a corresponding variation in the feeling; but each system should certainly have a law, an ordonnance within itself, and there ought to be an equilibrium between the whole. But none but a great poet should be allowed to write irregular stanzas. Their tempting facility, which promises to give freedom to thought, does in reality save the trouble of thinking.

Congreve had produced three comedies in as many years, the only important results of that leisure and freedom from care which the Minister had bestowed upon him. Nearly two years elapsed between the representation of "Love for Love," and that of the "Mourning Bride," his single tragedy, which was more rapturously received than any product of his comic muse. The critics have not confirmed the sentence of the theatre. Yet the Mourning Bride is assuredly the effort of no common ability. It contains a passage which Johnson pronounced superior to any single speech in Shakspeare, and which appears to us more *poetical* than any thing in Rowe or Otway. But poetry seldom saves a new play, though it sometimes happens, that a *beauty*, which has become a common place, adds greatly to the reputation of an actor in an established piece.

Perhaps the great success of the "Mourning Bride" might be owing, in no small measure, to astonishment. Mankind are always pleased to wonder for a while, though they are soon tired of wondering. A tragedy by an author of so gay and comic a turn as Congreve, was something to wonder at. Moreover, tragedies are in general more favourably received than comedies in their first run. It is a rare thing for a serious drama to be hissed off the stage. Truly has Terence spoken it :—

"Tantum majus oneris habet comedia, quantum minus veniæ."
Comedy has so much the more of difficulty, as it has less of allowance.

Not long after the appearance of the "Mourning Bride," Jeremy Collier * produced his celebrated strictures on the *profaneness and*

---

* Jeremy Collier was born at Stow Qui, in Cambridgeshire, September 23d, 1630. His father was a learned divine and linguist, and some time master of the Free School at Ipswich. His family was of Yorkshire. His education was at Ipswich, and Caius College, Cambridge. He took his Master's degree in 1676, was ordained Deacon in

immorality of the English stage, and Congreve, among other and yet more grievous offenders, was severely handled for the licence of his pen.

the same year, and Priest in 1677, by Dr. Henry Compton, Bishop of London, who has been mentioned as the first Bishop of noble birth after the Reformation. Collier was first domestic chaplain at Knowle, in Kent, on the establishment of the Countess Dowager of Dorset; then Rector of Ampton, in Suffolk, a small preferment, which he resigned after holding it about six years; came to London, and was made Preacher at Lincoln's Inn. How far his orthodoxy allowed him to comply with James's measures we cannot tell; certainly his loyalty did not allow him to acknowledge the Revolution Government. He became a stubborn non-juror, and a determined controversialist. Almost immediately after James's departure, he broke a lance with Burnet, in a pamphlet entitled " *The Desertion Discussed, in a Letter to a Country Gentleman,*" in which he labours to prove what we hope no honest man that has glanced at the facts with half an eye will now dispute, that James's retreat was occasioned by a well-grounded apprehension of personal danger; and that, therefore, he could not truly be said to have abdicated his throne. Here we thoroughly agree with honest Jeremy, whom we believe, though a perilously mistaken man, to have erred in head, not heart, and to have been an honour to that Church for which he would gladly have suffered martyrdom. That his understanding was not of the most lucid order, was in some sort to his credit, for it removes all reasonable doubt of his sincerity. His opinions being promulgated with little caution, and with none of that rhetorical artifice which utters sedition in hypothetical propositions, soon attracted the notice of a government too recently established to allow its legality to be discussed with impunity. Collier, and Newton, another non-juring clergyman, were arrested at Romney Marsh, in Kent, on suspicion of holding intercourse with the disaffected over the channel. No evidence, however, was found to convict them, and they were discharged on bail. But liberty, obtained by an implied admission of an authority which he thought usurped, was far less comfortable to Jeremy's conscience, than the durance which made him a sufferer for an exiled King. He went before the Lord Chief Justice Holt, withdrew his recognisance, and was committed to the King's Bench, but shortly after discharged freely, at the request of many friends, and perhaps by the good sense of Justice Holt, who might easily conceive, that a prisoner for conscience sake is more dangerous to a government founded on opinion than the busiest agitator at large. Neither fear nor favour, however, quieted the zealous high-churchman, who continued to pour forth pamphlets as quick as he could write them, all which are now forgotten. It was in vain that Collier was the foe of the " *glorious and immortal,*"—that he was, in some judgments, the martyr, in others the enemy and disturber of his church. His name would hardly have been remembered, but for his controversy with play-wrights and players.

One of his proceedings, however, was so bold and singular, that it has gained him a place in that important department of history which relates to the last stage of the law. When Sir John Friend and Sir William Perkins were executed for the assassination plot, Collier, together with Cook and Snatt, divines of like principles, publicly absolved and blessed the criminals on the scaffold. This, which was probably meant only to assert, by an extraordinary and overt act, the absolving power of the priesthood, was construed into an avowed approval of assassination. Of course a prosecution followed. Snatt and Cook were sent to Newgate, but after a time discharged without a trial: Collier, who scrupled to give bail, absconded, and was outlawed, an

He would have done wisely had he, like Dryden, at once admitted the justice of the charge. But he was young, conscious of talent, elated

incapacity under which he laboured to the end of his life. The two Archbishops, and ten Bishops, published a strong declaration in censure of his conduct with regard to the absolution. He replied again and again, with the perseverence of one determined to have the last word. Yet, though seldom disengaged from controversy, he found time to compose many works of a more peaceful character; some of which were essays, in which he concentrated the results of his meditations, and some ponderous dictionaries and histories, in which he treasured the fruits of his reading. Perhaps polemic writing was to him an agreeable excitement, a healthful exercise, a game which, however it was played, pleased him with the conceit of winning, and never impaired the health of his body or, the innermost peace of his soul. His essays, though not much read at present, have had their admirers, and comprehend a range of subjects, the mere selection of which proves that Collier possessed that essential of an active, exploring mind, a sympathy with all human interests. On the business of the grave, and on the pleasures of the gay, he often looked with anger, but seldom with indifference. Those essays, some of which are dialogues, others set discourses, and some translations from the fathers, treat of clothes, duelling, music, and the spleen,—the office of a chaplain, the immateriality of the soul, and the weakness of human reason. It was in the year 1698 that he published "*A short View of the Immorality and Profaneness of the English Stage, together with the Sense of Antiquity on this Argument.*" As usual, the weakest part of the work is that in which he attempts to shame the moderns by ancient example. If more moral sentences might be extracted from Plautus or Terence than from Vanburgh or Congreve, it may well be doubted whether the general tendency of their writings be much better. We are glad, however, that Jeremy admits the comparative purity of the elder English drama, and even alleges the authority of Ben Jonson and Fletcher against the immoral pretences of their successors. On the whole, it is probable that the main merit of Collier was that of calling the question into the *Court of Conscience*. There might be much coarseness, much pedantry, much bigotry in his pleadings; but yet the goodness of his cause, and the unanswerable nature of his evidence, secured him the victory.

Congreve was not the only culprit that spake in his own defence. Vanburgh, whose Relapse and Provoked Wife had been marked objects of Collier's animadversions, produced "A Short Vindication" of those plays. Collier made a point of answering his answerers—a task which many polemics think it prudent to decline. His pamphlets on this subject alone make up a pretty thick volume.

We have mentioned in the text, that by thus appearing as the champion of morality, he softened the animosities which his politics had occasioned: and he might very probably have completely reconciled himself to the government, and risen to high preferment, if he had been so disposed. But whether he had invincible hopes of the restoration of the old order of things, or, as we believe, had made his error guardian of his faith and conscience, he continued a schismatic from horror of schism, and a bad subject through excess of loyalty. Yet to the honour of the non-jurors be it spoken, they were assertors of church liberty. If they were wrong in their sentiments as to the constituents of a church, they maintained the sacred right of the church to dispose of its own offices, without interference of the civil power. Accordingly, Dr. George Hicks, who had been consecrated by the deprived Bishops of Norwich, Ely, and Peterborough, under the obsolete title of Suffragan of Thetford, in 1694, con-with success, and probably unconscious of ill intent. He attempted an answer, which only brought upon him a fresh castigation. In truth, his defence was as feeble as his cause was indefensible.*

ferred episcopal ordination on Collier in 1713, a period when the negociations at Utrecht, the discords of the English Ministry, and the supposed bias of Queen Anne, had revived the spirits of the Jacobites; but as this ceremony did not give him a Bishop's power on earth, it passed over unnoticed by the ruling party. Collier did not die till 1726, when he expired on the 26th of April, in the 76th year of his age, and was buried in St. Pancras church-yard.

Besides the works we have mentioned above, he was author of an Historical Dictionary, chiefly taken from Moreri, which, like many other old books, may sometimes be found in libraries where you would least expect it, among the few books of a small tradesman, or the chance gathered assemblage of odd volumes which a wet day produces from the cupboard of a country inn. Moreri was himself a very inaccurate compiler, and perhaps Collier has not materially diminished his blunders. The Ecclesiastical History of our author we cannot pretend to have read. On such a subject his peculiar opinions must have been more than usually active. Mr. Dibdin tells us that it might once be had for the price of waste paper, but that the days of *book-vandalism* are passed—so much the worse for poor book-worms. There are few branches of learning on which even well-educated Englishmen are so ill-informed as upon ecclesiastical history, surely the most interesting that a christian or a philosopher can study. Southey's " Book of the Church " will go far to remove this reproach as far as England and the Church of England are concerned.

* " I cannot think it reasonable, that because Mr. Collier is pleased to write one chapter of immodesty, and another of profaneness, that therefore every expression traduced by him under those heads shall be condemned as obscene and profane immediately, and without further enquiry. Perhaps Mr. Collier is acquainted with the *Deceptio visus*, and presents objects to the view through a stained glass : things may appear seemingly profane, when in reality they are only seen through a profane medium, and the true colour is dissembled by the help of a sophistical varnish : therefore, I demand the privilege of the Habeas Corpus and to appear before a just judge, in an uncounterfeit light."

This is a weak resistance, a puny attempt at pleasantry, unworthy of one of Congreve's wit-woulds. The following sophistry, though shallow enough, is rather more ingenious :—

" Because Mr. Collier, in his chapter of the profaneness of the stage, has founded great part of his accusation upon the liberty which poets take of using some words in their plays which have been sometimes employed by the translators of the Holy Scriptures; I desire that the following distinction may be admitted, viz.: that when words are applied to sacred things, and with a design to treat of sacred things, they ought to be understood accordingly; but when they are otherwise applied, the diversity of the subject gives a diversity of signification; and in truth, he might as well except against the common use of the alphabet in poetry, because the same letters are necessary to the spelling of words which are mentioned in Sacred Writ."

But the disposition of a drowning man to catch at a straw was never more pitiably betrayed than in what follows :—

" It may not be impertinent to take notice of a very common expedient which is

While we gladly acknowledge the excellent scope and general justice of Collier's reproofs, we may be allowed to doubt whether the effect of his admonitions was as great and sudden as some have supposed. He has been complimented as the purifier of comedy, and the great reformer of that stage which he purposed not to reform, but to overthrow. He certainly excited a great sensation, and gained both the King and the people to his side. William, educated in the strictness of Presbyterian discipline, and enured to the sobriety of Dutch manners, was so well pleased with the old non-juror's boldness, that he interfered to mitigate the severity of those laws which Collier's Jacobite principles had induced him to offend. Even the police were aroused by the crying scandal. Betterton and Mrs. Brucegirdle were fined for pronouncing profane and indecent words on the stage; and Colley Cibber tells us that comedy grew modest. The authors and actors might be upon their guard while public opinion, that Argus with a hundred drowsy eyes, was half awakened to their enormities; and many *well-meaning* people, roused by the indignant commentaries of Collier, blushed to find what they had not blushed at before. But, with few exceptions, the dramatists shewed as little amendment in their subsequent productions, as contrition in their angry replies. It was not in Collier's power to create a new idea of wit, or to erect a new standard of reputation; and while vice might be called wit without loss of reputation, it would never want auditors who stood well with the world. The worst of the old plays continued to be acted for many years after the date of Collier's diatribe; the new ones were a little more decent, but not a jot more moral.

Whatever refinement may have taken place in the public taste for diversion (and doubtless the improvement is considerable), is to be

made use of to recommend the instruction of our plays, which is this: after the action of the play is over, and the delights of the representation at an end, there is generally care taken that the morals of the whole shall be summed up and delivered to the audience, in the very last and concluding lines of the poem. The intention of this is, that the delight of the representation may not so strongly possess the minds of the audience as to make them forget or oversee the instruction: it is the last thing said, that it may make the last impression; and it is always comprehended in a few lines, and put into rhyme, that it may be easy and engaging to the memory."

And so, the whole tendency of five acts of intrigue, lying, adultery, and double-entendre, was to be corrected by a few couplets of jingling morality, spoken to the pit when the curtain was falling! This is a death-bed repentance with a vengeance.

Congreve's answer to Collier was addressed, in the form of letters, to Walter Moyle, Esq. and entitled, "*Amendments of Mr. Collier's false and imperfect Citations from the Old Bachelor, Double Dealer, Love for Love, and the Mourning Bride, by the Author of those Plays.*"

ascribed to other causes than the severity of satirists, or even the fulminations of the pulpit. The chief of these are, the general good education of females, the purifying influences of female society, the higher
value set upon the domestic affections, the greater freedom of choice in
marriage, and the more frequent intercourse between the religious and
the fashionable world.

It has been surmised, without much reason, that the reproof of
Collier alienated Congreve from the stage. Yet he produced another
comedy, written with infinite labour, but without any regard to the
censor's admonitions. The reception of this play fell far below his
expectations; and if we may credit the account given in the "Lives
of the Poets," published under the name of Theophilus Cibber, his
disappointment betrayed him into a folly more ludicrous than any that
he ridiculed on the scene. According to this incredible anecdote, he
rushed upon the stage in a passion, and "desired the audience to save
themselves the trouble of shewing their dislike, for he never intended
to write again for the theatre, nor submit his works again to the censure of impotent critics." The audience must surely have concluded
that he had undertaken to play the fool of the comedy himself, and
that for once the fool *was* "a fool indeed." But Congreve had too much
sense and too much pride to have acted thus, however keenly he might
resent the stupidity of the many-headed monster. The tale may safely
be set down as one of "the weak inventions" which a poor slave of the
ink-horn is ever ready to believe and promulgate of a rich, caressed,
and pensioned author. Nothing disposes the humours so strongly to
the acetic fermentation of envy, as the hopeless, heartless drudgery of
the brain; and Envy is more credulous than Love, Fear, Superstition,
even Vanity itself.

Congreve, however, was mortified at the dulness of his critics, and
provoked that all the *labor limæ* had been thrown away. But no man
should ever expect to profit in purse or reputation by superfluous pains-
taking. That very polish, that diligent selection and considerate
collocation of words, that tight-lacing of sentences into symmetry, that
exquisite propriety of each part and particle of the whole, which make
" The Way of the World " * so perfect a model of acuminated satire,

---

* "But little of it was prepared for that general taste which seems now to be predominant in the palates of our audience. Those characters which are meant to be
ridiculed in most of our comedies, are of fools so gross, that in my humble opinion
they should rather disturb than divert the well-natured and reflective part of an
audience: they are rather objects of charity than contempt, and instead of moving
our mirth, they ought very often to excite our compassion. This reflection moved
me to design some characters which should seem ridiculous, not so much through a

detract more from scenic illusion than they add to histrionic effect. The dialogue of this play is no more akin to actual conversation, than the quick step of an opera dancer to the haste of pursuit or terror. No actor could give it the unpremeditated air of common speech. But there is another and more serious obstacle to the success of the "Way of the World" as an acting play. It has no moral interest. There is no one person in the *dramatis personæ* for whom it is possible to care. Vice may be, and too often has been, made interesting; but cold-hearted, unprincipled villainy never can. The conduct of every character is so thoroughly and so equally contemptible, that however you suspend the moral code of judgment, you cannot sympathise in the success, or exult in the defeat of any.

With all these abatements, it is impossible to read this comedy without wonder and admiration; but it is an admiration altogether intellectual, by which no man is made better.

This was Congreve's last appearance on the stage. Perhaps he had already outlived that sleepless activity of animal spirits which made his work delightful to himself, and thought he had fully earned the commendation of Dryden.—

> Well, then, the promis'd hour is come at last;
> The present age of wit obscures the past:
> Strong were our sires, and as they fought they writ,
> Conquering with force of arms, and dint of wit;
> Theirs was the giant race, before the flood;
> And thus, when Charles return'd, our empire stood.
> Like Janus, he the stubborn soil manur'd,
> With rules of husbandry the rankness cur'd,
> Tam'd us to manners when the stage was rude,
> And boisterous English wit with art induced.
> Our age was cultivated thus at length,
> But what we gain'd in skill, we lost in strength.
> Our builders were with want of genius curst;
> The second temple was not like the first;
> Till you, the best Vitruvius, came at length;
> Our beauties equal, but excel our strength.

natural folly (which is incorrigible, and therefore not proper for the stage), as through an affected wit—a wit which, at the same time that it is affected, is also false. As there is some difficulty in the formation of a character of this nature, so there is some hazard which attends the progress of its success on the stage; for many come to a play so overcharged with criticism, that they very often let fly their censure when, through their rashness, they have mistaken their aim. This I had occasion lately to observe; for this play had been acted two or three days before some of these hasty judges could distinguish between the character of a wit-would and a wit."—*Dedication.*

WILLIAM CONGREVE.

Firm Doric pillars found your solid base,
The fair Corinthian crowns the higher space ;
Thus all below is strength, and all above is grace.
In easy dialogue is Fletcher's praise;
He mov'd the mind, but had no power to raise.
Great Jonson did by strength of judgment please,
Yet doubling Fletcher's force, he wants his ease.
In diff'ring talents both adorn'd their age ;
One for the study, t'other for the stage.
But both to Congreve justly shall submit,
One match'd in judgment, both o'er-match'd in wit.
In him all beauties of this age we see,
Etheredge his courtship, Southern's purity,
The satire, wit, and strength of manly Wicherly.
All this in blooming youth you have achieved,
Nor are your foil'd contemporaries griev'd :
So much the sweetness of your manners move,
We cannot envy you, because we love.
Fabius might joy in Scipio, when he saw
A beardless consul made against the law,
And join his suffrage to the votes of Rome,
Though he with Hannibal was overcome.
Thus old Romano bow'd to Raphael's fame,
And scholar to the youth he taught became.
    Oh that your brows my laurel had sustain'd;
Well had I been depos'd if you had reign'd !
The father had descended for the son,
For only you are lineal to the throne.
Thus when the state one Edward did depose,
A greater Edward in his room arose.
But now, not I, but poetry is curs'd,
For Tom the second reigns like Tom the first.
But let 'em not mistake my patron's part,
Nor call his charity their own desert.
Yet this I prophesy ; thou shalt be seen,
(Tho' with some short parenthesis between),
High on the throne of Wit, and seated there,
Not mine (that's little) but thy laurel wear.
Thy first attempt an early promise made,
That early promise this has more than paid,
So bold, yet so judiciously you dare,
That your least praise is to be regular.
Time, place, and action may with pains be wrought,
But genius must be born, and never can be taught ;
This is your portion ; this your native store ;
Heav'n, that but once was prodigal before,
To Shakspeare gave as much, she could not give him more.
    Maintain your post; that's all the fame you need,
For 'tis impossible you should proceed :

> Already I am worn with cares and age,
> And just abandoning th' ungrateful stage;
> Unprofitably kept at Heav'ns expense,
> I live a rent charge on his providence;
> But you, whom every muse and grace adorn,
> Whom I foresee to better fortunes born,
> Be kind to my remains, and oh! defend
> Against your judgment your departed friend.
> Let not th' insulting foe my fame pursue,
> But shade those laurels which descend to you;
> And take for tribute what these lines express;
> You merit more, nor could my love do. less

Congreve was almost as happy in the commendations of his brother authors, as in the favours of ministers, and the smiles of great ladies. Dennis, whose disease was not a plethora of complaisance, declared " that Congreve left the stage early, and comedy left it with him." Though he no longer exposed himself to the brunt of a theatrical audience, he still kept his name awake by the production of occasional poems, which were highly praised in their day, but their day has long been past. They were written in the height of the fashion, and fashion was then a more potent arbitress of reputation than now. The world of literature was then the town: the town took its cue from the court, and the court echoed the decisions of some " scribbling peer," some Lord of the Miscellanies." George the Second's Queen, Caroline, seems to have been the last personage who, by the mere prerogative of rank, could bring a book into vogue.

The latter years of Congreve furnish little or nothing worth recording. Though he never took a very active part in politics, he ranked with the Whigs, and remained constant to his first patron, Halifax. Hence there was some fear lest, on the change of Queen Anne's Ministry, in 1710, he might be deprived of his places. Several persons of consequence made interest with Harley, the new Secretary, and Mæcenas elect, that he might not be disturbed. But the Minister would not have it thought that the Poet owed his immunity to any interest but that of the Muses, and answered the mediators in the words of Virgil :—

> Non obtusa adeo gestamus pectora Teucri
> Nec tam aversus equos Tyriâ Sol jungit ab urbe.

The Tories, whose best virtue is their generosity, suffered Congreve to retain his emoluments without imposing any conditions; and he, by holding them, did not conceive himself to have incurred an obligation to be ungrateful. He signalized his adherence to the ousted party in the very year of their defeat, by dedicating a collection of his works to the Ex-Minister Halifax. His fidelity was rewarded, on the return of his friends to power, with an additional place, which made his income altogether £1200 a year.   The ideas of poetry and poverty have been so long and so inveterately connected, even in the minds of Poets themselves, that it is no great wonder if Congreve, in his affluence, chose to forget that he had ever exercised a craft so rarely profitable, or felt a proud reluctance to be reckoned with writers by trade.   There are few anecdotes which have been more frequently repeated than that of Congreve's interview with Voltaire.   The Frenchman, whose ambition was the literary supremacy of the age, was much surprised that Congreve should listen coldly to the praises of his own works, speak of them as trifles beneath him, and desire to be visited only as a gentleman living retired, and at his ease.   "Had you been so unfortunate," replied Voltaire, "as to be only a gentleman, I should not have visited you at all."   The retort was just in itself : but it is somewhat harsh to censure Congreve for *vanity* and *contemptible affectation*.   A man is not necessarily ashamed, or affecting to be ashamed, of his occupation, past or present, because he does not choose to make it the ground of his acceptance in society.   Our author on this occasion has found an able vindicator in Mason.   In fact, Congreve had gained from literature whatever literature could give him ; opulence, applause, the empire of wit, and the conversation of the great.   Pope, by laying the translated Iliad at his feet, had acknowledged him to be the chief poet of his time.   Thus it was the fortune of Congreve to receive honour from the veteran bard of the generation before him, and from the young aspirant upon whom the hopes of the next were settled.   Though he retired long before his death from the field where alone he had reaped true glory, he did not outlive his reputation.   He had the more singular felicity to be commended by most, and maligned by none.

Yet his latter years were not without affliction.   Cataracts in his eyes terminated in total blindness, and he was a martyr to the gout, from which he vainly sought relief by a visit to Bath.   An overturn in his chariot made his case hopeless.   He returned to London, and expired at his house (situate where now stands Holland House) on the 29th of January, 1728-9.   He was buried in Westminster Abbey, where a monument was erected to his memory, by Henrietta, Duchess of Marlborough.   This lady, the daughter of the great Duke, and wife of Lord Godolphin, was so warmly attached to Congreve, that, if the common report be true, his loss must have disordered her brain.   It is said that she had his image moulded in wax, of the size of life— talked to it as if living, helped it at table to the same dishes which the deceased was known to prefer, and had an imaginary sore on its leg attended with all the care of surgery.   There is no possibility of setting limits to madness, but this tale bears marks of gross exaggeration. Most likely it originated in the report of some discarded waiting maid, who *thought* she had some time or other overheard her lady talking to Mr. Congreve's bust.

The conduct of Congreve in leaving £10,000, the amassings of a close economy, to this Duchess, has been severely reprehended. If his relations were poor, he had certainly much better have bestowed his fortune on the poor than on the wealthy. Still, it was not by inheritance from parents, nor by aid of kinsfolk, that he became rich. To the great he owed his property, and to the great he returned it. He offended no rule of justice by so doing.

From a rapid survey of his life and character, he seems to have been one of those indifferent children of the earth " whom the world cannot hate ; " who are neither too good nor too bad for the present state of existence, and who may fairly expect their portion here. The darkest— at least the most enduring—stain on his memory, is the immorality of his writings ; but this was the vice of the time, and his comedies are considerably more decorous than those of his predecessors. They are too cold to be mischievous ; they keep the brain in too incessant inaction to allow the passions to kindle. For those who search into the powers of intellect, the combinations of thought which may be produced by volition, the plays of Congreve may form a profitable study, But their time is fled—on the stage they will be received no more ; and of the devotees of light reading, such as could read them without disgust would probably peruse them with little pleasure.*

* It is reported, that in the latter part of his life he expressed much disapprobation of some part of his works. But as this disapprobation was expressed in the presence of a Quaker, it is hard to say how much of it was contrition, and how much politeness. He left several small legacies, and £200 to Mrs. Bracegirdle, the object of his youthful gallantry. Dr. Johnson's critique on Congreve is one of his happiest.

DR. FOTHERGILL.

In a very entertaining little essay, prefixed, we believe, by the late Dr. Beddoes, of Bristol, to an edition of the works of John Brown, is a classification of physicians, according to the Linnæan method,—as the *canting doctor*, the *wheedling doctor*, the *Adonis doctor*, and the *bully quack doctor*; which last genus and species is exemplified by that eminent Yorkshire worthy, and great benefactor to the University of Oxford, Dr. John Radcliffe. But we do not recollect any mention of the Quaker philanthropist doctor. Yet such a one was John Fothergill, a man who rather lives in the gratitude of mankind for the good that he did, than in the archives of science for the facts he discovered, the phænomena he explained, or the theories he constructed.

John Fothergill, the father of our subject, was a member of the society of Friends, and seems to have had considerable influence among his brethren, and, like many of that public-spirited community, who make a point of conscience of whatever they engage in, a keen politician. In the year 1734 he took a very active part in the contested election for Yorkshire, and in concert with Joseph Storr, wrote a circular letter to the society, lamenting that some of them had given votes *inconsistent with unity and good report*, and recommending to their favour Sir Rowland Winn and Cholmondeley Turner. Whether these candidates were conspicuous for opposition to the war which was then raging on the continent, or for advocacy of a general distribution of political privilege, or were distinguished from their opponents by sobriety and sanctity of demeanor, or what other claims they had to the support of the Friends, we are unable to determine.

John Fothergill the elder, after travelling all over America, settled at Knaresborough as a brewer, was successful, so as to enable him to retire from business to a small farm at Carr-End, near Richmond, where his son John was born in 1712, either on the 8th of March or the 12th of October. He was the second son of his father. The eldest, Alexander, studied the law, and inherited the family estate. Joseph, the third, was an ironmonger at Stockport, in Cheshire. Samuel, the youngest, went to America, and became a celebrated Quaker preacher. Anne, the only daughter, became the companion of her brother John, and survived him.

John received his early education under his maternal grandfather, Thomas Houghton, a gentleman of fortune in Cheshire, and afterwards at the school of Sedburgh. His classical attainments were at least respectable, as appears from some of his medical works in Latin. As the principles in which he was educated shut him out from the English Universities, while the turn of his mind disinclined him to the active pursuits of commerce, he chose the medical profession, the only profession in which a Quaker can expect to rise, or indeed can engage, in strict accordance with the spirit of his religion. He was apprenticed to Benjamin Bartlet,* surgeon and apothecary, of Bradford, in the year 1718, and served out the full term of seven years, whereby he gained a very intimate acquaintance with the practical part of pharmacy, and probably with the routine of general practice. An apothecary's apprentice is often called to attend upon the poorest of the poor ; he has to exercise much patience ; whatever time he can devote to mental cultivation, or the higher branches of medical science, must be taken from his hours of relaxation or of sleep : if his disposition be indolent, his faculties obtuse, or his master unconscientious, he may very easily pass over the seven years without learning any thing more than the manual part of the trade. But, on the other hand, where a disposition to improvement meets with a master willing to afford instruction, and the opportunities of experience, the youth who goes through this troublesome probation has some advantages over him who passes from the general studies of the University to the School of Medicine.

Young Fothergill removed to London October 20th,† 1736, and was for two years the pupil of Dr. (afterwards Sir Edward) Wilmot, at St. Thomas's Hospital. Thus prepared with a solid foundation, he went to the University of Edinburgh, which was then just rising into repute ‡ as a medical seminary. He graduated in 1736. His inaugural

* Chalmer's Biographical Dictionary. Dr. Elliott calls Fothergill's master *Barclay*, and states that he afterwards removed to London, and resided at the corner of Featherstone Buildings. Dr. Elliott omits all mention of Fothergill's studying under Dr. Wilmot.

† This date bespeaks the precision of a Friend. Does it specify the expiration of his indentures ? or his arrival in London ?

‡ Dr. Fothergill, in his " Essay on the Character of the late Alexander Russell, M. D." thus states the origin of that succession of medical teachers which for more than a century have attracted so much youthful talent to the northern metropolis :—
" Though there had long been Professorships for Medicine in that place," (Edin-

thesis, " De emeticorum·usu in variis morbis tractandis " was republished in a collection of Theses by Dr. Smellie, a sufficient acknow-

burgh) " and several attempts had been made to introduce a general course of medical instruction, it was not till about the year 1720 that this University distinguished itself. Several gentlemen, who had studied under Boerhaave, with a view to revive the study of medicine in their native country, where it had formerly flourished, qualified themselves for the purpose of giving courses of public lectures on every branch of their profession. The celebrated Monro taught anatomy, after having studied it for several years under the ablest masters then in Europe,—Dr. Douglas, of London; Albinus the elder, of Leyden; and Winslow, at Paris. The *theory* of physic was assigned to the amiable, the humane Dr. Sinclair; Drs. Rutherford and Innes chose the *practice*; chemistry was allotted to Dr. Plummer; and the teaching the *materia medica*, together with *botany* (of which last he was appointed King's Professor), devolved upon the learned and indefatigable Alston. The city of Edinburgh favoured the generous design, added to the salaries allotted from the crown, and provided as suitable conveniences as the place would at that time afford.

"They had no sooner opened their respective Professorships, than many students of their own nation, some from England, from Ireland, and not long after from the plantations likewise, flocked thither. This stimulated the Professors to exert their great talents with the utmost energy; Professor Monro's class soon became numerous, and the anatomy of the bones, of the nerves, and his other pieces, will long remain as testimonies of his great abilities, when the grateful regard of the multitude of those who studied under him, and were witnesses of his singular attention to instruct and encourage his pupils, as well as to act the part of a parent to every stranger, fails of expression. With what grace and elegance, with what minuteness and precision, would the humane, the inimitable Dr. Sinclair explain the institutes of the master (Boerhaave) whose nervous simplicity he studied to exemplify, though not with servile imitation. Where he differed in opinion with that great man, with what diffidence would he offer his own? Ever the student's friend, and their example, in a noble simplicity of manners, and a conduct becoming the gentleman and the physician."

Dr. Fothergill proceeds to allot appropriate praises to Rutherford, Plummer, the "laborious Alston," "the learned, the able, the laborious Innes," &c. It is always pleasant to hear a man praising his instructors, and acknowledging intellectual obligations. But when one undertakes to review a whole generation of worthies, it is by no means easy to find a peculiar praise for each. Panegyric is certainly not the genius of the English people, nor of the English language. The *Eloges* and *Oraisons funèbres* of the French are so far superior to the British manufacture, that no wonder they should be often smuggled under the imperfect disguise of an Anglo-Gallic translation. As we shall have few opportunities of quoting from Dr. Fothergill's writings, most of which are either professional, or of temporary interest, we offer the above extract as a specimen of his style, which, though not ground to the fine edge of discriminative eulogy, is very useful, good, vernacular English, fit for plain statement, honest sense, and clear reasoning. The individual to whose memory the Essay in question was devoted, was Alexander Russell, author of the " History of Aleppo," a book of high reputation in the class to which it belongs. He was the son of a Scotch advocate, who was remarkable for having reared a family of seven boys to man's estate, in virtue and obedience, without ever striking a blow or using a harsh word,—a fact so contrary to the theories of education then prevalent, that the relator

ledgement of its medical merit. In style it is much less barbarous than the common run of medical Latinity.

seems to anticipate incredulity. After completing his medical studies under the best masters to be found in his native city, Dr. Alexander Russell went to Turkey, and, in 1740, settled at Aleppo, at the earnest desire of the British Factory. He speedily made himself master of the native languages, and cultivated the acquaintance of the native practitioners, who were very numerous, very ignorant, but not always incapable of the instruction which Dr. Russell was ready to impart. Nothing enables a man so quickly to acquire importance in a strange land, among a half-civilized people, as a skill in the healing arts. Medicine, and especially surgery, should be a necessary qualification of every missionary. In a little time, *the English Doctor* was the most indispensable person in Aleppo, consulted by all the tribes that compose the many-lingoed, many-garbed, and many-coloured population of an Oriental city,—Franks, Armenians, Maronites, Jews, Greeks, even by the Turks themselves. "In this instance they forgot that he was an unbeliever, remitted of their usual contempt for strangers, and not only beheld him with respect, but courted his friendship, and placed unlimited confidence in his opinion." But his influence with the Pacha was wonderful. "Seldom would the Pacha determine any intricate affair, respecting not only commerce, but even the interior police of his government, without consulting his physician and friend, and as seldom deviated from the opinion he proposed; and so singular was the character of the ruler's friendship for his confidante that he gave him the full credit of every popular and merciful act, reserving to himself only the gloomy prerogative of punishment, which he took care to exercise in the Doctor's absence. Even when he thought fit to spare of his own proper motion, lest his clemency should render him less dreaded, he always ascribed the remission or mitigation of the penalty to the suggestion of the English Doctor. Whence the English Doctor was occasionally surprised and overpowered with the thanks of respited wretches, who really owed him no obligation. Sometimes the Pacha went so far as to confess a kind of subjection to his physician, and tell an offender, that in his opinion he deserved death, but that he *durst* not order it, for the English Doctor insisted on mercy." It would be curious to know by what means Russell acquired and retained so uncommon an interest. Despots are extreme in all things,—

Not more a storm their hate than gratitude.

A physician may, by a timely application, changes a state of corporeal agony to that ease which, contrasted with contiguous suffering, is more delightful than any positive pleasure. This to any mind must appear a great good—to an untaught predestinarian a miraculous boon. Even brutes are capable of grateful passions towards those who rescue them from pain, when they can connect the cure with the agent. Who has not read of Androcles and the lion? a story so beautiful, and withal so possible, that we would fain believe it true. It would be very easy for a man possessed but of a moderate degree of medical or chemical knowledge, to persuade a Pacha that he possessed supernatural or prophetic powers; but the influence founded on fraud or fear is ever insecure, and Russell remained in favour as long as his Moslem patron continued to rule Aleppo. The gratitude of the Pacha appeared in some pleasing instances, particularly in sending costly presents to the Doctor's aged father. "But for your father," said he, "I should not have known your assistance." Nor did Russell's estimation fade away under the succeeding Pachas, one of whom,

4 T

From Edinburgh he went to Leyden, a University then much frequented by English students, both in Law, Medicine, and Arts. Here he made but a short stay, but travelled for some time on the continent, chiefly with a view to professional improvement, visiting the celebrated baths of Aix-la-Chapelle, and the Spa. He returned to England, and commenced practice in London about 1740, in the 29th year of his age. That he took so long a time to prepare himself for the active duties of his profession, proves that his circumstances must have secured him from necessity; but he was doubtless nurtured in frugal maxims and self-denying habits. His first habitation was in

an old man, who died at Aleppo, made him the depositary of his most important secrets.

The Doctor's fame extending throughout the Turkish empire, was more than once likely to expose him to the dangerous honour of a summons to Constantinople in time of plague. The name of Russell procured for his brother Patrick, who followed him to Aleppo, a courteous reception wherever he arrived in the Levant.

On his return from Aleppo, Dr. Russell visited the most famous lazarettos to which he could have access, inquired into their structure, the government they were under, and the precautions used to prevent the spread of the pestilence. His thorough and experienced acquaintance with the plague, the symptoms and treatment of which English physicians in general have had a long and blessed opportunity of not knowing, pointed him out to government, at the end of 1757, when reports were rife of the plague at Lisbon, as a fit person to consult on the most effective means of excluding the infection. He was summoned before the Privy Council, and gave great satisfaction by the fulness and pertinence of his answers, which he was ordered to commit to writing. Whatever his medical works may be, it is to his " Natural History of Aleppo " that he is indebted for whatever hold he may retain on the public memory. It is a book that still keeps its authority, though so many travellers have since traversed the plains of Syria, and did much to remove many false and antiquated notions of Oriental manners and Ottoman policy.

Russell, in the latter part of his life, was a vigorous assertor of the rights of the Licentiates against the Fellows of the College of Physicians. The same spirit which in the church has given rise to High Churchmen and Low Churchmen, Episcopalians, Presbyterians, and Independents, has long existed in the medical world, and the contest has been carried on perhaps in as ill a temper—sometimes with almost equal scurrility; but happily the points at issue do not require so much blasphemy.

Dr. Alexander Russell returned to England, after an absence of fifteen years, in 1755, was chosen Physician to St. Thomas's Hospital in 1759, and died in 1770. Among pharmacopœists and medical botanists he is noted as the first who brought to England the seeds of the true Scammony, in procuring which he had no small trouble from the ignorance or knavery of the Arabs, who brought him twenty sorts of seeds before the right, no doubt unwilling to give up a patent which nature had bestowed on the east. Dr. Fothergill also ascribes to him the first introduction of the *Andrachne*, a species of Arbutus, highly ornamental. But according to Rees's Cyclopædia, this shrub was cultivated as early as 1734, at Eltham, by Dr. Sherrard, probably the Consul Sherrard, who preceded Dr. Russell at Aleppo.

White Hart Court, Lombard Street. He did not set up a carriage on speculation, but for some time visited his patients on foot.

Dr. Johnson has remarked, that "an interesting book might be written on the fortune of physicians." And most true it is, that physicians must ever depend upon fortunate accidents for the foundation of their fame. The absence of a predecessor, the successful recommendation of a retiring favourite, the happy result of a single case, may have opened the way to affluence, when it seemed to be closed against all concerted endeavours. It may be doubted whether the mere reputation of science, or the good opinion of professional brethren, are available to bring a young man into notice. Some dash into celebrity by the unlikeliest means imaginable. 'Tis said that cowardice, in mere blind desperation, sometimes does the work of heroism in the field. Ignorance sometimes blunders into a cure by experiments which nothing but success could save from the imputation of manslaughter. An ugly visage, a blunt manner, a fluency of oaths, a braggart contempt of learning, perpetual quarrels with rival practitioners, a cynical snarling at every thing and every body, do occasionally succeed, especially with the poor, and the ignorant wealthy. Now and then we have known a drunken doctor have an uncommon run. Others have found their account in jacobinism or infidelity. We need not allude to quackeries more specifically professional, any further than to remark that their success is chiefly with the very low, and with the very high; with those who have never learned to think, and those who cannot bear the trouble of thinking. The poor man listens to the hasty empiric because he finds sickness more grievous than death is terrible; the rich, through extreme eagerness to live and enjoy, gripes at an offer of health on easier terms than established maxims warrant. Both rich and poor had rather believe the process of healing altogether unintelligible, than acknowledge that it is intelligible, but that they themselves do not understand it.

But even the worthier members of the faculty, who refrain from quackeries of every description, require something else besides a knowledge of diseases and remedies, to make their knowledge effectual either for their own or their patients' benefit. Of these exoteric qualifications, some are outward and visible; as a good gentlemanly person, not alarmingly handsome (for the Adonis Doctor, though he has a fair opening to a wealthy marriage, seldom greatly prospers in the way of business), with an address to suit,—that is to say, a genteel self-possession and subdued politeness, not of the very last polish—a slow, low, and regular tone of voice (here Dr. Fothergill's Quaker habits must have been an excellent preparative), and such an even flow of spirits as neither to be dejected by the sight of pain and the weight of responsibility, nor to offend the anxious and the suffering by an unsympathetic hilarity. The dress should be neat, and rather above than below par in costliness. The distinguishing costume of the faculty has now almost totally disappeared; the periwig has followed the furred gown, and the gold-headed cane is as much out of date as the serpent-wreathed staff of Æscalapius. This is doubtless a great relief to the professors; for no *civil* uniform is pleasant to wear, and even the military scarlet or naval blue give their wearers a painfully dazzling superiority. But the modern levelling of garments makes the streets and assemblies horridly unpicturesque, has done a serious injury to the stage, and left to every professional man (under a Bishop, or head of a house) the puzzling decision how to dress himself. Here, too, Dr. Fothergill was lucky in his religious denomination. In his earliest days the wig and ruffles were still in vogue, but he retained the simple garb of a *Friend*, not however so as to make its peculiarities obtrusive.

In fine, the young physician should carry a something of his profession in his outward man, but yet so that nobody should be able to say what it was. Some practitioners, in the ardour of their noviciate, talk of cases, dissections, and post mortem examinations, in every mixed company. This is very injudicious. Few ailing persons like to have their complaints made a general topic of discussion, however fond they may be of talking about them themselves :—

> Some people use their health (an ugly trick)
> In telling you how oft they have been sick,

As Cowper saith. It is a still uglier trick to tell how often other people have been sick. Besides, it clearly proves that the narrator has a paucity both of patients and ideas. Medical students sometimes think it very knowing to discuss offensive or equivocal topics with a solemn slyness and technical diction, shewing themselves abundantly satisfied with their superiority to the weak-stomached superstition of delicacy. This is by no means commendable at any age, but after twenty is intolerable. All slang, and knowingness, and slyness should, and generally will, exclude a young practioner from every respectable family.

But, far more than all definable proprieties of demeanor, the effects of which are chiefly negative, there are certain inward gifts, more akin to genius than to talent—to intuition than to rationation—which make the physician prosper, and deserve to prosper. Medicine is not, like practical geometry, or the doctrine of projectiles, an application of an abstract, demonstrable science, in which a certain result may be drawn from certain data, or in which the disturbing forces can be calculated with an approximation to exactness. It is a tentative art, to succeed in which demands a quickness of eye, tact, thought, and invention, which are not to be learned by study, nor without a connatural aptitude, to be acquired by experience. And it is the possession of this *sense*, exercised by patient observation, and fortified with a just reliance on the *vis medicatrix*, the self-adjusting tendency of nature, that constitutes the physician, as imagination constitutes the poet, and brings it to pass, that sometimes an old apothecary, not very far removed from an *old woman*, whose ordinary conversation partakes largely of the character of twaddle, who can seldom give any rational account of a case or prescription, acquires a reputation of infallibility, as if he had made a truce with death,—while men of talent and erudition are admired and neglected. The truth is, that there is a good deal of the mysterious in whatever is practical. It is not only in the concerns of the spirit that man walks by faith. Wherever there is life there is a mystery.

But neither genius nor science will avail the physician, if he want confidence in himself, and cannot create a confidence in others. He must also, by persuasion or authority, obtain a mastery over his patients, and over all about them. The occasional success of *bullying* doctors arises from the fear they inspire, which enforces a strict observation of their directions. A medical man stands in the situation of a father confessor. He has to extract truth from reluctant penitents; he has to inflict severe penance on peccant nature. But to this end, the sarcastic coarseness of a bully is far less effectual than the mild firmness of a Quaker. Some have ascribed the success of Dr. Fothergill to the novelty of a Quaker doctor. But this was, in fact, nothing new. There were two physicians of the same persuasion practising in London at the commencement of his career. Nor was his rise by any means sudden. He sought no sinister paths to popularity. His beneficence, great as it was, was never speculative. He proportioned his givings to his earnings. Without any remarkable brilliancy of talent, without any striking originality of practice, he gained the confidence of those who needed his assistance, chiefly by convincing them that he wished to do them good for their own sakes.

The medical profession, in respect of the spirit in which they pursue their occupation, may be divided into four classes, corresponding to four classes of clerical teachers : 1st, Those who have been put into the profession, or chosen it at random, because they must be something— loungers who feel their business a toil and a constraint, who at best only desire to escape disgrace and make a living—correlative to the gentlemen in orders, and the drudging curates,—a very unprofitable race

when gentlemen, a very unhappy and mischievous one when otherwise.
2d. Those who pursue their trade eagerly and diligently for money or
advancement—correspondent to the preferment hunters of the church,
and the popular preachers and *Tartuffes* of all denominations, who will
generally be respectable, or otherwise, as their rank and connections
give them more or less of character to lose. 3d. The votaries of science,
to whom knowledge is an ultimate object, and practice chiefly valued
as the means of increasing and certifying knowledge—correspondent to
the speculative theologians—the students of religious learning—a class
highly estimable and necessary, who answer their vocation well, and
dignify their rank, whatever it may be: and 4th, The philanthropists,
to whom knowledge is only a secondary object, valued as it is the
means of abating pain and preserving life—correlative to those christian
teachers and pastors who are animated with the true and faithful love
of souls. Among these, it is delightful to find men of all ranks—but
rank with them is nothing: these are illuminated with a light, in
which there may be many colours, but there is no darkness. To this
class did Fothergill belong. Yet he, too, was a lover of knowledge for
its own sake: a careful investigator of nature, whether she displayed
herself in the marvellous human frame, or in the multitudinous varieties of plants, shells, minerals:—glad, when he could, to discover a use
in her works, and glad at all times to acknowledge them the works of
God.

"The uniformity of a professional life," says one of Dr. Fothergill's
biographers, "is seldom interrupted: it therefore furnishes few particulars worthy of being recorded. The transactions of one day seldom
differ from those of another. In Dr. Fothergill's case, perhaps, there
was as little variety as ever fell to the share of any one man. His
popularity continued undiminished as long as his health and strength
would allow him to attend on his patients; and during a long series
of years his diligence was unabated."

This is in some measure true. Yet if the circumstances of a professional life make but a dull biography, they might furnish very
interesting auto-biographies. Every day adds something to their
knowledge of mankind. They behold human nature as it were *stripped
and whipped*. It would be truly delightful to read the private minutes
of a leech like Fothergill, whose eyes were purged by the euphrasy of
benevolence, and to trace the steps, the ramifications of practice, by
which he advanced from comparative obscurity to eminence. But no
such precious records have fallen under our cognizance.

In 1744, Dr. Fothergill was admitted a licentiate of the College of
Physicians at London, and about the same time was chosen a member

of the Royal Society, then flourishing under the auspices of Martin Folkes.* This proves that he had already distinguished himself by studies not strictly professional. He was a frequent contributor to the Philosophical Transactions. In 1744 he printed " *Observations on a case published in the last Volume of the Medical Essays, &c. of recovering a man dead in appearance.*" The suspension of animation arose from the noxious steam of coals in the pit ; he had lain between half an hour and three quarters, and was resuscitated by inflating the lungs with the natural breath, rubbing, &c. From the language of this essay it would seem that the experiment of distending the lungs was then new, and that the art of resuscitation was in its infancy. The Doctor proposes that experiments should be made on the bodies of hanged malefactors. We cannot suspect that he, or any other christian thought a thief should be hanged twice. At different times he contributed— an essay on the origin of Amber, by no means as full or satisfactory as it might have been—a review of Gmelin's account of Siberia, and other papers, which shew how much natural philosophy, geography, &c. have

---

* Martin Folkes was the son of an eminent lawyer and bencher of Gray's Inn, that most sylvan of all inns of court, whose ancient trees and venerable walks remind one more of the groves of Academus than Christ Church meadow itself. No man under sixty should be allowed to enter therein, unless those youths could be revived who performed in the masques of Fletcher and Jonson, when the men of law held high festival before Eliza and our James. Well, but Martin Folkes was born in Queen-street, Lincoln's-inn-Fields, on the 29th of October, 1690. From the age of nine to sixteen, he was under the tuition of the learned son of the erudite Lewis Capel, some-time Hebrew professor at Saumur, who came to England when that university was suppressed in 1695. After making great proficiency in Greek and Latin, he was entered of Clare Hall, Cambridge, in 1707. His progress in mathematics was wonderful for that period; and at twenty-two he was elected into the Royal Society, an honour which has never ceased to be coveted, notwithstanding the abuse and ridicule that has been constantly thrown on that learned body, even when Sir Isaac Newton was its head. Folkes was chosen a member of the council in 1716, when he made a communication relative to the eclipse of a fixed star in Gemni by the body of Jupiter. In October 1717, at the memorable royal visit, of which we have given so full an account in our life of Bentley, Martin was made Master of Arts by the University of Cambridge. A little while after he had the much higher honour of being appointed by Sir Isaac Newton himself a vice-president of the Royal Society. On the death of Sir Isaac, in 1727, he was a candidate for the Presidentship of the Society, and gained several respectable votes, though the election fell on Sir Hans Sloane; but on the death of Sir Hans, he attained that honour. He was also a distinguished antiquary, member of the Antiquarian Society, and of the French Academy of Sciences. He was a great encourager of the fine arts, the friend and patron of Hogarth, by whom his portrait was painted. It is the picture of open-hearted English honesty and hospitality, but does not indicate much intellect. He married an actress, a course less usual then than at present, and died of the palsy in 1754.

improved in the last half century. The Doctor's style is in the highest degree familiar and conversational, free from pedantry and vulgarism, but not remarkable for strength and liveliness. Though a truly religious man, he did not imitate the elder medical writers in interlarding his professional writings with Scripture texts or theological discussion: nor is there any of the Quaker in his compositions, except a general plainness, and absence of ornament. Many of his occasional tracts were printed in the "Medical Observations and Inquiries," a work of which only six volumes were published.

In 1748, he published the longest and most important of all his writings, "An Account of the Putrid Sore Throat," a form of disease then newly imported into England, though Dr. Fothergill establishes its identity with the Garrotillo* or gallows disease of the Spaniards, and the morbus strangulatorius of the Italian writers, which first appeared in Spain in 1610, and from thence spread to Malta, Sicily, Otranto, Apulia, Calabria, and the Campagna, in the space of a few years; and breaking out in Naples, in 1618, ravaged the country for upwards of twenty years, leaving many a prolific mother childless, for the pest was particularly obnoxious to children. Such an epicure in cruelty was this malady, as to select black-eyed girls for its peculiar victims. From its fatality to infants, it was called by Marcus Aurelius Severinus, Paedanchone Loimodes—the pestiferous Choke-babe. Dr. Fothergill, in the historical part of the tract, shews very considerable reading, for he quotes Johannes Andreas Sgambatus, Johannes Baptista Cortesius, Johannes Antonius Anguilloni, (physician in chief to the Maltese Gallies,) Ludovicus Mercatus, physician to Philip the Second, and to Charles the Third, and other of the illustrious obscure, of whom, though not wholly unacquainted with the backs and titles of the ordinary contents of a medical library, we never chanced to hear or read elsewhere. Yet in this display of research there is no pedantry. It was a real comfort to those who were alarmed by the appearance of a new disease, to be informed that the same malady had visited and quitted other countries in other times: for it adds to the despondency of sickness, and the terror of death itself, when the pain and peril seem strange, and unconformable to the regular course of nature.

* "Ab Hispanis Garrotillo appellatur, ut eadem patiantur Anginâ laborantes quæ facinorosi homines, cum injecto cir cum collem funestrangulantur. Epist. R. Moreau ad Th. Barth. Epis. Med. cent. I. p. 336. We cannot congratulate Monsieur Moreau on the conciseness with which he has latinized the operation of hanging, nor should we suppose that a sufficient number of sufferers in the Garrotillo had compared notes with the facinorosi homines in question to ascertain the identity of their sensations.

This morbus strangulatorius made its first attack on the English in 1739. While the poor only suffered, it spread little alarm; but when the two only sons of the Honourable Henry Pelham fell victims to its severity, a panic took possession of the higher orders. But the cases becoming rare, the apprehension subsided. As in most infections, the latter seizures were much less virulent than the earlier ones. "It began, however, to show itself again in 1742, but not so general as to render it the subject of much public discourse; for though such of the faculty as were in most extensive practice met with it now and then, in the city especially, it remained unknown to the greatest part of practitioners." In the winter of 1746 it broke out again with great violence, particularly at Bromley, in Middlesex. All remedies seemed vain: many families were left without one child out of many, and houses that had rung with the mirth of childhood, became silent and gloomy in a little week. After a time, the violence of the disorder abated, but it still continued to occur frequently, particularly in London. Though children were most subject to the infliction, adults did not always escape. Girls were more commonly attacked than boys, women than men, and the feeble than the robust. In the treatment of this complaint Dr. Fothergill was highly successful. At the suggestion of Dr. Letherland, he prescribed a much more genial and strengthening regimen than had before been usual, administering cordials, tonics, and alexipharmics; as bark, contrayerva,* aromatics, carminatives, &c.; nor did he forbid the moderate use of wine.—In what may be considered as the peroration of the essay, he makes the following recapitulation:—

1st. That the *sore throat attended with ulcers* seems to be accompanied with a strong disposition to putrefaction, which affects the habit in general, but the fauces and the parts contiguous in particular. And it seems not unreasonable to suppose,

2. That the cause of this tendency is a putrid virus, or miasma sui generis, introduced into the habit by contagion, principally by means of the breath of the person affected.

3. That this virus, or contagious matter, produces effects more or

---

* Contrayerva is a South American plant, introduced into Europe by Sir Francis Drake, in 1581. The name signifies *counter-poison*; its juice is strong poison, and was formerly used by the Peruvians to envenom their arrows. It was formerly esteemed a most powerful antidote and preservative; but its reputation has fallen off, and it is used only as a gentle stimulant. There is another sort, produced in Virginia, called Serpentaria, from its supposed efficacy against the bites of serpents. It is very aromatic, and by some accounted equal to the Peruvian contrayerva.— *Rees' Cyclopædia.*

less pernicious, according to the quantity and nature of the infection, and as the subject is disposed to receive or suffer by it.

4. That putrefactive and malignant diseases in common admit of the most sensible and secure relief from discharges of the peccant matter, either upon the skin in general, or on particular parts of the body.

5. That the redness and cutaneous effervescence in the present case may be considered as an eruption of like nature, and therefore to be promoted by such methods as have proved successful in similar diseases.

6. That a cordial, alexipharmic, warm regimen has been found by experience to be of the most use in such cases; and that bleeding, purging, and antiphlogistics, liberally employed, either retard or wholly prevent these discharges.

Therefore, as to expel the morbific matter seems to be the design of nature, to promote this design by the methods that are approved by experience in similar cases, is the duty of the physician.

This treatise was highly approved, and went through many editions. It is but fair to state, that Dr. Fothergill's merit in regard to this disorder was not that of an original discoverer, but that he owed much to the communications of Drs. Leatherland and Sylvester,—especially to the former, who with singular modesty or generosity forbad his name to be mentioned in the work.

We have entered somewhat largely into the subject of this essay, because the hopes of parents are perhaps more frequently and more cruelly cut off by diseases of the throat, than by any other cause. That murderous affection, the croop, which suffocates many a sweet infant, does not appear to have been much known half a century ago. The rise, abatement, and disappearance of diseases is a curious phenomenon in the history of nature. Is there any work extant on medical chronology?

In 1753, Dr. Fothergill was chosen a member of the Antiquarian Society; and in 1754, a Fellow of the College of Physicians at Edinburgh. He was also one of the earliest members of the American Philosophical Society, instituted at Philadelphia; and in 1776, when a medical society was founded at Paris by the King of France, he was one of a select number of foreign physicians whom the society thought proper to honour with their diploma.

Neither increasing wealth nor spreading fame ever alienated him from the body of christians from whom he sprung, and among whom he had been brought up. The society of Friends looked with affectionate esteem, and it may be with excusable pride, on their famous doctor; and he took a lively interest in whatever concerned the discipline and economy of their church. He was frequently employed by the meeting to which he belonged, to compose the annual letter to the Friends at their great Whitsuntide council. He also drew up the congratulatory address of his brethren on the accession of George the Third, in which he expressed himself like a man of this world. Really liberal, in the best and only true sense of the world, he valued the outward insignia of his religious connection as they were the means of strengthening the bands of union ; but he did not think it necessary to obtrude peculiarities of speech or opinion in his dealings with those who were without the pale.

Though mild by nature, and pacific from principle, he was by no means a man to sit down under injustice. Thinking that the Fellows of the College of Physicians not only assumed too much superiority over the Licentiates, but that they were inclined to lower the character of the latter by introducing unqualified persons among them, he took a warm interest in the contest between the *upper* and *lower* houses (so to express it) of the profession. Of this dispute we can give no better account than is contained in the preface to the "Essay on the Character of Alexander Russell," which is as follows :—

"A few years ago it was reported that the College of Physicians in London had it under consideration to admit persons desirous of practising physic, as Licentiates, upon an examination in English. This was done, as it was supposed, to introduce into this rank men of little or no education, in order to depreciate the characters of many who were in some esteem with the public.

"An attempt of this nature could not but alarm those who were immediately to be affected by it, and who felt the designed indignity. Several of these met together, compared the accounts they had received, and found there was too much truth in the reports, to suffer them any longer to remain inattentive to designs so prejudicial. It was resolved to call the Licentiates in general together, to acquaint them with their situation, and to act in concert for their general safety. But this was not all ; those who had embarked in this affair had at heart not only the honour of their profession, but its public utility ; not only to emancipate themselves from an authority which appeared to them in the light of a usurpation, but to establish the faculty upon a solid and liberal foundation. How far their endeavours may succeed is uncertain. But of one thing they are sure : they promote harmony among themselves ; excite to an honourable emulation ; and whatever may be their fate, will give proof, by the rectitude of their conduct, and an exertion of their abilities, that they are not unworthy of the highest honours of their profession."

Should the question be considered according to modern maxims, it is probable that more would be found to approve the design of the College, in throwing open the gates of the profession to such as could shew the requisite professional knowledge in their own tongue, rather than the jealousy of the Licentiates, who were for shutting out all who could not give the pass-word in Latin. The University of Edinburgh have lately made a similar concession to the spirit of the time; and though the measure may probably make certain Fluelless, who stickle for the primitive discipline, the "Roman Disciplines," shake their heads, and sigh out a "Fuimus Troes," we do not hear that the College is suspected of an intention to *swamp* the profession. But it is probable that the Licentiates, uneasy under the invidious distinctions of the Fellows, caught eagerly at the first departure from established custom, to revolt against a superiority which had nothing but custom to rest upon. There were serious thoughts of bringing the matter to a legal decision, and Dr. Fothergill subscribed £500 for the purpose. No trial, however, took place; but the union of the Licentiates assumed a purely literary and scientific character, and continued to assemble once a month, for the sake of reading medical papers, and conversing on the prevailing diseases, and other subjects of professional interest. On the death of Sir William Duncan, Bart. Dr. Fothergill was unanimously elected President of this meeting, and so continued to the time of his death. After the fashion of the French Academie, the deceased members were honoured with panegyrical orations. The "Essay on the Character of the late Alexander Russel" was spoken on one of these occasions.

No man can expect to pass through this world in perfect quiet. Fothergill, though his life was on the main a life of tranquility, was for a short time disagreeably embroiled with a man of his own persuasion, whom the Friends had been the principal means of bringing into notice. About the year 1766 flourished one Samuel Leeds, by education a brush-maker, by transmutation (of the Edinburgh College) an M. D. and by present profession Physician of the London Hospital, an appointment which he owed to the recommendation of some eminent *Quakers.* Fothergill, in a conversation on Doctor Leeds' rise in the world, said ominously, "Take care that he does no mischief." Leeds soon betrayed so much ignorance, that the Governors of the Hospital, to remedy their past precipitancy, passed a resolution, "that no physician should continue to officiate in that Hospital who had not undergone an examination at the College of Physicians." Leeds, unwilling to resign his emoluments, made the experiment, and was plucked. In his anger and disappointment he heard of the boding speech of Dr. Fothergill, and either thought, or pretended to think, that the resolution of the Hospital, which had subjected him to the disgrace of rejection, had been caused by it. He accordingly made it the ground of complaint before the Society. " These inoffensive people, who are averse to the litigious proceedings that vex and ruin so many of their fellow citizens, referred the charge, after their manner, to a certain number of arbitrators. Five persons were appointed for this purpose, and three of the number awarded £500 damages to Dr. Leeds, after refusing to hear Dr. Fothergill's principal evidence. The two other arbitrators, with great propriety, protested against the award; and after much altercation in the Society, Dr. Leeds moved the Court of King's Bench to shew cause why the rule for the recovery of the damages should be made absolute. Lord Mansfield, after hearing the evidence and counsel on the part of Dr. Leeds, refused to hear Dr. Fothergill's counsel; because, he observed, the evidence on the part of Dr. Leeds's arbitrators was sufficient to prove the illegality and injustice of their own award : the learned and noble judge further added, that Dr. Fothergill did no more than his duty in saying what he was charged with; and that he would not have acted as an honest man if he had said less." In fine, Dr. Leeds retreated to the sphere of a simple apothecary, and settled at Ipswich.

With these exceptions, Dr. Fothergill was seldom or never engaged in conflict or controversy with his brethren of the healing craft. He was, on the other hand, a liberal auxiliary to those who needed recommendation and protection, and was so far from feeling jealousy at the appearance of a rival in physic of his own religious persuasion, that Dr. Chorley, a young Quaker physician, was admitted into his house as an inmate, and introduced to a considerable practice : he might, indeed, have inherited the whole connection of his patron had he survived him, but his course was cut short, and he died under Dr. Fothergill's roof.

It is probable that Fothergill was on terms of intimacy with Dr. Mead; for in the Philosophical Transactions, No. 487, is a tract, in excellent Latin, addressed by our author to the Doctor, then Vice-President of the Royal Society.* The subject is a case of ruptured

---

* De Diaphragmate fisso, et mutatis quorundam Viscerum Sedibus, in Cadavere Puellae decem mensium observatis, Epistola Richardo Mead.

A learned wit once told a large assembly of medical gentlemen that they had no excuse for writing bad Latin, when they might find so much good in Celsus. Celsus is, indeed, an excellent writer, and might be read with great advantage by all who wish to learn Latin in earnest, as a model of didactic prose. But Celsus will not supply phrases for all the occasions of modern medicine; and, moreover, a physician who makes the history of his profession his study, must have so much to do with barbarous Latin, that it is a wonder if his own escape infection.

diaphragm occurring in a female infant of ten months old; but it is singular enough, that Fothergill expresses himself in the Latin tongue with a picturesque force, a vividness, an eloquent ardour, which he never ventures upon in his English compositions.

As his years and his wealth increased, he thought himself entitled to occasional respites from the press of his vocation, and to indulge those tastes which pointed out his natural recreations. He left his house in the city, and began to reside in Harpur Street, near Leon Square, which continued to be his town abode till his death. In 1672 he purchased a pleasant retreat near Upton, in Essex, to which he used to retire at the end of the week, and employed himself in laying out and cultivating one of the first botanic gardens in Europe. The hot-houses and green-houses extended 260 feet, all covered with glass. Whatever plant had obtained a place in the Materia Medica, or promised to be of service in physic or manufactures, or was any way remarkable for its rarity, beauty, or physiological habits, was sought out and purchased without regard to expense, and no pains were spared in the culture. Dr. Fothergill entertained a hope that the medicinal plants of the East might, in general, be successfully cultivated in the British Settlements of North America, or in the West India Islands, and by that means an unadulterated article be provided for the European market, a result hardly to be expected till the world grows honest. At that time even the learned of Europe were but imperfectly informed respecting the origin and preparation of many imported commodities. Long as musk has been celebrated both as a perfume and as a remedy, it is only of late years that there has been any accurate description of the animal producing it; and of the drug-producing plants, few had been described with such accuracy as to enable a botanist to recognize them. Even yet, the enlightened English have but vague notions of the trees which furnish the fancy woods in their cabinets, the shrubs

---

To write pure and elegant Latin even in an academic exercise, the highest object of which is to accommodate old words to new meanings, is by no means a common accomplishment; but when you really have any thing to say, you must be a very good scholar, and a man of strong sense and some imagination, if you can say it naturally in Latin.

Latin is now, in England at least, bonâ fide a dead language; it is no longer an organ of thought, or of vital communication; and the efforts of those who attempt to talk or compose in it, are like those of the worker in Mosaic, who would make an inanimated collection of fragments imitate life. But it should be remembered, that the period of its decease has been antedated many a century. The Latin of the middle ages was to all intents and purposes a living language. It was the medium by which the learned thought: it was the vehicle of religion and science: it made one nation of western christendom.

which contribute to the luxury of their tables, or supply the "juleps and catholians" which the consequences of luxury make necessary.

Botany, we have already mentioned, was Dr. Fothergill's favourite relaxation; and in regard to his professional researches, his attention was particularly turned to the Materia Medica. He was at great pains to procure accounts of the Cortex Winteranus,* and of the tree that produces the Terra Japonica (catechu). He had correspondents in all parts of the world, who were continually furnishing him with new plants, shells, and insects. But his great assistant and congenial friend in his investigations of nature, was that honour to Westmorland, Peter Collinson.† From 1751 to 1756, he was a constant correspondent to

---

* The original discovery of the Cortex Winteranus, or Winter's Bark, was a collateral consequence of Sir Francis Drake's voyage. Captain John Winter, who sailed with Sir Francis in the year 1577, as commander of the Elizabeth, destined for the South Seas, but after entering the Streights or Magellan, stress of weather obliged him to put back, and on some part of the coast of the Streight he collected a quantity of an aromatic and medicinal bark, which Clarias named after him, Cortex Winteranus. Though the trees producing it were noticed by many succeeding voyagers to those parts, as Van Nort in 1600, and Handasyd in 1691, yet the bark was frequently confounded with the Canella alba of the West Indies, and the black Cinnamon of Virginia. (See the account of Amada and Barlow's discovery of Virginia, in Hackluyt, vol. 3, p. 246.) Captain Wallis, in 1768, gathered a quantity of the true Cortex Winteranus; and Dr. Solander and Sir Joseph Banks, in the following year, drew up the first correct botanical account of the tree, which they found on the Streight le Maire, and in Tierra del Fuego. It is a large forest tree, sometimes exceeding fifty feet in height. Its outward bark is on the trunk grey, and very little wrinkled; on the branches quite smooth and green. By the accounts of Captain Wallis, and the minute botanical description of Dr. Solander, it must be very beautiful; the branches curving upwards so as to form an elegant oval head, the leaves large, eliptical, evergreen, of a dark, shining, laurel-like verdure above, and a pale bluish colour underneath; the flowers small, white, and delicate, but evanescent. Captain Wallis made an unsuccessful attempt to propagate it in the Falkland Isles. When first discovered, the bark was celebrated as an antiscorbutic, but it does not appear to have kept its place in the pharmacopœa. It is astringent, aromatic, with something of a cinnamon flavour, but much less *palatable.*

† Peter Collinson was of an ancient and honourable Westmorland family, a stock still growing in that land of lakes, from which, *ni fallor,* sprung the late Septimus Collinson, Provost of Queen's College, Oxon, and Margaret Professor of Divinity. Peter, who was born in the parish of Staveley, hard by the "river-lake Winander," while yet a boy, discovered the passion of a naturalist. The wonderful economy of nature in the metamorphoses of insects, strongly attracted his juvenile attention; and it was his recreation, his play, to hunt for those minute animals, so marvellous in their conformations, and in some instances so human in their architecture and their civil polity, so more than human in their prophetic instincts. Nor was he less curious in examining the varieties of vegetable life: though his commercial occupation carried him young to London, he found opportunities to cull and arrange the plants which

the Gentleman's Magazine. His contributions were chiefly on the weather, and diseases, and were designed to induce other physicians to

grow in the vicinity of the metropolis; he found access to the best gardens, and early began to form a hortus siccus. As he grew up, he entered into a partnership with his brother James, "in a business that did not always require their presence together. They lived in great harmony, and reciprocally afforded to each other opportunities for their respective pursuits. Both, however, had a strong relish for horticulture and planting, and both had acquired a just conception of rural elegance."

Congeniality of pursuits, and manners peculiarly pleasing, soon made him the friend of Derham, Dale, Woodward, Sir Hans Sloane, and others, whose enthusiastic devotion to natural knowledge excited the ridicule of Pope, Swift, and the rest of the Scriblerus club, only to prove how impotent is all wit against sincere goodness and true philosophy. In fact, the ill effects of satire have been as much exaggerated as its moral benefits. Satire on virtue or on knowledge never diminished the number of the virtuous or of the learned; at worst, it only flatters the self-complacency of the vicious and the ignorant. Whom has the "Tale of a Tub" either cured of fanaticism or alienated from piety? Who ever renounced mathematics or natural philosophy, in apprehension of being taken for a Laputan?

Peter Collinson was elected a Fellow of the Royal Society in 1728, and proved a most useful member, not only by the information he contributed from his personal stock to the general fund, but by his extensive correspondence. His mercantile affairs being connected much with foreigners, he turned this necessary intercourse to the benefit of science. To him Franklin communicated his earliest discoveries in electricity. As much of his commercial engagements were with America, he kept up a constant epistolary intercourse with the colonies, and felt a peculiar anxiety for their welfare. From a letter addressed by Franklin to Michael Collinson, Esq. it appears "that in 1730, a subscription library being set afoot in Philadelphia, he encouraged the design by making several very valuable presents to it, and procuring others from his friends; and as the Library Company had a considerable sum arising annually, to be laid out in books, and needed a judicious friend in London to transact the business for them, he voluntarily and cheerfully undertook that service, and executed it for more than thirty years successively, assisting in the choice of books, and taking the whole care of collecting and shipping them, without ever charging or accepting any consideration for his trouble. The success of this library," continues Franklin, "(greatly owing to his countenance and good advice), encouraged the erecting others in different places on the same plan, and it is supposed that there are now upwards of thirty subsisting in the several colonies, which have contributed greatly to the spreading of useful knowledge in that part of the world; the books he recommended being all of that kind, and the catalogue of this first library being much respected and followed by those libraries that succeeded. During the same time he transmitted to the directors of the library the earliest accounts of every new European improvement in agriculture and in the arts, and every philosophical discovery; among which, in 1745, he sent over an account of the new German experiments in electricity, together with a glass tube, and some directions for using it, so as to repeat those experiments. *This was the first notice I had of that curious subject, which I afterwards prosecuted with some diligence.*" Thus it was to Collinson's suggestions that the modern science of electricity in some measure is indebted for its origin.

For the Americans he appears to have felt a singular affection. He was never

supply the like materials for Meteorological and Nosological History. Finding that his example had not the intended effect, he discontinued his communications, on these heads at least; but he was a frequent writer in public papers on subjects of public utility, lending his pen to the aid of every improvement and every good work. It is said, that his papers of this kind, if collected, would fill many volumes. He wrote upwards of a hundred letters to the Gazetteer on the new pavement. He was one of those happy men, who are interested about every thing, and anxious about nothing. He was somewhat of a projector, and spared not words or money to promote what he esteemed beneficial. But, content with the ample income which his practice afforded, he never speculated in improvement, therefore his donations never impoverished him.

Many anecdotes of his beneficence remain, but three must suffice in this place. The object of the first was a poor clergyman, a class who, considering the rank they are expected to support, the expense of their education, and the wealth of their more opulent brethren, which operates as a direct tax upon the laborious and slenderly-provided, may be called the poorest of the poor. This door-keeper of the Temple

---

weary of giving them good advice. Did he regard them as his fellow Englishmen, or did he foresee that they were to become a great and rival nation? He constantly urged the Virginians, in particular, to make a better use of their soil, "to bethink themselves in time of a more permanent staple than a plant whose consumption only depends on custom and caprice, and this custom daily declining." His suggestion would at least beautify their country. "Vines," said he, "will thrive well in your country; but imitate nature in their cultivation; don't keep them close to the ground, as we are forced to do in this and other northern European climates, for the sake of a little sun and heat to ripen the grape; your summer heats exceed, as much as ours fall short; allow them, therefore, longer stems, let them he trained to, and supported by trees, and *hide their fruit among the foliage*, as in the warmer countries of Europe." From the picturesque eye which he evinced in this and other short touches, and from his enamoured attachment to plants, we doubt not that Peter Collinson, had he possessed or acquired the accomplishment of verse, might have written a very respectable Georgic. Gardening, indeed, was his hobby. He had correspondents in all parts of Europe, in America, in Asia, even at Pekin, and they all sought to oblige him by presents of rare seeds. Had he been a monarch, a present of seeds would have purchased his alliance.

Having arrived at his 75th year with little sickness, barring an occasional attack of gout, he died of a painful malady frequently incident to old age, at the seat of Lord Petre, in Essex, on the 11th of August, 1768. Inclosed in his will was found a paper, importing, "that he hoped he should leave behind him a good name, which he valued more than riches: that he had endeavoured not to live uselessly; and that all his days, he constantly aimed to be a friend to mankind."

A very minute life of Collinson is in Kippis's Biographia Britannica, a work which ought not to have concluded at the 5th volume.

(how much better off is a college porter!) was seated in London on a curacy of fifty pounds per annum, with a wife and a numerous family. An epidemical disease, which was at that time prevalent, seized upon his wife and five of his children: in this scene of distress be looked towards Fothergill—perhaps the sick matron herself put faith in him— but how was the fee to be raised? Every guinea had already to perform the work of two, and a poor curate with a large family has no hopes in contingency. The turns of the market, the increase of business, peace or war—nothing promises him anything. Very possibly this curate may have had a patron once (the only lever that can raise a churchman from the dust), but many a man, somewhat above legal pauperism, has given deadly offence by having a large family. In general, patrons are lost by nothing so hopelessly as by an imprudent marriage, an offence which parents, who alone have a right to be angry, are for the most part the readiest to forgive. Yet, if the poor London curate had no patron, he had a friend, who lent him a guinea, and introduced him to Dr. Fothergill. They attended at the usual hour of audience, gave an account of the several cases, and after some consultation offered the fee, which was rejected; but a note was taken of the clergyman's residence. The Doctor called assiduously the next and every succeeding day, till his attendance became unnecessary. The curate anxious to display his gratitude, or perhaps thinking that his cloth was stained by a debt to a schismatic, pinched or starved up a sum, which he proffered to the Doctor, with many apologies for his inability to do more. Fothergill put it back gently, and at the same time slid ten guineas into the curate's hand, bidding him to remember where he had a friend in case of future need. It is agreeable to record that the poor clergyman afterwards attained church preferment to the value of one hundred pounds a year, a hungry stipend enough for the servant of an aristocratic church, but still twice as good as fifty.

This was a kind act of the doctor, but we believe such kindnesses of the medical profession to be by no means rare. Seeing much of that distress which would fain hide itself, and which should therefore be relieved in secret, they perform many good deeds which others do not, not from disinclination to well-doing, but because the occasions do not cross their path. And few indeed are those who will hunt misery out of its lurking places into the light of consolation. Perhaps this anecdote has been repeated the oftener on account of the sectarian relations of the parties as Quaker and Parsons. The scene would make an excellent subject for a good humoured humorous painting. *

Could the curate in the midst of his gratitude forbear discontented reflections on the disproportionate regard of men for their souls and for their bodies, as exemplified in the wordly condition of the Leech and of the Pastor. *

* The miseries of the *inferior* clergy, (a phrase which we hope is, or will be banished from all good society) are not now what they were when they furnished conversation to Parson Adams at the country inn: but there are still numbers, who, if above penury, are not above care. This is the point to which the emoluments of a christian minister should always be raised, and which they never need surmount.

The pictures of poverty and wretchedness drawn by some writers on the church in the earlier ages of protestanism almost exceed belief, and yet they must have been matters of public notoriety, if true. Thus discourseth old Thomas Drant in his famous Spittle Sermon: "Howbeit, I am not ignorant how many a poor minister of these times is like *Elizas.* (*Elisha*, See 2 Kings, c. iv. verse 10.) He had not pen, nor ink, nor table, nor candlestick, but as his hosts allowed him; and these poor God's men must be helped by their host or hosts, or one friend or another, with coat and cap, and cup and candle, and study and table, or else they shall be harbourless and helpless, and needs must I further yet say, that in many a poor scholar in the universities, Christ himself is full of hunger and necessity. These be the noble sons of the prophets, and most apt of all others to be the builders of God's temple; yet have I seen many a good wit many a long day kept low and lean, or to be made broken with hunger and abject with poverty. I do not know the liberality of *this city* towards both these places, only this I can say, that less than the tenth part of that which is nothing but surfeit and sickness to the great excessive eaters of this town, would cherish and cheer up hungry and thirsty Christ in those his hunger starved members right well." Some in this age will be surprised, if not offended at the boldness with which this old divine appropriates to the clergy of his own church the declaration of the Saviour— "I was hungry and ye gave me no meat, I was thirsty and ye gave me no drink," and "inasmuch as ye did it not to one of the least of these, ye did it not to me." And still more at his imputing to the glorified Lord an instinct state of extenuation and inanition. His reproaching the city for gluttony is less remarkable, though few modern clergy would have been so very plain in the presence of the civic authorities, or so coursely graphic in his delineations. "Lord here is the rich glutton to be seen up and down and round about the town. Their horses *chew* and *sper* upon gold and silver, and their mules go under rich velvet. Dogs are dear unto them, and feed much daintily. Here is scarcely anything in the upper sort, but many a foolish Nabal scruping and scoutching, eating and drinking, and suddenly and unworthily dying. The eyes of Judah are said to be red with drinking, but much of this people have their faces fire-red with continual quaffing and carousing. Sodom and Gomorrah were said to be full of bread, but these Londoners are more than full, for they are even bursten with banquetting, and sore and sick with surfeiting. Lord, thou whistlest to them and they hear thee not; thou sendest thy plague among them, and they mind thee not. Lord, we are lean; Lord, we are faint; Lord, we are miserable; Lord, we are thy members. Lord, therefore, thou art lean; Lord, thou art faint; Lord, thou art miserable!!"

The sermon from which this extract is taken was preached about 1569. Drant was the first metrical translator of Horace in the English language. Refined Critics have pretended to be much offended with the tragi-comedy of the stage. What would they say to the tragi-comedy of the pulpit, and yet there is in many ancient discourses such an incongruous mixture of sublimity.

The quaintness of the pulpit was gradually reformed, but the poverty of the country parsons, and we might add, of the city parsons also, long continued to be complained

Yet Fothergill had calls upon his benevolence from the less favoured members of his own calling; among these was Dr. Gowin Knight, a man of learning and merit, but whether, like Arbuthnot, he

Knew his art but not his trade,

or whether the course of events was adverse beyond his skill to reconcile,

of. The treatise ascribed to Exchard, and entitled "The grounds and occasions of the Contempt of the Clergy inquired into," published in 1670, paints the condition of a small beneficed clergyman, as little superior to that of Hogarth's "Distressed Poet." The chief of his thoughts and his main business must be to study how to live that week; how he shall have bread for his family; whose sow has lately pigged; when will come the next rejoicing goose, or the next cheerful basket of apples? How far to Lammas or offerings? When shall we have another christening, and who is likely to marry or die? These are very reasonable considerations, and worthy a man's thoughts, for a family cannot be maintained by texts and contexts, and the child that lies crying in the cradle, will not be satisfied without a little milk, and perhaps sugar.

"But suppose he does get into a little hole over the oven, with a lock to it, called a study, towards the latter end of the week, one may very near guess what is his first thought when he comes there: viz. that the last kilderkin of drink is near departed; and that he has but one poor single groat in the house, and there is judgment and execution ready to come out against it, for butter and eggs. Now sir, can any one think that a man thus racked and tortured, can be seriously intent half an hour to continue anything that might be of real advantage to his people? Beside, perhaps that week he has met with some dismal crosses, and most undoing misfortunes. There was a scurvy conditioned scrole that broke his pasture, and ploughed up the best part of his glebe: and a little after that came a couple of spiteful ill-favoured crows, and trampled down the little remaining grass. Another day, having but four chickens, sweep comes the kite, and carries away the fattest and hopefullest of all the brood. Then, after all this comes the jack-daws and starlings, idle birds they are, and they scattered and carried away from his thin thatched house forty or fifty of the best straws, and to make him completely unhappy, after all these afflictions, another day that he had a pair of breeches on, he suffered very much in carefully lifting over his leg. But we'll grant that he meets not with any of these such frightful disorders, but that he goes into his study with a mind as calm as the evening: for all that, upon Sunday, we must be content even with what God shall please to send us. For, as for books, he is for want of money so moderately furnished, that except it be a small Geneva Bible, so small as it will not be desired to lie open of itself, together with small concordance thereunto belonging, as also a book for all kinds of Latin sentences, called Polyantheœ, with some exposition upon the Catechism, (a portion of which is to be got by heart, and to be put off for his own), and perhaps *Mr. Caryl upon Pineda*, Mr. Dodd upon the Commandments, and Mr. Clarke's Lives of Famous Men, such as Mr. Carter of Norwich that used to eat such abundance of pudden; besides, I say, there is scarce any thing to be found but a budget of old stitched sermons hung up behind the door, with a few broken girts, two or three yards of whipcord, and perhaps a hammer and saw to prevent delapidations." Allowing for the strain of burlesque and exaggeration which pervades this glaring description of the cases and comforts of a small vicar in the seventeenth century, these passages exhibit a degree of misery which we should have hoped had never existed in a church so often reproached with its exhorbitant riches.

he was weighed down with poverty and embarrassment, and knew not how to help himself; he turned to Fothergill with a heavy heart and timid asking eye, expecting no more than the means to ward off a pressing assault of penury, an importunate and threatening dun, or an old and merciful creditor as poor as himself, or it may be, he was at a loss for the morrow's meal. We do not correctly remember whether he made any direct application to Fothergill or not, but however the doctor understood his need, talked cheerfully to him, and in fine, gave him a piece of paper, which he probably supposed to be a five pound note, but which turned out to be a check for £1000. In what a new state of existence, what a renovation of youth and hope must this poor man have felt at that moment.

But Fothergill was not only beneficent, he was munificent. In his charity he had regard chiefly to necessity; and as necessity is rarely to be found in that fold of Christians of which he was a member, his donations were freely given to the needy of all denominations. But the remarkable instances of *munificence* which we are about to mention had a more especial reference to the interest of the Society of Friends. These were, his patronage of Anthony Parver, and the part he took in the foundation and endowment of Ackworth School.

Anthony Parver was a Quaker, poorer and less educated than most of his brethren, by trade a shoe maker. Can any one assign a reason why so many shoe makers have become eminent for their genius or their enthusiasm? The employment is still, often solitary, and allows a man to be meditative. Anthony Parver as he worked with his awl, was over-mastered with an idea that he was called and commanded to translate the Scriptures. His faith attributed the impulse, whose origin he could not trace in his own will, or in the concatenation of his human thoughts, to the Divine Spirit. But if he was an enthusiast, he was an enthusiast of much sanity; for he sought the accomplishment of his end by the necessary means, and did not begin to translate till he had mastered the original tongues. We know not what assistance he received in this great undertaking, which was commenced when he had long outlived the years of physical docility; but if it be true, as stated, that he began with the Hebrew first (and it was the natural course to occur to his mind), he must have had some, for there was then no Hebrew and English lexicon or grammar. However he did acquire a competent knowledge of the Hebrew, Chaldee, and Syriac. He afterwards learned Greek, and Latin last of all. But still he could not have accomplished his purpose without pecuniary aid, and that aid was liberally afforded by Dr. Fothergill, at whose sole expense, Parver's Translation of the Old and New Testaments, with notes critical and explanatory, in two volumes folio, was printed, and appeared in 1765. The cost of the work is stated at not less than £200. A short account of this extraordinary effort of faith and perseverance may be found in Southey's Omniana. It is said to be remarkable for a close adherance to the Hebrew idiom. It has not apparently attracted as much notice among biblical scholars as the curiosity, to say no more, of its production would seem to challenge. We never saw it but once, and that was in the library of a *Friend.** We doubt, indeed, whether any new translation, however learned, exact, or truly orthodox, will ever appear to English Christians to be the real Bible. The language of the authorized version is the perfection of English, and it can never be written again, for the language of prose is one of the few things in which the English have really degenerated. Our tongue has lost its holiness.

The peculiarities of the Quaker discipline, and the rigid purity in which it requires the youth of that church to be educated, render it essential to their consistency to have seminaries proper to themselves. They do not, indeed, require colleges, for they have no priesthood, no order that is especially their own, requiring a certificate of qualification, but they needed a school, where they might see their children reared to a stature of intellect commensurate to their station, their duties, and their intellectual desires. This desideratum Dr. Fothergill was anxious to supply, and he availed himself of the first opening that offered to make a beginning. We cannot record the conception and nativity of Ackworth better than in the words of Dr. Hird, related by Dr. Elliot. "On his return from Cheshire, through Yorkshire, in the year 1778, he did me the favour of being my guest a few days, during which time he was visited by many of his friends in those parts. In one of these interviews, the conversation turned on an institution at Gildersome, a small establishment for the education of poor children amongst the society. The Doctor was inquiring into its state and management, and how far it might serve for a larger undertaking. A just description being given of it, with the following remark, that not only this but all others, however laudable the motives from which they took their rise, must fail of success without a constant superintending care, and unremitting attention to the first great object of the institution; this idea was exemplified by the then present state of the Foundling Hospital at Ackworth, which, although originating from the most humane principle, and erected at a vast expense, was, from repeated inattentions to the first design, in danger of delapidation, and ready for public sale." The

* The late Charles Lloyd, banker, of Birmingham, a man whom I should be thankful to Heaven for having known.

relation struck the Doctor forcibly. "Why may not this," said he, " serve the very purpose I am in pursuit of?" To be short, the building and an estate of thirty acres of land were purchased, improved, and furnished by subscription. The Doctor set a generous example, by his own contribution, and a permanent endowment by his will in perpetuity.

It is the duty, and therefore the right of every religious body to educate their own children in their own principles. A national *religious* education which could comprehend all sects must be the organ of a new and impracticable heresy, and could only be maintained by inforcing a body of negative cannons more multitudinous than all the articles of faith, of all the orthodoxies, and heterodoxies that have sprung up since man took upon himself to improve revelation. Reading, writing, and arithmetic may be taught without instructing the pupils in any theological creed, and it is better so to do, than to teach a creed which, by the universal agreement of all sects, denominations and churches is a *caput mortuum* without life, truth, authority, or efficiency. We therefore think the Quakers right in founding schools for themselves ; and we are always glad to see the Catholics, the Methodists, the Arminians, or the Socinians doing the same. They ought not to find fault if the Episcopalians follow their example. But we must return to the Doctor, only observing, *en passant,* that his liberality to Ackworth has not been thrown away. More than one *poet* has been trained at that seminary. It is sufficient to mention William Howitt, Jeremiah Wiffin, and (we believe) Bernard Burton.

Dr. Fothergill's constitution was not of the most robust order, and as he advanced in years he found a temporary secession from the toil and anxiety of consultation necessary to recruit his health and spirits. His villa at Upton was too near London to allow of his calculating upon many weeks of repose there. He ever retained an affection for Cheshire, his grandfather's country, and the land of his opening thought, which induced him to make it the scene of his summer retirement. During the latter years of his life he used to spend the interval from July to September at Lea Hall, a pleasant seat in the neighbourhood of Middlewich, the property of Sir John Leicester, of whom he rented it from year to year. In this vicinity he is still remembered with gratitude. His arrival was always a joyful æra to the poor, to the sick, and to the circle of his friends. He never took fees during his vacation, but went every week to Middlewich, and prescribed gratis to all who came, at an inn. Such men are not readily forgotten. It was a goood omen or as good, to meet him on his morning rides. When in town, his ordinary practice was computed to amount to £7000 a year, but on some occasions it much exceeded that sum. In the year 1775 and

1776, when an influenza prevailed, he numbered, on an average, sixty patients a day, and his practice was supposed worth £8000 annually. His property at his death was estimated at £80,000. He was doubtless a fortunate as well as a good man. Among his services to literature, we must not omit his patronage of the voyager Sidney Parkinson, the introduction to whose voyage he drew up himself.

About two years before his death, he was afflicted with a troublesome disorder, which he mistook at first for irregular gout; though he never earned that gentlemanlike disease, taking much exercise, and was remarkably abstemious, seldom exceeding two glasses of wine after dinner or supper. His pains are said to have been aggravated, and perhaps his dissolution hastened, by his extreme delicacy. In his last illness he was attended by Dr. Warren, Dr. Watson, Dr. Reynolds, and Mr. Pott, whose efforts produced a temporary relief; but the symptoms returned with increased violence, and finally terminated his existence on the 26th of December, 1780, in the 69th year of his age, at his house in Harpur Street.

On the 5th of January following, his remains were deposited in the Friends' burial ground, at Winchmore Hill. Though only ten coaches were ordered to convey his relations and more immediate connections, upwards of seventy carriages attended the funeral, and some Friends came from a distance of a hundred miles to pay the last token of respect, to a man who had made their garb and discipline so honourable in the world's eye.

Dying a bachelor, he left the bulk of his property to his sister, who was joined with Mr. Chorley in the executorship. By his will he directed that his collections in Natural History should be offered to Dr. Hunter, at 500l. less than the valuation. The doctor purchased them for 1200l. His choice selection of English portraits which he bought for 80l. sold for 200 guineas; the house at Upton brought 1000l.

As a professional man he was principally noted for the intuitive skill with which he divined the true character of a disease—when the diagnosis was most perplexing, and administered the remedy which the idiosyncracy of the case required. He was well-grounded in medical learning, not given to novelties; a careful observer of facts—and one that practised his art at once with the caution and the courage of benevolence.

In politics he was the friend of peace and liberty; in religion, he was firm to the principle in which he was brought up. Neither wealth nor science, nor his own philosophical liberality, nor his widely extended friendship, ever estranged *him from* the simple piety of a Quaker.

END OF VOL. I.

HISTORICAL AND CHRONOLOGICAL INDEX.

ANDREW MARVELL.

RICHARD BENTLEY.

THOMAS LORD FAIRFAX.

JAMES, SEVENTH EARL OF DERBY.

LADY ANNE CLIFFORD.

ROGER ASCHAM.

JOHN FISHER.

THE REV. WILLIAM MASON.

SIR RICHARD ARKWRIGHT.

WILLIAM ROSCOE.

CAPTAIN COOK.

WILLIAM CONGREVE.

DR. JOHN FOTHERGILL.

Check Out More Titles From HardPress Classics Series In this collection we are offering thousands of classic and hard to find books. This series spans a vast array of subjects – so you are bound to find something of interest to enjoy reading and learning about.

Subjects:
Architecture
Art
Biography & Autobiography
Body, Mind &Spirit
Children & Young Adult
Dramas
Education
Fiction
History
Language Arts & Disciplines
Law
Literary Collections
Music
Poetry
Psychology
Science
…and many more.

Visit us at www.hardpress.net

CPSIA information can be obtained
at www.ICGtesting.com
Printed in the USA
BVHW060551280819
556854BV00001B/105/P